CROSSROADS TO ISLAM

Negev Archeological Project for Study of
Ancient Arab Desert Culture

CROSSROADS TO ISLAM

*The Origins of the Arab Religion
and the Arab State*

Yehuda D. Nevo and Judith Koren

Prometheus Books
59 John Glenn Drive
Amherst, New York 14228-2197

Published 2003 by Prometheus Books

Inquiries should be addressed to
Prometheus Books
59 John Glenn Drive
Amherst, New York 14228–2197
VOICE: 716–691–0133, ext. 207
FAX: 716–564–2711
WWW.PROMETHEUSBOOKS.COM

07 06 05 04 03 5 4 3 2 1

Library of Congress Cataloging-in-Publication Data

Nevo, Yehuda D.
Crossroads to Islam : the origins of the Arab religion and the Arab state / Yehuda D. Nevo and Judith Koren.
p. cm. — (Islamic studies)
Includes bibliographical references and index.
ISBN 1–59102–083–2 (cloth)
I. Islam—Origin. 2. Islam—History. 3. Arabs—Religion—History. 4. Arabian Peninsula—History. 5. Byzantine Empire—History—527–1081. I. Koren, Judith, 1948– II. Title. III. Islamic studies (Amherst, N.Y.)

BP55.N48 2003
297'.09'021—dc21

2003050003

Printed in the United States of America on acid-free paper

CONTENTS

Appendices

Maps

ACKNOWLEDGMENTS

The publication of this book was greatly delayed by the tragic and untimely death after long illness of its principal author, Yehuda D. Nevo. Now that it has at last come to press, it is a pleasure to acknowledge the help of the many people who contributed, in many and various ways, to its completion, giving generously of their time and attention. Professor Shlomo Pines unfailingly found time for discussion, and extended to us the hospitality of his home. Professor Sebastian Brock received from us, out of the blue, the material on the 7th-century Syriac sources, read it promptly, and sent us a detailed critique full of useful notes. Professor Philip Grierson, whom we placed in the same predicament regarding the material on the Byzantine and Arab coins, likewise answered our questions and added many helpful comments. Drs. Lawrence Conrad, Patricia Crone, Gerald Hawting and Robert Hoyland devoted hours, on their visits to Jerusalem, to discussions which we found fruitful. Dr. Crone, especially, took a great interest in the progress of our work and was always willing to argue the viewpoint of the opposition; and Dr. Hawting read, and commented closely on, early versions of many of the chapters. Robert Hoyland sent us early drafts of chapters of his doctoral thesis as they became available, as well as the finished thesis, all of which was of great help to our analysis of the contemporary non-Arab literary sources. Professor Amnon Ben-Tor of the Department of Archaeology of the Hebrew University, as well as other colleagues from the Department, was always ready to discuss the archaeological findings. Finally, Ibn Warraq took an interest in the research as this book neared completion; his encouragement and enthusiasm is gratefully acknowledged.

It is a pleasure also to thank those who helped in material ways. Work on the deciphering and dating of the four hundred inscriptions transcribed during 1981–1982, and an additional two hundred found in later years, was partly funded by the Department of Islamic Studies of the Hebrew University of Jerusalem, and by a research grant from the Israel Academy of Sciences and Humanities. In this regard we owe a special debt to Professor M. J. Kister, who, although himself a lifelong "traditionalist," furthered the research for this book, and work on the inscriptions, in every way possible: discussions, advice, help in deciphering difficult inscriptions, invitations to Yehuda Nevo to speak at conferences, and help with funding. In 1985 the Center for Social Studies of the Blaustein Institute for Desert Research at Ben-Gurion College, Sede Boqer, appointed Yehuda Nevo as Research Fellow, and from then until his death in 1992 provided working space for the project close to the areas studied, and some financial support. We owe especial thanks to Professor Emmanuel Marx, then head of the Center, for thus placing the Center's facilities at his disposal. And the members of Kibbutz Sede Boqer, which is situated very close to the main archaeological site, accepted Yehuda Nevo as a guest from 1983 until his death in 1992, thereby also greatly aiding the archaeological fieldwork. But he always considered that his greatest debt was to Dalia Heftman, for her unfailing encouragement and support over many years. It was Dalia, also, who handled all the technical side of preparing the manuscript and graphics for press: without her great technical skill and countless hours of effort, it would not have appeared in its present form.

Finally, Judith Koren would like to thank her family, for stoically bearing, over the years, the impediments to daily life that this work entailed. And finally, the University of Haifa Library, for making available to her, as a visiting researcher, the library's excellent collection, without which this book could not have been written.

Introduction:
The Traditional Account and Its Problems

The study of the 7th-century Arab takeover of the East and of the early decades of Islam has until recently been based almost exclusively on the Muslim sources. The earliest works of this huge literature date only from the mid to late 2nd/8th century, 100 to 150 years after the events they describe; nonetheless most Western scholars have accepted as factual the picture they draw of the pre-Islamic era (the Jāhiliyyah), the rise of Islam, and the subsequent centrally directed Arab invasion of the Byzantine and Persian Empires. According to this historical framework, many nomadic tribes inhabited the pre-Islamic Arabian Peninsula, and an extensive trade network, whose hub was Mecca, resulted in the rise of the peninsula as a political power. Political affairs in the Jāhilī period, both intra-peninsular and vis-à-vis the outside world, thus centered on the Ḥijāz. After conversion to Islam, the nomadic tribes of the peninsula supplied thousands of warriors for the invasion of Syria-Palestine, Persia, and Egypt. The decision to invade these lands was taken by Abū Bakr in Madīnah after Islam had prevailed throughout Arabia: he directed the campaigns from Madīnah, appointed the leaders of the various Arab forces, and sent each to fulfill a given task in a particular area. The Muslim sources tend to stress the religious aspects of the invasion, and the later ones provide detailed accounts, presented as verbatim reports of eyewitnesses or early authorities, of the course of the invasion and its battles, some of which involved vast numbers of warriors on both sides.

There are, of course, problems in interpreting and collocating such vast amounts of material. For instance, Western historians tend to be suspicious of the traditions' religious pedigree. They stress that the invading Arabs were in search of spoil or tribute and never actually intended a conquest: the pious phrases woven into descriptions of the goods and captives to be gained in an encounter may be accepted as later literary embellishments. There is also the problem of which details to accept as historical, for the Muslim sources usually provide several conflicting versions of an event, such as when, where, and how a battle was fought or a city surrendered, or who was the commander in a particular engagement. Nonetheless, the most common Western position remains that the Muslim account, if not quite straight historical fact, is at least a collection of sometimes conflicting sources from which the historical facts may be distilled: the grains of truth have merely to be separated from the chaff. Hill (1971), for instance, argues that although bias has contaminated the ᶜAbbāsid sources' treatment of "legal, fiscal, sectarian, and theological matters," there was no reason to falsify military facts. Therefore, although reports of the invasion suffer from "ignorance and indifference," they do not suffer bias: real historical matter may be extracted from them.[1]

Western scholars who accept the historicity of the Muslim sources have therefore devoted considerable effort to reconstructing the progress of the conquest from the many conflicting and contradictory details reported. A good example is Donner (1981). Donner considers that the difficulties of integrating the Muslim sources' contradictions into a plausible historical narrative stem chiefly from their lack of a chronological framework. This he attempts to provide, by dividing the conquest of al-Šām into two stages. The first object, he suggests—before the actual invasion of al-Šām—was to take control of the northern peninsula: the Wādī Ṣirḥān–Tabuk–al-ᶜUla (Madāʾin Ṣalīḥ) area. Abū Bakr therefore sent Xālid bn Saᶜīd bn al-ᶜĀṣ[2] "towards Syria"—i.e., into this area—with instructions "to bring the Arab-speaking tribal groups with whom he made contact under control."[3] Xālid bn al-Walīd was sent with similar instructions to Iraq. After securing the

1. Hill (1971), p. 23.

2. For Xālid bn Saᶜīd bn al-ᶜĀṣ bn Umayyah bn ᶜAbd Šams al-Umawī see Ibn Ḥajar, *Iṣābah*, 1.406 no. 2167. The obscure role in the first phase of the invasion which the traditions ascribe to him may hint at a real historical personality, though his date and the political context of his activity have yet to be investigated.

3. Donner (1981), p. 113 para. 2.

northern peninsula, the next task was to gain control of the nomadic Arab tribes in the Byzantine provinces of Palaestina III and Arabia, the interface areas with the *oikoumenē*: i.e., the Negev, the Trans-Jordanian mountain ridge from the Balqāʾ to the Jūlān, and the Ḥawrān towards Damascus. ʿAmr bn al-ʾĀṣ, in Donner's view, seems to have been responsible for the Negev, and to have gained control of the Central Negev, even though "it is his raids on a few villages near Gaza[4] that are recorded in the sources."[5] At this point the Arabs could have reached any place south of Caesarea in no more than four days; but in fact they left Palestine alone.

The second phase of the invasion, according to Donner, was a thrust along the interface area into the Jūlān–Ḥawrān–Damascus region, and the capture (usually by siege) of the Syrian towns: Faḥl, Bayṣān, Tiberias, Bostra (Buṣrà), Damascus, Baʿlabakk, and Ḥimṣ. In the course of these operations, the Arab forces clashed with the Byzantine army along the East Bank from the Balqāʾ (Moab) to the Yarmūk River, and along the Jordan valley at Faḥl, Bayṣān, and Tiberias. Donner has no doubt that the accounts of the battles are valid, i.e., that "the Islamic armies engaged elements of the Byzantine army several times and delivered serious defeats to them at the Yarmūk, at Ajnādayn, and at Faḥl,"[6] and that the outcome was "the decisive defeat of the Byzantine armies in the second phase" and "the collapse of Byzantine power."[7]

The Traditional Account, as retold by Donner, makes considerable sense; and to formulate a coherent, plausible narrative out of a vast array of conflicting details is quite an achievement. It does not, however, demonstrate that any of the conflicting accounts are "true"; and the question, indeed, is not whether the traditions can be moulded to make sense, but whether they are demonstrably historical. Arguments such as Hill's, mentioned above, that the reports of the invasion suffer not from

---

4. The villages in the vicinity of Gaza could be what we label the Negev "cities." The Roman-Byzantine texts referred to them (except Elusa) as villages, *komei*. We also know from the Nessana papyri that the western fringe of the Central Negev (Sobata, Nessana, Elusa) was included in the Gaza administrative district. The archaeological survey of the area conducted by various archaeologists during recent decades has shown that the north-western Central Negev was quite densely inhabited, and several large sites have been found so far to testify to this.

5. Donner (1981), p. 116 para. 4.

6. Ibid., p. 146 para. 4.

7. Ibid., pp. 148, 149 para. 1.

willful bias but only from the "ignorance and indifference" of their transmitters shed little light on this problem, for it is difficult to ascribe to ignorance and indifference the typical problems encountered in the sources—and especially the existence of several conflicting reports of the same event: different commanders for the same assignment, which is set in different sequences of events and/or on different dates. It is more likely that ignorance and indifference on the transmitter's part would keep the original information unaffected. Transmitters, collectors, or harmonizers of traditions who are not familiar with a certain aspect of the information they have received, and have no reason to falsify it, will not invent different "facts" (commanders, sequences, etc.); they will just repeat the information given to them, trying to copy the names, dates, and sequences of events as accurately as possible. So if, for example, Abū ᶜUbaydah was the commander-in-chief of the al-Šām theatre (and there is no known reason to distort this "non-controversial" information), the ignorance or indifference of the transmitters will not explain why at least four other names were recorded as holding this same post at the same time.[8]

Faced thus with several conflicting reports of the same event, some scholars have adopted a more critical stance. Already in the 19th century Goldziher (1889) sensed that no strong case exists for accepting the data in the Muslim sources as deriving from the period which they describe; but little attention was paid to his view at that time. Much later, Schacht (1950) argued for the late date of origin of many laws supposedly instituted by Muḥammad based on the Qurʾān, the implication being that the Qurʾān itself is a late compilation. Nearly three decades after Schacht, Wansbrough's source criticism of the Arab literature[9] led him to the conclusion that the Qurʾān is a late compilation of *logia* generated over a period of time by one or more sectarian communities,[10] and that the Muslim sources are compilations of stories embroidered around central themes, of didactic

---

8. Of course, as Hawting has pointed out to us (private communication, November 23, 1987), if Abū ᶜUbaydah were *not* the commander, one could easily see why he should be substituted for some less notable figure. This still leaves us with four or five contenders for the same position.

9. Wansbrough, J. (1977) and (1978).

10. In fact the Qurʾān as we have it cannot be dated, outside the framework of the traditional account of history found in the Muslim literature, to the 7th century. Wansbrough considers that it was canonized at the end of the 2nd/8th century or early in the 3rd/9th.

material, and of exegesis. Little of the supposedly historical facts in them, Wansbrough suggested, should be accorded the status of history—i.e., they arose no earlier than the sources that record them. In a brief but, as always, conceptually condensed lecture[11] he has also summarized the basic problem which his previous works documented at length: no external evidence corroborates the accounts found in a late, literary corpus whose authors had a vested interest in the historicity of the accounts they transmitted. Western scholars who accept the historicity of those accounts are, in Wansbrough's view, proceeding on the basis of nothing more than "a tacitly shared paradigm, that is, an assumption that the literature in question has documentary value."[12] But in fact, Wansbrough maintains, it does not: the sources are literary rather than historical, and should be analyzed and interpreted by the methods of literary criticism.[13]

Crone (1987) has done just that for one basic tenet of the Traditional Account: the belief that an important international trading network existed, centered on Mecca, whose inhabitants derived from it not only their living but considerable wealth and a preeminent position in peninsular politics. Crone's study demonstrates that the Muslim sources themselves do not ascribe to the Ḥijāz any share in the luxury transit trade; they mention only trade in bare necessities such as leather or cheap woolen cloth. None of the different versions in the sources supports the conclusions derived from them by early Western scholars and accepted ever since. Crone concludes that the Ḥijāzis in general, and the Meccans in particular, did not control any international trade routes, nor could they have made much of a living from trade. Moreover, the variant accounts in the Muslim sources conflict with each other to such an extent as to suggest that their writers did not in fact know much about either 7th-century Ḥijāzī or more specifically Meccan trade. It makes considerably more sense, Crone argues, to regard them all as storytellers' fabrications; for an analysis of the different accounts of Meccan trade in the Muslim sources leads to the conclusion that there was no continuous transmission of historical information through the three generations or so between the time described and the mid-2nd/8th century recording of its history. Thus "it was the storytellers who created the tradition";[14] or if it was not, at least not all the tales can be true and we do

11. Wansbrough, J. (1987).
12. Ibid., p. 10.
13. Ibid., pp. 14–15.
14. Crone (1987), p. 225.

not know which to discard and which to accept: "indeed, the very theme of trade could be legendary."[15]

Bashear (1984, 1985), going one step further, has argued that many of the events in the life of the Prophet reported in the Muslim sources are in fact retrojections into the past of later incidents, e.g., some from the life of the mid- to late 7th-century "prophet" Muḥammad bn al-Ḥanafiyyah.

Whether or not they accept Bashear's arguments, proponents of the source-critical method of analysis would agree that the Muslim sources' accounts of both the Jāhilī period and the conquest are unacceptable as historical fact. The descriptions of battles, for instance—such as the Battle of the Yarmūk—are composed of stereotypes, narrative *topoi* often recounted in a fixed manner, and topography so general as to be useless for identification of the site of battle.[16] There is, too, a suspicious parallel between the biblical account of the conquest of Canaan and the traditional Muslim account of the conquest of al-Šām. In both accounts, the great religious leader (Moses or Muḥammad) starts the process of invasion but dies before the goal is reached; his close friend (Joshua or Abū Bakr) continues the military campaign.

These problems illustrate, in an extreme form, a dilemma familiar to most historians. The problems associated with the derivation of historical facts from written sources, even those dating from the period they describe, have been extensively debated in the literature of historical methodology.[17] The basic problem with the use of a written source is that, while purporting to tell us "what really happened," it actually tells us only what the author *thought had happened* or *wanted to believe had happened* or *wanted others to believe had happened.*[18] What we make of it depends, then, on how much we

---

15. Ibid., p. 114. Cf. also Peters (1988) on the lack of evidence for Meccan trade in contemporary non-Arab sources.

16. Thus the description of the battle of the Yarmūk contains nothing which might differentiate it from the other fantastic battle-legends: the topography of the river area could fit almost any river in the region, while the allusions to the fatal precipice and lethal torrents are useless for ascertaining the site.

17. For a useful discussion and basic bibliography, see Crawford (1983), Ch. 1 and pp. 75–79.

18. For a discussion of methodological problems with reference to use of the Arab literature, see Wansbrough (1987); Koren and Nevo (1991). For further comments on the aims of medieval chronicle-writers see below, Part II Chapter 2; for an analysis of the attitude of one (late 8th-century) chronicler cf. also Witakowski (1987), pp. 138–41, 170–72.

know of the author's knowledge and intentions—and very often we know little or nothing of them. Moreover, even the most consciously unbiased account is necessarily the result of the author's personality, intelligence, powers of reasoning and drawing conclusions, and his view of history, which dictates his choice of what to omit, what to include, and how to present it. Often we have little way of knowing if a written account, *taken by itself*, is history or simply literature. That it reads easily and "makes sense" is no help: the fact that it looks easy to get history out of a written source indicates that its author has devoted considerable *literary* effort to his work, but not that the account is necessarily "true." Our problem, moreover, is not just that of getting history out of an author's text, for we almost never have the author's original text. We count ourselves lucky to have a copy made a few centuries after the original and usually a few copies removed from it; sometimes we have only a quotation from one source, now lost, in a later one, or a later work which claims to be based on an earlier.

The complicated transmission history of a document does not merely introduce scribal errors, but also more insidious diversions from and even perversions of the original. This is because a copyist who "knows" what happened—often, in his own opinion, demonstrably better than the writer of the contemporary document—will, even unconsciously, alter the older text in ways that accord with his "knowledge." We are therefore faced with transmitters who interpret the older text—by adding, subtracting, or substituting a word, a phrase, or a gloss here and there—without even realizing that they are thereby altering the meaning of the document being copied. In the field of Arab studies an example would be a copyist, or an author quoting from an earlier text, who used the term "Muslim" where the original had "Hagarene" or "Ishmaelite" or "Saracen," or replaced an original "the Prophet" by "Muḥammad," or who identified an unnamed battle as one of those known to have been fought, and added to the account: "This was the Battle of such-and-such." If the older document does not survive independently of this copy or quotation, it is nearly impossible to detect such tampering with it.

All of the above applies to contemporary texts: those written by people who lived through the events they describe, or at least not far from them in either time or place. The farther one gets from the events described, the more dubious the account must become. An account by a Syrian living through the Arab invasion and describing what he sees is one thing. It is not necessarily history: it is more likely to be a combination of sermon, prophecy, and religious moralizing; but it is at least the interpretation of an eyewitness. An account by an Armenian living fifty years later is something else. Even though the late 7th-century Armenian chronicler Sebeos tells us that his account is based on the reports of prisoners of war brought back from Syria, he can record only the tales of old men remembering the events of their youth, or reports made to him closer to the time of the events, as he himself remembered them fifty years later. These memories in turn reach us with, of course, the probable changes wrought by successions of copyists who "knew" more details of the story than Sebeos. Yet even Sebeos, from our vantage point, is an approximately contemporary source compared to the great body of Muslim literature, which did not start to be composed until the 2nd/8th century.

The present study, then, sides with Schacht-Wansbrough-Bashear (though perhaps none of the three would have liked to see his name *murakkab* in such a scholarly trinity). They and others have argued, from a critical reexamination of the Muslim sources, that most of the material in them relating to the 7th century needs to be radically reinterpreted or discarded altogether *as historical fact*. (Of course these sources are still evidence for the currency, at the time they were written, of a particular view of the past, or a desire to promulgate a particular view of the past, among a particular sector of the population or in a particular geographical area). We argue that postcontemporary sources cannot, per se, be accepted at face value, but must be checked against contemporary evidence. This evidence may include written accounts, preferably several from different places, so as to cancel out the personal biases and shortcomings of a single author or culture. But even better are material remains from the period in question. A rock inscription presents no problems of transmission history. Similarly, an archaeological site represents what people did, not what a more or less contemporary author and/or his later copiers thought they did or wanted others to believe they did. The slogans on coins proclaim what the State thought or wanted others to think at the date on the coin, distilled to essence in a formula and again with no copyists' interpretations; and the coins minted in a town or region can reveal who controlled that town or region at the time they were minted. All of these types of evidence are inherently more reliable than even contemporary written sources. Historians of other areas and periods routinely utilize them in the course of their research.[19] That they have so far been little utilized is a result of

---

19. For a good account of how to obtain history from archaeology, see Alcock (1971), Ch. 6.

the unusual character (from the historian's viewpoint) of Arab studies, which have frequently been confined very largely to the literary works of the Arabs themselves.

Of course, material evidence presents its own problems. For a start, only a fraction of it survives and only a fraction of that is discovered, and which fraction we have is usually a matter of chance. But then this is true also of written sources. Secondly, material evidence appears to require a much greater effort of interpretation than written sources do. Archaeological remains do not explain themselves. They are like pieces of a jigsaw puzzle: it is up to us to fit them together or suggest missing links between them, and explain the meaning of each. But it is preferable to have to do this oneself, knowing all the hypotheses and reasonable conjectures that went into composing the picture, than to be faced with a written account which incorporates fact and hypothesis into one integral whole, so that is no longer possible to separate out what the author originally heard from what he made of it. Raw, unsieved evidence is preferable to that selected according to unknown criteria and glued together with unknown conjectures.

In our opinion, then, the most reliable sources available for studying the early history of Islam and the Arab State are *material remains*: the results of archaeological surveys and excavations, epigraphy, and coins. More problematic, but still valuable, are *literary sources contemporary with the events they describe*. These two types of evidence may be used together, the description of events in contemporary documents being checked against the picture derived from the material remains. If details in a literary account contradict evidence from material remains, the latter is to be preferred: it is not likely that the archaeological evidence is "lying," while it is quite likely that the detail in the literary source is a later interpolation or change introduced by someone who believed the view of history current at the time that this copy of the text was made, or at some earlier time in the course of its transmission history. Where there is no corroborating material evidence, contemporary literary accounts are acceptable as evidence, but must be used with caution.

Non-contemporary literary sources are, in our opinion, inadmissable as historical evidence. If one has no source of knowledge of the 7th century except texts written in the 9th century or later, one cannot know anything about the 7th century: one can only know what people in the 9th century or later believed about the 7th.

The uselessness of works later than say, the late 1st/7th or early 2nd/8th centuries holds true for the literature of other peoples no less than the Muslim. We see little point in examining post–8th-century sources such as

Michael the Syrian, for instance, since their descriptions of 7th-century history are inevitably colored by the Traditional Account. The only trustworthy written accounts of 7th-century events from any region, then, are pre-ᶜAbbāsid: preferably 7th-century, and at the latest not post–mid-8th.

The contemporary and near-contemporary evidence, both literary and material, presents a picture of the Arab takeover of the Middle East, and of the rise of Islam, so far removed from that in the Muslim literature (and in all the other literary sources based on it) that no reconciliation is possible.[20] One is forced to choose between two incompatible paradigms: either to reject the main outline of the Traditional Account as *history*, and to formulate an alternative version based on the contemporary evidence, or to turn a blind eye to the latter and to work solely within the universe of discourse of the Muslim sources. In our opinion, the latter course is the study of literature, not history.

The picture of the Arab conquest of the Near East, and of the early Arab State, which emerges from the contemporary (non-Arab) literary accounts and from the archaeological, epigraphical, and numismatic evidence, and which will be argued in this book, may be summarized as follows:

- The Arabs took over the eastern provinces of the Byzantine Empire without a struggle, because Byzantium had already decided not to defend them, and had effectively withdrawn from the area long before the Arab takeover [Part I Chapter 2: the Byzantine East on the Eve of Invasion]. There were no major battles; at most, there were skirmishes with local troops called up by a local *patrikios* [Part II Chapter 1: The Takeover].
- The Arabs were pagan at the time of the takeover. Soon afterwards some

20. The demography of the pre-Islamic Arabian Peninsula is a good example. In sharp contrast to the demographic proliferation described by the Arabic literature (*ᶜayyam, ᶜaġānī* etc.) and the picture given by the Muslim sources of a well-populated pre-Islamic peninsula, economically and politically dominated by a Ḥijāz enjoying far-flung trading links, our non-Muslim sources of information indicate a sparse, widely-scattered peninsular population with a very low economic level. The peninsula, excluding of course the Yemen and Haḍramawt, was then as now a parched desert, which could supply only the barest sustenance to societies at a very low level of existence, and the peninsular nomads, this evidence suggests, were few and by any standard extremely poor.

or all of the ruling élite adopted a very simple form of monotheism with Judaeo-Christian overtones, which gradually, over some 100–150 years, developed into Islam. Many Arabs, however, remained pagan throughout the 1st/7th century, and an active pagan Arab cult existed in the Negev desert until abolished in the second half of the 2nd/8th century by the ᶜAbbāsids. This cult, and not that of the 6th-century Ḥijāz, provided the basis for the descriptions of "Jāhilī" paganism extant in the Muslim literature[21] [Part III Chapter 1: The Religious Background].

- Muḥammad is not a historical figure, and his official biography is a product of the age in which it was written (the 2nd century A.H.). Muḥammad entered the official religion only ca. 71/690, and the very few passing references to him in earlier literary sources should be regarded as later interpolations by copiers who knew the Traditional Account. It is much more difficult to explain why, if he existed and played the central role accorded him in the Traditional Account, there are no references to him before 71/690 not only in the popular inscriptions but also where they should have been obligatory: on the coins and in the official pronouncements of the Arab State [Part III Chapter 3: The Chosen Prophet].
- The Qur᾽ān is a late compilation; it was not canonized until the end of the 2nd century A.H. or perhaps early in the 3rd. This conclusion, reached by Schacht and Wansbrough, is supported by an analysis of extant rock inscriptions and an examination of the references to the Arab religion in the works of the peoples with whom they came in contact [Part III Chapters 5 and 6].

In presenting our reading of 7th-century history we find it necessary to encompass a much wider framework than usual. For instance, the information on the Arab religion throughout the 1st century A.H. to be gleaned from the reports of those with whom the Arabs came into contact, and from the archaeological, epigraphical, and numismatic evidence left by the Arabs themselves, differs profoundly from the Traditional Account. But in order to evaluate it, we must set it within the general pagan and monotheistic background of those years and regions to which it relates. Similarly, in the political sphere, the Arab takeover of Byzantium's

21. Cf. Nevo and Koren (1990).

eastern provinces cannot be understood without fitting it into the continuum of the region's history. This means starting from the 4th or 5th century, not the 7th. For, as stated above, the wider contemporary evidence suggests that far from fighting furiously to retain her eastern provinces, Byzantium did not seriously intend to defend them, and had not so intended since at least the mid-5th century.[22] And while the non-Arab literary sources, those written by the inhabitants of those provinces, certainly reveal a transfer of power from Byzantine to Arab rule, it is difficult to conclude from them that their writers had been subjected to an organized invasion and conquest.

This leads us to state our position on acceptance of an *argumentum e silentio*. If one's universe of discourse is defined as *how* an event took place, not *whether* it did, accounts which do not mention that event are worth very little. Since historians usually study what happened, rather than what did not, they seek the "positive" evidence of at least one unshakeable contemporary account, and tend to slight the value of "negative" evidence, such as inferences from the fact that many sources include no account of the event they are studying. But if one is trying to ascertain whether the event took place at all, the situation is different. One unshakeable contemporary account would settle the question, and the fact that there is none, if demonstrable, becomes "positive" evidence. For evidence more "positive" than that cannot exist: obviously, no contemporary source will tell us, for instance, "the Arabs are not Muslim yet," or "the Battle of the Yarmūk did not take place." They tell only what they see; so they say, for example, "the Arabs are pagan," and they do not mention the battle at all. Thus the lack of a reference to an event such as a great battle, in accounts covering the years and region where it was supposed to have happened, written by contemporaries who lived in the country concerned, and who do mention events of much lesser import, constitutes evidence in support of the hypothesis that the event did not take place. The "traditional" school tends to reinterpret this evidence: the Christian writers cannot really mean that the invading Arabs were pagan—the word must in this case mean 'Muslim'; the undated, unnamed battle, briefly described by the late 7th-century Armenian chronicler, Sebeos, must be the Battle of the Yarmūk; and so forth. The *argumentum e silentio* is thus, perhaps, an invitation to those who accept the

22. This point is discussed at length in Part I Chapter 2, "The Byzantine East on the Eve of Invasion."

Traditional Account to produce one piece of clearcut *contemporary* evidence to support their version of history.

The *argumentum e silentio* applies to the archaeological, epigraphic, and numismatic evidence no less than to the literary sources. In all these fields, the Traditional Account leads us to expect to find a certain set of phenomena in a certain area and time, and in fact we find something quite different. For instance, there have been extensive surveys of the Ḥijāz and the northern Arabian Peninsula by teams of Arab and Western archaeologists over the last few decades. They have found no evidence to corroborate the Traditional Account, even though they were expressly looking for it. In fact they have found few signs of any extensive occupation of the Ḥijāz during the 7th century C.E. They did indeed find sites from the Hellenistic, Nabatean, Roman, and even Byzantine periods, and have excavated a few of them. But no 6th- or 7th-century sites have been found which accord even partially with the descriptions of the Jāhilī Ḥijāz in the Muslim sources. In particular, no archaeological remains of pagan cult centers have been found in either Trans-Jordan or the Ḥijāz, nor any signs of Jewish settlement at Madīnah, Xaybar, or Wādī al-Qurà.[23] This contradicts the detailed descriptions in the Traditional Account regarding the demographic composition of the pre-Islamic Ḥijāz; but technically it is an *argumentum e silentio*. One may always suspend judgment, waiting for the revelations of that unknown manuscript or undiscovered site.

Others before us have raised doubts; but they have tended, as said, to adopt the view that the early decades of the Arab State and the first 150 years or so of the Arab religion are unreconstructable. We on the other hand suggest that, though much remains to be done, the evidence we do have—including some not previously available, such as the archaeological and epigraphical findings in the Negev—is sufficient to enable a preliminary attempt at reconstruction. Our own reconstruction combines

---

23. Of course no archaeological excavations have been carried out in the major religious centers, Mecca and Madīnah. This in no way affects the argument. The remains of a whole period will be found in any site which was occupied during the period in question. For example, the Biblical period in Palestine was well attested, archaeologically, long before excavations were carried out in Jerusalem; many other sites yielded archaeological evidence of it. This is not the case in the Ḥijāz and Trans-Jordan, where the phenomena, pagan and Jewish, described in the Muslim sources as characterizing the Jāhiliyyah simply do not appear in the archaeological record. Cf. Part I Chapter 4, note 4.

this existing evidence with our interpretation of the general political background. It is our hope that this study may stimulate some students of historical processes to ask those questions which the current paradigm finds unnecessary, or to go out and look for evidence for or against the view here presented.

Part I

The Background

Ah, what avails the classic bent
And what the cultured word
Against the undoctored incident
That actually occurred?

Rudyard Kipling

1

The Foundering of Empire

In the third decade of the 7th century Arab tribesmen took possession of the eastern provinces of the Byzantine Empire. This would appear to be no mean feat, and the obvious question is, why did they win? The classical Muslim literature portrays a series of pitched battles against the forces of a mighty power, and ascribes the Arab success to their newfound faith. They won, in short, because God was on their side. The current Western version suggests that the Arabs won because the Byzantine Empire had been weakened and impoverished, first by Justinian's partially successful but exhausting attempts to regain the western provinces and then by the Persian wars of the early 7th century. Heraclius conquered the Persians but was left in no state to withstand the Arabs.

Archaeological work over the past decade and a half, together with evidence from literary sources, suggests that neither of these views is accurate. An examination of Byzantium's actions in her eastern provinces indicates that she had already decided, long before Justinian, not to defend militarily the regions south of Antioch. From the late 4th to the early 6th century, imperial troops were gradually withdrawn. They were replaced, if at all, by local militia and Arab garrisons, who were themselves demobilized in the mid-6th century. In many cases they were not replaced: along the whole of the eastern *limes*, forts were abandoned. Defense was increasingly transferred to Arab tribes organized as *foederati* ("allies"). By the early 7th century, both before and especially after the 7th-century Persian wars, Byzantium's eastern provinces existed in a military and political limbo.

This gradual process of military withdrawal will be examined in Chapter 2. But while it is feasible to document a series of actions which can best be accounted for by postulating such a decision, it is not so easy to suggest reasons for it. The historical documents that might shed light on the subject (for instance, the Byzantine state archives) are lacking; and archaeological remains attest the results of decisions, not the reasons for them. Our own explanation of Byzantium's attitude to her eastern provinces, and her consequent decision to give them up, is based on our view of political processes in general. The rest of this chapter summarizes our interpretation; the detailed arguments for it are presented in the remaining chapters of Part I.

According to our interpretation of political processes, the attitude of a state or empire to its provinces is determined by the interplay of forces between the various sectors which make up the state's political élite. Since the interests of different élites almost invariably conflict to a greater or lesser extent, a state's actions will be determined by the interests of that or those élite(s) which enjoy a dominant political influence on the policy-formulating sectors of the civil service or state bureaucracy. This view leaves little room for the emperor as the originator or pursuer of major long-term policies. In the case of Byzantium, at least, the emperor was indeed often little more than a figurehead. His secure position was only a façade; behind the pomp and circumstance, he was constantly faced with plots, intrigues, and revolts, especially during the earlier centuries, before the right of succession became better established.[1] From the 4th century C.E. to the end of the Byzantine Empire, nearly two-thirds of the emperors ascended to the throne as a result of revolution, deposing the one before them; and more revolutions failed than succeeded. The emperors who came to the throne in this manner were often from low walks of life—peasants or artisans—and of slight education if any. So although in theory all decisions depended on the emperor, this was clearly no more than propaganda for mass consumption. His role in determining policy was in practice slight, for policy formulation requires information, and he was dependent for that information upon the civil service.

The imperial civil service was "extremely costly, highly traditional in its methods, often corrupt" but nonetheless usually efficient.[2] Its corruption

1. Diehl (1957), p. 137.
2. Baynes and Moss, eds. (1961), Baynes' Introduction, p. xxiv.

indicates that its members were mostly concerned with advancing their own personal careers and wealth; and this meant that it could easily be used as an instrument for implementing the wishes of the rich and powerful: those members of élite sectors who had the wealth and the political influence to impress their wishes upon the civil service's policy-formulating stratum. The top government posts were held by such men, usually members of the great families, with a fixed relationship between office and social rank. These powerful ministers, and the top levels of the Byzantine civil service, together with their family and social ties, constituted a de facto ruling élite which both determined and maintained the consistent enactment of policy.

One key task of the civil service, then as now, was to sift the information to be presented to the emperor: to separate the important from the trivial, to formulate possible policies, and to present them to the emperor for decision. These included not just short-term responses to particular events, but long-term policies; and the bureaucratic machine's view of what information was relevant and should be forwarded to the emperor was governed by the policies which it itself had formulated in response to the pressures of the dominant élites. The bureaucracy not only supplied the emperor with information, but effectively shielded him from what it did not want him to know. In theory the emperor was all-powerful; in practice he had little possibility of making decisions which countered the policies formulated by the civil service. Those policies would have been the ones deemed desirable by the dominant élites.

An empire is acquired through the actions of individual members of those élites to whom territorial expansion will bring wealth and power (for instance, generals, or members of families who may expect to supply provincial governors). In the early stages of empire-building, enough wealth may accrue to enough members of enough élite sectors to ensure a consensus in favour of continued expansion. But the very process of enrichment and provincial administration changes the nature of the mother state: the economy diversifies, its complexity increases, and the structure of its ruling élites changes accordingly. Each élite sector strives to increase its own wealth and influence; depending on its sources of wealth, this may or may not require an empire. The main division of dominant interests becomes that between those whose wealth and political influence derive from empire (e.g., holders of posts in provincial governments, or the contractors and suppliers of goods and services to the provinces) and those who acquire these assets by other means (e.g., commerce, including the control of customs and other taxes, and finance). The former tend to be proponents of empire-building, whereas the latter have nothing to gain from further augmenting the masses of human beings who fall under the direct jurisdiction and responsibility of the mother state. The time comes when the scales of political influence tip in favor of those élites whose wealth and power do not derive from *rule over* the empire and who see the provinces (or colonies) as liabilities. In their opinion, the center of the political system should not be burdened with the business of checking and manipulating and catering to great multitudes of strangers living in faraway countries; it is far more profitable to let them govern themselves, to loan their governments money, and to trade with them.[3] Once the influence of sectors that hold these views becomes dominant, the policy of the state will shift in that direction.

Having made such a decision, the state faces two major problems. One is how to continue to control the foreign sources of wealth, and to ensure that no other state becomes strong enough to challenge her right to do so, without having to be responsible for the foreign population and to finance its administration. One possible solution is to divide the areas to be divested into many petty kingdoms and hand them over (or allow control of them to pass) to many different tribal or national groups, mutually hostile and divided by race and religion. Another is to hand them over to tribal élites who see themselves as imperial clients, and to maintain their client status by cultural, political, and financial means. Byzantium adopted several variations and different combinations of these solutions.

The other problem is how to shed the "white man's burden" of political responsibility for and administrative management of the provinces, in the face of opposition from minority but still vocal and powerful elements at home, without causing turmoil or even civil war in the mother state. One strategy could be to achieve a consensus among the different élites. This, however, is rarely practicable. There are always "empire-builders," élite sectors whose position derives from governing the provinces, rather than trading with them or loaning money to them; these sectors are, naturally, unlikely to compromise. Another strategy, one with a better chance of success, is to avoid proclaiming a policy of ending direct administration of the provinces, and instead to demonstrate de facto inability to retain control of them. The state sheds the provinces very regretfully, because she has no

3. The empire was also not averse to finding a pretext for war with small states which had amassed wealth. The result of such a war was a license to plunder the state concerned, before signing with it a peace treaty exacting tribute for many years. The wealth of a province, on the other hand, was milked more by the provincial governor than the empire.

choice. Since this method minimizes the risks of civil war within the mother state, it is the one most likely to be adopted.

This is a long-term solution, and is costly in both time and human lives. That is no reason to reject it. History does not reveal any great concern on the part of ruling élites to avoid political decisions which would cost the lives of soldiers, or for that matter of the general population. As for time, the process of detaching provinces is in any case a slow business, compared with annexing them. Shrinkage is a more difficult strategic goal than expansion, and to shrink successfully is a much slower and more subtle process than to expand. This is essentially because an empire changes every society which it encompasses, and it is impossible just to stop taking responsibility for such societies without causing their physical and social disintegration. So the process of shedding unwanted provinces requires long, complex, and painstaking preparations; without them, either the provinces or the mother state are likely to sink into anarchy or civil war. The final act of dissociation from the provinces—the barbarian invasion, the popular rebellion—which history records as the sole reason for it, is actually only the tip of the iceberg. The rest of the iceberg is hidden in the classified papers of the state archives, if indeed it is documented at all. A province, or satellite state, is never lost overnight, nor abandoned in a few months. Outsiders simply do not see the years, decades, and even centuries of preparations that have gone into enabling the final public act of separation.

A key point in determining Byzantium's strategy regarding her eastern provinces was that the East was rich and quite densely populated. The cities were numerous and prosperous, the economy in general and trade in particular were developed, and wealth was quite evenly spread. We suggest that Byzantium saw the East as an important source of her future wealth. The Byzantine aim in the East was therefore to keep the area intact and prosperous while transferring control; to keep it at an economic level that would enable its active participation in trade profitable to Byzantium, while turning its day to day government over to others. Byzantium therefore had to be careful, while demonstrating her inability to retain control of the eastern provinces and de facto withdrawing from them, to avoid abandoning them to anarchy. Skillful diplomacy was required.

Diplomacy is the art of creating situations. If events are caused by chance and necessity, it is the task of the diplomatic machine to ensure that the role of chance is negligible and the demands of necessity overwhelming. Long-term diplomatic goals are achieved by creating situations that force a sociopolitical response in the required direction. If, with all this in mind, we analyze what actually happened in the early centuries of the Byzantine

Empire, we can derive a list of the strategies the empire used to shed responsibility for the unwanted provinces. The main strategies this analysis reveals are as follows:

- **Transfer local government to the local civil and religious élites.** This was not as simple as it sounds. The East's evenly spread prosperity meant that there was no single aristocratic élite of great wealth and influence, to whom power could easily be transferred: "While Gaul and Italy fell into the hands of half a dozen great clans, ten families at least competed for influence round Antioch alone. The gains of a Greek civic magnate remained limited to his locality, and the city itself remained the focus of his energies."[4] Any plans that included keeping the East prosperous would have to preserve this situation. Fostering local civil élites was therefore a complex undertaking, though the attempt was made, especially towards the end of the transition period, and the population was given enough autonomy to manage its own day-to-day affairs at the local/municipal level. A more promising line of attack, perhaps, was to utilize the governing ability of an organized church. Like the civil élites, the local church was encouraged, indeed often forced by persecution, to become organizationally independent of the imperial Orthodox Church and to develop its own leadership.
- **Foster religious differences between different local groups.** In addition to fostering local autonomy, national identity was defined in terms of religious affiliation. The local church was defined as schismatic or heretical; this enabled Byzantium to absolve herself of the responsibility she would otherwise have had towards a Christian population. Where possible, several local religions or religious variants were fostered; for if a local, organized church was to inherit local loyalties, there would have to be one or more local organized churches competing with the Melkite for allegiance. Similarly, if populations were to be separated along lines of religious differences, there would have to exist variants of religion over which to dispute. These considerations led to an imperial interest in fostering both religious schism and local autonomy, in which local politics were inseparable from the local religious context. The result was to split the population into different sectors, each controlling dissent within itself while being openly or covertly hostile towards the rest. This strategy

4. Brown (1971), p. 43.

minimized the danger that the different religious communities would combine to form a common mainstream culture and society which could compete for supremacy with the mother state.

- **Alienate the local population from the emperor and his administration.** The population was brought to regard the empire and its administrators as foreign bodies, obeyed out of expediency but generally hated. Such a relationship between the empire and its constituent peoples made the latter the emperor's subjects, rather than compatriots with reciprocity of expectations and a common identity.
- **Borders in flames: foster constant border troubles.** In the many border clashes with the Persians, the initiative in engineering hostilities usually came from the Byzantine side. For constant border troubles encourage the would-be empire-builders to switch from attack to defense: to think of preserving what they have, rather than continuing to annex territory and thereby harnessing the state to an ever heavier load. Border troubles have the added advantage of demonstrating that the state is incapable of defending the provinces. This connects with another strategy:
- **Populate the border areas with "barbarians":** barbarian tribes that cause trouble and barbarian "allies" to deal with them. **Acculturate these barbarian tribes on the borders,** so that when the empire withdraws and control passes to them, they will be up to the task of maintaining law and order.

In engineering results according to this long-term policy, Byzantium's main tools were money and diplomacy. Intense diplomatic activity, including formal treaties with valuable allies, was a Byzantine hallmark throughout her history.[5] Money was an especially valuable diplomatic tool. The richest state in the world in her time, Byzantium used her wealth not only to overwhelm foreign ambassadors with the splendor of her court,[6] but in many other practical ways. For instance,

> Justinian kept all the neighboring barbarian kings in imperial pay; he granted annual subsidies and gave magnificent presents to the Hun princes of the Crimea, Arab emirs of the Syrian marches, Berber chieftains of

---

5. See Diehl (1957), pp. 60–68 for details.

6. For details and examples, a useful compilation may be found in Hendy (1985), p. 268.

> North Africa, the rulers of far Abyssinia, of the Lombards, Gepids, Heruls, and Avars, Iberians ... and Lazes.[7]

This was not Justinian's private policy; it was a mainstay of Byzantine diplomacy throughout the ages. Examples may be found in Procopius regarding Justinian,[8] and in the *Continuation of Theophanes* regarding Theophilus. Constantine Porphyrogenitus[9] records a list of gifts intended for the king of Italy, Hugh of Provence, in 935, to induce him to fight against other Italian princes, and Anna Comnena records those sent by Alexius I to the German emperor Henry IV in 1083. Basil II used the method to induce ʿAḍud al-Dawlah to renew a truce in 983, as did Constantine IX to al-Mustanṣir in 1045.[10] Alexis Comnenus used the same means in his dealings with the barons of the First Crusade.[11] And the same principle of keeping client states dependent by financial means had been used by Rome of the late Republic, though she tended to do it by keeping them in her debt rather than directly financing them. All the emperors granted subsidy payments to the barbarians in both East and West. Theodosius, for instance, subsidized Alaric; the emperors from Justinian to Heraclius subsidized the Ġassānids and the Beduin tribesmen of the northern Arabian Peninsula, and those before them subsidized a series of Arab allies—*foederati*—from at least the 4th century on. While the subsidies were being paid, such tribes functioned as protectors of the empire, not attackers. They supplied soldiers to the army as part of the agreement,[12] and they acted as buffers between the empire and "untamed" barbarians beyond the frontier. But the real effect of the subsidies was seen when they were suddenly and inexplicably withdrawn—as they were, inevitably, just when the empire could apparently least defend itself against the anger and frustration thus unleashed.

In the eastern provinces with which this book is concerned, the Byzantine preparations for withdrawal in accordance with this general strategy can be traced from the early 4th century C.E. The Tetrarchy seems to have been the time when the change in the dominant political strategy occurred: when the major policy decisions were made to stop direct

---

7. Diehl (1957), p. 55.
8. Procopius, *History of the Wars,* II.xxviii.44.
9. *De Caerimoniis,* II.44.
10. The above examples were collected by Hendy (1985), pp. 268–69.
11. Diehl (1957), p. 55.
12. Ibid., p. 60; Heather (1986), p. 290.

administration of the provinces. From then on we can trace, over a period of about three hundred years, the remarkably consistent implementation of this policy in the East: to make the local population hate the emperor and his representatives; to foster an alternative, locally based form of government; to prepare outsiders ("barbarians") to assume responsibility for the areas concerned; and finally to allow them in to take over. The method of fostering hatred was religious persecution; the alternative form of administration was the hierarchy of a church which was carefully encouraged to identify itself in local, "national" terms, and the outsiders were the Arabs.

The remaining chapters of Part I examine the working-out of this policy. Chapter 2 considers the evidence for Byzantine de facto military and administrative withdrawal in the East, and the transfer of military dominance to Arab tribes. Chapter 3 deals with the strategy of fostering local religions and religious élites, and of transferring administration to the local church and élites, many of whom were also ethnically Arab. Chapter 4 examines in more detail the Arab population of the Arabian Peninsula and al-Šām (Syria–Palestine–Trans-Jordan), and the Byzantine policy of importing Arabs from the peninsula and from areas under Persian control into the desert interface areas between al-Šām and the peninsula.

2

The Byzantine East on the Eve of Invasion

The imperial decision not to defend the eastern provinces, which was taken, we consider, during the Tetrarchy, found its first expression at the end of the 3rd century C.E., when Diocletian redivided the provincial borders. **Map I.2.1** shows the area before his reforms. The central province of Syria Palaestina (which had been called Judaea until the Bar-Kochba revolt) included an area from the Golan (Gaulanitis) in the north to a line between al-ᶜAriš and the Dead Sea at Wādī al-Mujīb in the south, and from the Trans-Jordanian highlands in the east to the Mediterranean. North of Syria-Palaestina lay Syria; east and south of it, Arabia, a vast province which included the Negev, ᶜAravah, the mountains of Edom and Moab, and the area shading into the desert to the east. Arabia was essentially the interface area between the fertile areas of Palaestina and the desert nomads. Diocletian split Arabia into two, and transferred its southern half—the Negev, ᶜAravah and southern Trans-Jordan—to Provincia Syria-Palaestina. At the same time he extended the remaining northern half to the north and east, including in it the Bashan (Batanaea) and Ḥawrān (Auranitis: see **map I.2.2**). The areas transferred to Syria-Palaestina were placed under the military control of the *dux Palaestinae*, stationed at Aila (ᶜAqabah) with one legion, the tenth. The new Provincia Arabia was the military responsibility of the *dux Arabiae* with two legions, the third and the fourth.

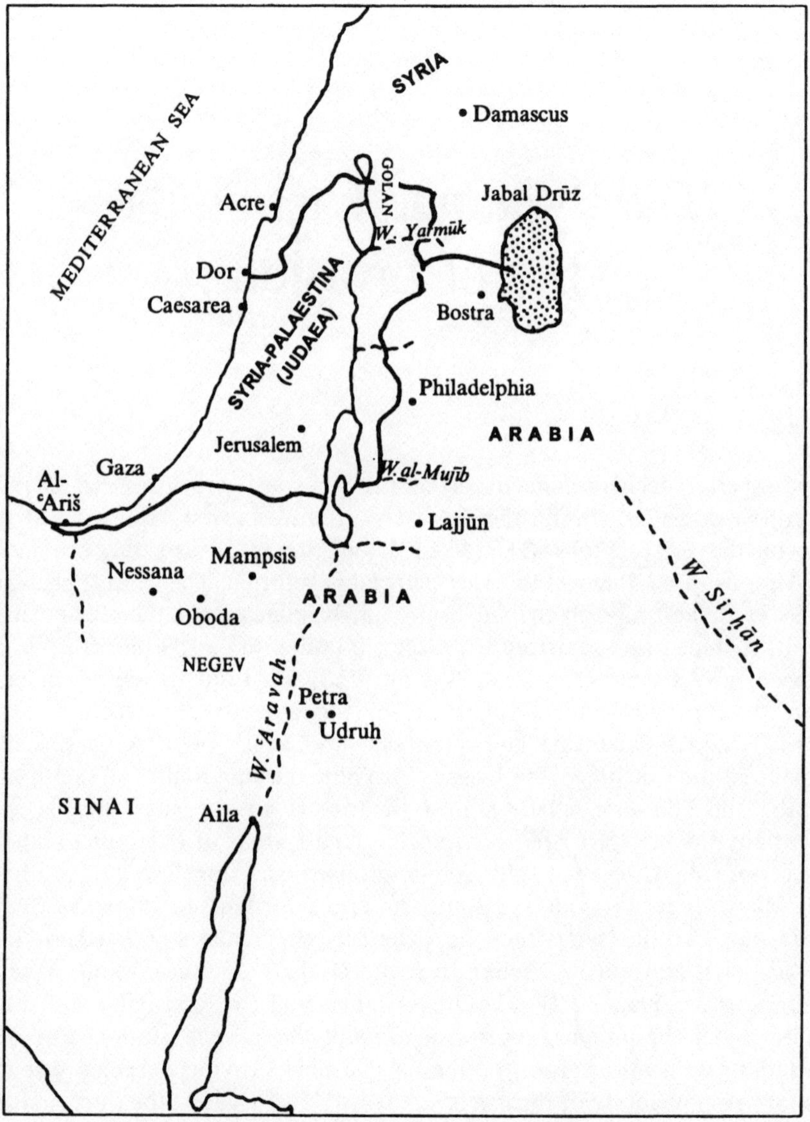

Map I.2.1. The pre-Diocletianic provincial borders.

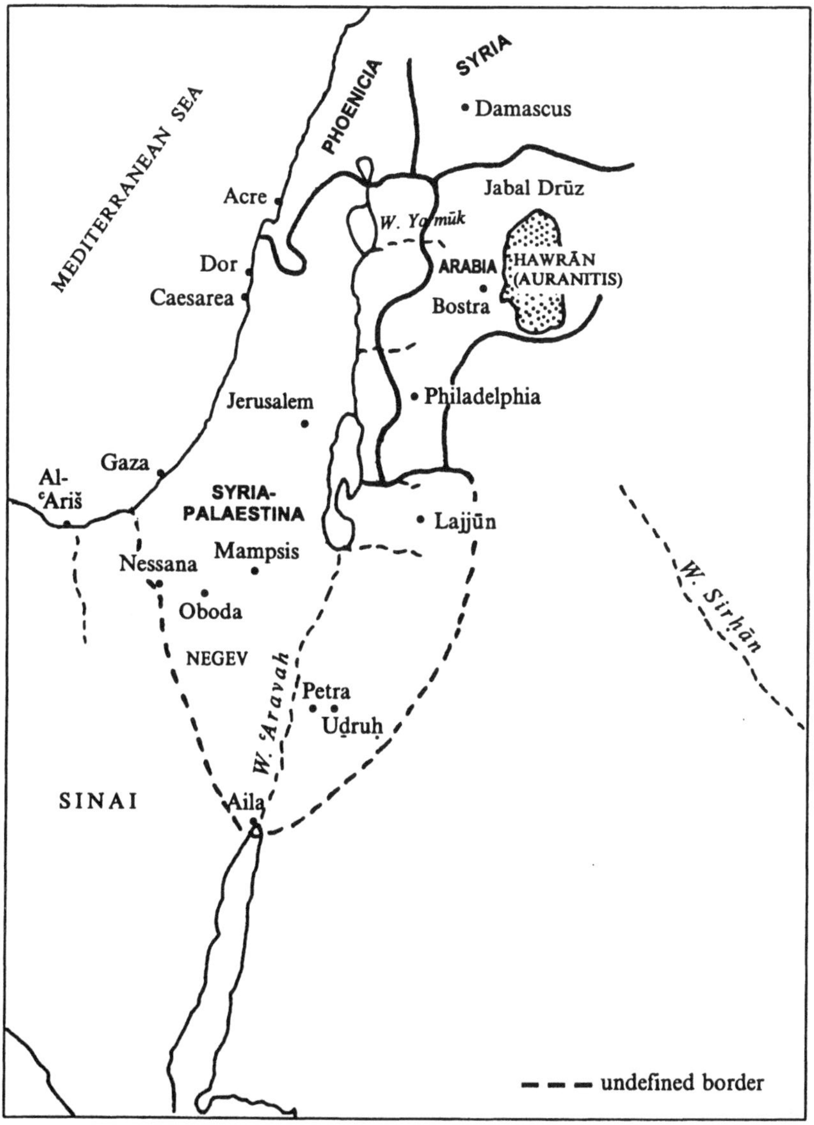

Map I.2.2. The provincial border after Diocletian's changes.

Major administrative changes are not undertaken lightly, without compelling reasons. We understand those detailed above as signaling the beginning of a new Arab policy on the part of the empire. The division defined two interface areas between the *oikoumenē* and the desert, one to the south and one to the northeast. Diocletian's changes weakened military control of the southern interface area between the Byzantine provinces and the northern peninsula, by removing it from the military sphere of control of the *dux Arabiae* and his two legions, and leaving it with only one, and that stationed at Aila. The area which the *dux Palaestinae* was now expected to control with one legion was larger than that controlled by the *dux Arabiae* with two.

In the mid- or late 4th century[1] Byzantium split Syria-Palaestina into a northern province, renamed Palaestina, and a southern one, Palaestina Salutaris (**Map I.2.3**). Around 425 C.E. she defined the whole area as Palaestina, but divided it into three small provinces. Palaestina I (Prima) was the central region, Palaestina II (Secunda) the northern region, with its capital at Scythopolis (modern Beit She'an), and Palaestina III (Tertia) the southern, the area formerly called Palaestina Salutaris (**Map I.2.4**). The main result of these two changes was to include the southern interface area in a separate province, Palaestina III. As we shall discuss below, most of Palaestina III was not seriously defended.

In the early 6th century, when the Emperor Anastasius made peace after the Ġassānid and Kindite attacks of 498–502,[2] Byzantium adopted the tribal confederations of Kindah and Ġassān as *foederati*, officially independent "allies." The Kindite chief, al-Ḥariṯ (Arethas), received the title of phylarch of Palestine,[3] and the Ġassānid, who was probably called Jabalah (Gabalos), became phylarch of Arabia and perhaps also of Phoenicia Libanensis to the north.[4] Initially, then, the two confederations may have

1. The accepted date is 358 C.E.; Mayerson (1988) argues quite convincingly that the change was probably later, ca. 390–393 C.E.

2. These may have been linked. Shahîd suggests that the Kindites attacked in 498 C.E. following an appeal for help from the Ġassānid chief, who attacked Palestine (Palaestina III) and was defeated by the *dux Palaestinae*, Romanus (Shahîd [1989], pp. 121, 125–29). The reason for the Ġassānid attack, Shahîd speculates, was Anastasius' refusal to renew the lucrative treaty that the previous Ġassānid chief, Imruʾ al-Qays, who died in 498, had had with Leo I.

3. Theophanes, *Chronographia*, vol. I.141, 143–44. We do not know which Palaestina is meant; Shahîd conjectures that it may have been Palaestina III (Kawar [1960], p. 60).

4. The title of phylarch implied control of the Arabs living in the provinces concerned, not of territory as such.

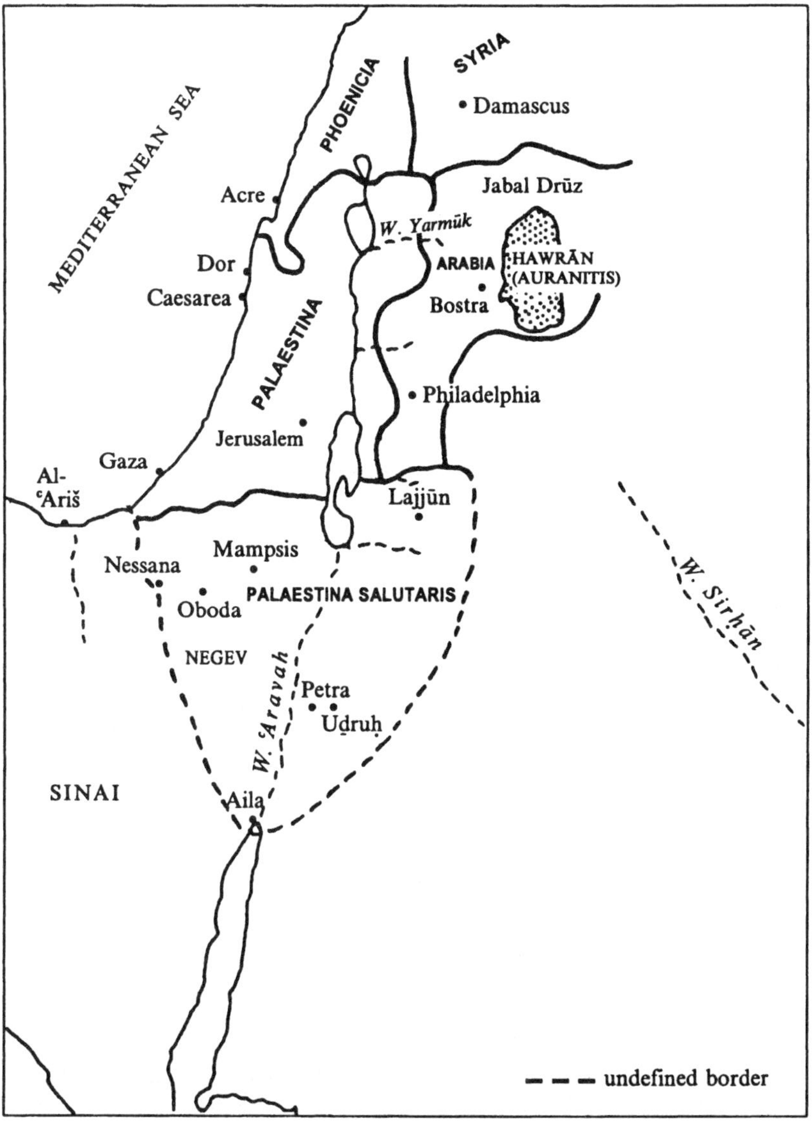

Map I.2.3. The provincial borders in the late 4th century C.E.

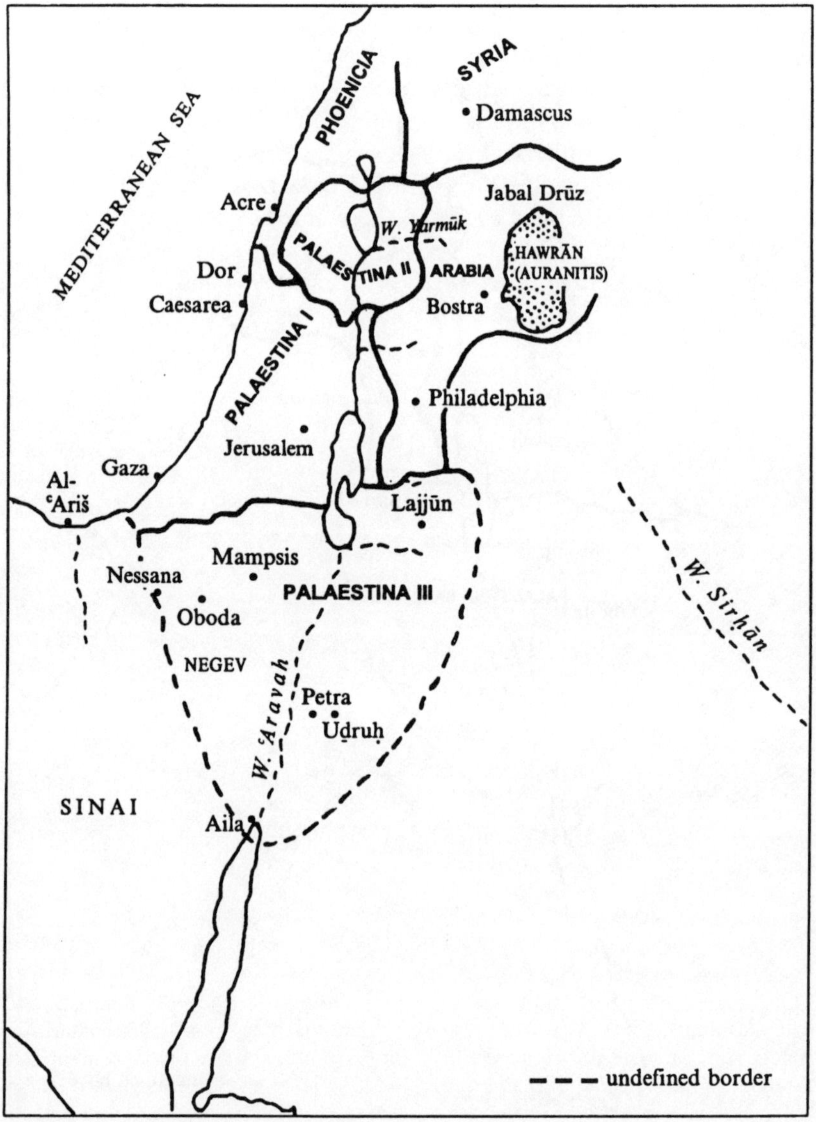

Map I.2.4. The provincial borders in the 5th century, after ca. 425 C.E.

been seen as of equal importance, jointly replacing Salīḥ as the main Byzantine federates in the border area. But by the time al-Ḥarīṯ the Kindite died in 528 C.E., Byzantine policy had shifted decidedly in favor of the Ġassānids.[5] In 530 or 531, within two or three years of al-Ḥarīṯ the Kindite's death, Byzantium created a kingdom (*basilea*) of Ġassān in the northern interface area along the Syrian border and around Provincia Arabia, raising the Ġassānid chief (another al-Ḥarīṯ: al-Ḥarīṯ bn Jabalah, probably the son of the previous Ġassānid chief) to the status of a king. This kingdom became responsible for frontier security along the whole of the eastern *limes*, from the Euphrates to Trans-Jordan.[6] It also seems to have gradually assumed at least some administrative functions. For instance, we know that in 578 al-Munḏir, the Ġassānid king, had an administrator (*epitropos*) called Flavios Seos. H. Kennedy (1985) concludes that the Ġassānids "ran something of a parallel administration" with the Byzantines, at least in northern Provincia Arabia, around Bostra the capital.[7]

At the same time as al-Ḥarīṯ bn Jabalah was made king of the *basilea* of Ġassān, Abū Karīb bn Jabalah, who was most probably al-Ḥarīṯ's brother,[8] was appointed phylarch of the northwest peninsular region, around Tabūk. This new phylarchy supposedly reached up to the Wādī Sirḥān and, as S. Smith (1954) quite convincingly suggests, as far as the southern border of Palaestina III around Aila (ᶜAqabah).[9] Its capital was named Phoinikon, "palm grove," a name that fits any of the region's few large oases; it is convenient to use this name, as Smith does, for the whole phylarchy.[10]

---

5. It is not impossible that al-Ḥarīṯ the Kindite's death was the result of this shift in policy: John Malalas relates that he was forced to flee to the desert after quarreling with the *dux Palaestinae*, and was killed by the Laxmids (*Chronographia* [Bonn], pp. 434–35). That Byzantium engineered the quarrel is of course pure conjecture, but this merely places it on an equal footing with the explanations offered by other students of this region and period, so slight are the known facts.

6. Parker (1986b), p. 652.

7. Kennedy, H. (1985), p. 174.

8. Cf. the dam inscription of Abraha at Mārib, translation given by Smith, S. (1954), p. 440; and ibid., p. 443. The Muslim sources relate that the "king" of Dumat al-Jandal (= Phoinikon?: see note 10) was a member of the Ġassānids and was probably in touch with Byzantium. (Sirah 2:526; al-Balaḏurī, *Anṣāb*, 382; Waqidī, 403. We are indebted to Simon [1989], p. 134 n. 108 for these references.)

9. Smith, S. (1954), p. 443.

10. Simon (1989), p. 134 n. 108 points out that Hartmann's *Die arabische Frage* identifies the oasis of Phoinikon with Dumat al-Jandal, modern al-Jawf at the southern end of the Wādī Sirḥān.

Thus by 530–531 the whole interface area, from the Syrian desert to the northwest peninsula, was under the control of Ġassān and Phoinikon, whose leaders were chosen by Byzantium from the same family.[11] Concomitantly, Byzantium weakened the kingdom of Kindah by persuading its ruler, Qays, the grandson of al-Ḥarīṯ the Kindite, to divide his kingdom between his two brothers, and himself come north to Palaestina, where he was given the title of Hegemon of the Palaestinas and disappeared from history.[12] The Kindite confederacy had already begun to break up upon al-Ḥarīṯ the Kindite's death, with the rebellion against Kindite overlordship of the tribe of Maᶜadd.[13] Qays' departure with a large part of his tribe probably struck the final blow.[14] This weakening or perhaps even abolishment of Kindah must undoubtedly have strengthened the phylarchy of Phoinikon.

The function allotted to Ġassān and Phoinikon was political as much as, if not more than, military. However, the Byzantine attitude to the two phylarchies differed. Ġassān was a Byzantine client state, but Phoinikon, though recognised as a phylarchy, was the emperor's personal property. Officially it had been given to him as a personal gift by the local chief, who earned thereby the title of phylarch, and was described as a desolate, remote, and utterly useless stretch of desert with no potential interest for the empire.[15] This formal definition is contradicted by Phoinikon's 6th-century history. For instance, its phylarch sent an embassy to the meeting at Mārib in era year 657 (ca. C.E. 539)[16] which was attended by delegations from the two empires, the Byzantine and Sassanian, and their three major phylarchies—Ġassān, Phoinikon and Ḥīrah.[17] Its phylarchic "dynasties" were also changed, not without appropriate imperial concern

11. Smith (1954), p. 464 gives 527 as the date of appointment of al-Ḥarīṯ and Abū Karīb as phylarchs; Parker (1979) gives it as about 530, and Shahîd also prefers a date between 528 and 531 (Kawar [1960], p. 66).

12. Kawar (1960), pp. 66–70. The source for the little we know of Qays the Kindite is an abstract made by the Patriarch Photius in the 9th century of the account by Nonnosus, who, like his father Abram, was Justinian's special ambassador to Qays.

13. Kawar (1960) and (1960a), relying on Procopius, *History*, I.xx.9–10.

14. Compare the fate of Ġassān when it outlived its usefulness to Byzantium some three quarters of a century later (see below, p. 45).

15. Procopius, *Wars*, I.xix.8–14; q.b. Smith (1954), p. 428.

16. Smith, S. (1954), pp. 441, 443, 447.

17. The delegations are listed in the Mārib dam inscription, ibid., p. 440.

and intervention.[18] But on the basis of the officially declared view of its worthlessness, Phoinikon was never incorporated into the empire. It was therefore not a Byzantine province, and was unrestricted by any official pact or allegiance sworn to the emperor; its chief was nobody's vassal. On certain occasions he acted in accordance with Byzantine interests; on others Phoinikon, or bands which should be regarded as under Phoinikon's control, harassed the Trans-Jordanian border of Palaestina III and the southern border of Provincia Arabia. Such attacks probably increased with the declining Byzantine presence in the late 6th century. Phoinikon-controlled units may also have led forays into the Negev.[19]

Thus a new geopolitical factor, Phoinikon, was deliberately introduced in the northern peninsular area, from Wādī Sirḥān to Tabūk and southward to al-ᶜUlā. It had a special status as an independent, recognized Arab polity situated in a formidable geopolitical and strategic position, and it participated actively in the area during the 6th century, both diplomatically and militarily. Although it was officially independent, and even on occasion anti-Byzantine, it was de facto controlled by Constantinople. More remarkable still, the empire further enhanced its special status by *subordinating the Arabs living in Palaestina III to the phylarch of Phoinikon.* (This is why S. Smith deduces that Phoinikon adjoined the southern border of Palaestina III.[20]) Abū Karīb was named phylarch of Palestine by Justinian;[21] as Smith notes, this means that he was put in control of the Saracens in Palestine, i.e., of the *Arab inhabitants*, not of the provincial administration.[22] The empire, then, granted the Arabs living within its borders, in the Negev and southern Trans-Jordan, a unique status: not citizens or subjects, but what we may call "imperial guests"—guests whose allegiance was defined de jure(!) as belonging to Phoinikon, a foreign entity beyond official imperial administrative reach.

The reorganization of the Byzantine provinces resulted in the establishment of new (and essentially Arab) political authorities along the interface

---

18. Ibid., pp. 444–45.

19. Cf. the archaeological history of the eastern Negev towns of Mampsis (Kurnub, now Mamshit) and Oboda (ᶜAbdeh, now ᶜAvdat), that suffered to some extent during the end of the 6th and beginning of the 7th century; Mampsis was perhaps sacked and burnt ca. 600 C.E.

20. Smith, S. (1954), p. 443.

21. Parker (1979), p. 266.

22. Smith, S. (1954), p. 443.

area from the Negev up through Trans-Jordan to the Jūlān and Ḥawrān. Within and just beyond the imperial borders was Ġassān, a nominally independent Arab state, facing the Laxmid buffer state of Ḥīrah on the Sassanian side of the border area, along the middle Euphrates. Further south, in the northern reaches of the Arabian Peninsula and extending right up to the head of the Gulf of Eilat/ᶜAqabah, the phylarchy of Phoinikon controlled the passages to and from Arabia into Sinai, the Negev, and Trans-Jordan. Its position also enabled it to affect the middle Euphrates and Ḥīrah, by peninsular roads leading far away from the imperially guarded border roads.

In short, at the end of the 6th century Palestine, Lebanon, Syria and Iraq were surrounded by five Arab provinces/phylarchies: Ġassān, Laxm/Ḥīrah, Phoinikon, Palaestina III, and Arabia.[23] The two last-mentioned were governed by a Byzantine official (who may well have been an Arab); the others were ruled by Arabs with varying allegiances and degrees of autonomy. All five political entities shared a large, sometimes even predominantly Arab population of recently-settled or still-nomadic desert tribes in addition to the Arabs among the older-established settled population.[24] The southernmost of them, Phoinikon, was for all practical purposes an independent north-peninsular power, controlling both the peninsular Arabs and those of Palaestina III.

DEFENSE AND BORDER CONTROL

During the 4th and 5th centuries, concomitant with this geopolitical reorganization, Byzantium gradually demilitarized the eastern and southern *limes* (border area).[25] She reduced the imperial army in Syria-Palestine (and

---

23. Lebanon had its own foreign military custodians acting on behalf of the emperor—the 'Mardaites' (Vasiliev [1952], I:215 para. 3). It is noteworthy that they too, like the Ġassā nids, were withdrawn by the Byzantines as soon as the Arabs approached that area. The time was the reign of Justinian II (66–76/685–95), i.e., during ᶜAbd al-Malik's crucial first ten years.

24. For discussion of this point, see Part I Chapter 4, "The Demographic Background."

25. There is some dispute regarding the meaning of the term *limes*. It is often taken to mean a fortified frontier defense line, but Isaac (1988) and (1990) argues that it meant "border district," and was a geographical and administrative term, not a military one (see also Isaac [1986], p. 384). Similarly, Whittaker (1994) argues that in the Roman Empire a frontier was conceived of as an unorganized, indeterminate, vague area whose limits were

Egypt) to *limitanei* ("border forces") with inferior military capabilities, and increasingly transferred to the local Arab population the responsibility for defense of the eastern and southeastern *limes*: the entire area from Syria through Trans-Jordan to the Gulf of ʿAqabah and northern Arabian Peninsula. In the 6th century Justinian finally disbanded the vestiges of the imperial army, and transferred total responsibility for defense to the Arab buffer state of Ġassān, whose area of control was essentially in the northern part of the *limes*, leaving the southern sector defended only by small federate tribes whose very existence is scarcely mentioned and has to be inferred from later events.[26]

The last major military works along this eastern border were constructed under Diocletian. They included repairing and building roads, and constructing forts along the main roads (the *Via Nova Traiana*, which ran along the ridge of the Jordanian hills, and the *Strata Diocletiana* thirty to seventy kilometers to the east, between the edge of the foothills and the open desert) and in the area of the *limes* between them.[27] A legionary base camp was established in the central sector of the *limes*, at Lajjūn, and another in the southern sector, at Uḏruḥ near Petra. Both appear to date from the early 4th century, and probably formed part of the Diocletianic defense system.[28] They were, however, only about twenty percent the size of Principate legionary fortresses, and were designed to hold about two thousand men each, a considerable reduction from the full legionary size of five thousand to six thousand men or even the reduced size of three thousand.[29] The other

never clearly demarcated. We accept Isaac's and Whittaker's views, and use the term "the eastern *limes*" to mean the interface zone between the Syro-Jordanian desert and the Byzantine *oikoumenē*. This interface zone ran from the Euphrates southeast via the Palmyra region, and then south through the Ḥawrān and Trans-Jordan down to the Red Sea at ʿAqabah. For most of its length it was far from the actual Byzantine-Sassanian border, which ran along the Euphrates.

26. E.g., the fact that Byzantium stopped a subsidy payment to tribes in this sector in 632 C.E. implies that she had been paying them until that date (see below, p. 49).

27. Parker (1986b), pp. 643–45.

28. Bowersock (1976), pp. 226–27 argues an early 6th-century date for Uḏruḥ, whereas Killick (1986), p. 432 maintains that there is no archaeological evidence for a post-Trajanic (early 2nd-century) one. But Parker (1979), pp. 149–51, arguing a Diocletianic date on the basis of ceramic evidence plus a comparison with the Lajjūn fortress, is much the most convincing. Parker considers that the Ġassānids rebuilt or repaired the Uḏruḥ fortress in the 6th century; on this point see pp. 41–42.

29. Parker (1986b), p. 644.

forts were much smaller, in most cases only *quadriburgia* forty to sixty meters square, which could from the start have housed only small auxiliary units.[30] As noted elsewhere,[31] in the southern sector it is very difficult to distinguish between forts, fortified farmsteads, and large watchtowers.

After the Diocletianic fortifications were built, a considerable amount of construction continued in this eastern border zone throughout the 4th and 5th centuries. The result, revealed by archaeological surveys today,[32] was a fairly dense patchwork of forts or *burgia* along the main roads, watchtowers in the hills, and a network of subsidiary roads connecting them all. But it is not at all clear how far this indicates frontier defense activities on the part of the Roman army, or indeed the presence of a competent Roman army at all. There is a good deal of evidence that once an area was considered secure, the army was diverted to police duties (guarding against robbers, safeguarding roads, and providing escorts to caravans and pilgrims, etc.), and to this end was split up into many small units stationed in towns and villages and especially along roads.[33] This was the case in southern Syria-Palaestina from the Diocletianic period.[34] Many small watchtowers and forts along roads were essentially police stations, and the *burgi* especially, and also larger forts, served as hostels for travelers. A few extant inscriptions from Syria and Arabia record the building of *castri* explicitly for this purpose.[35] This activity of policing lines of communication occurred whether the road was far from a frontier, as in the eastern desert of Egypt, or near one, as in the eastern *limes* area of Syria-Palaestina; and the same construction pattern of forts and signal towers occurs in both. Thus the system of watchtowers, forts, and roads along the eastern *limes* is more probably evidence of peace and quiet along the frontier, freeing the army for police work, than of a need for frontier defense.

This is the more likely, because in the Byzantine period this eastern border was relatively quiet. It was never the scene of a serious military campaign, and was of secondary military importance to the empire. Throughout this period Persia was interested in peaceful relations with

---

30. Ibid., pp. 643–44.
31. Part I Chapter 4, "The Demographic Background," pp. 76–77.
32. See the works of Killick and especially Parker in the bibliography.
33. Isaac (1986), pp. 386–91.
34. Avi-Yonah (1974), p. 94, based on the *Notitia Dignitatum* and Sozimus 2.34.
35. Isaac (1986), p. 391. Parker (1986b), p. 639 agrees that the *burgi* served this function, despite his general tendency to adhere to military models.

Byzantium, and the provocations which led to the not infrequent outbursts of hostility came from the Byzantine side. Many of the settlements in the central and southern sectors of the eastern *limes* were unwalled, suggesting that Beduin raids were also not much of a threat. Raids there undoubtedly were, but these do not justify, and in any case cannot be controlled by, large-scale military defense systems. Small forts ten to twenty kilometers apart, even accompanied by a system of watchtowers, are of little use against marauding Beduin. Raiders move at night, when a watchtower garrison cannot see them; and even if the garrison had heard something, it is doubtful they could have passed on much specific information.

Parker's team in fact experimented with signaling between forts and watchtowers in the Lajjūn area.[36] They found daytime signaling to be impractical: light reflected from mirrors could not be seen from far enough away, and smoke signals tended to be dissipated by wind. Night-time signaling with torches was more successful, in that the torches could be seen up to ten kilometers away; but *what* could be signaled is more doubtful. When Parker published the first results of the signaling experiment, the detailed logs of it had not yet been analyzed. Thus although his report notes that "most posts reported successful reception and transmission of messages" (using a simple code to convey the approximate strength of the supposed attackers), his team had not yet verified that the message as interpreted at the receiving end in fact tallied with the message sent. In later publications Parker did not return to the results of the signaling experiment. At the very least this means that we do not know whether information could be accurately transmitted; and it may hint that the posts' logs, when analyzed, did not reveal results clear or positive enough to be further reported. In any case, at night the watchposts would not have had much information to send, beyond the mere fact of an intrusion. Indeed the watchtower garrisons—if such they were—would have been in a most frustrating situation: by day, when they could see what was happening, they could not signal; by night, when they could signal, they could not see. So their signal could convey the bare fact that something had happened, but not the size or position of the raiding party, for during the day this information could not be sent, and during the night, whether sendable or not, it could not be learnt.

Even if a fort, receiving a signal of some sort, sent out a patrol, it would

36. Parker (1983), p. 228.

have been unlikely to intercept a small, fast-moving band of raiders. Whereas if the intruders were not raiders, but a larger (and therefore slower) army unit, the limited garrison of the small forts might have found them but would probably not have been able to stop them. In both cases it made much more sense to rely on the *foederati*, both to control potential raiders within the province and to stop outsiders penetrating into it. All these considerations lead us to conclude that the eastern *limes* was not, and was not intended to be, a military barrier. Indeed, as Isaac also points out, in the East the term *limes* came into use only in the 4th century, and then as a geographic and administrative term, not a military one: "*limes* was not a concept used to describe the physical organization of the army."[37]

From as early as the mid-4th century, the Diocletianic fortifications along the eastern *limes* began to be abandoned. The army units stationed in the area were systematically reduced in both size and quality, and by the end of the 5th century most of the forts were no longer garrisoned.[38] The small forts at Fityān, Yassir, and Bašīr were abandoned before 500 C.E.; as far as excavation can tell, in all three cases the process was peaceful. The watchtowers in the central sector had been oriented towards Fityān; thus when the fort was abandoned, whatever signaling system may have been operational became ineffective, whether or not the watchtowers continued to be garrisoned. In fact the watchtowers not connected with settlements seem to have been abandoned before the fort was: of the nine watchtowers that Parker surveyed in the central sector of the *limes*, "all were abandoned by ca. 400."[39] After the earthquake of 363 C.E. damaged the Lajjūn legionary camp, only half its barracks were rebuilt.[40] Thus although it had been built for a two-thousand–man legion in the early 4th century, by only a few decades later its actual military strength could not have exceeded one thousand. Its garrison may of course have been reduced long before the earthquake; indeed it may never have housed a legion even of the reduced size for which it was built. In any case, even if two thousand men were initially stationed there, they were there for only a few decades at most.

By the 5th century the garrison of the Lajjūn camp appears to have been rather run-down, and military discipline very lax (for instance, there is some

---

37. Isaac (1986), p. 384.
38. Parker (1979), p. 130.
39. Parker (1987), ii:816.
40. Ibid.

evidence that soldiers' families were living inside the fortress).[41] In 500 C.E. another earthquake damaged the fort. This time it was not rebuilt, and following a third earthquake in 551 it was finally abandoned. During this last half-century the fort was in ruins, and it is therefore unlikely that it was occupied by a military unit. More probably the inhabitants were civilian "squatters."[42] The same was probably true also of the few less important forts that remained occupied at this date. If the occupants were not civilians, they were probably not regular army units but *limitanei* and/or Arab *foederati*. MacAdam (1986a) concludes that some of the Ḥawrān forts seem to have become "monastic establishments" in the 5th to 6th centuries C.E.,[43] and notes that by the start of the 6th century "there are almost no epigraphic references to Byzantine military activities" in this region.[44] At Umm al-Jimāl, farther to the north, the late Roman fort was converted to civilian use in the 5th century, its military function being transferred to a much smaller barracks, built in 411/412 C.E.[45] From the end of the 5th century, at least, the fort was an abandoned ruin. The city walls, however, were repaired during the 6th century, and so was the small barracks; but it is uncertain whether the barracks' inhabitants were soldiers or civilians. The building may well have been converted to civilian use after the rise of the Ġassānids.[46]

Some of the watchtowers farther to the south remained occupied until the late 5th century, and during the 4th to 5th centuries several forts were also built in this southern sector.[47] In these centuries there was a civilian settlement at Uḏruḥ, but it is not clear if the legionary camp there was garrisoned. The gateway in the south wall of the camp was repaired several times, apparently between the 4th and 6th centuries, which implies, as Killick argues, "continued use of the fortifications up to the end of the Byzantine period."[48] However, it is very unlikely that the fort was *garrisoned*, since the structures inside it disappeared during this same

41. Ibid., pp. 818–19.

42. Parker (1983), p. 230. Parker elsewhere suggests (Parker [1988], p. 186) that Justinian may have demobilized the garrison of Lajjūn ca. 530 C.E.

43. MacAdam (1986a), p. 536.

44. Ibid., p. 540.

45. De Vries (1985), p. 249.

46. Ibid., p. 255.

47. Parker (1979), pp. 131–83.

48. Killick (1986), p. 432.

period, most probably because they were raided for building stone.[49] Thus continued use of the fortifications does not necessarily imply the presence of a *military garrison*; it is more likely that the population of Uḏruḥ used them as a place of refuge in time of need. This would explain why the outer walls were left intact and the gateway repaired, even while the stones of the inside structures were gradually removed (probably, as said, for reuse elsewhere). In the early 6th century the camp was partially rebuilt, and Parker suggests that it and the few other camps occupied at this date in the southern sector (Kiṯarah and Xaldah) were garrisoned, not by the Byzantine army but by the Ġassānids.[50] This suggestion attempts to resolve the question of what military or quasi-military presence could have been in the area, considering that it was demonstrably not the Byzantine army. However, the Ġassānids were only just being established as *foederati* at this time, and Ġassān was further to the north. It is in our opinion more likely that repaired and/or manned fortresses in the southern sector of the *limes* reflect the presence of other Arab *foederati* in this sector and right down to ᶜAqabah, including the Wādī Sirḥān leading to Phoinikon.

The replacement of regular army units by local Arabs can also be traced during this period. Some regular army units, especially high-quality ones, were withdrawn in the 4th century. Others had been Arab from the start. From the information in the *Notitia Dignitatum* regarding the army in the East[51] it can be calculated that sixty percent of the military units in Palaestina, and sixty-seven percent of those in Arabia, were mounted on either horses or camels.[52] The names of many of these units reveal their Arab composition (e.g., *equites Thamudeni...* or *cohors III felix Arabum*). In addition, the units called *indigenae* ("locally recruited"), about half the total number of mounted units, were also presumably Arab.[53] They must have been recruited mainly from nomad tribes, like the *foederati*, whereas the *limitanei* probably came mostly from the settled (and at least partly Arab) peasant population.

Gradually, the responsibility for border defense was moved to the Arab *foederati*. At first a phylarch was paired with a *dux* in each province, and he

49. Parker (1979), pp. 131–83.

50. Ibid., p. 186.

51. Parker (1987), ii:809–10. The *Notitia Dignitatum*'s eastern information dates from 400 C.E., but is generally agreed to reflect the composition of the army since Diocletian's re-organization. It lists only units of the regular army, not *foederati*.

52. Parker (1986b), p. 644.

53. Parker (1987), ii:809–10.

and his men were paid regular subsidies.[54] But after the peace treaty with Persia of 532 C.E., Byzantine forces were further reduced, and the main responsibility for frontier defense over the whole area from the Euphrates to southern Trans-Jordan, the interface with the northern Arabian Peninsula, was transferred to the *foederati*.[55] Chief among these were the Ġassānids; but since Ġassān was in the northern sector and its main task was to counter—and eventually destroy—the Persian buffer state of Ḥīrah, other smaller Arab tribes had almost certainly been adopted as *foederati*, as the regular Byzantine army was phased out, to guard the southern sector and Wādī Sirḥān, the approach route from Phoinikon. These southern *foederati* may well have been the same tribes that were previously recruited into the *indigenae* mounted units of the regular Byzantine army formerly stationed in the *limes* area. Such tribes, containing men exposed to the rudiments of Byzantine civilization and trained in warfare, would have made very suitable *foederati*. They would in any case have had to be subsidized in some fashion, to prevent them from raiding when the army pay they had formerly received ceased to arrive. Of the regular army, only the *limitanei* remained, and they gradually degenerated into a largely hereditary peasant militia: required to raise their food by farming their own land, undersupplied, understrength, underpaid, and only sporadically drilled.[56] These, the last vestiges of Roman troops, were demobilized by Justinian.

Procopius says that Justinian increased the importance of the Ġassānids at the expense of the *duces* because the old system of pairing Roman military *duces* with Arab phylarchs separately in each province had failed to deal with the pro-Persian Laxmid confederacy.[57] It must have been self-evident that the old system had failed; but to increase the importance of the Ġassānids and dismiss the *duces* was not the only possible reaction, nor was it a purely military one. It was, rather, a political decision. One could go farther and suggest that once a policy decision had been taken to hand control of the eastern *limes* over to the Ġassānids, a real or perceived lack of

---

54. Parker (1979), p. 263.
55. Ibid., p. 264.
56. Ibid., p. 263. A law of 423 indicates that farming lands had already been assigned to the garrisons of the border forces at some previous time, and forbids others to take them from the soldiers (*Codex Theodosianus* 7.15.2); a law of 443 mentions that these lands belong to the *limitanei* "according to ancient regulation" and forbids also the imposition of taxes on them (*Cod. Theod. Nov.*, 24.4).
57. *Persian War* I.17.45–48.

military success against the Laxmids was a very convenient pretext for implementing that decision.

Procopius elsewhere says the *limitanei* were disbanded for reasons of cost.[58] But the *limitanei* had been allowed to deteriorate for a long time by now. They were so seriously underfinanced that it is doubtful if Justinian saved much by disbanding them, and militarily it made little difference whether he did or not. His action is thus much more easily read as a political declaration that the imperial army was officially no longer responsible for border defense.[59]

Thus the military duties usually carried out by the regular army were gradually transferred to Arab *foederati*, tribesmen militarily organized and under the command of phylarchs appointed by Byzantium. These duties included not only border security and the "police work" of safeguarding roads and villages and protecting the area from raids by desert tribes, but also the collection of taxes. The main tax levied in the provinces was the *annona militaris*, a yearly levy in kind (wheat, oil, and fodder) which Diocletian had formed out of several irregularly imposed special taxes, and which was intended to feed the army and civil bureaucracy in the area in which it was collected.[60] Thus the local army units who had collected it on behalf of the provincial authorities charged with this duty were also those who had consumed it. As the regular army withdrew and the *foederati* took over their duties, the collection of the *annona militaris* must have passed from the former to the latter. Presumably the tax was counted as part of the Byzantine subsidy to the *foederati*. In any case, the result of this situation was that the settled population became accustomed, already in the 6th century, to paying taxes to Arab tribesmen: the *foederati*, who were the only imperial military forces left in the area.

It is sometimes suggested that the undermanning of the *limes* should be

---

58. *Secret History* xxiv.12–14.

59. Parker (1979), p. 268. H. Kennedy (1985) comes to similar conclusions regarding the cessation of Byzantine interest in the area, independently of Parker's work which he does not cite: cf. Kennedy (1985), esp. pp. 166–67, 180–81.

60. Bury (1958) 1:46–47. The tax rate for a given year was calculated by estimating the supplies needed for the army units stationed in that area (in units of *annonae*, one *annona* being the amount needed to support a regular soldier; officers received several *annonae* according to rank) and dividing it by the number of productive land-units (Weber and Wildavsky [1986], pp. 112–13). This method was established under Diocletian and remained basically unchanged for several centuries (ibid.).

attributed to the depredations of the bubonic plague, which started in 542 C.E. in Pelusium in Egypt and swept through the eastern provinces, reaching Constantinople in 543;[61] there were further outbreaks in Constantinople in 558 and 573–74, and in the West in 570–71.[62] About a third of the population is reported to have died. The toll was greatest in the coastal cities; in sparsely populated desert areas the disease petered out, so that desert garrisons should not have been greatly affected; but the suggestion is that the garrisons in towns would have been much reduced, and that soldiers would have had to be withdrawn from the less-affected *limes* areas to replace those in the cities and elsewhere in the empire. The problem with this argument is that the evidence for withdrawal from the military installations along the *limes* comes from the mid-4th through the 5th centuries (as discussed above, most of the forts had already been abandoned by 500 C.E.), whereas there were no recorded outbreaks of plague from the mid-4th century[63] to that of 542–43.

By the end of Justinian's reign (mid-6th century) Byzantium was no longer investing in the upkeep of her eastern provinces. Civilian building in the cities had rarely been initiated or paid for by the imperial authorities even in earlier times; where it was, this was almost always following a petition by the city (such as to rebuild after a disaster) or because of personal contacts at court or direct patronage by a member of the imperial family.[64] Most of the public buildings in the provincial towns, Isaac argues, were in fact financed by the local inhabitants: "The fact that constructing and repairing public buildings became one of the numerous compulsory and unpaid personal services established by law, like maintaining roads or transporting clothes for the army, shows clearly that the imperial government did not expect to pay for it."[65] From the Persian invasion of 540 on, even the military buildings seem to have been financed by the local population, not the imperial government.[66] In Syria and the northern half of

61. The chief source for this outbreak is Procopius, *History of the Wars*, ii.22–23; a full list of sources may be found in Bury (1958), 2:62 n. 1–4.

62. Jones, A.H.M. (1964), 1:288.

63. The latest recorded outbreak in the 4th century was in 370–71, before Diocletian's reign.

64. Isaac (1990), Ch. 8, esp. pp. 369–71.

65. Ibid., p. 369.

66. Kennedy, H. (1985), pp. 166–67, 180–81. For instance, along the fringes of the Syrian desert there is evidence for "local landowners, probably supported by ... alliances with the neighbouring nomads, taking over responsibility for security in the area" (p. 167).

the eastern *limes* defense was mainly in the hands of Arabs. In the southern half of the eastern *limes*, the only military presence was that of the small federate tribes supplementing the Ġassānids farther to the north.

In the late 6th century the Emperor Maurice decided to dismantle the Ġassānid kingdom. As Caesar and general in the Persian campaign of 581 he accused al-Mundir, the Ġassānid phylarch, of treachery, and as emperor abolished the Ġassānid buffer state in 584. The Ġassānid confederation disintegrated into its fifteen constituent tribes, and as Frend notes, "Rome lost a powerful ally in her struggle with Persia, and even more important, the protection of her south-east frontier from raids of hostile Arabs."[67]

From the Arab literature on the invasion it would appear that by the early 7th century Byzantium had drawn her de facto borderline from west to east approximately at Antioch, and stationed her forces behind it.[68] Militarily, the area south of this line was undefended by the empire. In the later 6th century the Byzantines also withdrew northwards from their *civilian* settlements in al-Šām (the Arabic term for the Syria-Palestine area), leaving a limited imperial presence in a few selected towns. Parker sees this as a response to the insecure situation produced by the military withdrawal: "This growing level of insecurity along the Arabian frontier is reflected by the low number of sites occupied in the ... sixth and early seventh

67. Frend (1972), p. 330.

68. Cf. Brockelman (1948), pp. 52–53, or any standard history of the invasion, based on the Muslim literary sources. The Muslim literature is concerned to emphasize the strength of the opposition defeated by the Arab forces, and we do not consider the detailed accounts of the battles with the Byzantine army given in it to be historical. However, it is interesting that the traditions the Muslim historians pieced together referred overwhelmingly to the north rather than the south as the area where the Byzantine army was encountered. There were a few skirmishes in the south, probably with local militia (e.g., the Battle of Dāṯin); but the main engagements with Byzantine forces—the Battle of Faḥl, the siege of Damascus, the battle for Ḥimṣ, and the Battle of the Yarmūk—took place in the north. According to the standard Muslim account, the Byzantine army which fought at the Yarmūk had to be assembled from widely scattered areas and from other provinces. The Emperor Heraclius led the campaigns from Ḥimṣ in 634; after his defeat at the Battle of the Yarmūk he retreated to Antioch and sailed from that city (Ṭabarī, *Taʾrīx*, 3.441: in Wustenfeld, 1:2155). As noted, we do not accept as historical the account of the Battle of the Yarmūk in the Muslim classical literature; but we point out that any remembrance of the deployment of the Byzantine army the Muslim sources may preserve indicates that it was confined to the north, even beyond the borders of Palestine. This is also the picture that accords with the archaeological evidence given above.

centuries."[69] We, on the other hand, consider that both the civilian and military withdrawals were implementations of Byzantine policy, rather than the one being dependent upon the other. We would also suggest that the Sassanian onslaught was the result of the Byzantine army's withdrawal rather than vice versa. The evidence presented above suggests that the Byzantine withdrawal began at least a hundred years before the Sassanians started their forays into the empire's domains in 604, and the state of the empire's defenses in the East must have been an open invitation. In any case, the ease with which the Persians overran al-Šām indicates that Byzantine military control of Syria-Palestine (and also Egypt) was slight, and this is supported by the archaeological evidence.

Further indirect evidence of Byzantine de facto abandonment of al-Šām may be found in the Nessana papyri. The Greek papyri date from 460 to 630 C.E.[70] Until the 7th century, the Nessana scribes recorded their names in Greek, following normal Byzantine Chancery convention. But already in 601 C.E. they had abandoned this practice: in the eight papyri dated from 601 to 630 C.E., the scribes used the Arabic forms of their names, instead of the Greek. No other nonimperial influence may be discerned in the papyri: we cannot point to any new political factor which might have influenced the scribes. We see, rather, a withering of the old imperial chancery conventions, which provides an additional argument for the view that Byzantine influence and control had already waned considerably in the area—in this case the northwestern Negev—before the Persian interlude.[71]

The Persian occupation was a strange historical event. The Sassanians had come into conflict with Byzantium chiefly in the north. Their wars had been border wars in northern Mesopotamia and focusing on control of Armenia. But in the early 7th century Sassanian strategy changed. From 604 on, they sent many small warparties out in many different directions. For the first two to three years they engaged in border forays, capturing towns and plundering along the Byzantine side of the frontier, and then returning to Persia. Thus they instigated spasms of inroads into Byzantine territory, sometimes winning and sometimes losing, but never engaging in a decisive battle. In 606 they moved through Mesopotamia and turned their attention southwards, towards Syria, Palestine, and Phoenicia, capturing Jerusalem in

69. Parker (1983), p. 230.
70. Published in Colt I and III.
71. We owe this point to Avraham Negev, private communication.

614.[72] This is in sharp contrast to the northwesterly direction of their previous conflicts with Byzantium. We suggest that the change in direction of the Sassanian offensives was a natural result of Byzantium's withdrawal of forces from the area. The Armenian chronicler Sebeos says that the towns in the path of the Sassanian army, from Edessa to Antioch, surrendered without resisting, "not seeing from where might come their deliverance."[73] This, if reliable, is further evidence that Byzantine forces were not available in northern Syria. The accumulated Sassanian successes demonstrated that Byzantium was unable to defend her eastern provinces. But the Sassanians never *controlled* all the occupied territories as provinces of their expanded kingdom. Although the Byzantine provinces of Syria, Palaestina and Arabia had nominally been conquered, vast areas of them were clear of a Persian presence.

In 622–628, a renewed Byzantine offensive under Heraclius demonstrated just how insecure was the Sassanian control of captured Byzantine territory. Heraclius struck through Armenia into Persia itself, never bothering to enter Palestine and southern Syria.[74] In one major battle near Ctesiphon (628 C.E.) Heraclius destroyed the Persian army, killed the king, and entered the capital. He appointed a new king—a member of the Persian royal house who would be loyal to Byzantium—and left. In effect he had destroyed Sassanian military power, leaving the civil administration intact. The Arabs, when they came, found the Persian Empire to be but a slight military deterrent, even though administratively it was still functioning unimpaired. And along the eastern *limes* the Arab *foederati* continued their duties, and continued to receive Byzantine subsidies.

The renewal of Byzantine overlordship in the eastern provinces was marked by religious ceremonial: the True Cross was brought back to rest in Jerusalem (in 630), churches were rebuilt, and so on. But politically matters were different. Byzantium did not reenter all the "liberated areas," and Byzantine control was slight. Al-Šām was not returned to its 6th-century state of some degree of control from the imperial center. Although the imperial presence did continue to be felt—to a greater degree in areas deemed important to the empire (the northern areas, around Antioch) and

---

72. For a more detailed account of the course of the Persian campaigns, see *Cambridge Medieval History*, II:9:285–99.

73. Sebeos, ed. F. Macler (1904), Ch. 23, p. 61.

74. Ibid., pp. 293–99.

less compellingly in the other areas—a real imperial army was not stationed there, and the border area was not regarrisoned or militarily strengthened with Byzantine troops. Since the Ġassānid kingdom had been abolished a generation before, control of security on the southeastern frontier remained in the hands of the small *foederati*: individual tribes who received imperial subsidies. Byzantium now withdrew this last vestige of overt control. In 632 C.E. she stopped the subsidy payments to the tribes of the Maᶜan area. This action in the south, and the break-up of Ġassān in the north, should be seen as two documented examples of a general Byzantine policy of abandoning the defense of the whole eastern *limes*.[75] This entire area, then, was left in the hands of Arab tribes who until now, as *foederati*, had been accustomed to funding from Byzantium.

Historians who believe that Byzantium was seriously trying to defend her eastern provinces are forced to a dubious conclusion: that she truly considered feasible a defense based on Arab tribesmen, barely supplemented by a dwindling, underpaid militia and mostly ungarrisoned forts in advanced stages of disrepair. Since this viewpoint is untenable, they propose that Justinian's campaigns had depleted the treasury, and Byzantium could therefore not afford to pay for her defense needs. Byzantine sources themselves tend to cite this reason. If this theory is true, however, it must be one of the very few examples in the history of the world when a nation—any nation—has abandoned the defense of territory she considered worth defending because of a lack of funds. Had Syria been important, she would not have been exposed to such dangers for such a reason. There is, besides, considerable evidence that Byzantium's financial distress was not as great as she claimed. She did not cut back on the size of her army, and continued to expend vast sums on it in bounties and pay. Clearly she believed that she had the funds available. But she did not station these troops along the eastern *limes*. Instead, she relied on the support of numerous Arab tribal groups, which was also a very costly affair, involving large payments of gold coin from time to time. Yet despite these ongoing drains on the treasury,

---

75. It has also been seen (following the account in Theophanes, *Chronographia*, 1.335–36) as the misguided decision of a minor official, e.g., Kaegi (1981), p. 134: "A eunuch in the bureaucracy refused to pay the Arab mercenaries on the Palestinian frontier their usual annual sum ... exclaiming that Heraclius scarcely had sufficient money to pay his own regular soldiers." But minor officials do not make such policy decisions on their own. The decision to stop subsidizing the "Arab mercenaries" probably was in the hands of the bureaucracy, not of the emperor in person; but it was undoubtedly official Byzantine policy.

Heraclius' eldest son Constantine was able in 641 to provide a total of sixty-six thousand *nomismata* as a reserve to buy army support for his young son Constans II against the claims of Heraclius' second wife Martina and her two sons.[76] Constantine died in 641 C.E., the same year as his father, after only about three months on the throne,[77] so the amount he put aside for Constans II must have been taken from reserves left by Heraclius. Money was, then, quite readily available despite the drains of the Persian wars and Heraclius's reputation for indigence. The sum was, moreover, in addition to the large payments in gold made to the army in that same year.[78]

It is therefore difficult to attribute Byzantium's actions in the eastern provinces to indigence. We read them, rather, as the implementation of a consistent policy. Byzantium had long before decided not to retain control of the provinces, and her military and administrative actions throughout the 4th to early 7th centuries were a progressive implementation of that decision. Stopping subsidy payments to the Arab tribes was merely the last step in this long process.

---

76. Kaegi (1981), p. 155, relying on Nikephoros, *Hist. syn.*, 28.24–29.7. The amount was initially fifty thousand *nomismata*, later supplemented by another sixteen thousand.

77. Sebeos, *Histoire*, Ch. 32, gives the length of Constantine's reign as only a few days, an error corrected by Macler (p. 103 n. 3). It was rumored that Martina poisoned him (Theophanes 331, 341), but his provision for his son's claim on the throne suggests that he knew his health was failing; cf. Herrin (1987), p. 215.

78. Hendy (1985), pp. 625–26.

3

The Role of the Church

The de facto withdrawal of the army from the eastern provinces, discussed in the last chapter, was but one aspect of Byzantium's implementation of the decision not to retain control of them. A second aspect was the fostering of local élites who would be able to take over day-to-day administration, at least at the local level of the towns and their territories. Once the withdrawal of the army was well under way, Byzantium turned her attention towards encouraging autonomy in the local political élites. Local autonomy was based, among other things, on local religions, and especially on local variants of Christianity. This policy therefore led Byzantium to foster the development of a local church independent of the official Melkite (Chalcedonian Orthodox) church in the eastern provinces.

The history of eastern Christianity is usually explained as a long, drawn-out imperial attempt to suppress heresy, an attempt which finally failed owing to a long series of tactical blunders. We propose a different inter-pretation of the facts: that it was imperial policy to foster heresy. The existence of a loyal Orthodox majority vowing allegiance to the emperor would make it very difficult for Byzantium to give up control, since this would mean abandoning the faithful to "barbarians." Moreover, a heretical or schismatic church would find itself forced to develop its own organization separate from that of the imperial church, and would then be in a position to take over day-to-day administration of the population in the provinces as Byzantium withdrew. For both reasons, then, it would be in Byzantium's political interest, if she had decided not to defend her eastern provinces, to foster the development of a heretical or schismatic church which favored independence from the empire, and which she could disavow with few religious repercussions; and to prevent its reconciliation with Chalcedonian Orthodoxy.[1] This is precisely what she did.

Once the empire had adopted Christianity as the state religion, she decided what was Orthodox and what heretical. Her tools were councils, synodic conventions, and imperial silence and deafness, and she used them to good effect. Ecumenical councils, ostensibly convened to settle theological controversies, actually resulted in the proliferation of different sects, all claiming to be the one true Christianity. This effect did not pass unnoticed: Zacharias of Mitylene in the 6th century complained that "under the pretext of suppressing the heresy of Eutyches, Chalcedon had established and increased that of Nestorius, and that by substituting one heresy for another it had divided and confused the whole Christian world."[2]

By the mid-6th century the aim had been substantially achieved. Rome and New Rome were ecumenical, i.e., each regarded the other as a sister church (though erring and misguided), and accepted that together they formed the Universal Church. The East had been divided among several nonecumenical national churches—the Nestorian (eastern Syriac), Monophysite (Western Syriac or Jacobine), Coptic, and Armenian. The latter two were also, essentially, local manifestations of Monophysitism. By the time the openly pro-Monophysite empress Theodora died in 548 C.E., Monophysitism was the national religion in South Arabia, East Africa, Nobatia (Nubia), Egypt, Syria (except for Jerusalem), Armenia, and Mesopotamia. By the time Theodora's fervently Chalcedonian husband, Justinian, died in 565, Monophysitism had been extended to the Blemmyes of the desert east of the Nile, and not long thereafter, to the southern Nilotic kingdom of Alwah.[3] Iraq, Persia, and areas further east were Nestorian.[4] Only in

---

1. Chalcedonianism strictly speaking should mean only the doctrine, now called Dyophysitism, accepted by the Council of Chalcedon in 451 C.E. In practice it meant whatever Byzantium declared to be Orthodox at that particular time. Thus during the Monotheletic episode "Chalcedonian," like "Melkite," implied acceptance of Monotheletism; before and after it both terms meant "Dyophysite."

2. Zacharias Rhetor, q.b. Frend (1972), p. 148. Frend calls this a summary of contemporary public opinion.

3. Frend (1972), pp. 299–300.

4. In the 7th century Nestorianism did achieve some importance also in the Arabian Peninsula and the interface areas with al-Šām—if not in the greater geopolitical affairs to be discussed below, then at least among the local inhabitants; but Monophysitism was the foremost deviant creed in al-Šām.

Jerusalem and the small Nilotic kingdom of Makurrah[5] was a dominant Chalcedonian enclave preserved.

This policy was not, for obvious reasons, openly stated; but it was pursued de facto. Even Justin I (518–527), who persecuted the Monophysite church in the Byzantine East, supported its spread among the Arabs, sending Syrian Monophysite missionaries via the desert oases and the Red Sea coast of the Arabian Peninsula all the way down to the Yemen. Frend hypothesizes that he must have had no choice: "The pro-Western and Chalcedonian emperor was obliged to make use of the good offices of anti-Chalcedonians to develop relations with the peoples beyond his southern frontiers."[6] However, there seems to be no reason why the emperor should be obliged to use Monophysites as missionaries if he had preferred to distribute a different form of Christianity in those areas.[7] When war broke out in the Yemen in 523 between the "Jewish" (i.e., Judaic) king Yūsūf d̲ū Nuwās and the newly converted Monophysite Christians, Justin went to the latter's aid by inciting the king of Axum (Ethiopia) to invade South Arabia. The king promised to do so if Justin would provide the ships, which he did. Thus, using Axum as a front, Justin made it clear to all concerned that Monophysites in the Yemen were not to be interfered with. Additional effects of the move were to strengthen Monophysitism in the Najrān highlands and to threaten the Ḥijāz, and perhaps also Mesopotamia via Ḥaḍramawt.[8]

The Orthodox Justin I, then, played a large part in establishing Monophysitism as the local, national non-Chalcedonian church of the Arab kingdoms bordering the eastern provinces. Within those provinces, it was Justin who forced the Monophysites, through persecution, to break with the empire and establish an autonomous church. His equally Orthodox successor, Justinian, continued this policy of strengthening Monophysitism

---

5. Makurrah, sandwiched between the Monophysitic kingdoms of Nobatia to the north and Alwah to the south, did not stay Chalcedonian for long. At some point between 560 and 710 it united with Nobatia to form one Monophysitic kingdom, and may have converted to Monophysitism before the union (Frend [1972], p. 301).

6. Frend (1972), p. 306.

7. Indeed a few years later the next emperor, Justinian, demonstrated his public commitment to Orthodoxy by sending a Chalcedonian mission to the Nubians. It was, predictably, ill-fated, as is discussed below.

8. The "ecclesiastical policy" of the empire may be seen as the historical context for the notorious stories about the Ethiopian period in the history of South Arabia and its repercussions in the Ḥijāzi traditions.

within the eastern provinces and extending it beyond them. John of Ephesus gleefully relates how the Empress Theodora outwitted her husband and tricked the *dux* of the Thebaid into allowing her own Monophysite embassy to reach and convert the Nobatae (Nubians), while delaying Justinian's Chalcedonian mission to them.[9] This pretty and oft-retold story undoubtedly represents the official version of events put out for public consumption, and may be relied upon about as much as modern presidential press releases. Here—and not only here—Theodora acted as Justinian's accomplice rather than his adversary, enabling the emperor's public image to be staunchly Orthodox even while the needs of diplomatic policy dictated a pro-Monophysite strategy de facto. The Nubian king, Silko, having adopted Monophysitism, fought with and converted the Blemmyes, the desert tribes to the east of the Nile—with the help of Narsus, Justinian's general.[10] It is highly unlikely that Narsus's orders came from Theodora.

It must be stressed that only minimal doctrinal differences separated Monophysitism from the officially sanctioned Chalcedonian faith. The leading theologian of the Monophysite movement, Severus (ca. 464–538 C.E.), patriarch of Antioch from 512 until deposed by Justin I in 518, held a doctrine close to Chalcedonian teaching, and his only divergence from orthodoxy may have been terminological.[11] Nor did the Monophysites themselves regard their belief as grounds for either a religious schism or a political break with the empire: they considered themselves its obedient subjects, and believed there was "a providential association between church and empire, foreshadowing the time when all men would be Christians under a Christian emperor."[12] Ever hopeful that the emperor would repudiate Chalcedon, they persisted in being loyal to him, and were loath to set up an independent church hierarchy.[13] The Monophysite leadership was finally forced to do so by persecution coupled with an imperial refusal to allow the Monophysite bishops to ordain lower orders of clergy. Only after about ten years of such treatment, lasting from the deposition of Severus by

---

9. John of Ephesus, *Hist. Eccl.* II.iv.6–7; translation given in Bury (1958), 2:328–29.

10. Frend (1972), p. 299.

11. Cf. *ODCC*, "Severus," p. 1266; "Monophysitism," p. 932 col.1. Other Monophysite movements, especially the Julianists, were more extreme; but it was on the Severan movement that the national church of the eastern provinces (Syria, Palaestina, and Arabia) was founded.

12. Frend (1972), p. 76.

13. Ibid., p. 79.

Justin I in 518 until 529–530 C.E., two years into the reign of Justinian, did the Monophysite bishops give in to popular concern regarding the lack of lower clergy, and bow to the pressure to ordain them without imperial consent. They then did so on such a scale that, as Frend points out, "Even if the number of ordinations, 170,000, is greatly exaggerated, the foundations of a Severan church extending through the whole of the Roman east had been laid."[14] As soon as this result occurred, Justinian stopped persecuting the Monophysites (in 530/531), restoring monks to their monasteries, but not bishops to their sees. An independent Monophysite church had indeed been founded, but its grassroots organization needed fostering, and this could be achieved by the return of the monks. However, the new church needed to be kept on its toes by some indication of persecution; so the bishops were kept in exile. It could be foreseen that this would not actually hurt the Monophysite cause, since the bishops had likewise been in exile while engaged in the ordination of thousands of priests and deacons.

In the winter of 534–535 the emperor invited Severus to Constantinople. It was a very fruitful visit for Monophysitism: he converted Anthimus, Patriarch of Constantinople, to his cause. Since the Patriarch of Alexandria, Theodosius, was already a Monophysite, this brought the three major eastern patriarchs into the Monophysite fold.

Once the Monophysite movement was strongly enough established, the next step was to force it to break completely with Chalcedon. From this point of view, the condemnation and excommunication of Severus and the immediately ensuing persecution of 536–538 C.E. was totally expectable, and it had the desired effect: a complete break between Severan Monophysites and Byzantine Orthodoxy. The emperor continued to posture as "peace-loving" and to demonstrate efforts to prevent the break; but by refusing to compromise on the issue of Chalcedon itself, he ensured that a reconciliation would not be achieved. The end result was that

> *However fine might be the difference* between neo-Chalcedonianism and Severan Monophysitism, the latter was not in communion with the church. In addition, among the Severans the hatreds and fears aroused by ... the persecutions ... could not be washed away. Monophysitism had become *despite itself* a schismatic movement.[15]

---

14. Ibid., p. 161.
15. Ibid., p. 275, emphasis added.

Nonetheless Byzantium continued to protect the top leaders of the Monophysite movement, and allowed them to continue the work of organization. Thus although the edict of 536 banned the Monophysite leaders and their supporters from Constantinople and all other major imperial cities, the Patriarch Theodosius and his followers resided in the palace of Hormisdas, in Constantinople, from then until his death in 566. During all this time "his authority was unchallenged ... and the canons which he promulgated provided the basis for the law of the new church."[16] It is commonly supposed that he was Theodora's protégé,[17] but Theodora died in 548, and yet Theodosius continued for another eighteen years, in her absence and under Justinian's very nose, to establish the legal foundations for the whole Monophysite hierarchy, including canons for clergy ministering in Constantinople itself.

In 542, under pretext of a request from al-Ḥarīṯ bn Jabalah, the king of the Ġassānid Arabs, and at the urging of Theodora, two Monophysite metropolitans were consecrated in the East. One was Jacob Baradaeus, who became the metropolitan of Edessa, the other Theodore, bishop of Bostra (Buṣrà) in Provincia Arabia, who became the metropolitan of Arabia.[18] Theodore seems to have stayed initially with the Ġassānids, fulfilling their request for religious leadership. Later he took up residence in al-Ḥīrah among the Arabs allied with the Persians. But Jacob turned his attention to missionary work and to further establishing the Monophysite religious leadership. He and others consecrated twenty-seven metropolitans and a claimed one hundred thousand clergy all over the East. By the time Jacob Baradaeus died, his Syrian Jacobite church had an assured existence.[19]

In the same year as the consecration of the two Metropolitans, 542 C.E., Justinian commissioned John of Ephesus to convert the remaining pagans in the diocese of Asia. John was a known, if moderate, Monophysite. As a result of Justinian's choice of missionary, seventy thousand people were added to the Monophysite church and ninety-eight new churches and twelve monasteries were built for them. And when John clashed with

16. Ibid., p. 288.

17. As we saw above, the responsibility for fostering Monophysitism could be attributed to the openly pro-Monophysitic empress.

18. Atiya (1968), p. 181, quoting Honigmann (1951), pp. 161–64.

19. Ibid., pp. 183–84.

the impeccably Orthodox bishop of Tralles over a missionary center which the bishop wanted for his own use, Justinian sided with John.[20]

John of Ephesus later replaced Theodosius as the eminent Monophysite leader resident in Constantinople. Like Theodosius, he remained there until his death, ca. 585/86. This period included three years of Maurice's reign, even though Maurice resumed persecution of the Monophysites upon his accession in 582.

Maurice's persecution, like those before it, showed the Monophysites that they could not look to Byzantium for reconciliation, much less overt help; yet their essential organization was not touched, and their leader was allowed to provide his leadership from the capital itself. Near the end of Maurice's reign, a massacre of monks at Edessa in 599 had the same effect as the burning alive of a few Severan supporters had had in the persecutions of 536/37: it "left the emperor with the worst of popular reputations through-out the east."[21] The net effect was to cut any remaining ties between the imperial government and the inhabitants of the eastern provinces, on the eve of the annexation of the East by the Persians.

The main religious effect of the Persian interlude (614–628) was to oust the remaining Chalcedonians, including the patriarch of Jerusalem, till now a Chalcedonian enclave, and replace them by Monophysites.[22] Moreover, the Persian emperor, Xusraū, seemed to be acting in accordance with a definite policy: "to give the Monophysites the status of majority religion in the conquered provinces of Syria, Palestine and parts of Asia Minor, while maintaining the Nestorians in this role among the Christians in Persia."[23] This had two effects, apart from removing the Chalcedonians: it strengthened the Monophysite church, and it showed the Monophysites (and Nestorians) that a non-Christian ruler did not necessarily persecute them and could thus be preferable to a Chalcedonian, who did. Why the Persian emperor should do all this is, however, problematic, since he was a protégé of Maurice, who had put him on the Persian throne in 590. Since Xusraū

---

20. Frend (1972), p. 286, based on John of EphesusIII.37. This episode illustrates not only the imperial policy of spreading Monophysitism in the East, but also the considerable number of people who still remained pagan in the 6th century (cf. Shahîd [1989], p. 136 + n.12). And this in Asia, which was much nearer to the Byzantine capital than the diocese of Oriens (we owe this point to Robert Hoyland).

21. Frend (1972), p. 334.

22. Ibid., p. 336.

23. Ibid., p. 337.

himself was not a Christian of any persuasion, there would seem to be no reason for him to attack the Chalcedonians selectively, or to favor either the Monophysites or the Nestorians at their expense. If, however, it was Byzantine policy to establish in the East deviant sects estranged from Chalcedonian Orthodoxy, Xusraū's actions cease to be surprising—he was carrying out the wishes of his patron. Note that Xusraū *expelled* the Chalcedonians: he did not kill them, nor did he persecute them while effectively leaving them where they were (as Byzantium did to the Monophysites). He just made sure that they were out of the way:

> ... on the capture of a city, the Chalcedonian bishop was *expelled and replaced* [by a Nestorian or Monophysite]. Not even Chalcedonians of the standing of the Patriarch Zacharias of Jerusalem were spared, and *he, together with 35,000 Chalcedonians* ... was transported to Ctesiphon when Jerusalem fell on 5 May 614.[24]

When the Arabs took control of Syria, it was almost totally Monophysite.

During the 5th and especially the 6th centuries, while Monophysitism was being established as the dominant religion of al-Šām, many functions of leadership and local administration were gradually transferred to the Monophysite church and specifically to the bishops. In Justinian's reign this process was largely completed: bishops not only exercised a legal jurisdiction paralleling civil magistrates, but had also taken over many duties formerly under civil jurisdiction, especially those concerned with the management of funds allocated for public works and for providing for the local population.[25] MacAdam (1986), discussing the Lejā and Ḥawrān (then northern Provincia Arabia), argues that the church grew in power and influence from the 5th to the 7th centuries, gradually subsuming both the titles and the administrative functions of the imperial officials. There is no evidence for activity on the part of Byzantine village officials in this area during this period: political power passed from the provincial administration to the church officials and the Christian Arab (Ġassānid) phylarchs.[26]

In central Trans-Jordan many new churches were built and old ones beautified (for instance, by the addition of mosaic floors) in the second half

---

24. Frend (1972), p. 336, emphasis added.
25. *Cod. Just.* I.4.26, 530 C.E.; Frend (1972), p. 76.
26. MacAdam (1986), p. 225.

of the 6th century.[27] Someone was spending a lot of money on churches; but the dedications mention not the Byzantine authorities, but the local clergy and élite families. These were, then, presumably the donors.[28] The latter may have been a new élite, for their names, Piccirillo remarks, are only recorded "at this stage in the village." It is interesting that some village families, and members of the clergy, were rich enough to finance extensive church building projects, and it is not beyond the bounds of speculation that Byzantium chose to channel funds into the development and establishment of the clergy and a civilian élite, rather than to fund civilian projects directly.

Civil administration in the eastern Roman provinces was now very largely a function of the church. Clerics frequently took part in local and regional politics, and in al-Šām during the Persian occupation, in areas where the Persian presence was felt, the local church, it seems, represented the Christian population vis à vis the ruling unbelievers, very much the same as in Merovingian France at the same time. It is very likely that from the turn of the 7th century the local (Monophysite) church in al-Šām formed the only organized leadership of the majority of the population.

MONOTHELETISM

Heraclius's proposal in 622 or 624 C.E.[29] of the doctrine which later became known as Monotheletism is usually regarded as an attempt to reestablish unity with the estranged Monophysite church, in order to preserve political support during the campaigns against the Persians.[30] We read it, rather, as a step towards the final aim of abandoning responsibility for the Christians in the areas which Byzantium had decided not to defend.

Although exact Christological formulae are of little concern to us here, we shall not be able to follow the course of events without a brief mention of them. The official position of the Byzantine church since the Council of Chalcedon (451 C.E.) was that Christ had two natures, divine and human. This doctrine is today known as Dyophysitism. The Monophysite position

---

27. Piccirillo (1985), reporting on the excavation of churches in the villages of Nebo, Rihad, and Massuh.

28. Ibid., p. 261.

29. For 622 C.E. see Atiyah (1968), p. 76; for 624, *ODCC*, p. 932 col. 2.

30. Thus for instance Vasiliev (1952), p. 222.

was that Christ had but one nature, in which the divine and the human were miraculously and perfectly fused. The proposed compromise position consisted of accepting that Christ had two substances or natures, the human and the divine, but only one "mode of activity" (*mia energeia*). The Monophysitic patriarchs of Antioch and Alexandria, and Patriarch Sergius of Constantinople, accepted this formula, but Sophronius, a Palestinian monk, opposed it vigorously and with great theological skill. Although his arguments obstructed Heraclius's apparent aim of conciliation, it was after he began to air them abroad that he was appointed, in late 633 or early 634, to the influential position of patriarch of Jerusalem. This is the more remarkable in that Sergius of Constantinople, using his authority as patriarch, had a few months earlier ordered Sophronius to keep silent on the subject; but after his appointment as patriarch of Jerusalem Sophronius considered himself freed from this obligation of obedience and bound to provide guidance for his flock in so important a matter, so that he took up the issue once more.

In response to this threat, Sergius of Constantinople drew the Roman pope, Honorius, into the controversy. Honorius supported the Byzantine position in two letters, in which he substituted for the phrase *mia energeia* the concept of *en thelema*: "one will." This new terminology was used in the first official pronouncement of Monotheletism, the *Ecthesis* or Exposition of Faith, issued by Heraclius in 638.[31] Thus the main result of Sophronius's appointment as patriarch of Jerusalem was to rally support for Monotheletism among the Chalcedonians. Sophronius himself, an old man of nearly eighty when appointed patriarch, died some three or four years later,[32] and the remaining Chalcedonians in the East found that to be Orthodox was, by definition, to be a Monothelete. Thus in the East, both the Orthodox and the Monophysite churches accepted Monotheletism, the former as part of the Orthodox faith, the latter as a bearable compromise position.

When Heraclius first proposed Monotheletism, in 622 or 624 C.E., the Arab takeover of the eastern provinces was just beginning. In 632 he stopped subsidizing the *foederati* in the Maᶜan area, along the southern half

31. For brevity we will use the name Monotheletism to refer to this doctrine from the time Heraclius first proposed his conciliatory announcement of 622/624, though it was not called by that name until the *Ecthesis* was issued in 638 C.E.

32. Thus Eutychius, *Annales* II.289 (Arabic 281). The date of Sophronius' death is uncertain; various authors give it as 636, 637 or 638.

of the eastern *limes*.[33] By the time he issued the *Ecthesis* in 638 and achieved acceptance of the doctrine in the East, the Arabs were essentially in control of al-Šām. The result of the religious policy which Byzantium pursued during these crucial years was to remove the remaining vestiges of Chalcedonianism from the eastern provinces, by unifying both churches, Orthodox and Monophysite, in acceptance of a non-Chalcedonian position.

Whereas in the provinces of Syria and Palaestina Byzantium based acceptance of the new doctrine on persuasion, in Egypt she based it on force. Already in 631, long before the *Ecthesis*, Heraclius appointed Cyrus, originally the bishop of Phasis near the Black Sea and a staunch supporter of the emperor's religious policy, as Chalcedonian patriarch of Alexandria and prefect of Egypt. This dual role, which gave him unprecedented power in an important province, would remain his provided he succeeded in converting the Copts to Monotheletism. The proviso had the expectable effect—for ten years he was one of the worst tyrants in Egyptian history:

> Cyrus's visitations of the cities and villages in the Delta and the Valley left behind a trail of terror. Flogging, imprisonment and killing were coupled with confiscation of property and of sacred church utensils .... Every vestige of loyalty to Constantinople was obliterated by the behaviour of the imperial patriarch, who pursued Coptic prelates and Coptic nationalists until they paid lip service to his imperial faith or lost their lives.[34]

The lip service was apparently extensive, and together with Cyrus's ecstatic reports[35] has given historians the impression that he enjoyed a very real success in converting the urban Copts.[36] But the main purpose in unleashing Cyrus on the Copts, we suggest, was not to secure their conversion. Extreme persecution merely hardens opposition; in the provinces where Byzantium really wanted Monotheletism to be accepted, she used gentler methods. The point was rather to fan resistance to imperial policies, and hatred of the empire. In Egypt as in al-Šām, the local

---

33. See Part I Chapter 2: The Byzantine East on the Eve of Invasion, p. 49.

34. Atiyah (1968), p. 76.

35. "There was rejoicing at the peace of the holy churches in all the Christ-loving city of the Alexandrians and its surroundings as far as the clouds, and beyond these among the heavenly orders." J.D. Mansi, *Sacrorum Conciliorum Amplissima Collectio*, II, col. 561–64; q.b. Moorhead (1981), p. 582.

36. E.g., Moorhead (1981), p. 583; *ODCC*, "Monotheletism."

national church welcomed the transfer of power to the Arabs as an end to oppression.

For two or three generations, all through the initial period when the Orthodox Christians, at least, still looked to Byzantium for political guidance and hoped for her return,[37] Monotheletism was kept alive, first by Heraclius's *Ecthesis*, and then by Constans II's issue, some ten years later, of the *Typos* forbidding discussion of the subject (a certain way of ensuring continued interest in it). Then in 680 C.E., when the former Byzantine Christians were beginning to accept the permanence of Arab rule, Byzantium convened the Sixth Ecumenical Council and reverted to a Chalcedonian position: Orthodoxy meant Dyophysitism. This settled a religious controversy between Byzantium and the West, for the pope who succeeded Honorius, Severinus, had not accepted Monotheletism, and neither had his successors. But politically the Council was aimed at the East. With this decision Byzantium spurned any hopes of reconciliation the Monophysites may have held, and cast off also the Melkites of her former eastern provinces, who found the doctrine that had been officially "Chalcedonian" for the preceding half-century now finally rejected and themselves suddenly branded as heretics. What Vasiliev records as an unintended by-product of political miscalculation was, in our view, the intended political message of the Council:

> The decision of the sixth council proved to Syria, Palestine and Egypt that Constantinople had abandoned the desire to find a path for religious conciliation with the provinces which no longer formed part of the Byzantine empire.[38]

In 638 there had been good reason for the Melkites of the eastern provinces to revise their beliefs to accord with the imperial position. This was no longer the case in 680. They knew that Byzantium would not return; what she considered Orthodox was increasingly irrelevant to them. Byzantium, however, took no chances. Unlike the Orthodox population of the empire, those of her former eastern provinces were not given the chance to accept the new version of Orthodoxy; the break was final. For Byzantium henceforth refused any *official* contact with the organized

---

37. This is discussed in Part II Chapter 4: The Foundation of the Arab State, pp. 154–56.

38. Vasiliev (1952), I:224.

Christian churches of the east, including the Melkite. Trade, pilgrimage, and "imperial diplomatic missions" which "conducted their business without reference to the local church"[39]—these continued. But all official contact with the eastern churches was restricted. Griffith (1985), surveying the official church documents, both local and patriarchal, of the first two centuries of Arab rule, concludes that the local churches simply did not know what was happening in Byzantium or the West, and even important Byzantine affairs received no mention in the historical documents of the eastern patriarchates.[40] This means, he suggests, that although travelers from the areas of Arab rule reached Byzantium, she did not allow them to return: "Few if any ... ever came back to the Holy Land to inform their *confrères* about ecclesiastical affairs in Byzantium. Certainly documentary sources for the historian were wanting."[41] We would prefer to differentiate between official and unofficial "knowledge"—what they had heard, and official communications received through official channels. It is unlikely that the patriarchs, or even the bishops, really heard nothing of church affairs—there were many ways of acquiring unofficial information, from rumors to talks with the traders or pilgrims who arrived regularly at Alexandria or Antioch. But the point was that official, documented communiqués had ceased, and they could not include unofficial hearsay in church documents. Information not officially received in writing through official church channels was not usable for official church purposes. This is the reason, we suggest, why no mention was made in patriarchal documents of matters about which they should have been officially informed—and were not.

This policy of isolating the eastern churches from official contact with Byzantium was especially noticeable in the decades following the Sixth Ecumenical Council. Though Griffith sees it as a reaction to ʿAbd al-Malik's decision "to assimilate the body politic in the conquered areas to an Arabic and Islamic manner of public life,"[42] in our estimation the date is more precisely fixed by the remarks of Eutychius of Alexandria (876–940): "The names of the patriarchs of Constantinople have not reached me since

39. Griffith (1985), p. 31.
40. Ibid., pp. 24–25 + notes 8, 9 for sources.
41. Ibid., p. 28.
42. Ibid., pp. 26–27.

Theodorus died."[43] Theodorus had died in 679, less than a year before the Sixth Council and four years before ᶜAbd al-Malik was officially proclaimed caliph. By "have not reached me" Eutychius means, in our opinion, that there had been no official notification, not that he really did not know who the current patriarch of Constantinople was. Alexandria, then, was included in the list of recipients of official imperial church announcements in 679, but not since.

The same policy of allowing no contact with the churches of the former eastern provinces continued to be enforced in matters great and small. For instance, in order to be canonically legitimate the Second Council of Nicaea, in 787 (171 A.H.) required attendance by the eastern patriarchs or at least their legates. But Byzantium did not invite representatives from the East; instead she chose "proxies" from among the refugees living in Constantinople, who read at the Council a letter from a patriarch of Jerusalem then dead for twenty years.[44] There are even some accounts of letters sent by Byzantine ecclesiastical figures to the eastern patriarchs and to Palestinian monasteries, none of which ever seems to have reached the East.[45] Of the two possible explanations for this, it seems less likely that the church figures were lying when they claimed to have written the letters, and more likely that state censorship ensured they were not sent or did not arrive.

Our conclusion from the above is that Byzantium was well informed of events among the Christians in the East, but took care not to reestablish open, official links with them, especially after she had made it clear, in the Sixth Council of 680 C.E., that she was renouncing her responsibility towards them and they should consider themselves to be on their own.[46]

Thus Monotheletism was the vehicle for the final open dissociation of the East from the empire. We would suggest that the date of the Sixth Ecumenical Council—61/680—was likewise determined by political rather

43. Eutychius, *Annales, CSCO* vols. I and II, 1906 and 1909, li. 49; reference given in Griffith (1985), p. 26, note 11.

44. Griffith (1985), p. 30.

45. Ibid., p. 29 + notes 28, 29 for sources.

46. This does not mean that she never gave them any *financial* aid. An imperial policy that could indirectly finance the construction of mosques in Damascus and Madīnah (cf. Part II Chapter 4: The Foundation of the Arab State, p. 161–62) could certainly indirectly finance, for example, the upkeep of churches. This question is quite separate from that of *political responsibility* for the Christian population.

than religious considerations. This was the year of Muᶜāwiyah's death. Although Muᶜāwiyah had officially assumed the title of caliph only in 41/661, he had in fact taken control within a few years of the Arab takeover, and, first as governor and then as caliph, had been the actual ruler of the former Byzantine provinces ever since.[47] At his death there was no clear successor, and a few years of interregnum and civil war ensued until ᶜAbd al-Malik became caliph. This, if ever, was a time when the Christians of the East might expect Byzantium to reclaim her lost territory for Christendom. The Sixth Council was Byzantium's way of announcing the futility of such hopes.[48] In 680 C.E., the year of Muᶜāwiyah's death, the empire effected via the Sixth Ecumenical Council the final break with her former eastern provinces.

---

47. Cf. Part II Chapter 4: the Foundation of the Arab State.

48. Muᶜāwiyah had been in control for forty years and must have been over sixty years old. He was, by the standards of the time, an old man whose death could be expected in the not too distant future. That he had no clear successor was also known, and the probable results of this situation would be clear to any observer of the political scene. It is perfectly possible that Byzantium completed the lengthy preparations needed for an Ecumenical Council in advance, so that it could be convened as quickly as possible when the political moment was ripe: when Muᶜāwiyah was dead or close to death.

4

The Demographic Background

THE POPULATION OF THE ARAB PENINSULA

The Muslim traditions depict the Arabian Peninsula as filled with roaming nomadic tribes who, after conversion to Islam, supplied thousands of warriors for the conquest of al-Šām, Iraq, and Egypt. This view does not bear close scrutiny. Most of the peninsula (excluding of course its southern coastal region) is a parched desert which, judging from the material remains so far discovered, was never densely inhabited and whose population was not only sparse but extremely poor by any standard at any historical time.[1] It is true that we have few hard facts about the peninsula's pre-Islamic societies and political groupings. Not enough archaeological work has been done, so that our main source of information is epigraphic; and the inscriptions, by and large, are brief and uninformative. But even the little information discovered so far cannot be reconciled with the traditional Muslim account of peninsular society and, within it, the relative importance of the Ḥijāz.

---

1. Excluding immigrant populations in a particular place, e.g., from South Arabia (Dedanites at al-ᶜUlā), Syria-Palestine (Nabateans in Madāʾin Ṣāliḥ) or even, perhaps, Mesopotamians (Nabonaid in Taymāʾ). This is the essence of the *Quṣayy* tradition, too: the immigration of Syrian groups ("tribes") into the Peninsula, introducing an advanced economy, cult, and modes of living.

During the early centuries of the first millenium B.C.E., a densely populated urban civilization developed in South Arabia (Yemen to Ḥaḍramawt). In the Hellenistic period (end of the 4th to the 1st centuries B.C.E.), and perhaps starting already at the end of the previous Persian period, this Sabaean society expanded its interests towards Egypt. These interests were based on the frankincense trade, about which much has been written but few hard facts are known. The earliest known trade route led up the eastern side of the peninsula, along the shores of the Arabian Gulf to southern Iraq (i.e., Babylon). Later, in Hellenistic times, there arose the western trade route, the "Dedan Route." This ran from Najrān along the western coast of the peninsula, bypassing the East African coastal routes until, at an unknown point, it crossed the Red Sea. The little that we know about this northward expansion of South Arabian mercantile interests derives from the findings at al-ᶜUlā (Dedan, south-west of Egra, Madāʾin Ṣāliḥ), where a Sabaean colony dating from the Hellenistic period has been discovered. Al-ᶜUlā is, however, situated rather deep inland and can by no means be considered a coastal site. It may have been a trading station with Sabaean warehouses, a resting place for the weary caravans before proceeding north towards Palestine and Syria or east towards Iraq. In any case we may accept that the reason for the Sabaean presence up there in the northwest Ḥijāz was the long-distance South Arabian trade. Other South Arabian remains inside the peninsula, both archaeological and epigraphical, are very limited. They do not occur generally all over the peninsula, but are confined to short periods—almost to certain years—and to specific sites.[2] In other words, the coastal South Arabian cultures did not colonize or spread into the inner peninsula; at most, they established more or less isolated outposts inside the peninsula in specific places at specific times, and presumably for specific purposes.

The inner peninsula, in stark contrast to the highly developed cultures of the south, was inhabited by economically primitive Beduin-type cultures. Their presence is revealed by thousands of rock inscriptions in various epigraphic peninsular language (EPLs): the northern and central peninsular dialects known as Ṯamūdian, Ṣafaitic and Liḥyanite.[3] These inscriptions

2. Important excavations were carried out during the 1980s–1990s at Qaryat al-Faw in Wādī Dawsir near Sulayl: published at intervals in *Qaryat al-Faw*.

3. For a general survey of this field, see the Introduction in Oxtoby (1968); for an important contribution and bibliography, see Winnett and Harding (1978). Research tends

occur all over the peninsula and in its extensions towards the Fertile Crescent: the Syro-Jordanian desert and, in smaller numbers, the Negev. The epigraphic record starts, at the earliest, in the 6th century B.C.E., almost contemporaneously with the Sabaean site at al-ᶜUlā, and even this dating is subject to considerable doubt; but the peninsular societies clearly existed for some time before they started to leave inscriptions. Thus the Ṯamūd, the peninsular Arab people whose inscriptions are considered to be the earliest (spanning from ca. the 6th century B.C.E. to the 4th or possibly the 5th century C.E.) are already mentioned in the annals of the Assyrian king Sargon II about 715 B.C.E.

The epigraphic record continues for nearly a thousand years. During this time, despite the fundamental developments which meanwhile shaped the Fertile Crescent and its neighbors, the Arabian peninsular cultures show no signs of development. As far as we can tell from the archaeological and epigraphic record, they never rose above the lowest economic level, nor did the pattern of their lives, society, and culture change throughout this period, right down to the disappearance of their archaeological and epigraphic traces around the 4th or, more probably, the 5th century C.E. Despite extensive surveys over wide areas, no signs of Ṯamūdian or Ṣafaitic settlement—or, for that matter, 6th century Jāhilī (pre-Islamic) settlement either—have yet been discovered at any site;[4] the major material traces are

---

to be scattered in several journals, but there are clusters of papers in *ADAJ* 27 (1983) and earlier volumes.

4. For an illustration of how this lack of evidence appears in the literature, see King (1991), a survey of the archaeological evidence for settlement patterns in the Arabian peninsula. Faced with the contradiction between the Traditional Account of settlements in the Jāhiliyyah period and the almost total lack of any archaeological evidence for them, King tries to resolve the paradox by an initial, openly stated premise that the settlement patterns of the last two centuries "would probably hold good as a pattern over much of the past two millenia," a layer of constant surmise ("it seems reasonable to imagine that ..."), and a resort to the Muslim literature, whose descriptions are indeed far more forthcoming than any that archaeology can provide. Nonetheless King is careful to make it clear what is surmise or reliance on the Muslim traditions, and what is archaeological evidence, noting, for example, the complete lack of evidence for settlement at Taymāᵓ despite its place in the Muslim traditions. Indeed, the only area mentioned in this article where any archaeological evidence has been found for settlement in the two or three centuries before Islam is Najrān in South Arabia. Some pottery which King was able to identify as chronologically Byzantine (i.e., one assumes, 4th to 7th century C.E.) was also found in the southern Tihāmah. Late Byzantine ribbed sherds have been found at Aṯar in the southern Tihāmah, and possibly Byzantine ones at Sirrīn nearby (Zarins and Awad

the fifty cairns published by Winnett and Harding (1978).[5] Until about the 6th century C.E. we have no evidence indicating a substantial influence of the South Arabian culture on the other peninsular societies, or important relationships between them. It would thus appear that the presence of primitive Beduin-type cultures in the inner peninsula is a completely different phenomenon from the development of the sophisticated South Arabian culture. The Beduin did adopt the existing South Arabian script when they came to write, rather than inventing a new one. But that fact apart, the archaeological and epigraphic evidence does not indicate any important cultural contact between the peninsular Beduin and the South Arabian caravans moving through their territory along the trade routes, or the permanent trading stations they may have established, such as al-ᶜUlā and Qaryat al-Faw.

There is also some linguistic evidence that the Beduin of the inner peninsula were unrelated to the people of the South Arabian cultures. As Ephᶜal reminds us: "the distribution and use of the term 'Arabs' indicates that it was originally a northern concept exclusive to the cup of the Fertile Crescent and to northern Arabia."[6] The people of the developed South Arabian kingdoms were not called "Arabs": the term *ᵓᶜrb* or *ᶜrbn* is never so much as hinted at in connection with the southern kingdoms in any of the

---

[1985], p. 83, 85). However, one should note that King's assertion that "the excavations at al-Rabadha ... have shown that the place was settled from well before the coming of Islam" is not in fact borne out by the report of the al-Rabaḏa excavations to which he refers (al-Rašidi [1986], where the evidence for 7th-century settlement comes from the Muslim sources, not the archaeological remains; the earliest datable remains are from the 90s/710s). The evidence from the 1985–1987 excavation seasons, which King says identified "a pre-Islamic element ... concentrated on the northern side of the site," has not been published to date. Furthermore, the use of the vague term "pre-Islamic" implies that this element cannot be dated, or at least not to the Byzantine period, i.e., the few centuries immediately preceding the Islamic. In Jordan, where remains *are* datable to the Byzantine period, King has no hesitation in saying so (e.g., King, Lenzen, and Rollefson [1983], pp. 408, 412; King [1983], p. 328). Zarins and Awad could similarly ascribe the pottery from the southern Tihāmah to the Byzantine period. It is therefore significant that the findings from the Ḥijāz and northern peninsula are described only as "pre-Islamic," a term so general (3rd century B.C.E.? 4th century C.E.?) as to be meaningless.

5. For a careful excavation of one such cairn, see also Harding (1953); it yielded nothing but two skeletons and the bare minimum of essential personal artifacts: a knife with the man, and wool yarn, a mirror, and eyebrow tweezers with the woman.

6. Ephᶜal (1982), p. 9.

thousands of extant Epigraphic South Arabian inscriptions. When it is first used—not before the 1st century C.E. in the kingdom of Sheba and the 3rd century C.E. in Ḥaḍramawt—it refers to "Beduin who came into contact with the kingdoms either as auxiliary troops or enemies."[7]

Thus the Arab population of the northern and central peninsula and the Ḥijāz was neither numerous nor economically advanced. It consisted, like the populations of the more northern desert areas which connected the peninsula to the *oikoumenē*, of Beduin-type tribes; in fact many tribes probably migrated seasonally between the northern Syrian desert and the northern Arabian Peninsula, as Beduin tribes have continued to do down to modern times.

THE ARAB POPULATION OF THE *OIKOUMENĒ*

Many Arabs had settled in the Fertile Crescent long before the Roman Conquest. Like many other segments—Aramaic-speaking Jews and Samaritans, Greeks, and others—they formed a distinguishable and deeply rooted element of the population in late antiquity. But they were concentrated in the interface provinces of Palaestina III and Arabia; the heartland of the *oikoumenē*, coastal and central Syria and Palaestina, was settled mainly by an Aramaic-speaking population with a Rūmī, Greek-speaking élite. Of course some Arabs (we do not know how many) settled there too, but there is no evidence that they penetrated into the secular urban élite, i.e., that they had any influence on the management of daily life. In the written sources, both epigraphic and literary, they are well-nigh invisible: we can identify in these sources Samaritan, Jewish, Christian-Aramaic, and Greek ethnic layers, but no Arabic layer, nor do we find Arab names in the Greek-Aramaic inscriptions from these areas. Where Arabs are mentioned, they are *Ṭayyāyê*: Beduin raiders from the desert.

THE POPULATION OF THE INTERFACE AREAS

Whereas we have no sign of an important Arab population in the heartland of the *oikoumenē*, we have ample evidence for both a settled and a nomadic one in the interface provinces. And from the 4th to the 6th century,

---

7. Ibid., p. 8.

Byzantium augmented both strata, the settled Arab and the nomadic, in the interface areas. Some nomadic Arabs were settled on the fringes of the *oikoumenē*. The rate of settlement was intensified during the 6th century, and over this period they were established in Trans-Jordan, Syria, and the Jazīrah region as a permanent and imperially recognized segment of the population. They were involved, in some areas and to a certain extent, in the political, military, and clerical framework of al-Šām, and they developed their own élite groups.[8] The Arab population of important centers such as Damascus, Baᶜlabakk or Ḥimṣ, while Byzantine, were also Arabs, and they maintained their Arab identity unobscured.

From the 4th century on, Byzantium deliberately imported tribes into both the *oikoumenē* and the desert interface areas between Syria Palaestina and the Euphrates.[9] By the early 7th century C.E., Arabs, both settled and nomadic, were living in many areas of al-Šām: southern Syria; many valleys of central Syria, such as the Biqaᶜ; some regions of Palestine; many northern Syrian and Euphrates towns, such as Ḥimṣ (Emesa), Harran, and Edessa, where they had established dynasties; and the northern Syrian steppe.[10] An overview of the archaeological evidence in Jordan concludes that in the Byzantine period "the settled population was continuously increasing" and inscriptions show that most of the population was Arab.[11] The peak of sedentarization in Jordan was the 6th and 7th centuries C.E.[12] And Vasiliev

---

8. In the 5th century Sozomenus stated, from personal knowledge, that among the Arabs were many bishops who served as priests over villages (*Hist. Eccl.* VII.19.330, lines 14–15). Shahîd sees these as settled Byzantine (Rūmī) Arabs, not *foederati* (Shahîd [1989], p. 178). The Arab *foederati* sent bishops to the Latrocinium of Ephesus in 449 and to the Council of Chalcedon in 451, though one cannot tell from their names whether these bishops, like their flocks, were Arabs (Shahîd [1989], pp. 216–221). The Negev/Palaestina III, however, sent several bishops with recognizably Arab names to the Council of Ephesus in 431 C.E. and the Synod at Constantinople in 449 (Shahîd [1989], p. 225); and three bishops with recognizably Arab names attended the Council of Chalcedon. Adrian Reeland recorded in 1714, in his commentary on Palestinian towns, three names of bishops of Elusa who attended ecumenical councils: ᶜAbdallah, "Aretas" (= Ḥarīṯ), and "Zenobius" (Reeland [1714], pp. 756–57). Cf. Mayerson (1983). At the end of the 5th century, in 494 C.E., an Arab, Elias, was elected patriarch of Jerusalem, in which capacity he served till 516 (Shahîd [1989], p. 196). It is at any rate clear, from the number of names of Arab bishops that have been preserved, that there must have been many Arab bishops in Syria as a whole.

9. This policy is examined in detail below.

10. Donner (1981), p. 95 para. 2.

11. Piccirillo (1985), p. 259.

12. Ibid., p. 260.

considers that "the Lives of the Syro-Palestinian saints ... clearly reveal ... that, in the pre-Islamic period, the Arabs formed the principal part of the local population."[13] But while all the other elements in the population were sedentary, and their demographic hinterland lay somewhere among urban and rural peoples, the Arab segment was in close and continuing contact and kin relationships with the nomadic Arabs whose demographic hinterland stretched into the peninsula. Indeed, perhaps the continuance of similar ethnic traits in the populations of the peninsula and the *oikoumenē* over a period of a thousand years can be explained only by such interactions.

The contact between the two related populations presumably occurred mainly in the extensions of the peninsula into the *oikoumenē*: the Syrian and Trans-Jordanian desert and the south Jordanian mountain ridges, areas where numerous inscriptions in Epigraphic Peninsular Languages have been found. Along their eastern borders, the ancient route from the peninsula via Trans-Jordan or Wādī Sirḥān up to Damascus provided access from the peninsula and interface areas to the whole of al-Šām. There was a strong Arab population on both sides of these borders, and unrestricted open channels of demographic movement from the northern peninsula deep into Syria.[14] This was augmented by the Byzantine policy implemented from the 4th century on, of importing Arab tribes.

The tribes imported by Byzantium came both from the northern Arabian Peninsula and from areas under Persian control. Some remained nomadic and were adopted, as *foederati*, into the border defense/patrol system; others were settled within the *limes* area and the eastern fringe of the *oikoumenē*. Many of these tribes adopted Christianity, which usually means only that their chief converted; presumably Byzantium made this a condition of the move. The inducements to move which were offered the tribes included titles for the chief (phylarch, *patrikios*, "King of the Arabs") and no doubt generous subsidies. It is reasonable to suggest that some tribes, which had formerly been Persian clients or allies, were persuaded to change sides mainly because Byzantium offered larger subsidies than they had been getting from the Persians.

---

13. Vasiliev (1955), p. 309; we would phrase it as "a considerable part," since it is arguable whether Arabs were a majority.

14. Avraham Negev has pointed out the relations between the populations who left the Nabataean and those who left the Ṯamūdian-Ṣafaitic epigraphical texts in the Negev and eastwards into the northern regions of the peninsula (Negev [1986], pp. 149–50, "postscript"). His interesting observations require further elaboration and research.

Throughout the 4th to 6th centuries Persia was interested in maintaining peaceful relations with Byzantium, seeing the two powers as allied against the common threat of invasion of central Asian tribes along the two empires' mutual Caucasian border. She repeatedly urged treaties, which Byzantium repeatedly broke, and only resorted to attack as a result of Byzantine provocation, after the failure of extended diplomatic efforts.[15] In many cases, however, the provocations concerned a Byzantine-induced change of sides by Arab tribes formerly allied to Persia. These imperial initiatives, for the sake of which Byzantium was repeatedly willing to risk war or at least border campaigns with Persia, make sense if seen in the context of a conscious Byzantine decision to attract an Arab population, both civilian and quasi-military, to her side of the eastern border area.[16]

Imruʾ al-Qays, an Arab chief buried at Namarah (Nemara), in Roman territory, in 328, is perhaps a very early example of this policy. His titles included *al-Badʾ*, "the founder," and "king of the Arabs." Since the name Imruʾ al-Qays was borne by more than one Laxmid chief, it is possible that this Imruʾ al-Qays was a/the founder of the Laxmid dynasty, and was originally allied to Persia but went over to Rome.[17] We are on more certain ground with Mavia, the queen who led a major revolt of Arab tribes against Rome soon after 376 C.E. She was either already Christian or accepted Christianity at this time,[18] and demanded, as a condition of making peace, that a locally famous Christian holy man named Moses be appointed bishop to her people. Here as in many other instances, the conversion of the leader made the tribe nominally Christian, but it actually remained pagan to a greater or smaller degree for some time, for the bishop is said to have worked to convert many of Mavia's tribespeople. Mavia cemented her

---

15. Rubin, Z. (1986), pp. 678–79.

16. For a fuller discussion of the transfer of Arab tribes to this area by Byzantium, see Nevo (1991).

17. Smith (1954), pp. 441–42; for a detailed discussion see Shahîd (1984a), pp. 31–52. For his funerary inscription, see Beeston (1979).

18. Religious reasons may have been a factor in the revolt, but always secondary to political and economic factors. Thus Mavia's final revolt in 383 C.E., whose failure destroyed her nominally Orthodox Tanūxid *foederati*, was a response to Theodosius's refusal to grant her the favorable terms and treaty renegotiations considered customary on the accession of a new emperor, even while he granted them to the Arian Goths against which Tanūx had fought on the empire's behalf in the recent Gothic wars (Shahîd [1984], pp. 536–37).

switch to the Roman side by marrying her daughter to Victor, the commander-in-chief of the Roman army.[19]

In the late 4th century Byzantium conferred the status of Roman *foederati* on the tribe or confederacy of Salīḥ, and entrusted it with control of the border area.

At the turn of the 5th century, Byzantium was paying regular subsidies to the Persian king Yezdegird I (399–420); part of the money may have been used for Yezdegird's own payments to the Arabs of al-Ḥīrah, with tacit Byzantine approval. At least, a Byzantine envoy once intervened to patch up a quarrel affecting relations between Yezdegird and al-Mundir, the Laxmid chief.[20] This suggests that the Persian policy of using Arab client kings to secure the border was consistent with Byzantine policy in that area. This did not prevent Byzantium from trying to attract Persian Arab tribes to her own side. She did so by increasing her blatant Christian missionary activity on the Persian side of the frontier, and then providing a haven of freedom from religious persecution to any convert who crossed the border.[21] We read this as a continuation of the Byzantine policy of enticing Arab tribes away from Persia by promises of large subsidies and fancy titles, and settling them in Byzantine border areas. We see the missionary activity as essentially a pretext; now as before, conversion to Christianity was not the *reason* for their move, but a Byzantine *condition* of it. The chief who found it worth his while to change sides had to formally profess Christianity in the local version, usually Monophysite. One point of this requirement was that Byzantium could then refuse Persian extradition requests, despite the peace treaties between the two powers, on the grounds that the defectors were religious refugees. Clearly this was just a pretext: as discussed in the last chapter, Byzantium was quite ready to abandon the local Christian population when it served her political interests to do so,[22] on the grounds that they were not Orthodox but Monophysite schismatics.

---

19. Our knowledge of Mavia comes mainly from one late 4th-century and three early 5th-century church historians (Rufinus, Socrates, Sozomenus, and Theodoret, respectively). The main source for her revolt is Sozomenus, *Eccles. Hist.* IV.38; discussed extensively by Shahîd (1984a), pp. 139–58. The marriage of her daughter to Victor is mentioned only in Socrates; cf. Shahîd's interesting but rather far-reaching analysis of it, ibid., pp. 158–64. For a full list of sources, see Vasiliev (1955), p. 307 n. 3.

20. Rubin, Z. (1986), p. 679.

21. Ibid., p. 680.

22. In 680 C.E. at the Sixth Ecumenical Council.

The Persians were apparently furious, and ordered their Arab client tribes to prevent Christian converts from fleeing to Byzantine territory. One chief they chose for the task, whose name is preserved as Aspebetos,[23] is portrayed as having been sympathetic to the Christians from the start; and at some point he and his son Terebon crossed to the Byzantine side and then converted. Aspebetos assumed the name Petrus and became bishop of the "camp-dwellers": the converted Arabs, especially those living in a settlement three hours east of Jerusalem, called the *Parembolē* (i.e., camp, enclosure) which had been organized for them by the missionary St. Euthymius.[24]

Whatever one may think of the Persian choice of cat to watch the mice, it is clear both that Aspebetos' move was precoordinated with the Byzantine officials who welcomed him upon arrival,[25] and that this was not the defection of a single man, but of a tribal leader with his tribe. Aspebetos's tribe seems to have settled down rather than remaining nomad and integrating into a military framework as Salīḥ did. It is probable that one inducement for Aspebetos's decision was Byzantium's offer of the position of bishop, giving him religious as well as secular authority.

Incidents such as the one just cited led, finally, to the Byzantine-Persian war of 421–422. One clause of the treaty which ended this war stipulated that neither side would accept the Arab allies of the other.[26] Byzantium did not keep this treaty either, for twenty years later she had established a defense system along the border, based on fortifying frontier towns and setting up "imperial households" capable of maintaining garrisons in the border area.[27] In other words, she had populated the Syro-Jordanian desert with Arab tribes, given their chiefs titles, and entrusted them with border defense. Z. Rubin (1986) rightly sees this as just another name for the old policy of wooing Arab tribes away from Persia and settling them on the Byzantine side of the border. So did Persia, for she called it a breach

---

23. Isaac (1990), p. 246 and Shahîd (1984a), p. 119 n. 5 point out that this was in fact a Persian title, *spabadh*, not a name.

24. Rubin, Z. (1986), p. 680 + n. 5, p. 690 for source and discussion of it; Vasiliev (1955), p. 310. Aspebetos/Petrus participated in the Council of Ephesus in 431; that he was an Arab is known from the account in Cyril of Scythopolis (Shahîd [1984a], p. 333 n. 16).

25. Rubin, Z. (1986), p. 680.

26. Ibid., p. 681.

27. Ibid., p. 683.

of the treaty of 422, and it was one of the causes of the Persian invasion of 441.[28]

Thirty years later, in 473, the Byzantine emperor Leo I signed an alliance with another Arab chief, Amorcesos (Imruᵓ al-Qays), who is generally identified with the Imruᵓ al-Qays *al-bitrīq* mentioned by Hišām bn al-Kalbī.[29] If, as Smith (1954) thinks, he was related to the Laxmids of al-Ḥīrah, we have here another case of Byzantium stealing Persian allies. Imruᵓ al-Qays was rewarded with the title of *patrikios* (*al-bitrīq*). As expected, he converted to Christianity; this was given as the reason why Leo entertained him in Constantinople with such honors that the Byzantine nobles took offense,[30] culminating in granting him the title of phylarch.

In 502–503 an Arab chief called ᶜAdīd, previously a Persian client, also crossed sides to Byzantium with his tribe.[31] In the early 6th century Byzantium first fought against, and then adopted as *foederati*, the confederations of Kindah and Ġassān.[32] Kindah was an east-central Arabian tribe, and the kingdom of Kindah was originally an offshoot of the southern peninsular kingdom of Ḥimyar, to which it remained subordinate. We do not know where the tribe of Ġassān originated, but it appears to have also come from the south, at least from a region closer to Kindah than the Syria-Arabia area. We know, however, that Byzantium established the Ġassānids in the northern border area, either when she made peace with them and gave their chief the title of phylarch, or at some point not long before. It follows that al-Ḥarīṯ the Kindite was also established in the general area of Palestine, i.e., that he and at least part of his tribe were imported from further south. This is borne out by the circumstances of his death in 528: having quarreled with the *dux* of Palaestina, he fled to the desert and was killed by al-Mundir the Laxmid.[33] The need to flee shows that he was living in an area controlled by the *dux* with whom he had quarreled.

Al-Ḥarīṯ's death left Byzantium without a phylarch for Palaestina.

---

28. The other was Byzantium's withholding of sums she was bound by agreement to pay towards fortifying and garrisoning the frontier against the tribes of Central Asia.

29. Smith (1954), pp. 443–44; Rubin, Z. (1986), p. 691 n. 10.

30. Vasiliev (1955), p. 313.

31. Vasiliev (1955), p. 13. Vasiliev phrases it that he "surrendered with all his troops and became a subject of the Greeks," a phraseology perhaps better in accord than ours with Byzantine propaganda.

32. See Part I Chapter 2.

33. John Malalas, *Chronographia* (Bonn), pp. 434–518; q.b. Kawar (1960), p. 60.

Justinian solved this problem—and, more importantly, several others connected with the politics of the Arabian Peninsula[34]—by persuading al-Ḥarīṯ's grandson Qays (Caïsus), the ruler of Kindah, to come north with a large number of followers and accept the "Hegemonia of the Palestines." What exactly this term signified is open to conjecture; Shahîd suggests that it was, on the one hand, a "more important appointment" than a phylarch but, on the other, that Qays' power was fictitious rather than real.[35] The political aspects have been discussed in Part I Chapter 2; from the viewpoint of the present discussion we note simply that when Byzantium was faced with the problem of how to dispose of Qays and weaken the kingdom of Kindah, the alternative she found the most attractive was to give him an important title and move him with a large number of his followers into the general area of Palaestina. This solution fitted in with the policy Byzantium had been implementing for a good two centuries.

So far we have given examples mainly of the importation of nomadic tribes, allied to Byzantium as *foederati*. There is also considerable evidence for *civilian* settlement of the whole eastern *limes* area. The 4th and 5th centuries were apparently a time of greatly increased prosperity in the interface areas. In the Negev, many wadis were terraced. In both Trans-Jordan and the Negev we find towns with imposing churches, indicating the investment of considerable funds during this period. Many large, unwalled settlements from the Byzantine period, and terraced hillsides, were found in a survey of an area thirty to fifty kilometers north, south, and east of Petra, in the southern sector of the eastern *limes*.[36] Such settlements, especially those on the edge of the desert, were of course associated with springs; they also had watchtowers.[37] In fact many of the watchtowers were associated with settlements, and though Killick, who reported on them, favors a military view of them as part of a border defense system, he himself acknowledges that there is little difference, in the field, between fort, fortified farmstead, and watchtower, and that there is often no evidence that a tower existed before the accompanying settlement.[38] In other words, the

34. Cf. Kawar (1960).

35. Kawar (1960), p. 69+n. 25.

36. Killick (1986), p. 438. Parker (1987) ii:812 reports that most settlements in this sector were in the hill country, west of the *Via Nova Traiana*, with only a handful east of it; Killick found settlements also towards the desert.

37. Killick (1986), p. 440.

38. Ibid.

archaeological record does not show that settlements grew up because an army post provided security; rather, the watchtowers were built when the settlement was, and presumably to serve its needs, not those of military border defense. Similarly, there was a "substantial increase" in settlements in the central sector in the 4th and 5th centuries, found by both Parker and the Central Moab Survey.[39] The Moabite plateau and plains of Madaba (the areas east of the Dead Sea) were quite heavily populated with both small settlements and towns. In the northern sector (southern Ḥawrān) there is also evidence of considerable settlement and agriculture, including wadi terracing, apparently from the Byzantine period.[40] Mosaic inscriptions in villages show that Trans-Jordan had at least eighteen bishoprics, though not all would have had the status of a city.

This archaeological evidence ties in with the references in our sources to Arabs being settled along the eastern interface areas. It is almost certain that the settlers in such villages and towns were Arabs, whether from desert tribes or veterans of the army, themselves originally recruited from nomadic tribesmen. Epigraphic evidence bears this out: along the fringes of the *oikoumenē*, from near Damascus, through the Syrian and Jordanian steppe areas bordering the desert, and down through the Trans-Jordanian highlands extending south to the Maᶜan region and beyond, people left Greek inscriptions preserving their Arab names. Judging from the epigraphic evidence, a large part—in some places most—of the settled urban and village population were Arab, and Christian.[41] The inhabitants of the Negev "cities" were likewise Greek-writing Christian Arabs.[42] In these areas the urban élite were also at least partly Arab. By the late 6th to early 7th century, a majority Arab Christian population existed in the towns and

39. Parker (1987), ii:811–812; Parker cites also evidence from preliminary reports of the Central Moab Survey, which were unavailable to us.

40. Kennedy, D. L.. (1982), pp. 331–41.

41. Cf. *GLIS*, III, Preface p. xiii, concluding that "a large number of the names in these inscriptions [from Syria and northern Provincia Arabia] are undoubtedly Semitic in their origin."

42. Negev (1976) identifies the names of the 4th- and early 5th- century keepers of the churches at Mampsis as "local Palestinian" or Egyptian rather than "Arab" or "Nabataean"; but the Christians of Nessana—at least those buried in the churches—bore Arabic names such as ᵓAmr bn Saad and (Stephan) bn Khalaph-Allah (both of whom died in 541 C.E.). The 5th-century bishops of Elusa had Nabataean names (Abdellas and Aretas) whereas the 6th-century ones had Arab and Greek ones (Zenobios and Petrus).

villages along a wide belt stretching from the Jazīrah through the Ḥawrān and Trans-Jordan to the Negev.

The settled, Christian Arab population of the interface areas, Provincia Arabia and Palaestina III, remained recognizably separate from the nomads of the interurban areas. These interurban desert tribes were sometimes nominally Christian and sometimes nominally pagan, but almost always, as we have noted, pagan de facto. This is indicated by the thousands of Ṯamūdian and Ṣafaitic rock inscriptions from this area, all of them pagan. Why did Byzantium pursue a long-term policy of importing and subsidizing a largely pagan Arab population in this area? There are, too, the vast number of structures built in these two provinces. Particularly striking is the relatively dense network of roads, towers, and forts, especially in the central and southern sectors. As discussed in Part I Chapter 2, they cannot be explained in terms of border defense. Undoubtedly there were Beduin raids, and as already noted, the forts served as police stations and overnight havens for travelers. But the total number of forts, towers, etc. built in the eastern *limes* during this period seems excessive compared to both the actual threat to security posed, and the chances of effectively countering it by such means.

Thus Byzantium invested vast sums, in a border area of secondary importance to the empire, on works whose military effectiveness is doubtful and whose quantity seems excessive in comparison to the type and degree of threats being faced along the border. And the same problem must be faced in the Negev. All over the Central Negev lie the remains of dykes and terraces in the wadis, and associated structures near them and on the surrounding hillsides. Most archaeologists consider them to date from the Nabataean period on, and interpret them as the work of families building runoff farms for themselves over several generations. This opinion, however, is based on impressions gained from very cursory examinations, since the structures have not been seriously studied; and from rainfall and runoff calculations. But the runoff calculations are seriously misleading: the runoff systems could in fact have achieved only marginal yields, sufficient for use as pasturage but not to support a population of sedentary farmers.[43] Detailed surveys and more limited excavations of some of these sites, carried out over several years, indicates that they did not in fact function as runoff systems

43. Nevo (1991); Ben-David (1988).

in the way the current theory suggests.[44] Furthermore, a detailed survey by the Israel Antiquities Authority estimates the area covered by dykes and terraces as approximately three hundred thousand dunams,[45] a considerable expansion from the original estimate, current when the "family farm" theory was formed, of about forty thousand dunams. Yet most of the construction and terracing work seems to have taken place, not gradually over several hundred years, but during a period of less than a century: in the ᶜAvdat area (eastern Central Negev) mainly in the mid-5th to mid-6th centuries, and in the Shivta area (western Central Negev) from the mid-6th century, less than a hundred years before the end of the Byzantine period.[46] It is highly unlikely that areas this size could have been dyked and terraced in so short a time by individual families. Moreover, even after terracing this area could not have supported reasonable cereal yields. The runoff farming model proposed by Evenari et al.[47] works under modern conditions, but does not fit the archaeological findings nor the agricultural methods available in late antiquity. Even the limited excavations of the sites carried out so far indicates that they did not function as runoff systems in the way the current theory suggests.[48] A different explanation seems to be required.

We suggest that the runoff systems were not isolated family farms, developed from Nabataean times on, but a large-scale, organized development of the Negev on the part of the Byzantine authorities.[49] They were intended, not to grow marketable quantities of grain, but to produce fodder (mainly barley) for sheep.[50] Camels, goats, and donkeys are an integral part of the nomadic ecosystem and can be pastured on the hillslopes, but sheep-

44. Nevo (1991).

45. Figures given by one of the survey archaeologists in his M.A. thesis: Haiman (1988), p. 94. A dunam is approximately a quarter of an acre.

46. Nevo (1991).

47. Evenari, Shanan, and Tadmor (1982).

48. See Nevo (1991) for a detailed discussion of all these points.

49. It is unclear if all the phenomena associated with the Negev agricultural project are contemporary. The dykes, terraces, and small buildings coded BFs in Nevo (1991) can be dated to the 5th and 6th centuries. The stone lines (interpreted by others, mistakenly in our opinion, as "runoff-ducts"), the mounds, and the walls encircling the dyke and terrace systems have not so far been dated, but they all seem to belong to the same period as the dykes.

50. The Beduin who sow wheat and barley in the Negev today, partly using those same runoff systems (and achieving pitifully low yields), are similarly growing fodder for their flocks.

raising in this area requires richer pasturage and watering holes or cisterns, items which do not naturally occur and must be specially provided. The dyke and terrace systems, and the many cisterns in the area, provided these basic needs. Sheep-raising was a financially much more attractive enterprise than growing grain. But the scale of the terraces, the engineering precision with which they were built, the vast quantities of material which had to be moved, and the amount of manpower required, all add up to a huge project which could only have been funded and successfully completed by a central authority enjoying considerable financial resources. This must have meant the central government.

We read events in these areas bordering the Byzantine provinces—the eastern *limes* from Syria to ᶜAqabah, and the Negev—as an attempt by Byzantium to "tame" elements of the desert "barbarians" by a process of acculturation. The datable remains found so far ascribe the project, in the ᶜAvdat area, to the second half of the 5th century C.E. and the first half of the 6th, and in the Shivta area to the east of it, to the second half of the 6th century on. But it is probable that the authorities defined this strategy and started the process already in the late 4th century or early 5th: archaeological findings represent "a moment in time," and it takes quite some time to get from the starting point of a process to a stage at which an archaeologist can recognize it. The Negev runoff systems were a centrally funded project intended to bring the "barbarian" nomadic tribes, both those already in the Negev and those attracted to it, under some degree of control and civilizing influence. The control was maintained by paying them to work on the construction projects, and the runoff systems thus constructed, while insufficient for agriculture proper, supported large-scale sheep rearing. Most of the sheep may have belonged to the state, which owned the land and the project and employed the tribesmen as shepherds, though the latter presumably grazed their own flocks as well as those of their employers. The government may also have granted grazing rights to selected chiefs or to others, according to political considerations. Most important of all, the tribesmen employed on the project were thereby brought into contact with Byzantine civilization, and acculturated to it over a long period.

But they were not converted to Christianity. Despite the huge sums being spent during this same period on ostentatious churches within the "Six Cities," not a single cross, nor any other sign of Christianity, has so far been found outside them. Some of the Christians in the *towns* bore pagan Arab names, which implies that they were first-generation Arab converts. But the pastoralists who lived between the cities remained, for the most part, pagan, as attested by the Ṣafaitic and Ṯamūdian inscriptions found all over the Negev and Trans-Jordan down to the 5th and perhaps 6th century.[51]

In the eastern *limes* area, the tribes imported into the area were similarly employed to build and repair roads, and to build structures of various kinds. Some of these served a useful function as police stations, hostels for travelers, and watchtowers near civilian settlements; some of them were in our opinion built mainly in order to employ the tribesmen whose continued presence in the area, and exposure to civilization, was a feature of Byzantine policy. Some of the Arabs incorporated into the military structure, either as *foederati* or as regular soldiers of locally recruited units, were apparently defined by Byzantium as new tribes, under leaders of her own choosing rather than traditional chiefs.[52] A good deal of the construction work was probably done, here as in the Negev, by young men who worked for short terms, earned some money, and returned to their desert tribes. This view fits well with our suggestion that the Arabs of Palaestina III were "imperial guests," not citizens, since their ruler was the phylarch of Phoinikon. By these means the authorities could in a short time put a large number of young men through a "training course" in basic Byzantine culture.

The archaeological evidence from the Negev suggests that Byzantium stopped paying the tribesmen employed in the ᶜAvdat area in the mid-6th century, and terminated the sheep-rearing project. This date is suggested by the pottery found in the few structures so far excavated, and by an archaeological estimate that it would have taken at least two centuries for the dykes, once abandoned, to have deteriorated to the point they had reached when the Arabs started to repair them in the 8th century.[53] The tribesmen formerly employed to herd the sheep were either allowed to remain in the area, supporting themselves and their flocks as best they could, or required to leave Byzantine territory. The archaeological evidence suggests that they left the ᶜAvdat area, but that work continued farther to the west, in the Shivta area. Even if they were allowed to stay, some would have left, and many probably crossed over to Phoinikon. Others probably moved eastwards within Palaestina III, joining up with the *foederati* in Trans-Jordan.

---

51. On the religious situation at this time, see Part III Chapter 1: The Religious Background. For pagan names among Christian converts: ibid., p. 176 + n. 10–13.

52. This point is discussed in Nevo (1991), Ch. 4.

53. The Arabs used the runoff systems, not for agriculture, but to provide grazing lands for breeding thoroughbred horses, judging from the rock drawings of mares with foals, and stallions with enlarged genitals, which date from the Arab period. Some of these drawings are reproduced in Nevo (1991), p. 105, fig. 3.1.

Part II

The Takeover and the Rise of the Arab State

And then the Ṭayyāyê appeared and took control of Syria and many other areas

Syriac Life of Maximus, ca. 662–680 C.E.

Part I outlined our reading of the policy and actions of the Byzantine Empire that culminated in the Arab takeover of the eastern Byzantine provinces. This reading was based on the archaeological and epigraphic evidence: an early Byzantine decision not to invest in maintaining control of her eastern provinces was followed by a cessation of first military and then civilian expenditure in them, and a gradual withdrawal of the army northwards. Concomitantly, Byzantium established a major Arab population in these provinces by bringing in tribes from the east and south, including some that had formerly owed allegiance to Persia. Some of these tribes she settled in the border areas of the *oikoumenē*; others remained nomadic and were formally allied to the empire as *foederati*, receiving subsidies in return for assuming the tasks previously performed by the regular army, which was being withdrawn. Meanwhile, Byzantium used religious persecution and intransigence to estrange the local Christian population, much against its will, from its imperial allegiance, and to force the local political and religious élites to become capable of functioning independently of the empire.

Part II examines the next stage of this process: the de facto assumption of power by Arabs as a result of the political and military vacuum created by the Byzantine withdrawal, culminating in the emergence of Muᶜāwiyah as ruler, and the establishment of an Arab state. The evidence for our reading of the sequence of events during these few decades is partly epigraphic and numismatic, and partly documentary: the contemporary writings of the local population that experienced the transfer of control.

1

The Takeover

The situation in the eastern Byzantine provinces ca. 630 C.E., as outlined in Part I, may be summarized as follows. In the heartland of the *oikoumenē* lived a settled Greek- and Aramaic-speaking Christian population. The majority were Monophysites, though Chalcedonian enclaves existed, notably at Caesarea and Jerusalem, even after the weakening of the Chalcedonian presence during the Persian occupation; and there was an unknown number of Nestorians, especially in the northern areas, towards and in the Jazīrah. In Provincia Arabia and Palaestina III, the interface areas between the Byzantine *oikoumenē* and the desert, two separate populations coexisted. In the towns and villages lived a Christian Rūmī population, of whom a large percentage, indeed probably the great majority, were ethnically Arab, though assimilated into Byzantine culture to a greater or lesser degree. They had been settled by Byzantium in Provincia Arabia from the 4th century on, a process which reached a peak at the end of the 6th and start of the 7th centuries, towards the end of Byzantine rule. The élite in these towns were probably also Arab, though this is not always discernable, since most of them had adopted Greek Christian names. Distinct from this settled Arab population were the nomadic or semi-nomadic tribes, till now *foederati* receiving Byzantine subsidies. These too had been imported by Byzantium, from Persian-controlled areas to the east and from the desert to the south. They were organized as quasi-military units under phylarchs appointed by Byzantium, and were accustomed to perform the roles normally undertaken by the regular army, which had been gradually transferred to them over the preceding two centuries as the regular army was withdrawn: border security, the "police work" of safeguarding their areas from raids by tribes from farther out in the desert, and the collection of the *annona militaris*. Apart from the payments in kind provided by collection of the *annona*, of course, the chiefs of the *foederati* had also been receiving direct subsidy payments in gold.

Then, at the turn of the 7th century, the largest group of *foederati*—the Ġassānids—were disbanded, their kingdom annulled, and their subsidies stopped. Subsidies to *foederati* in the southern areas of the *limes* were discontinued somewhat later, after the Persian wars. One might expect that the former *foederati* would vent their rage upon the Rūmī population in the form of indiscriminate raiding, but there is no sign that this happened. The *foederati* remained by and large in their assigned territories, and as far as we can tell from the contemporary archaeological and epigraphic evidence, they at first went on doing exactly what they had been doing previously: collecting taxes in kind from the local population, and undertaking in return to safeguard the area from desert raiders. Whereas as *foederati* they had collected the *annona militaris* ostensibly on behalf of the provincial authorities, they now levied *xuwwah* payments directly for themselves. The distinction was largely academic, and it is doubtful if the local population felt much difference. The amount levied, for instance, probably did not rise, or not by much; otherwise complaints would have filtered into the contemporary Syriac literature.

It is probable, since the *foederati* had been organized as tribes, that each tribe had been responsible for safeguarding, and collecting taxes from, its own tribal area, and that they had not encroached on each others' territory. Skirmishes and raids on each others' camps may indeed have occurred in the past, and probably continued to occur and possibly increased as the realization of the lack of an overt Byzantine presence grew and the tribes vied for dominance. But these took place, if they did at all, in the desert areas beyond the *oikoumenē*, doing no or very little damage to the settled population. Nor could raiding by outside tribes have increased very much. Of course there had always been intermittent raiding by desert tribes, which it was the task of the *foederati* to prevent; and since the 5th century, at least, the towns had closed their fortified gates at night and maintained a certain level of alertness, being exposed to attacks from both Arabs and others. But there cannot have been a situation in which raiding by desert Beduin increased uncontrollably, with the former *foederati* either doing nothing to counter it or joining the raiders. Nor could the *foederati* have turned to large-scale raiding in revenge for the loss of their subsidies, nor competed with each other to such an extent that tribes encroached on each other's territories, so that settlements who formerly had paid their taxes to one unit now found themselves faced with repeated demands for payment to several different ones. If the settled population had been faced with demands greater than they could pay—such as repeated raids, or a succession of former *foederati* demanding "taxes" already paid to others—they would have abandoned their villages and sought protection in the larger towns or deeper into the *oikoumenē*. Such abandonment of agricultural land because of an inability to pay taxes did, after all, occur frequently throughout the period.[1] And had rival tribes, left to themselves without the controlling hand of the empire, decided to fight for supremacy in settled areas, the same result would have ensued. But the archaeological record shows us that this simply did not happen. No destruction or abandonment of villages, no reduction in the settled or farmed areas, no diminishing of the population, accompanied the changeover from Byzantine to Arab rule. Both the physical remains (housing, household utensils, etc.) and the literary descriptions of daily life, show that the modestly comfortable standard of living achieved under Byzantine rule continued unchanged into the Umayyad period: no change

---

1. Various reasons have been suggested for the widespread abandonment of agricultural land in the later Roman Empire: exhaustion of the soil, deforestation of the hills leading to denudation of the agricultural land below them, a shortage of manpower, and taxation. A. H. M. Jones discusses the question and concludes that taxation was the major factor; it was also the reason usually given by contemporaries (Jones [1964], 2:816–21). Thus in Africa, where all land paid tax at the same high rate, a third to a half was deserted by the first quarter of the 5th century, whereas in Syria, where land was elaborately classified according to potential yield, with different tax rates for each class, only about a sixth was. As MacMullen (1988) points out, a lot of this may have been marginal land which someone tried and failed to farm, thereby getting it first listed in the land registers and then marked as "deserted" when the would-be farmer gave up the attempt a few years later (Macmullen [1988], p. 44). The archaeological evidence cited in Part I Chapter 2, and later in the present chapter, shows that villages in Syria in fact prospered in the 5th to 7th centuries C.E. However, failed attempts to farm marginal land cannot explain the high rate of abandonment in Africa compared to that in Syria, nor the lands abandoned in Egypt, where "marginal" and "exhausted" land scarcely existed: either land received rich silt deposits from the yearly Nile floods, or it was desert. One may also note that much of the "marginal land" referred to by MacMullen would probably have been farmable if the tax burden had been lighter: farming it was probably not so much impossible as unprofitable, and those who tried may well have simply miscalculated the taxes that would be demanded. The tax burden fell heaviest on small tenant farmers, for the senatorial class and rich landlords had the money and influence to bribe their way out of their obligations, or to accumulate tax arrears which would eventually be written off (Jones [1964], I:465, 467; MacMullen [1988], p. 42).

for the worse, and little deterioration in public order, preceded the Arabs' ascendancy.

The inscriptions from what is now Jordan, for instance, show that settlement in these fringe areas reached a peak in the 6th and 7th centuries C.E.;[2] and in the northern part of Provincia Arabia a basic pattern of "a grid of towns and cities radiating from Bostra and the Jebel Druze," with their accompanying villages, was established in the Roman period, was greatly increased and to a large extent demilitarized in the Byzantine, and continued without a break into the early decades of Umayyad rule.[3] It was in fact the norm for occupation of the villages along the fringes of the desert to continue without interruption from the Byzantine into the Umayyad period.[4] King notes that "the usual pattern" revealed in the archaeological remains is for a Roman period of occupation to be "followed by a Byzantine and Umayyad continuum."[5] Yet it is villages such as these, on probably marginal lands along the desert fringe, which would have been most affected by the upheavals and lawlessness of a conquest, and most vulnerable to the depredations of raiders and demands for repeated *xuwwah* payments, had there been any.

Not only in the area surveyed by King, but throughout southern Syria and Jordan (Provincia Arabia), we have a uniform picture of continued rural and urban occupation.[6] Of eighteen sites in Jordan, representative of those on which considerable archaeological work has been carried out, only two were abandoned; occupation of the rest continued uninterruptedly from the Byzantine through the Umayyad period.[7] In the Ḥawrān, occupation was continuous from the Byzantine period until the start of the ʿAbbāsid.[8] At Rihab and Ḥirbat al-Samra, Christians dedicated new churches around 635 C.E[9] This would put the start of construction before the Arab takeover; what is interesting is that these churches were completed in the middle of the conquest period. Life, apparently, went on as normal; or as Schick puts

---

2. Piccirillo (1985), p. 260.
3. De Vries (1985), esp. pp. 249, 251.
4. King (1983), p. 385, reporting on the 1981 season of archaeological work in Jordan.
5. Ibid., p. 408.
6. Sauer (1982); King (1983a).
7. Sauer (1982), p. 330.
8. MacAdam (1986a), p. 536.
9. Schick (1987), p. 7.

it, the Christian inhabitants of Syria "were unconcerned with the fact that they were being conquered."[10] In Palaestina, too, Christians continued to build new churches both during and immediately after the conquest period, for instance in ᶜAvdat, Bet Guvrin, and Jerusalem.[11]

It is true that the larger towns underwent considerable change and declined in grandeur and sometimes also in size. The well-planned classical city, with its wide streets and colonnades, public squares, baths, and theaters, became the medieval city of narrow, winding lanes, its once open spaces filled in by private houses and shops. To ascribe this change of fortune to the Arab conquest is tempting, but inaccurate. In Syria and Arabia the change started in the last century of Byzantine rule, a century before the Arab takeover.[12] A study of Bayṣān, the provincial capital, and Gerasa[13] reveals the same situation: the turning point seems to have been the mid-6th century. After the first half of the 6th century we have no evidence for new public buildings, and existing ones ceased to be maintained. The imperial administration, then, stopped constructing and maintaining public buildings in the towns in the 6th century, after having stopped the construction and maintenance of fortifications in the 4th and 5th.[14] The usurpation of public spaces by private citizens, especially shopkeepers, started in the later 6th century, well before the Persian conquest—let alone the Arab—and continued as an unbroken trend into the Umayyad period. Archaeologically it is "almost impossible to make a distinction between the periods before and after 636–640."[15] There are no visible signs of the conquest in the former provincial capital.[16]

The smaller towns, which had no classical plan to begin with, do not show any change. Places such as Umm al-Jimāl, Sama, Umm al-Quttayn,

10. Ibid.

11. Ibid., p. 8.

12. Kennedy, H. (1985, 1985a).

13. Tsafrir (1991).

14. H. Kennedy (1985 and 1985a) attributes the decline of the larger—and especially coastal—towns to the bubonic plague of the 540s on. This was probably one factor; but it does not explain the *political* aspect: why Byzantium populated these provinces with Arab tribes already from the 4th century on, stopped building and maintaining fortifications in the 4th and 5th centuries, and appointed the Ġassānids as de facto rulers in the early 6th century. The cessation of building activity in the towns from the mid-6th century was, in our opinion, one more step in the same direction.

15. Tsafrir (1991), p. 21.

16. Ibid., p. 19.

Madaba near the Dead Sea, and many others, started as small, moderately prosperous agricultural communities, and as far as the archaeological record can tell they continued with no change into the Umayyad period.[17] At Umm al-Jimāl the characteristic activity of the early decades of Arab rule was "the continued use and maintenance of Late Byzantine structures"—including public structures such as the east gate, the main aqueduct from the northeast, which was extended to the southern side of the city, and the remodeling of at least one of the fourteen Byzantine churches.[18] The *actual transition* from the Byzantine to the Arab period cannot be distinguished in the archaeological record. H. Kennedy surmises that such communities "felt they were merely exchanging one group of semi-nomad Arab protectors for another."[19] We suggest that there was not even this much change: they in fact kept the same "group of semi-nomad Arab protectors" that they had had before.

Only towards the south, around the southern Dead Sea and northern ʿAravah (the Ġawr), do the Roman and Byzantine remains not continue into the early Umayyad period.[20] This may indicate that the early Umayyad state was not interested in this region. Similarly, the Central Moab and Wādī Ḥesa surveys found little Umayyad pottery, whereas it was quite well attested in the East Jordan Valley survey.[21]

The material evidence indicates, then, that the transfer of power from the Byzantine Empire to the Arabs was not accompanied by any great disruption of daily life, or a degree of lawlessness that the population found it difficult to cope with. This leads us to conclude that the former *foederati* remained by and large in their assigned territories, and while we do not know if they exacted the same amount from the local population as they always had, it is clear that they did not exact very much more. They remained controlled, which means that their chiefs remained in control.

Such control requires money. Tribal societies are not internally cohesive: they are built up of successive units, from the extended household through the clan or subtribe and the tribe to the federation. The head of each group in such a social organization expects to receive payment in

17. Kennedy, H. (1985), pp. 178–79.
18. De Vries (1985), p. 251.
19. Kennedy, H. (1985), pp. 179–80.
20. Ibid.
21. Sauer (1982), p. 351.

money and/or kind from the chief above him. Thus a federation or tribe of any size is composed of loosely connected tribes or bands with little real cohesion, based on a reluctant dependency on the biggest chief, who distributes the wealth. If a group's share is not forthcoming, its members will look for a more generous overlord—or an alternative source of funding. If there are no chiefs with sufficient means to buy allegiance, the confederacy or tribe disintegrates, each band splintering off to raid independently.

From the viewpoint of a tribal chief or the head of a federation, then, plundering is a high-risk enterprise, because it tends to bring about the federation's breakup. Raiders can get along very well on the basis of each band for itself; they do not need an overall leader, as long as the proceeds of raiding support them. Thus as money flows directly into the pockets of every small commander, the leader of the confederacy has a great problem in maintaining internal order and discipline. He can do so only if he continues to dispose of very considerable funds, which make it more worthwhile for the lesser chiefs to continue their participation in the tribe or confederation than to leave it and raid for themselves. Had the tribal leaders had no access to large amounts of money, the *foederati* would have broken up into uncontrolled bands of raiders. The result would have been the large-scale abandonment of villages by the rural population which Byzantium had so painstakingly settled in the area, and economic crises in the towns overwhelmed by refugees from the countryside and cut off from access to commerce.

That this would indeed happen was a very real possibility. We know today that the effect of Beduin rule over a sedentary population is to eliminate all the more sophisticated and subtle systems which keep urban societies and their rural hinterland alive and prosperous. This is not the Beduin's intention—they would prefer to keep the population prosperous and taxpaying. The leadership of the Beduin confederations is concerned by the rapid deterioration of municipal services and facilities, since they see their incomes diminishing and they themselves, impoverished, losing the means necessary to attract smaller tribes to join their confederacy or tribal league. But the deterioration inevitably occurs, because the Beduin tribes are not cohesive enough to ensure that paying taxes to one band will guarantee freedom from plunder and/or tribute demands by another. And no faction is interested, or able, to cooperate with municipal authorities to ensure the smooth working of local administration, upkeep of the roads, and so on. Just a short period of Beduin rule is therefore enough to reduce the population in numbers and in the quality of its leadership (élite), and to curtail commercial activities until only the unsophisticated and cheap merchandise needed by primitive rural and pastoral people is marketed. Palestine in the 18th century is an example of what would have happened to Syria and Palaestina in the 7th, if the Arab tribes had enjoyed uncontrolled rule for only a decade or so. But the literary, epigraphical, and archaeological evidence from all over the *oikoumenē* shows that no such deterioration happened.

The conclusion is that the leaders of the former *foederati* had access to considerable sources of funds; and the only source of money was the central government, the same government which had officially stopped subsidizing them. In other words, though the Byzantine Empire had decided not to retain control of the eastern provinces, she did not intend to abandon either her strong economic interest in the area, or, for the moment, its Christian population. It was in her interest to ensure that the partly acculturated Arab tribes to whom she was transferring responsibility would destroy neither the rule of law and order, nor the social and economic infrastructure. She therefore needed to continue to control them, even while publicly announcing that she was no longer paying subsidies and that they would have to fend for themselves. In other words, we suggest that she did not actually discontinue the subsidy payments, but merely moved them from the open to the covert sphere of diplomacy. Since the payments were unofficial, no records of them would have been made. But only such a system of continued payment to the tribal leaders in the area can explain the uninterrupted occupation and continuing prosperity of the population throughout the interface area during the changeover to Arab rule.

This stage—the de facto control of the rural areas of Provincia Arabia by Byzantium's former Arab *foederati*, and direct taxation by them of the local population—may be regarded as the "First Stage" in the takeover of the eastern Byzantine provinces. The next stage, we surmise, was the emergence among the Arab tribes of "strongmen" eager for wider dominance. One of these was Muᶜāwiyah. Since he won the contest, we do not know who most of the others were.[22] What we do know is that

22. The only contender for supremacy against Muᶜāwiyah of whom we have reliable knowledge is ᶜAlī, whom Muᶜāwiyah fought at the Battle of Ṣiffīn (36/657). The Muslim traditions provide a wealth of names, both of the caliphs before Muᶜāwiyah, and of field commanders. But the historicity of the four first caliphs is highly suspect, and the commanders are placed within an impossible historical framework—the unified conquest commanded from the Ḥijāz—so that we can make little history out of the

Mu^cāwiyah's power base was the Damascus area; that he relied for his power, not on the settled Arab population but on the desert tribes; and that among these were some whom he imported (as had the Byzantine government before him) from the south.[23] By ca. 640 C.E. he had amassed enough power to be acknowledged as governor of Syria. In our opinion he was ruler of Syria, for there is no evidence outside the ᶜAbbāsid sources that the Rāšidūn caliphs actually ruled, i.e., that there was any all-Arab ruler before Muᶜāwiyah.

It is improbable that all the tribes, either former *foederati* or desert tribes from the south, at once declared allegiance to Muᶜāwiyah. The leaders of the phylarchy of Phoinikon may themselves have tried to gain a political and military advantage and to challenge Muᶜāwiyah for control. We do not know the relationship between the tribes of Provincia Arabia—the former *foederati*—and those from Phoinikon, but given all that has been said above, it must be assumed that there was friction between them. However, the leaders of the "southern" tribes clearly failed, for Phoinikon did not become the political center of the Arab rulers of the East.

Just as the rural areas continued to pay the *annona militaris* to the *foederati*, so too did the towns. The Byzantine withdrawal meant that authority within the towns rested with the local *patrikios* and the church: there was no larger framework of Byzantine control. The *patrikioi* thus had no real alternative to paying what the Arabs demanded: they had no possibility of resisting with only the manpower they could raise from the town and the villages on its territory. So the demand for payment would normally develop into negotiations, ending with an agreement on terms. What actually happened at Tabūk and Ayla cannot be known, but even the Muslim traditions stress the fact that the invaders did not *conquer* any walled town in Syrian territory. They portray the towns as coming to terms, agreeing to pay tribute in various forms.[24] This same reality is evident also during the later phase of the Arab advance eastward (the Arab campaign of 31/651 in Xūrasān up to Merw), as Shaban points out:

---

occurrence of names in the Muslim sources. It is likely that the tales of the Riddah campaigns are back-projections of events that occurred in the period leading up to Ṣiffīn.

23. This does not mean the Yemen, but the northern peninsula area: see below, "The Tribes of the South" pp. 100–101. A discussion of Muᶜāwiyah's power base is given in Part II Chapter 4.

24. Hill (1971) lists the terms of surrender of the various towns, as portrayed in the Muslim sources.

> Deprived of the support of a central government, the helpless local leaders of the districts and towns of Khurasan found it expedient to conclude separate peace treaties with the conquerors. Accordingly, the Arabs received an annual tribute and in return undertook not to interfere in any way with the existing administrative, social and economic structure of the area.[25]

According to our interpretation, what the towns actually paid to the Arabs was the *annona militaris* they had formerly paid to Byzantium. When the Arabs wrote the history of the takeover period and set it within the framework of a great conquest, they interpreted and described these payments as tribute.

CASE STUDY: THE BATTLE OF DĀṮIN

An early engagement, which we would regard as a clash with local garrison troops,[26] was the Battle of Dāṯin. We will use it as an example of how our own reading of events differs from the traditional Western approach.

The Arabic sources relate that Dāṯin and al-ᶜArabah, two consecutive battles which took place on the same day in early February 12/634, were the first engagements in Syria between the Muslim forces and the Byzantine army.[27] The accounts in the Arabic sources are, as usual, confused and contradictory regarding details, but it can be ascertained from them that Dāṯin was at first regarded as a minor battle, until magnified by retelling and the introduction of folkloric elements. After combining these accounts with reports in Byzantine sources (Theophanes and Nikephorus) concerning difficulties with the Arabs whose subsidies had been stopped, and reports in Syriac chronicles preserving accounts of what appears to be the same engagement, we may gain the following general picture of events. The

25. Shaban (1971), p. 172.

26. As does Donner (1981). Regarding his analysis of the stages of the conquest according to the classical Muslim literature, see our Introduction.

27. The following sources amassed by Conrad (1987) preserve accounts of the event or reports which can be linked to it: Theophanes, *Chronographia*, 335.23–36.3; 336.14–20. Nikephorus, *Historia syntomos*, 23.13–24.2. The Syriac *Chronicon 724*, 147.25–148.3. *Chronicon ad annum 1234*, I.241.7–242.16. Eutychius, *Naẓm al-jawhar*, II.9.18–11.10. Muslim sources: Al-Balāḏuri, *Futuḥ al-buldān*, 109.7–13 and 13–16. Al-Azdī, *Futuḥ al-Šām*, 44.8–18. Al-Ṭabarī, *Taʾrīx*, III.406.16–19 (= de Goeje 1/208).

Byzantines cut off the regular subsidies of the tribesmen in the interface area; these sought some means of reprisal. Such reprisal included showing raiders from farther away the route to the Gaza area. A raiding party approached Dāṯin, a village somewhere near Gaza,[28] and entered into the usual negotiations regarding tribute with the local *patrikios*, whose name is recorded as Sergios. For some reason, however, the negotiations broke down,[29] and Sergios then decided to fight. He apparently had a small band of regular troops, which he supplemented by conscripting a local militia; the Byzantine force is given as anything from three hundred to five thousand men. The Arabs laid an ambush for them and killed most of the force, including its commander Sergios.

The Arab accounts refer to the Byzantine commander as the *patrikios* of Gaza, or simply as the leader of the Byzantine forces; and they make it clear that this was a local affair. They relate it as an early success of ᶜAmr bn al-ᶜĀṣ on his way to Syria. The Syriac *Chronicon ad annum 1234*, which is considered to preserve the 9th-century account of Dionysius of Tellmaḥre, refers to the Byzantine leader as Sergios, the *patrikios* of Caesarea, and has him issue forth to battle from that city with five thousand conscripts. The early 9th-century Byzantine source, Nikephorus, whose account is easily the most imaginative of them all, refers to Sergios as the *dux orientis* (!), and reports that the commander killed in this battle was not Sergios, but his successor in this post.

Where the sources preserve such widely different accounts of the same event, any reconstruction is open to question. It is, however, possible to adopt the majority view of the sources that the "battle" was a minor affair (as the Arabic versions explicitly say) at the local level, involving the *patrikios* of Gaza. The (Monophysite) Syriac sources tend to raise the size of the Byzantine force and the rank of its commander, presumably in order to magnify this defeat of their religious opponents (the Chalcedonians). With all this we agree. The traditional Western view, however, also accepts that this was one of the battles fought by ᶜAmr bn al-ᶜĀṣ, and that he enlisted local Arab tribesmen as part of a conscious policy of recruiting most of his forces locally, which Abu Bakr had decided upon before sending ᶜAmr

28. Even this is uncertain. Al-Azdī's *Futuḥ al-Šām* identifies Dāṯin as Dothan, a village in the north between Megiddo and Baysān. (We are grateful to Robert Hoyland for drawing our attention to this.)

29. This gave the later Arab historians the opportunity of supplying reasons, such as the zeal for conquest of the Muslim invaders, who could not be bought off.

north.[30] We, to the contrary, see it as a local affair caused by a town official's decision to resist paying taxes to tribesmen no longer (apparently) backed by imperial authority, or possibly as the result of his decision to resist raiders.[31] We see the attribution of the victory to ᶜAmr bn al-ᶜĀṣ as a later embellishment which turned a local skirmish into one of the early successes of a famous commander.

Another point of general agreement is that the *patrikios*, whether or not he had a small core of regular troops, had to rely mainly on conscripting the local inhabitants. Byzantium sent no further forces. This fits with the view proposed here, that after about a century and a half of gradual withdrawal there were none available; and in any case Byzantium simply had no intention of sending any. In view of all that has already been argued regarding Byzantine policy, it makes sense to read this battle in one of two ways. Most probably, as said above, it was a purely local initiative on the part of the *patrikios* of Gaza, and Byzantium pointedly refrained from sending aid. Another possibility is that Byzantium engineered the battle—sending a local militia and its commander to their deaths in the process—as a demonstration that she could no longer defend her territory against even a small force.

In our view, the military significance of the engagement lay in demonstrating, not the prowess of the Arab tribes, but Byzantium's policy towards them. Its influence on local Syrian attitudes was undoubtedly great, for Dāṯin showed that *Byzantium did not intend to retain control*—or, according to the viewpoint that Byzantium took care to promulgate, that she was unable to do so. It would not be surprising if other towns and districts took the hint: there was no point in fighting, for they were on their own. The only possible course of action was to come to terms with the Arabs, and pay what they demanded.

THE TRIBES OF THE SOUTH

The Traditional Account of the invasion and conquest mentions the Yemenis as the best warriors: easily regimented into military troops and very

30. E.g., Donner (1981) and Mayerson (1964), though they differ in their interpretation of where the battle was fought.

31. Conrad (1987) has shown that Mayerson's attribution of it to Pharan cannot be accurate, and suggests a view not far removed from ours: that the Muslim sources in fact preserve an account of a raid on the Gaza region by tribesmen angry at nonpayment of their usual subsidies.

easily disciplined, in obvious contrast to the other Arabs, who were considered unruly barbarians. This was explained by South Arabia's long history of urban society organized into well-administered kingdoms, in which the population was constantly recruited to serve in either construction projects or warfare. But according to the scheme detailed here, these warriors did not in fact come from the area we call Yemen. As Bashear (1989a) has shown, the term *al-Yaman*, "the South," originally referred to the northern peninsula (the area defined by Byzantium as Phoinikon) and possibly even to Edom (in Byzantine terms, southern Provincia Arabia). It was thus the area south of the Byzantine *oikoumenē*, or alternately, *south of al-Šām*.[32] The tribes of Edom were, as we know, partly acculturated former Byzantine *foederati*, and at least nominally Christian; those of the desert, including Phoinikon, were independent and largely pagan nomads. It is these tribes, we suggest, that Muᶜāwiyah brought up to southern Syria and allied to himself in the process of establishing his power base, along with local Syrian tribes, of which the confederacy of Qudaᶜah may have been the largest.[33] So *Yamaniyyat al-Šām* ("the *Yamanis* of *al-Šām*") does not mean tribes from South Arabia, but north peninsular people, including the tribes of Palaestina III, who had assembled in al-Šām in considerable numbers.[34] Northwest of *al-Yaman* was *atraf al-Šām*, i.e., the southern Negev and southern Trans-Jordan. We may conclude that the geographical nomenclature was as follows: *al-Šām, atraf al-Šām* (the Syrian-Jordanian deserts), and *al-Yaman* (southern Provincia Arabia, southern Palaestina III, and Phoinikon). It is of course possible that tribes from Phoinikon had penetrated into the Negev and the Euphrates area, just as we surmise above that they did into Provincia Arabia, and that as Muᶜāwiyah gained control he integrated them into the tribal power base he was creating.

---

32. Bashear (1989a), pp. 327–44, esp. pp. 333–36, 341. The identification of the term with southwestern Arabia arose only in the late 2nd century or early 3rd century A.H., when the view that the reference point was the Kaᶜbah and that *al-Yaman* was therefore *to the south of Mecca* gained prominence.

33. Crone (1980), p. 30.

34. Of course in the period between the takeover and the writing of the first accounts 150 years later, tribes from South Arabia could well have been settled in al-Šām, and have been included in the list of tribes from *Yamaniyyat al-Šām*. Equally, tribes from the north of the peninsula, who had reached al-Šām in the takeover years, could have been settled also in the Yemen. By the time of the first extant accounts, tribes described as *Yamaniyyat al-Šām* could be found also in the Yemen; this tells us little about their distribution in the early 7th century.

We suggest that the notorious confusion, contradictions, and obscurity in the military details of the invasion of al-Šām were the result of the very nature of the takeover. It was *not* a well-organized offensive, controlled from headquarters in Madīnah or anywhere else. There never was a planned invasion which could be described as a sequence of military events with the commission and dismissal of commanders by the Arab king-caliph. The stories of the invasion were originally just *ayyam* traditions, i.e., stories of individual encounters told as independent events. The events behind such accounts, whether real or legendary, were not at the time perceived as parts of a wider "Historical Event"; they were local or group recollections of the past, and not articles recorded by chroniclers. Had there been chronicles or contemporaneous documents, it would have been less easy to confuse the details so hopelessly. And the initial lack of an Arab headquarters that controlled the operations of the various tribes is one reason why there were no documents.

There is no way of telling which of the events described in the traditions, and classified by Donner as the First Stage of the invasion, actually took place around this time. They could equally well be *ayyam* accounts of 6th-century events; they could also refer to events of later date. The same may be said of the commanders whose names are recorded. For instance, the Arab traditions about ᶜAmr bn al-ᶜĀṣ, his raid into the Negev, and his "headquarters" in Ġamr al-ᶜArabat, could be accepted on the grounds of archaeological evidence in the area during the 6th or 7th centuries C.E.; but on epigraphical and numismatic grounds he should be placed not earlier than the latter half of the 7th century C.E., i.e., several decades after the takeover.[35] Thus stories and memories of events from a period of a hundred years may have been compressed into the account of the conquest.[36] The archaeological evidence indicates that the takeover period was not characterized by indiscriminate raiding: the tribes were controlled, we think by covert funding from Byzantium, at least until they transferred their allegiance and began to receive their funding from Muᶜāwiyah.

35. See for example the paleographic and epigraphical arguments in Nevo (1989), for a date in the 70s/690s or later for an inscription commemorating a *mowla* of ᶜAmr bn al-ᶜĀṣ in the Negev town of Ruḥayba (Reḥovot ba-Negev).

36. One may speculate that some, at least, of these tales actually derive from Sassanian stories of engagements with Byzantine forces during the first years of the Persian-Byzantine wars of the early 7th century. Such heroic tales must have gone the rounds of the Persian storytellers, and may well have been recorded, sooner or later.

2

Political Events
The Evidence of Contemporary Texts

The peoples over whom the Arabs assumed control had a long tradition of literary activity, and left chronicles and religious writings (sermons, saints' lives, letters from church officials, and so on) dating from the time of the Arab takeover and the immediately following decades. This literature has scarcely been used as source material for the history of the takeover and the early Arab state, perhaps partly because it says so little on the subject compared to the vast detail found in the Muslim sources from the late 8th century C.E. on. This is a pity, for the non-Arab sources reflect the period in light of a completely different wavelength and from a different angle.

Like the Muslim sources, the contemporary non-Arab ones present many problems of reliability and interpretation. Most of them, as said, are not primarily historical but religious in nature; even the chronicle-writers took pains to reveal to which sect they belonged, and one of their reasons for composing the chronicle was religious. The accurate recording of historical events was no part of the purpose of a religious text; indeed our modern ethic concerning the need for an accurate factual transmission of history is conspicuously absent from them.[1] And even when the source is apparently factual, reading history from it can be hazardous. For instance,

1. Rather than recording *wie es eigentlich gewesen war*, they were "moral teachers using

we have letters of the Nestorian Catholicos Isho^cyahb III (d. 39/659) discounting a claim by the clergy of Nineveh that the new rulers favored the Monophysites and this was why the Nestorians had lost ground to them. We do not have their letter making this claim, but we have Isho^cyahb's reply that the losses were the fault of the local clergy, and it was untrue that the Arabs had helped the Monophysites.[2] It is not hard to imagine how our view of Church history would change, if we possessed the letter(s) of the Nineveh clergy and not Isho^cyahb's reply. As it is, each side had its own reasons for the claims it made, and it is difficult to know if Isho^cyahb's reprimand to his clergy was any closer to the historical truth than the clergy's complaint. Accounts of persecution and atrocities committed are another example: very little historical fact can be derived from general, unspecified complaints of hardship in literature of this type, for it is biased by its authors' intentions and perceived readership, and these and other factors are not usually known to us.[3]

So if we wish to use these works as historical sources, we face several questions. Firstly, what factual historical content, if any, can we extract from the text—for instance, regarding the Arabs' assumption of control, their behavior as rulers, and how they actually treated the Christians? For as Brock notes, "Each of the three main communities, Chalcedonian, Monophysite and Nestorian, came to provide their own particular interpretation of these events."[4] Secondly, can we date the events referred to, and are they past, contemporary with the author, or future as in the eschatological apocalyptic works? For their authors were accustomed to use past events as *exempla* for present ones, and those of both past and present, for the future. Thirdly, which church's parochial historiography are we reading, and how might the viewpoint presented distort the information given? For these works, even the chronicles, were written within the specific cultural and religious framework of a particular sect, and their open or hidden agenda was the religious guidance and edification of members of that sect.

---

historical argument" (Witakowski [1987], p. 172; arguing specifically for the Pseudo-Dionysius of Tellmaḥre: pp. 170–71).

2. Brock (1982), pp. 16. The religious aspects of Isho^cyahb's letter are discussed in Part III Chapter 2.

3. The problem of deriving history from written sources is discussed further in the Introduction.

4. Brock (1982), p. 10 para. 2.

Two main methods were employed to this end: *reprimanding* and *thanksgiving*. To reprimand was an essential part of the guidance of believers, and both Jews and all the various Christian sects practiced it in a variety of literary genres. The pattern was familiar: a natural or social mishap would be elaborated into a disaster, which would serve as a token of God's wrath at the believers' erring behavior. The community would be reprimanded for sinning and thereby bringing God's punishment upon His otherwise beloved people. Sophronius, Patriarch of Jerusalem, was following an already well-worn path when he ascribed the Arabs' prevention of the Christmas procession of 634 C.E. to the iniquity of his flock: "But we, for our many sins and gravest errors, have been rendered unfit to ... direct our course [to Bethlehem] ...."[5] So was Jacob of Edessa (d. 708 C.E.): "Christ has delivered us up because of [our] many sins and iniquities and subjected us to the hard yoke of the Arabians."[6]

To reprimand the state was also a common theme, especially among the non-Chalcedonian sects: the ruler had wickedly disobeyed God's will, and was consequently visited with affliction, in the shape of his own disease and/or death, a calamity which befell an area under his rule, or a military failure such as the loss of a battle or of part of his territories. In this way divine intervention secured also vengeance for the sufferings inflicted by the ruler on his subjects, the believers in the True Faith. For this divine intervention, God's people owed Him thanks, and thus the other side of the same coin was thanksgiving to God for the punishment of the wicked (i.e., the ruler or the other Christian sects and, less often, other religions such as the Jews). Thus writings whose main function was to reprimand and to give thanks could be the reaction to any untoward occurrence: social strife, natural catastrophes, frightening rumors, and political changes; and the authors of these works tended to present history as a series of very dramatic events, each designated by Providence to serve as a lesson to mankind.

Given this framework, and assuming the truth of the descriptions in the Muslim sources—an organized Arab invasion resulting, after a series of great battles, in a conquest—we would expect to find accounts of the course of the invasion, and especially the battles, in the contemporary writings of the peoples conquered. But we find relatively little, and what there is tends to be vague references or generalized comment rather than detailed

5. Sophronius' Christmas sermon for 634 C.E..; Latin text, *PG* 87 col. 3205 lines 48ff.
6. Jacob of Edessa, *Scholion* on I Kings xiv:21 etc., in Phillips (1864).

descriptions of events.[7] Syriac sources down to the early 8th century do not describe the invasion itself; and later sources which do, such as the 12th-century chronicle of Michael the Syrian,[8] the 13th-century chronicle of Bar-Hebraeus,[9] or those parts of the lost 9th-century chronicle of Dionysius of Tellmaḥre which were incorporated into Bar-Hebraeus's chronicle, reproduce the traditional Muslim account which they copy faithfully from an Arab source.[10] The scarcity of reference in the contemporary sources is surprising, for the battles recorded in the ᶜAbbāsid accounts would have provided many a moral for a Nestorian or Monophysite pen. Yet no extant contemporary or near-contemporary writer availed himself of the opportunity they afforded: only the *fact of Byzantine loss* of the provinces was pressed into service to support religious lessons. Thus John bar Penkayê, a Nestorian (fl. 680s–700), saw the loss of the Roman provinces as God's punishment for Chalcedonian and Monophysite heresy;[11] the Monophysites, as punishment for Byzantine (Chalcedonian) church policy. The Chalcedonian Anastasius the Sinaite (late 7th century) attributed it to Constans II's pro-Monotheletic policy and his mistreatment of the pope.[12] The same attitudes are to be found, centuries later, in the chronicle of Michael the Syrian and the *Chronicon ad annum 1234*.[13] But the contemporary sources make no use of any of the great battles to draw such conclusions; indeed there is scarcely a mention of them.

7. For a highly useful annotated bibliography of all Syriac sources with any historical bearing on the 7th century, see Brock (1976). The much more comprehensive compilation of notes on Syriac authors and their works, by Chabot (1934), only confirms that Brock has indeed omitted nothing of relevance. Hoyland (1997) is now the most comprehensive list and discussion of contemporary references to the Early Arab religion. It unfortunately reached us late in the preparation of this book for press.

8. Ed. by Chabot (1901).

9. Ed. by Budge (1932).

10. Bar-Hebraeus takes his material on events concerning the Arabs almost exclusively from Ṭabarī. Hoyland (1991) analyzes the parts of the lost chronicle of Dionysius of Tellmaḥre (818–845) incorporated into Bar-Hebraeus, and demonstrates that Dionysius also copied whole paragraphs from the Muslim sources, especially Al-Azdī, whose phrases he sometimes translates word for word (Hoyland [1991], pp. 222–24 + table of correspondences in Appendix I).

11. Bar Penkayê, chs. 14–15; German translation in Abramowski (1940), pp. 5ff. French in Mingana (1907). Hoyland (1997) dates his chronicle to 687–88 on internal evidence.

12. Kaegi (1969), pp. 142–43. The point is made also by Brock (1982), p. 11.

13. Brock (1982), pp. 10–11.

This is in sharp contrast to the information about earlier wars recorded by contemporary writers both secular and religious. The Chronicle of Joshua the Stylite, for instance, which covers the years 395 to 506 C.E., shows what detailed information a religious source could include about battles, sieges, ambushes, and raids when there was something to relate.[14] Works from the immediate preconquest years also provide good accounts of current events, even when these were only incidental to the reason for writing. For instance, the Life of the Nestorian R. bar ᶜIdtâ (d. 612 C.E.)[15] refers to confrontations between the Persians and the Romans, though these are far from being important to the narrative. And Antiochus of Mar Saba, in a letter written some time during the years 614–628 C.E.,[16] relates at length an Arab raid on his monastery during which the Arabs tortured and killed the monks in an attempt to discover where valuables were hidden. But when, a few years later, the Arabs replaced both the Byzantine and the Sassanian empires, and supposedly introduced into the religious battlefield a new, unheard-of contender for the title of True Faith, the events marking their political and religious progress were slighted in the writings of the people we would have expected to be most intimately concerned. Thus the Life of Maruṯâ, a biography from the time of the Arab invasion into Syria,[17] devotes only a few words to the campaigns of Heraclius and of the Arabs; and the Life of R. Hormizd,[18] who lived through the takeover period, comes no closer to a description of political events than a passing reference to one ᶜAlī, governor of Mosul, whose son Hormizd cures. The "Khuzestan Chronicle," an anonymous chronicle written between 50/670 and 60/680, which purports to be a history of the church,[19] contains so many descriptions of events of the Roman-Persian wars that Brock describes it

---

14. The Chronicle of Joshua the Stylite is preserved in the Pseudo-Dionysius of Tellmaḥre (Vat. Libr. no. Syr. 162, folios 65–86, publ. Chabot [1895]), into which it was apparently incorporated in its entirety.

15. Budge (1902).

16. Migne, *PG* 89, cols. 1421–28. It was probably written not long after the removal of the True Cross to Persia in 614 C.E., an event mentioned in the letter, though it could have been written any time from then till the Persians were defeated in 628. After that date the reason for writing—to send a summary of Scripture to a monk hiding from the Persians—would no longer have applied. We are grateful to Robert Hoyland for drawing our attention to this letter.

17. Nau (1909a).

18. Also published in Budge (1902).

19. Nöldeke (1893).

as a chronicle on the end of the Sassanids,[20] but it has very little on the Arab conquest, and that mostly in a concluding summary.

In fact, in contrast to the raiding lamented by Antiochus of Mar Saba during the Persian period, throughout the Arab takeover period life seems to have continued with little untoward disturbance in the monasteries responsible for most of the literary output. To take an example provided by Brock, which sums up the atmosphere:

> On 24 December 633 at a monastery outside Damascus, a sumptuous Gospel manuscript was completed, miraculously to survive the turbulent events of the next few years, to give us some hint of the *lack of awareness of the storm clouds over the horizon.*[21]

It is true that this is still three years before the accepted date of the Battle of the Yarmūk, which, as the Traditional Account has it, shattered the imperial army and stripped al-Šām of all protection from the predatory Muslim hordes. But if we believe the Traditional Account, then other clouds had already heralded the storm. There was the Battle of Muʾtah in 8/629 in southern Syria, described as an engagement between Byzantine forces and an Arab party venturing north from the peninsula.[22] In 12/633, the very year at whose end the Gospel manuscript was completed, there are reports of battles at Dāṯin[23] and al-ʿArabah. In that year, too, came the conquest of southern Mesopotamia, which should remind us that according to the traditions the oncoming Arab forces were fighting battles in several arenas besides al-Šām. December 24, 633 C.E. was therefore, if we accept the Traditio-nal Account, the end of the fourth year of open warfare between the peninsular Muslims and the two empires, the Byzantine and the Persian, a year in which two battles had been fought and Mesopotamia conquered. So it is difficult to explain the local population's lack of awareness as due to the clouds being still over the horizon. If the Traditional Account is true, the thunder was crashing all around them.

And according to the Traditional Account, three more years of warfare followed, bringing the great Battle of Ajnādayn (13/634), the fall of Damascus (14/635), and finally the Battle of the Yarmūk (15/636), which resulted in the withdrawal of the defeated empire to the north, leaving

---

20. Brock (1976), p. 23 no. 13.
21. Brock (1982), p. 9 para. 3, emphasis added.
22. See Conrad (1990), "The Battle of Muʾta."
23. Discussed in the previous chapter.

southern Syria and Palestine to the Arabs. Yet both during these years and after them, the local writers recorded very few references to these tumultuous events in their nonhistorical works, and not much more in the chronicles. No description of specific events *of the conquest* can be found in the region's contemporary extra-Muslim literature[24] until much later, when the Syriac and Greek authors began to borrow from the by-now-established Muslim historiography. The closest we get to a specific description is the work of Sebeos, an Armenian historian writing in the late 7th century.[25] He has two accounts of battles which modern scholars have assumed to be those of the Yarmūk and Qadisiyyah. These, like the garbled echoes in the Khuzestan Chronicle, will be considered later in this chapter. In the 7th-century Syriac and Greek literature we have not even the little that we find in Sebeos. It is the much less "dramatic" fact of *Arab rule* which the contemporary writers mobilize to teach the lesson of divine wrath or divine grace.

This situation should at least suggest the possibility that the fact of Arab rule was the most dramatic event available: there had simply been nothing more dramatic or catastrophic on which to focus in the process of changing rulers. That, in our opinion, is the most likely explanation why the plain fact of Byzantium's loss of the East was a favorite "divine punishment" theme of non-Chalcedonian works, while they make no use of the empire's loss of battles.

Because there is this vacuum in the contemporary texts, it is very easy for even the most careful scholar who accepts the Traditional Account to read it into them unawares—as even Brock does, for instance, when he remarks that in the Monophysite sources "the Arab invasions are seen primarily as a punishment ...."[26] In fact the passages to which he refers do not mention *invasions*, but only the *loss of the provinces by Byzantium*, seen as God's punishment for the persecution of the Monophysites. The "Ishmaelites" are seen as God's agents in effecting this punishment, but *how* they did it we cannot tell. Of the invasions and the battles that Byzantium lost there is no sign.

There is also the problem that relatively few sources have survived from the 7th century, and the accounts of the relevant years may be missing from

---

24. The anonymous scribble on a Gospel flyleaf published by Nöldeke (1875) is undated and not, in our opinion, contemporary. We discuss it later in this chapter.

25. Sebeos, *Histoire d'Héraclius*, tr. to French and ed. by Macler (1904).

26. Brock (1982), p. 10.

those that have. There is, for example, a "Maronite Chronicle" from the mid-40s/660s,[27] but the surviving portions do not cover the invasion period; they start with the war between ʿAlī and Muʿāwiyah. The Chronicle (chronological charts) of Jacob of Edessa (19–90/640–708) survives only down to 632 C.E., and even that only in a 10th- or 11th-century manuscript.[28] It is ascribed by Elias of Nisibis (11th century) to 691–692 C.E., and by Theodosius of Edessa to 685–692 C.E.,[29] but there is no internal evidence to limit its date, so that it could have been written at any time up to Jacob's death in 708. It will be discussed later in this chapter.

A later 8th-century source is the Pseudo-Dionysius of Tellmaḥre,[30] compiled in the monastery of Zuqnīn in Mesopotamia around 158/775,[31] but it contains only very brief entries for the 7th century. In any case we have already moved beyond the years when we could hope to discover "what really happened," for by this period the earliest extant Arab Taʾrīx literature was being either compiled or rewritten. Thus the Pseudo-Dionysius faithfully reproduces the account found in the Arab sources.

But despite all, some contemporary comments on the Arab takeover of al-Šām have survived, and they are intriguing both for what they say, and, perhaps even more, for what they do not. We will now discuss these sources in turn. We stress that this chapter deals only with the political aspects—references to religion in these sources will be discussed in Part III.

There is, to start with, a marginal comment in Syriac by an unknown author on the flyleaf of a 6th-century Syriac Gospel manuscript. The handwriting is a barely decipherable scrawl lapsing frequently into illegibility. Of the twenty-nine lines, the first six and last four or five are unreadable; the remaining seventeen or eighteen have been published with a German translation and a commentary by Nöldeke (1875), and in a new

---

27. Brock (1976), p. 19.

28. Ms. BL Add. 14.685, folios 1–23, of which folio 23, pp. 324–27, covers the 7th century. For a translation into English see Palmer (1993), text no. 5. There were at least two continuators of Jacob's Chronicle, for Michael the Syrian found entries down to 709/10 C.E., and himself continued it further.

29. Hoyland (1997), p. 164.

30. Chabot (1895). Chabot's mistaken identification of this chronicle as that of Dionysius of Tellmaḥre follows Assemani. Only one fragment of the real chronicle of Dionysius of Tellmaḥre survives, but parts of it were incorporated into the *Chronography* of Elias of Nisibis (975–1050), the Chronicle of Bar-Hebraeus (1226–1286), and the *Chronicon ad annum 1234*.

31. For date and authorship see Witakowski (1987), p. 90ff.; and Hoyland (1997), pp. 409–14.

reading with English translation by Palmer (1993). We give here Palmer's version, noting where Nöldeke differs from him. Square brackets enclose unreadable words which the editor guesses from the context.

7 ... appeared ... and the Rhomaeans ...[32]
8 And in January they took the word for their lives[33]
9 [the sons of] Emesa, and many villages were ruined with killing by
10 [the partisans of][34] Muḥammad, and a great number of people were killed and captives
11 [were taken] from Galilee as far as Beth ...
12 [...] and those Arabs pitched camp beside [Damascus?][35] ...
13 [...] and we saw (?)[36] everywhe[re] ...
14 and olive oil which they brought and [...] them. And on the t[wenty-][37]
15 [six]th of May[38] went S[ac[ellar]ius] [39] ... cattle[40]
16 [...] from the vicinity of Emesa,[41] and the Rhomaeans chased them [...]
17 [...] and on the tenth
18 [of August] the Rhomaeans fled from the vicinity of Damascus [...]
19 many [people], some 10,000. And at the turn
20 [of the ye]ar[42] the Rhomaeans came. On the twentieth of August in the year n[ine hundred]

---

32. Nöldeke could not read the first seven lines, and while Palmer gives them, not enough of the first six are decipherable to be worth giving here.

33. According to Palmer, a technical term for a surrender agreement.

34. Conjectured by Palmer.

35. Nöldeke's conjecture.

36. Palmer's reading; Brock comments: could be "we rejoiced"; Nöldeke read "were seen."

37. Brock comments that the whole line is very uncertain.

38. Or possibly "of August."

39. Different people could read different parts of "Sacellarius." Hoyland (1997), p. 117 read Saq[īlā]rā and compares with Theophanes's mention of Theodore the treasurer (*sakellarios*) who defeated the Saracens at Emesa and drove them as far as Damascus.

40. Cattle: Brock comments that the word could be "as usual."

41. Brock finds the reading "Emesa" only "just possible" and no more likely than several other possible restorations.

42. This is a literal translation. Nöldeke translates "in another year" but the Syriac expression usually meant "the next year." If the month last referred to (l. 18) was indeed Ab (August), this could have meant after only one or two months: the Syrian Christian new year started on September 1 or October 1, depending on the writer's sect. However, the fact that the date of August 20, 947 (of the Seleucid era) follows this reference to the next year implies that 947 was "the next year," i.e., that the events reported in lines 8–19 took place in 946 (635 C.E.).

21 [and forty-] seven[43] there gathered in Gabitha
22 [...] the Rhomaeans and a great many people were ki[lled of]
23 [the R]homaeans, [s]ome fifty thousand [...]
24 [...] in the year nine hundred[44] and for[ty-eight]
....
....
29 .... and the Romans were troubled.[45]

Nöldeke has no doubt that the fragment preserves the comments of a contemporary Syrian,[46] and on the strength of the general area (west of the Ḥawrān), and the number of the slain, he identifies the battle referred to as the Yarmūk, even though Gabīṯâ was a considerable distance from the site of that battle (about 20 kilometers north of the valley of the Yarmūk):

> Denn dass die Schlacht bei Gabhithâ mit der am Jarmûk identisch ist, kann keinem Zweifel unterliegen. Es handelt sich ja hier bei dem Syrer um eine Entscheidungsschlacht, in der 50.000 Römer umkamen; das kann nur die Schlacht sein, in welcher nach den Arabern 70.000 Römer gefallen sind. Auch ist in jener Gegend (im Westen des Ḥaurân) weiter kein grosser Zusammenstoss gewesen als der am Jarmûk.

Palmer agrees, and furthermore sees a reference to the Battle of Ajnādayn in lines 9–10, concluding that "[it is] likely, to my mind, that there were not three, but two initial Arab victories in Palestine: one near Gaza, to be identified with al-Ajnādayn, and one near Gabitha, to be conflated with the Battle of the Yarmūk."[47] This despite the fact that lines 9–10 do not mention a battle, and their context is northern: Emesa, Galilee and possibly Damascus, not the vicinity of Gaza.[48] Moreover, lines 8–19 trace events from January to August, and the year in question is most probably 946, i.e., 635 C.E., the year before 947 (the date given in lines 20–21; see n. 40 above); the alternative interpretation is that it is 947, i.e.,

43. Of the Seleucid era, i.e., 636 C.E.
44. Brock finds the reading "nine hundred" very uncertain.
45. Not in Palmer; given by Nöldeke.
46. Nöldeke (1875), p. 79.
47. Palmer (1993), p. 29.
48. It is of interest that the area concerned is the north: Syria and Galilee, since the evidence of the early Arab coins, examined in the next chapter, also suggests that the Arab assumption of control in al-Šām was originally confined to the north.

636 C.E. It is difficult to see lines 8–19 as referring to the events of two years, 634–35, as Palmer surmises they do in order to read into them the Battle of Ajnādayn (634 C.E.). In short, both Nöldeke's and Palmer's interpretations follow the familiar process of scholarship within an accepted paradigm which one does not question—one takes a new piece of information and fits it into the established framework as best one can. There is, however, nothing in the fragment itself which dates it to the actual years whose events it records. Palmer believes that the author was an eyewitness, basically on the strength of the word "we saw" or "we rejoiced" in line 13. However, Nöldeke read this as the passive, "were seen."

In our opinion Brock rightly queries the description "contemporary" accorded the fragment by Nöldeke (and Palmer).[49] Firstly, the readable portion covers, in an orderly chronological progression, the events of at least two to three years, 635–637/38 C.E., and it is both preceded and followed by several unreadable lines which probably extended the time span even more. The date in line 24, "in the year 94[..]," which Nöldeke tentatively assumes to be a reference to 947, the date of the battle given two lines before, could equally well be the start of a new section, and indeed Palmer conjectures that it refers to the following year, 948. This reading has some logic to it, for there are another five lines to the end of the passage, and the phrase following them, "the Romans were troubled," scarcely describes their reaction to the loss of a decisive battle. For all we know, the five unreadable lines may have taken the account even later than 948. Secondly, many events are reported, and those for which the most details are given are the earliest mentioned (in the readable portion), the events of the year 635 or 636 C.E. (946 or 947), not those nearest in time to when the author was writing. This does not suggest the hurried recording of the writer's own immediate experience. In an eyewitness account we would expect the opposite emphasis: greater attention to the most recent events which the writer has just experienced, and especially to the most momentous ones, i.e., the battle.

We therefore consider this fragment to have been copied from an already existing text, and suggest that Nöldeke's initial comment, namely that one might expect to find on a Gospel flyleaf something such as the trial

49. Brock (1976), p. 18. Donner (1981), p. 144 also prefers to reserve judgment, considering the fragment's illegibility and the lack of information concerning its provenance; so also Hoyland (1997), p. 117, though with some regret.

of a new pen, comes much closer to the truth than the vision of a fleeing Christian scribbling hurried impressions in a time of turmoil.

In any case an account covering several years must have been composed some time after the events described, and who can tell whether the "some time" was five years, or fifty, or more? The point is not trivial. A date must be assigned to the fragment before we can consider it as evidence, and obviously this can only be done from external data—our knowledge of the events of the various times in which it could have been written. In practice this means fitting it into the current paradigm (assuming that one accepts it), as Nöldeke and Palmer do. However, to fit it into one paradigm is no more valid than to fit it into another. According to the Traditional Account, this scribble could have been written at the time of the conquest (if we allow that the writer knew of the Battle of the Yarmūk under a different name and in a rather different place). According to the theory set forth in this book, it could not have been. And though we are not now considering religious references, since we discuss religious development only in Part III, we may perhaps mention here that in our opinion the reference to Muḥammad dates it as post–ca. 70–71/690, and the mention of a great battle also dates it to not earlier than the later 7th century. That it differs from the Traditional Account concerning the name of the battle and the number of the dead only fits it the better into the confused versions current at that time. The point is that the fragment's date is unknown, whereas the most important aspect of an account, for the purpose of supporting or rejecting a particular view of the Arab takeover, is its date. Since the theory one accepts must be used to date the fragment, it cannot then itself be used to verify that theory.

In the *Doctrina Iacobi nuper baptizati*, set in the year 634 C.E. and probably written not long afterwards, appears a reference to an unnamed "false prophet coming with the Saracens," which most scholars accept as a reference to Muḥammad. We dispute this identification, but postpone a detailed analysis of this source to our discussion of the religious references in the contemporary sources (Part III Chapter 2).

The earliest securely dated references to local events connected with the Arabs come from Sophronius, Patriarch of Jerusalem. The first is in a synodical letter which can be dated by internal references to the first half of 634 C.E.[50] At the end of this letter he expresses his hope that God will enable the empire:

---

50. Hoyland (1997), p. 69.

> To break the pride of all the barbarians, and especially of the Saracens who, on account of our sins, have now risen up against us unexpectedly and ravage all ... with impious and godless audacity ... [may Christ] quickly quell their mad insolence and deliver these vile creatures, as before, to be the footstool of our God-given emperors.[51]

The situation this describes is that those same Arab tribes who were formerly subservient to, and perhaps in the service of, the emperor are now out of control. Exactly what their former relationship with the empire was, depends on what Sophronius meant by "the footstool of the emperors" (not that he was striving for precision). But clearly there was a subservient relationship; the Arabs described here have not suddenly smashed into the civilized world from somewhere far beyond it. They were around all the time; but they used to be tame and now are running wild.

By Christmas of 634 C.E. (13 A.H.) Sophronius is considerably more troubled. His problem is documented at length in his Christmas sermon for that year, which survives in two Greek manuscripts and in a Latin translation dating from the 16th century.[52] Much of the sermon revolves around the fact that people cannot go to Bethlehem—cannot even safely go outside the city walls of Jerusalem—for fear of the Arabs; therefore the traditional Christmas procession cannot be held and the Christmas service cannot be celebrated in the Church of the Nativity. The Christians, who so greatly desire free passage to Bethlehem, can only gaze upon her from afar. This sermon is sometimes taken as evidence that the Arabs had already captured Bethlehem and an organized invasion was well under way; but the text does not support this view. For while Sophronius, like other religious writers, sees the situation as a punishment for sin, he does not see it as a calamity presaging the end of the world. His point is not that impious infidels have captured the holy places of Bethlehem—as it assuredly would have been, had the Arabs done so—but that the Christians of Jerusalem cannot themselves get near them. Thus he compares their situation with that of Adam cast out of Paradise, able to look back at it but not return;[53] of Moses, shown the Promised Land but forbidden to enter it;[54] and especially of David, longing for

51. Sophronius, *Ep. Synodica*, *PG* 87, 3197D–3200A; tr. in Hoyland (1997), p. 69.
52. Greek text: Usener (1886); Latin translation: *PL* 87 cols. 3201–12.
53. Gen. 3:24.
54. Deut. 32:52.

water from the well of Bethlehem but prevented by the Philistines from reaching it.[55]

The sermon's actual references to Arabs and Bethlehem are as follows (our translation is from the Latin, with a discussion of the points at which it differs significantly from the Greek original):

> But we for our many sins and gravest errors have been rendered unfit to contemplate these things or to direct our course there, and are forbidden to approach, but are compelled against our will to remain at home; not bound, to be sure, by physical chains, but deterred and fettered by fear of the Saracens.[56]

> And we are thus punished today [i.e., as Adam was], since we have at hand the city of Bethlehem, which received God, but nonetheless are not permitted to enter it ... frightened by the sword of the savage and most barbarous Saracens, full of every cruelty. [This sword] ... banishes us from that happy sight, and compels us to remain at home, without further advance.[57]

> If then we do the will of our Father, and constantly maintain the Orthodox faith and truth, we will easily remove the Ishmaelite sword, and turn aside the Saracen dagger, and break the Hagarene bow, and see holy Bethlehem, long unseen.[58]

> ... For we have close [to us] the place in which God ... appeared ... yet notwithstanding we are not strong enough to hasten there.[59]

In the next passage, the Latin translation differs significantly from the Greek original. It reads:

> ... For [David] too, just like us, was prevented by fear of enemies from going to sacred Bethlehem and drinking the longed-for water.... Because at that time too, just as now, a Philistine position was besieging Bethlehem; and the same thing that frightened him away and prevented him from reaching divine Bethlehem, now prevents us and frightens us away from

55. 1 Chron. 11:16–19.

56. Sophronius: Christmas sermon. Latin: *PL* 87 col. 3205 lines 48–54; Greek: Usener (1886) 506, lines 31ff.

57. Ibid. Latin: *PL* 87 col. 3206 lines 24–37; Greek: Usener (1886), p. 507 lines 23–24.

58. Ibid. Latin: *PL* 87 col. 3207 lines 25–31; Greek: Usener (1886), p. 508 lines 28ff.

59. Ibid. Latin: *PL* 87 col. 3209 lines 8–11.

obtaining [our desire]. ... He could not at that time reach that God-bearing city, because of the hostile steel of the Philistines, who then held Bethlehem under siege.[60]

The Latin here twice refers to a siege of Bethlehem, but in the Greek original[61] the first reference, which explicitly links a Philistine siege of Bethlehem with the current situation, is missing altogether, and even the second, which refers only to events in David's time, is doubtful. In the first reference, where the Latin gives *Philistaeorum statio Bethleem obsidebat*—"a position of the Philistines was besieging Bethlehem"—the Greek has: *hoti kai tote, phēsin, katha kai nun tōn Sarakēnōn, en Bēthleem tōn allophylōn ēn to hypostēma* "for then, too, a position of the Philistines [was] at Bethlehem, just as now of the Saracens."[62] In the second, where the Latin has *obsessum tenebat*—"was holding besieged"—the Greek has *proskathēmenon,* from *pros* + *kathemai.* In classical Greek this compound would indeed have meant "to besiege";[63] but this meaning did not transfer to New Testament and patristic Greek.[64] The more probable meaning is therefore that conveyed by the two words *pros* and *kathemai*—to sit or be settled relative to something.[65] We would suggest the translation "a Philistine position was stationed in the neighborhood of Bethlehem" or perhaps "stationed before Bethlehem," i.e., from the viewpoint of a Jerusalemite, near Bethlehem on the road between it and Jerusalem. Sophronius, in fact, keeps closely to the Biblical description, which was that a Philistine position was "at" Bethlehem, and David's captains had to break through the Philistines in order to get to the well of Bethlehem, which was at the city gate.[66] Those are the events that Sophronius chooses to liken to the current situation.

In the next—and last—passage referring to the Arabs, the Latin again differs from the Greek. The Latin reads:

---

60. Ibid. Latin: *PL* 87 col. 3210 line 51–col. 3211 line 12.

61. Usener (1886), p. 514 para. 2.

62. Kaegi (1969) twice translates "the slime of the gentiles/Saracens" instead of "a military position of the gentiles/Saracens." We have not been able to discover the basis for this translation.

63. Cf. the entry in Liddell and Scott (1849).

64. It is not listed in either Lampe (1961) or GENT.

65. Cf. Lampe *pros* p. 1163 col. 2; *kathemai* p. 689 col. 1.

66. I. Chron. 11:16–18.

> For a position of the impious Hagarenes, as formerly of the Philistines, is in like manner, as said, occupying and besieging illustrious Bethlehem, nor does it allow any passage to her whatsoever. For it threatens slaughter and destruction, if anyone should dare to go out to that holy city, and approach our most sacred and most beloved Bethlehem. Wherefore shut inside the gates of this city, not in the holy Church of the Nativity of God, we meet and publicly celebrate this festival.[67]

The difference is in the first sentence. Where the Latin has *etenim impiorum Agarenorum statio aeque nunc, ut dictum est, illustrem Bethleem occupat et obsidet, ut quondam Philistaeorum,* the Greek reads: *Sarakēnōn gar atheōn nun to hypostēma hōs allophylōn tote, tēn thespasian Bēthleem pareilēphe*: "a position of the godless Saracens has now, as the Philistines before, taken[68] divine Bethlehem."[69]

In what sense should we understand "has taken" here? Sophronius proceeds to develop from this statement, yet again, the point around which his whole sermon has revolved: the Christians cannot reach Bethlehem for the Christmas ceremonies. He does not make the point that the godless infidels now hold the most sacred shrines of Christendom—neither here nor elsewhere in the sermon. But is it possible that, the Arabs having recently captured the Holy Places of Bethlehem, the Patriarch of Jerusalem should devote his entire Christmas sermon to lamenting only that he and his congregation cannot go there? If the Arabs were really in possession of the Church of the Holy Nativity—or if Sophronius thought they probably might be—he would be quoting Lamentations, not Chronicles; he would be comparing the desecration of the church with that of the Temple. His whole sermon would revolve around a different focal point. The scribe of the Greek manuscript, who added a heading, likewise understood that Sophronius was talking of a time when "the Saracens, out of control and destructive, were rebelling," not of a time when they were in possession of the holy places of Bethlehem. But the 16th-century translator into Latin saw a problem. He did not know whether to translate *pareilēphe* as "was besieging" (which would make sense but which it cannot mean) or as "has captured/occupied" (which it might be construed to mean, except that

---

67. Latin: *PL* 87, col. 3212, lines 28–39; Greek: Usener (1886), p. 514 lines 24–32.

68. *Pareilēphe* from *paralambāno*: to take (by force or treachery); cf. Liddell and Scott (1849).

69. Usener (1886), p. 514, lines 24–25.

Sophronius's attitude, given such a case, is incomprehensible). So he gave both options; and he added a note at the start of his translation, referring to the Saracens *qui per id tempus oppidum Bethleem vel occuparant vel certe obsessum tenebant*: "who at that time were either occupying or certainly besieging the town of Bethlehem"—the Arabs, he apparently reasoned, must have done one or the other, and when writing note 1 to column 3201 he had thought it was the first; but by the time he wrote note 2 a column later he had apparently concluded that he could not tell which.

Our own reading of this passage, in the context of the whole sermon, is that the Arabs had neither occupied nor besieged Bethlehem, but had *taken the town from the Christians of Jerusalem* by preventing their access to it. The picture is consistent throughout the sermon: the problem is simply that the Christians cannot travel from Jerusalem to Bethlehem. The reason, as Sophronius explicitly says, is that a band of Arabs, positioned somewhere near Bethlehem, is preventing them from entering it.

It was not the first time that Sophronius had been prevented by Arabs from reaching a city. In 619 C.E., when he brought the body of his friend John Moschus from Rome to Palestine for burial at Mount Sinai, he was barred by a Saracen "incursion" from reaching Ashqelon (and thence Sinai), and had to take the body to Jerusalem instead.[70] That the Saracens were preventing him from reaching a city did not mean that they had "taken" it in 619; nor did it in 634.

Sophronius's description of the situation in fact fits our proposed model better than it fits the Traditional Account. Let us surmise that a group of former *foederati* had demanded taxes/tribute from Jerusalem, and that the negotiations had not been satisfactorily concluded by Christmas. The Arabs then took the opportunity to apply pressure, by denying passage to the traditional Christmas procession from Jerusalem to Bethlehem.[71] They did so by the simple method of placing an armed contingent near the entrance to Bethlehem: a situation indeed very similar to the Biblical one to which

---

70. Biography of John Moschus in Migne, *PL* 74, col. 121; q.b. Vasiliev (1955), p. 316.

71. It is also possible that the town from which money was demanded was not Jerusalem but Bethlehem. We consider Jerusalem more likely, since the method of applying pressure—stopping the Christmas Procession—affected the Jerusalem Christians far more than it affected those of Bethlehem (who, after all, could continue to hold the Christmas Mass in the Church of the Holy Nativity), and because Sophronius says that the Jerusalemites could not leave their city at all, not just that they could not enter Bethlehem.

Sophronius compares it. Quite possibly they also stationed a position on the Jerusalem-Bethlehem road near Jerusalem, since Sophronius laments not only that the Christians of Jerusalem cannot enter Bethlehem, but also that they cannot leave their own city. This is not a siege in the military sense, and Sophronius does not say it was; but his 16th-century translator into Latin quite naturally read the Traditional Account back into Sophronius's words.

The Christian community of Jerusalem whom Sophronius addresses, reading between the lines, would also have understood what Sophronius did not say: where is the Byzantine army, that one contingent of Arabs near the Bethlehem gate can prevent the Christmas procession? In David's time it took only three "mighty men" to break through the Philistines; but nowadays the emperor cannot supply even one.

A few years later—probably in 636 or 637—Sophronius digresses at the end of his sermon at the Feast of the Epiphany to give a long list of Arab atrocities:

> Why do barbarian raids abound? Why are the troops of the Saracens attacking us? Why has there been so much destruction and plunder? Why have churches been pulled down? ... Why is the cross mocked? Why is Christ ... blasphemed by pagan mouths? ... The vengeful and God-hating Saracens, the abomination of desolation clearly foretold to us by the prophets, overrun the places which are not allowed to them, plunder cities, devastate fields, burn down villages, set on fire the holy churches, overturn the sacred monasteries, oppose the Byzantine armies arrayed against them, and in fighting ... add victory to victory. Moreover they are raised up more and more against us and increase their blasphemy of Christ and the Church and utter wicked blasphemies against God.[72]

The reason, of course, is Christian transgression: "We ... first insulted the gift [of baptism] and first defiled the purification, and in this way grieved Christ ... and prompted Him to be angry with us."[73]

There is much that is puzzling about this account. Firstly, it occurs at the end of a sermon on Jesus' baptism by John, and has no apparent connection with the themes of that sermon. Secondly, it describes events

---

72. Sophronius, *Holy Baptism*, pp. 166–67, tr. in Hoyland (1997), pp. 72–73, q.v. for the original manuscript, to which we did not have access.

73. Ibid.

which we know (from the archaeological record and from other sources) did not happen: with the possible exception of a few isolated incidents, churches were not burnt or pulled down nor monasteries destroyed, and in this initial period the Arabs did not object to the Cross as a symbol used by Christians. Thirdly, the language used is not typical of Sophronius's attitude to the Arabs. When they were preventing the Christmas procession and his congregation could neither leave Jerusalem nor enter Bethlehem, he "merely" called them godless barbarians. Now that he is listing their general misdeeds, which do not affect his congregation so nearly, he uses much stronger words: God-hating God-fighters whose leader is the devil. The general atmosphere and feel of the passage accords with Christian descriptions from much later times. We have no information on the date of the manuscript or its transmission history, but suggest that either the entire section was tacked on to Sophronius's sermon at a later date, or that his initial rhetorical question, "Why do barbarian raids abound?" was considerably embellished by a later transcriber who knew the Traditional Account and therefore "knew" better than Sophronius what the prophesied "abomination of desolation" entailed.

During this same decade—the 630s—Maximus the Confessor wrote two extant letters containing possible references to the Arab intruders. The first is actually not a reference to Arabs at all, though it has sometimes been seen as one. It was written in Africa and is datable to 632 C.E. on the basis of an additional fragment discovered by Devreese, which relates a forced conversion of the Jews of Africa at Easter of that year.[74] In it Maximus refers to the terrible bites of the "wolves of Arabia." However, 632 C.E. is too early for this to be a reference to the invasion of the Traditional Account, especially in a letter written from Africa, and it is difficult to know what Maximus was in fact talking about, if indeed he intended an allusion to contemporary events. The phrase, as Migne points out, comes from Habbakkuk 1:8, "the Chaldaeans ... fiercer than the wolves of Arabia." If Maximus intended to remind his recipient of the Chaldaeans, i.e., the Babylonians, he may have been thinking of the depredations of the Persians, whom Heraclius had defeated only a few years before. However, immediately after mentioning "the wolves of Arabia" Maximus notes that the correct reading is not "Arabia" but "the west." This is fine as com-

74. Epistle no. 8 in *PG* 91, col. 439–446; Devreese (1937). Our thanks to Robert Hoyland for drawing our attention to this letter and to Devreese's article.

mentary on Habbakkuk,[75] but scarcely lends itself to a reference to either the Arabs or the Persians. Maximus solves our dilemma by explaining that these wolves are really the sins of the flesh, which overwhelm the divine laws of the spirit. In short, we have here a Biblical allusion supporting a metaphor for sin. If Maximus intended a reference to Arabs, it was only in general terms; and his inclusion of the gloss "i.e., of the west" indicates that he did not intend such a reference and wished to steer his reader away from the idea.

The second letter,[76] written some time during the years 634–640 C.E. (13–19 A.H.), is much clearer:

> What could be more piteous or fearful to those who are now suffering than to see a barbarous people of the desert overrun a foreign land as though it were their own ...?[77]

Maximus' phrasing is highly interesting: what most arouses his sentiments is not the emergence of a non-Christian religion, of which he makes no mention, but the "barbarous" origin of the newcomers, and the fact that they took control swiftly and almost effortlessly: they "overran" the area "as though it were their own." This implies that the Arabs were not required to wrest the area by force from the hands of an empire determined to protect it—because of a political vacuum, the previous owner being already absent de facto, they could take control as if it were already theirs. It is this feeling of defenselessness, the absence of the expected protector, which moves Maximus to label the events especially "piteous" and "fearful."[78]

The Syriac *Life* of Maximus, written (by a Monothelete vehemently

---

75. The original Hebrew is *zeʾevē ʿerev*, "wolves of the evening," i.e., the west, the direction of the setting sun. The translation "the wolves of Arabia" results from reading it, with changed vocalization, as *zeʾevē ʿarav*. Maximus notes in his gloss that the latter translation is incorrect; the correct version is "wolves of the west."

76. *PG* 91, cols. 530–44.

77. *PG* 91 col. 539–40; tr. from Kaegi (1969), p. 142.

78. The passage continues with a reference to the Jews: "... and [to see] the Jewish people, now delighting in murder, and yet they suppose themselves to be worshipping God." "The Jewish people" is often taken to be a reference to the Arabs, but this is very uncertain. The Greek is extremely difficult and the Latin is none too accurate a translation. It could equally be taken at face value: the Jews, says Maximus, who claim to worship God, are in actual fact "ungodly" enough to delight in the Arab conquest of a Christian land (scarcely surprising, in view of their treatment by the Christians, such as the forced conversion Maximus himself described in Epistle 8.)

opposed to Maximus the Dyothelete) ca. 662–680 C.E.,[79] sums up the transfer of power to the Arabs in one sentence: "the Arabs [*Ṭayyāyê*] appeared and took control of Syria and many other areas."[80] The choice of wording here is significant: *ᵓeštallaṭ(w)*, "took control," *not* "conquered."[81] Maximus then emerged from hiding, because "the land was in the control of the Arabs and there was no longer anyone to restrain and nullify his [heretical—Dyotheletic] doctrine." The date of this event can be ascertained as ca. 17/638.[82]

The next link in the chain is a sermon of St. Anastasius the Sinaite dating probably from the last decade of the 7th century.[83] Anastasius gives a condensed account of the Arab conquests, but it is a strangely garbled one. He is writing only about fifty years after the events he describes; yet he records that "the desert dweller Amalek rose up to strike us, Christ's people," resulting in the "fall of the Roman army"—all during the reign of Constans II (d. 48/668), when, also, the Battles of Gaḇīṯâ, Yarmūk and "Daṯemōn" occurred, followed by "the capture and burning of the cities of Palestine, even Caesarea and Jerusalem." Despite this hopelessly muddled chronology, Anastasius does record a main outline which accords with the facts we know: that the Arabs came from the desert areas, and took over first Palestine, then Egypt, and then "the Mediterranean lands and islands."

How are we to explain Anastasius's confusion over the dates and chronology of battles, fifty years afterwards? Hoyland conjectures that "religious convictions and remoteness in time have distorted the sequence of events,"[84] but this seems extreme. Anastasius was born in Cyprus in the

---

79. Cf. discussion in Brock (1973), pp. 335–36.

80. Brock (1973), p. 317 §17, Syriac, p. 310 §17.

81. The semantic field of the root *š.l.ṭ.* (followed by *b* or *ᶜal*) is to rule, bear sway, be in authority over, be in charge of (*CSD*, 579 col. 1); but *not* to conquer, to overcome, which would be rendered by the root *z.k.y./ᵓ.*, as in, "He went forth conquering and to conquer": *n:faq kaḏ zākê ᵓaykanâ d:nezkê.*

82. He had been in hiding—"confined to a small cell," i.e., probably in a monastery—since ca. 13/634 for fear of "the emperor and the patriarchs who had anathematized his teaching." The patriarchs in question all died in the period 634–638 C.E. So by 638 C.E. nobody was left to restrain him from teaching: the emperor no longer ruled the province and the patriarchs were all dead.

83. Presented by Kaegi (1969), pp. 142–43; see also the translation in Hoyland (1993), p. 102 + n. 165 for date.

84. Hoyland (1993), p. 102.

early 7th century, and may have had to leave as a result of the Arab conquest of Cyprus in 649[85]—at which time he would certainly have known that the Arabs had long before established themselves as rulers of Syria. Yet when recalling this period in his sermon, he is hopelessly confused about what happened when. Now the information he records must have reached him from some source, and his use of it in a sermon implies that he could expect it to be not unknown also to his listeners. But he shows no sign of having access to an *ordered history*, such as would be extant less than a hundred years later. It is tempting to wonder whether what he and his listeners did have access to were the Arab *oral traditions* out of which, in part, the Traditional Account would later be fashioned. In this connection it is worth recalling that Anastasius travelled extensively throughout the region for many years, including periods spent in Damascus and Jerusalem, among other places, before returning to the monastery of Mount Sinai around 680 C.E. The Christian population lived at close quarters with the non-Christian Arabs; so close that there was large-scale conversion and intermarrying (aspects which will be discussed in Part III Chapter 2). There is no reason why they should not have heard the stories arising among them; indeed, it would be surprising if they had not. Anastasius on his travels had ample opportunity to hear them too. These stories, we suggest, mentioned the names of battles, but with no specific dates, simply as "tales of the conquest." Anastasius was thus free to assign to them the dates most convenient to himself, e.g., to present the "fall of the Roman army" as God's punishment for Constans II's mistreatment of Pope Martin I (this was in fact the main point of the sermon)—without any danger of his listeners knowing, and almost certainly without knowing himself, that it was supposed to have taken place in the 630s. We may, then, have here a tantalizing glimpse of the sort of stories and traditions that were making the rounds among the Arabs, concerning how their ancestors defeated the Byzantine army. It is interesting that one of the few historical references to events of the conquest in the anonymous (Khuzestan) chronicle of 50–60/670–680,[86] mentioned above, similarly concerns the fall of the Roman army:

> The Roman emperor Heraclius ... sent ... a great army against them, whose

---

85. Ibid., p. 92 + n. 124.
86. Hoyland (1997), p. 185 dates it to the 660s.

> leader was called Sakellarios, but the Arabs defeated them, annihilated more than 100,000 Romans and killed their leader.[87]

Here the emperor is named correctly, but imagination is given full rein concerning the number of casualties. This chronicle also describes the Arabs in terms reminiscent of folktale: "numerous as the sand on the beach," "before whom neither wall nor door remained standing, neither weapon nor shield"; but as far as actual fact is concerned, it simply states briefly that "they became rulers of the whole land of the Persians" and that they killed, among "countless" other Persians, the general Rustam. No set battle is mentioned, but the Arabs are depicted as destroying all the troops that Yezdegird sends against them.[88]

We may draw the conclusion from accounts of this nature that stories about battles and the prowess of the Arabs, set into a vague historical framework—that they took Persia and Syria, then Egypt—were probably common by the second half of the 7th century. They provided material for Anastasius, the Khuzestan Chronicle, and the Armenian Sebeos.

Sebeos's *History of Heraclius* ends in 41/662 with Muᶜāwiyah's assumption of the caliphate. This date is therefore a terminus a quo for the work; since Sebeos represents Muᶜāwiyah as bringing unprecedented peace to the Arabs, it was probably written before the interregnum following Muᶜāwiyah's death in 61/680.[89] Sebeos includes in Chapter 30 of his *History*, which covers the events from the first appearance of the Ishmaelites to the early 640s, two accounts of battles. Neither are provided with either date or name, but they are taken to be those of the Yarmūk and of Qadisiyyah. The latter is only a very short reference: the Persians reached a village called Herthican, with the Arabs close on their heels; "the battle started and the Persian army fled before the Arabs, who pursued them and put them to the sword. There perished the general Rstom ..."—and he names several others, mostly Armenians. The only reason for identifying this as the Battle of Qadisiyyah would seem to be that Sebeos says that a

87. From the German translation in Nöldeke (1893), p. 45.

88. Nöldeke (1893), p. 33; see Hoyland (1997), pp. 186–87 for a newer translation.

89. Even this is not conclusive evidence, for strife following Muᶜāwiyah's death does not contradict the point that there was none during his life; if anything, it strengthens it. Yet one would have expected Sebeos to mention that the peace of Muᶜāwiyah's reign did not last beyond his death, had he known it at the time of writing.

Persian general, Rustam, was killed in it, and the Traditional Account assigns this event to the Battle of Qadisiyyah.

The other account goes as follows:

> Having arrived at the Jordan, [a Greek army of ca. seventy thousand men] crossed it and penetrated into Arabia; leaving their camp on the banks of the river, they went on foot against the [enemy] army. [The Ishmaelites] placed part of their army in ambush, here and there, and arranged most of their tents around the camp site. Then they placed the herds of camels around the camp and the tents, and tied their legs with ropes. That was the setup of their camp. As for the Greeks, tired from the march, they could scarcely start setting up their camp; they started to fall upon [the Ishmaelites], when those in hiding suddenly emerged from their retreat and fell upon them. A terror inspired by the Lord took hold of the Greek army; they turned their backs to flee before them. But they could not flee because of the depth of the sand, in which they sank up to their knees, while the enemy pursued them, a sword in their backs, and they were greatly hampered by the heat of the sun. All the officers fell. The number of the dead exceeded two thousand. Only a few managed to save themselves by flight and find a refuge. The [Ishmaelites], after crossing the Jordan, camped at Jericho.[90]

Sebeos continues with an account of how the inhabitants of Jerusalem that very night sent the True Cross and treasures from the churches to Constantinople for safe keeping, and then surrendered to the Arabs.

Clearly, Sebeos has heard of a battle, but his account is very incoherent and disordered. For a start, as Macler points out, the True Cross and other treasures were supposedly sent to Constantinople in 635 C.E., which was a year *before* the Battle of the Yarmūk. Moreover Jerusalem did not surrender, according to the Traditional Account, until 17/638, two years after the Yarmūk, and following a siege lasting nine or ten months. Secondly, Sebeos's numbers are inconsistent, for a total of two thousand killed out of an army of seventy thousand does not leave only "a few"—unless Sebeos meant that two thousand officers were killed, and did not bother to count the rank and file. This however is not too important, for his numbers, like those of most accounts, are clearly very untrustworthy in any

90. Sebeos, ed. Macler (1904), Ch. 30; our translation from Macler's French.

case. Thirdly, the account of the start of the battle—that the Greeks were so tired from the march that they could scarcely set up their camp, so they attacked the Arabs instead—does not make sense. But since Sebeos usually does not specify which side he is referring to, and this information is supplied by Macler, we suspect that Sebeos actually meant it the other way around: that the Ishmaelites, having made their preparations in advance, fell upon the Greeks as soon as the latter arrived, while the Greeks were still tired from the march and before they could even start setting up their camp. None of this is too problematical.

The serious problems concern the topography of the area where this battle was supposed to have taken place. The Jordan flows through a rift valley, on the eastern edge of which rise steep mountains, through which the Yarmūk cuts a narrow canyon. Between the river and the mountains there is room for an army to pitch its camp; but they would have had a stiff climb before finding a site for a battle. Sebeos also describes their moves as if the border between Palaestina and Arabia was the Jordan, whereas in fact in this region it was about thirty kilometers east of it; and he implies that the battle took place near Jericho, which is actually about ninety kilometers, as the crow flies, from the confluence of the Yarmūk and the Jordan. It is, moreover, difficult to find any sand—let alone knee-deep sand—in the Jordan rift valley, the canyon of the Yarmūk or nearby areas of the Trans-Jordanian mountains.

Both this account, and Sebeos's description of the course of the Arab conquest of al-Šām in general, suggest that he had little knowledge of the events of this period. The general plan is biblical—the reconquest of the land of Israel by the new children of Abraham. Any attempt to derive history from Sebeos's account of the early campaigns has to be very selective. One can say for sure only that he knew the Arabs had taken the area from the Byzantines and had heard some tales or rumors of battles. At the end of Chapter 30 he states that he heard of "these deeds" from Arab prisoners who had been eyewitnesses; but he is probably here referring to the "deeds" immediately preceding this statement: the accounts of later Ishmaelite incursions against various places with which the chapter ends. Since Sebeos was probably writing around forty years after the Arabs took control of al-Šām, it is highly unlikely that he had really talked to eyewitnesses of that event. He gives an account of only one of the battles connected in the Traditional Account with the conquest of al-Šām, and that account seems to be confused either with rumors of other battles in sandier areas, or with what Sebeos thought Arabia ought to look like, or both.

Sebeos's account, then, is no clearer than that of St. Anastasius. He knows that the Arabs came out of the desert and overran first Palestine, then Persia; but his framework is Biblical and his chronology muddled (though quite different from Anastasius's).[91] His battle description, like Anastasius's, could easily derive from the Arab tales and battle songs which, starting from the facts of skirmishes and minor engagements which could have taken place at any time during the preceding century, and proceeding by extolling the exploits of their warriors and magnifying the forces over which they prevailed, had arrived by the later 7th century at tales of battles between huge armies, which were later institutionalized (not without many contradictions) into the official Arab history. Accounts such as these, and not eyewitness reports, are what Sebeos would have heard if he had asked Arab prisoners of war about the conquest of Palestine in the 660s–670s.

Not all writers were convinced that the Arabs had won by force of arms. Also in the late 7th century[92] John bar Penkayê adduced the very fact of the Arabs' victory against the empire as proof of divine intervention:

> But we should not consider their coming naively. In fact it was an act of God. ... So as they came by God's order, they won so to speak two kingdoms without combat and without battle, like a log pulled out of the fire, without implements of war and without human devices. Thus God gave them the victory .... How otherwise, apart from God's help, could naked men, riding without armour or shield, have been able to win ...?[93]

It was of course, as the sources already referred to demonstrate, commonplace to present the downfall of the Byzantine empire as God's punishment for Christian wrongdoing. The case is probably overstated in order to prove the point; but no amount of overstatement can reconcile the idea of winning two kingdoms "without combat and without battle" with the Traditional Account.

---

91. Hoyland (1997), p. 128 also dismisses Sebeos's account of the Arab conquests as unreliable because it is "heavily influenced by Biblical conceptions and terminology."

92. The accepted range of dates is the late 7th to early 8th centuries; Hoyland (1997), p. 200 dates the work to 687–688 C.E.

93. Bar Penkayê, Bk. XIV; German tr. in Abramowski (1940), pp. 5–6; French in Mingana (1907). This is an interesting early statement of a *topos* which was especially developed in the Muslim literature: that of "those who came from the harsh, barren desert land." This could take two forms: the Arabs might themselves relate that the invaders, their forefathers, were "naked" barbarians from the desert, or, more commonly, they would relate that the *Byzantines* discounted and derided them as mere uncultured barbarians, the weakest of the weak.

Jacob (also called James) of Edessa (19–90/640–708; bishop of Edessa 684–688) composed a set of chronological charts intended to continue those of Eusebius. Only fragments remain, covering the 7th century only down to 631 C.E. The manuscript itself dates from the 10th or 11th century.[94] Elias of Nisibis (975–1050 C.E.) tells us that Jacob wrote the work in 1003 A.G. (72–73/691–692); Michael the Syrian (12th century) cites Theodosius of Edessa to the same effect. However, Michael had access to Jacob's charts down to 710 C.E. Jacob died in 708 C.E., so obviously someone continued his work after his death. Michael himself appears to have thought that Jacob probably wrote the charts himself down to his death, and only after that did someone else continue them.[95] The alternative is to accept that someone else continued the work for sixteen years during which Jacob was still alive. We would advise caution, and consider that the work cannot be dated more closely than the two decades 690–710 C.E. It is quite likely that its composition extended over several years, so that the parts dealing with the Arab takeover period were probably composed in the 690s.

The manuscript is arranged in three columns. A central column gives the dates of rule of the rulers of Rome/Byzantium and Persia. To the right of this are notices of church events, and to the left of it, notices of secular events. A notice can extend over several lines, so that it is not usually possible to equate a secular event with one specific year. There are three notices relevant to our subject:

1. In the right-hand column, beside the years 293 and 294 since Constantine (i.e., 617–18 and 618–19 C.E.) is the comment "and Muḥammad goes down on commercial business [or: "for trade"] to the lands of Palestine and of the Arabias and of Phoenicia and of the Tyrians." It is followed by a notice of a solar eclipse which Palmer equates with that of September 2, 620 and Hoyland with that of November 4, 617.
2. The notice: "The kingdom of the Arabians [*arbayê*], those whom we call *ṭayyāyê*, began when Heraclius, king of the Romans, was in his 11th year and Khusrau, king of the Persians, was in his 31st year [i.e., 620–21 C.E.]".
3. The notice beside years 301 and 302 since Constantine [i.e., 625–26

94. *BL* Add. 14:685, f-23, pp. 324–27; tr. + commentary in Palmer (1993), pp. 47–50.

95. Michael the Syrian II.XVII, 450/482–83. For a discussion of the dating see Hoyland (1997), p. 164 + n. 78, accepting 692 or possibly 693 as the date of Jacob's original work.

and 626–27 C.E.]: "The Arabs began to carry out raids in the land of Palestine."[96]

Jacob, then, writing in the 690s, knew of Arab raids in the 620s. Whether he knew of battles in the 630s we cannot tell, since his original chronicle for those years has not survived except as reworked source material in much later writers. He also gives a reasonably accurate date for the start of the Arab era, which was well established by his time. Clearly, however, he does not equate Muḥammad with the Arab religion—there is no indication that the Muḥammad who went down to Syria for trading purposes was an Arab prophet—nor the start of the Arab era with a religious event. Rather, he seems to have assumed that the Arab era, like the Greek and Roman ones, must have been reckoned from the first year of rule of a king, presumably their first king. Since the Arabs reckoned from 622 C.E., their first king must have started to rule in that year.[97]

In the central column giving the dates of rulers there is the entry for 932 A.G. (=622 C.E.): "Muḥammad, the first king of the Arabs, began to reign, 7 years." Similarly there is a note for 939 A.G. (=629 C.E.): "No. 2 of the Arabs, Abū Bakr, 2 yrs 7 months." This implies that Jacob had heard of Muḥammad and his importance to the Arabs, but again, not in a religious context. It is interesting that the very short Syrian chronicle *Ad Annum 705*[98] preserved in a late 9th-century manuscript, also regards Muḥammad as the first Arab king, and accords him a seven-year reign (followed by Abū Bakr for two years and "ᵓUmūr" for twelve). The chronicle *Ad Annum 724*, preserved at the end of an 8th-century manuscript, allots Muḥammad ten years as king, Abū Bakr two years and six months, and ᶜŪmar ten years and three months; there are some signs that it is a translation from an Arabic original.[99] There is another reference in a Syriac source from 726 C.E. to Muḥammad having reigned as king for ten years.[100] It would appear that in the 690s the name Muḥammad was known to some Christians as that of the first king of the Arabs, not as the Arab Prophet; by 724 the length of his

96. Jacob of Edessa, *Chronicle*, p. 326; collected by Hoyland (1997), p. 165.

97. Papyri and inscriptions use the Arab era from the 640s C.E. on, but without ever explaining what event they are counting from.

98. Tr. in Hoyland (1997), p. 394.

99. Translation and commentary: ibid., pp. 395–96; Palmer (1993), text no. 8.

100. In John of Litarba, who corrected Jacob's reference to seven years in his last chronicle, finished in 726 C.E.; mentioned in Palmer (1993), pp. 43–44.

reign had stabilized at ten years, and the information about the other Arab kings had reached the form found in the Traditional Account. However, by 724 other Christian writers certainly knew that Muḥammad was the Arab Prophet; during the period from the 690s to the 720s there appears to have been some confusion among the Christians as to what exactly his role had been.

It is difficult to reconcile the entry in the central column for 622 C.E., "Muḥammad the first king of the Arabs," with the notice against the years 617–619 C.E., "Muḥammad goes down for trade...." If Jacob wrote both notices, did he conceive of the first Arab king as a trader? Or did he think he was referring to two different Muḥammads? Why is there no indication who the trader was, especially as this notice is several years before Muḥammad the king started to rule? The usual implication of such a casual mention is that everyone already knew who he was. As we shall see (in Part III Chapter 3), this would most probably have been true of the Arab population in the 690s, for Muḥammad was officially proclaimed the Arab Prophet in 71–72/690–692; but we have little indication that the Christians were aware of Muḥammad's existence and significance at this time. Given the structure of Jacob's charts, we cannot tell if the notice was written by Jacob or added at a later date in the free space in the side column, perhaps by whoever continued the work down to 710 C.E.

John bar Penkayê, whose description of "naked men" winning two kingdoms "without combat and without battle" was discussed above, is also interesting for his portrayal of the political situation during the early years of Arab rule. He portrays the Arabs as being internally divided and subject to conflict until Muᶜāwiyah finally brought peace. John says, in effect, that Muᶜāwiyah was the *first Arab ruler to control the area effectively and bring it under the rule of one man*:

> Henceforth, since Muᶜāwiyah came to power, this peace has been current in the world, the like of which neither we nor our fathers nor our fathers' fathers have ever heard or seen.[101]

Sebeos, writing around the same time, gives as mentioned a similar picture of Muᶜāwiyah. Regarding the 30s/650s, he says:

> Much blood flowed in the Ishmaelite army, through the massacre of great

101. Bar Penkayê, Bk. XV, tr. from Abramowski (1940), p. 8.

> numbers, because the sad work of war compelled them to kill each other. And they had no respite from the sword, captivity, violent combat on land and sea, until Muᶜāwiyah became powerful and overcame them all. When he had submitted them to himself, he ruled over all the possessions of the children of Ishmael, and made peace with them all.[102]

The idea that Muᶜāwiyah was the first to rule over all the lands taken by the Arabs is of course at odds with the Traditional Account. But it accords well with other historical evidence, such as that of the coins.[103] It also accords with the fact—noted by Brock—that the local population did not at first conceive of the takeover as a permanent political change, certainly not in the years before Muᶜāwiyah's rule, the years the Traditional Account divides between the Rašidūn caliphs. In the absence of dramatic events such as are detailed in the Muslim traditions, the fact that Arab rule was here to stay only became clear with the passage of time. And it took even longer to conceive of Arab rule as Arab empire (*malkūṯâ*), i.e., to equate the new political order with those it replaced. For, as Brock points out,[104] the new rulers did not resemble the Sassanid or Byzantine emperors. Thus those who referred to the Book of Daniel for an explanation of contemporary events, such as the writer of the *Doctrina Jacobi nuper baptizati*, mentioned above, still interpreted the Fourth Beast (Dan. ch. 7) as Rome. Indeed they may well have given the new Arab polity the title of *malkūṯâ*—kingdom—only because they were used to thinking in Biblical terms.[105] In fact, in view of the paucity of sources from the 30s–60s/650s–680s and the evidence of Sebeos, one of the few that we do have (from the end of this period), it is quite possible that the perception of Arab rule as a lasting, incontrovertible fact, was only firmly established ca. 40/660, i.e., after Muᶜāwiyah emerged from the ᶜAlid-Sufyānī conflict as undisputed ruler. This recognition also found less conscious expression; thus the Nestorian Synod called by the Patriarch George in 57/676 recorded its date as "in this fifty-seventh year of the empire of the Arabs,"[106] without

---

102. Sebeos ed. Macler (1904), Ch. 38; our translation from Macler's French, p. 149.
103. To be discussed in the next chapter.
104. Brock (1982), p. 20 para. 2.
105. For this point, again, we are indebted to Brock (1982).
106. Chabot (1902), text 1:216, tr. 2:482: *l:šultanayâ d:Ṭayyāyê*: "l'empire des Arabes."

referring to any other era; earlier Syriac texts preferred to date events in terms of the Seleucid era.[107]

Non-Chalcedonian writers were much more willing than the Chalcedonians to accept that the new rulers were here to stay. For the latter, the Byzantine loss of the provinces was very difficult to explain within the religious *Weltanschauung* of heaven-sent punishment for evils committed. Thus Sebeos, a Monophysite, interpreted Daniel's "fourth beast" as the kingdom of Ishmael,[108] replacing thereby the formerly accepted interpretation that the "fourth beast" was Rome. Whereas the author of the *Pseudo-Methodius*, a 7th-century apocalypse attributed to Methodius of Olympus (d. 312 C.E.) but probably written ca. 690,[109] remained a loyal Byzantine Christian and confidently predicted and joyously looked forward to the ultimate triumph of the Byzantine emperor—just as Sophronius had in 13/634.[110]

We should, however, be very careful how we rephrase these authors' message. Kaegi, for instance, paraphrases Sebeos as accepting that the "Islamic empire" is here to stay.[111] But Sebeos never mentions Islam—he talks only of the *Kingdom of Ishmael.* In fact, the term he consistently uses for the Arabs is "Ishmaelites" or "sons of Ishmael"; once he also calls them "the sons of Abraham, who were born of Hagar and of Keturah: Ishmael."[112] Sebeos also alludes to "the great and terrible desert from which the storm of these nations surged." But we cannot conclude from this that he witnessed a great conquest. The description is sandwiched between the explanation that the Arabs were sent by God as a punishment for His people's sins, and a quotation from Daniel 7, that favorite mainstay of the apocalyptic vision, which is presented as a summary of what actually

---

107. There is also the bilingual papyrus from Nessana (Colt III, papyrus no. 60), which gives the date as "the month of November of the third indiction, year 54 according to the Arabs."

108. Q.b. Kaegi (1969), p. 146.

109. Brock (1976) dates it to 65–73/685–692 on internal evidence, and Hoyland (1997), p. 64 + n. 17, to ca. 690, but Alexander (1985) argues that it was probably written in the 650s in Mesopotamia. Like other works, it gives no details of the Arab conquest. The Arabs are portrayed as hordes of cruel barbarians, sent as God's punishment for the Christians' (lavishly detailed) sexual license.

110. Kaegi (1969), p. 145.

111. Ibid., p. 147.

112. Sebeos ed. Macler (1904), Ch. 34; our translation from Macler's French, p. 130.

happened. The reference to a storm is itself inserted so as to accord with biblical prophesy:

> The storm in question passed through Babylon but unleashed itself also upon all the countries ... and on the nations who live in the great desert, where [live?] the children of Abraham who were born of Hagar and of Keturah.[113] ... It [i.e., the storm] came from the great and enormous desert, where Moses and the children of Israel had lived,[114] following the word of the prophet: "Like a strong wind he will come from the south, coming from the desert, from a fearful place,"[115] that means from the great and terrible desert, from where the storm of these nations surged and occupied the whole earth. ... And that which was said was carried out: [whereupon he quotes Dan. 7].[116]

To sum up the evidence regarding the *political* events: the local written sources down to the early 8th century do not provide any evidence that a planned invasion of Arabs from the peninsula occurred, and that great and dramatic battles ensued which crushed the Byzantine army and vanquished the empire. What we do have is many descriptions of "barbarous" people "from the desert": *Ṭayyāyê*, Ishmaelites, *Mhaggarê*. The first two names occur prior to the 7th century,[117] and none of them indicates a specifically peninsular origin. Thus the most usual word for "Arab" in the Syriac sources, *ṭayyāyê*, had long been applied to all the desert dwellers in any part of the interface area, from the northern regions of the Syrian desert down. Nowhere, either, do we find any mention of *Islam*, although the identity between "Arab" and "Muslim" is so self-evident to scholars brought up on the Traditional Account that the terms "Islam" and "Muslim," and derivatives of them, tend to creep into translations.[118] But Brock carefully sums up the real situation: "sources best anchored in the [later decades of the] seventh century suggest that there was greater awareness that a new empire (*malkūṯâ*) had arisen, than that a new religion

113. Gen. 25.

114. Deut. 1:19.

115. Is. 21:1.

116. Sebeos ed. Macler (1904), Ch. 34, our translation from Macler's French, p. 130.

117. See also Mayerson (1986), p. 36 col. 2.

118. Hoyland (1997) consistently translates *mhaggarê* as "Muslim" in order to differentiate it from *ṭayyāyê*, which he translates "Arab," but this also begs the question we are trying to elucidate, and is misleading in cases where he does not also give the original term.

had been born."[119] As discussed above, these texts do not describe the process of gaining political control; and considering their use of political events to fuel the contemporary apocalyptic vision, the fact that there was no apocalyptic exploitation of the tremendous events of the conquest itself, i.e., the great battles (as distinct from apocalyptic exploitation of the fact that the Arabs gained control and Byzantium lost it), strongly suggests that there was little to exploit. The earliest Arab event described in contemporary literary works is the war between Muᶜāwiyah and ᶜAlī (36/657).[120] No caliph's name before Muᶜāwiyah is mentioned in the early manuscripts (as distinct from the later ones dating from the 9th century or later, whose report of 7th-century history is based on the Traditional Account). And battles such as Dāṯin and al-ᶜArabah or Muʾtah, which are supposed to have taken place in the early part of the period, are not reported in texts written close in time to the supposed date of these events.[121]

Perhaps there was indeed a great invasion, with battle after battle between tens of thousands of opposing soldiers, over the course of several years (629 to 636). But if there were, it would seem that, *at the time*, nobody noticed.

---

119. Brock (1982), p. 13.

120. E.g., in the "Maronite Chronicle" of the 8th or 9th century, which was actually composed in the mid-40s/660s (Brock [1976], pp. 18–19); and the Life of Maximus the Confessor (Brock [1973], p. 319 §25).

121. Conrad (1987) and (1990) respectively.

3

The Evidence of the Coins

It will by now be clear that we have very little *contemporary* documentary evidence regarding the political situation in al-Šām during the early period of the Arab takeover and Muᶜāwiyah's rise to power. The Arab accounts are all much later, while the non-Arab contemporary sources, surveyed in the last chapter, refer to the Arabs' assumption of control but not to their political organization. There is, however, considerable contemporary numismatic evidence. Historians of the period have not, so far, paid much attention to coins, and this is a pity, for both their iconography and epigraphy can provide evidence of historical events and official opinions in a given place at a given time. It follows that an examination of the early Arab coins can lead us towards a certain degree of historical reconstruction.

Coins, then, can provide valuable evidence; but many difficulties complicate its evaluation, especially in our field of study. Firstly, relatively little is known about the early Arab coins. Compared with the amount of study that has been devoted to the Byzantine coins contemporary with them, study of the Arab ones has been fragmentary and is still in a relatively preliminary stage.[1] Moreover, the aspects of concern to numismatists are quite different from those which interest historians, so that even the little we

1. The material in the works of authorities such as Walker (1956) and Grierson (1982) makes this point abundantly clear.

do know is rarely utilized as evidence for or against a view of the period's history.[2] Secondly, a single coin cannot as a rule provide reliable evidence; and even a hoard of coins needs careful and specialist study to fit it into its correct historical context—study which, as stated, has often been lacking. Thirdly, many coins never become available for study. Our thanks are due to the many serious and responsible collectors and numismatists who have made available the information so far published; unfortunately not all coins reach such collectors. Those which do not are, of course, rarely if ever published, and the most basic information regarding their original provenance—the site and date of the context in which they were found—is never disclosed or soon lost. Finally, even when the coins are published, the method of publication is unsuited to the needs of systematic study. Coins are usually published, not on the basis of common characteristics, but as collections: those which have been found together, or have common ownership, or are being offered for sale together. There are important and rare or unique items which have been published only in auction catalogs, and others which are buried in the appendices of reports on archaeological excavations, or as solitary papers in any imaginable (and some unimaginable) publications. It is therefore necessary to sift through many volumes of widely different types of publications in order to collect systematic information regarding any specific feature of the coins themselves. This characteristic of the literature makes a thorough study of it immensely time-consuming, perhaps even practically impossible.

All of the above urges caution in the use of numismatic data as historical evidence, especially by those who are not themselves numismatists.[3] It should in any case be accepted that numismatic data are insufficient as the *primary* type of evidence on which to ground a historical theory; but they are useful in corroborating evidence from other sources. We consider that the numismatic evidence regarding the Arab takeover, so far as we have it, is consistent with the theory here proposed. And the legends on the Arab coins are particularly important as evidence for both the political and the religious situation, simply because the other epigraphical evidence available to us is relatively slight—a mere handful of royal inscriptions, and personal

---

2. Bates (1986) has also pointed out the lack of *historical* study of numismatic evidence, and urged the task upon historians.

3. This is the place to thank Mr. Shraga Qedar for the time he so generously devoted to our numismatic education, even though he frowned upon the use we made of it.

rock graffiti which while more numerous are each very brief. These official and personal inscriptions in any case provide evidence mainly regarding religious development, not political (we discuss them in Part III). The early Arab coins, then, are our chief source of contemporary evidence regarding the formation of the new Arab state.

THE PRE-MOHAMMEDAN ARAB-BYZANTINE COINS

The first coins minted in al-Šām after the Arab takeover are imitations of earlier Byzantine ones, and for this reason are known as Arab-Byzantine coins. The issues with which we are concerned, from the first decades of Arab rule,[4] are all copper coins. Unlike later issues they bear no Mohammedan religious texts,[5] and we therefore refer to them in this book as pre-Mohammedan Arab-Byzantine coins. No date or ruler's name is given on them, so that it is very difficult to establish their chronology or to date them with any certainty. On the other hand, the name of a town is (usually) recorded—presumably their mint town, or more likely the town where they were to be distributed. However, the towns recorded, e.g., Gerasa, Scythopolis (Bayṣān), and Tiberias, were not mint towns in Byzantine times. The coins were initially about the same size as their Byzantine prototypes, though they could be thicker and consequently heavier; and they were often, though not always, of coarser workmanship. As time went on, however, they became smaller and thinner, so that the relative size and thickness of a coin provides some indication of its position within the chronological sequence. Grierson (1982) puts them in a rough chronological order which we accept; but his terminology is not differentiated enough for our purposes, since he calls all coins between the Byzantine issues and the post-Reform epigraphic issues of ʿAbd al-Malik "transitional." We therefore present his chronology, but with a finer subdivision of terms.

---

4. This attribution follows Walker (1956). Bates (1986) would date the pre-Standing Caliph copper coins much later, but we consider his arguments unconvincing; we discuss the point later in this chapter. We are grateful to Philip Grierson for drawing our attention to Bates's important article.

5. "Mohammedan" is not a synonym for "Muslim" but denotes a particular set of religious formulae and the corresponding stage in religious development towards Islam—a subject to be taken up in Part III.

Precursors

The earliest coins ("Precursors") come from Scythopolis and Gerasa (the latter was unknown when Grierson [1982] went to press). The name of the town is inscribed in Greek. Their Byzantine prototype is the Nicomedian issues of Justin II—i.e., coins from the mid-6th century C.E., which were common in Palestine. The quality of these early Arab-Byzantine coins is very uneven—some are much cruder than others, and are often regarded as "blundered imitations" of the better-quality Arab-Byzantine coins. This, however, is a hypothesis, and as such is open to query. There are, after all, coins of ʿAbd al-Malik which seem closer in technical quality to these "imitations" than to the better-quality issues.[6] There was in general little consistency in the quality of copper coins, and even official Byzantine mints could produce coins of widely varying technical quality in different issues—in fact Bates (1986) considers these Arab coins to be *superior* in workmanship to their Byzantine prototypes.[7] Obviously there is room for a wide range of judgment on this point. We cannot, then, be reasonably sure that a poor-quality issue is a "blundered imitation" of a better one, or even that they were produced by different mints.

On some of these coins, including those considered among the earliest,[8] Arab inscriptions were overstruck, e.g., *jayyid, ṭayyib,* and *wafā* or *jayyiz*: the meanings, "good" or "whole," are assurances that the coins may be accepted as legal tender in a particular area. We also find *fils ḥaqq* (legal fils) on copper coins. The conclusion this invites is that these coins were overstruck because people hesitated to use them. Whether this was indeed the reason for overstriking will be discussed later.

As already mentioned, it is very difficult to date the Precursors. One coin, however, is dated *XII (i.e., XXII),[9] which on a Byzantine coin would mean the twenty-second year of the emperor's reign. Since the figures shown are Justin II and Sophia, and there was no such year of Justin II's reign, Grierson accepts this as further evidence that the coins are not Byzantine.[10] But he does not discuss what era is referred to; in general, he considers the Precursors to have been issued during the Persian period, in the 620s C.E.,

---

6. Cf. Grierson (1982), p. 135 and plate 34.
7. Bates (1986), p. 250.
8. Walker (1956). pp. xviii, 2, 6–8.
9. Grierson (1982) no. 612, plate 34; also reproduced in Walker (1956) no. G1, p. 44 and plate IX. Both interpret this form of the date as meaning XXII.
10. Grierson (1982), p. 145.

because of their high weight compared to the main sequence of coins, the absence of an Arabic inscription, and the existence of a half-follis.[11] However, it is difficult to see why the weight would confine these coins to so early a date. It is true that they weigh approximately the same as their Byzantine prototypes,[12] whereas the main-sequence pre-Mohammedan Arab-Byzantine copper coins weigh half that or less.[13] It would thus seem to be a valid conclusion that the Precursors are earlier than the main sequence; but this does not mean that they date from the Persian period. A case could be made for such a date, if it could be shown that these coins were actually modeled on Persian ones, at least regarding their weight. But there are almost no Persian copper coins with which to compare these folles: the Persians minted almost nothing but silver. In any case, no Persian coins of any metal circulated in Palestine, so that it is most unlikely that copper coins for circulation there would have been modeled on Persian ones, even if any had been minted.[14]

Regarding the absence of an Arabic inscription on them: some of the main-sequence pre-Mohammedan coins also lack such an inscription, and Grierson dates them to the A.H. 50s/670s or later, rejecting Walker's proposal of the A.H. 20s/640s on as too early.

On these two counts at least, then, we can see no reason for a date as early as the Persian period. We would tentatively suggest that the date 22 may refer to the new Arab era, i.e., A.H. 22/642–43, which was a year or two after Muᶜāwiyah had been acknowledged as governor of al-Šām. This fits nicely with the fact that the earliest surviving record of a date in terms of the Arab era is on a papyrus also dated A.H. 22. Some of the Precursors may well be earlier than this dated coin. We would set the type in general in the A.H. 10s/630s and the early 20s/640s.

Main sequence

After the initial issues of Scythopolis and Gerasa, coins (still all copper) were issued mainly by Ḥimṣ, Baᶜlabakk, Damascus, and Tiberias, with one rare issue from Ṭarṭūs. They may be divided into five types according to the

11. Ibid.

12. The precursors weigh 10–11 grams, one weighs 14.64 grams, compared with 9–12 grams for most Byzantine folles from Justinian to Heraclius listed in Grierson (1982); Whitting (1973) pp. 111–12 gives 13.5 grams as the average weight for the folles of Justin II.

13. The great majority fall within the range of 3–5 grams.

14. We are indebted for this point to Grierson (private communication June 27, 1987).

iconography of their obverse, but it is very difficult to date them relative to each other. The Byzantine prototype, where identifiable, is of course dated, but this can give only a terminus a quo for dating the Arab imitations, since the Arab coin may have been issued considerably later than the date of its Byzantine prototype. The five varieties Grierson lists are as follows:[15]

a) Three standing figures: the prototype is a Heraclean coin dating from A.H. 15–18/636–39 or 17–21/638–41.[16]
b) Facing bust: prototype of Constans II, A.H. 20s/640s.
c) Seated figure holding transverse scepter: no clear prototype.
d) Standing figure: prototype of Constans II's first decade, ca. A.H. 20–30/641–50.
e) Two seated figures:[17] no clear prototype.

One may therefore hypothesize that type b) is a little later than type a), and it is rather more probable that type d) is later still; but no firm conclusions are possible.

These coins were frequently overstruck with Arabic assurances; and Greek words for "good" (e.g., *kalon*) may also appear together with the Arabic ones. The name of the town, when written in Arabic, is in the local Semitic form, not the Byzantine Greek form, and coins also appear that were struck from the start in both Greek and Arabic (as opposed to being struck in Greek and then overstruck in Arabic), with the Byzantine form of the town's name being given in Greek, and the local form in Arabic (e.g., Emesa and Ḥimṣ). But there is still no date, or ruler's name, on the coins, and we do not know who minted them. At this point the pre-Mohammedan coins merge into the Mohammedan ones, in the sense that Christian iconography starts to be removed from the figures and later still Mohammedan legends appear.

There is still considerable disagreement over the dating of these pre-Mohammedan copper coins. Walker (1956) dates them all to the A.H. 20s/640s onwards, whereas Grierson inclines to consider them together with the Mohammedan coins, some of which are dated, and assigns them all to the

---

15. The reader is referred to Grierson (1982), pp. 145–46 and plate 34 for a fuller description.

16. Bates (1986), p. 240 and notes 11–12.

17. Grierson has "standing figures" in the text, but this must be a typographical error, for the plate clearly shows them seated.

A.H. 50s or 60s/670s or 680s. One reason for this is his view that the copper coins minted before the conquest would only then be wearing out. Bates also prefers a late date, largely on the basis of conjecture as to the expected behavior of the Arab invaders. He finds it hard to believe that the early Arab coinage started from the time of the conquest: it is "extremely unlikely," he considers, that the Arabs began to mint coins as soon as they arrived, and "improbable" that they did so before ᶜAbd al-Malik. Moreover, if they started so early, he reasons, the coins must have been minted over a period of fifty to sixty years (ca. 15 or 20 to ca. 70–75 A.H.), which he finds improbable. He therefore sees them as "the copper parallels of the earliest gold and silver coins of Damascus ... and probably to be put in the years A.H. 72–74/692–694."[18]

Part of Bates's reasoning addresses political considerations, and will be discussed when we come to analyze the political events of the takeover years, later in this chapter. We do not consider the arguments for a late date to be convincing. Firstly, as we suggest below in our discussion of the evidence derivable from the coins, we consider that they were minted not only for economic reasons but also, and in the case of the Precursors primarily, for political and symbolic ones. And if their function was to make a political statement, whether or not the issues already in circulation were wearing out would have been irrelevant. Secondly, neither the argument from economic need nor that from the probable political actions of the new rulers uses the evidence of coins minted in the Sassanian areas. These were usually dated, and from them we learn that in the east, at least, coins were being minted throughout the Sufyānid period, from A.H. 31 on. They include coins from A.H. 44/661–62 with Muᶜāwiyah's name on them, and others with the names of Sufyānid governors. Since, then, Muᶜāwiyah minted coins in the east, it is not so very unlikely that he did so also in al-Šām, where he was much more firmly in control. It is much more likely that Walker's view is correct, and the pre-Mohammedan Arab-Byzantine coins date from the first decades of Arab rule. We consider, then, that the Precursor and pre-Mohammedan coins were issued under Muᶜāwiyah during the period ca.[19] A.H. 20–60/640–680.

18. Bates (1986), pp. 250–51.

19. Our dating cannot claim precision; all dates here are approximate, unless explicitly stated otherwise.

MOHAMMEDAN PRE-REFORM COINS

These are later issues and were minted at a much larger number of towns from a much wider geographic area. There are two main types:

1. A gold issue whose iconography is still clearly Byzantine: its obverse resembles type a) above (three standing figures bearing wands), and its reverse is a figure modified from the Byzantine "cross on steps."[20] Accompanying this iconography are religious legends on the obverse which mention Muḥammad.[21] Grierson (1982) dates this issue to the early A.H. 70s/690s, immediately preceding dated coins minted from A.H. 74/693 on.
2. The common issues of pre-Reform Mohammedan coins. These may be divided into two types according to their iconography:
   a) The obverse bears the figure known as the Twin Caliphs, and the reverse, an uncial M (as on Byzantine folles).
   b) The obverse bears the figure known as the Standing Caliph;[22] the reverse may be either a cursive m modified version of the Byzantine "cross on steps."

It is plausible that the Twin Caliphs type may have started a little earlier than the Standing Caliph type; the latter certainly continued later. The inscriptions on both are purely in Arabic, and include Mohammedan legends (e.g. "There is no God but Allāh alone; Muḥammad [is the/a] messenger of Allāh"). Some coins also bear the name of ᶜAbd al-Malik, and there is no doubt that all of them date from his reign.

Gold coins of the Standing Caliph type, with Mohammedan inscriptions on their reverse, were also minted; they are dated, and all come from the years A.H. 74–77/693–694. We may therefore reasonably assign the copper coins of the same type also to this period: i.e., the reign of ᶜAbd al-Malik, up to his reform of the coinage in A.H. 77/696–97, when purely epigraphic coins were introduced. Bates (1986) uses historical and epigraphic evidence to date the start of the gold (and silver) Standing Caliph type to

20. The modifications made to the cross will be discussed in Part III Chapter 4, in connection with religious development.

21. For the introduction of Mohammedanism into the Arab religion, see Part III Chapters 3–4.

22. Described in Walker (1956), p. xxviii ff., civ and plates VI-VIII; Grierson (1982), p. 146; cf. also al-Ḥadīdī (1975), pp. 9–14.

A.H. 72,[23] and we accept his arguments. Like us, he dates the copper Standing Caliph coins to the same period.

GEOGRAPHICAL AND POLITICAL CONSIDERATIONS

Map II.3.1 indicates both the provenance of the various types of pre-Reform coins, and the lines of the Arab advance according to the Traditional Account. The Muslim traditions themselves lead to the conclusion that the Arabs initially took control around the edges of al-Šām. They came from the interface areas (*aṭrāf al-Šām*) and encountered the towns on the edge of the *oikoumenē*: Gaza (the Battle of Dāṯin?); Jerusalem and Bethlehem; Bayṣān and Tiberias; Damascus and Ḥimṣ. Though there are southern and central towns on this list, most of those mentioned are northern, and the general impression is that the initial center of activity was not in the areas nearest to the Arabian Peninsula, but in northern Palestine–central Syria. For instance, while the Battle of Dāṯin may represent an incident in southern Palestine (if indeed Dāṯin was near Gaza and not near Bayṣān in the north), it appears in the Arab versions as a minor affair. (We have already argued above, in Part II Chapter 1, that its main import probably lay in the clear indication it gave that Byzantium did not intend to retain control of the area). Sophronius's Christmas sermon notwithstanding, Jerusalem did not come under Arab control in the early years of the Takeover: the Traditional Account gives the date as 15–17/636–638, and we would put it even later than that. The towns from Bayṣān and Gerasa northwards, on the other hand, are recorded in the Traditional Account as falling to the Arabs during the first years of the Takeover.

The numismatic evidence provides some support for this reading of the Traditional Account. The earliest Arab-Byzantine coins, the Precursors, were minted at Bayṣān and Gerasa. The main sequence of what we call pre-Mohammedan coins were minted in several towns from Tiberias in the south up to Ḥimṣ and Ṭarṭūs in central Syria. Whatever it was that was happening as the Arabs assumed control, the coins suggest that it was happening in northern Palestine up through central Syria.

If we examine the coins of this early period more closely, an interesting sequence emerges. Counting each type of coin from each town as a separate

23. Bates (1986), pp. 246–49.

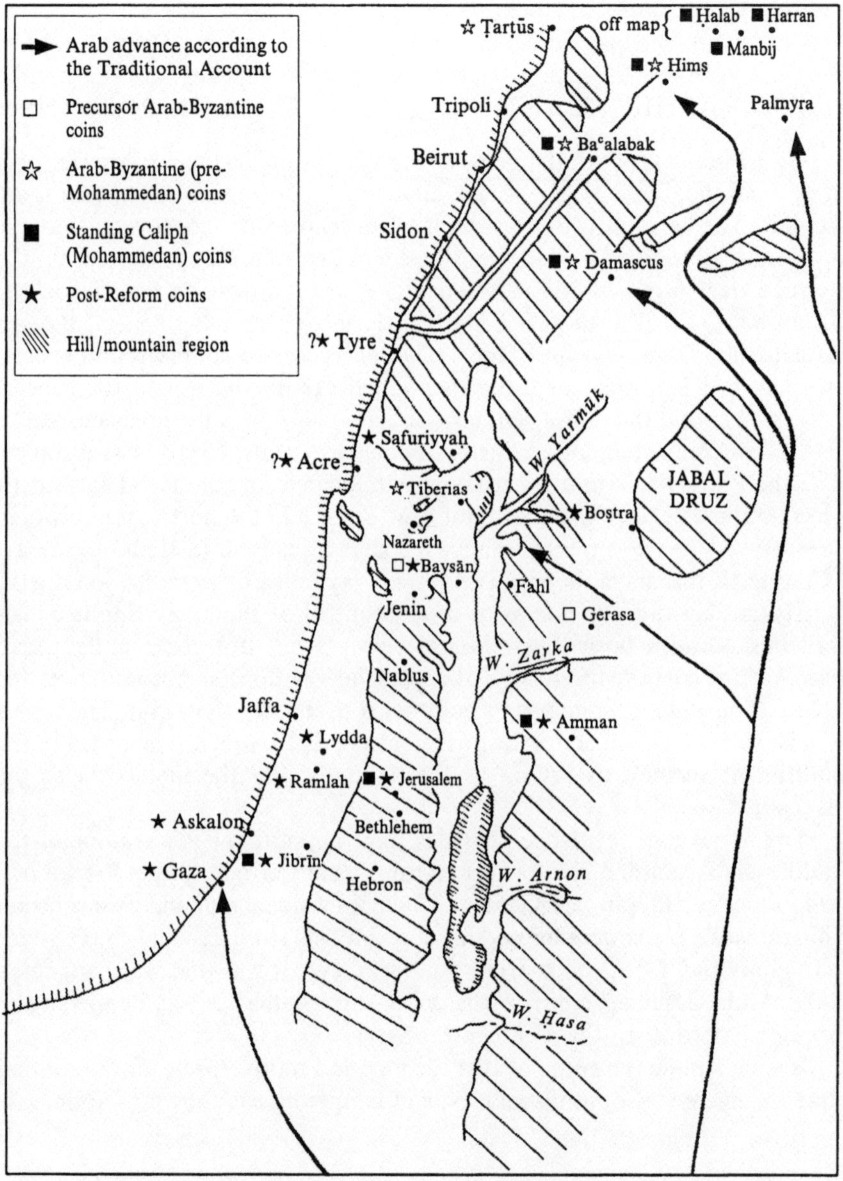

Map II.3.1: Mint towns of Arab-Byzantine coins.

issue, we know to date of thirteen different issues of Precursor and pre-Mohammedan Arab-Byzantine coins. Most of the coins of each type come from one town, with the occasional rare issue from a neighboring town. The only type for which this is not true is Grierson's type d), which was minted in most of the towns which minted coins under Muᶜāwiyah as governor or caliph. The start of the series can be chronologically arranged, in that the Precursors are definitely earlier than the pre-Mohammedan type a), which itself imitates an earlier prototype than the other pre-Mohammedan coins. The interesting fact then emerges that this is also a *geographical* distribution, with the more southerly towns named on the earlier coins. **Table II.3.1** plots the different types of Precursors and pre-Mohammedan coins against their mint towns, arranged in geographical order, south to north.

Table II.3.1: Pre-Mohammedan Arab-Byzantine coins, ordered by mint name, south to north

		Precursor	Pre-Mohammedan (Grierson's types a–e)				
Mint Name:	Total Issues:	p 2	a 1	c 1	e 2	b 2	d 5
Gerasa/Jaraš		p*					
Bayṣān		p*					
Tiberias			a*				d**
Damascus				c*	e**		d***
Baᶜlabakk					e***		d**
Ḥimṣ						b***	d***
Ṭarṭūs						b**	
No name							d***

Letters a–e: issues described in text.
* = sole issue of this type
** = rare issue of this type
*** = predominant or very common issue of this type
p = Precursors

We would suggest that type d) is indeed the latest of the series, representing a stage when a more centralized government existed, and imposed greater uniformity on the process of minting coins. The question is then, when did this happen? The coins of type d) cannot be earlier than 641–650 C.E., the date of their Byzantine prototype, and they may well have started to be minted considerably later than that. Given this consideration, and the fact that the pre-Mohammedan coins cover the whole period from the 10s/630s to ca. 61/680, it is quite likely that this stage of a more centralized government with wider control was reached only after the Battle of Ṣiffīn (36/657).

So during the thirty years or so preceding Muᶜāwiyah's assumption of the caliphate in 41/661, the towns of northern al-Šām (but not others) began to issue coins. Gerasa and Bayṣān, in the south of this area, were the earliest to do so, and an analysis of the coin issues suggests that the practice then spread gradually northwards throughout this period. In fact so many towns produced early Arab coins, in contrast to the Byzantine practice of establishing only a very few central mints, that the main reason for them all cannot have been simply the need for coinage. The issue of coins by towns which had not been allowed to do so in Byzantine times was, rather, a clear political declaration of some kind of autonomy, or freedom from Byzantine rule,[24] and we consider the pre-Mohammedan coin series to be signposts on the road of Byzantine withdrawal. We recall that after the Persian interlude, Byzantium did not return to al-Šām in more than a token sense, but gradually established the border at Antioch. Day-to-day administration of a town and the surrounding territory subordinate to it was in the hands of the Rūmī municipal élite—the *patrikioi* and their supporters—and they were encouraged to be independent. The (Monophysite) church clergy and administration also had a considerable degree of influence.[25]

It was just at this stage that various towns—which had not been Byzantine mint towns—started to issue their own coins. While this is a declaration of a more or less considerable degree of autonomy, it does not indicate rebellion or a declaration of independence by the *patrikioi*; rather, it is a symbolic act. Coins issued in one town were not confined to use in that

---

24. Donner (1986), p. 290 similarly acknowledges the political ramifications of minting coins: "Indeed, we might consider the very act of issuing coins to be a declaration of autonomy and independence, even in the case of [the] earliest coins"—though he assumes the coins were issued by a central political factor, "the new regime," and therefore reflect "its" claim to independence and autonomy from Byzantium.

25. See part I Chapter 2: The Byzantine East on the Eve of Invasion, and Chapter 3: The Role of the Church.

town, and would gradually find their way throughout the area. Coins from a town which had not been a mint town of the Byzantine empire therefore made a political statement to the province: that the town concerned was no longer bound de facto by the strictures of central rule, and its *patrikios* considered himself free to increase his own sphere of control as much as he could (even though he continued to recognize the emperor's sovereignty de jure).

The technical aspects of starting to mint coins were not, however, so simple. Making dies and minting from them is a highly skilled art, and it is unlikely that the necessary expertise was available in a town which had not previously minted coins, at least not since late Roman times. It can be argued that the closure of the Byzantine mint at Antioch in 610 C.E.[26] would have released several hundred mint workers onto the job market, and these would have been available for employment by the towns. But the towns started to mint coins some twenty to thirty years after the Antioch mint was closed, and it seems most unlikely that by that time many former mint workers were still available. We cannot, then, simply assume that coins marked "Scythopolis" were really minted there. It was not unheard of to mint in one place for distribution in another.[27] Moreover, some of these early coins of Scythopolis and Gerasa are so similar that they may well have been minted from the same die,[28] and rather than postulating that Scythopolis minted coins for Gerasa or vice versa, it makes more sense to conclude that coins for both towns were minted somewhere else. We suggest, then, that Byzantium supplied the Rūmī élite of various towns with a visible sign of their increasing independence, in the form of a municipal coinage, minted at a Byzantine mint for distribution to the towns.[29] This

---

26. Whitting (1973), p. 68.

27. Compare Jungfleisch's claim (*Bull. de l'Inst. d'Egypte* XXXI [1949], p. 111, referred to by Walker [1956], p. lxiii), that the excavation of the Arab mint of Wāsiṭ, which together with Damascus was the major mint of the late 1st—early 2nd century A.H., revealed a large stock of newly minted *dirhams* with the Arabic legends "struck in al-Andalus" and "struck in Ifriḳiya." Walker comments: "Apparently they were all products of the mint of Wāsiṭ ready to be dispatched to the West. If true, the evidence would completely support Maḳrizi's statement"—which was that under Hišām and Walīd II the sole mint for *dirhams* was Wāsiṭ. (The passage from Makrizi is from an unpublished manuscript, quoted by Walker, p. lxiii.)

28. Cf. Bates (1986), p. 250, lines 3–5 from bottom.

29. We may mention here, as an aside, that the practice of putting the town's name on coins makes a great deal of sense if it is not the place where the coins were actually minted, but

interpretation—that the coins were minted by Byzantium for the different towns and supplied to them as a way of making a *political statement* that they were no longer under Byzantine control—fits in nicely with Bates' point, referred to above, that the pre-Mohammedan copper coins "are few in number and very similar in style, and often die-linked to each other."[30] Bates argues from these facts that they could not have been minted continuously over a period of fifty or sixty years, from the time of the conquest to the appearance of the Mohammedan issues in the 70s A.H.; therefore they should be dated to the few years immediately prior to the Mohammedan (Standing Caliph) issues. These same attributes, however—few types, similar styles, and die-links between coins bearing different mint names—equally support our suggestion. Each issue could indeed have been brief, of only a few years' duration, since it was a political act rather than an economic necessity: the declaration that the town concerned was no longer under Byzantine jurisdiction or that it was under Arab control. Yet the total issues of all the towns could have spanned, discontinuously, the whole period of Muᶜāwiyah's rule.[31]

The towns continued to govern themselves much as they had before. Initially, at least, the *patrikioi*—i.e., the Rūmī élite—would have been left in control. Nevertheless, after quite a short time the coins began to be overstruck with Arabic (and often also Greek) confirmations that they were legal tender. To understand this development, we should remember that every new ruler, Byzantine and Arab, issued his own coins; but this did not mean that he would inevitably recall the old ones, or that they ceased to be recognized as valid. He might simply confirm the validity of the old ones—in general, not by overstriking them—and they would continue

---

the place to which they should be sent. Among other factors, it made it unlikely that towns along the route would "appropriate" a shipment of coinage intended for somewhere else.

30. Bates (1986), p. 250.

31. Moshe Sharon has suggested that the towns issued these coins from purely economic considerations—to provide a supply of low-denomination coins sufficient for the daily needs of the local population (private communication, May 1988). This could have been one factor, but not, we think, the most important one. Otherwise it is difficult to understand why relatively few towns did in fact issue coins during these first decades, and why those that did are all concentrated in a specific geographical area, from Gerasa in the south to Ṭarṭūs in the north. Why did important towns such as ᶜAmmān, Bayt Jibrīn, and Caesarea, the former Byzantine capital, not to mention Jerusalem, not feel the need to supply the basic daily requirements of their populations?

to circulate. Thus in the towns of al-Šām there would have been many different coins in circulation—various Byzantine issues from perhaps the past hundred years, as well as the new municipal folles. People were used to handling different issues of coins, and in particular, they were used to folles of widely differing weights and types—especially after the wide variations in the folles of Heraclius's reign. Why, then, should some of them have been overstruck? The reason for overstriking cannot have been to confirm that the new Arab rulers continued to allow the use of these coins, precisely because it was the *new* issues—not older ones of the Byzantine era, still in circulation—that were overstruck. In addition, overstriking in order to validate a coin implies that coins not so validated were not legal tender, a position which would have upset the whole system. It is, besides, opposed to everything we know about early Arab administrative practice, which indicates that the Arabs consistently tried to allow life to be administered just as it had been, making as few changes as possible.

There are two other possible reasons. The first is that people might regard the coins as counterfeit. Grierson (1982) seems to favor this view, because of the crude workmanship of some of them. However, such assurances were struck on many pre-Mohammedan coins, including ones of perfectly good workmanship, not only on the cruder types of Precursors, so that this reason seems insufficient. The other explanation, and the one we favor, is political: overstriking was a public declaration that the authorization of the Arab rulers was now required on coins issued by the towns. It thus indicates a further stage in the consolidation of Arab control over the area, including the "internal affairs" of the towns.

The use of Arabic as well as—or instead of—Greek was also a symbolic act. In al-Šām in these early years of Arab rule most of the population would not have been literate in Arabic: educated people, i.e., those who could read at all, knew Greek and/or Syriac. To use Arabic on coins was, therefore, more a way of declaring that it was now an official language, than of telling people that the coins were valid for use. The medium—the use of Arabic—was the message.

Judging from the coins, then, Muᶜāwiyah controlled only the northern towns, from Bayṣān to Ḥimṣ, not those of central Palestine. Not till ᶜAbd al-Malik's time were coins minted over a wider area, both to the south of the initial region, in central Palestine (ᶜAmmān; Īlyā, i.e., Jerusalem; Bayt Jibrīn) and to the north of it, in northern Syria (Ḥalab, Manbij, Ḥarrān). In fact, only under ᶜAbd al-Malik were coins minted in any of the five northern provinces: al-Jazīrah (northern Mesopotamia), Arminiyyah (the Caucasus region), Mosul, Arran, and Aḏarbayjan.[32] Not till even later—not before the turn of the 8th century C.E.—were coins minted in the other towns of Palestine, such as Gaza, Askalon, and Lydda. If all of al-Šām came under Arab control from the Battle of the Yarmūk in 636 C.E., this time distribution requires an explanation, for we would expect some of the more important Palestinian towns, at least—notably Jerusalem—to have minted coins in this early period, given that many much less important towns did so. The time distribution of the coins suggests, rather, that the assumption of control was gradual, and that Muᶜāwiyah controlled only the northern towns of al-Šām (Bayṣān to Ḥimṣ), not those of central Palestine. The five northern provinces listed above, according to this reading, did not come completely under the caliph's control until ᶜAbd al-Malik, who put them all under the unified control of his brother, Muḥammad bn Marwān.

THE SASSANIAN ARENA

The Sassanian polity ended in A.H. 31/651, when Yezdigird III was killed at Merw. In the Persian as in the Byzantine areas, the contemporary evidence regarding the Takeover and the first decades of Arab rule is mainly numismatic. Like the Arab-Byzantine coins, the Arab-Sassanian ones are a continuation of Sassanian issues and continue to portray the bust of a Sassanian monarch (a *kisrà*). The issues imitated were those of Xusraū II (590–628 C.E.), large numbers of which were in common use throughout the Persian empire. Unlike the early Arab-Byzantine coins, these early Arab-Sassanian ones are for the most part dated[33] and record the names of their mints. Despite this fact, assigning a date to an Arab-Sassanian coin can be quite complex. This is partly because of the difficult Pehlevi script employed, and partly because the date can often refer to more than one of the three partly overlapping eras: the Arab (A.H.), Yezdigird (Y.E.), and post-Yezdigird (P.Y.E.). It is not always easy to decide which era was intended. We shall not go into this question here, since the dates of the coins mentioned in this chapter are not in doubt. However, problems do occur with the dating of the coins bearing religious legends, so that when we come to discuss the religious

32. Bates (1986), p. 237.

33. For this reason, too they can provide useful evidence regarding the diachronic sequence of religious texts in their legends. This aspect is discussed in the section "Prophethood and Guidance" of Part III Chapter 4.

information on the coins (in Part III Chapter 3) we shall have to examine the question of dating Arab-Sassanian coins in more detail.

The earliest Arab-Sassanian coin is from the mint of Ḏārābjird and is dated Y.E. 20 (=A.H. 31/651).[34] The earliest coins with Arabic legends are from Merv, dated A.H. 31, i.e., the same year. The legend is *jayyid* (= "good"), as on the Arab-Byzantine coins, and we consider that, here as there, it indicated less that the currency was suitable for market use than that confirmation to this effect by the Arab ruler was required. During the decade from Y.E. 20–31, i.e., A.H. 31/651 to A.H. 42/662, the religious legend *bism Allāh*, in Arabic, appears on Arab-Sassanian coins struck at various mints all over the former Sassanian realm. It provides evidence for Arab control of a political entity still recognizably Sassanian in appearance. But no ruler's or governor's name appears on the coins until the early 40s/660s. Coins issued by three different governors[35] appear in A.H. 41/661–62; coins bearing Muᶜāwiyah's name, in A.H. 44/664–65, three years after his final accession to the caliphate. Later, ᶜAbd al-Malik's name appears, and the coins continue to bear the caliph's or a governor's name down to 83 A.H., near the end of ᶜAbd al-Malik's reign.[36]

From a historical point of view, the interesting aspect of the coins of this period is their silence regarding the pre-Sufyānid rulers; and the two dates, A.H. 31/651 for the first dated Arab-Sassanian coins, and A.H. 41/661 for the earliest coin bearing any Arab ruler's name, provide a pair of chronological parentheses marking the Sufyānid-ᶜAlid struggle for the ascendancy. As far as numismatics can tell the story, it was Muᶜāwiyah who, while still governor of Syria, conquered the Sassanian realm. In this connection, the occurrence of pre-Mohammedan (Arab-Byzantine) coins of types a) and b), bearing Pehlevi legends, is of interest. Grierson considers that the legends on these coins limit their possible provenance—i.e., that they were "evidently struck in Persia with Pehlevi inscriptions."[37] But another possibility is that this was a Damascene issue (of Muᶜāwiyah), intended to be circulated in areas once under Sassanian control and now in

34. Walker (1941), p. 25 no. 35.

35. Ziyād bn Abū Sufyān, Samurrah bn Jundab, and ᶜAbdallah bn Ziyād.

36. Walker (1941), pp. xxvi, 23, 125–26. Both Sufyānī and Marwānī governors were commemorated on coins; all told, thirty-five Arab governors' names appear in the coinage of this particular type. There are also issues of pretenders to the caliphate, the Zubayrites, their lieutenants, and other "rebels," which are of great historical value.

37. Grierson (1982), p. 145 (a).

Sufyānid hands. For comparison, we know that some Marwānī Arab-Sassanian coins were struck in Damascus.[38]

The epigraphy of the contemporary coins, then, provides no evidence to corroborate the version of history in the Traditional Account, namely that ᶜUṯmān conquered the Sassanian realm. Neither ᶜUṯmān nor any of the earlier commanders and governors are mentioned.[39] This silence regarding the names of early commanders fits in much better with our suggestion that until Muᶜāwiyah there was nobody to mention. Until A.H. 41/661 the Arabs operated as *foederati*. After the battle of Ṣiffīn, Muᶜāwiyah was recognized as the unified ruler of the whole area, and his name then appears on the coins. In fact Muᶜāwiyah, whose name is known from coins, inscriptions (one in Arabic and one in Greek), and written sources such as Sebeos, John of Phenek, and the *Life* of Maximus the Confessor,[40] is the first historical Arab ruler to be fully archaeologically and epigraphically attested.

---

38. Walker (1941), p. 23 no. N1 (A.H. 73/692), on reverse *dmšq*; p. 23 no. DD1.

39. Still less, of course, does it support the traditional dates for the conquest of the Sassanian realm: the Battle of Nihavand and the conquest of Rayy (21/642) together with the founding of Arab towns, Baṣrah (A.H. 16/637 according to the Traditional Account) and Kufah (17/638).

40. These sources were discussed in the previous chapter.

4

The Foundation of the Arab State: A Suggested Reconstruction

The evidence presented so far is consistent with the following schematic framework. The Byzantine military withdrawal from al-Šām and later de facto withdrawal from civilian administration, detailed in Part I, were both complete by the end of the 6th century C.E. There ensued a period of power struggles in a political vacuum, which we may call Phase I of the Arab takeover. It started in the years following the Persian occupation of al-Šām, when the towns of Syria and northern Palestine publicly announced the lack of central control by minting their own coins. These numismatic declarations of autonomy started at Jeraš (Gerasa) and Bayṣān in the 10s/630s, and gradually moved northwards to Ḥimṣ and Ṭarṭūs, not far from the line decided upon by Byzantium as her frontier, which ran east-west approximately at Antioch. Meanwhile the empire's former Arab *foederati* announced that they were now in control; they continued to demand taxes ("tribute") from the countryside and the towns, but in their own name rather than that of their former masters. Various chiefs gradually aspired to widen their sphere of control beyond their former territories, and desert tribes from, for example, Phoinikon may also have sought to exploit the Byzantine withdrawal.

A power struggle ensued between the heads of the various tribal groups, and most probably also between them and influential families among the local Arab population, who now also saw their chance for political control. Each faction vied for control of territory and of the tribute from the towns. The Sufyānids emerged uppermost from these years, but it would seem that

Muᶜāwiyah spent most of his first two decades, A.H. 20–40/641–660, continuing to amass support and gradually taking control of the Sassanid areas from his base in Damascus. This period of gradually widening and consolidating his control we may call Phase II of the Arab takeover. It was concluded by Muᶜāwiyah's defeat of his main rivals at the battle of Ṣiffīn, and recognition of him as caliph of the whole area. This we may call Phase III of the takeover: the establishment by one leader of control over al-Šām, and a unified Arab conquest of Egypt and Iraq.[1]

There have been some studies of Muᶜāwiyah's administrative system[2] and diplomatic methods.[3] He seems to have been especially skilled at arousing and keeping the support of various local élites,[4] and his power base rested on a "confederation" of tribes personally loyal to him. Some of them were probably former members of the Ġassānid confederation; others were defined as *yamanī*, which as we have seen[5] probably meant that they came from southern Provincia Arabia, Palaestina III, and Phoinikon. Muᶜāwiyah based his method of control on personal links with tribal leaders (*ašrāf*), and on appointing a small number of governors connected by family ties to himself or to his immediate entourage. Military administration was based on tribal units, and where necessary (as in Kufah, newly settled by desert tribes) he formed new tribal units corresponding to civic divisions. Already in 638 Kufah was divided into sevenths, each seventh being a "tribe." This procedure merely continued the old Roman practice—cf. the division of Bostra into twelve tribes, two at least of which had Greek names, Zeus and Romana; or the nine tribal names of Jaraš (Zeus, Artemis, Leto, Hadrianē, etc.).[6] The *ašrāf*, or tribal leaders, were appointed by Muᶜāwiyah or his representative, usually but not necessarily from the hereditary chiefly families, and there was rivalry for nomination. The chiefs "commanded their units in times of war and were responsible for them in times of peace,"[7] and

1. It is probable that Muᶜwiyah was not responsible for the conquest of Egypt. Although the only undoubtedly historical competitor for supremacy whose name we know is ᶜAlī, there must have been many others, one of whom could have diverted his attention to Egypt, perhaps on seeing his chances of success in al-Šām diminishing.
2. Crone (1980), Ch. 3.
3. Hasson, Isaac (1982), esp. Ch. 1.
4. Ibid., passim, esp. Ch. 1.
5. Pp. 100–101.
6. MacAdam (1986), pp. 101–102.
7. Crone (1980), p. 31.

their position depended on their acceptability to both the tribe and the authorities. There was a hierarchy among the various tribal units, and the funding which greased the whole system came from the provincial governor. This latter, who had both financial and military power in his province and was always related somehow to the caliph, would meet regularly with the most important *ašrāf* at his *majlis*—tribal meetings—where among other matters he handed out generous payments. Each such *šarīf* then repeated the process at his own *majlis* for the lesser *ašrāf* who owed allegiance to him, and so on down to the smallest unit. The result was to preserve the tribal organization of society, and leave responsibility for tribal control in the hands of the tribal chiefs. Even when new administrative units were created and men chosen by the authorities were placed in charge of them, this was done within a framework of new 'tribes' and *ašrāf*.

At the same time, the tribesmen and chiefs were effectively kept apart from the older established population. They were settled, if at all, in new towns, not existing ones (and even these in Iraq, not in al-Šām), and prevented from access to any significant position within the civil administration. This is because these posts were awarded by the governor, and most of them went to his relatives. Nonetheless, a limited number of relatively unimportant posts were, at the governor's discretion, awarded to *ašrāf*, and they could also aspire to marriage ties with the governor's family or relatives. Thus the *ašrāf*, while in practice never achieving any significant position of power within the state administration, could constantly hope for it, and were bound in loyalty to the governor as their only source both of funds and of hopes for social advancement.[8]

Muᶜāwiyah, then, relied for power on desert tribes, and on his own family or members of small tribes whom he allied to his family by marriage, and from among whom the provincial governors were chosen. He did not rely on the settled Rūmī population: he did not recruit them to the army and they did not take part in the inter-Arab quarrels which plagued the long period during which he was consolidating control, up until the Battle of Ṣiffīn (36/657). And the tribal Arabs did not interfere in the organization, civic administration, and daily life of the settled population, which continued to administer itself just as it had under Byzantium.

Muᶜāwiyah's situation probably more closely resembled that of a feudal overlord than any modern notion of ruler. Moreover, the areas that inter-

8. Crone (1980), pp. 30–33.

ested him were more to the north and east of Damascus than to the south. The only evidence for control of the Palestinian towns comes, as usual, from the Traditional Account, which provides a wealth of contradictory reports regarding the dates, commanders, methods, and terms involved in the capture of any given place.[9] Even here, northern towns figure more prominently, apart from Jerusalem (nobody, it seems, could consider leaving a record that did not include an account of the capture of Jerusalem). But the central part of Palestine, the old, established *oikoumenē* where there were few Arabs in the population, from Bayṣān to Gaza and ᶜAmmān to Bayt Jibrīn, shows little sign of having been under Muᶜāwiyah's control; certainly not before the Battle of Ṣiffīn. We have no external corroboration of the Traditional Account regarding the political situation in central Palestine during Muᶜā wiyah's governorship and caliphate; we cannot even tell whether he himself was interested in controlling that area. We do have evidence for his interest in the Negev area, from the bilingual (Greek and Arabic) papyri found at Nessana. But even here, that interest was apparently very selective. The last purely Byzantine papyrus at Nessana is dated October 7, 630 C.E., after which a gap of over forty years ensued before we have any dating from the time of Arab rule: the bilingual (Greek-Arabic) papyri start only in A.H. 54/674,[10] i.e., towards the end of Muᶜāwiyah's caliphate. During the following four years (A.H. 54–57/674–77) the Arab authorities demanded taxes in kind—wheat and olive oil—from Nessana, and probably also from the other towns of the Negev's northwest triangle, and their delivery to (presumably military) units stationed in the area. After 57 A.H. there is another gap of twelve years, until the next papyrus, which dates from ᶜAbd al-Malik's time, A.H. 69–70/689.[11] The short period covered by the papyri in Muᶜāwiyah's time may be misleading—it is quite possible that some papyri have been lost, and that Muᶜāwiyah was interested in the area for a longer period of time. But the general pattern of the evidence available so far supports the conclusion that Muᶜāwiyah attached military and administrative importance to the Negev for only a short time, and then only to the northwest fringes of it. It is possible that this was connected with his interests in Egypt: the Nessana area was part of the administrative district of Gaza, as the papyri explicitly state, and Nessana was an outpost between

9. Listed in Hill (1971), pp. 59–75; cf. our Introduction, pp. 2–4, and Part II Chapter 1, pp. 104–105 on the Traditional Account of the invasion.

10. P. Colt 60, in Colt III:178.

11. P. Colt 67, in Colt III.

Palestine and Egypt. Muᶜāwiyah would have found it necessary to station military units in this area. But in any case, we have very little evidence that the towns of central Palestine recognized Muᶜāwiyah as their ruler, or that he himself took much interest in them; the area to the east, in Mesopotamia, seems to have interested him more.[12]

Even in the mid-7th century, some twenty years after the start of the Takeover, Arab sovereignty and detachment from the empire was still incomplete. The coins of al-Šām testify to this by continuing consciously to follow Byzantine prototypes, and by refraining from putting dates and names of rulers on coins issued in the former Byzantine provinces, in contrast to their practice in the former Sassanian areas. The continuation of bilingual Greek-Arabic chancery conventions is another example of continued Byzantine influence. In fact, it is probable that the divergence of the Arab coins from Byzantine prototypes, which is gradual and can be observed phase by phase, marks not so much the augmentation of Arab strength and independence as the gradual withdrawal of Byzantine interest from the arena, as the new Arab state became firmly established. This process was not complete, we suggest, until ᶜAbd al-Malik established firm control.[13]

During this period—from the takeover up to ᶜAbd al-Malik, ca. A.H. 20–75/640–95—the Christian inhabitants of al-Šām either rejoiced in the empire's loss of her provinces or confidently expected Byzantium's return, according to religious persuasion; but all of them were in a politically delicate situation as they waited for several decades to learn their fate. Byzantium might yet decide, as the Melkites so fervently hoped, to reclaim her own; but meanwhile life went on and the local élites, at least, had to decide with whom to cast their lot. The decision was, as usual, expressed in religious terms. Allegiance to Byzantium was shown by adherence to the Orthodox version of Christianity, rather than to Monophysitism, the majority church; this included accepting Monotheletism during those years when Byzantium declared it to be the Orthodox creed.

---

12. How far he was interested in the northern areas is unclear. Armenia came under Arab control in 33/653, but was still acknowledged as Byzantine property, for which the Arabs paid a yearly tribute. The details of the conquest of Armenia are obscure, with contradictory accounts in the Armenian, Greek, and Arabic sources (Vasiliev [1952], p. 313).

13. At the end of this chapter we discuss evidence for Byzantine influence on the early Arab state.

Professing the official creed was a declaration of personal or group loyalty to the state, a way of keeping one's Byzantine identity—it was, in fact, the only way left. Lest it be objected that one's religion is a question of private belief, not of politics, we would here recall that the doctrinal differences between Orthodoxy and Severan Monophysitism (the creed of the dominant Monophysite Church) were slight, and may indeed have been mainly terminological.[14] Furthermore, both creeds had, albeit for different reasons, reluctantly accepted Monotheletism. In such circumstances, and considering the pressures the Melkite minority must have faced, it is probable that those who persisted in calling themselves Chalcedonians in al-Šām did so not only from religious conviction, but also in great measure to maintain their Byzantine identity.[15]

The uncertainty about the empire's intentions affected the relationship of the local urban population with the Arabs who became the de facto rulers.[16] For years al-Šām remained nominally under Byzantine suzerainty, while in fact the Arabs were in control and collected yearly taxes/tribute on the basis of treaties concluded with individual towns. The stories in the Muslim literature relate that the towns usually put a clause in the treaty stipulating that they were paying only for so long as they did not receive instructions from the emperor: for example, for three years, or until the messengers sent to *qayṣar* (the Byzantine emperor or his representative) should return with orders. If this reflects any reality, it means that the towns at this point still expected Byzantium to return, or at least thought such an event possible. They did not perceive the situation as a unified, clear-cut conquest by an Arab empire, and the larger towns, at least, kept their Byzantine identity. The *patrikios* of such a town may have foreseen the eventual superiority of the Arabs, but nonetheless held out for years, remaining nominally loyal to Byzantium in the hope that the emperor would settle the matter definitively, either by sending an armed force to rid the country of the Arabs, or by political means. The

14. Cf. Part I Chapter 3, p. 53 + n. 11.

15. Nubia is an example of such a Byzantine identity maintained by means of cultural relations with Byzantine Christianity, despite the fact that Nubia was outside the Byzantine polity. Cf. Frend (1980), pp. xxiii, 16.

16. While not *all* Orthodox Christians hoped to remain the emperor's subjects, and some may have been willing to see the Arabs as their political masters, even these would have liked to enjoy imperial recognition as brethren in faith, and some sign of Byzantine diplomatic concern, at least during the early period of the Takeover.

Rūmī élite in such towns would certainly have preferred this course of action, since divorce from Byzantium meant an end to their culture and way of life, and probably to their position as a ruling sector. But Byzantium did not reciprocate their loyalty. Throughout Muᶜāwiyah's rule, she left them suspended in their religiopolitical uncertainties. During this time, the Byzantine loyalists of al-Šām were awaiting an imperial decision—either to enforce Byzantine sovereignty or to acknowledge the fact of Arab sovereignty over the former Byzantine domain. At Muᶜāwiyah's death the Byzantine strategy was proclaimed—again, in theological terms—by the Sixth Ecumenical Council of 60/680 C.E. Its rejection of Monotheletism, previously defined as the official Chalcedonian faith, was a rejection of the Rūmī faction of the eastern provinces. Byzantium thereby declared that she had no intention of claiming the areas now under Arab control; hopes that the emperor would come to the rescue of his loyal subjects and save the holy places from the Arabs, were revealed as the merest fantasy. After 60/680 the Melkites had no more choice as to whether they wanted to retain their Rūmī identity—Byzantium was de facto out of al-Šām.

In 65/685, in the midst of a bellicose interregnum, ᶜAbd al-Malik came to power, and within a decade had established himself in firm control. With their fate finally decided by both the Byzantine decision and the appearance of a clear Arab ruler, those *patrikioi* who had previously held back from accepting the fact of Arab rule now weighed political expediency against unrewarded allegiance, and went over to the Arab side.

The transfer of allegiance to the Arabs on the part of many former Rūmī *patrikioi* and their factions was of course accompanied by much hesitation and interfactional conflict between the different sectors of the various municipal élites. This stage in the transfer of power is, we consider, reflected in the Arab sources. As Bashear (1985a) has shown, the Arab traditions (the *futūḥ* literature) concerning the conquest of al-Šām depict the "Byzantines" as divided into two main blocks: Rūm, i.e., Greek-speakers, and non-Rūm, i.e., non-Greek speakers of Byzantine allegiance. We accept Bashear's identification of the latter as mainly Byzantine Arabs, for the towns mentioned in the traditions, and those to which Bashear refers, were in the northern interface areas (Bostra and north of it), where, as we have seen, a large percentage of the population were Arabs. Bashear's source analysis further divides the Rūm into two subsectors: the Greek Byzantines, who were Orthodox (i.e., Chalcedonian, first Dyophysite and then Monotheletic), and their non-Orthodox supporters, who were allied with them during the confrontation with the invading Arabs, but split with them over the question of whether to transfer allegiance to the Arabs after the Sixth Ecumenical Council and ᶜAbd al-Malik's assumption of power. The *futūḥ* literature pictures the Takeover as a conflict between the previous ruling sectors of Šamī society, and the Arabs who eventually ousted the Rūmī segment and replaced it with an Arab-only ruling élite. Bashear (1985a) suggests that the Traditional Account's stories of messengers whom Muḥammad sent to the different areas (Diḥyā al-Kalbī to al-Šām, Šujaᶜ bn Wahb to the Ġassānids, and so on) were, like many events in the life of the Prophet, retrojections of events from ᶜAbd al-Malik's day. This suggestion seems quite plausible, and fits well into the scheme of events here suggested. ᶜAbd al-Malik by means of such messengers sought the political allegiance of the Byzantine Arabs, who were among the élite factions in many towns in the interface area. As usual, politics were expressed in religious terms: he urged the *patrikioi* to give up their Byzantine faith (i.e., allegiance) and accept the prophet and the state religion which ᶜAbd al-Malik was even then starting to introduce[17] (i.e., to transfer allegiance to the Arab ruler). A *patrikios* thus solicited by ᶜAbd al-Malik's messengers may himself have been amenable to their suggestions; but he did not always manage to convince the die-hard Rūmī faction of his town to accept his judgment. He therefore continued to lead the Rūmī opposition to Arab rule, and he also continued to fear for his and his followers' lives at the hands of the Rūm, for wishing to convert. For the Byzantine loyalists were still fighting a strenuous rearguard action against the change of fortune that threatened to destroy their political status on the local level as it had on the regional. They still clung desperately to their Melkite (and, therefore, Monotheletic) allegiance. Those who showed signs of going over to the new de facto rulers were prime targets of Rūmī anger; it is not surprising that they were afraid for their lives.

Hiraql is a typical example of this situation.[18] He declined the invitation, "fearing for his life and property [*mulk*]," but others, say the traditions, accepted. One was Ḍuġātir (meaning of title/name uncertain) who confessed his change of faith publicly, and was killed by the Rūm as a result.[19] And the *Futūḥ al-Šām* (Pseudo-Wāqidī) relates that ᶜAẓīm Buṣrà

17. This subject is discussed in Part III.

18. "Hiraql's dilemma" is an attested *topos* in the *futūḥ* literature, e.g., Ibn Kaṯīr, *Bidaya* 3.266, q.b. Bashear (1985a) n. 244. As Bashear makes clear ([1985a] and summary in [1985b], pp. 2–3), the terms *Hiraql* and *qayṣar* cannot mean the Byzantine Emperor Heraclius, but the leader of the Rūm, i.e., in the place to which Diḥya was sent.

19. Ibn Kaṯīr, *Bidaya* 3.266, q.b. Bashear (1985a), n. 254.

faced the same dilemma, so much so that even when the Arabs emerged victorious and concluded a *ṣulḥ* agreement with the city, he himself did not wish to stay "with them" (the people of the city) but to accompany the Arabs, and he returned to Buṣrà (to be appointed as the Arab principal of the town) only afterwards, when Buṣrà became an Arab-controlled municipality. ᶜAẓīm Buṣrà, too, was afraid for his life.

This of course is a literary *topos*, not a historical report. Nonetheless it may be based on an element of historical fact: that ᶜAbd al-Malik sought by diplomatic means to persuade the remaining Byzantine loyalists who were ethnically Arab to switch allegiance to himself.

In ca. 77–79/696–99 ᶜAbd al-Malik reformed the coinage of the Arab state, abolishing all Byzantine traces from the designs of coins. The point of his reform is usually taken to be religious: to replace the coins' iconography, forbidden by Islam, with religious formulae. But in fact the post-Reform coinage is not totally nonfigurative: the designs on the copper/bronze issues include depictions of birds, small animals (e.g., the hare), and what seem to be vessels strangely resembling those depicted on ancient Jewish coins, in which they are assumed to be articles of the temple cult (e.g., the *menorah*). However, they indicate a clear break with the Arab-Byzantine coins of the past: no Byzantine resemblance can be found on the post-Reform coins. This is explicit evidence for the declaration of independence, an independence which the coins had never before proclaimed.[20]

An examination of the level of trade between Byzantium and the new Arab state similarly points to the 680s–690s (ᶜAbd al-Malik and Justinian II) as the time when Arab independence from Byzantium first started to be announced. Despite the classic Pirennian thesis, Byzantine continued to trade with the Arabs after the Takeover, being both a large consumer of luxury goods and the main channel for trade between the Arabs and the West. Where Pirennians see an "almost permanent state of war in the eastern and central Mediterranean" which made regular trade "impossible" for 250 years,[21] others see only isolated local damage from raids and campaigns in specific places, separated by long intervals during which

---

20. There is also a coin dating from 75/694–95, during the few years of experimentation before the Reform, on which the usual reverse emblem of a Byzantine coin, the cross-on-steps, is replaced by a "*miḥrāb* and lance" (Miles [1952]). Like the post-Reform coins, this iconographic one consciously aims to replace Byzantine religious/state symbolism with an "equivalent" Arab symbol, i.e., to assert independence from things Byzantine.

21. Ashtor (1976), pp. 103–104.

any damage could easily have been repaired.[22] This latter view, that there was probably little dislocation of trade around the Mediterranean in the first half-century after the Arab conquest, is undoubtedly much closer to the truth. Sporadic attacks on a port at intervals of several years do not make trade impossible in the intervening period. Cyprus was raided in 648 and 654, but remained an important transit halt for ships between Egypt and Syria, and Constantinople, both between and after the raids.[23] The raids on Sicily and parts of the Aegean in 652 and 669 similarly did not halt their trade activities. Both Egypt and Syria prospered in the 7th century despite the sporadic raids on coastal cities; moreover, trade between them and Byzantium was freer than before. In distinct contrast to earlier regulation, Byzantium did not restrict or apply a quota to imports from Egypt and Syria; shipmasters in the later 7th century could pick up cargo from wherever they wished.[24] Byzantium controlled the central Mediterranean, the Aegean, and the Black Sea, and Byzantine ships visited Alexandria and the Syrian ports. And since the Arab rulers continued the Byzantine administrative and commercial arrangements, control of much of this trade remained in the hands of the Christian communities.[25]

But from the 680s C.E., Byzantium instituted a new economic policy. At first sight it looked like a naval blockade against trade with the Arabs in the Mediterranean; in actual fact it was a calculated policy of cutting out towns not under Byzantine control and routing as much trade as possible through Byzantine ports, where it would pay considerable state taxes. Such a policy had already been used to channel trade through Luni on the Ligurian coast of Italy, cutting out Genoa; in the 680s Byzantium expanded it by establishing Cherson as the port of entry for Crimean trade (a situation unwillingly agreed to by the Khazars); and in the early 8th century she established Constantinople and Salonika as those for Bulgarian trade (in a treaty of 716 C.E.) and Trebizond on the Black Sea as that for trade from the eastern Arab empire (a situation attested only from somewhat later, but which may well have started also in 716).[26] The advantage of using

22. E.g., Lewis (1951), pp. 78–87.
23. Ibid.
24. Ibid., p. 83.
25. Adelson (1962), p. 49.
26. Lewis (1969), p. 48; Lewis (1951), pp. 91–96.

Trebizond was that it forced all goods to pass through Constantinople and pay taxes also there (ten percent import duty, ten percent reexport duty, shipping fees in the Dardanelles, and port dues). Byzantium thus established her own ports, and especially Constantinople, as transit centers for as much international trade as possible: through Trebizond (and then Constantinople), the luxury goods of the Far East and those of the eastern Arab empire, and through Constantinople, the goods of the western Arab lands such as Syria, whose merchants were encouraged to come to Constantinople and set up permanent trading colonies.

This policy could be explained purely in economic terms; but of course it also had a diplomatic side. By curtailing the movement of her own subjects (merchants and ships' crews) to the Arab empire, and instead forcing foreign merchants to come to her, Byzantium also reduced the likelihood of incidents requiring diplomatic intervention concerning Byzantine subjects in foreign ports. If friction occurred, it would be between foreign merchants and the Byzantine authorities in Byzantine towns, a situation where Byzantium would be in control. This was a quiet way of declaring a Byzantine policy of nonintervention, or at least of minimizing the need for intervention, in events happening in the territories now controlled by the Arabs.

Byzantium's economic power and her high level of trade with the Arab state—trade which was economically vital to both sides—could be expected to result in a strong Byzantine cultural influence on the new Arab state, and in considerable diplomatic contact between them. Besides that, if Byzantium intended the Arabs to take over the administration of the East, as this study argues, and used the familiar means of gold and diplomacy to control them, we should expect to find some evidence for relations and influence, probably covert, between Byzantium and the new Arab rulers. Those who accept the traditional view of the Arab conquest, on the other hand, find it natural that such relations should have been absent altogether.

Although there are few historical sources for the Umayyad period, there is some evidence for quite a high degree of Byzantine influence on the Umayyads. Gibb (1958) has pointed out several indications of such influence. Firstly, it is well known that the bureaucracy after the Takeover continued to be staffed by the same officials who had held their posts under the Byzantines. These officials must have had some influence on the caliphate, and its extent should not be underestimated. Byzantine methods of administration and revenue collection continued; until ʿAbd al-Malik's reform, the coinage was Byzantine in design; road maintenance continued, including the Roman custom of setting up milestones. The state monopoly on fine cloth production in Syrian cities, and papyrus production in Alexandria, was continued by the new Arab rulers.[27] Even in matters of ceremony, as Gibb (1958) puts it, "there was a slow process of small adjustment to Byzantine practice."[28] Gibb considers, however, that "the most striking legacy of the imperial heritage ... is ... the Umayyad policy of erecting imperial religious monuments."[29] These monuments are the Dome of the Rock, Walīd's mosque in Damascus, and that of Madīnah. The earliest of these, the Dome of the Rock, is especially Byzantine in character.

Byzantine influence did not stop at providing the inspiration. Later Muslim sources relate the tradition that al-Walīd "requested and obtained the aid of the Greek emperor for the decoration of the Prophet's Mosque at Medina and the Great Mosque at Damascus."[30] Gibb accepts the historicity of this tradition, and his arguments appear convincing.[31] He adds to it the statement, in the *History of Madīnah* composed in 814 C.E. by the Medinan scholar, Ibn Zabāla,[32] that in response to al-Walīd's request the Greek emperor sent mosaic cubes, ten or twenty workmen, and eighty thousand dinars to aid in building the Prophet Mosque in Madīnah.[33] Gibb concludes, from all the sources he brings, that "the Greek emperor did in fact supply some workmen in mosaics, along with mosaic cubes, for both the mosques of Medina and Damascus, and sent also money or gold for the work on the mosque of Medina at least."[34] This means that although al-Walīd confiscated a church to make way for his mosque, and openly proclaimed the fact in his inscription in it, he maintained normal diplomatic relations with Byzantium. As another indication of this, he is also reported to have sent the emperor a gift of a load of pepper worth twenty thousand

27. Lewis (1951), p. 79.
28. Gibb (1958), pp. 223–24.
29. Ibid., p. 224.
30. The sources are al-Ṭabarī and al-Maqdisī, cited in full by Gibb, ibid., p. 225.
31. Another school regards the head of the Byzantines (*ṣāḥib al-Rūm*), from whom the aid was requested, as meaning the leader of the Greek Melkites in Syria, i.e., the Syrian Christian leader; and that it was he who sent workmen and aid to build the mosque. See Gibb (1958), pp. 226–28 for a discussion of the controversy.
32. This work has not survived, but extracts have been preserved by direct quotation in much later works. Cf. Gibb (1958), pp. 228–29.
33. Ibid., p. 229.
34. Ibid.

dinars.[35] Faced with evidence such as this, Gibb concludes that the loudly proclaimed Umayyad view of Byzantium as the Enemy was a political front, a matter of public policy. It served the purpose of rallying the people around the caliph, and the attacks on Byzantium and later seasonal raids served the same function as army exercises and war games do today.[36]

It is harder for Gibb to understand the reasons for the Umayyad acceptance of Byzantine influence. He postulates that they wanted to conquer Byzantium, and being new in the political arena, copied the Grand Master. Only when, after A.H. 101/718, they decided that they could not conquer Byzantium, did their outlook turn to the east, a change seen in the reign of Hišām (107–125/725–43), and in the islamizing policies of ᶜUmar II. The Byzantines, meanwhile, Gibb maintains, were trying to pretend that the conquest had never really happened, and that events in the East were as much under control as in the West:

> At the Byzantine court, one may suspect, a formal pretence was maintained that the caliphs were just another group of barbarian invaders who had seized some of the provinces of the empire, and were disregarding their proper status as vassal princes. Hence the indignation of Justinian II when ᶜAbd al-Malik infringed the imperial privilege of striking gold coinage.[37]

But the fact of Byzantine influence on the new Arab polity should occasion no surprise, for the latter was, essentially, a client state. Indeed, the Arab payment of tribute to Byzantium was a theoretical recognition of Byzantine overlordship of Syria and Egypt. It was no "formal pretence" that the Arab state was on a par with barbarian kingdoms established elsewhere—from the empire's point of view, it was the simple truth. Both ᶜAbd al-Malik's reform of the coinage and Justinian II's public attitude to this reform were as much a political front as the rest of the Byzantine-Umayyad declarations of enmity and seasonal warfare, which, as Gibb has already concluded, were for public consumption only. And the relations between Byzantium and al-Walīd, mentioned above, show that even after ᶜAbd al-Malik, the Umayyads continued to be, de facto, a Byzantine client state.

---

35. Recorded in *Futūḥ Miṣr*, a 9th-century work by Ibn ᶜAbd al-Ḥakam; q.b. Gibb (1958), p. 231.

36. Gibb (1958), p. 222.

37. Ibid., p. 232.

Nor did the "conflict" between Byzantium and the Arab rulers of her erstwhile provinces stop the pilgrim traffic to the Holy Land. Throughout the whole period from the Takeover to the Crusades, Christian pilgrims of every nationality continued to flow to al-Šām in general and Jerusalem in particular.[38] The enriching influence on Mesopotamia of the trade route to Trebizond, as opposed to the Byzantine economic blockade of the Syrian coastal ports, probably resulted in shifting the center of wealth to Mesopotamia, which may help to explain why the ᶜAbbāsids moved the political center from Syria to Mesopotamia when they came to power in the mid-2nd/8th century.[39]

---

38. Wilkinson (1977); q.b. Griffith (1985), p. 23. This flow of pilgrims had of course nothing to do with the receipt or nonreceipt of official Byzantine information through official channels (cf. Part I Chapter 3). But it does make it hard to believe that the eastern Church really did not know what she proclaimed officially not to have heard.

39. Lewis (1951), p. 95. Similarly, Lewis sees the Byzantine economic blockade as an important element in the 2nd/8th-century decline of Egypt and North Africa.

Part III
The Arab Religion

ʿAllāh, Lord of Moses and Jesus, forgive ʿAbd-Allāh

late 7th-century Kufic "Basic Text" inscription, Sede Boqer

ʿAllāh! Incline towards Your messenger and servant, Jesus son of Miriam

Dome of the Rock inscription

We have striven to separate the political aspects of the rise of the Arab state, discussed in the preceding chapters, from the rise of Islam. For in our opinion the Arab state preceded the Arab religion; indeed Islam arose partly, at least, in response to the new state's need for its own state religion. At the time of the takeover, many of the Arab tribesmen were pagan, and paganism survived among Arabic-speaking populations in some areas of the new empire down to the mid-2nd/8th century. The official state religion arose from a general, basic form of monotheism, was influenced by different strands of monotheistic belief current at the time in different parts of the newly acquired empire, and evolved through the declaration of an Arab prophet into Islam. This stage was not reached till late Marwānid times, and was formalized only in the early ᶜAbbāsid period. Part III presents evidence and arguments for this view of religious development.

1

The Religious Background

PAGANISM

The connection between the paganism of the Arab population in the Byzantine Near East, and the religion of the Arabs who took over control of al-Šām, has yet to be seriously investigated. It is of course well-known that the Muslim traditions refer to paganism as the dominant pre-Islamic—Jāhilī—religion of the Ḥijāz, and indeed of the whole peninsula. They also state that elements of pagan ritual were adopted into Islam, and describe pagan sanctuaries. Because of these descriptions, those who accept as historical the traditional Muslim accounts of the conquest have sought evidence for pre-Islamic Arab paganism not in al-Šām, but in the Arabian Peninsula, and especially the Ḥijāz. Indeed, no other region seemed likely to provide such evidence. For with the exception of a few localities such as Ḥarrān, paganism was considered almost extinct in the Byzantine provinces by this time, some three hundred years after Christianity had become the official faith of the empire.

Over the last few decades, teams of local and Western archaeologists have carried out large-scale, systematic archaeological surveys and excavations in the Ḥijāz, the peninsula, and the Jordanian desert. Their findings are regularly published in the archaeological literature;[1] but the results are very

1. The swiftest publication of the archaeological work in these areas is reported in the Lebanese, Jordanian, and Saudi Arabian journals *Abḥāt, ADAJ,* and *Aṭlāl,* respectively.

different from those we might have expected. Hellenistic, Roman, Nabataean, and early Byzantine remains have been found in these areas, as have many pagan inscriptions in various peninsular dialects from the first few centuries C.E. But the finds include no remains of local Arab cultures from the 6th and early 7th centuries,[2] with the exception of some Ṯamūdian and Ṣafaitic cairns (tumuli) in the Jordanian desert, accompanied by inscriptions but no indications of settlement.[3] The first signs of Classical Arabic in the area are inscriptions from the Ṭāᵓif area in the Ḥijāz, which start only in the 40s A.H. (and include one by Muᶜāwiyah dated 58 A.H.).[4] Most disconcerting of all, the entire area has yielded no Jāhilī pagan sites, or inscriptions in Classical Arabic, dating from the 6th and 7th centuries, and specifically, no pagan sanctuaries such as those described in the Muslim sources. This lack contrasts markedly with the thousands of pagan inscriptions in Ṯamūdian and Ṣafaitic and other dialects found in these areas down to the 5th or even 6th centuries C.E. Judging from the archaeology and epigraphy of the Middle East in general, the pagans did not use Classical Arabic. Judging from the archaeology and epigraphy of the Ḥijāz in particular, the pagan cults described in the Muslim sources were not a Ḥijāzī phenomenon. Further field work in these areas is undoubtedly necessary, especially in the Arabian Peninsula. Nonetheless, if the Traditional Account were historical, and did describe 6th- and early 7th-century Ḥijāzī society, then the work already done should have revealed at least some points of correlation with it. In their absence, we must once again search elsewhere for traces of pre-Islamic paganism.

The Arabs were a distinct sector of the urban population in the "cities" of the Negev. Culturally these urban Arabs were Byzantine, part of the empire, and the texts they left behind them were written in Greek and reflect the imperial religion: local forms of Roman-Hellenistic paganism

2. Cf. the discussion in the Introduction n. 22, and Part I Chapter 4, n. 4.

3. Winnett and Harding (1978).

4. The following such inscriptions have been published: from Wādī Šamiyyah, dated 40/660, in *Aṯlāl* 1 (1977): plate 49; from Wādī Šabīl, dated 46/666, in Grohman (1962), inscription no. Z 212; from al-Xašnah, dated 56/675, in *Aṯlāl* 1 (1977): plate 50; Muᶜāwiyah's dam inscription near Ṭāᵓif, dated 58/678, in Grohmann (1962) p. 56, inscription no. Z 68. For evidence regarding the construction projects in this area, see Khan and Mughannam (1982). Livingston et al. (1985) announced the discovery of about five hundred additional Kufic inscriptions from the peninsula; the earliest dated one in their announcement is from 40/660.

at first,[5] and Christianity later. Archaeologically it is easy to follow the transition from Roman paganism to Byzantine Christianity in these six Negev "cities." Each was the size of a large village, having as its nucleus at least two impressive churches, well built and richly adorned with marble and mosaics. The textual remains, all in Greek, come from the churches, tombstones, dedication inscriptions, and papyri.[6] Christian devotion is obvious from the many crucifix marks painted in ocher on the walls of the houses, such as the subterranean dwellings of Oboda (ᶜAvdat). The archaeological remains and inscriptions give the impression that within the Negev "cities," from the 5th century on, Christianity was the only observable faith.

We do not know to which particular sect these Negev Christian Arabs belonged; we may surmise that, as in Syria and the Palaestinas to the north of them, they were predominantly Monophysite. However, as Vasiliev remarks, it is hard to believe that the Arabs were interested in, or understood, the subtle differences between the various Christological positions.[7] Their conversion had a more material basis: it was required of Byzantine subjects, especially of those serving in the army or receiving government salaries. And despite the importance of Christianity, it is well known that paganism was not dead in the Negev or in adjacent areas. If, for instance, following Shahîd and Mayerson, we accept the authenticity at least of the information on the desert Arabs in Nilus's *Narrationes*,[8] his account of the massacre by raiding Saracens of Christian monks near Sinai implies that there were pagan Arab tribes in Sinai in the early 5th century, who had, and sometimes violated, treaties regulating conduct with the Byzantine *oikoumenē*. The publishers of the Nessana papyri concluded that Christianity was only introduced into Nessana soon after 400 C.E. and spread slowly throughout the 5th century.[9] The process of conversion was certainly not complete by the 6th century in the Negev towns, as indeed it was not in places closer to the heart of the empire. As we noted in Part I Chapter 3, in the 6th century John of Ephesus converted seventy thousand pagans in Asia Minor to (Monophysite) Christianity, and undoubtedly he did not reach

5. E.g., Negev (1981), p. 15, Greek inscription no. 3, from ᶜAbdah/ᶜAvdat, an invocation to Zeus Oboda commemorating four Nabataean Arabs.

6. See Colt I and III and Negev (1981).

7. Vasiliev (1955), p. 309.

8. Shahîd (1989), pp. 134–36; Mayerson (1963), pp. 161–64; Mayerson (1975), pp. 51–58.

9. Colt III:15.

them all. If such a sizeable number of people were still pagan so near the Byzantine capital, at least a similar percentage of the population, if not more, may be expected to have remained pagan in the farther reaches of the empire, along the interface with the desert.

The names recorded in Christian inscriptions from the Negev "cities" support this view. Not only in the 5th century but also in the 6th, some of the Christians bore names indicating that they were first-generation converts from paganism.[10] Those who bore theophoric pagan names: ᶜAbd al-Ga (servant of Ga) for a man or ᵓAmat Ga (maid of Ga) for a woman, must have been born to pagan parents. Such names occur in pious Christian texts or in a list of donors to an ecclesiastical building.[11] Their bearers were clearly not required to adopt Christian names upon conversion; but they gave their children Greek (i.e., Christian) names or religiously inoffensive Arab ones.[12] Mixed Greek/Arabic names of Christians therefore also occur, such as the woman of unknown age, Azonene bint Abba, or the twelve-year-old Stephan bn Khalaph-Allāh, who died in 541 of the plague and were buried in the North Church of Nessana.[13] We cannot draw firm conclusions as to whether the Arabic-named fathers of such people were born Christian or pagan.

Outside the towns there is little evidence of Christianity among the Arab tribes of the Negev. Almost no Greek inscriptions have been found there; but many in the Nabatean, Ṯamūdian and Ṣafaitic languages are scattered throughout the desert, mostly on rocks in the open, indicating that peninsular tribes also inhabited the Negev, just as the Nabataeans penetrated the peninsula as far south as Qaryat al-Faw.[14] Archaeologically we can map

---

10. There are also some enigmatic hints of a possible pagan mixing with Negev Arab Christianity. For instance, the ancient Nabataean pagan symbol of the bull's head was combined with the crucifix on the walls and ceiling of the burial/cult cave at Oboda.

11. For the Greek epigraphical evidence in the "six cities" see Colt I & III, and especially Negev (1981).

12. The Christian Arabs in modern Israel today follow the same practice, giving their children either religiously neutral Arab names or else, very commonly, specifically "Christian" ones such as Thomas, Edward, Rosa, or Emily.

13. Negev (1976), p. 407, referring to epitaphs published in Colt I, nos. 114 and 112 respectively.

14. There are no pagan inscriptions in Classical Arabic. The first inscriptions of any sort in what seems to be a close variety of that language appear in the early 6th century, in bi- and trilingual (Syriac/Greek/Arabic) inscriptions on church lintels in northern Syria (Zebed, Ḥarrān, and elsewhere; reproduced in Grohmann [1971], p. 16, figs. 7a-d.

the occupation of the Negev at large and the ᶜAravah, with some interruptions, from the middle of the second millenium B.C.E. right through to the end of the first millenium C.E. Apart from the culturally assimilated town dwellers of the Roman-Byzantine period, the Negev in the different periods shared the same demographic composition as the northern Ḥijāz: Midianites, Amalekites, Nabataeans, Ṯamūdians, and Ṣafaitic Arabs.[15] All these Arabs were of course pagan. An extensive survey carried out in 1985 by one of the present authors (YN)[16] provided evidence that a local Arab tradition of worshipping stones (i.e., stelae) continued without interruption in the Negev from at least the 1st century B.C.E. to the 8th century C.E. During this entire period, pagan Arabs inhabited the central Negev; their shrines and the stone stelae they worshipped have survived to provide explicit archaeological evidence of their cult. This confirms Patrich's conjecture[17] that the Nabataean religion continued "an ancient Arab tradition of worshipping stelae," and that Arab tribes in the Negev, Sinai and the Arabian Peninsula continued to do so long after the Nabateans.[18] In 1988–89, Y. Nevo excavated four of the small, square buildings associated with the Negev runoff systems, and cleaned a section through a fifth,[19] and found them to be, not storehouses as usually thought, but cult shrines. They are datable by pottery found in situ to the 5th–6th centuries C.E.; and they are clearly pagan. Some of their features resemble those of the larger pagan cult centers in the Negev, to be discussed below. Some had a raised

---

Note especially inscription d from Jebel Usays, a historical Ġassānid text). The first Classical Arabic inscriptions in the peninsula date from the 40s A.H., from near Ṭāᵓif (see n. 4 above), and their religious content is monotheistic but not Islamic.

15. For archaeological evidence of the demographic contact of South Palestine with the northern Ḥijāz (W. al-Qurayyah) already in the second millenium B.C.E., see Rothenberg and Glass (1981).

16. Unpublished due to lack of funds and Yehuda Nevo's death.

17. Patrich (1982), pp. 103–104.

18. Of course the Nabataean Arabs did not disappear into thin air with the destruction of their kingdom. Some degree of demographic continuity from the Nabataean period into later centuries is attested by the occurrence of Nabataean and Nabataean-derived names among the Negev Arabs in the 5th to 7th centuries (Negev [1981]). Another remembrance of the Nabataean past can perhaps be observed in the continuation of floral motifs in the earliest Muslim pottery decoration, which thematically and stylistically can be associated with the famous classical Nabatean pottery decoration (Rosen-Ayalon [1987]).

19. Sites HB-BF1, BF2, BF3, BF4, all excavated during 1988, and BF7 (sectioned). For the archaeological report of these excavations and surveys of other similar structures, and wider evidence for paganism in the Negev in the Byzantine period, see Nevo (1991).

threshold; and from the walls protruded stones, which were worn smooth and shiny from being touched (an aspect of pagan worship mentioned in the Muslim traditions).[20] At some point in the 6th century they were carefully filled in to above entrance level with a layer of earth and stones. The care with which this was done, and the lack of damage to the buildings, suggests that the worshippers themselves (ritually?) filled in the shrines before abandoning them. The pagans, then, appear to have left peacefully, not to have been driven out or forced to convert. In Part I Chapter 4 we suggested that they left because the Byzantine authorities stopped subsidizing them in the mid-6th century. But clearly paganism was being openly practiced by the desert Arab tribes in Byzantine territory in the 5th and early 6th centuries. If further excavation should reveal that many of the buildings associated with the runoff systems in the Negev were pagan shrines, as the first five investigated have all been found to be, we will have to conclude that the Beduin tribes inhabiting the Negev outside of the "Six Cities" were overwhelmingly pagan.[21]

At some point after the shrines were filled in and abandoned, they were all methodically destroyed, even those in the most remote places. The walls were completely pulled down; the rubble fell on top of the layer of earth and stones previously used to fill in the shrines.[22] But it is highly improbable that the pagans still left in the area converted. Nor did paganism die out in the 7th century with the advent of Islam. Pagans must have formed a considerable part of the population all through the first two centuries of the Muslim era; for the pagan cult reemerges in a pagan revival which took place, so it seems, under Hišām (A.H. 105–25/724–43), when scores of new pagan cult centers were built in the central Negev. Over fifty sites of this kind have been discovered to date. One small site has been wholly excavated,[23] and the largest, at Sede Boqer, has been partially excavated, but the others have not been studied further. Even so, the archaeological evidence we do have provides a fascinating glimpse of the Negev paganism

20. Alī, J. (1970), p. 232.

21. For the whole question of paganism among the desert tribes in this period see also Nevo (1991).

22. We have no way of dating this final destruction. It could have been the work of the church authorities in the 6th century, soon after the shrines were abandoned, but it was most probably the work of the Arabs in the 8th century, when the large pagan cult centers in the Negev were shut down (see below). This point is discussed in Nevo (1991), Ch. 5.

23. Structure BZ2, reported in Nevo (1991), Ch. 2.

of this period. In contrast to the lack of archaeological evidence for the Jāhilī cult in the Arabian Peninsula, the pagan remains found in the Negev so far correlate very highly with the descriptions of the Jāhilī pagan sanctuaries in the Muslim sources, and largely verify the Muslim accounts regarding both the topography of the sites and the layout of the buildings on them.[24] The essential difference is that, according to the evidence now available, the time and place in which this pagan cult existed was not the pre-Islamic Ḥijāz, but the central Negev of the 2nd/8th century.

The sites in the Negev were discovered long before the 1985 survey; they have been known for several decades from surface surveys, and included in the reports of surveys in the archaeological literature. But they were mistakenly thought to be Byzantine or early Arab settlements. Their cult nature was not discovered until the largest of them, Sede Boqer, was systematically investigated and found to be pagan, and following this the systematic survey of the Negev sites was undertaken in 1985 and later. Thus the mere fact of their existence has long been known, even though their nature was not understood.[25] But as stated earlier, from the peninsula, despite several decades of intensive field work, we do not have even reports of any archaeological findings which might prove, upon reexamination, to be cult centers wrongly interpreted.

In order to demonstrate the close correlation between the Negev cult centers and the Jāhilī sanctuaries described in the Muslim sources, we will describe briefly the site at Sede Boqer, which is the largest of the over fifty such sites discovered so far in the Negev. Only about twenty-five percent of the site has been excavated so far, but this includes separate areas chosen systematically from over the entire site, along the whole length of the wadi (where most of the buildings were concentrated), and all over the adjoining ridge. The evidence from them all presents a uniform picture which conforms to that given by the main area excavated.

---

24. The full report of the excavations at the large cult site of Sede Boqer has not been published due to lack of funds and Yehuda Nevo's death; a brief description is given below. For the Muslim accounts see Hawting (1982) and (1984) as well as Rubin, U. (1986). For a description of specific aspects and a comparison between the Muslim accounts and the Sede Boqer site, see Nevo and Koren (1990).

25. The new interpretation of the findings from both Y. Nevo's excavations and other sites is far from being accepted by all archaeologists. Many still consider these sites to have been agricultural settlements or those of herders.

The Cult Center at Sede Boqer

Only cult buildings have been discovered at Sede Boqer to date: no regular dwelling places have been found, either in the surface survey or in the areas so far excavated. This suggests that the worshippers were nomads or semi-nomads, living in tents as the Beduin do today, who would come to the cult center for relatively short periods, at intervals or on specific occasions. The buildings are square units clustered together in a small area, usually on the lower hill slopes and extending right into the bed of the wadi. Some buildings standing alone are also scattered over the main ridge. A similar topographical arrangement has been found in almost all the contemporary pagan sites of the central Negev. Most of these structures were originally about 1.6 meters high—i.e., less than the height of a man—and none was covered by a hard roof. They contain offering shelves; wall niches, also used for offerings (the remnants of offerings were found in and around them); and recesses in the walls, either deliberately constructed (semicircular, apsidal, or *miḥrāb*-like) or formed after the wall was built by pulling out stones. They seem to be the precursors of the *miḥrāb*, or the successors of the earlier "holy of holies" common in pagan (and Israelite) shrines since days immemorial. Other types of structures include high places: round and apparently solid platforms about 2.5 meters in diameter and 0.7 to 1 meter in height, standing alone or combined with another structure to make a high place complex. Finally there are closed units: rooms with no entrance of any kind. A platform accompanies one of them. The platforms were not altars for sacrifices, for no fire was ever set on any found so far.

Stelae occur frequently in central Negev sites from the Nabataean and Byzantine-Arab periods. At Sede Boqer they were erected upright as part of the door (*not* as regular doorposts), and some were found leaning against the wall or on a heap of stones near the entrance.[26] There were also small, single stelae, each set in a "dwelling," i.e., a small round or square stone construction protecting the stela. None bore an inscription. The top of a few were pierced with one or two holes, a familiar feature also of stelae from other places and periods. They may well be the *anṣāb* of the Arab traditions, or just the "stones" which it is forbidden to worship.

Quite early in the chronological sequence an enclosure was built on the central hillock of the site, on the summit of the ridge. It is close to a concen-

---

26. For a more detailed description of the stelae at the Sede Boqer site, see Nevo and Koren (1990), pp. 34–36 + Fig. 7.

tration of cupmarks arranged in a circle. We consider it most likely that the cupmarks indicate pagan occupation of the hilltop. There was also a typically pagan unit adjoining one wall of the enclosure. But the enclosure itself was probably made by a different group of people, monotheist in religion. This point will be discussed in the section on the various monotheist sects.

Around or soon after 165/781, and probably when or not long after the site ceased to be used, a mosque was built on the summit of the ridge, and the enclosure was eventually annexed to it. So far three other pagan sites have been found in the central Negev where a mosque was added at a later date.[27] In two cases (sites MB and MC) the topographical plan is similar to that at Sede Boqer, i.e., the pagan buildings are on the lower slopes, extending into the wadi, whereas the mosque was built on the hilltop. In the third case, site KA, the mosque was added to the pagan site itself, to the east of the stela-flanked entrance to a well-built enclosure of the pagan shrine.

A notable aspect of the cult at these sites was the ritual destruction of vessels, presumably those used in the cult rites. Vessels of pottery, of soft black stone, of hard stone, and milling and grinding implements of expensive imported stones (sandstones, basalt, granite, etc.) were all intentionally and systematically broken into small pieces and then scattered. In and near the special places set aside for presenting offerings were found also glass vessels and pottery lamps, all broken, together with a variety of other offerings: small pieces of marble and gemstone, eggshells, seashells, and pieces of iron and copper. The number of hand millstones—a symbol of life and home—that suffered this fate is especially remarkable. The general custom of destroying ritual vessels is, however, familiar: its purpose is either to avoid later contamination of what has become pure and sacred through cult use, or to destroy unclean vessels whose use in sacred service is forbidden. Potlatch (i.e., the ritual destruction of wealth) is also a possible explanation.

Because of this ritual, the pottery was usually found outside its loci of

---

27. Site MB, map 1:50,000 Sede Boqer, sheet no. 18-IV, Ḥorbat Ḥatsats, Israel grid reference 1367.0336; site MC, map 1:50,000 Har-Ardon, sheet no. 22-I, Israel grid reference 1406.0163; site KA in N. Laᶜanah, map 1:50,000 Har-Ḥamran, sheet no. 18-IV, Israel grid ref. 1159.0131. Site KA was partially excavated by Nahlieli and Israel (1987). Other archaeologists have reported finding many other mosques, but only the three here mentioned, in our opinion, present convincing evidence of having been a mosque.

implementation, deliberately broken into small pieces, widely scattered, and mixed with ashes in ash concentrations. The pottery (and the stone) findings were therefore most disappointing: it was practically impossible to match pieces and to restore a vessel. It is, however, clear that very few types of vessels were in fact used, mainly storage jars and cooking pots.[28] These types of pottery reflect the activities of a cult center, not those of households where people live. Bowls, jugs and juglets, craters, and the like were all limited in number, types, and sizes, whereas if normal kitchen and household activities are carried out, many different sizes and types of all these implements characterize the pottery assemblage. The very limited scope of this assemblage at Sede Boqer, and the negligible quantity of important Arab ceramic products (e.g., glazed dishes), indicate both the specific and limited requirements of a cult center, and the low economic level of the cult's adherents.

Both the *physical* aspects of the pagan site at Sede Boqer (and of the other pagan sites, as far as we can tell from the surface survey) and the *ceremonial* aspects reconstructable from the design and layout of the buildings, closely match the Muslim descriptions of the Jāhilī cult. The only major point of difference is in the sacrificial aspects of the cult. The Muslim sources state that the pagans practiced animal sacrifice to their idols, and indeed imply that most meat for human consumption was ritually slaughtered. But the Negev pagans did not sacrifice animals to their gods. No bones of small animals (chickens, rabbits, and the like) have been found at Sede Boqer, and only negligible numbers of larger ones (goats or sheep, and camels). In fact there are so few bones, compared to the normal refuse of a dwelling site, that they could be those of animals that died a natural death, not of ones butchered for meat. It is clear that meat was not a staple item of the people's diet, and very likely that they did not eat meat at all. This is a most unpagan attribute. The late 1st/7th-century Christian sources, to be discussed in the next chapter, refer routinely to animal sacrifice and subsequent feasts among the pagan Arabs who settled in the Fertile Crescent, so it is clear that this more expectable pagan behavior was common in other Arab groups. The reasons for the apparent avoidance of

---

28. Our inability to reassemble the fragments does not prevent us from ascertaining the types of vessels used. Archaeological typology is based on such characteristics as degree of rim curvature, degree of curvature of side fragments, handle types, etc., which may be identified even from small pieces of vessels.

animal sacrifice among the Negev pagans are unknown. They may have been influenced by one of the monotheistic creeds which, as we shall see, penetrated the Negev.

The pagan site at Sede Boqer was active until the second half of the 2nd century A.H. At some time not earlier than A.H. 152/769–770[29] it was abandoned peacefully: the whole site was cleaned, covered with layers of ash, lime, and sterile earth, and then filled in with earth and stones in an unhurried, orderly, and indeed possibly ritual fashion, just as its predecessors were two centuries before.[30] There was no destruction of stelae or buildings, though some of the ritual entrances were desecrated by splitting the threshold stone, overthrowing stelae, or removing them from their former positions. When the process was complete, the low, roofless buildings had been completely buried. In this respect they differed from the 6th-century shrines, which were filled inside to about the level of their raised thresholds, but looked from the outside the same as before: buildings complete with roofs and arches. This difference may explain why the shrines abandoned in the 8th century escaped the violent secondary destruction inflicted, obviously by religious opponents (probably 8th-century Muslims), on those from the Byzantine period discussed above.

The burial of the Sede Boqer site marks the end of a centuries-old religious tradition among the Arabs of the Negev, and probably elsewhere too. Its date means that the final period of paganism overlapped with the propagation of Islam—or what ultimately became Islam—for 1½ to 2 centuries. During this period paganism existed openly in the Negev; over fifty pagan cult centers were periodically visited and pagan ceremonies performed in them.

A cult, especially an architecturally prominent cult with so many centers of worship, could not have existed in a barren desert area such as the central Negev without the government's knowledge. Such knowledge implies at least acquiescence, if not approval, simply because a desert population is not self-sufficient: it depends economically on contact with the *oikoumenē*. Had the central authorities opposed the existence of pagans in the desert, it would have been easy enough to eradicate them, even without the use of force, by preventing such economic contact. But this did not

29. See the section on dating, below.
30. See p. 178 above.

happen; as discussed in the next section, the pagan cult centers continued to exist openly until about the 170s A.H. We argue in the following chapters that the Marwānids actively introduced and propagated the new state religion which developed into Islam, and one interpretation of the late date of destruction of the Negev pagan shrines is that they did not wish to terminate pagan activity while this process was underway. The ᶜAbbāsids, however (possibly the caliph al-Mahdī), introduced a new policy which had no place for the ancient Arab cult.

Dating—Pottery and Coins

Three styles of pottery occur at Sede Boqer: Byzantine (6th century C.E., still in vogue in the 7th–8th century), Arab-Byzantine (developed at the very end of the 6th century and the first half of the 7th), and Early Arab or Umayyad, which presumably started to appear in the mid-7th century, and continued to be produced for another two hundred years.[31] This is a typical example of a transitional phase assemblage: an older culture (here Byzantine) is being replaced by a newer one (Arab). Because of this, and because we presently lack a satisfactory chronology for Umayyad pottery in general, we cannot use the pottery to date the site's period of active use with any precision. The coins found in situ, however, provide very clear evidence. They all date to after ᶜAbd al-Malik's reform of the coinage in A.H. 77–78/696–98, and two have governors' names in their legends. One is the little-known Marwānid governor Marwān bn Bišr (end 1st century A.H.), and the other is Muḥammad bn Saᶜīd (A.H. 152–57/769–773), governor of Egypt in al-Manṣūr's day (136–158/754–775). These coins were discovered under the earth and stones with which the buildings were filled, either on the floor itself, or in the earth layer immediately over the floor; other coins were found in debris and over the ground surface. The few whole, or almost whole, vessels were found in situ under the same heavy layer of earth and stones. The coins, and these few vessels, therefore date from the last point in time when the units were open and active, with people walking on the floors, so that they give us a terminus a quo for the site's closure. This means that the cult center was in use during the Marwānid period, and on into the ᶜAbbāsid; it could not have been

31. Early Umayyad pottery is very difficult to date, and no sure chronology for it has so far been established.

buried much before ca. A.H. 160, and a date up to ten years later than this is quite probable.

Dating is also difficult because Sede Boqer is a single-stratum site: there are no stratified floors. In such a case diachronic ordering of the architectural and ceramic evidence is difficult and uncertain. There can be no doubt that buildings underwent constructional changes; walls were dismantled, rooms added to existing clusters, and changes made to existing rooms. These activities are evidence for the passage of time, but because the modifications stretch horizontally, and there is almost no vertical accumulation above floor level (which is here usually the flat rock surface), this passage of time is difficult to measure. Nevertheless, considering all the architectural evidence at hand, the excavators consider that the areas so far uncovered at Sede Boqer were occupied, either continuously or at intervals, for something under a hundred years. This estimate is undoubtedly impressionistic; yet it would be difficult to allow much longer than sixty years for the use of any individual structure at the site without conflicting with the pattern of accumulation of archaeological remains.[32] Since the pagan structures were covered up ca. A.H. 160–170, these considerations give us ca. 100–110/720–730, or a little before, for the founding of the pagan site. However, as we shall see below, the site was in use by a different, monotheistic Arab population from ca. the 70s–80s A.H. (ᶜAbd al-Malik's reign on).

To sum up: the archaeological evidence which has gradually accumulated indicates that what the Muslim sources describe as the Jāhilī pagan cult of the Ḥijāz closely resembles the pagan cult of the Arabs of the Negev. The considerable archaeological activity of the past several decades has failed to find any evidence for a pagan cult in the Ḥijāz such as is described in the Muslim sources, whereas a cult very similar to those descriptions did exist in the Negev. And the archaeological remains indicate that this cult experienced a considerable revival in Marwānid times, from the reign of Hišām, until the pagan centers were methodically and unhurriedly closed down in the late 2nd/8th century.

---

32. The buildings were not very strong or well-built, but there is no sign that they had to be repaired (as distinct from altered or added to) during the life of the site; and the accumulated layer of refuse and dust is very thin. On both points, the figure of sixty years, if inaccurate, is probably an overestimation rather than the opposite.

MONOTHEISTIC SECTS

The material presented so far may have implied that the entire Arab population of al-Šām and the desert interface areas professed either paganism or one of the dominant forms of Christianity. Such an impression would be inaccurate. Apart from the better known forms of Christianity (such as Monophysitism, Nestorianism, and whatever Byzantium currently proclaimed to be Orthodox), a number of other monotheistic creeds existed in the area, most with a long history behind them. We consider that the form of monotheism that became Islam developed out of this monotheistic background, and that several sources contributed to its development. The next sections of this chapter survey the creeds which left their mark on the new faith.

Abrahamism

In several sources, Christian, Jewish, and Muslim, we find evidence that throughout the first centuries C.E. there existed a form of monotheism which emphasized Abraham as founder of the religion and exemplary model. Many of these sources have been discussed by Pines, on whose work we largely rely in the following account. The earliest is Tertullian (ca. 160–230 C.E.), who disputes with a group who want to follow the example of Abraham;[33] he tries to convince them of the error of their ways by asking if they propose, therefore, to practice bigamy and circumcision. Pines considers that these Abrahamists "probably lived in the second century."[34] Later on there is Sozomenus, who lived in Gaza and seems to have had considerable knowledge of the Arab tribes. In his *Ecclesiastical History*, written 443–450 C.E., he describes a form of "Ishmaelite monotheism" which he considers to be identical to the pre-Mosaic religion of the Hebrews. The Ishmaelites' present religion, he concludes, is a corruption of that monotheism due to the influence of their pagan neighbors over a long period of time.[35] Sozomenus further relates that some of the Arabs who had thus fallen from the purity of their original religion into pagan ways learnt

---

33. *De Monogamia*, Corpus Christianorum, Ser. Lat. II, *Tert. Opera*, pars II, pp. 1235–36; q.b. Pines (1984), p. 143.

34. Pines (1984), p. 143 n. 37.

35. Pines (1990), p. 189, quoting Sozomenus, *Eccl. Hist.* 299 (this source is also considered by Cook [1983], p. 81).

more recently from the Jews of their descent from Abraham, and consequently adopted Jewish laws and customs, so that "many among them have a Jewish way of life." Finally, they have now also begun to adopt Christianity as a result of coming into contact with priests and monks.[36] Sebeos, the Armenian historian, writing in the second half of the 1st/7th century, has a similar account of the Arabs learning of their descent from Abraham from the Jews.[37]

In the works of the Neo-Platonic philosopher Isidorus, as quoted by Photius, we find a reference to Marinos, a Samaritan of the second half of the 5th century C.E., who converted to paganism and eventually became the head of the Athenian Academy. Isidorus is quoted as stating that Marinos "gave up their creed [i.e., Samaritanism], since it deviated from Abraham's religion and introduced innovations in it."[38] Marinos then—probably at a later point in time—"fell in love with paganism." For Isidorus, then, the religion of Abraham was a definite creed which one could compare with, for instance, Samaritanism; and some regarded it as the "original" religion, from which others had deviated.

In the *Book of Jubilees*, an apocryphal Jewish work preserved by Christians, a religion of Abraham is outlined which he is said to have imposed on all his sons and grandsons—which, obviously, means also the Arabs.[39]

In the Qur᾿ān Abraham far outweighs Ishmael in importance; the Christians may call the Arabs Ishmaelites, but Ishmael's importance to the Arabs themselves lies in enabling them to trace their descent from Abraham. Abraham himself, says the Qur᾿ān, was neither a Jew nor a Christian, but a *ḥanīf*,[40] a term denoting a class of pre-Islamic believers in one God, who are neither Jewish nor Christian.[41] They follow the religion of Abraham and are portrayed as the forerunners of Islam: "In truth the people that are the

---

36. Ibid.

37. Sebeos, ed. Macler (1904), Ch. 30. An English translation may be found in Crone and Cook (1977), pp. 6–7; and cf. our discussion in the next chapter of the evidence in Sebeos regarding the Arab newcomers' religion.

38. Q.b. Pines (1990), p. 188. For the Greek original and the translation Pines uses, see Stern (1980), pp. 673–74.

39. Cook (1983), p. 80.

40. Q.2:60.

41. There is epigraphical evidence for the existence of such a sect; our term for it is Indeterminate Monotheism. However, the inscriptions which exhibit Indeterminate Monotheism do not prove that its adherents especially venerated Abraham.

closest to Abraham are those who followed him, and this prophet and those who believe."[42] In keeping with this, the Qur'ān records that the Prophet was told, in a divine revelation, to follow the religion of Abraham.[43] It is a central tenet of the Muslim literature that Islam is the continuation of this original religion of Abraham, the *ḥanifiyyah*. Thus in the *Sīrah*, Salmān the Persian after long wanderings finally learnt that "a prophet was about to arise who would be sent with the religion of Abraham."[44] Zayd bn ʿAmr, the prototypical *ḥanīf*, rebuked his people for paganism but "accepted neither Judaism nor Christianity... saying that he worshipped the God of Abraham."[45] And he, like Salmān, after a long search for the religion of Abraham, found a Christian monk who prophesied the imminent arrival of a new prophet who "will be sent with the *ḥanifiyyah*, the religion of Abraham." Islamic tradition maintains that adherents to this creed—personified and typified in the figure of Zayd bn ʿAmr—lived in both Mecca and Yaṯrib before Muḥammad. It is clear from the Qur'ān that Abraham was the first *ḥanīf*, and that ḥanifites are followers of the religion of Abraham.

The exact etymology of this term *ḥanīf* has been a matter of dispute. Crone and Cook (1977) derive it from the Syriac *ḥanpê*, which usually meant pagan.[46] Pines comments that it cannot be so derived, and suggests that it was the Arabic form of the disparaging Hebrew term *ḥanef*, applied to all the sects of which Rabbinic Judaism disapproved—Nazareans, Judeo-Christians, Gnostics, and, Pines would add, Abrahamists.[47] The Qur'ānic use of it seems to concentrate on the latter, and far from denigrating them, extolls them as preservers of the original, true knowledge of God in a sea of pagans—a situation akin, in fact, to that of Abraham himself.

It is not surprising that the Arabs, having accepted the account of their ethnic origins found in Genesis, should be particularly drawn to a form of monotheism claiming for itself direct, uncorrupted descent from the "original" religion of their ancestor Abraham. Textual evidence that such a creed did in fact exist has been given above. There is also a body of epigraphical evidence from the Negev, in the form of a highly unusual

42. Q.3:6.
43. Q.16:124; Pines (1984), p. 143.
44. Guillaume (1955), p. 96.
45. Ibid., p. 99.
46. We discuss this term in Part III Chapter 2 below.
47. Pines (1990), pp. 192–94.

frequency of occurrence of the name Abraham (Abraamos, Abraamios, etc.) in the 6th-century Negev Greek texts, both inscriptions and papyri:

> The name Abraamios, completely absent at Oboda, occurs 74 times at Nessana. Otherwise the name is quite rare in the Christian world. It should be noted that at Nessana about one half of the persons bearing the name Abraham were born to fathers who were of specifically Nabatean-Semitic names.... The earliest occurrence of this name at Nessana goes back to 512 C.E., and in this way Abraham of Elusa antedates that of Nessana by 57 years.[48]

The keeper of the East Church at Mampsis was also Abraham—his name appears in the inscriptions of the mosaic floor, along with those of the builders of the church.[49] Negev, who excavated the church, dates its construction to the second half of the 4th century C.E.[50] The prevalence of the name Abraham in the 6th-century Negev contrasts markedly with the Palestinian and Syrian Greek inscriptions, where the name is infrequent: Negev considers that we must regard it as unusual among Christians in this period.[51] When it does appear, however, it usually—perhaps always—indicates a Semitic origin.[52] While the study of names is but an auxiliary aid, it can indicate a particular ethnic or religious grouping, and this may have been the case here. As we have seen, some at least of the Negev Christians must have been recent converts from paganism, even in the early 6th century. This itself might explain why they preferentially adopted the name of Abraham, the archetype of the convert: the first man to abandon pagan society and worship God. It is equally possible that the converts to Christianity in the Negev included many who were already "Abrahamists," and that this explains why they gave the name Abraham to their sons with unusual frequency. The adherents to the religion of Abraham, it seems, showed a preference for living in the region to which Hagar fled and where Ishmael dwelt—traditionally considered to be the west-southwest corner of the northern Negev, the Gaza-Elusa-Nessana area.

Thus the Negev Arabs in particular seem to have been drawn to

48. Negev (1981), p. 76.
49. Negev (1976), p. 412.
50. Ibid., pp. 402–404, 411.
51. Private communication, November 22, 1982.
52. E.g., GLIS III:4.

Abrahamism as a form of Monotheism that specifically expressed their own ethnic identity: an especially Arab creed. The new Arab religion that arose in the 7th century borrowed from Abrahamism, and built upon it, in a successful attempt to embody an Arab identity and thereby claim Arab allegiance. For instance, the Kaᶜaba, a pagan sanctuary, was incorporated into the new religion via a tradition linking it with Abraham. It is probably because of this ethnic link, this provision of a pedigree, that Abrahamism was incorporated into what became Islam. The other elements of Arab Monotheism are northern, whereas Abrahamism, as stated, appears to have been a specifically Negev sect, insofar as we can tell from the archaeological and epigraphic evidence. From the literary evidence we can tell very little about geographical provenance. We may recall that the writer who shows the greatest knowledge of Abrahamism is Sozomenus, who came from Gaza, and argue that this familiarity results from living close to the people whose beliefs he describes. But it is doubtful if we should be considered justified in so doing, did we not have other evidence for their existence in the Negev.

Judeo-Christianity

The Arabs who, according to Sozomenus, reverted to the pre-Mosaic belief of their forefathers under Jewish influence were not the only Abrahamists. An especial stress on Abraham, and reverence for him, was also an important element of Judeo-Christianity. But this Abrahamism is only one of the many similarities between the Judeo-Christians and Islam. Many have pointed out the parallels, and the conclusion that Judeo-Christianity was probably a major influence on the emergence of Islam is now fairly widely held among Western scholars.[53] But few have investigated the link between the two. The most extensive work has been done by Pines, and it is on his accounts that we mainly rely.[54]

The Judeo-Christians classed themselves as Jews, and maintained that

---

53. To the list given in Pines (1984), p. 144, we may add Cook (1983), a popular account which refers casually to this influence as an accepted fact in his popular account; and also Wansbrough (1978), passim.

54. Pines's articles are listed in the bibliography. Schoeps has addressed specifically the early centuries of Judeo-Christianity, especially the 1st and 2nd centuries C.E., and his work is therefore of less direct relevance to the present study; but see Schoeps (1964), pp. 107–10 for a summary of the comparison.

Jesus was a human prophet whose mission was to restore the original form of the Jewish religion, but that Paul and his followers had corrupted his message. The best-known Judeo-Christian sects are the Ebionites and the Nazarenes or Minae, but the term could include anyone who called himself a Jew yet accepted Jesus as a prophet, so there were almost certainly other Judeo-Christian sects in the Middle East of the first Christian centuries, sects of which we know little today. No known Judeo-Christian sect granted Jesus any actual divinity, though some allowed a supernatural element in his birth. The Christian writers classed them as "Jews who believe,"[55] and Eusebius tells us that from the foundation of the Church until Hadrian's siege of Jerusalem, "the whole Church [of Jerusalem] consisted of faithful Hebrews."[56] This implies that the Christian congregation in Jerusalem was wholly, or almost wholly, composed of converts from Judaism, who regarded themselves as Jews who had accepted Jesus. There is some evidence of a bitter struggle for supremacy between the Judeo-Christian and Pauline versions of Christianity during the first century C.E. and even later, and that

> as late as the first half of the third century the status of "the Catholic doctrine" was not as yet recognized in Syria as indubitably superior to that of the Jewish Christians who lived in that country, and that in certain regions these sectarians had a preponderant position.[57]

But finally Pauline Christianity gained the upper hand, and the Judeo-Christians of Syria-Palestine, and especially Jerusalem, had to flee. Some probably "went underground," outwardly professing adherence to orthodox Christian doctrine; others sought a more liberal religious atmosphere. They found it in the Sassanian Empire, especially Nisibis, a Nestorian center. Pines suggests that there are some signs that they lived, more or less clandestinely, among the Nestorians.[58] For instance, a Jewish work, the *Tōldōt Yeshū*, attributes to Nestorius some beliefs and teachings shared by the Judeo-Christians.[59] If early Nestorianism shared the views of the late

---

55. Cf. Pines (1984), p. 135–37.
56. Eusebius, *Eccles. Hist.* IV.5.2.
57. Pines (1966), pp. 38–39, summarizing the view of G. Strecker in W. Bauer, *Rechtglaübigkeit und Ketzerei im ältesten Christentum* (Tübingen, Germany: 1904).
58. Pines (1966), p. 43.
59. Publ. by S. Krauss in: *Das Leben Jesus nach jüdischen Quellen* (Berlin: 1902); ref. from Pines (1966), p. 41.

8th-century Nestorian patriarch, Timothy, who implied in a discussion with the caliph al-Mahdī that human knowledge cannot tell which is the true religion,[60] the Judeo-Christians could have lived quite easily among them. (The presence of Judeo-Christians among the Nestorians might further help to explain why Nestorius was denounced by the Council of Ephesus as a Jew.)

Memories of the flight from Jerusalem echo in a Judeo-Christian text incorporated into a 10th-century work of anti-Christian polemic, ostensibly by the Muslim author ᶜAbd al-Jabbār. Pines demonstrates that this text is a reworking, with interpolations by ᶜAbd al-Jabbār, of several polemical texts and historical accounts which must date from much earlier, "reflecting the views and traditions of a Jewish Christian community."[61] From their polemics, Pines dates all the texts preserved in al-Jabbār's work to the late 4th to 6th centuries;[62] from historical considerations, he thinks it "more than probable" that most were composed some time between the 5th and early 7th centuries, and in any case before the Muslim conquest.[63] They were almost certainly written in Syriac, which clearly colors al-Jabbār's Arabic, and very probably in Mesopotamia. The most interesting of them, for our purposes, is "a relation of the fortunes of the first Christian Community of Jerusalem from the death of Jesus till the flight of its members..."[64] They fled, the text implies,[65] to the district of Mosul and perhaps also to the Ḥarrān region. But some Judeo-Christians probably continued to exist in Jerusalem, and perhaps more generally in Syria-Palestine, after the flight. For in the later 7th century Arculf, a bishop from Gaul who visited the Holy Land sometime between A.H. 59/679 and 69/688, mentions the existence of a community of "believing Jews"—i.e., Jews who believed in Jesus, variously referred to as *Iudaei credentes*, "believing Jews," and *Iudaei Christiani*, "Christian Jews"—in Jerusalem at that time.[66] Nonetheless it is

60. Pines (1966), p. 37 n. 139.
61. Ibid., p. 1.
62. Ibid., p. 32, 34–35.
63. Ibid., p. 35.
64. Ibid., p. 14. The full translation of this text is on pp. 14–19.
65. Ibid., p. 15.
66. The account is preserved in Adomnan of Iona's *De Locis Sanctis*; the translation by Wilkinson (1977) is quoted in Pines (1984), pp. 145–46. A complete—but less precise—translation of the account of Arculf's pilgrimage, may be found in Vol. III of the *Library of the Palestine Pilgrims' Text Society* (New York: AMS Press, 1971).

more probable, given what has been said above, that the Arabs absorbed Judeo-Christian ideas in northern Mesopotamia.

Our knowledge of Judeo-Christian beliefs comes largely from the pseudo-Clementine *Homilies*, which probably date from the second half of the 4th century C.E., and the pseudo-Clementine *Recognitiones*, written perhaps slightly later. Both these works are possibly or probably based on earlier material. The parallels with Islam have been discussed at length by Pines,[67] and the following are those that seem most pertinent to our account.

• The belief that Jesus was not the son of God or part of the Godhead, but a prophet subordinate to Him.

• The use of 'knowledge' versus 'ignorance' to define *membership in the community*. Members are not 'believers' (as in Pauline Christianity), nor 'practitioners' (as in Rabbinical Judaism), but 'men of knowledge', and access to membership of the community is by *being taught*. This attitude is clear in Islam also. Already in the *Sīrah* Jews are regarded as "people of the scriptures and knowledge" (*ᶜilm*), and similarly knowledge is what distinguishes the Muslims from the pre-Muslim Arabs.[68]

• The emphasis on Abraham as the first 'man of knowledge.' This knowledge of the True God had been conferred on him first by an angel and then by the 'True Prophet' sent by God. This point was also combined with the Biblical accounts of ethnic origin to provide support for the correctness of the sect's beliefs: the Judeo-Christians distinguished between Ishmael, Abraham's elder son, born when he was in a 'state of ignorance,' and Isaac, born when he was in a 'state of knowledge.' From this it followed that the Jews—to whom the Judeo-Christians considered themselves to belong—were 'people of knowledge,' whereas the Arabs were ignorant regarding the true faith. The implication was that they are congenitally condemned to remain in this state of ignorance. As Pines points out,[69] the story in Gen. 15–16 does not really support the claim that Abraham was 'ignorant' of God when Ishmael was born, and some distortion of the Biblical account is required to reach that conclusion. The Arabs—and the Persians—were

67. Pines (1966), pp. 11–13; Pines (1984), pp. 144–45; Pines (1990), pp. 182–86.
68. Guillaume (1955), pp. 93, 136.
69. Pines (1990), pp. 185–86.

singled out for this proof of congenital ignorance, and the reason, as Pines postulates, is most probably that these were the peoples among whom the Judeo-Christians lived, and whose inferiority to themselves they were therefore at pains to demonstrate.

• The direction faced in prayer—towards Jerusalem—which was also the direction of the first *qiblah*.

• Denial of the crucifixion (a belief held by several heretical sects). The sect whose treatise was preserved in ᶜAbd al-Jabbār's work found both the cross and the crucifix repugnant,[70] and this attitude was probably common among the Judeo-Christians.

• The high esteem accorded to an Original Language in which God spoke to His messengers. The Judeo-Christians thus esteemed Hebrew, the language in which God spoke to Abraham and Moses.[71] Islam accords even higher esteem to Arabic as the Original Language, and that in which God spoke to Muḥammad.

• The belief that Pauline Christianity (specifically, Paul himself) had corrupted the message relayed via Jesus from God.

• Insistence on the observance of the Mosaic law, circumcision, and Sabbath observance.

• The acceptance of the Pentateuchal prophets alone, especially Moses and of course Abraham, and also Noah and Lot. This was a position shared also by the Samaritans. But Crone and Cook may be correct in asserting that the Arabs borrowed it from the latter rather than from the Judeo-Christians,[72] since it goes together with acceptance of the Pentateuch alone from the Old Testament, which seems to have been, in the 7th century C.E., a position held only by the Samaritans. We recall in this regard that the suppression of a major Samaritan revolt in Syria-Palestine in 529 C.E. resulted in the mass flight of Samaritans to Persia.[73] There

70. Pines (1966), p. 29.

71. The esteem accorded Hebrew as the Holy Language by Rabbinical Judaism does not match the emphasis and extremity of the Judeo-Christian attitude.

72. Crone and Cook (1977), pp. 14–15.

73. Smith (1954), p. 444.

was therefore a large Samaritan community there, just as there were many Judeo-Christians.

From the 5th century C.E., as discussed above, we have evidence of a cult of Abraham in the Negev, in the form of an extraordinary frequency of occurrence of Abraham as a baptismal name, especially in records from Nessana (from 512 C.E.) and Elusa (from 454). Shortly before this time, Sozomenus tells us that the Arabs learnt of their Abrahamic descent via Ishmael from the Jews, from whom some of them consequently adopted a "Jewish way of life" in accordance with what they considered to be the "religion of Abraham." In the second half of the 7th century C.E., the Armenian chronicle ascribed to Sebeos relates the same tradition. Crone and Cook (1977) see this as evidence for an initial pact, or de facto cooperation, between the invading Arabs and the Jews, whereas Pines (1990) concludes that the "Jews" were Judeo-Christians. We accept Pines's view, and suggest that these Arabs were influenced by Judeo-Christians not in the Ḥijāz, but in al-Šām and in Persia, where Judeo-Christians were living among the Nestorian community. There is no reason not to accept a Samaritan contribution, too, to the general weave of religious ideas; but clearly the main religious influence on the Arabs came from the Judeo-Christians. The area in which this cross-fertilization occurred was probably Mesopotamia, where there were centers of Judeo-Christians, Nestorians and Samaritans, with whom both the indigenous and the newly arrived Arabs would have come into contact.

The development of Islam from a primitive Arab monotheistic creed with Judeo-Christian attributes may be traced in the Arabic monotheistic inscriptions; and especially, in some detail and apparent chronological order, in those discovered over the past decades in the central Negev. The Negev, then, is our final stop in our survey of monotheistic sects, and our stepping stone to an account of the stages of development of Islam.

Early Arab Indeterminate Monotheism

We stated above that the pagan inscriptions in the Peninsular Epigraphical Languages died out during the 5th or perhaps the 6th century C.E.; but this does not mean that the Arabs stopped writing on the desert rocks. There are, indeed, no more pagan inscriptions; but starting from the mid-1st/7th century we find monotheistic rock inscriptions in the same general desert areas where once the pagans wrote: Iraq, Syria, Jordan, the Negev, and the Arabian Peninsula. The earliest dated ones are from the 40s/660s, from the Ṭāʾif area; and many similar ones were inscribed throughout these regions during the early, formative period of Islam, down to the end of the 2nd century A.H. Hundreds have been found in the Negev alone;[74] it is highly probable that many thousands exist. Unlike the pagan inscriptions, they are all in Classical Arabic and in the Kufic script. But their most striking feature is the religion they express: a creed which cannot be classified as either Christianity or Judaism, though it contains elements acceptable to both, and which initially exhibits not a trace of Islam. In the earliest inscriptions, those of the mid- to late 1st/7th century, it is a very strict, simple monotheism, which then developed over a period of time into something recognizably Islamic. Because the initial creed exhibited in these inscriptions lacks distinguishing features which would enable one to class it with a known religion, we call it *Indeterminate Monotheism*.

These popular inscriptions are private supplications, written by ordinary people or by scribes on their behalf, and intended to affect the writer's destiny, or to record some private event or emotion. Such texts reveal which aspects of the religion had meaning for the writer, and indicate its current state of development in the popular conception. Thus we may, for instance, discover something about the popular form of the religion in Hišām's time (A.H. 105–125/724–743) from groups of dated inscriptions in the Negev, and near Damascus, and one inscription near Ḥimṣ, even though we have no representative declaration of faith by the caliph himself, that would show us the official form of the religion in his days. We should remember, however, that private inscriptions could include only the stock phrases their owner or the scribe had learnt—for instance, in religious texts from which he learnt to read and write. The expressions used reflect the faith and choice of wording of the scribe; we cannot tell whether they also reflect the beliefs of the inscription's owner. Nor is it clear whether the scribes' language reflects official directives as to what constituted suitable religious phrases. Moreover, we can only tentatively tell what the writer (owner or scribe) actually understood by the phrases he inscribed. The meanings of words and formulae were topics of fierce dispute, and the members of two or more sects could use the same texts, each imbuing them with their own meaning, each sure that only they had the *ᶜilm*. But despite all these difficulties, the popular inscriptions reveal more faithfully than any other extant source the forms of belief current among their writers. Our main analysis of these inscriptions is given in Chapter 5; here we give only the brief outline necessary to sketch in this part of the religious background.

---

74. About four hundred of the Negev inscriptions have been published in Nevo, Cohen, and Heftman (1993) (usually referred to as *AAIN*).

On the basis of religious content the inscriptions may be divided into three classes, which we call Basic Texts, Mohammedan, and Muslim.[75] This is also a rough chronological division, in that the demonstrably Muslim inscriptions are definitely the latest and the Basic Texts the earliest to appear, though Basic Texts continued to be inscribed for a long time after their first appearance. The Basic Texts exhibit Indeterminate Monotheism. The Mohammedan class adds the Prophet Muḥammad to this basic creed, but lacks some other aspects of Muslim theology, which appear only in the latest class.

The Basic Texts. These occur throughout the Negev—and the Middle East in general—from the mid-1st century (40–60 A.H.) on, right down into the later Muslim periods. The first dated inscriptions are from ca. 40/660, from the Ḥijāz around Ṭā'if. Their most prominent feature, as already stated, is the lack of any indication of a specific creed: not Islam, Christianity, or Judaism. Neither Muḥammad nor the Tawḥīd are men-tioned; and they do not engage in the polemics which are the heart of the later, Muslim texts. The only deity is Allāh/Allāhummah (*'allhm*), also referred to as *rabb/rabbī*. Many words and phrases used in this class, though by no means all, appear also in Mohammedan inscriptions, but the literary and religious contexts in which they appear are different in the two classes.[76]

Some of the Basic Texts exhibit a distinct language and content: for instance, the very common formula *ḥayy-an wa-mayyit-an*,[77] the eulogizing of Allāh with epithets many of which, but not all, are among those later classified as Beautiful Names; the use of the phrase "Lord of Creation" as a concluding phrase, and the definition of God as "Lord of Moses and Jesus" (*rabb Mūsà wa-ᶜĪsà* or *rabb ᶜĪsà wa-Mūsà*), occasionally as a concluding phrase[78] but usually as an opening one.[79] While many Mohammedan and Muslim texts use *rabb Mūsà wa-ᶜĪsà* as a concluding phrase, its use in an inscription containing no indication of Mohammedan or Muslim belief is

---

75. For examples of representative inscriptions from each class, see the Appendix of Inscriptions.

76. For the analyses of the various classes of inscriptions, see Chapter 5 below.

77. E.g., nos. MA 406(7), MA 419(8), and MA451(8). For inscriptions referred to here and not included in the Appendix, see *AAIN*.

78. E.g., MA 4900(27).

79. MA 4204A(14), MA 4340(22), MA 4210(16), MA 4269(19), MA 4508(25), and MA 4516(26).

remarkable, especially when it occurs in an opening phrase, for this position usually indicates the writer's definition of God.[80] In these circumstances, this formula implies Judeo-Christian beliefs; but we cannot separate the *rabb Mūsà wa-ᶜĪsà* group too sharply from the other Basic Texts, for their theology, this phrase excepted, is very similar to that of the other inscriptions,[81] and most named owners of inscriptions in this group left others which exhibit simple Indeterminate Monotheism. One of the Basic Text inscriptions[82] is dated 85 A.H. (704 C.E.); some of the others, from literary considerations, we would place somewhat earlier, but the language of the group in general is more developed than that of the inscriptions from the Ṭāʾif area of the 40s–60s A.H., and it is very unlikely that they date from before ᶜAbd al-Malik's reign. We would date them, from linguistic considerations plus the one date we have, 85 A.H., to the late 60s to 80s A.H. (late 680s to first decade of the 8th century C.E.). Many of them were inscribed by or on behalf of a small group of people whose names recur.

As said, many of the expressions and formulae in the Basic Texts continued in use for a long time and may be found also in inscriptions whose religious content is clearly Mohammedan or Muslim. Other formulae, however, seem to have died out or developed over time into other forms. An example is the *kull ḏanb* ("all his trangressions") complex, discussed in Chapter 5 below.

The monotheistic creed expressed in the Basic Texts was very unsophisticated and limited in both intellectual content and development of detail. What made the greatest impression on its believers was the doctrine that all men are inevitably sinners, dependent on God's grace for protection from punishment for their sins. There is no reference to an Arab Prophet, whether Muḥammad or anyone else; God is defined by reference to the prophets Moses/Jesus/Aaron/Abraham only. There is no indication of a knowledge of, or concern about, the hereafter in the Muslim sense. *Baᶜṯ* and *nār* are not mentioned, and in the few references to *al-jannah* the context makes it doubtful if the term means paradise. Essentially the only religious notions that emerge from these inscriptions concern *human*

---

80. Cf. Chapter 5 below, the section titled, "Muḥammad the Prophet and the Definition of God."

81. See discussion in Chapter 5 below.

82. MA 4265(19).

sin, punishable in ways unexplained but greatly feared; and divine pardon. Both were relevant only during this life: death was not considered a continuation.[83]

Despite the pervading, desperate preoccupation with sin, it is clear that the Basic Texts cannot be classified as any variety of Christianity. In contrast to the Greek inscriptions—including those made under early Arab rule, such as that in the Ḥammat Gader baths, and bilingual Greek-Arabic papyri—these Arabic inscriptions are never accompanied by the sign of the cross. A few cases have been found outside the Negev where inscriptions were accompanied by crosses, but they are of later date.[84] And there is never any mention of the Trinity: no Father, no Son, and no Holy Ghost. Moreover, the definition of Allāh as "Lord of Moses and Jesus" denies Jesus any divinity and relegates him to the same level as God's other messengers. Nor, despite Old Testament elements, is there any trace of Rabbinic Judaism in these Arab Monotheistic texts. But the definition of God as "Lord of Moses and Jesus" indicates to us a definite Judeo-Christian influence.

The Mohammedan inscriptions. These are Marwānid: the earliest dated one is from A.H. 112/730–31 (Hišām's reign), and they continued until replaced by Muslim inscriptions. Although some expressions found in the earlier texts continued in use, the structure and conceptual universe of the Mohammedan inscriptions are very different from the earlier ones. The pervading atmosphere of fear of punishment for transgressions is replaced by optimism and the expectation of Allāh's favors. Here for the first time in *popular* (as distinct from royal) inscriptions, we find references to Muḥammad the Prophet, though he is clearly capable of sinning like anyone else, for the inscriptions request pardon for him. There is no sign of belief in the Muslim tenet of Muḥammad as *maʿaṣūm*—incapable of sinning. A cluster of other concepts, such as *ṣirāt mustaqīm*, 'the Right Way'; *hudà*, 'guidance'; and *jahd*, 'exertion' (on Allāh's behalf), also make their first appearance in popular texts at this time. The supplicants also request *al-jannah*, but again, the context makes it doubtful if this means paradise.

---

83. All these points are discussed in Chapter 5 below.

84. Grohmann (1962), no. 176 from Tunaiṯilah, 350 km south-southeast of Ṭāʾif, west of southern Xaybar.

The Muslim inscriptions. These fall into two distinct groups according to date: the early Muslim inscriptions, dating from the 160s–170s A.H., and the later Muslim inscriptions, from the end of the 3rd century A.H. Both sets of Muslim inscriptions differ from the Mohammedan ones in idiom and conceptual content: again, we find in them concepts not previously attested in popular inscriptions. These include the Muslim form of the paradise-hell-resurrection conceptual complex; Allāh as patron; and the idea that a believer should "bear witness" to Allāh as a way of announcing his faith. Words from the root *š.h.d.* do appear in one or possibly two Mohammedan inscriptions,[85] but it is in the Muslim groups that the concept of testifying one's faith becomes commonplace.

How far the popular inscriptions reflect the official religion is a different question; but the fact that common people felt free to make signed inscriptions, some placed beside desert paths where those who traveled that route could be expected to see them, shows that the state at least tolerated their beliefs and religious concepts.

THE RELATIONSHIP BETWEEN THE MONOTHEISTS AND THE PAGANS

As we saw above, the Negev pagans did not sacrifice animals to their gods, and ate little if any meat. This may have been simply because they were desert nomads, but it may also indicate the influence of a monotheistic sect. It might seem obvious that the monotheistic inscriptions represent a completely different phenomenon from the pagan cult centers, and it is true that in most cases the two are found at different sites. How much interaction was there between the two populations, monotheist and pagan, which existed, in the Negev at least, in the same general area at the same time? In several instances, only a few hundred meters or less separate collections of monotheistic rock inscriptions from an apparently contemporary pagan site. Perhaps this still does not require us to postulate interaction between the pagans who used the cult center, and the monotheists who engraved the rock inscriptions. But at two places found so far (and again, further work could find more) the monotheistic rock inscriptions occupy the same site as a

---

85. HS 3155, dated 117 (735 C.E.), and MM 107, which may be Mohammedan or Muslim.

contemporaneous pagan cult center—i.e., the pagans were using their cult center or sanctuary during the same time period as the monotheists were engraving invocations to their own god at the same place. One of these sites is Sede Boqer; the other is a much smaller one (coded SK) a few kilometers away. When the pagans first started to build at Sede Boqer, the site apparently was already frequented by monotheists, and there must have been some relationship between the two groups.

That relationship was apparently complex. The site of Sede Boqer was perhaps a *ḥaram* venerated by both religions. The monotheists engraved there literally hundreds of religious invocations, each carefully and painstakingly incised into the rock with considerable effort and in many cases also care for aesthetic form; and the pagans chose to build in the same place their largest sanctuary. We can establish that the monotheists were the first to arrive at the site. The earliest dated monotheistic inscription is from A.H. 85/704. Other inscriptions from this site, though undated, appear from text analysis to be somewhat earlier, but the total number of Basic Text inscriptions found at Sede Boqer, and the limited number of people who left them, does not suggest a time span much longer than ten or fifteen years. This leads to the conclusion that the monotheists probably first started inscribing at the Sede Boqer site ca. 70/689 or a little later.[86] The pagan remains start approximately in Hišām's day (ca. 105/724) or a little earlier, as discussed above, so that the pagans founded their cult center perhaps twenty to forty years after the monotheists had adopted the site.[87]

The archaeological evidence also shows that the pagan buildings and the monotheistic rock inscriptions at Sede Boqer are not part of the same cult phenomenon. Inscribed building stones were in secondary use, i.e., rocks already bearing inscriptions had been quarried for use as

---

86. Tentative as this timetable may be, it fits in well with the epigraphic evidence and with historical considerations. The Nessana Greek-Arabic papyri show that during the 50s of the 1st century A.H. the more fertile and inhabited northwestern area of the Negev (the Elusa-Nessana-Ruḥaybah triangle) was incorporated into the Sufyānī taxation system as part of the administrative region of Gaza. But Sufyānī interest in the area was restricted to imposing taxes (of wheat and oil), and was short-lived. Evidence for it ends in the year A.H. 57/Febuary 677, and a dozen years passed before renewed Arab (now Marwānid) interest is recorded in 69–70/689.

87. These dates may be compared with the following facts: Muᶜāwiyah died in A.H. 60/680; ᶜAbd al-Malik became caliph in 65/685, but his reign was at first insecure. The date of its consolidation may be taken as 75/694, when Ḥajjāj took command in Iraq.

building materials. Few of the monotheistic inscriptions were very close to the pagan buildings, and those were probably made before the buildings were constructed.

In contrast to the pattern described above, monotheistic inscriptions seem to have been deliberately set inside the enclosure built on the summit of the ridge. But this enclosure is quite early in the archaeological sequence, and its relationship to the two cults is uncertain. Its northern corner was built upon an inscription, which may argue in favor of its construction by the pagans. On the other hand, the fact that many—perhaps most—of the numerous inscriptions on the rock floor of the enclosure were deliberately set inside it is an argument for its construction by the monotheists. Building upon the inscriptions of coreligionists was clearly not unthinkable, for the mosque eventually built on the summit of the ridge also covered clusters of inscriptions, some of them obviously Muslim. And the enclosure's position on the top of the ridge was a surprising choice, if it were a pagan building. One would, in general, expect a building in that topographical location to be monotheistic, not pagan. Not only at Sede Boqer, but at other sites too, the pagans characteristically avoided the summit: they built on the slopes of the hill, sometimes extending right into the wadi, whereas the monotheists wrote everywhere, including the sides and summit of the ridge. At Sede Boqer there are a few marks of pagan activity on the summit of the ridge too: the cupmarks near the enclosure are probably pagan in origin, and a pagan unit was attached to the enclosure's east wall.[88] But the enclosure itself was annexed to the mosque. Topography, then, argues for a continuum of outlook between the builders of the enclosure at Sede Boqer, and the later builders of the mosque, regarding the proper position of religious buildings—an outlook which was not characteristic of the pagans. This suggests that the monotheists built the enclosure, though the pagans seem to have later juxtaposed to it a unit of their own.

One thing is clear: the pagan complex could not have been built without the knowledge, and at least indifference, if not approval, of the central authorities; nor could the monotheists, who were clearly non-Muslim, have developed their religion in the desert had the central government opposed their presence there. But this does not tell us what the monotheists were. A retreat community? Religiopolitical exiles? And similarly we do not know

---

88. Areas D2 and D4.

why the pagans built their largest cultural complex at Sede Boqer, already frequented by monotheists. Was it with the active encouragement of the government, which hoped by these means to assist their conversion? Or was it purely a question of chance, each side having its own reasons for regarding the site as holy, and avoiding as far as possible the members of the other camp? Or does the explanation lie elsewhere, in the many Negev sites as yet unexcavated?

Whatever the pagans' attitude to the monotheists, the latter were clearly uncompromising in their rejection of paganism. Nowhere in the monotheistic inscriptions, from the earliest on, is there any pagan influence. In most cases where a population converts, remnants of earlier values and linguistic usage, and names, at least, from the preconversion period, linger on for a while. Thus, as we have seen, the Christian (Greek) texts from the Negev record pagan names such as ᶜAbd al-Ga or ᵓAmat Ga among the believers; but unless the Beautiful Names were originally epithets of idols, not even a single pagan (i.e., theophoric) personal name among the monotheistic community has been recorded in Arabic monotheistic texts from the Basic Texts onwards. One possible explanation is that the Indeterminate Monotheists of the Negev were not converts from among the indigenous pagans, but a different group of people, who were already monotheists when they penetrated into (or retreated to, or possibly were exiled to) the desert. They came from elsewhere; and we have argued above that the Arabs probably first came into contact with this form of monotheism in Mesopotamia, or perhaps, less probably, in al-Šām, after the Takeover.

In any event, towards the end of occupation of the Sede Boqer site the inscriptions assume a Muslim character. The mosque, as said, was built on top of several such, which together form a group. One inscription in this group is dated 160 A.H. This means that the mosque was built when, or at most a very few years after, the pagan buildings were buried—an event already dated on different grounds to 160–170. Some of the other early Muslim inscriptions in the Negev are also dated, the dates being 164 and 170.[89] We thus have two independent dating methods, both of which indicate that the pagan site was closed down a few decades after

89. 164 A.H.: inscription YT 9000 (not published in *AAIN*), set beside a path and visible from it. 170 A.H.: inscription ST 640(34), set in a ruined pagan shrine facing the path and visible to those passing along the path beside the building.

the ᶜAbbāsids came to power, and a few years after Islam began to appear in the Negev.[90]

The rock inscriptions briefly surveyed above (and analyzed in Chapter 5 below) show the popular form of the Arab religion at various stages of development. For the official form, there is evidence from milestones, coins, protocols, and royal inscriptions.[91] The royal inscriptions are public declarations by the ruler concerning what constitutes the official faith, inscribed in a prominent place. It is much to be regretted that there are so few royal inscriptions from the 1st century A.H.; for they provide us with a studied, carefully worded formulation of officially accepted religious belief, which had received the caliph's considered approval. They represent the religious premises of the political center—the state religion,[92] and are therefore of relatively greater value for a study of religion than the texts of protocols and coins, which are much shorter and more limited to set formulae. But we have very few: Muᶜāwiyah's dam inscription from Ṭāʾif, dated 58/678; one from a bridge at Fusṭāṭ in Egypt built by ᶜAbd al-Malik's brother, ᶜAbd al-Azīz, dated 69/688; the inscription in the Dome of the Rock, dated 72 A.H.; the "ᶜAqabah inscription" on a mountain road straightened by ᶜAbd al-Malik, dated 73 or 83 A.H.; that in the Umayyad mosque of Damascus, and the ᶜAbbāsid Prophet Mosque at Madīnah. The earliest of these, the Ṭāʾif and Fusṭāṭ inscriptions, demonstrate Indeterminate Monotheism; the ᶜAqabah, Dome of the Rock, and Damascus mosque

---

90. It would appear that the introduction of ᶜAbbāsid Islam into the Central Negev was not entirely problem-free, for soon after the mosque was built at Sede Boqer an attempt was made to destroy it by tearing stones from the walls. Little damage was caused, but the animosity felt, and the physical absence of the mosque-builders (Muslims) from the site after the mosque was constructed, is clearly attested. In this connection, it is of interest that following the decade of considerable Muslim activity, 160–170 A.H., we have no further Muslim inscriptions from the Negev until the end of the 3rd century A.H.—300/912. They then reappear in a different region: the northwestern central Negev (Nessana area).

91. There are also early Arabic and bilingual Greek-Arabic papyri, but they are of little use as evidence for the official religion, since they are chancery documents and their religious content, not surprisingly, is slight. The earliest is PERF 558 from Egypt, dated 22/643, reproduced in Grohmann (1952), pp. 113–14.

92. For this reason, too—the importance attached to the religious content of the text—the Marwānid rulers were careful to put their Mohammedan formulae on their papyrus protocols and coins in both Arabic and an imperial lingua franca—Greek or Latin, depending on the area.

inscriptions are Mohammedan. (All are discussed in Chapter 4 below). In general, the form of religion evidenced in the Negev popular inscriptions lags behind religious development in the official, royal ones. One possible explanation for this is that it took time for the beliefs adopted as the state religion and propagated by the caliph to be accepted by the general population, or to percolate into this remote desert area. This in turn suggests that the government was content to let it percolate at its own rate, rather than taking steps to ensure the general population's adherence to the new official religion. This whole question of religious development will be examined more fully in the following chapters.

SUMMARY

There existed, then, in the areas occupied by the Arabs, several monotheistic creeds besides Rabbinic Judaism and the various Christian churches. Samaritanism existed not only in al-Šām but also, the evidence suggests, in Iraq. Judeo-Christian sects may still have existed in al-Šām, and almost certainly existed in Iraq (Mesopotamia). And the form of belief we have called Abrahamism seems to have been especially prevalent in the Negev—though perhaps not there alone—and to have appealed particularly to the Arabs. But until the discovery of the Negev inscriptions and pagan sites, we had no contemporary evidence of *how* the Arab religion arose, nor any archaeological remains of the pagan culture which the Arab sources describe. For although Judaic and Christian notions are everywhere in the Muslim sources, nonetheless "what they do not, and cannot, provide is an account of the 'Islamic' community during the 150 years or so between the first Arab conquests and the appearance, with the sīrah-maghāzī narratives, of the earliest Islamic literature."[93] After all, the extant Arabic literary sources give us the Traditional Account, which crystallized later. Now, however, the findings of the Negev survey and the excavations at Sede Boqer, combined with other evidence such as that of the Arab coins and protocols, enable us to reconstruct some of the missing links in the development of the Arab religion from a simple, basic form of Judeo-Christian monotheism to full-fledged Islam. The following chapters examine this development.

---

93. Wansbrough (1978), p. 119.

2

Religious Events: The Evidence of Contemporary Texts

This chapter examines references to the Arabs' religion in works dating from the first century of Arab rule. Our examination leads us to the conclusion that there were, at least from ca. 20/640 on, two different types of belief current among the newcomers. The mass of the Arabs seem to have been pagan, and continued to be so for a long time. The élite who came to power, however, adopted a monotheistic form of belief.[1] This was not Islam, but the very basic, undifferentiated faith which we call Indeterminate Monotheism. Both these religions—paganism and Indeterminate Monotheism—were discerned by the inhabitants of the areas the Arabs occupied, and contemporary non-Arab sources refer now to paganism, now to monotheism, depending on the stratum of the population about whom they write. Texts referring to members of the Arab élite provide evidence that their religion was monotheistic, though not Islam. Texts dealing with the general population of recently arrived Arabs refer to them as pagan. This chapter examines these two types of references in two sections, one on the references to paganism and one on the references to

1. We include here not only Muʿāwiyah, his governors, and others who achieved positions of power and influence under him, but also his opponents who claimed that power for themselves.

monotheism. The one religion the texts do not describe is Islam; and until the 70s/690s they do not mention Muḥammad.

REFERENCES TO AN ARAB PROPHET IN EARLY 7TH-CENTURY TEXTS

There is, it will be objected, one early text which refers to an unnamed Arab prophet. It is an anti-Jewish tract, the *Doctrina Jacobi nuper baptizati*, set in the year 634 C.E. and probably written within a few years of that date. The relevant passage purports to be a letter from a Palestinian Jew named Abraham:

> A false prophet has appeared among the Saracens.... They say that the prophet has appeared coming with the Saracens, and is proclaiming the advent of the anointed one who is to come. I, Abraham, ... referred the matter to an old man very well-versed in the Scriptures. I asked him: "What is your view, master and teacher, of the prophet who has appeared among the Saracens?" He replied, groaning mightily: "He is an imposter. Do the prophets come with sword and chariot?"... So I, Abraham, made enquiries, and was told by those who had met him: "There is no truth to be found in the so-called prophet, only bloodshed; for he says he has the keys of paradise, which is incredible."[2]

This has generally been accepted as a reference to Muḥammad—thus Kaegi (1969) and Crone and Cook.[3] Indeed the latter argued that the information in the *Doctrina Jacobi* concerning the "false prophet" preserves an older, more historical set of facts about Muḥammad, which later Islam suppressed because of its Judeo-Messianism: that he was alive at the time of the invasion, personally led it, proclaimed himself to be the heralder of the (Jewish) Messiah, and claimed to hold the keys of Paradise.

The *Doctrina Jacobi* does clearly refer to a Saracen prophet who accompanied a group of Arabs and claimed to herald the Messiah and to hold the keys of Paradise. Whether he was a historical figure—i.e., whether someone who called himself a prophet and claimed to hold the keys

---

2. *Doctrina Jacobi*, q.b. Crone and Cook (1977), pp. 3–4. For a longer quotation and a slightly different translation see also Hoyland (1977), p. 57.

3. Crone and Cook (1977), pp. 3–6.

of paradise really accompanied a group of Arabs—cannot be decided on the basis of the evidence we have. The question is, why should one identify the reference in the *Doctrina Jacobi* with Muḥammad? If he existed, he clearly fitted into the general Judaic and Christian monotheistic background, as shown by the *motifs* of 'the anointed one' and 'the keys of Paradise' connected with him. Moreover, it is more likely that his message was proclaimed in Aramaic than in Arabic, for if his proclamations worried people, they must have been in a language widely understood by both the Jews and the Christians in the area. Little attention would have been paid in this area to prophesies in Arabic. If so, the group he was associated with had arisen locally. Thirdly, the fact—if fact it was—that a group of the Arabs were accompanied by a monotheistic—Judaic or Christian—prophet, tells us little about that group's religion. It could have been any form of monotheism; and indeed it accords much more with Jewish, Judeo-Christian, or even Christian belief than it does with Islam. On all these counts, the *Doctrina* provides no support for the identification of this prophet with Muḥammad. In fact if one thing is clear, it is that the account in the *Doctrina Jacobi* does not describe the Muḥammad that we know. The Arab Prophet of the Traditional Account does not "proclaim the advent of the anointed who is to come"—rather, if anything, he proclaims that the *hour* is nigh.[4] The Arab Prophet, even in the earliest literature extant, does not have the keys of Paradise. And Muḥammad was not alive, in the Islamic version of history, at the time of the conquest. Crone and Cook acknowledge that "this testimony is of course irreconcilable with the Islamic account of the Prophet's career"[5]—and conclude from this fact that we have here older material—"a stratum of belief older than the Islamic tradition itself"[6]—which "proves" that the true, historical Muḥammad led the invading Arabs, proclaimed the advent of the Messiah, and claimed to hold the keys of paradise. However, the only reason for regarding this material as the original, true version of Islamic history is the a priori identification of the prophet here mentioned as Muḥammad.[7]

---

4. Kister (1962).

5. Crone and Cook (1977), p. 4.

6. Ibid.

7. The corroborating evidence adduced by Crone and Cook does not help. The Byzantine oath of abjuration of Islam (ibid., note 6 to p. 3) is apparently a 9th-century compilation, and the "group of traditions, in which keys of paradise are sublimated into harmless metaphor" is undated.

Yet if this material proves anything, it is that the prophet of the *Doctrina Jacobi* cannot be Muḥammad. He could more easily be almost anybody else: prophethood was, to use Wansbrough's terms,[8] a monotheistic constant: a basic belief, concrete examples of which arose in the area in every monotheistic religion, the specific manifestation of course differing from religion to religion.[9] In those troubled years there can have been no shortage of such prophets, appealing to the various Christian and Jewish sects.

An example of such a reference, which Crone and Cook adduce as contemporary evidence, occurs in the *Secrets of Rabbi Simon ben Yoḥay*. This apocalyptic work has been shown by Graetz to be mainly mid-8th century C.E., written during the conflict that ended the Umayyad caliphate—the only exception is a passage added later.[10] It includes a messianic interpretation of the Arab conquest, including a passing reference to an Ishmaelite prophet:

> When he saw the kingdom of Ishmael that was coming, he began to say: "Was it not enough, what the wicked kingdom of Edom [i.e., Rome/Byzantium] has done to us, but [we deserve] the kingdom of Ishmael too?" [Meṭaṭron the angel replied:] "Do not fear, son of Man, for the Almighty only brings the kingdom of Ishmael in order to deliver you from this wicked one [Edom, i.e., Byzantium]. He raises up over them [the Ishmaelites] a prophet according to His will and He will conquer the land for them and they will come and restore it to greatness, and there will be great terror between them and the sons of Esau" [i.e., the Byzantines]. Rabbi Simon answered him and said: "How [is it known] that they are our salvation?" He [Meṭaṭron] said to him: "Did not the prophet Isaiah say that he saw a chariot with a pair of horsemen etc.?[11] Why did he put the chariot of asses before the chariot of camels, when he should rather have said 'a chariot of camels and a chariot of asses'—because when he, the rider on the camel, goes forth, the kingdom will arise through the rider on an ass? [No, rather because] the chariot of asses, since he [the Messiah] rides upon an ass, shows that they [the Ishmaelites, represented by the

8. Wansbrough (1987), p. 11.
9. Even the traditional Muslim account has its prophets of the *riddah* campaigns.
10. Lewis, B. (1950), p. 309.
11. Isaiah xxi.7: regarding possible translations see Hoyland (1997), p. 309 n. 159.

chariot of camels] are a salvation for Israel, like the salvation of the rider on an ass."[12]

Crone and Cook argue that the *Secrets* probably derives from "an earlier apocalypse written soon after the events to which it refers" because "the messiah belongs at the end of an apocalypse and not in the middle." We find this simply unconvincing. They refer for support to the discussion of the *Secrets* in Lewis's "An Apocalyptic Vision of Islamic History"[13]—but in fact Lewis does not there suggest that the *Secrets* are based on an earlier apocalypse. Rather, he is concurring with the opinion that another, related but later work—the *Prayer of R. Simon ben Yoḥay*, datable to the time of the Crusades[14]—is based on an earlier one (i.e., on the *Secrets*):

> Kaufman has suggested that the whole of this passage [one just quoted from the Prayer] is based on a fragment of an earlier apocalypse, dating from the time of the conquests, the author of which saw in the rise and spread of Islam itself the preliminaries of redemption.... A comparison of the three versions[15] and of the variants of the *Secrets* tends to confirm this hypothesis, and to show that, while the text in the *Secrets* expresses a Messianic hope from these events, the others are subsequent and probably independent reflections of disillusionment.[16]

Clearly, for Lewis, the *Secrets* is the earliest apocalypse of those being compared. We have in fact no evidence for a version written "soon after the events to which it refers." Moreover, where Crone and Cook understand "the rider on a camel" to be "the prophet"[17] Hoyland and Lewis understand

12. Translation from Hoyland (1997), pp. 309–10. Crone and Cook (1977) used the translation in Lewis (1950), but it is incorrect in several details. We prefer also Hoyland's interpretation of the second half of this very difficult text, though the general meaning is the same in Lewis's translation: the association of (the Messiah's) ass with (the Ishmaelites') camel shows that the Ishmaelites are bringing salvation to Israel.

13. Lewis (1950), p. 323.

14. Variously assigned to the 10th to 13th centuries; cf. discussion in Lewis (1950).

15. The third version is that preserved in the *Midrash of the Ten Kings*, also ascribed to Rabbi Simon; it appears to be later than the Secrets although it may be based on a version of the *Secrets* no longer extant, which is different from the one we have. See Lewis (1950) for a translation; also Hoyland (1997), p. 308 + n. 156.

16. Lewis (1950), p. 323.

17. Crone and Cook (1977), p. 5 n. 14.

it as a more general reference to the Ishmaelites: the fact that they deliver Israel from the yoke of Edom is the salvation referred to.

We are left, then, with a mid–8th-century text that refers to an Arab prophet coming with the Ishmaelites. Such an occurrence in a text of this date should occasion no surprise, just as it proves nothing.[18] In fact, as Brock (1982) reminds us, only a few late chronicles provide any details of Muḥammad's early career—those written after the Traditional Account had already been formulated. Furthermore, the Christians who came into contact with the newcomers and lived side by side with them did not, apparently, learn from them anything of Islam for more than two generations. Byzantine literature (including Syrian Chalcedonian) displays no knowledge of Islamic teachings until the early 8th century.[19] Syriac authors recognize Islam as a new religion only late in the day; as Brock points out, "it was perhaps only with Dionysios of Tellmaḥre (d. 231/845) that we really get a full awareness of Islam as a new religion."[20] In fact not one early Syriac or Greek source describes the Arabs of the early 7th century as Muslims. Various reasons for this have been proposed; none fits the case as well as the simple proposition that the 7th-century Christians did not discern Islam because it was not there to discern.

EVIDENCE FOR PAGANISM AMONG THE ARABS

Sophronius, who lamented Arab control of the Jerusalem-Bethlehem road in his 634 C.E. Christmas sermon,[21] certainly did not consider the Arabs to be of any religious persuasion. As Kaegi points out, "He did not mention Muḥammad. In his view, the Arabs were simply terrible, godless invaders without any religious impulse."[22] Kaegi's explanation is that "many of the

18. Regarding Crone and Cook's claim that the references in the *Secrets* to the Kenite of Num. 24:21 "are intelligible only as the residue of an alternative messianic interpretation of the conquest" and that the different messianic interpretations indicate independent and presumably earlier apocalypses from which the *Secrets* are derived (pp. 35–37), see Hoyland's comment that this fails "to take into account the style of midrashic exposition whereby a Biblical quotation will be adduced, then various digressions indulged in before the quotation is again considered" (Hoyland [1997], p. 312 n. 164).

19. Meyendorff (1964), p. 115.

20. Brock (1982), p. 21.

21. Discussed in Part II Chapter 2 above as evidence for the political situation.

22. Kaegi (1969), p. 140. Note that Sophronius himself nowhere refers to these Arabs

invading tribesmen only recently had been converted from paganism to Islam and probably had only a slight or no understanding of Muḥammad's religious message."[23] The facts fit even better if we do not have to postulate that the tribesmen had been converted to Islam. If the Arabs of whom Sophronius complained were still pagan, and Muḥammad yet unknown, the fact that Sophronius mentioned neither their Prophet nor their religion ceases to require explanation.

The crucial point in our interpretation of Syriac references to the Arabs' religion is the meaning of the word *ḥanpê*, especially in 7th-century texts. The standard dictionary definition for this term is 'pagan' or 'godless,' and it has been so rendered in the texts to be brought as evidence. Thus it was used, for instance, to refer to Zoroastrians, to non-Christian sects, and to animists of various kinds. In the *pešiṭṭâ* it means 'pagans.' It was also a normal term for the invading Arabs. This potentially enlightening fact is inexplicable in terms of the Traditional Account, and writers striving to understand this use of *ḥanpê* explain it as a derogatory term for 'Muslim.'

Such a usage is not prima facie unlikely. After all, other words meaning 'pagan' were used of the Muslims in later times, especially in Europe: "In the Middle Ages a Muslim was called *paganus, paien* in the *Chanson de Roland, paynim* in Medieval English."[24] The term *ḥanpê* was also used of Muslims (and Manicheans) in Syriac Christian apologetic treatises in ʿAbbāsid times: Theodore bar-Koni (late 2nd/8th to early 3rd/9th century) is an example. Similarly, Nonnus of Nisibus (mid-2nd/9th century) referred to Muslims as "recent" or "present-day" *ḥanpê*.[25] Presumably the qualification was intended to distinguish them from the people formerly indicated by the word *ḥanpê*, i.e., pagans. Griffith considers that the Syriac writers used the term *ḥanpê*, which "in general may be said to mean 'pagan' or 'heathen'"[26] because they were aware that it was cognate with the Arabic term *ḥanīf*. This is probably true of the 9th-century texts he is considering, but cannot be true of the 7th-century ones. He suggests that *ḥanpê* "really" meant 'non-Christian' rather than specifically 'pagan,' and was therefore available as a

---

as *invaders*—here again, a modern scholar is unconsciously reading the Traditional Account back into the ancient text.

23. Ibid.

24. Pines (1990), n. 36.

25. A. van Roey, *Nonnus de Nisibe, traité apologetique*, Louvain, 1948, pp. 9, 12; q.b. Griffith (1980), p. 118.

26. Griffith (1980), p. 118.

term for Muslims, and that the Christian writers preferred using it because of the nuisance potential inherent in its linguistic relationship to *ḥanīf*.[27] This argument, however, is circular. It is postulated that *ḥanpê* could not have meant 'pagan' since it was applied to Muslims, but must have meant 'non-Christian.' The "fact" that it meant 'non-Christian' then explains why it was applied to Muslims. There is no explanation given as to why, if it meant 'non-Christian,' it was not used of other monotheists such as the Jews. Furthermore, the examples Griffith brings do not support his case: they are actually arguing that since *ḥanīf* is cognate to *ḥanpê*, it must mean 'idol-worshipper,' as in al-Kindī's apology (late 9th or 10th century):

> Abraham used to worship the idol, i.e., the one named al-ᶜUzzā in Ḥarrān, as a *ḥanīf*, as you agree, O you *ḥanīf*.... He abandoned *al-ḥanifiyyah*, which is the worship of idols, and became a monotheist.... Therefore we find *al-ḥanifiyyah* in God's revealed scriptures as a name for the worship of idols.[28]

The author of the al-Kindī letter is well aware of the tenets of Muslim belief, and with the above argument is merely goading his opponents.

Even later on, in the 10th to 11th centuries, there are a few cases where Muslims continue to be referred to as *ḥanpê*. An outstanding example is the account in the Chronicle of Elias, Metropolitan of Nisibis of how a certain Ignatius "became a pagan in the house of the Saracen Caliph and was called Abū Muslim and took many wives."[29] This chronicle dates from 1019, nearly three hundred years after the Takeover. It presents a thoroughly "traditional" account based on the Arab sources; and it reflects the changes that had taken place in the religious character of the area. It would not be surprising if by the 11th century the semantic field of *ḥanpê* had drastically changed; bringing it into line with the near-contemporary use of *paynim, paien*, etc. in medieval Europe.

The simplest explanation for the situation in the Syriac Christian texts from the ᶜAbbāsid period is that their writers used the term *ḥanpê* for the Arabs because they always had—ever since the 7th century. They were perfectly aware that the Arabs were not pagan, and had a good understanding, as Griffith demonstrates, of Muslim belief. They were likewise

---

27. Ibid., p. 120.

28. Q.b. Griffith (1980), p. 120; for the date of the al-Kindī / al-Hašimī letters see ibid., pp. 106–107.

29. Brooks and Chabot (1909–10), p. 111 of Latin transl. = p. 227 of Syriac.

perfectly aware that *ḥanpê* meant 'pagan' or 'idol-worshipper.' The more conciliatory, such as Nonnus of Nisibus, tried to smooth out the dissonance by qualifying the term *ḥanpê* ("present-day" as distinct from the old type). The more aggressive took pleasure in goading their religious opponents: he who calls himself a *ḥanīf*, which is the same as a *ḥanpê*, they gleefully say, acknowledges that he is an idol-worshipper. But none of this explains why the Arabs were originally called *ḥanpê* in the 7th century, a period when *ḥanpê* normally meant 'pagans.'[30] The only reason for reinterpreting it when it refers to the Arabs is the existence of the Traditional Account. So when Jacob of Edessa considers the treatment of someone who *haggar w-ʾaḥnap*—converted to the Arabs' religion and became a pagan[31]—our conclusion is that the two were perceived to be the same. And if *ḥanpê* was used as the normal term for the invading Arabs, the simplest explanation is that they were perceived to be pagans. If we choose to explain the term away as meaning 'Muslim,' we still have to explain why the writers of this period never used the term 'Muslim,' not even in a derogatory sense or as an alternative for *ḥanpê* or together with it; and why they did not see any of the components of Islam, nor learn anything of Muslim teachings, until the early 8th century.

The Monotheletic author of the *Life of* (the Dyothelete) *Maximus the Confessor*—of whom he naturally sternly disapproves—relates that after the Arabs had taken control of Syria, Maximus was able to come out of hiding and preach openly there, "because heresy is accustomed to join forces with paganism."[32] This expression differentiates between the two as clearly as it links them: they may find it expedient to join forces, but whereas Maximus is a heretic, the Arabs are pagans. Nor does "paganism" here mean 'anything non-Christian,' as Brock, like Griffith later, is forced to suggest. It had a specific meaning. The author is not calling the Arabs names, but mentioning, almost as an aside, a known fact: the Arabs were pagans, and therefore indifferent to Christian sectarian disputes.[33] They therefore allowed "heretic" churches to profess and preach their faiths openly. The "heretics" took advantage of the opportunity to join forces with

30. Pines, private communication, October 28, 1986.

31. *Responsa*, no. 21, I.238.

32. Brock (1973), p. 317, §18.

33. Or for that matter Christian-Jewish ones, as Bar Penkayê laments: "The believer was not known from a Jew."

the pagans in order to gain power and influence at the expense of the Chalcedonians.[34]

The Nestorian Catholicos Ishoᶜyahb III (d. A.H. 39–40/659) makes it quite clear that initially the Arabs (*ṭayyāyê mahggrayê*) did not discriminate between the various Christian sects, nor did they pressure Christians to convert:

> But those Arabs to whom God has granted the sovereignty of the earth at this time ... not only do they not attack the Christian religion, but truly they protect our faith, honor the priests and holy places of our Lord, and confer favors on the church and cloisters.[35]

Such claims by converts, he says in a furious letter to a bishop in Mazūn, i.e., Oman,[36] where the Christians had converted to an extent that he calls "wholesale apostasy," are just an excuse to hide the fact that the real reason for their conversion was financial. In the case of the Mazūnites, they had been required to pay half their belongings if they remained Christian; Ishoᶜyahb presents this as a small price to pay, and maintains that he cannot understand how it could have induced them to convert, since he notes that no other pressure to do so was put upon them:[37]

> Why then should your Mazūnites forsake their faith on account of them? Especially since the Arabs, as the Mazūnites themselves acknowledge, did not compel them to forsake their religion, but ordered them to give up only half of their possessions to preserve their faith.[38]

Ishoᶜyahb does not characterize the Arab religion; but he refers in the letter to "the pagans" as opposed to "the Christians." The reasons for the

---

34. This of course is the Chalcedonian viewpoint. We also find Nestorians making this charge against Monophysites, as will be discussed below.

35. Duval (1905), p. 251, our translation from Duval's Latin.

36. Brock and many other scholars accept Braun's long-standing suggestion that the Syriac *Marunayê* was a substitution for *Mazunayê*—the people of Mazūn, i.e., Oman. Nau (1904) suggested that the original reading, which would mean 'Marunites,' could refer to the people of Marūn, a town in the region of Mahrah, east of Ḥaḍramawt and south of the peninsula of Qaṭar.

37. Duval (1905), pp. 248–51.

38. Ibid., p. 251, our translation from Duval's Latin. This letter is also translated in Hoyland (1997), pp. 180–81.

Arabs' desire to convert to paganism the Christians of the southern areas, as opposed to their lack of such religious zeal, according to Isho^cyahb, in the main Nestorian areas, are discussed later in this section.

How long the Arabs' indifference lasted, we are not sure. Soon after Maximus began to preach the Dyophysite doctrine in Syria, he was forced to flee to Africa, where we find him congregating with others in a like situation. The year was ca. 20/641. From then on, they fled before the oncoming Arabs, first to Sicily and the other Mediterranean islands, and finally to Rome, which became a center for non-Chalcedonian refugees, including Nestorians, from the areas under Arab control. This phenomenon indicates that some sects were now less welcome to the Arab rulers than others, which in itself suggests that a change may have been occurring in the attitude of the ruling élite towards the different Christian sects. However, the Nestorian patriarch Isho^{c}yahb III remained on excellent terms with the authorities,[39] and there is no sign of any anti-Christian feeling per se. We do not know the reasons for the change of Arab policy regarding the non-Chalcedonian sects, if such there was; but it was assuredly caused by political rather than purely religious considerations.

Thirty or forty years later Athanasius II, Syrian Orthodox patriarch during the years 64–67/684–86, in a letter to the priests under his jurisdiction addressed the question of how to deal with the increasing number of Christians who participated in the sacrificial rites of the *ḥanpê*,[40] and, especially, with the Christian women who intermarried with them:

> Christians ... take part unrestrainedly with the pagans in their festivals ... and some unfortunate women unite themselves with the pagans.... [I]n short they all eat, making no distinction, any of the pagans' [sacrificial] victims, forgetting thus ... the orders and exhortations of the Apostles ... to shun fornication, the [flesh of] strangled [animals], blood, and food from pagan sacrifices.
>
> ... [E]xhort them, reprimand them, warn them, and especially the women united with such men, to keep themselves from food [derived] from their

39. Brock (1982), p. 16; Hoyland (1997), p. 182.

40. The term used throughout the letter is *ḥanpê*. The copyist of the manuscript gave this letter the heading: "that a Christian should not eat of the sacrifices of the *mhaggrāyê*," and it is possible, as Nau suggested, that this note was added by Jacob of Edessa: see Hoyland (1997), pp. 147–48 + n. 109.

sacrifices, from strangled [meat], and from their forbidden congregations. But they should strive with all their might to baptise the children born of their union with them. If you find women who conduct themselves in this fittingly Christian manner, you should not cut them off from participating in the holy mysteries [i.e., Communion], only because they are married to pagans openly and of their own accord.[41]

Having disposed of this subject, Athanasius then turns to another which has been troubling him:

[N]one of the Orthodox priests should knowingly and willingly give holy baptism or Communion to Nestorians, Julians, or any other heretics.[42]

The text is quite explicit. The local Arab population is pagan, and they are holding pagan rites.[43] Athanasius is faced with a gradual drift to paganism of the Christian population, resulting partly from intermarriage, especially between Arab pagan men and Christian women. He urges his clergy to combat it quietly but firmly, and to do their best to keep as many people Christian as possible. The Church has, also, to combat heresies of various kinds, and her policy towards heretics is quite different: there must be no compromise.

Eight or ten years earlier, the Nestorian Synod called in 56/676 to rectify the lax state of Christian affairs in "the islands of the south" had found it necessary to address precisely the same problem of a drift to paganism, and had been considerably more uncompromising in attitude:

Women who once believed in Christ and wish to live a Christian life must keep themselves with all their might from a union with the pagans.... Therefore, Christian women must absolutely avoid living with pagans; and the woman who dares to do so must be removed from the Church.[44]

Another problem was the acceptance by the men of the Christian community of the pagan custom of taking several wives:

41. Nau (1909), pp. 128–30.

42. Ibid.

43. Even if we agree with Hoyland (1997), p. 149 that "sacrifice" could equally well be translated "ritually slaughtered meat," there is no way to reconcile Muslim ritual slaughter with the repeated reference to "strangling."

44. Chabot (1902), *Synodicon Orientale*, Syriac text p. 224, French translation p. 488.

> Those who are listed among the ranks of the faithful must distance themselves from the pagan custom of taking two wives ... seeing that they were once sanctified by Christ's baptism and separated from the worship of impurity which takes place among peoples [who are] strangers to the fear of God.... If, then, there are men who in their folly scorn this, and in addition to their legitimate wife, dare to take others, from far or near, free or slaves, under the name of concubines or otherwise, and if, having been warned to change their impure practice, they do not obey, or they promise to correct [their behavior] and do not, they must be deprived of all Christian honor.[45]

Christians must also be prevented from adopting pagan funeral customs, such as the adornment of the corpse with rich clothing, and the use of loud lamentations in mourning:

> The Christian dead must be buried in a Christian manner, not after the manner of pagans. Now, it is a pagan custom to wrap the dead in rich and precious clothing, and to make ... loud lamentations regarding them, which is the sign of those with no faith [or: those who do not believe]. This is why we have decreed ... that Christians are not permitted to bury their dead in silk cloth or in precious clothing; but they must be buried, with the hope of believers, in simple clothes of no great price. Those lamentations made by hysterical women in the funeral houses must also be stopped.[46]

The reference to taking two wives could apply to both paganism and Islam; but to dress the corpse in rich and precious clothing is a practice as far removed from Islam as from Christianity, whereas the inclusion of this and other requirements for a comfortable life in the next world was an important component of pagan religions.[47] As for the pagan custom of loud wailing by women mourners (sometimes paid professionals) at funerals: Muḥammad, according to the Traditional Account, also tried to put an end to it. The practice continues to this day.

If we read these texts without forcing upon them the interpretations required by a priori acceptance of the traditional Muslim account, we must

---

45. Ibid., Canon 16.
46. Ibid., Canon 18, Syriac text p. 225, French translation p. 489.
47. Even Hoyland, who believes that *ḥanpê* in these examples must mean "non-Christian" in general and that the writers were referring to Muslims, concedes here that there must have been "pagan vestiges in East Arabia." (Hoyland [1997], p. 194).

conclude that at the time of Athanasius II and the Nestorian Synod, forty to fifty years after the Arabs took control, and during the end of Muᶜāwiyah's caliphate and the start of ᶜAbd al-Malik's, a considerable section of the Arab population was still pagan; and paganism was also increasingly attractive to the Christians. It is the contention of the present work that this in fact accurately describes the situation among the general population, though not among the élite, who for political reasons had accepted a form of monotheism.

When we compare the attitudes to apostasy and intermarriage of the Nestorian (East Syrian) patriarch Ishoᶜyahb, the Nestorian Synod of 676, and the Monophysite (West Syrian) patriarch Athanasius, an interesting pattern emerges. The West Syrian Church took a very much "softer" line on the question than did the East Syrian. Athanasius, the West Syrian patriarch, urges his priests to act with discretion and circumspection, in an attempt to retain within the church as many souls as possible—both the originally Christian women, and their offspring, the children of pagan fathers. As another instance of the same attitude, we may note also Jacob of Edessa's late 7th-/early 8th-century dispensation of the need to rebaptize Christians who became pagans or *mhaggrāyê* and then reverted to Christianity.[48] The East Syrian attitude is harder to explain. Ishoᶜyahb in a passion of rhetoric claims not to understand how the Christians of Mazūn could sell their souls for money, and a mere half their possessions at that. But he must have been aware that a fine of half one's total possessions was a far different matter from the normal poll tax, and in fact, despite his protestations to the contrary, constituted severe pressure to convert. This pressure was apparently applied only to the Christians of the south (Mazūn, as noted, was either Oman or the Gulf coast of the peninsula, east of Ḥaḍramawt): we may accept Ishoᶜyahb's account of the favorable treatment enjoyed by the Christians of his own area. It is interesting to speculate that the Christians of these southern areas were mainly Arabs with close kinship ties to the tribes of the peninsula and the interface areas, and that for this reason the policy of the Arab élite regarding them differed significantly from their policy towards the (mainly non-Arab) Christians of the north. In areas where the Christian population was not predominantly Arab, they were not interfered with; but in areas that were overwhelmingly Arab, they should be assimilated into the general

48. *Responsa* I, nos. 15, 21.

post-Takeover Arab population, which involved adopting their religion. The reason, however, was not missionary zeal on the part of the invading Arabs, but a political decision to encourage assimilation of all Arabs, old and new, into a uniform population.

Around the 30s/650s, Ishoᶜyahb III denounced the Christians who thus assimilated, though he did not lay down a Church policy regarding them. By 676 the Nestorians had such a policy: Christian women who married pagans would be thrown out of the church. Such a totally uncompromising attitude effectively cut off the Christians' escape route from apostasy by burning the bridge back to Christianity the moment they had crossed it. This is, in effect, a de facto acquiescence to Christian Arab assimilation into the religion of the Arab majority.[49] Interestingly, the Synod of 676 also stated that its decisions applied specifically to the Gulf area—the "islands of the sea," which must refer to the Persian Gulf, since Nestorian jurisdiction in Persia did not extend to any other sea.

The official Nestorian policy formulated by 676 C.E. thus made it very difficult for many Christians in the southern areas either to stay in the Church or to return once they had left. It is tempting to speculate that this was the result of some political bargaining behind the scenes, between the heads of the Nestorian Church and the new rulers: if the former would give up the Christian Arabs of the peripheral southern lands, and let them assimilate with the newcomers, the church would be rewarded by favorable treatment in the areas more central to her interests, and by influence where it counted. It is, in this connection, highly interesting that the Nestorian Church did indeed gradually rise in influence to such an extent that Nestorians were important advisers to the early ᶜAbbāsids at the court of Baghdad. No such idea can be traced in the Arabs' relations with the Monophysites of Syria and Palaestina; and this church, as we have seen, was considerably more concerned to do whatever it could, by means of

---

49. We surmise that the Church was especially concerned about the intermarriage of Christian women and pagan Arab men, and does not mention the marriage of Christian men to pagan Arab women, for two reasons. Firstly, social status was defined by the man's social position, so that Christian parents had good reason to try to marry their daughters into the ranks of the Arabs whereas Arab parents had little reason to marry their daughters to Christians, so that such marriages must have been rare. Secondly, in both the Christian and Arab societies the children of the marriage belonged to the father's community, so that marriage of women out of the Christian community meant that their children were also lost; if it occurred, as it apparently did, on a large scale, the Christian community was in danger of assimilation within a generation.

considerable concessions, to preserve its congregation. It is at least possible that this was because it had nothing to gain by acquiescing in the loss of any part of it.

EVIDENCE FOR ARAB MONOTHEISM IN THE 7TH AND EARLY 8TH CENTURIES

So far we have presented evidence for the thesis that the newcomers were pagan. Nonetheless, mixed with the accounts of paganism we find other references to the Arabs' religion, which indicate that while it was not anything we would call Muslim, it was not pagan either. We may start to trace this strand of the weave with the interesting and often referred-to story in the late (13th-century) chronicle of Bar Hebraeus. Here we find a tradition regarding Heraclius's views on the Arabs who had defeated him. Having questioned "all the bishops, and the chiefs of the priests, and the rest of the satraps" concerning the Arabs, and heard at length the reply of each, he summed up the discussion thus:

> They are remote from the darkness, inasmuch as they have rejected the worship of idols, and they worship One God. But they lack the perfectly clear light because of their remoteness from the light and because of their imperfect knowledge of our Christian Faith and Orthodox Confession.[50]

The Arabs are here characterized as a monotheistic people, who have abandoned paganism and whose faith is a very imperfect form of Christianity. The story, as Brock says, is probably apocryphal; but it is not necessarily as late as Brock thinks. He would place it later than the 7th century, since in that century there was little awareness on the part of the Christians that a new religion had been born.[51] We would place it around the mid-7th century for exactly the same reason—because the story in Bar Hebraeus contains nothing that would indicate the birth of a new religion, much less Islam. It is inconceivable that Islam could have been described in these terms. The description does, however, fit the simple belief in "One God" that we call Indeterminate Monotheism. If it were later than the mid-7th century, we would expect to find in it an awareness that the new Arab

50. Budge (1932), p. 90.
51. Brock (1982), p. 13.

rulers were supposed to have been the proponents of an entirely new religion incompatible with Christianity.[52] For instance, the first major non-Christian aspect of the Arabs' religion—Mohammedanism—would already have existed.

The Discussion between the Patriarch John and the Emir

An account of a meeting held on Sunday, May 9th between a Monophysite patriarch and an Arab governor referred to as "the emir" has survived in a letter in a manuscript dated 876 C.E.[53] Nau, who published and translated it,[54] considered that it took place somewhere in Syria, and identified the patriarch as John I, 635–48 C.E., and the emir as ᶜAmr bn al-ᶜĀṣ. The text itself does not name either of the protagonists; the name John is given in the explanatory heading of the letter, added by the editor of the manuscript; and its position in the manuscript shows that he regarded it as pertaining to events before 93/712.[55] The identification of the emir is derived from a separate, very short account of the meeting in Michael the Syrian, where the emir is called Amru bn Saᶜad. If we accept the name John, the only candidate, as Nau points out, is John I; if we accept the name Amru and the identification with ᶜAmr bn al-ᶜĀṣ, the most probable date is 18/639. The other possibility is 23/644, when ᶜAmr bn al-ᶜĀṣ was, according to the Traditional Account, in Egypt. Later scholars have argued that the Amru concerned was the governor of Ḥimṣ, and the date was indeed 644.[56] We

---

52. It is interesting that the translation given by Brock himself is: "They are deprived of the perfect light, in that they *still* fall short of complete illumination in the light of our Christian faith..." (Brock [1982], p. 13, emphasis added). This suggests that the Arabs were perceived as being at an intermediate state on the way to Christianity: they had at least forsaken paganism and adopted monotheism, but they still had some way to go.

53. The analysis of this text owes much to a discussion with Professor Shlomo Pines, Jerusalem, December 6, 1986.

54. Nau (1915).

55. Ibid., introduction.

56. For a discussion regarding the date, see Nau (1915), p. 227 n. 3. Lammens (1919) discusses the identity of the emir, and suggests that Michael the Syrian's ᶜAmru bn Saᶜad was in fact Saᶜīd bn ᶜAmīr, governor-elect of the Ḥimṣ district from 641 C.E. This, he argues, fits much better both the administrative rather than military nature of the issues involved, and what we know of the characters of the two candidates for the role. He therefore argues that the date should be 644. Crone and Cook give (from Ṭabarī) the name of this governor of Ḥimṣ as ᶜUmayr bn Saᶜad al-Anṣārī, thus supporting Lammens's conclusion, and would likewise fix the date as 644 C.E. (Crone and Cook [1977], p. 162 n. 11).

cannot, however, accept these identifications uncritically. The compiler or editor of the collection, who supplied the heading, was none too exact; thus he describes the letter as written by the patriarch when it actually purports to be written by someone in his retinue who was present at the meeting. The account in Michael the Syrian is, of course, late, and its content is very different. The letter tells of a formal meeting between the Arab governor and the leaders of the two main sects, Monophysite and Chalcedonian, each with a large retinue. The former had been empowered by the emir to speak on behalf of all the Christians (presumably as leader of the majority sect), and the Chalcedonians had therefore prearranged with him that, as general spokesman, he would present a common front and hide their differences. One main point of the writer's presentation is that the patriarch kept the bargain, thereby earning the esteem of all, Chalcedonian and Monophysite alike. Michael the Syrian, by contrast, tells of a probably private meeting between the emir and the patriarch (no one else is mentioned as being present), the main result of which was the commissioning by the former of an Arabic translation of the Gospel by the latter. The point, then, is to relate how the Gospel came to be translated into Arabic. This translation is not mentioned in the letter. It is therefore preferable not to accept our sources' identification of the protagonists a priori, nor to transfer an identification in one source to the other, but to rely on content analysis of the letter itself to determine the date, and from this, the names of the chief actors.

The letter's main points of interest to our discussion include

a) A Christological discussion: was Jesus God, or the Son of God, and how could the two identities coexist?

b) The fact that the Arabs accept the Pentateuch, and Abraham and Moses as prophets, but not the rest of the Old Testament or the other prophets.

c) The laws the Christians are to be governed by: do they have their own laws, or should they be judged by those of the Arabs?

Several aspects are worth noting here. Firstly, the emir is interested in finding out about Christian belief, not in proving Christianity to be the wrong faith. He is certainly not a Muslim. He shows no knowledge of, or adherence to, Islam, and mentions neither Muḥammad, Islam, nor the Qurʾān. Secondly, he requests, as evidence for the divinity of Christ, "the opinion and the faith of Abraham and of Moses"[57]—accepting, as stated,

57. Nau (1915), p. 259.

only the Pentateuch (not the New Testament) as Holy Writ, and Abraham and Moses (not Jesus) as prophets. This fact was already known to the Christians, for early in the meeting the patriarch remarks that "the Law [i.e., the Pentateuch] ... is accepted by us Christians and by you *Mahaggrê* and by the Jews, and the Samaritans."[58] The patriarch professes himself ready and able to bring evidence for the divinity of Christ from all the prophets and the sages and from all the Holy Books, but the emir is unwilling to accept testimony from any source but the Pentateuch, or any prophet but Moses: "And the illustrious emir did not accept the (words) of the prophets, but called for Moses to show him that Christ is God."[59] This is a position adopted by various non-Rabbinic Jewish sects. The emir's position regarding scripture is either Judeo-Christian or, as Crone and Cook have pointed out,[60] Samaritan.

The discussion regarding the laws of the Christians, which comes last in the meeting and after which it breaks up, is in our opinion the main reason for it. It is easy to misread this discussion as a dispute over the foundation of legal authority, in which the emir maintains that the laws of a community must be written in their holy books—if they are not, the community should be defined as lacking adequate legal provisions; and the patriarch maintains that a community can equally well be governed by laws based on its holy books and in their spirit (i.e., canonical decisions)—as in the case of the Christians. But in fact this is not the point. The emir wants to know whether the Christians have enough, and sufficiently detailed, laws to enable them to govern their community. If so, they may judge themselves; if not, they must be judged by the Arab law which is now the law of the land. He *assumes* that the Christians' laws will be found in their holy books:

> The illustrious emir said: "I demand of you to do one of three [*sic*] things: either to show me that your laws are written in the Gospel, and to conduct yourselves according to them, or to adhere to the Hagarene law" (Mahgrâ).[61]

The patriarch explains that the Christians' laws are not written in the Gospel, but yet do exist, and are based on it and in its spirit: the Christians

58. Ibid., p. 257.
59. Ibid., p. 260.
60. Crone and Cook (1977), pp. 14–15.
61. Nau (1915), p. 262.

do indeed have laws sufficiently detailed to enable them to govern themselves according to them. The meeting here comes to an end:

> And when our father had replied that we have laws, we Christians, which are just and right, which accord with the teaching and the precepts of the Gospel and the canons of the Apostles and the laws of the Church, the meeting of this first day was dissolved upon this (point), and we have not so far managed to appear before him again.[62]

We are thus not informed whether the emir accepts this position.[63]

What conclusions may we arrive at concerning the date of the meeting? The Christological discussion could be anywhere in the 7th century. The crucial point, to our mind, is the discussion regarding the laws of the Christians. The emir tells them to prove that they have laws sufficient for their needs, or else to accept his laws. This is the implementation of an administrative decision: that communities which have until now (presumably) governed themselves, and can prove themselves capable of doing so, should be allowed to continue to do so. Only communities with no law of their own (and, presumably, intercommunity disputes) should be judged by the Arabs. The Arab governor is the one empowered to decide which communities are included in which category; a community, needless to say, is defined in religious terms.

The time this fits is clearly the period when the Arabs were setting up an administrative procedure for al-Šām, i.e., deciding what parts of the old order to accept and what to change. They are here discussing legal procedures, with the aim of changing only what was absolutely necessary: current procedures which could be proved to be workable should be left alone. This attitude to legal procedure accords with their similar attitude to administrative procedure, i.e., their continuation of the Byzantine administration largely unchanged. We can, therefore, place the document, not in

62. Ibid.

63. Hoyland considers that the religious aspects of this text are "a later (probably early-mid-8th century) literary work composed from earlier disputes" which "cannot be depended upon for a picture of 7th century Islam" (private communication, June 11, 1992). In Hoyland (1997), pp. 464–65 he opts for the early 8th century. He does, however, agree that there was probably an actual meeting, most probably in either 639 or 644, and that the emir's main concern was the legal question: can the Christians be relied upon to govern themselves? The present authors are struck by the aspects of the religious dispute which do *not* reflect Islam, not even Islam as we think it was in the early 8th century.

the first few years of the Takeover, when the situation was till confused, but within a few years of the establishment of a central authority over al-Šām—within the first few years of Muᶜāwiyah's taking control with the official title of governor. We therefore conclude, like those who have discussed this text before us, but on entirely different grounds, that the date must have been 23/644, i.e., in the years immediately following Muᶜāwiyah's assumption of control, not 18/639, which was just before he did so. This means that the patriarch was indeed John I, and there is no reason not to accept the view put forward in Lammens (1919) and in Crone and Cook (1977) that the emir was the governor of the administrative district of Ḥimṣ. From this it follows that the name preserved in Michael the Syrian is reasonably accurate.

The date of 22–23/644 also accords well with the religious aspect of the colloquium. We postulate that Muᶜāwiyah, around the time of assuming the position of governor, adopted the form of monotheistic belief we call Indeterminate Monotheism, and that this became the official faith of the élite. The fact that the Arab emir was known to accept the Pentateuch and Moses, but no other Old Testament books or prophets, indicates that a non-Rabbinic Jewish sect (Judeo-Christian or Samaritan) influenced this monotheism. This accords very well with the traditions regarding Jewish influence on the origins of Islam (once the later harmonization with the Life of Muḥammad has been stripped away).

We conclude, then, that the meeting was probably historical, that it occurred when Muᶜāwiyah had assumed control in al-Šām, and that its main purpose was to establish whether the Christians formed a well-regulated community which could safely be left to govern itself, as long as the disputes to be judged were between Christians. This explains why the Monophysites and Chalcedonians united in a common front. The latter, of course, felt themselves to be in a position of weakness, since the right of speech in the name of the Christians had been granted to the rival sect. The former, however, also had a good reason for agreeing to hide their differences. Had the emir realized that the Christians did not all accept the same canonical decisions, i.e., that not only did the *faith* differ, but that there was *no one set of Christian laws accepted by all Christians,* there was a very real danger he might decide that the Christian community was not capable of governing itself; all the Christians, Monophysites and Chalcedonians alike, would then find themselves subject to the laws of the Arabs. We should note, too, that the emir is interested to treat all the Christians as one group; he does not want to distinguish between sects, though he is aware that they exist. This too accords with what we would expect of him, if his aim was efficient administrative practice.

In this document the Qurʾān is conspicuous by its absence. The emir refers to the "laws of the *mhaggrê*" without specifying that they are laid down by the Arabs' sacred scripture: if they are in a scripture, it is the Pentateuch, not the Qurʾān. This omission is not easily glossed over. It is inconceivable that a Muslim emir, disputing Christology with a Christian, should disregard the Qurʾānic view of Jesus and instead demand proof of Jesus' divinity from the Pentateuch. It is also strange that he should assume that a community's laws must be included in their gospel. Such an assumption reflects the conceptual background of Judaism, not early Islam, for the Qurʾān in fact contains very little law, and even after it was canonized it was not at first regarded as a repository of legal rulings; this was a later development.

> Muḥammedan law did not derive directly from the Koran but developed ... out of popular and administrative practice under the Umaiyads, and this practice often diverged from the intentions and even the explicit wording of the Koran.... [A]part from the most elementary rules, norms derived from the Koran were introduced into Muḥammedan law almost invariably at a secondary stage. This applies not only to those branches of law which are not covered in detail by the Koranic legislation—if we may use this term of the essentially ethical and only incidentally legal body of maxims contained in the Koran—but to family law, the law of inheritance, and even cult and ritual.[64]

The explanation we offer for both these points is that the emir disregarded the Qurʾān because it did not yet exist; and the emir's belief was not Islam, but a form of basic monotheism with Judeo-Christian affiliations.

Although we do not learn, in this document, whether the emir accepted the Christians' claim that they were capable of ruling themselves, the sequel may be found, some thirty years later, in the Canons of the Nestorian Synod of 56/676.[65] Canon 6 states that

> Legal proceedings and quarrels between Christians must be judged within

---

64. Schacht (1950), pp. 224–25.
65. Chabot (1902).

> the church; let them not go outside, *like those who have no law*; let them be judged in the presence of judges designated by the bishop.[66]

This clearly shows that the right of the Church to act as judge of the Christian community is not disputed. The problem addressed by the canon is that the Christians themselves do not always seek to be judged by their clergy, as is right and proper, but take their disputes outside, to the Arab judges. Such a canon could not have been promulgated, still less acted upon, without official approval. It indicates that the Church's right to judge disputes between Christians was officially accepted by the administration.

The Arab Monotheism as described in later 7th-century and 8th-century texts

Sebeos, writing probably in the 670s, records that Muᶜāwiyah sent a letter to Constantine in 651, which included the following text:

> If you wish to live in peace ... renounce your vain religion, in which you have been brought up since infancy. Renounce this Jesus and convert to the great God whom I serve, the God of our father Abraham.... If not, how will this Jesus whom you call Christ, who was not even able to save himself from the Jews, be able to save you from my hands?[67]

While this is undoubtedly only what Sebeos imagined would have been written in such a letter, it does indicate that at the time he wrote, the religion of the Arab ruler was seen as Abrahamism—a belief in the God of Abraham—not as anything more specific. It is hard to envisage a call to a Christian to convert to Islam that did not include the demand to acknowledge that God has no companion, and that Muḥammad is His messenger.

It is hard, too, to reconcile this account with that in chapter 30, where "Muḥammad, a merchant" is mentioned as the prophet of the Arabs who "taught them to know the God of Abraham." The Jews, says Sebeos, had already told the Arabs of their descent from Abraham. But they had succeeded in convincing them only partially: "They could not convince

66. Chabot (1902), Syriac text, p. 219, French translation, p. 484, emphasis added.
67. Sebeos, ed. Macler (1904), pp. 139–40, our translation from Macler's French.

the whole mass of the people, because their religions were different." Muḥammad, however, rallied all the Arabs to belief in the God of Abraham, and told them that God had promised "this land to the Children of Abraham. When He favored the Jews, He gave it to them; He would now give it to the other Children of Abraham, the Arabs." The Arabs then divided themselves into twelve tribes, placed a thousand of the twelve thousand Jews in each tribe to act as guides, and started the invasion. This account is obviously unhistorical; its one saving grace, for a modern historian sifting through haystacks to find a needle of firm evidence, is that it mentions Muḥammad by name. Unfortunately the account of Muḥammad's role makes most sense as a later explanation added by a copyist who saw that Sebeos did not know what he was talking about. It was not true that the Jews had partially converted the Arabs—they were all of one faith and Muḥammad had converted them. It was not true that they had invaded the Byzantine territories in order to help their brethren the Jews against Heraclius, as Sebeos relates: Muḥammad had taught them that Palaestina belonged to them by right. Certainly it is difficult to see why, if Sebeos knew anything of Islam, and had earlier written of Muḥammad the Arab Prophet, he would put in Muᶜāwiyah's mouth a religious challenge to the Byzantine Emperor that included no reference to Muḥammad and defined the Arab faith only as belief in the God of Abraham.[68]

John bar Penkayê, whose views on the nature of the Arab takeover were given in Part II Chapter 2, confirms that the propagation of a new religion in the conquered territories was not a concern of the new rulers; they required only payment of taxes, and apart from that there was complete religious freedom: "Among the Arabs are not a few Christians,

68. There is apparently only one manuscript, on the basis of which two editions were published in the 19th century. Both include three parts or books. Of these, the first is obviously not the work of Sebeos; it has been translated under the name *Pseudo-Agathange* (Macler [1904], p. x). The second is a compilation of works by two other known authors, one of whom wrote until 1004. Only the third book is accepted to be by Sebeos. (In fact the very identification of this work with the "History of Heraclius" of the Bishop Sebeos, mentioned by medieval historians, is unlikely, so that we call the author Sebeos only for the sake of brevity, not accuracy: cf. Hoyland [1997], p. 124 + n. 27). This tells us, at the very least, that the sole manuscript we have was written at least three centuries after Sebeos wrote, and probably more than that, since it includes as Sebeos's work a piece by an author who was still writing in 1004: if his work could be misattributed to Sebeos, the copyist who made that mistake probably himself lived considerably after the time when this late 10th–early 11th-century author wrote.

some belonging to the heretics [i.e., Monophysites] and some to us [i.e., Nestorians]."[69]

The *Pseudo-Methodius*, which may be dated ca. 70/690 on internal evidence,[70] refers to the Arabs as the sons of Ishmael and as destroyers, but does not mention Islam. Kaegi's conclusion that its author "looked forward to the ultimate triumph of the Byzantine emperor and the eradication of the Arabs and Islam"[71] therefore suffers from the unconscious tendency, already referred to, to treat the terms "Arabs" and "Islam" as synonymous. The author does indeed foresee—and of course deplore—widespread conversion to the Arabs' faith: "Few from many will be left over who are Christians." But he does not mention what that faith is. His concern is that Christians will "deny the true faith ... and put themselves on a par with unbelievers"—it is of little concern to him what form the unbelief takes. Once again, however, the use of the term "apostasy," not "heresy," connotes that it is not a heretical form of Christianity. The description of widespread apostasy to the Arabs' religion fits the description of sources from the 650s to 680s C.E. concerning a serious loss of Christians to paganism,[72] but could also refer to apostasy to Arab monotheism. This contrasts with early 8th-century texts, where the description of the Arab religion leaves no room for doubt: what is being described is clearly Mohammedan.

The feeling one gets from reading these references to the Arabs and their religion in chronological order is that the early 690s were the years of decision. Up until then, the élite had been monotheistic but there was no pressure to convert to this monotheism: the general Arab population could, if they wished, continue to be pagan, and Christian Arab communities which were to be assimilated into the "new" Arabs could be converted to paganism. But by the end of the 7th or early 8th century the Christian writers clearly perceived the Arab religion to be what we call Mohammedan. We connect this change to the adoption of a state religion with the proclamation of Muḥammad as Prophet in 72/691–92 in the Dome of the Rock inscription, a subject to be discussed in the next chapter.

There are also signs that in the 690s the attitude of the ruling élite to Christianity became more intransigent. Anastasius of Sinai (d. ca. 700 C.E.)

---

69. Brock (1982), p. 17 para. 2 + n. 53.
70. See Part II Chapter 2 n. 109 on its date.
71. Kaegi (1969), p. 145.
72. See the section on Arab paganism above.

wrote a guide for the faithful to aid in refuting heresies; it is most probably datable to the 690s.[73] His view of the Arab religion centers on the Christological dispute—the Arabs accuse the Christians of believing in two gods, and take the Christian belief in a son of God literally, to mean that "God has carnally begotten a son."[74] He also wrote two collections of stories: the second of these, compiled ca. 71/690, was intended to be a spiritual aid to Christian slaves of Arab masters. One of these stories relates the martyrdom of George the Black, a Christian child enslaved by a Saracen in Damascus, who denied the Christian faith at the age of eight, but reconverted on reaching adulthood. He was betrayed to his master by another "Christ-hating apostate." The master requested that George pray with him; when George refused, he was killed.[75] Another story tells of Euphemia, the Christian maid of a Saracen woman, also in Damascus, whose mistress would beat her every time she returned from taking communion, yet the maid remained steadfast in her faith. There is no mention of what the religion of the Arab master or mistress was. Hoyland would date George's martyrdom to the 650s, reckoning that George would have been taken prisoner in the 640s and would have been a slave for about ten years before he reconverted. But there is no indication of what area George came from, at what age he was captured, or how long he managed to be a Christian in secret before he was found out. The intolerance to Christianity shown in the story is much more typical of the period between ʿAbd al-Malik and Walīd: the period when Anastasius wrote it. The story of Euphemia certainly is related as contemporary. It is also arguable that Anastasius compiled his anthologies when he did—towards the end of the 7th century—because this was the time when hostility to Christians was increasing. Previously, Christian slaves had been allowed to practice their religion, but it was becoming more and more difficult to do so. The point, then, is not that a Christian was or was not martyred at some indefinite past date, but that the Christian slaves in the 690s needed spiritual support to face the new pressures being brought on them to convert.

The situation in Egypt was similar. When ʿAbd al-Malik appointed his brother ʿAbd al-Azīz governor of Egypt in 65/685, he made ʿAbd al-Azīz's

73. Hoyland (1997), pp. 92–93.
74. Ibid., p. 94.
75. Hoyland (1997), p. 351.

scribe, the Copt Athanasius, ʿAbd al-Azīz's general manager and invested final authority in him, on account of ʿAbd al-Azīz's youth. ʿAbd al-Azīz was on good terms with the Christian community, and especially with its patriarchs, first John of Samanud (686–689) and then Isaac of Rakoti. However, at some time during Isaac's patriarchate (i.e., after 68–69/689), ʿAbd al-Azīz ordered all crosses in Egypt to be broken, and followed this by affixing to the doors of all the churches the announcement: "Muḥammad is the great messenger *(al-rasūl al-kabīr)* who is God's, and Jesus too is the messenger of God. God does not beget and is not begotten."[76] He also invited the patriarch Isaac to dinner and requested him not to make the sign of the cross before eating.[77]

The earliest use of the term "Muslim" occurs at the end of the Chronicle of the Coptic bishop, John of Nikiu, written in Egypt in the 70s/690s:

> And now many of the Egyptians who had been false Christians denied the holy orthodox faith and lifegiving baptism, and embraced the religion of the Moslem, the enemies of God, and accepted the detestable doctrine of the beast, this is, Mohammed, and they erred together with those idolaters, and took arms in their hands and fought against the Christians. And one of them ... embraced the faith of Islam ... and persecuted the Christians.[78]

Kaegi accepts this as proof that "as far as he [i.e., John] was concerned, Islam was indeed a new religion, and a hateful one, and not at all another heresy."[79]

The problem here is that we have inherited John of Nikiu's Chronicle in such an indirect form that it is difficult to rely on it at all for an account of the Arab conquest, let alone to base any theory on its precise use of terms. The text as we have it is in Ethiopic, and the manuscript itself records that it is a translation made in 1602 from an Arabic version. Textual analysis of the forms of names, and transliterations of some other words, reveals that the original was probably written in Greek, with possibly some parts in

76. Hoyland (1997), p. 151, based on the *Life of Isaac of Rakoti and the Christian Arabic History of the Patriarchs of the Coptic Church of Alexandria*. For the significance of the Mohammedan formula, see Part III Chapter 4.

77. Ibid.

78. *Chronicle of John of Nikiu*, Ch. 121:10–11; tr. in Church (1916), p. 201.

79. Kaegi (1969), p. 148.

Coptic.[80] We do not have this original version. The date of the translation into Arabic is unknown and the Arabic version has likewise not survived. All we have is the 1602 Ethiopic version, which purports to be a faithful translation of the Arabic. The translator into Arabic affixed to the beginning of the manuscript a list of chapters and summary of their contents; in this list, where the terms are his and not John of Nikiu's, the term consistently used for the Arabs is "the Muslim" (for the Byzantines it is "the Roman"). It is significant that the terms "Muslim" and "Islam" used by the translator into Arabic are not found in Arabic texts before the 70s/690s. The term "Islam" was first used by ʿAbd al-Malik in the Dome of the Rock, 72/691, but as we shall argue in Part III Chapter 4, "The Official Faith," it almost certainly did not have then the meaning it later acquired, i.e., as an official term for the Arabs' religion. The term "Muslim" is later still: it does not appear in any pre-ʿAbbāsid Arabic texts, including official inscriptions, popular graffiti, coins, and protocols. It is thus highly probable that the Arabic translation was made considerably later than the date of the original manuscript, after the Traditional Account of Arab history and the origins of Islam had become accepted. It is therefore in no way surprising that the Arabic translator (who was obviously a Christian) used the terms "Muslim" and "Islam" in translating references to the Arabs and their religion.[81] We have no way of telling what terms John of Nikiu used; whatever they were, they have been "translated." Similarly, the use of the terms "the religion of the Muslim, the enemies of God," "the detestable doctrine of ... Mohammed," "the faith of Islam," and "these idolators," all together and referring to the same religion, cannot be late 7th century. The terms "Muslim" and "Islam" were not yet used by the Arabs themselves, let alone by onlookers. The only interpretation that makes linguistic sense of this passage is that our Christian translator into Arabic, living considerably later than John, has substituted polemic for precision, and like many another copier and translator of manuscripts before and after him, has helped John along in his laudatory condemnation of the damned by adding a few choice terms from his own time to the religious description(s) he found in the original. It is an interesting exercise to try to discern which terms are

80. Hoyland (1997), p. 152 + n. 126 considers it more likely to have been written in Coptic.

81. As we have seen, modern scholars tend to do the same when translating Syriac texts today.

the translator's and which are John's. As stated, "the faith of Islam" cannot be John's, since the use of this term as a name for the religion had not yet been introduced by the Arabs themselves. The term "Muslim" must also be a result of the Arabic translation. The phrase "the detestable doctrine of ... Mohammed" may very possibly be in the original, since at the time of writing, Muḥammad had already been proclaimed in the Dome of the Rock. The few times that the term "the Ishmaelites" are used may also be original. "Those idolaters" may be an original description of the Arabs as pagans, but it is more likely to date from the time when 'pagan' had become a derogatory term for 'Muslim': it is the only use of it in the Chronicle as a term for the Arabs.[82] But it is one thing to use external evidence regarding the development of the Arabs' religion in the 7th century, as an aid in the critical examination of John of Nikiu's Chronicle. It is quite another to use the Chronicle as evidence for accepting or rejecting any view of the Arabs' religion at the time of the conquest: that would seem to be impossible, in view of the manuscript's history. We must therefore reject Kaegi's conclusions regarding John of Nikiu's view of the Arabs' religion: we cannot tell what he thought of it.

Jacob of Edessa (d. ca. 89/708), in an undated letter whose main purpose is to prove the Davidic descent of Mary, notes:

> That the Messiah is of Davidic descent, everyone professes, the Jews, the *Mahgrayê* and the Christians ... the *Mahgrayê* too, though they do not wish to say that this true Messiah, who came and is acknowledged by the Christians, is God and the Son of God, they nevertheless confess firmly that he is the true Messiah who was to come.... [O]n this they have no dispute with us, but rather with the Jews.... [But] they do not assent to call the Messiah God or Son of God.[83]

This Judeo-Christian view of Jesus was obviously well-established in Arab monotheism; we consider it to be the earliest core of the new Arab religion.

---

82. Hoyland (1997), p. 156 also considers that the manuscript has probably suffered "distortion and tampering," and that many of the expressions in it for the Arabs and their religion are "questionable," including the reference to Muḥammad and the term "Muslims," which he notes does not occur elsewhere in Christian texts until 775 C.E.

83. Crone and Cook (1977), p. 11; Hoyland (1997), p. 166. Hoyland follows his normal practice in translating *mahgrayê* in this passage as "Muslims," which here somewhat begs the point.

We come now to John of Damascus, writing in the early decades of the 8th century, who, in Meyendorff's words, "usually heads every list of Christian anti-Moslem polemicists."[84] Meyendorff demonstrates, and other scholars agree, that of the four works connected with John of Damascus that deal with Islam, two were most probably written by Abū Qurrah, who lived in the late 8th century under the ʿAbbāsids, and one is in Arabic and so far unpublished. We are left with a chapter of the *De Haeresibus*. In this work the religion of the Arabs is called "the deceptive error of the Ishmaelites" which "appeared in the time of Heraclius," i.e., in the early 7th century. No mention is made of any link between an Arab conquest and this heresy, nor of the new faith having been brought in from the outside. It could equally, from John's description, have appeared in the general area of Syria-Palaestina, where he saw it.

We see little relevance, for the purposes of this study, in the dispute as to whether the Arab faith described by John should really be called a new religion or a Christian heresy; by the time he wrote, after the reign of Walīd (86–97/705–715), that faith had separated from Christianity. How well John knew what he was describing is of greater interest than what he called it.[85] Similarly, though he knew the Arab religion had arisen in the early 7th century, he is obviously describing it as he himself knew it. How well did he know it? The question of John of Damascus's degree of familiarity with the Arab rulers and their religion is a subject of considerable controversy among scholars. His date of birth is unknown. He came of a Syrian Christian family which had apparently served the government in official positions concerned with financial administration, under both the Byzantines and the Arabs, and John continued in this tradition. At some point he retired to the monastery of Mar Saba, in the desert a few miles from Jerusalem, where he spent the rest of his days; he died ca. 749/750 C.E. The details—when and for how long he served where—are unknown. At one extreme, he could have retired to the monastery before 96/715, at around the age of forty and after about fifteen years in government service, and died in his seventies.[86] At the other, he retired not before 105/724, in his sixties and after perhaps thirty-five years of

84. Meyendorff (1964), p. 116.

85. Hoyland (1997), pp. 484–85 points out that the word "heresy" in any case is used with the meaning "false belief": the list of a hundred heresies includes twenty beliefs that are pre-Christian, among them Hellenism and Judaism.

86. Chase (1958), introduction, pp. xii, xviii.

government service, and died in his late eighties or early nineties.[87] Those scholars who stress his familiarity with the Arab world, such as Sahas, emphasize the high rank and importance of his father's position, which John apparently inherited,[88] and present him as integrated into the Muslim community. The opposing camp, represented here by Meyendorff, maintains that his position was relatively uninfluential—that of collecting taxes from the Christian community—that knowledge of his life is anyway based on a late (11th-century) and untrustworthy source, and that his writings give the impression that he lived in a Christian-Byzantine ghetto and knew little about Islam.[89] On the whole, an examination of the evidence marshalled by the opposing sides in this dispute leads us to the conclusion that the information regarding John of Damascus's life and family background is probably authentic. It is based on several sources, including Eutychius (d. 940) and al-Balāḏurī (d. 892), not just on an 11th-century Life. Moreover, he was anathemized during the iconoclastic controversy as "Saracen-minded." Since this epithet usually indicated an opponent of the icons, and John was a staunch defender of them, it seems reasonable to accept Sahas's conclusion that it was applied in his case "in order to emphasize John of Damascus's affinity with the Muslim world, in terms of his environment, his family, and his personal contact with the Muslims."[90]

The general picture we receive, then, is of a man deeply involved in the administrative processes of the Arab state, moving among its élite, and certainly in a position to become conversant with the tenets of their religion—all of which is not necessarily incompatible with Meyendorff's assertion that "in mind and heart John still lives in Byzantium."[91]

The *De Haeresibus* itself is the second part of the *Fount of Knowledge*, written at the request of Cosmas, Bishop of Maiuma and dedicated to him. Since Cosmas became bishop in 125/743, we may date the *Fount* to the period 743–50 C.E.[92] It could be argued that John's knowledge of the Arabs'

---

87. This is the view adopted by Sahas (1972), pp. 38–45.

88. Sahas (1972), pp. 7–8, 17–19, 26–29.

89. Meyendorff (1964), esp. pp. 117–18.

90. Sahas (1972), p. 13.

91. Meyendorff (1964), p. 118. John's position may be seen as that of any political or spiritual exile, whose unfulfillable desire to live in different circumstances does not preclude him from taking an active part in the society in which he actually finds himself.

92. It is interesting that most of the *De Haeresibus* is not John's work, but a compilation from other, earlier sources; and the heresies described after the "deceptive error

religion reflects it as it was before he retired; but he was not out of touch with the outside world even after his retirement, for he was ordained as a priest in 726 and left the monastery several times to serve in that capacity in Jerusalem.

The text of the *De Haeresibus* reveals that John was familiar with many Arab traditions, and part but not all of the Qur'ān. In our opinion, it supports Meyendorff's conclusions that John knew only the *sūrahs* he paraphrased (nos. 2–5), plus some locutions which also appear in the Qur'ān but probably antedate it. Sahas's attempts to show that he had a detailed knowledge of the whole Qur'ān are somewhat far-fetched, and do not refute the supposition that what John actually knew were some of the stories and ideas on which the Qur'ān was also based, or from which it was compiled. The most interesting aspect of John's account, to us, is that he relates to the Qur'ānic material as separate "books," not as one book, and that he presents a story called "The Camel of God" as one of these books:

> As has been related, this Muḥammad wrote many ridiculous books, to each one of which he set a title. For example, there is the book On Woman [*sūrah* 4].... Then there is the book of The Camel of God.... Again, in the book of The Table [*sūrah* 5] ... and again, in the book of The Heifer [*sūrah* 2]....[93]

The story of the Camel of God is not in the Qur'ān, though there are casual references to it in Q.vii:73, 77 and Q.xci:13–14. Yet not only does John present it in parallel with *surahs* from the Qur'ān, he in fact devotes more attention to it (for the purposes of ridicule) than to any canonical *sūrah*. But there would have been no point in this extended ridicule, if the Arabs themselves had already excluded this story from their Scripture. This implies that the Qur'ān had not yet been canonized, and that John was referring to separate "books" of material from which the Qur'ān was later compiled ("The Camel of God" being excluded from the canon), not directly to the Qur'ān in its final form. So although the religion described by John of Damascus had some writings and many *logia*, it seems very unlikely that these had been codified into the Qur'ān.

---

of the Ishmaelites" have also been discounted by various scholars as either later than John, or separate works. About the only part of the *De Haeresibus* which all agree to be John's work is the description of the Ishmaelite religion.

93. *De Haeresibus*, transl. Chase (1958), pp. 157–59.

Close in time to the *De Haeresibus* is a letter purporting to be from Leo III to the Caliph ᶜUmar II, who ruled only three years, 99–102/717–720. It shows a much wider knowledge of Islam than other contemporary works, though it discusses it very little, being primarily a defense of Christianity against charges made by ᶜUmar, and only secondarily an attack on Islam. Whether it should be considered as earlier than John of Damascus's work, or contemporary with it, depends on whether the letter is accepted as authentic, itself a matter of much dispute and still unresolved. The earliest source, Levond's Armenian text, cannot be earlier than the late 8th century, and dates later still have been proposed for it. The later, Latin version differs from it considerably, and we are forced to assume that they are independent recensions of a presumed Greek earlier version which has not come down to us.[94] It is also possible that the letter was not in fact written by Leo, but by a later writer who knew the tradition that such a letter existed and what it should have said.

The most important points arising from the letter, from the viewpoint of the present subject, are as follows. Firstly, Leo never mentions the Qurᵓān by that name, nor, in the Armenian version, does he quote from it.[95] He makes many points, each of which the editor—not Leo himself—refers to an appropriate *sūrah* of the Qurᵓān. Considering that Leo grew up on the northern border-area of Syria and, according to one source, was bilingual in Greek and Arabic, he was well-placed both to hear the oral traditions of the Arabs and to know about their holy book. But we cannot tell from Leo's letter (or from ᶜUmar's as paraphrased in Levond) whether he is drawing on the Qurᵓān, or on oral tradition and knowledge of the theological controversies occupying the Arab theologians at the time. On the whole, Levond's text supports the conclusion that Leo is mentioning points about which he has heard, not quoting directly. Leo refers to the Qurᵓān only twice—both times in a discussion of its *compilation:*

---

94. The Armenian text has been translated by Jeffery (1944). The reader is referred to pp. 270–76 and 331–32 of Jeffery's article for a discussion of the evidence regarding authenticity. Meyendorff (1964) finds Jeffery's arguments in favor of authenticity "quite convincing," in fact more so than Jeffery himself, who adopts a neutral stand. Hoyland (1997), pp. 490–94 argues for the late 8th century date, but considers that "some of the material in the text" is from the early 8th century, though other parts are late 8th century (pp. 496–500).

95. The Latin has one rather inaccurate quotation from *Sūrah* 5, prompting Jeffery to remark that "his knowledge of the Quranic passage is probably from oral tradition" (Jeffery [1944], p. 315 n. 68).

> [Y]ou admit that we say that it [the Gospel] was written by God... as you pretend for your Furqan, although we know that it was ᶜUmar [i.e., the second caliph], Abū Turāb [i.e., ᶜAlī] and Salman the Persian, who composed that.[96]

> As for your [book], you have already given us examples of such falsifications, and one knows, among others, of a certain Ḥajjāj, named by you as Governor of Persia, who had men gather up your ancient books, which he replaced by others composed by himself, according to his taste, and which he propagated everywhere in your nation... From this destruction, nevertheless, there escaped a few of the works of Abū Turāb, for Ḥajjāj could not make them disappear completely.[97]

Clearly there were traditions among the Christians regarding different versions of the Qurʾān, or the texts from which it was compiled, which seem to have been connected with the Marwānid-ᶜAlid rivalry, and/or with the religiopolitical struggles which took place during the Sufyānī-Marwānī interregnum (Second Civil War), mainly in Iraq and the Ḥijāz, where al-Ḥajjāj bn Yūsuf was instrumental in consolidating the Marwānid ascendancy. Jeffery examines the evidence in both Christian and Arab sources and concludes that "some revision of the text, as well as clarification by division and pointing, was undertaken by al-Ḥajjāj, and that this was known to the Christians of that day."[98] It seems probable, then, that when the letter was written the material from which the Qurʾān was drawn (*logia, pericopae*, etc.) had only recently been assembled and may not have been in its final form; and that it was not commonly known by the name Qurʾān.

In view of the fact that John of Damascus also quotes only from *sūrahs* 2–5, it is highly interesting that Leo too shows a much greater knowledge of these than of the others. There are in all thirty points in Leo's letter which Jeffery characterizes as references to *sūrahs* 2–5; two of them may be regarded as doubtful—i.e., Jeffery calls them "apparent" references, or not Leo but Jeffery himself refers to them in discussing the text. There are twenty-six references to all the other *sūrahs* combined, fourteen of them in the "doubtful" category. The text leaves a very strong impression that its writer may well have known a written version of *sūrahs* 2–5, but otherwise

---

96. Jeffery (1944), p. 292.
97. Ibid., p. 298; cf. note 48 for Jeffery's commentary on this passage.
98. Ibid., p. 315 n. 68.

was relying on "hearsay"—oral and/or written *logia* which also found their way into the Qurʾān.

The second main point to note is that Leo refers many times to Muḥammad, both by name and as "your legislator," and once as "the head of your religion." He cannot of course be conceded the title "Prophet," and is characterized as the man who laid down the laws by which the adherents to this false religion live. This reference to Muḥammad as the Arabs' lawgiver is evidence in favor of a late date for the letter. As Schacht has demonstrated,

> the first considerable body of legal traditions from the Prophet originated towards the middle of the second century, in opposition to slightly earlier traditions from Companions and other authorities and to the "living tradition" of the ancient schools of law; ... The evidence of legal traditions carries us back to about the year 100 A.H. only; at that time Islamic legal thought started from late Umaiyad administrative and popular practice.[99]

Schacht's findings are not surprising in the light of the theory that Muḥammad the Prophet was himself introduced at a late date; but the point here is that Schacht's date (mid-2nd century A.H.) would place a document referring to Muḥammad as the Muslims' "lawgiver" not earlier than thirty or forty years after the purported date of Leo's letter, and probably later still. This would make it, at least, contemporary with the *De Haeresibus*. While leaving the question unsettled, the present work inclines to favor such a late date, for the reasons given above.

Finally, we have a Nestorian account of a debate between a monk of Bet Ḥale and an Arab, a follower of the "Emir Maslama."[100] It appears to have been written ca. 710–740 C.E.[101] If so, it is roughly contemporary with the two preceding sources. It refers to a debate about "our scriptures and their qūrān"; the Arab notes that "we observe the commandments of Mūḥmd and the sacrifices of Abraham." The actual information regarding the Arab's religion is very slight: the "dispute" is a literary fabrication in which the Arab's task is purely to ask questions and accept the truth of the monk's answers, and hence of Christianity. The most interesting point is the

---

99. Schacht (1950), pp. 4–5. The reader is referred to the whole of this work for the basis of these conclusions.

100. Described and partially translated by Hoyland (1997), pp. 465–72.

101. Regarding the date of this work, see Hoyland (1997), p. 472.

monk's reply to the question, why do Christians adore the Cross "when he did not give you such a commandment in his Gospel?" The monk replies:

> I think that for you, too, not all your laws and commandments are in the Qur'ān which Muḥammad taught you; rather there are some which he taught you from the Qur'ān, and some are in *sūrat albaqrah* and in *gygy* and in *twrh*. So also we, some commandments the Lord taught us, some the Holy Spirit uttered through the mouths of its servants the Apostles, and some [were made known] by means of teachers who directed and showed us the Way of Life and the Path of Light.[102]

This is the earliest reference from non-Muslim sources to a book called the Qur'ān. And like John of Damascus, the monk knows of several books from which the Muslims derive their laws. Whereas the text in John of Damascus does not explicitly say that Muḥammad's "many ridiculous books" are separate rather than part of a single compilation—though that would be the most normal way to understand the phrase—the monk makes it absolutely clear that these books are mutually exclusive: *sūrat albaqrah* (now Q.ii) is not, for him, part of the Qur'ān. It is a text as separate from the Qur'ān as the *twrh* (i.e., the Torah) and *gygy* (which Hoyland understands to refer to the Gospel).

CONCLUSION

Putting the evidence of this chapter together with that presented in Part II, we may suggest the following outline of events. The Arabs who took control of Syria-Palestine around 17/638 were a mixture of former Byzantine *foederati* from the *limes* area, augmented by other tribes from Palaestina III and Phoinikon. Some of the former *foederati* were at least nominally Christian, but many of the Arabs, especially those from farther afield, were pagan. They were joined, as soon as the winds of change became apparent, by local Arabs, some of whom were Christians of various persuasions, and others members of other creeds existing in the area. There was initially no overall control by one Arab leader; but by around 20–21/640, Muᶜāwiyah was in control of at least the northern areas of al-Šām.

102. Monk of Bet Ḥale, *Disputation*, tr. in Hoyland (1997), p. 471.

Muʿāwiyah now found himself in a position of some political complexity. The superpower of the day was Byzantium, and it was inconceivable that he could maintain control without contact of some kind with the Byzantine empire. From both the Arab and Byzantine point of view, contact was necessary; but Byzantium made it clear that her condition for allowing Arab control of her former eastern provinces, and for maintaining contact with the Arabs, was that the ruling élite, at least, should accept a form of monotheism. The eastern provinces, with their Christians, would not be delivered into the hands of pagans.

The new élite, then, were faced with the political necessity of professing some form of monotheism. From Byzantium's point of view, this monotheism should not be Orthodox Christianity. Melkites would recognize the empire's jurisdiction (as indeed the Melkite population insisted on doing until late in the 7th century); Byzantium was intent on giving up direct administrative control. Similarly, the religion could not be one of the local forms of Christianity—Monophysitism or Nestorianism—for that would invite an alliance between the population and the new rulers which might quickly threaten Byzantine supremacy. But the Arabs also had conditions of their own, which the form of monotheism they adopted would have to meet. Firstly, it had to distinguish them from other peoples, not merge them into them; for the Umayyads, in marked contrast to the ʿAbbāsids, had an ethnocentric view of the Arabs' place in their new countries, and seem to have envisaged a national Arab State. Secondly, the new religion would have to fit in with what they already "knew" of their relationship to other monotheistic peoples—i.e., their status as "Ishmaelites" and descent from Abraham. What creed could fulfill all these requirements?

The Arabs eventually adopted Judeo-Christianity, which was indeed a near-perfect solution to the above problem. At the time of the Takeover, however, it was apparently not a suitable option. We should remember that the established Arab population of al-Šām—the Byzantine Arabs—were already Christian, and could not be expected to convert to a different, "heretical" form of Christianity any more than the non-Arab Christians of al-Šām would. Arab conversion to the new religion, then, would occur, if at all, among the pagan tribesmen from the interface areas. This meant that it must be as free as possible from the subtle Christological disputes and philosophical hairsplitting that formed the basis for the differentiation between most Christian sects. To pagans fresh from the desert, these Christological controversies must have been incomprehensible. The form of monotheism chosen was therefore no version of Christianity, but the creed we call Indeterminate Monotheism—a very simple belief in a single God, already current among some at least of the desert tribes. Byzantium impressed upon the Arab élites the necessity of adopting this religion; and they did so out of political expediency.

We can therefore distinguish at least three broad religious groups in the population of the Takeover period:

- The urban élite of the towns was Rūmī in culture and initially, at least, in political affiliation, and the urban population was largely Christian. While it included many Christian Arabs, there were very few *newcomers* among its ranks. This urban élite, having agreed to recognize Arab sovereignty at least provisionally, and to pay taxes, were left to govern their towns and their religious communities very much as before.
- The tribal leaders who became the Arab ruling élite, and from among whose ranks Muᶜāwiyah emerged, adopted a very basic form of monotheism, possibly influenced by Samaritan and/or Judeo-Christian positions. This ruling élite continued to employ the services of the Christian officials of the former Byzantine administration, so that the Syrian urban Christian élite effectively ran not only the towns but also the state, and Byzantine administrative practices continued essentially unchanged. In time the religion of the ruling élite became more Judeo-Christian in character; in Muᶜāwiyah's time it was either Judeo-Christianity or very much influenced by Judeo-Christian beliefs, and probably also by the Abrahamites, and/or by the importance which the Judeo-Christians attached to Abraham.
- The general Arab population of newcomers, however, were pagan and tribal. They must have included a large number of different groups, each with its own dialect, manners, and religious customs. But they were all pagan, and all essentially non-Byzantine in character. These were the pagans whom the indigenous Syriac-speaking rural and urban population encountered daily.

We have seen indications that where it was decided to cut an existing Christian population from its erstwhile cultural roots and merge it into a newly-arrived Arab one, this goal was achieved by encouraging conversion to paganism. It is also possible that paganism had remained latent in the nonurban areas of the former Persian empire, far from imperial influence, throughout the Christian era, and that the nonurban population of these areas conceived of Christianity as a mode of worship, not as a complete theological system. Whether or not this was so, the fact is that this rural Christian population, which included many Arabs, exposed to an active pagan cult among the newcomers, showed itself to be vulnerable and susceptible, and began to convert in numbers that varied from a slow drift to "wholesale apostasy." The alarm of the church authorities at this situation is vividly conveyed in the sources that have survived from this time. With the old barriers between the Byzantine and Persian empires now nonexistent, intersectarian Christian competition also intensified, as the Monophysites expanded into northern Mesopotamia,[103] and this too is reflected in the sources, such as the letters of Catholicos Ishoᶜyahb III. In this atmosphere of competition, the Arab rulers were perceived as the guarantors of success. It is no wonder that Ishoᶜyahb took a "very positive attitude" towards them and strove to keep on good terms with them.[104]

At the turn of the 8th century, around 81/700, Christian writers who came into contact with the élite of the Arab state saw its official religion as a form of Christian heresy. At the same time the Christian clergy in the field, such as the bishops, were still struggling with the fact that a large part of the Arab population was pagan, and that many (Arab?) Christians were finding their example enticing.

Muᶜāwiyah died in 60/680, and in 65/684 ᶜAbd al-Malik became caliph. It took him several years to establish firm control, a process completed around 72/692. As soon as his reign was assured, he took the next religious step: he proclaimed a national Arab Prophet, and thereby founded Mohammedanism. Within a few years, the official attitude to Christianity hardened, and pressure began to be brought on Christians to convert. The Arab Prophet, and the creed centered on him, are the subject of the next two chapters.

---

103. Brock (1982), p. 15.
104. Ibid.

3

The Chosen Prophet

When ᶜAbd al-Malik became caliph the official Arab religion was still, as far as we know, the Indeterminate Monotheism found in dated inscriptions from the 40s/660s, the best known of which is probably Muᶜāwiyah's dam inscription at Ṭāᵓif (58/678).[1] But this situation was to be short-lived. Within a few years of assuming the caliphate, ᶜAbd al-Malik began to develop the state religion in a new direction: the adoption of an Arab prophet.

Muḥammad the Prophet makes his first dated public appearance with the three words *Muḥammad rasūl Allāh* on an Arab-Sassanian coin of Xālid bn ᶜAbdallāh, struck in Damascus in 71/690–91.[2] A year later he became, with ᶜĪsà (Jesus), a central protagonist of ᶜAbd al-Malik's inscription in the Dome of the Rock in Jerusalem, dated in the inscription itself to 72/691–92.[3]

---

1. *RCEA* 1 inscr. no. 8; Grohmann (1962), pp. 56–57; Miles (1948), pp. 102ff.

2. Walker (1941), p. 108, coin no. 213. Xālid could perhaps have brought the coin with him when he returned to Baṣrah from Damascus after the Marwānids succeeded in defeating the Zubayrites in the province of ᶜIrāq.

3. This is usually taken to be the date of completion of the building. Blair (1992), pp. 67–70 argues persuasively that ᶜAbd al-Malik was most unlikely to have been free to start major construction work in Jerusalem before 72 A.H. (for instance, he began to mint coins in Syria only in that year, following his return from ᶜIrāq), and that this date should therefore be understood as the date he ordered the building to be erected, i.e., as a terminus a quo. The date of completion would then be several years—perhaps even a decade—later.

Before 71 A.H. he is not mentioned; after 72 A.H. he is an obligatory part of every official proclamation.

The evidence for this statement is mainly numismatic; and since the early coins of al-Šām are undated and do not bear religious legends,[4] they are of little use for the purposes of dating Muḥammad's appearance.[5] The Arab-Sassanian coins, however, do usually bear dates, and provide valuable evidence regarding the official use of religious formulae, and especially the introduction of Muḥammad.

Although dates were usually struck on the Arab-Sassanian coins, it is no simple matter to date them. Firstly, dates in Arabic are the exception: even on coins bearing names of political figures and religious texts in Arabic, the names of the mints and the dates are, as a rule, written in the difficult Aramaic-Pehlevi script and may therefore pose problems of decipherment. After the date has been deciphered, the problem of era remains to be solved.[6] The Sassanian monarchs dated their coins from the year of their succession, not by reference to an external era; Xusraū's own issues therefore bear dates from 1 to 39. The Arab imitations of Xusraū's coins, which still bear his name, are dated from 21 to 50, and it is not always clear to which era the date refers. Three eras were in use: the Arab (A.H.), the Yezdigird (Y.E.: from the ascension of Yezdigird III in 632 C.E. on), and the Tabaristān or post-Yezdigird era (P.Y.E., from 651 C.E., the date of Yezdigird's death). The Yezdigird era should have ended in 651; but since he was the last Sassanian ruler, it continued to be used after his death. The alternative, equally attractive to Iranian patriots, was to start a new era from the year following Yezdigird's death (Y.E. 21/32 A.H.), even though there was no Sassanian king. Most of the ʿAbbāsid coins of Tabaristān use

4. The undated bronze coins bearing the legends *xalīfat Allāh* and/or *rasūl Allāh*, which Walker assigned to the Sufyānid period, have been redated to the time of ʿAbd al-Malik (Bates [1976], p. 23). Of course the fact that a caliph's official coinage did *not* include a reference to the Prophet is as significant as the fact that it did—it does at least indicate that the state's official religious propaganda was not interested in proclaiming this form of belief.

5. But they can tell us of the political events of the takeover and the early period of Arab rule, an aspect examined in Part II Chapter 3.

6. The following information on the various eras comes from Walker (1941), pp. xxvii–xxviii.

this third era, and it is therefore usually called the Tabaristān era; but it was not confined to use in Tabaristān, and Walker therefore favors the non-geographic term 'post-Yezdigird era' instead.

So from 632 to 651 C.E., a date on an Arab-Sassanian coin could be either A.H. or Y.E.; from 651, it could be any of the three. The following conversion table[7] sums up the situation:

P.Y.E.	Y.E.	A.H.	C.E.
–	20	31	651 Aug. 24
11	31	42	662 Apr. 26
21	41	52/53	672

As Walker points out, it is not always easy to discover which era was meant: "All three eras are actually used in the case of some governors, though apparently not all at the same mint."[8] Ascription of a coin to an era is usually based on what we know of historical events in each of the possible years, and on the biography of the governor (e.g., his known dates of governorship) or other personage named on the coin. The "Biographical Sketches" in Walker (1941) provide several good examples of the complicated way in which such considerations, often biographical, influence the decision as to what era was intended on a given Arab-Sassanian coin. In some cases the date could still be either A.H. or Y.E., or even, occasionally, P.Y.E.

With this caveat in mind, we may turn to an examination of the religious legends on the Arab-Sassanian coins. **Table III.3.1** lists the different formulae, and gives the dates of all 7th-century Arab-Sassanian coins that bore each formula.

Table III.3.1 provides several instances where the era of a coin's date is far from clear. Usually it is assumed in such cases that the Arab era was intended, unless historical or biographical considerations rule out the resulting date. In most cases, the precise date matters little to the present enquiry. This is the case, for instance, in the "pre-Mohammedan era," i.e., during the decades when only general monotheistic formulae were employed on coins. Similarly, dates from the 70s on fall within the "Mohammedan era" whether the era is read as A.H. or Y.E., so that it is no surprise to find

7. Based on the table in ibid., pp. 237–38.
8. Walker (1941), p. xxviii.

Table III.3.1. Main Religious Texts on Arab-Sassanian coins
(Compiled from information in Walker [1941])

Text	Years	Notes
bism Allāh	21	Y.E. = A.H. 32/652; P.Y.E. = A.H. 52/672
	25	
	26 (×2)*	Y.E. = A.H. 36/659; P.Y.E. = A.H. 57/656
	28	
	29 (×2)	
	30 (×5)	
	31 (×2)	
	32	Miles takes as A.H. 35/655
	37	
	38 (?)	
	40	
	47	Y.E. = A.H. 59/678; P.Y.E. = A.H. 79/698
	Continue down to Ḥajjāj	
bism Allāh rabbī ("in the name of Allāh my Lord")	26	Really struck in 50 (Walker's note p. 13, no. Zam. 1)
	35	This is Walker's no. Zam. 1
	38 (?)	
	39	
	41	
	42	
	45	
	48 (×4)	Sistān
	48	Merw
	49 (×3)	
	50	
	51	(Yr. 48?)
	54	
	63	
rabbī Allāh ("My Lord is Allāh")	37	Y.E. = A.H. 48/668; P.Y.E. = A.H. 69/688
Allāh wa-rabbī ʿwr/ bism Allāh rabbī	61(?)	Y.E. = A.H. 73/692; P.Y.E. = A.H. 94/712

* "×2" means "occurs twice."

Text	Years	Notes
bism Allāh al-malik ("in the name of Allāh the King")	31 or 32	If 31, Y.E. = A.H. 42/662; P.Y.E. = 63/683
	45	
	47	Y.E. = A.H. 59/678; P.Y.E. = A.H. 79/698
Muḥammad rasūl Allāh bism Allāh	66	Y.E.? = A.H. 78; ᶜAbd al-Malik bn ᶜAbdallāh
	71	A.H.: Xālid bn ᶜAbdallāh
	74	A.H.: Xālid bn ᶜAbdallāh
In Arabic on obverse: bism Allāh al-ᶜAzīz *In Persian on reverse*: lā ilah illā Allāh waḥdahu Muḥammad rasūl Allāh	72	A.H.: ᶜAbd al-ᶜAzīz bn ᶜAbdallāh*

* This is the first occurrence of the *Tawḥīd* on a Persian coin; the reference to Muḥammad had been introduced only a year earlier. Mochiri, who published this coin,[9] suggests that Pehlevi was used because Arabic was still unfamiliar in Sistān: the common language was Persian, the chancery language also Persian in the Pehlevi script.[10] We consider that the choice of the local language for the new formulae suggests that the authorities intended them to be widely understood.

bism Allāh lā ilah	76	A.H.? Ḥajjāj bn Yūsuf
illā Allāh waḥdahu	77	A.H.? Ḥajjāj bn Yūsuf
Muḥammad rasūl Allāh	78	A.H.? Ḥajjāj bn Yūsuf
	79	A.H.? Ḥajjāj bn Yūsuf

the formula *Muḥammad rasūl Allāh* on coins from these years. But when we ask at what date this formula first appeared on a coin, it becomes of prime importance to which era the date on the coin refers.

The earliest dates on coins mentioning the Prophet Muḥammad are 66 (a coin of the governor ᶜAbd al-Malik bn ᶜAbdallāh) and 71 (a coin of the governor Xālid bn ᶜAbdallāh, in power intermittently, 70–75 A.H.). The latter was issued in Damascus by a Marwānid official. The era must be A.H. to accord with the governor's period of office, and this presents no historical difficulty: 71 A.H. was after ᶜAbd al-Malik had defeated most of

9. Mochiri (1981).
10. Ibid., p. 172.

the Zubayrite opposition in the province of ᶜIrāq, and only a year before the date of the Dome of the Rock.[11] The coin dated 66, however, raises several problems.[12] If this date means 66 A.H., it is a unique example of a Mohammedan inscription from any source, numismatic or other, prior to the 70s A.H. Moreover, 66 A.H., the second year after ᶜAbd al-Malik's accession, was a most inopportune moment to introduce a major religious change. The new caliph was preoccupied with the interregnum wars and in his worst situation vis-à-vis his many opponents; his grip on his realm was at its weakest. Besides, the coin was struck at Bišāpūr in the province of Fars. But after 64 A.H. the provinces bordering the Persian Gulf, from Baṣrah at the head of the Gulf to Kirmān and Zaranj north of the Straits of Hormuz, were controlled by anti-Marwānid factors. **Map III.3.1** plots the coins minted in this region from the late 50s to 72 A.H. It shows that between 64 and 71 A.H. no Umayyad governor was firmly enough in control to mint coins in this area. The mint towns in the vicinity of Bišāpūr were held by the Zubayrites: Baṣrah, Ardašir-Xurrah, and Dārābjird from 65; Istaxr from either 63 or 66 (the date on the coin in question is uncertain). Bišāpūr itself was held by the Zubayrites from at least 67 to 70 A.H. Finally, the governor named on this coin, ᶜAbd al-Malik ibn ᶜAbdallāh, is mentioned in Ṭabarī's *Annals* as having been appointed governor of Baṣrah in 64/65 A.H., after ᶜUbaydullāh bn Ziyād was driven out.[13] But he can have held office only very briefly, for two more governors, an Umayyad and a Zubayrite, had succeeded him and been replaced in their turn by 65 A.H.[14] We know nothing of him apart from Ṭabarī's brief mention,[15] but Walker concludes from this coin that he was in charge of Fars after leaving Baṣrah. Clearly he was governor of Fars when he minted this coin, but the question remains whether he held this office in 66 A.H., when Xūzistān, Fars, and Kirmān were all Zubayrite-controlled, or in 66 Y.E., i.e., 78 A.H., when the area was firmly controlled for ᶜAbd al-Malik by Ḥajjāj. As Map III.3.1 demonstrates, it is difficult to believe that a Marwānid official could have

11. Regarding whether this date represents the start of construction or the date of completion of the building, see n. 3 above.

12. Walker (1941), p. 97, no. Sch. 5.

13. Q.b. Walker (1941), p. liv.

14. Ibid., pp. liv–lv.

15. Crone and Hinds (1986), accepting the date 66 as A.H. = 685/86 C.E., refer to him as a "pro-Zubayrid governor" (p. 25). We consider this most unlikely, for the reasons given in this chapter. No other Zubayrite coins mention Muḥammad, whereas once ᶜAbd al-Malik had decided to use this slogan it quickly became ubiquitous.

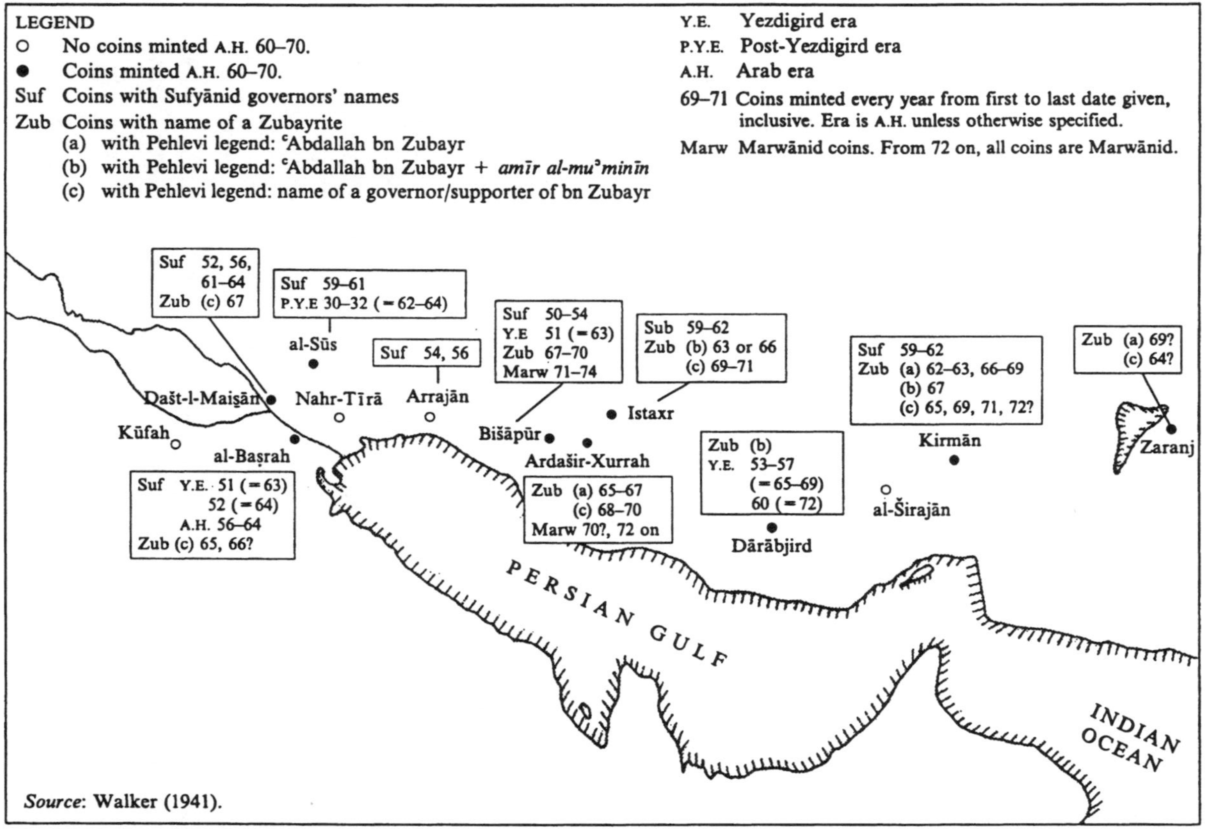
LEGEND
○ No coins minted A.H. 60–70.
● Coins minted A.H. 60–70.
Suf Coins with Sufyānid governors' names
Zub Coins with name of a Zubayrite
(a) with Pehlevi legend: ʿAbdallah bn Zubayr
(b) with Pehlevi legend: ʿAbdallah bn Zubayr + *amīr al-muʾminīn*
(c) with Pehlevi legend: name of a governor/supporter of bn Zubayr
Y.E. Yezdigird era
P.Y.E. Post-Yezdigird era
A.H. Arab era
69–71 Coins minted every year from first to last date given, inclusive. Era is A.H. unless otherwise specified.
Marw Marwānid coins. From 72 on, all coins are Marwānid.
Suf 52, 56, 61–64 Zub (c) 67
Suf 59–61 P.Y.E 30–32 (= 62–64)
al-Sūs
Suf 54, 56
Suf 50–54 Y.E 51 (= 63) Zub 67–70 Marw 71–74
Sub 59–62 Zub (b) 63 or 66 (c) 69–71
Suf 59–62 Zub (a) 62–63, 66–69 (b) 67 (c) 65, 69, 71, 72?
Zub (a) 69? (c) 64?
Dašt-l-Maisān
Nahr-Tīrā
Arrajān
Istaxr
Kūfah
al-Baṣrah
Bišāpūr
Ardašir-Xurrah
Kirmān
Zaranj
Suf Y.E. 51 (= 63) 52 (= 64) A.H. 56–64 Zub (c) 65, 66?
Zub (a) 65–67 (c) 68–70 Marw 70?, 72 on
Zub (b) Y.E. 53–57 (= 65–69) 60 (= 72)
al-Širajān
Dārābjird
PERSIAN GULF
INDIAN OCEAN
Source: Walker (1941).

Map III.3.1. Minting activities around Bišāpūr.

struck any coins, let alone coins with a radically new religious formula, in Bišāpūr in 66 A.H.

The date on the coin was written in Pehlevi, and we are not competent to offer an opinion regarding its transcription or translation as 66. But assuming that the reading is accurate, we consider that for the reasons given above, the era must be Y.E., corresponding to 78 A.H. This date accords much better with the history of the area in the 60s–70s A.H., and with all the other evidence, numismatic and epigraphic, pointing to ca. 70 as the date of adoption of Mohammedanism by the ruler(s) of the Arab polity.

One other coin bears a problematic date (and it too, as it happens, was minted at Bišāpūr). It was issued by the Umayyad governor ᶜUbaydullāh bn Ziyād (gov. 53–67 A.H.)[16] and is dated 53. Since Ibn Ziyād held office for a long time, this could be either 53 A.H. or 53 Y.E. = 65 A.H. We consider it to be almost certainly from 53 A.H. Firstly, this is in the "main sequence" of Sufyānī coins, whereas no other Sufyānī coins at all were minted by any governor in this entire area after 64 A.H., so that the date of Y.E. 53/65 A.H. is inherently most unlikely. Even more to the point, although ᶜUbaydullāh was officially governor till his death in 67 A.H., he was in fact driven out of the province of ᶜIrāq into Syria by popular opposition in 64 A.H., after the death of the caliph Yazīd.[17] It is therefore very problematic to date a coin issued by him to 65 A.H.

These considerations lead to the conclusion that no Sufyānī governor held effective power in the provinces to the north of the Persian Gulf between 65 and 70–71 A.H.; during this period the whole area was controlled by the Zubayrites. Both the pre-65 A.H. Sufyānid coins, and those issued by Ibn al-Zubayr and his supporters, bear general monotheistic formulae only; specifically, none of them mentions Muḥammad. The first coin to do so was minted in 71 A.H., in ᶜAbd al-Malik's own capital city of Damascus, after he had quashed the Zubayrite rebellion; and it was followed a year later by the Dome of the Rock inscription. We see this as the introduction of the concept "Muḥammad Messenger of God" into the official religion.

The nonnumismatic contemporary evidence also fails to place Muḥammad prior to ᶜAbd al-Malik's day. The local Christian sources from the 1st century A.H.[18] show little awareness of his existence. The reference to

16. Walker (1941), p. 55, coin no. 76.

17. Ibid., p. xlvii.

18. These were discussed in the previous chapter.

an invading prophet in the *Doctrina Jacobi* must, as argued in the previous chapter, be seen as quite separate from the traditions that Muḥammad led the invading Arabs. Such traditions may well have grown up around Muḥammad after he was introduced: they are not recorded before the early 8th century.[19] They were then available to be incorporated into 8th-century sources, such as the *Secrets of Rabbi Simon ben Yoḥay*, together with other material which saw the Arab takeover in Messianic and apocalyptic terms. The Syrian chronicles from the end of the 7th and early 8th centuries mention Muḥammad as the first Arab king, but know nothing of his role as prophet.[20] The Sufyānid inscriptions indicate only Indeterminate Monotheism, as do the two surviving pre-Marwānid tombstones and the official papyri.[21] But if the Arabs lacked a national prophet, they clearly needed one. The Jews had a national and religious leader and prophet in Moses, and the Christians identified and defined themselves via belief in Jesus. The Arabs still had no sense of identity or allegiance above the tribal level; but the founding of a national state requires a national identity. And in this period, that identity would inevitably have to be stated in religious terms. To ʿAbd al-Malik, the lack of an Arab parallel to the Jewish and Christian prophets would have been painfully obvious.

That lack was the more acute, in that the Arabs also had no pedigree, in an area and among peoples where lineage was of great importance. The Jews could point to a history preserved in the Old Testament, which traced their descent from Abraham, their occupation of the land from the time of Moses, and by divine right. The Byzantine élite (the Rūm) regarded themselves as Greeks, and could trace their "national" history back to Alexander the Great. The Christians in general considered themselves the successors of the Jews (Israelites). But the Arabs, as an ethnic group, had no history to display. Their descent from Abraham, of which they had learnt from the Jews, was a start, but being through a slave woman it made them inferior to the Jews; and they could point to no stamp of divine approval for a separate Arab religion or an Arab state. This deficit was only corrected with the *Sīrah*; but ʿAbd al-Malik laid the foundations for an Arab history,

---

19. The earliest in the list given in Crone and Cook (1977), p. 152 n. 7, dates from the reign of Hišām.

20. Jacob of Edessa's chronological charts, *Chron. ad annum 705*, and *Chron. ad annum 724* are all discussed in the previous chapter.

21. Cf. Crone and Hinds (1986), p. 24. We discuss the evidence of official documents and inscriptions in the next two chapters.

too, when he supplied the Arabs with a national prophet of their own, through whom to experience the unity of a common identity and to express their allegiance to the newly emergent state.

All this is of course totally at odds with the biography of Muḥammad, the Ḥijāzī preconquest founder of Islam, related in such detail in the Muslim literature. But as many Western scholars have pointed out, the road to acceptance of this biography as historical fact is strewn with the boulders of imprecision and contradiction. The first account of the Prophet's life is the *al-Maġāzī wā-al-ṣīyār Sīrah*[22] of Ibn Isḥāq (d. A.H. 150/767[23]), which survives only in the form imparted by Ibn Hišām's (d. 213/828 or 218/834[24]) extensive editing at the end of the 2nd century A.H. In Ibn Isḥāq's time—and even, it seems, in Ibn Hišām's—there was no generally accepted History of the Prophet, and neither his age nor his date of birth were undisputed. This can be, and has been, supported by an analysis of the traditions regarding him. The Traditional Account maintains that Muḥammad was forty when he was called to act as God's prophet, and that he was born in the Year of the Elephant, the year in which the Ethiopian Abraha led an expedition into the Ḥijāz. This would result in a birthdate of ca. 570 C.E., since chronological calculations would place the date of his call to prophethood at ca. 610 C.E. There are many problems with this chronology. Conrad (1987) has collected the views of scholars on the subject, all leading to the conclusion that it is impossible to accept the Traditional Account on this point, since the *Sīrah* is hopelessly confused regarding Muḥammad's date of birth, age at the time of various events, and early life in general. In fact "well into the second century A.H. scholarly opinion on the birthdate of the Prophet displayed a range of variance of 85 years"[25]—from which Conrad concludes that *sīrah* studies were still in a state of flux till then. The earliest extant reference to his birthdate (if the *isnād* can be accepted) is from Zurā rah bn Awfā, who died in A.H. 93/712, and though closest in time to the event it is describing, it gives the most general date of all: that the Prophet was born within the same *qarn* (120-year period) as the year in which Yazīd

---

22. On the name of Ibn Isḥāq's original work, and on *maġāzī*, *ṣīyār*, and *sīrah* as technical terms, see Hinds (1983).

23. This is the usually accepted date, though references to other dates from 151 to 154 A.H. occur. See Hinds (1983), p. 59 n. 6.

24. See Khoury (1983), p. 8 + n. 5 for Ibn Hišām's dates.

25. Conrad (1987), p. 239.

bn Muᶜāwiyah died (64/683).[26] This means that he could have been born in the mid-6th century—or as late as the mid-7th.

There are also problems with the Year of the Elephant. Conrad points out that it was considered "sufficiently significant to make it the starting-point for a new chronology of subsequent occurrences in Arabia, so that we commonly find reports dating events from a certain number of years after the *ᶜĀm al-fīl*."[27] It is therefore not itself anchored by reference to any other independently dated event; but modern scholarship tends to place Abraha's expedition in 552 C.E., not 570.[28] This would make Muḥammad nearly sixty when called to the prophethood—or, more likely, it means we must abandon the claim that he was born in the Year of the Elephant. We then have no way of knowing his date of birth. Moreover, Conrad argues convincingly that in the Jewish, Christian, and even pre-Islamic Arabian traditions (as later in the Islamic), the number forty had symbolic signif-icance: to say that Muḥammad was forty when called to the prophethood was but a way of indicating that he was well-qualified for his mission, being of the "age of understanding" and at the peak of his powers.[29] There was in fact no other reason to state how old he was: an individual's exact age was of little social significance, and therefore not generally remembered with any precision.

Our problems do not end at Muḥammad's birth. Not just that one date, but the whole chronology of his life, survives in a form so confused and contradictory that the *sīrah* literature fails to collate it, and manages to resolve difficulties only by a very high-handed and arbitrary approach.[30] If we ask, did the Prophet Muḥammad in fact exist in the early 7th century?—the *sīrah* literature cannot resolve the question. If he was not a mythological

26. Ibid., p. 235.

27. Ibid., p. 226.

28. Ibid., pp. 227–28, 237.

29. Ibid., pp. 230–37. In this connection it is interesting to note that Auxentius, bishop of Durostorum and a pupil of Ulfila's, writing of Ulfila in a letter, mentions three times the "forty years of his bishopric." Yet other evidence indicates that Ulfila was bishop of the Goths for either forty-four or forty-six years. This has occasioned much dispute as to whether we may or may not accept the possibility of inaccuracy on Auxentius's part (cf. Thompson [1966], pp. xv–xvi and n. 2). It would seem that we have here another example of the use of forty as a general concept, perhaps in this case with a conscious Biblical parallel of the "forty years in the wilderness" variety.

30. Surveyed briefly by Conrad in *Theophanes*, pp. 15–16; eagerly pointed out by Lammens (1911), "L'âge de Mahomet"; and see Jones, J.M.B. (1957); Wansbrough (1977).

figure, at least his actual history could not easily be rooted in that period. In fact even a cursory reading of the *Sīrah* gives the strong impression that one of the main reasons for writing it was to provide an external referent for the Qur᾿ān's obscure allusions, and vice versa, to create a History of the Prophet that would match the allusions in the Qur᾿ān.[31] For although the terms "the Prophet" and "the Messenger of God," alone or in combination, are all-pervasive in the Qur᾿ān, its central named religious figure is not Muḥammad, who is mentioned only four times,[32] but Moses. As Wansbrough points out, "the scriptural [i.e., Qur᾿ānic] material may be enlisted to support the particular position of Moses in the prophetical hierarchy, but hardly that of Muḥammad."[33] It is difficult to glean from the Qur᾿ān any historical or biographical information regarding him, in sharp contrast to the position of Moses in the Old Testament.[34] The biography has to be supplied separately, a task first undertaken by Ibn Isḥāq and his generation[35] and thereafter engaging the minds of generations of scholars. Wansbrough, again, puts his finger on the disparity:

> Unlike the Hexateuch, from which could be inferred at least the outlines of a historical portrait of Moses, the role of the Qur᾿ān in the delineation of an Arabian prophet was peripheral: evidence of divine communication but not report of its circumstances.... The very notion of biographical data in the Qur᾿ān depends upon exegetical principles derived from material external to the canon.[36]

The Qur᾿ānic account has two main features: the constant reference to an unnamed prophet, and a Judeo-Christian theological outlook.[37] If we examine the Qur᾿ān without prior acceptance of the Traditional Account, it is difficult to avoid the conclusion that the material collected in it is, or was originally, the work of some Judeo-Christian sect(s) who acknowledged a prophet, defined as the messenger of God, who had been sent to warn them of the dangers of unbelief and to guide the Community of the Faithful on

---

31. Cf. Wansbrough (1977), Ch. 2, esp. pp. 57ff.; pp. 121–29.

32. The four instances where the name or term Muḥammad occurs in the Qur᾿ān will be discussed later in this chapter.

33. Wansbrough (1977), p. 56.

34. Or indeed to that of any other prophet, including the Arab prophets of Q7.

35. See Hinds (1983), p. 60 for a list of early scholars (d. 154/770 to end of 8th century) to whom is attributed a work on *maġāzī*.

36. Wansbrough (1977), p. 56.

37. Cf. Part III Chapter 1, section titled, "Judeo-Christianity."

the right path (just as He had guided Abraham). That they referred to this prophet by title rather than name does not imply that he was a concept rather than a specific person; it may have been accepted terminology in a sectarian community.[38] This Judeo-Christian community whose beliefs were incorporated into the Arab Scripture may have existed in ʿAbd al-Malik's time. As noted in Part III Chapter 1 above, Adomnanis's *De Locis Sanctis* includes Arculf's account of a community of *Iudaei Christiani* that existed in Jerusalem at the time of his visit some time during the decade 59–69/679–88.[39] But we have no reason to suppose that they were either numerous or important. It is also possible that ʿAbd al-Malik adopted into the state religion, not the views of a community that currently existed (either in Jerusalem or elsewhere), but those in the writings of a sect which had existed in the past (probably in Jerusalem or Mesopotamia).[40]

The introduction of the Prophet into the state religion does not of course imply his immediate acceptance by the population. At least one peripheral community absorbed the Judeo-Christian theology without the prophet: the Basic Text inscriptions from Sede Boqer which define God as "Lord of Moses and Jesus" breathe not a word about a Messenger of God. As noted in Part III Chapter 1, Mohammedanism is attested in the desert popular inscriptions only from about the time of Hišām, some forty years after the Dome of the Rock inscription.

There are several possible reasons for this time gap. It could be that the Indeterminate Monotheists of Sede Boqer were stubborn adherents to the old creed, who resisted Mohammedanism for a generation before finally merging, in Hišām's reign, with the mainstream of accepted belief. One might also suggest that it simply took time for the new official faith of the state to percolate down from the élite to those who wrote the popular inscriptions. However, a creed only takes forty years to percolate down to the common people if the rulers of the state do not care whether or not they accept it. Similarly, adherents of the old form of belief can continue to proclaim their existence openly for forty years after the introduction of a

---

38. The Qumrān sect, for instance, also referred to their spiritual leader by title only—the Teacher of Righteousness (*mōreh ha-ṣedeq*)—which similarly does not mean that he did not exist in the flesh.

39. For this form of Adomnan's name and the date of his *De Locis Sanctis*, see Wilkinson (1977), pp. 9–10. Pines (1984), p. 145 argues for a date between 679 and 683 for the journey itself; Wilkinson will allow any date between 679 and 688; Hoyland (1977), pp. 220–21 prefers the 670s for the journey, and the early 680s for the writing of the report.

40. Cf. the discussion of Judeo-Christianity in Part III Chapter 1.

new one only if the state is not especially concerned to enforce the new faith on the population. If the state had been interested to spread Mohammedanism among the general population, it would have declared other forms of belief "heretical" and made Mohammedan formulae obligatory. Whether or not the people privately accepted the change, signed religious declarations which did not include such formulae would have ceased to be inscribed practically overnight. So a more exact formulation of the situation, in our view, is that the official declarations of faith on the coins and the Dome of the Rock inscription gave notice that Mohammedanism was now the official state religion, but the state was not initially concerned to promulgate it among the general population.

Whether or not ᶜAbd al-Malik's subjects accepted the official state religion, they would at least have understood the cryptic slogan *Muḥammad rasūl Allāh* in the Dome of the Rock, for prophecy was, as Wansbrough puts it, a "monotheistic constant," and any monotheist would be familiar with the idea of such a Messenger of God as a concept whose embodiment was an ever-present possibility. ᶜAbd al-Malik, in providing such an embodiment, added a sorely-needed component to the state religion. In the process he added one important contribution of his own: that the prophet was *muḥammad*. We do not state that *muḥammad* was, at this early stage, the prophet's name, for it is impossible to tell from the formula *muḥammad rasūl Allāh* whether the word *muḥammad* is in fact a name or an epithet. To understand this point, we must consider the word's etymology.

In terms of the Traditional Account, such a pursuit is superfluous. It has already been well established that *muḥammad* is a passive form of the root *ḥ.m.d.*, meaning "the praised one." But this meaning is part of the Muslim tradition and may be considered as another *tafsīr* of an accepted scriptural item; here as elsewhere, if we do not wish to accept uncritically the Traditional Account, we must begin again.

TO PRAISE

In the traditional Muslim lexicography, surveyed and summarized by Lane,[41] the root *ḥ.m.d.*, from which the Prophet's name is derived, is understood

41. Lane, *ḥ.m.d.*, p. 638 col. 3: "a praiseworthy quality" ... "a quality for which one is praised," ... "He praised, eulogized, or commended him, spoke well of him." ... "*Ḥamada* also implies admiration: and it implies the magnifying, or honouring, of the object thereof."

to generate words with the meaning 'praise.' But this lexicography is based on prior acceptance of the Traditional Account. It also accepts as axiomatic that Arabic preserves features of the earliest strata of 'Semitic,' and is therefore a treasure-house of proto-Semitic phenomena. Being, a priori, an exemplum, it is not subjected to the rigorous scrutiny and questioning which a language usually undergoes at the hands of modern Western linguistics. In contrast to this attitude, Wansbrough has pointed out that the activities of exegesis and polemics—which scarcely started before the 2nd/8th centuries—shaped religious thinking;[42] in the process, the semantic fields of the religious vocabulary were also defined. The works of Muslim Arabic lexicography, of which Lane is a prime example, record the results of this process, not, as the Traditional viewpoint asserts, the pristine meanings of *Ursemitisch*. To set the record straight is a vast undertaking, reserved for those better qualified than ourselves; but if we wish to understand the pre-Islamic meaning of the name Muḥammad, we must apply modern linguistic methods of analysis at least to this one root.

The concept 'praise' is not primarily expressed in Semitic languages by *ḥ.m.d.*, but by *s/š.b.ḥ.*, a root which developed relatively late, and seems to be Aramaic in origin.[43] It denotes the verbal expression of devotion: declaring the divinity's greatness, perfection, justice, etc. Thus Q.15:98: *fa-sabbiḥ ... rabbika wa-kun min-al-sājidīna* means: "but do praise your Lord's ... and prostrate yourself in prayer." Similarly, in Biblical Hebrew this root means 'to acknowledge as good,' either morally, aesthetically or materially, i.e., to praise.[44] It occurs mainly with reference to God, and the main emphasis is on verbal acknowledgment, so that it can also mean 'to tell, speak etc.' of His goodness, greatness, etc.—i.e., to eulogize, as in Ps. 145:4, where the idea of speaking is paralleled by all the verbs in verses 4–7. In fact the Hebrew root *š.b.ḥ.* provides words with the various meanings 'praise,' 'bless,' and 'thank.' Similarly, in Arabic one of the lexically recorded meanings for this root is 'to pray,'[45] and there is also the meaning

---

42. Wansbrough (1977) and (1978), passim.

43. There are a total of sixteen words derived from the root *š.b.ḥ.* in the Old Testament. Hebrew words derived from this root occur in the later books: Ecclesiastes (two occurrences), Psalms (7), Proverbs (1), and 1 Chronicles (1); the Aramaic form occurs in Daniel (two occurrences).

44. In Biblical Hebrew the root *š.b.ḥ.* also has the meaning 'to calm, to still,' as in Ps. 89:9 and 65:7 (Heb.: 65:8). But this is not the meaning which concerns us here.

45. Lane, *tasbīḥ*, p. 1289 col. 3 quoting Q.3:41 (Lane: 36); one could add Q.20:130 = 50:39; Q.15:98; etc. One may surmise that this meaning may be connected with the less

'invocation of God' or 'supplication' or the like.[46] One of the prominent words derived from *s.b.ḥ.* is *tasbīḥ*, which signifies the declaration that God is devoid of, or far removed from, every imperfection, impurity, or evil.[47]

Whereas *s/š.b.ḥ.* expresses the concept 'to praise' in Semitic languages, the semantic field of *ḥ.m.d.*, by contrast, is 'to desire, covet, wish to have or to acquire for oneself.' A thing desired is, by logical extension, praiseworthy, but in Arabic *ḥ.m.d.* crossed the semantic boundary between 'desired' and 'praised' only later, as part of the *tafsīr*. In the Old Testament the former meaning is clear:[48]

> [This is] the hill [which] God desireth to dwell in (*ḥāmad ʾElohīm l:šibtō*) (Ps. 68:16 [Heb. :17]).
> And they covet fields (*ḥām:dū šādōt*) and take [them] by violence (Mich. 2:2).
> Thou shalt not covet thy neighbor's house, thou shalt not covet thy neighbor's wife ... (*lo taḥmōd*) (Ex. 20:17).

Words from this root occur in the Old Testament thirty-nine times, distributed in books of all the literary types, from the Pentateuch to Chronicles. This argues for the lexical antiquity of *ḥ.m.d.*; and indeed the root is also attested in Ugaritic epigraphical records since the middle of the second millenium B.C.E.:

> Baᶜal verily covets (them) [*bᶜl · ḥmdm · yḥmdm*][49]
> [to] Syria (and) the choicest of its cedars [*bšryn · mḥmd · arzh*] [when they went to bring wood and cedar for Baᶜal's palace][50]
> the hills [will yield] the choicest gold [*gbᶜm · mḥmd · ḫrṣ*][51]

---

frequent meaning of Biblical Hebrew—'to calm down, soothe, still'—as applied to the divinity or to a man in a position of power and influence; to appease and/or enlist the aid of a potentially dangerous power by recounting his merits.

46. Lane, *subḥat-on*, p. 1290 col. 2.

47. Lane, *tasbīḥ*, p. 1289 col. 2 §2 to col. 3.

48. Even today in modern Hebrew, following the older Biblical usage, words derived from *ḥ.m.d.* indicate a strong wish to possess, a desire to gain or acquire something; therefore adjectives from this root have meanings such as 'beautiful,' 'aesthetically pleasing,' etc., but not 'praised.'

49. Gordon (1955), vol. 3, text 75:I:38. In all the examples given here, the English translation is from Gordon, pp. 54, 33.

50. Ibid., text 51:VI:19, 21.

51. Ibid., text 51:V:78, also 51:V:101.

In the Phoenician (El-Amarna) texts from the 14th century B.C.E., *ḥ.m.d.* in various forms has the meaning of "desire, take possession of a desired object; something valuable; jealousy, envy."[52] And Zadok records names with the root *ḥ.m.d.* in cuneiform texts from the second half of the first millenium B.C.E.: *Ḫa-ma-da-ᵓ*, *Ḫa-ma-da-a-ni*, which "are derivable from Ḥ-M-D, 'desire, take pleasure in,' in Aramaic and Canaanite."[53] Another name, apparently of the same etymology, is *Ḫa-am-mi-du-u* (=Xammidū), and he refers also to the Nabataean name *Ḥmydw* and the Arab names *Ḥamīd, Ḥumayd* in an undated document which, however, is of the same general date as the other names, i.e., 500 B.C.E. to the turn of the era.

Zadok also refers, on the other hand, to the names *Ḫa-am-me-da-nu* and *Ḫa-me-du-ni*, deriving them from 'praise' (Arabic). But he does not explain this etymology, and has confirmed to us that, reading these as typical Arab names, he derived them from the customarily accepted meaning of their root.[54] Similarly, the glossary in Gordon (1955) lists: "*ḥmd*: Ar. *ḥamuda*, ESA *ḥmd* = 'to praise'"; but provides for this entry neither explanation nor example. Finally, Akkadian supplies one other case where *ḥ.m.d.* does not mean 'desire': some texts contain *ḫamādu*, meaning 'to be evasive'[55] and *ḫamdātu*, meaning 'evasions.'[56] This however is a different root, corresponding to the Arabic *ġ.m.d.*,[57] meaning 'to cover, prevent from seeing.'

Were it only a question of the etymology of the Prophet's name, it would be doubtful if we should search so far and so wide. But the meaning of *ḥ.m.d.* is crucial to an understanding of the original nature of the Prophet, and also for the correct interpretation of important religious formulae, such as *lahū al ḥamdu* and *li-llahi al-ḥamdu,* and expressions combining *s.b.ḥ. and ḥ.m.d.* in the same phrase or sentence, such as *yusabbiḥ bi-ḥamdihi.*

THE CHOSEN ONE

If the above interpretation of the root *ḥ.m.d.* is correct, it follows that *muḥammad* means not 'the praised one' but 'the one desired (and so chosen)

52. Jean and Hoftijzer, *DIS*, vol. 1, p. 90, *ḫmd.*
53. Zadok (1977), p. 118.
54. Zadok, private communication, December 7, 1987.
55. *CAD*, Ḫ, p. 58 col. 1.
56. Ibid., p. 66 col. 1.
57. Soden (1958), *ḥamādum*, p. 315 col. 1.

by God' to be His messenger. The *Sīrah* transfers this act of divine selection to the name itself, and assigns it the related meaning 'protected, favored.'[58] Other verbs with similar meanings are also commonly used of prophets in the Qur'ānic material. Thus Q.19:58, referring to Abraham, Isaac, Jacob, Moses, Aaron, Ishmael and Idris (Enoch): "These are they to whom Allāh showed favor from among the prophets, whom We guided and chose" (*wa-miman hadaynā wa-'ijtabaynā*). Q.6:88, also with reference to a list of prophets, uses these same two roots: "we chose them (*j.b.w/y.*) and guided them (*h.d.à.*) to a straight way"; and the preceding verse, Q.6:87, includes the concept of showing favor: "and to all we gave favor (*f.d.l.*) above the nations." The root *ṣ.f.à.* is also used of choosing a prophet, as in Q.3:33: "Allāh chose Adam and Noah, and the family of Abraham ..."; and *al-Muṣṭafà*, 'the chosen one,' or *Muṣṭafahu*, 'His chosen one, the elect'[59] are accepted terms for the Prophet Muḥammad. Such an epithet seems to have been an expected term for a Messenger of God—e.g., 'the chosen vessel,' *al-'inā'u al-muṣṭafà* (in Christian Arabic = St. Paul);[60] the use of *al-Muṣṭafà* may well reflect the original meaning of the word *muḥammad.*

To sum up: the linguistic evidence indicates that the word *muḥammad* meant not 'praised' but 'desired.' As such, it was a valid Arabic name for a child, without any apparent religious meaning, long before the Mohammedan era. But the texts as we have them indicate that at some point it was adopted into religious jargon, with the meaning, we would suggest, of 'the man desired by God [as His messenger]'—or, as English might translate this concept, 'the Chosen One.' The first evidence we have for such a usage is the coin of 71/691 and the Dome of the Rock inscription of 72/692. The term *muḥammad*, like the term *al-muṣṭafà*, was thus not intended to refer to a specific person, but to describe an attribute of the Messenger of God, and especially in such a way as to contrast him with Pauline Christian theology—he is only a human being, not a Son of God nor in any way divine; he can be anyone God chooses. In the absence, so far as we know to date, of any prior use of the term *muḥammad* for this concept, we consider that it was introduced around the time of the interregnum between the reigns of Muᶜāwiyah and ᶜAbd al-Malik, and that the latter linked it to the Judeo-Christian prophet whom he adopted. But since the word *muḥammad*

58. *Sīrah,* pp. 157–58, 356; cf. Wansbrough (1978), p. 48.
59. Lane, *ṣ.f.w.*, p. 1704 col. 1.
60. *Al-Munjid* 429.3.

was also a valid name, (though not, until then, a very common one), it was soon perceived as the prophet's name rather than as an attribute describing him. This conversion of the term *muḥammad* from epithet to name could well have happened very quickly, helped on by the fact that the terse phrasing in the Dome of the Rock inscription allows this interpretation. John of Damascus, who wrote his *De Haeresibus*[61] ca. 125–133/743–750, before the ᶜAbbāsids came to power, knew that a good deal of Qur'ānic material was associated with a "leader" whose *name* was Muḥammad. The transition from epithet to name must therefore have been made during the first half of the 2nd/8th century.

As is well known, in the Qur'ān the word *muḥammad*, referring to the Prophet, occurs only four times. For comparison, *rasūl Allāh* in its various forms (*rasūl, rasūluhu, rusūl*, etc.) occurs no less than 300 times; *nabī* 43 times; *Ibrāhīm* 79 times; *Mūsà* 136 times; *Hārūn* (Aaron) 20 times; *ᶜĪsà* 24 times; *Maryam* 34 times; *Ādam* 25 times; *Nūḥ* 33; and *Firᶜawn* (Pharaoh) 74 times. Moreover, no personal information accompanies the four occurrences of the word *muḥammad*: no mention of his family, his pedigree, or even his deeds, so that it makes as much sense to read the word as an epithet, "the one chosen/desired (by God)," as to read it as a name. Muḥammad's anonymity contrasts strongly with the Qur'ān's emphasis on the kinship affiliation of prophets with the peoples to whom they were sent: "We sent Noah unto his people (*qawm*)" (Q.7:59)—and Noah specifically tells them: "Do you wonder that a message/word should come to you from one of your own men?" (*ᶜalà rajul-en minkum*) (Q.7:63). Similarly, "unto ᶜĀd—their brother (*'axāhum*) Hūd (Q.7:65) and "their brother (*'axāhum*) Ṣāliḥ unto Ṯamūd" (Q.7:73). We interpret Muḥammad's anonymity as a sign that three of the four references to him entered the scriptural material before the Prophet had been provided with a biography, and very probably before the term *muḥammad* had been interpreted as the Prophet's name; the fourth reference we consider to be more probably a later addition.

The first occurrence of *Muḥammad* in the Qur'ān, according to the canonized order of the *sūrahs*, is Q.3:144:

> Muḥammad is nothing but a messenger (*wa-Muḥammad-on 'illā rasūl-on*), messengers have passed away before him. And if he should die or be killed, would you turn away on your heels?

---

61. Discussed in Part III Chapter 2.

With this we may compare Q.5:75:

> *al-Masīḥ* the son of Maryam is nothing but a messenger, messengers have passed away before him; and his mother (was) a righteous woman (*ṣidīqah*) and both used to eat food.

Muḥammad and Jesus are both portrayed in the familiar subordinationist terms derived from Judeo-Christianity. But the main point to note is Muḥammad's anonymity, in contrast to Jesus who is linked to his family, both here and elsewhere in the Qurʾān. The sentence could equally well be translated "the Chosen One is nothing but a messenger" (and mortal, not part of the Divinity).

The term *Muḥammad* next occurs in Q.33:40:

> Muḥammad was not the father of any man among you, but he (was) Allāh's messenger and *xātam*[62] of the prophets.

And in Q.47:2:

> Those who believe (*āmanū*) and do the proper things (*al-ṣāliḥāt*) and trust in what was revealed to Muḥammad (*wa-āmanū bi-mā nuzzila ʿalà Muḥammad-en*) which is the Truth (given) by their Lord, their evil deeds will be covered (= forgiven) and their state will be improved (*wa-ʾaṣlaḥa bā-lahum*).

Again, "Muḥammad" is not linked here to a particular man, with a family, birthplace, tribe, etc. The word could equally well be an attribute: 'the Desired/Chosen One'—i.e., he whom God desired as His messenger.

The fourth and last Qurʾānic reference to Muḥammad is in Q.48, *al-Fatḥ*, a short *sūrah* whose twenty-nine verses are rich in suggestive locutions. We consider this *sūrah* to have entered the Qurʾānic material later than those discussed above, for the following reasons:

- It contains two "official" pronouncements: one introduced on coins in 77 A.H. (and which also occurs in two other places in the Qurʾān): *huwa arsala rasūlahu bi-l-hudà wa-dīn al-ḥaqq li-yuẓhirahu ʿalà al-dīn kullihi*: "He sent His messenger with guidance and the religion of truth, that he may cause it to prevail over all [other] religions" (Q.48:28); and the other, immediately following it, which was introduced on coins in 71 A.H.: *Muḥammad rasūl Allāh*: Muḥammad is the Messenger of God (Q.48:29).

---

62. The meaning of *xātam al-nabiyyin* is still a topic of scholarly debate.

This suggests that it was formulated in an "official" environment. The same section continues: *wa-ᵓallaḏīna maᶜahu ᵓašiddaᵓu ᶜalà al-kuffār ruḥamāᵓu baynahum*: "and those with him are hard against the unbelievers and love each other" (Q.48:29). We see this, too, as an official pronouncement regarding the behavior expected of believers: to love other believers and act with intransigence against unbelievers. This attitude was not typical of the official faith before al-Walīd, as we shall see in the next chapter. These considerations, then, date this *sūrah* to any time from the early 2nd/8th century on.

- It includes the only references in the whole Qurᵓān to Mecca (Q.48:24) and to the Arabians (*al-ᵓaᶜarab*) (Q.48:11). This indicates that it was formulated in different circumstances from most of the Qurᵓān; and these references date it, in our opinion, to the time during which the *Sīrah* was composed or later, i.e., mid- to late 2nd/8th century.

One cannot tell whether Muḥammad is here intended as a proper name or an epithet, but given the general tone of the proclamation, and the probable late date of this *sūrah*, we consider the former to be more likely.

POSTSCRIPT: *Ḥ.M.D.* IN THE QURᵓĀN

If we accept the argument in this chapter, that the roots *s.b.ḥ.* and *ḥ.m.d.* had in Arabic the meanings they had in the other Semitic languages, we can gain a fresh understanding of their role in the Qurᵓān. This hypothesis implies that

- *s.b.ḥ.* meant in Arabic, as in Aramaic and Hebrew, 'to praise, laud, eulogize,' and this meaning did not change throughout the period during which the texts comprising the Qurᵓān were composed.
- *ḥ.m.d.*, already in the earliest stratum of texts, meant 'desire, will' (corresponding to the Greek *thelema*), i.e., God's ability to desire a thing and thereby cause it to be: "Whenever He decides to have anything, He only says to it 'be' and it shall become true": *wa-ᵓiḏa qaḍà ᵓamr-an fa-ᵓinnamā yaqūl lahū kun fa-yakūn* (Q.2:117).

The idea expressed by *ḥamd* meaning 'will' (*thelema*) is that only God may will or desire, since only He has the ability (*qadr*) to accomplish His desires; by the mere exercise of His will He has power over everything and accomplishes whatever He wishes (Q.2:117, quoted above; 3:47; 40:68; etc.).

The concept is seen clearly in Q.64:1:

> All (ye) that are in the sky and on earth—praise Allāh (*yusabbiḥu li-llāhi*). His is the sovereignty (*lahū al-mulk*) and (only) He desires/wills (*lahū al-ḥamdu*)—He is omnipotent (*ᶜalà kulli šayᵓ-en qadīr*).

Similarly, the angels' response to Allāh's decision to create human beings on earth has much more point when we recognize the intended contrast between their praise of His will, and the result they fear from His use of it:

> They said: would You make in it [the earth] a thing which will corrupt it and shed blood while (wa-) we are praising your will (*wa-naḥnu nusabbiḥu bi-ḥamdika*) and sanctifying You (*wa-nuqaddisu laka*)? (Q.2:30).[63]

It is instructive to look at the doublets in verses containing the expression *lahū al-ḥamdu*, for instance:

> *lahū al-ḥamdu wa-lahū al-ḥukm* (Q28:80): His is the will and His is the judgment/government/authority.
>
> *lahū al-ḥamdu wa-huwa al-ḥakīm al-ḥabīr* (Q.34:1): His is the will and He is the Judge, the Cognizant.
>
> *lahū al-mulk wa-lahū al-ḥamdu wa-huwa ᶜalà kulli šayᵓ-en qadīr* (Q.64:1): To Him belongs the sovereignty, and His is the will, and He is the Omnipotent.

The most frequent doublet comes from the root *ġ.n.y.* (self-contained, affluent, rich), and the doublet *ġniyy-an ḥamīd-an* is, in context, revealing:

> To Allāh (belongs) what is in the heavens and what is on earth. And we commanded those who already received the Book before you, [as we command] you: fear Allāh, and if you would abandon belief (*takfurū*)—to Allāh belongs all that is in the heavens and on earth and Allāh is *ġaniyy-an ḥamīd-an*, affluent and able [i.e., He achieves whatever He wills] (Q.4:131).

The will of Providence implies the power to accomplish what He wills;

---

63. We would understand *wa-nuqaddisu laka* to mean repeating the formula "Holy, holy, holy" (compare *takbīr* meaning to repeat the formula *Allāh akbar*). The angels of Q.2:30 derive from the conceptual world of Is. 6:3: "And one [of the seraphim] cried unto another and said, Holy, holy, holy [is] the Lord of hosts: the whole earth is full of His glory."

thus it is maintained by His power and might, i.e., His ability (what Christianity called *dynamis*) and action (*energeia*). The declaration *lahū al-ḥamdu wa-huwa ʿalà kulli šayʾ-en qadīr* ("His is the will and He [alone] is the Omnipotent") is a "subordinationist" formula for the divine power and control over all. The point of the verse is to refute the Trinity and promulgate God's singleness, and the subordination of all Creation—which itself is the outcome of His action, (*energeia*, Ar. *xalq*)—to His will (*thelema*, Ar. *ḥamd*) and strength and ability (*dynamis*, Ar. *qudrah*). This is the translation into Arabic of the vocabulary of Christian intersectarian dispute,[64] used to support a Judeo-Christian position.

---

64. Wansbrough (1978), p. 105 points to the use of standard Qurʾānic phrases such as *ṣirāṭ mustaqīm* in the Christian Sinaitic manuscript as evidence that the Qurʾānic vocabulary was employed also by Christians, and Griffith (1985a) argues that initially, in the late 8th to 9th centuries C.E., Christian Arabic was borrowing from the Muslim vocabulary. As polemic continued, Christian Arabic diverged from the Muslim, resulting in the formation of two distinct sectarian idioms: Muslim Arabic and Christian Arabic.

4

The Official Faith: Mohammedanism and Walīd's *ʾIslām*

The Chosen Messenger did not step alone onto the religious stage of the Dome of the Rock. In ʿAbd al-Malik's public proclamation of the state religion, *Muḥammad rasūl Allāh* was accompanied by two other new religious formulae: the *Tawḥīd*, and the definition of Jesus as *rasūl Allāh wa ʿAbduhu*—God's messenger and servant/worshipper. These three phrases together form a Triple Confession of Faith defining the advent into the development of the Arab religion of that discrete, distinctive phase which we designate Mohammedanism. We may summarize these formulae as follows:

1a. The "basic" *Tawḥīd: lā ilah illā Allāh waḥdahu*: "there is no God except Allāh alone." This is a discrete formula, with a variant form of *Allāh lā ilah illā huwa*. Pines (1984) has shown that *lā ilah illā Allāh* and *lā ilah illā huwa* are translations into Arabic of slogans used in Judeo-Christian polemic during the previous centuries.[1]

1. A Greek form of the *Tawḥīd*, namely *heis estin ho theos kai plēn autou ouk estin theos*—"God is One, there is no God except Him"—occurs in the pseudo-Clementine *Homilies*, XVI:7, 9; cf. Pines (1984), pp. 141–42.

1b. The "full" *Tawḥīd*: the above with the additional *lā šarīk lahu*: "He has no *šarīk*."[2] This is a gloss or clarifying addition to the *Tawḥīd*.

2. *Muḥammad rasūl Allāh*. What at first seems to be a fuller form: *Muḥammad rasūl Allāh wa-ʿabduhu*, is in fact a gloss clarifying the essential formula, just as *lā šarīk lahu* is.

3. The definition of Jesus as "Your messenger and servant/worshipper"—*rasūluka wa-ʿabduka*; Muḥammad was designated *ʿabd Allāh wa-rasūluhu*.[3]

Apart from these basic formulae, two other locutions indicate a Mohammedan conceptual environment:

A. Q.112: "Say, Allāh is One, Allāh is indivisible,[4] He begets not, nor was He begotten, and there is none comparable to Him." This formula is also present in the Dome of the Rock.

B. Q.9:33 (=61:9 = 48:28): "He has sent His messenger with the guidance and the religion of truth, that he may cause it to prevail over all [other] religions." This formula is not in the Dome of the Rock.

None of the elements listed above occurs in Arab monotheistic inscriptions of the Sufyānī period. From the period prior to 71 A.H. we possess religious texts, such as supplications, and commemorative texts with some religious content, such as Muʿāwiyah's dam inscription near Ṭāʾif of 58 A.H. (678 C.E.),[5] or the similar text of ʿAbd al-ʿAzīz, ʿAbd al-Malik's younger brother and governor of Egypt, on a bridge at Fusṭāṭ in Egypt dated 69 A.H. (688–89 C.E.), as well as many dated coins. They exhibit the same traits of Indeterminate Monotheism as the popular desert inscriptions from the same period, and provide little evidence that any such thing as a state religion existed when they were written. Neither Muḥammad himself, nor any Mohammedan phrases or formulae, appear in any official pronouncement—document, inscription, or coin—dated

---

2. *Šarīk* is usually rendered "associate" or "companion," but in our opinion this misses an important connotation not easily translated. For a discussion of the term, see below.

3. Dome of the Rock inscription A:22.

4. See comments on *ṣamad* below.

5. Published in *RCEA,* 1 inscr. no. 8; Miles (1948), p. 102f.; Grohmann (1962), pp. 56–57, inscr. Z 68; included in the Appendix of Inscriptions.

prior to 71/691.[6] This is an *argumentum e silentio* of considerable weight. For the Negev inscriptions were simply personal declarations; but those on coins and royal inscriptions were a public declaration of official state views, and their wording was not casually decided. Both the political and religious content of such a coin or inscription had been vetted by the state and granted official approval. Issuing coins is an important symbolic function of any political entity, one which requires careful consideration of all its aspects—iconic and epigraphic, political, and religious. This is especially the case when the political entity is new. If a religious formula appears on a coin, its wording has been carefully considered and its message is intentional. The conclusion the evidence invites is that before 71/691 no Mohammedan religious message was intended, for there was no mention of Muḥammad himself, nor any Mohammedan expressions. In other words, the *official* Arab religious confession included neither Muḥammad nor Mohammedan formulae in its repertoire of set phrases at this time; it included only what we have called Indeterminate Monotheism. But after 71/691 and all through the Marwānid dynasty, it was official policy to include Mohammedan phrases wherever religious formulae were employed. Thus ᶜAbd al-ᶜAzīz's bridge inscription of 69 A.H., exhibiting only Indeterminate Monotheism, contrasts with the declaration he had affixed to the doors of all the churches in Egypt at some point after 70 A.H.:[7] "Muḥammad is the great messenger (*al rasūl al-kabīr*) who is God's, and Jesus too is the messenger of God. God does not beget and is not begotten."[8] We read this proclamation as ᶜAbd al-ᶜAzīz's implementation of his brother the caliph's decision to adopt Mohammedanism as the state religion.

Mohammedanism is thus a previously unattested Marwānid introduction, formed by the imposition of new religious concepts onto a preexisting stratum of belief. The Dome of the Rock inscription suggests that ᶜAbd al-Malik held, or adopted, Judeo-Christian beliefs. To these he added the Prophet; and the result became—almost overnight!—the State's *only* form of official religious declaration, to be used in many kinds of formal

6. The numismatic evidence was discussed in the previous chapter. Regarding milestones see n. 9 below.

7. It is recorded as having taken place during the patriarchate of Isaac of Rakoti, who became Coptic Patriarch of Egypt in 689/70.

8. Text in Hoyland (1997); from the Christian Arabic *History of the Patriarchs of the Coptic Church of Alexandria.*

documents and inscriptions: coins, milestone inscriptions, public royal proclamations, and papyri protocols. In short, the state decided to formulate and officially declare the adoption of a state religion which might hold its own against those already competing for its subjects' allegiance, and especially against Christianity, the creed of Byzantium. The Dome of the Rock inscription is especially interesting as the first extensive declaration of this new faith.

THE THEOLOGY OF THE DOME OF THE ROCK

Religiously as well as geographically, the Dome of the Rock is a landmark. It was constructed in accordance with a policy emphasizing the importance of Jerusalem as the center of the new religion. One sign of this policy is ᶜAbd al-Malik's new "pilgrimage route" from Damascus via Tiberias and the Jordan Valley to Jericho and Jerusalem, and thence westward to the coast, to link up at Emmaus and Jaffa with the ancient Sea Way, the main coastal route between Egypt and the north. Four milestones have been found on this route. The two east of Jerusalem count miles "from Damascus," the two west of it, "from Īliyā," i.e., Jerusalem.[9] And then in Jerusalem itself, ᶜAbd al-Malik built a religious monument, designed to equal the fame of the Byzantine churches and proclaim aloud the state religion.

The site he chose is highly significant: on the Temple Mount, over the Temple ruins, and enclosing within itself the rock on which, said tradition, Abraham was to have sacrificed Isaac. So far, the foundation is Judaic, though it is very possible that ᶜAbd al-Malik chose this site for its connection

---

9. Only the lower parts of the four milestones are intact; we cannot tell how many lines of inscription have been lost. The surviving portions bear a standard official text; a "composite" version is given in the Appendix of Inscriptions. The milestones' only religious note is the reference to ᶜAbd al-Malik as *ᶜAbdallāh*, "Servant of God" and *Amīr al-muminīn*, "Commander of the Faithful," with the additional exclamation "God's love be upon him." They are devoid of Mohammedan phrases. Complete milestones from this period—and, ideally, ones with an exact date, not just a reference to the reigning caliph—might tell us much about the inception of ᶜAbd al-Malik's Jerusalem policy, and the precise date of his adoption of Mohammedanism. But the milestones so far discovered could be either pre-71 A.H. and non-Mohammedan, or post-71 A.H. and originally bearing Mohammedan opening phrases which have broken off. They are therefore of little use as evidence for the introduction of Mohammedanism.

with Abrahamism rather than Judaism. Equally, both aspects may have played a role—a viewpoint in keeping with the Judeo-Christian theology of the inscription.[10]

What ʿAbd al-Malik constructed on this site was not a mosque; architecturally, the Dome of the Rock cannot be so classified. The building has clear affinities with Byzantine religious architecture, while its octagonal shape emphasizes that it faces equally in all directions and in none—indicating that its planners defined the direction of prayer as towards the site upon which it itself stood.[11] In structure, then, it is not Muslim; but it *is* a major religious monument. Clearly, within a few years of his assumption of power—essentially as soon as his control was assured—ʿAbd al-Malik had decided that there was a need for a state religion.

The theology of the Dome of the Rock inscription is no more Muslim than the building which houses it. It runs around both sides of the octagonal arcade—the outward-facing side, and the inner side facing the holy rock. Because of the differing content of these two parts, we refer to them as the "Allāh text" and the "Christological text" respectively.[12] We cannot tell how much of each was already formulated when the groundwork for the Dome of the Rock was started a few years before its completion. But the two texts do not seem to have been planned together, as a unified whole, for their content, literary structure and design differ considerably.

The Christological text (Text B in the Appendix of Inscriptions) is a contribution to the ongoing dispute between Pauline and non-Trinitarian forms of Christianity regarding the nature of Jesus and of God. It adopts the extreme subordinationist position of Judeo-Christianity: that Jesus was of wholly human nature, *rasūl Allāh wa-ʿabduhu*—Allāh's messenger and His

---

10. Van Ess (1992), p. 101 discusses a Jewish belief that God rested upon His throne on this rock after the work of the Creation, and left His footprint upon it when He returned to heaven; and the evidence that this belief was adopted by the local Arabs into the Syrian variant of the religion, and later roundly condemned by the Ḥijāzis as anthropomorphism. This, Van Ess suggests, may have been a factor in ʿAbd al-Malik's choice of site for a building obviously intended as a counterpoint to the Christian Church of the Ascension, on the floor of which was a footprint left from Christ's Ascension.

11. Cf. Busse's comment (Busse 1981): "Der Felsendom ... ist das Werk byzantinischer und syrischer Architekten.... Seine vier Türen öffnen sich nach den vier Himmelsrichtungen und weisen den heiligen Fels als den Mittelpunkt des Kosmos aus."

12. The text of the Dome of the Rock inscription is given, with translation, in the Appendix of Inscriptions.

servant/worshipper. It also emphasizes the unity of God and denies the Trinity, dismissing centuries of dispute with a terse "do not say three ... for Allāh is One."[13] This text reproduces written *pericopae* with diacritical points,[14] which with one exception are known to us also from the Qur'ān. We suggest that both its content and its actual form were already part of a preexisting written literature or set of locutions belonging to a sect with obvious Judeo-Christian beliefs.

The Allāh text (Text A) is designed differently from the Christological. It is divided into verses, each ending with a rosette; and it contains only one instance of diacritical points. Few of its verses occur in the Qur'ān, and those that do, all come from one brief *sūrah,* Q.112. It is the Allāh text that introduces Muḥammad as Allāh's messenger—he does not appear in the Christological text—and the verses that mention Muḥammad are not in the Qur'ān. It also defines Allāh's nature in anti-Trinitarian terms: He was not born and does not beget. And it introduces the concept *širk* with the phrase *la šarīk lahu.* We consider that, unlike the Christological text which was assembled from existing *pericopae*, the Allāh text was composed specifically for the Dome of the Rock, and from there parts of it found their way into the Qur'ān. But its adoption into the Qur'ān was selective—the locutions including the term *Muḥammad* were omitted.

The Dome of the Rock text contains a number of words which became key terms in Muslim theology: the *tawḥīd, šarīk, ṣamad,* and indeed *'islām,* which also appears here. We suggest that these are technical terms whose reference is the Christological dispute: the Dome of the Rock was a rebuttal, in the language of intersectarian dispute, of the Trinitarian Christian position. In order to take part in this dispute, the new creed needed to define the relevant concepts in Arabic. The existing religious terminology was too imprecise for this purpose, and needed to be refined.[15] Thus the *tawḥīd* was introduced, with the meaning of asserting God's Oneness, paralleling

---

13. Paraphrasing the Dome of the Rock inscription B:4–5.

14. The style of the diacritical points—which are wide, similar in shape to those produced by the stylus used for writing on papyri—may also hint that the text was copied from a written source.

15. Compare the relative poverty of Syriac religious vocabulary in earlier centuries, which led Ephrem (4th century) to denote the union of natures in Christ by the word *mzag* (= 'mix'), and Philoxenus (early 6th century) to regret such an imprecision, caused by the fact that "our Syriac tongue is not accustomed to use the precise terms that are in currency with the Greeks" (*CSCO*, 231:51; q.b. Brock [1984], V:20).

the Rabbinic Hebrew *yiḥūd*, 'singularity,' as in the morning prayer: *ᵓeḥād w:ᵓēin k:yiḥūdō*: "One and nothing is like His singularity," or in the expression *l:yaḥed š:mō*: "to insist on His [lit.: His Name's] singularity."

But this concept alone was not specific enough for intersectarian dispute. For the Christians also accepted God's "Oneness," and resolved conflict between this belief and the position of Jesus via the doctrine of the Trinity. Trinitarian Christianity professed God's singleness, but not His indivisibility. To combat this theological position, a further term was needed; and this, we consider, was the reason for introducing the word *šarīk*. In the Christological text ᶜAbd al-Malik attacked the Christian view of Jesus; in the Allāh text, the attribution to God of a composite nature, which he saw as equivalent to associating companions with God. The concept of *širk*, then, was an Arabic equivalent of the Greek *synthetos*—compounding the singleness of God—familiar from inter-Christian polemic:[16] Christians were "syntheists"—*mušrikūn* in the language of the Qurᵓān. The phrase *la šarīk lahu* was thus a contribution to an old and familiar intersectarian Christian quarrel.

A related term is the adjective *ṣamad*, applied to Allāh in the verses preserved as Q.112. Traditional Muslim scholarship has reached no consensus regarding the meaning of this word. We suggest a derivation from a Semitic root which appears in Akkadian as *ṣamādu*, meaning 'to connect, bind, harness together, etc.' (it had related meanings in Ugaritic); and in Hebrew as *ṣ.m.d.*, with meanings such as 'to grasp firmly, to be knit together.' In the Dome of the Rock it is connected with the definition of Allāh as One: *Qul, huwa Allāha aḥad Allāh al ṣamad.* We therefore consider that the term *ṣamad* was here used to convey the concept 'indivisible.'

The word *taslīm* (root *s.l.m.*, expressing concepts of wholeness and of concord) is in our view an attempt to translate into Arabic a Christian method of expressing one's belief. Whereas *tawḥīd* referred to the singleness of God, *taslīm* referred to the wholeness, or unity, or internal concord, of God's community: it was, we suggest, the translation into Arabic of the Christian concept of *pax*. We would thus understand *salimū taslīm* to refer to a custom akin to the Christian ceremony of pronouncing the *pax nobiscum*.

The Christological text (Text B) contains an important passage also preserved in the Qurᵓān.[17] B17–18 (Q.3:18) declares God's singularity;

---

16. Lampe (1961), p. 1329 col. 2 §C-Theology, D-Christology.
17. B17–22—Q.3:18–19.

B19–22 (Q.3:19) contains two terms, *dīn* and *ᵓislām*, and a commentary on those who do not follow Allāh's wishes regarding them:

> Lo! *dīn* with Allāh is *ᵓislām*. Those who received the Book differed only after knowledge came to them, through envy/their own willfulness. Whoever denies the signs of Allāh, behold, Allāh is swift at reckoning.

The cognate root *š.l.m.* in Hebrew conveys the meaning 'whole, undivided.' The derivative *mušlam* (lit: made whole) means 'completed, finished' and also 'perfect.' Lane records for *s.l.m.* the meanings 'safe, secure; absolutely free from any kind of evil' (i.e., perfect).[18] We suggest that the connotation 'perfect' is a derivation from the earlier meaning of 'whole, undivided,' as it is in the cognate Hebrew. We would thus understand *ᵓislām*, at this stage in the development of the religious vocabulary, as meaning 'unity' or perhaps 'concord.' *Dīn* is usually translated 'religion,' and this is indeed one of its meanings. But it has many others, including 'a system of usages or rites, a mode of conduct' and 'the regulation of affairs.'[19] We suggest that this was its meaning here: 'the correct way of behaving,' or 'the conduct of affairs' (i.e., of the community), even though the alternative meaning, 'faith' or 'religion,' would also make sense. We base this suggestion on the remaining text of this passage, which is obviously intended as explanatory commentary to the first sentence. For the point it criticizes is *the growth of dissension in the community*. Allāh desires His community to be whole, to be unified. This was His intention also on the previous occasions when He granted knowledge of the truth to man, but the recipients of that knowledge, instead of remaining in one unified community, dissented among themselves and thus incurred Allāh's displeasure. And those who continue to deny the signs that Allāh desires a unified community may expect their punishment to be swift.

A community, of course, is defined in religious terms; but the point of this verse is nonetheless political rather than religious as such. In the wake of the interregnum and the civil wars (*fitnah*), ᶜAbd al-Malik is here making a plea for an end to dissension, for the community to cease its quarrels. He presents this as the wish of God: Allāh desires His community to be united—to avoid the error of the Christians, forever squabbling among themselves! "*Dīn* with *Allāh* is *ᵓislām*" thus means "the communal conduct

---

18. Lane, 1:1412ff.
19. Lane, 3:944 col. 2–3.

that Allāh desires is concord (or unity)." There is much more point to this verse when so read, and a much stronger reason for including it in the Dome of the Rock. The traditional reading of the first sentence—that "Islam ('surrender') is the religion of Allāh"—makes the rest of the verse something of a non sequitur.

The Dome of the Rock inscription, then, had several purposes. It called for an end to dissension, and for the population to unite into one community under their caliph, now firmly in control after several years of civil war. As the reason and justification—and framework—for this communal consensus, it presented an official religion: a form of Judeo-Christianity, with particular emphases. To this end it took issue with, and rejected, the tenets of Trinitarian Christianity. And finally, it set within this framework an element which became the focal point of that religion—the Arab Prophet.

PROPHETHOOD AND GUIDANCE

As we saw in the previous chapter, Mohammedan formulae appeared first on Arab-Sassanian coins, starting in 71 A.H.[20] Until ʿAbd al-Malik's reform of the coinage in 77 A.H., both the Arab-Sassanian and Arab-Byzantine coins bore only the brief slogan *Muḥammad rasūl Allāh* and/or the brief *tawḥīd* and the *basmalah*. After ʿAbd al-Malik's reform, from 77 A.H. on, the gold dinars minted in the East bore an extended formula composed of several parts, as follows:

1. The *Tawḥīd—lā ilah illā Allāh waḥdahu*—"There is no God but Allāh alone."
2. The addition *lā šarīk lahu*—"He has no companion."
3. *Muḥammad rasūl Allāh*
4. *Arsalahu bi-l-hudà wa-dīn al-ḥaqq*—"He sent him with the guidance and the religion of truth"
5. *Li-yuẓhirahu alà al-dīn kullihi*—"that he may cause it to prevail over all [other] religions."[21]

20. As discussed in the previous chapter, there is one coin dated 72 A.H. where the Arabic text is Indeterminate Monotheist, but the basic *tawḥīd* appears together with the phrase "Muḥammad is the Messenger of God" in Persian (not Arabic) on the reverse.

21. Walker (1956), pp. lv–lix.

All these elements have already been mentioned as standard Mohammedan formulae, and all but one were already included in the Dome of the Rock inscription. The exception is no. 4–5, a formula preserved in three different places in the Qur᾽ān—9:33, 61:9, and 48:28—but which does not occur in ᶜAbd al-Malik's inscription in the Dome of the Rock. It introduces the concept of *hudà*—'guidance.' It is worth noting that between 90 A.H., when gold dinars started to be minted in the West (North Africa and Spain), and 114 A.H., the Western form of this legend was more moderate, omitting parts 2 and 5;[22] after ca. 114 A.H. the Western coins adopted the Eastern legend. But the key phrase "He sent him with the guidance" occurs in both the Western and Eastern forms of the legend.

The concept of guidance from God—i.e., the idea that God sends a messenger to convey His precepts to His chosen community, and to guide them on the right path—was of course a part of the Judaic and Christian background. To judge from the locutions that found their way into the Qur᾽ān, it figured prominently in the Judeo-Christian concept of the role of a prophet. ᶜAbd al-Malik's opponent al-Muxtār seems to have drawn upon this or a related concept of an agent sent with guidance from God, for political ends, during the Kufan revolt in the first years of ᶜAbd al-Malik's reign. He used the name, and claimed—probably without justification—the support of Muḥammad bn al-Ḥanafiyyah, a son of ᶜAlī, in an attempt to raise followers for himself among the ᶜAlids. The point of interest for the present discussion is his claim that Muḥammad bn al-Ḥanafiyyah was the *Mahdī*. We cannot be sure what exactly al-Muxtār and his contemporaries understood by this word, but in later years, after the concept of the Prophet had become well defined, the *Mahdī* was an embodiment of the concept of guidance: one sent by God to guide the faithful in the way of truth. At the time of the Kufan opposition to ᶜAbd al-Malik, however, it could well have had prophetical overtones. Moreover, al-Muxtār's war cry invoked "*Ya Manṣūr*,"[23] i.e., "one aided or assisted [by God], especially against an enemy."[24] As a slogan, this proclaimed that al-Muxtār himself, and/or the *Mahdī*, i.e., Muḥammad bn al-Ḥanafiyyah, was favored by God.[25] Al-

22. Ibid., p. lvii.
23. Dixon (1971), p. 44 + n. 91, 92.
24. Lane, 8:2803, col. 3.
25. Dixon (1971), p. 44 considers this war cry to be an invocation of a Yemenite Messiah, designed to encourage Yemenite support for the rebellion. In our opinion this was probably a side issue.

Muxtār was thus inviting the attachment of both these concepts, *al-Mahdī* and *al-Manṣūr*, onto the person of Muḥammad bn al-Ḥanafiyyah: here was the man sent by God to guide the faithful, and the one enjoying God's aid against all enemies.

But al-Muxtār was defeated, and it was ᶜAbd al-Malik who finally took firm control of the empire; wherupon he introduced his own version of God's messenger to His community. ᶜAbd al-Malik did not adopt al-Muxtār's term *al-Mahdī*; but after he had added to the concept of God's Chosen Messenger the idea of guidance—first attested in the official religion, as noted, in 77 A.H.—the result approximated the concept of a Guide of the Community favored by God. And this function of conveying God's guidance to the faithful, as Wansbrough has already noted, became Muḥammad's role in Islamic salvation history.[26]

The official religion became that of the Prophet introduced by ᶜAbd al-Malik. But the ᶜAlid faction appears to have preserved the remembrance of the claims regarding Muḥammad bn al-Ḥanafiyyah; and when, in late Marwānid or early ᶜAbbāsid times, the composers of the Traditional Account needed biographical details to flesh out their Ḥijāzī Prophet, it was to Muḥammad bn al-Ḥanafiyyah that they turned. Bashear (1984) has shown that many of the events of the Prophet's life are retrojections of events of Muḥammad bn al-Ḥanafiyyah's life in the Ḥijāz. He was, after all, a pertinent figure to serve as an ᶜAbbāsid model for the Prophet: a son of ᶜAlī, a leader in the Ḥijāz, proclaimed as the *Mahdī* (even if this were, as the story goes, without his consent). Even his name was right—assuming it was in fact his personal name, not a title bestowed on him by his supporters. It is very difficult to ascertain whether Muḥammad bn al-Ḥanafiyyah's link with the ᶜAlids is fact or fiction—for instance, his name refers to his mother, and there is some dispute in the texts as to who and what she was, too. But after al-Muxtār had publicized the link for propaganda purposes, it mattered little whether it was real or imagined: by ᶜAbbāsid times it was a "fact" that could be built on. For the ᶜAbbāsids, Muḥammad bn al-Ḥanafiyyah was as near to the ideal figure for the prophetic role as they could hope to find. Bashear hints that Muḥammad bn al-Ḥanafiyyah "was" the Prophet Muḥammad, but we consider that this is probably too far-reaching a conclusion. There is little evidence that ᶜAbd al-Malik meant Muḥammad bn al-Ḥanafiyyah when he inscribed *muḥammad rasūl Allāh* in the Dome of the Rock, and it is not

26. Wansbrough (1977), p. 48.

inherently too likely that he would center the new state religion around an ᶜAlid. One could conceivably argue, in view of Muḥammad bn al-Ḥanafiyyah's studious avoidance of politics for as long as possible, and his repeated refusal to give his clear support to any side, that ᶜAbd al-Malik was making a grand bid for his support and the consequent chance to win the allegiance of the ᶜAlid faction. We, however, consider that events from the life of Muḥammad bn al-Ḥanafiyyah were only used at a later date to anchor the Prophet in history.

The concept of guidance had one more metamorphosis to undergo. The *Sīrah* gives a version of John 15:23–16:1 containing a reference to the Paraclete, which is then interpreted as a prophecy of Muḥammad's coming:

> But when the Comforter [*al-munḥamanna*] has come whom God will send to you from the Lord's presence, and the spirit of truth[27]... The *Munaḥḥemana* [*sic* Guillaume[28]] in Syriac is Muḥammad; in Greek he is the paraclete (*al-baraqlīṭs*), God bless and preserve him![29]

As Guillaume[30] and more recently Griffith[31] have pointed out, the term *Munaḥemana* for the Paraclete is found only in the Palestinian Syriac Lectionary, and means 'the comforter.' Ibn Isḥāq adds the information that the Syriac term *Munaḥemana* and the corresponding Greek term *parakletos* mean *Muḥammad.* In other words, all three, says the *Sīrah*, are terms in different languages for the same concept. The point of Ibn Isḥāq's comment is that the Paraclete foretold by the Christian scriptures is Muḥammad—he is the one whom God promised to send, who "will guide you into all truth":[32] the agent of God, whose function is to convey God's guidance to His religious community.

---

27. In the *Sīrah* this is *ruḥ al-qudus*, the Holy Spirit; but a variant is mentioned, *ruḥ al-qisṭ*, "spirit of truth" (*Sīrah* i:233 n. 4). Cf. Griffith (1985a), p. 139 + n. 44.

28. Guillaume (1955) uses the Syriac vocalization; in the *Sīrah* of course the vocalization is Arabic: *Munḥamanna.*

29. *Sīrah* i:233 = Guillaume (1955), p. 104. Guillaume transfers the benediction to follow "the *Munaḥḥemana*"; we have returned it to its place in the Arabic, at the end, following the term in all three languages, Arabic, Syriac, and Greek.

30. Guillaume (1955), p. 104 n. 1.

31. Griffith (1985a), p. 141.

32. John 16:13.

This is a hitherto unfamiliar use of the guidance concept. It is not employed, as in the Mohammedan formula "He sent him with the guidance and the religion of truth," simply to define Muḥammad's role within the new faith. It is, rather, an argument aimed at the Christian community. It suggests that at some unknown point in time between ʿAbd al-Malik's introduction of Muḥammad and the composition of the *Sīrah*, the new religious community tried to attract Christians by proclaiming that the Chosen Prophet had been foretold in the Gospel as the Paraclete. This view cannot be shown to have been *officially* adopted: it does not appear in any royal proclamation, nor in the canon of the Qurʾān. Possibly it circulated mainly in religious circles, among those approaching the Christians. When it did so, we cannot say, but two periods seem possible. The earlier is the time when the state was trying to win the Arab Christians over to the new religion. This suggests the reign of ʿAbd al-Malik, for with Walīd the state became intent on demonstrating that it was independent of the Christians and did not need them either religiously or politically. After Walīd it was clear that they no longer ran the state and did not need to be taken into account. The later period is the time when Muslim-Christian polemic arose: the equation of Muḥammad with the Paraclete would then have been part of the Muslim attempts to prove that Muḥammad was foretold in the Old and New Testaments, that the Christians had falsified Scripture, and so on. This would mean the late Marwānid or early ʿAbbāsid period, i.e., that the equation of Muḥammad with the Paraclete did not long precede its recording in the *Sīrah*.

In any case, this equation did enter the *Sīrah*, whence it influenced the whole Muslim tradition and became a staple of intersectarian polemic. Thus the letter purporting to be from the Byzantine Emperor Leo to Caliph ʿUmar, discussed in Part II Chapter 4, finds it necessary to refute the claim that the Paraclete was a prophecy regarding Muḥammad.[33] A refutation is found, too, in Timothy's *Apology* before al-Mahdī, and as Jeffery notes, "Almost every polemical writing in this field contains some account of the matter."[34]

33. Jeffery (1944), p. 293. The date of this letter is a subject of much dispute. In our discussion in Part III Chapter 2 we suggest that it is at least thirty years later than its purported date of 717–720 C.E., i.e., not before the mid-2nd/8th century.

34. Ibid., p. 293 n. 43.

PROTOCOLS AND LETTERS: PUBLIC DECLARATION, PRIVATE BELIEF

The papyri protocols and official inscriptions commemorating public works provide further evidence for religious development. They are much more matter-of-fact in their use of Mohammedan formulae, as one would expect of texts whose main purpose is not religious, but which are merely complying with state policy regarding the phrasing of the obligatory religious formulae.

A papyrus protocol was the identification written at the head of a papyrus roll at the factory. Its nature was obviously bureaucratic—to record when the roll was produced, by command of what official working for which caliph. There are no Arabic protocols from the Sufyānid period. The earliest are from the reign of ᶜAbd al-Malik and are not dated more precisely. The first surviving protocol with an exact date comes from 88 A.H.—Walīd's reign. Many, though not all, of the Marwānid protocols are bilingual, which reminds us that much of the papyrus manufactured was intended for export, and that even within the Arab realm, Arabic was only now replacing Greek as the official chancery language, and was perhaps not yet universally understood.

A papyrus protocol usually included a religious preamble, often quite lengthy. Balāḏurī noted that ᶜAbd al-Malik was the first caliph to use Islamic (i.e., Mohammedan) phrases in it, and that previously, Christian(!) formulae had been used.[35] This information is of great interest, since as stated no pre-Mohammedan Arab protocols have survived.

Typical examples of protocol texts follow. All are bilingual; our translation is from the Arabic.

1. From ᶜAbd al-Malik's reign, otherwise undated.[36]
   In the name of Allāh, the Compassionate, the Merciful,
   There is no God but Allāh alone.
   Muḥammad [is the] messenger of Allāh.

   The information concerning production of the roll of papyrus was given only in Greek.

35. Abbott (1938), p. 21 + n. 108.
36. Source: Grohmann (1924) vol. 1 pt. 2, p. xxxvii.

2. From 89/707 (Walīd).[37]
   In the name of Allāh, the Compassionate, the Merciful,
   There is no God but Allāh alone.
   Muḥammad [is the] messenger of Allāh.
   This is what the *ᵓamīr* [personal name] has ordained, may God keep him in good health.

3. From 98/716–17 (ᶜUmar II).[38]
   In the name of Allāh, the Compassionate, the Merciful,
   There is no God but Allāh alone; He has no *šarīk*.
   He did not beget and was not begotten, and nobody is like unto Him.
   Muḥammad [is the] messenger of God. He sent him with the guidance and the religion of truth.
   [This is] of [personal name], Servant of God, Commander of the Faithful.
   This is what the *ᵓamīr* [personal name] has ordained
   In the year ____
   Manufactured by order of [personal name].

The earliest surviving protocol that contains the "guidance" formula is dated 86 A.H., the first year of Walīd's reign. As discussed above, we consider that the appearance of this concept on the coins from 77 A.H.[39] marks its introduction into the official faith; we would therefore tentatively suggest that the very few protocols that have survived from ᶜAbd al-Malik's reign are pre-77 A.H. Since they do contain the basic Mohammedan formula, they must in this case be from the period 71–77 A.H. Another possibility, of course, is that ᶜAbd al-Malik was content to use the coins alone to publish his newest religious message; only in Walīd's time did anyone think—or feel the need—to use the protocols also to this end.

Especially interesting is the case of Qurrah bn Šarīk, governor of Egypt during the years 90–96/709–714. In the protocols which his subordinates inscribed on his behalf, the Mohammedan formulae appear in full. But some of his letters to Copts and Arabs under his jurisdiction also survive,[40] and

37. Source: ibid., p. xxxvi.
38. Source: ibid., pp. xlviii–xlix.
39. Walker (1956), pp. 84ff., nos. 186ff.
40. For the Arabic texts of Qurrah's papyri, see Becker (1911); Abbott (1938); Ragib (1981). For the Greek with an English translation, see Bell (1911–1913).

they never employ Mohammedan formulae. They do contain phrases indicating a strict monotheism with roots in the Judeo-Christian background. One is that version of the *tawḥīd* which Pines has shown to have arisen in Judeo-Christian polemic: *naḥmid Allāh alladī lā ilah illā huwa*: "We praise Allāh, there is no God but He."[41] The other is his normal closing formula to non-Arabs:[42] "Allāh is with him who follows the Guidance." Apart from these two expressions, Qurrah's letters contain only general religious phrases which had become part of the everyday language: "if God wills," "by God's command," "with God's help," "we hope in God," "with the fear of God," "we give thanks to God," and so on. Muḥammad is never mentioned. This suggests that at this time a clear distinction was made between official public pronouncements embodying the caliph's authority, and private belief. The protocols were public pronouncements in the same sense as a milestone inscription or that of the Dome of the Rock: anyone who bought a roll of papyrus would read them and accept their contents as the official view of the Arab State. But this obviously was not true of everything written. Chancery documents continued to be very meager in religious expressions of any kind. And letters—even those written by an administrator's scribes in his official capacity—were apparently considered private documents. As such, they were not required to express the official state religion, nor indeed any religious belief beyond what their writer himself felt moved to include. Qurrah's letters reveal that he was not, apparently, a Mohammedan. Similarly, no Mohammedan phrases or references to Muḥammad appear in the desert rock inscriptions—which reflect the popular belief—of the Sufyānid or early Marwānid periods. They start to appear only in Hišām's reign, forty years after ᶜAbd al-Malik's declaration of Mohammedanism as the official creed in the Dome of the Rock. Of course many members of the élite would have adopted Mohammedanism; but the case of Qurrah bn Šarīk suggests that those who did not were not prohibited from high office, provided they allowed Mohammedan formulae to be used where state policy required them.

To sum up: the formal Mohammedanism of official proclamations, including papyri protocols, contrasts with the non-Mohammedan nature of the desert rock inscriptions, the undefined monotheism of Qurrah bn Šarīk's

41. Cf. The discussion at the beginning of this chapter. Examples: Abbott (1938), pp. 47–48, no. 13756; pp. 42–43, no. 13757.

42. Abbott (1938), p. 40.

letters, and the religious content of contemporary chancery documents in general. This suggests that it took thirty or forty years from the time Mohammedanism was proclaimed the state religion, until it gained acceptance as the belief of the general population. Firm evidence for such acceptance appears only in Hišām's reign. As we suggested earlier, a probable reason for this was state indifference to the form of private belief held by the general population, as distinct from great state concern to define an official state religion.

PUBLIC INSCRIPTIONS

Apart from the Dome of the Rock inscription and other royal proclamations with primarily religious content, ᶜAbd al-Malik and later caliphs left on-site inscriptions commemorating public works. From ᶜAbd al-Malik's reign comes the *ᶜAqabah* (i.e., "winding road") inscription, so called because it concerns improvements made to a mountain road.[43] It was originally dated, but part of the date has broken off, leaving only the final word "three." Possible years of ᶜAbd al-Malik's reign are 73/692–93 or 83/702–703. As we would expect in a public declaration from either of these dates, the religious formulae are standard Mohammedan. We suspect that the date was 73, not 83, because the locution "He sent him with the guidance ..." (Q.9:33), adopted into the official faith in 77, is absent from it. We translate the full text as follows:

1–4: In the name of Allāh the Compassionate, the Merciful; there is no God but Allāh alone, He has no *šarīk*. Muḥammad [is the] messenger of Allāh.

4–9: ᶜAbd Allāh [=Servant of God] ᶜAbd al-Malik, *ʾAmīr al-Muʾminīn* [= Commander of the Faithful] ordered the straightening of this mountain road. It was made by Yaḥya b. al-___ in the month of Muḥarram of the year three [and seventy *or* and eighty].

With this we may contrast what were considered, in the pre-Mohammedan era, to be suitable religious phrases for a royal proclamation

43. DKI 176, publ. in Sharon (1966); the Arabic is given (with translation) in the Appendix of Inscriptions.

on a large construction. The first is Muᵓāwiyah's inscription on the Saysad dam near Ṭāᵓif, dated 58/678:[44]

1–3: This is the dam [belonging] to ᶜAbd Allāh [=the Servant of God] Muᶜāwiyah, *ᵓAmīr al-Muᵓminīn* [=Commander of the Faithful]. Abdallāh b. Ṣaxr built it with God's permission in the year 58.

4–6: Allāh! forgive the Servant of God, Muᶜāwiyah, *ᵓAmīr al-Muᵓminīn*. Confirm him in his position and help him, and let the faithful rejoice in him. ᶜAmr b. Janāb wrote it.

The second comes from an arch of a bridge over the great canal at Fusṭāṭ, Egypt, and is dated 69/688. The bridge was built by order of ᶜAbd al-Malik's brother, ᶜAbd al-ᶜAzīz:

This is the arch which ᶜAbd al-ᶜAzīz b. Marwān, the ᵓAmīr, ordered to be built. Allāh! Bless him in all his deeds, confirm his authority as You please, and make him greatly satisfied in himself and his household, amen! Saᶜd Abū Uṯmān built it and ᶜAbd al-Raḥmān wrote it in the month Ṣafar of the year 69.[45]

The Fusṭāṭ inscription predates the Dome of the Rock by only three years and the Mohammedan coin of 71 A.H. by only two, yet it is clearly non-Mohammedan. It bears a strong family resemblance to Muᶜāwiyah's inscription in layout and even phrasing: there is no *basmalah*; the information as to who ordered the construction work comes first, the supplication to Allāh in the middle, the scribe/engraver adds his name at the end. In both cases, the supplication includes a request for divine support of the emir's or caliph's temporal authority. Muᶜāwiyah's inscription is more obviously Indeterminate Monotheist, in that it asks God to forgive him, but both are clearly of the same genre. The ᶜAqabah inscription, like all since, continues to use the originally general titles *ᶜAbd Allāh* and *ᵓAmīr al-Muᵓminīn*, which occur also in the Indeterminate Monotheist texts; but otherwise it inhabits a different conceptual universe: that of the Dome of the Rock. In 69 A.H. the state religion evidenced in the Fusṭāṭ inscription was non-Mohammedan; it essentially differed little from that of Muᶜāwiyah and of the pre-Mohammedan inscriptions. In 71 A.H. it was

44. Our translation from the Arabic. Also given, with Arabic, in the Appendix of Inscriptions.

45. Source: *RCEA*, 1 (1931), inscr. no. 8; also given, with Arabic, in the Appendix of Inscriptions.

Mohammedan, and the ᶜAqabah text, which may be as early as 73 A.H., is an example of the standard Mohammedanism so pervasive in state pronouncements after 71 A.H., and so absent from them before that date.

Finally, one other aspect considered typical of Islam requires a comment: its hostility to the Cross. This, too, developed only with the introduction of Mohammedanism, and in our opinion derives from the Judeo-Christian foundation of the new creed.

THE ATTITUDE TO THE CROSS

The Byzantine cross *potens* precedes and ends the *Greek* text of bilingual chancery documents dating from Muᶜāwiyah's governorship and caliphate.[46] As is often noted, this use of the cross is a Byzantine chancery convention, and does not indicate Arab acceptance of it as a religious symbol. But, we would add, it does show that in Muᶜāwiyah's time no repugnance was officially felt for the cross, so that its use as a symbol was not actively prohibited. This fits well the chronology of the rock inscriptions established on literary and archaeological grounds: the Basic Text inscriptions, which reflect Indeterminate Monotheism, are the earliest, and start in Muᶜāwiyah's time. There was indeed no reason why Indeterminate Monotheists should actively object to the sign of the cross.

The same situation is reflected in the coins. The earliest Arab-Byzantine copper coins, the Precursors, which we see as dating from the 10s/30s and early 20s/640s,[47] include crosses with no defacement.[48] The main sequence of pre-Mohammedan Arab-Byzantine coins similarly includes many examples where no defacement of the cross was considered necessary.[49] These coins span Muᶜāwiyah's governorship and caliphate, ca. 20s–60s/640s–680s. We interpret this nonobjection to crosses on coins of the early Arab State as indicating either the continued recognition of Byzantine authority[50] or no objection to Christianity—probably both.

On the later pre-Mohammedan coins, this attitude to the cross already

---

46. Including the earliest, that prototypical example so often referred to here, PERF 558 of 22/643; and those in the Nessana papyri. Cf. Colt III: 60ff.
47. See Part II Chapter 3.
48. Grierson (1982), p. 145 + plate 34 nos. 612–14.
49. Ibid., pp. 145–46 + plate 34 nos. 617–20.
50. See Part III Chapter 2 on the political aspects of the Arab religion.

began to change. The pre-Mohammedan inscriptions of Sede Boqer show that starting around the 70s A.H., Judeo-Christian beliefs colored Indeterminate Monotheism, at least that of the Sede Boqer texts; and ᶜAbd al-Malik promulgated Judeo-Christian beliefs soon after consolidating his control. There is some evidence that an avoidance of the cross became part of official state policy even before Mohammedanism was formally introduced: there are some pre-Mohammedan coins on which the cross has been defaced. In one highly interesting issue[51] the obverse figure holds in its right hand—where the cruciform globus would be on a Byzantine coin—a symbol resembling a cross whose side arms have been bent upwards to form a Y-shape, the whole symbol resembling a Y-shaped three-pronged trident: ᛘ. The bottom of the figure is obliterated, so that one cannot tell if it was originally a globus. The prototypical cruciform scepter in the figure's left hand has been replaced by a staff resembling a shepherd's crook. On the reverse is a cursive m, and above it, where the cross should be, is the same trident-like symbol ᛘ. It looks as if here the cross was deformed by bending its side-arms. This is the only issue we have found where such a change was made. But it is notable that the standard decoration on the crown of the obverse figure(s) of Arab coins—what Walker calls a "triple ornament"—is a variant of this symbol, without the lower shaft: ѱ; and it fills the space occupied on the Byzantine prototypes by a cross above the crown(s).[52]

Another way of deforming the cross was to turn it into a T-shape, or to replace it with a different symbol entirely. These methods became common especially with the advent of the Mohammedan coins, i.e., those bearing Mohammedan legends. These are of two main types:

1. **Byzantine iconography:** an undated issue depicting on the obverse three standing figures holding wands, and on the reverse, a modified version of the Byzantine "cross on steps" (to be described below). The Byzantine prototype is "Heraclius and his sons," and in it the wands bear crosses—as of course does the reverse. Crosses do not remain anywhere on the Mohammedan version. The crosses on the wands were either omitted altogether, or replaced by a pellet (small ball). The cross of the "cross on steps" was either deformed into a T shape, or replaced by a pellet. Grierson (1982) dates the "three standing figures" issue to

51. Walker (1956), nos. 139, 152 and plate IX.
52. Ibid., plate X, most of the coins on that plate.

ca. 71–72/691, and regards it as experimental, the first stage towards ʿAbd al-Malik's reform.

2. **The "Caliph" types:** two variants may be distinguished:
   a. **The "Twin Caliphs" type:** coins depicting on the obverse two richly dressed standing figures. The reverse is an uncial M.
   b. **The "Standing Caliph" type:** coins depicting on the obverse a standing figure in magnificent dress wearing a sword. The reverse is either a cursive m, or a modified "Cross on Steps." This type continued later than the "Twin Caliphs" type, and probably also started a little later than it. All the "Standing Caliph" issues are dated 74–77/693–97.

The "Cross on Steps" was the normal reverse design of the Byzantine solidus. It consisted of three or four "steps" surmounted by a cross *potens*: ☩. By the 7th century C.E., the vertical arm of the cross had lengthened, so that it could be described as a cross on a pole. In the version on the Mohammedan coins the cross was deformed to a T or replaced by a circular object. On North African coins, the T-shape was more common. The forms I (implying removal of the two side arms of the original cross *potens*) and T (implying removal of the top arm) are both found.[53] On Šāmī coins, replacement by a circular object became the norm. This object was sometimes a round pellet, i.e., a small sphere; and sometimes it was a circle which formed, together with the pole, a symbol resembling the Greek letter φ (which however it clearly is not). It has been described as a pillar or scepter, and Grierson suggests that "it may represent nothing at all, since its main function was negative, that of not being a cross."[54] This seems to us unlikely, given the political nature of the act of issuing a new coin, and the importance attached to its iconography. It is much more likely that the cross was not simply obliterated, but replaced by a new symbol of some political or religious significance, whose exact meaning and derivation we do not know.[55] The pellet was a frequent symbol on Byzantine coinage, used at the ends of the side arms of the cross *potens*, for instance, or at the top of the

53. Ibid., plate X.
54. Grierson (1961), p. 244 n. 3.
55. It is worth noting that the crescent and star is a Sassanian religious symbol, which was also eventually replaced on coins, in a Mohammedan context, by a pellet or a small circle with a pellet in its center.

scepter;[56] and a symbol which may variously be regarded as a small globus or a large pellet could be inserted between the cross and the steps of the Byzantine "cross on steps."[57] It is also interesting that the symbols φ, ф, and ♁ for ф (on coins dated 674–681 C.E. = 54–62 A.H.) occur on Italian solidi, tremisses, and nummia of Constantine IV and Justinian II (668–695 C.E. = 48–76 A.H.).[58] It is thus possible that the symbol chosen to replace the cross—basically a circle or sphere—was one which already bore, for the Byzantines too, a meaning somehow connected with holiness. One may speculate that it was a visual expression of the unity, wholeness, and all-embracing nature of God.

Whether or not this was so, the pre-Reform Mohammedan coinage marks visually the development from the Sufyānid initial indifference to, and later avoidance of, specifically Christian formulae, to the Marwānid rejection of them, in order to assert a form of religion specific to the Arab polity. The sign of the cross became a target for disfigurement and later replacement with the symbol φ. The reform of the coinage marks the climax of this process of independence.[59]

The evidence amassed so far, then, indicates that it was only shortly before Mohammedan legends were first introduced that any objection was felt to the presence of crosses on official state coins; and that this happened approximately when ʿAbd al-Malik came to power. But after 72/691–92 and all through the Marwānid dynasty, crosses were no longer tolerated in official state proclamations (inscriptions or coins); and the new creed of Mohammedanism was apparent wherever official religious formulae were employed—on coins, milestone inscriptions, construction texts, and papyrus protocols.

---

56. E.g., Whitting (1973), p. 18 coin no. 7; p. 160 coin no. 249.

57. Cf. Grierson (1968), p. 97 table 10; Whitting (1973), p. 48 coins nos. 56, 57 (where the globus or pellet is *under* the steps).

58. Grierson (1968), pp. 122, 560, 606.

59. There is also a coin dated 75/694–95, from the years immediately preceding the Reform, which bears on its reverse, where one would expect the "cross on steps," a miḥrāb-and-lance (discussed in Miles [1952]). This is an interesting attempt to replace Byzantine state and religious imagery with an "equivalent" Arab symbol, before ʿAbd al-Malik finally decided in 77/696–97 to abandon visual symbolism and adopt a purely noniconographic coinage.

WALĪD'S *ᵓISLĀM*

One of Walīd's first acts on his accession to the caliphate in A.H. 86/705 was to confiscate St. John's Church in Damascus, pull down its inner walls, and convert it into a *masjid*.[60] Two inscriptions inside it celebrated this event.[61] For Walīd's contemporaries, its main significance may have been the declaration of official enmity against the Church;[62] for us, it is the religio-political content of the inscriptions.

The most obvious difference between ᶜAbd al-Malik's proclamation in the Dome of the Rock, and Walīd's in the Umayyad Mosque of Damascus, is the change of attitude towards Christianity. ᶜAbd al-Malik com-mented on Christological and Trinitarian issues from within the Christian polemical tradition, but was not anti-Christian; Walīd destroyed a church, built an Arab house of prayer on the site, and proclaimed the deed publicly. He thereby finalized the complete separation between Christianity and the new religion. With ᶜAbd al-Malik came intolerance specifically towards the sign of the cross but not necessarily towards Christians; a policy of principle aimed at offending, frightening, and degrading the Christians was introduced only with Walīd.[63] And while Walīd was not embarking on a holy war to bring more unbelievers, in general, to the Arab faith, there is some evidence that he was less indifferent when the unbelievers were Arabs. Thus it seems that a chief of the Christian Taġlib Arabs "was martyred on the ground

60. The term *masjid* in the early period meant, as in Aramaic, 'a place of prayer'; we prefer not to translate is as 'mosque,' a term which begs too many questions regarding the religion practiced there.

61. They are included in the Appendix of Inscriptions. The source for the text is *RCEA* inscr. no. 18, which is reproduced from Ibn Rustah, *al-ᶜAlaq al-nafīsah*, ed. de Goeje (1892), pp. 70–77. It designates the two inscriptions as (A) and (B). (A) is dated, in the text, Ḏulḥijjah 87/November 706. (B) is dated Ḏulqaᶜadah 86/November 705.

62. Until then the Umayyads had rarely converted churches: there are only three possible cases, at Samah, at Umm al-Surab, and the Numeranianos church at Umm al-Jimāl (Schick [1987], p. 8). The Christians extensively repaired churches and built new ones throughout the 7th century and even into the 8th (ibid., p. 8; Piccirillo [1984], pp. 333, 340).

63. Even then, the much-quoted tale of the martyrdom of St. Peter of Capitolias, probably datable to Walīd's last illness in 97/715, indicates that Peter had to go out of his way to force the Arabs to martyr him by publicly and repeatedly slandering Muḥammad as a false prophet. As Walīd said to him, "You are free to recognise as God Jesus who is a man ... but why insult our religion...?" (Hoyland [1997], pp. 354–60; Piccirillo [1984], p. 340 n. 17).

that it was shameful that the Chief of the Arabs should adore a cross."[64]

The second difference, and no less important, is the change of attitude to the official Arab religion. ᶜAbd al-Malik defined his faith by means of how it differed from Christian belief; al-Walīd felt no such need. His inscription does not mention either Jesus or Christianity, but substitutes for anti-Trinitarian dispute the brief threefold declaration: 1) our God is Allāh, we shall worship none but Him; 2) our prophet is Muḥammad; 3) our *dīn* is *ᵓislām*. Refusing terminological debate, he added to Judaism and Christianity a separate, third monotheistic religion. Replacing a church with a *masjid* was a public demonstration of this theological development.

The main political and religious message in the Damascus mosque inscriptions is embodied in the earlier text (called (B) in *RCEA*). It starts with a text which also appears in the Qurᵓān as Q.2:256:

> *lā ikrāha fī dīnī qad tabayyana al-rušdu min al-ġayyī* etc.: "There is no coercion in matters of *dīn*, as the right (way) is already distinct from the crooked. And he who denies nonsense [i.e., an erring creed] but trusts Allāh clings to a firm handhold never to give way" (our translation).

We have argued above, in discussing the inscription in the Dome of the Rock, that *dīn* meant 'the social order, the community' (defined of course as a religious community), rather than 'religion.' Just as we read ᶜAbd al-Malik's use of the word as social/political, so here we see Walīd as issuing a social/political ultimatum. "There is no coercion in matters of *dīn*" meant: "No one will tell you what community to belong to—you will not be forced to join the one sanctioned by the state." However, the message continued, since the right way is now distinct from the false, anyone should know enough to be able to choose it for himself, and to reject error, without the need for coercion. He who does so—i.e., who rejects Christianity and affiliates himself with the state religion—will not regret it. "Clings to a firm handhold never to give way" is a promise of material reward—those who make the right decision will find it worth their while. The implication, of course, is that those who do not, cannot expect such amenities of life as financial gain and professional or social advancement. In modern phrasing: those who have not yet declared their allegiance must now choose between the plain and the buttered side of the bread.

---

64. See Crone and Cook (1977), p. 121 + n. 10 for source.

This announcement is followed in the inscription by two lines of formulae—the basic formulae of the state religion:

- The *tawḥīd* + *lā šarīk lahu,* introduced by ᶜAbd al-Malik
- Walīd's addition "and we shall worship only Him"
- The threefold proclamation, "Our Lord is Allāh alone; our *dīn* is *ᵓislām*; our Prophet is Muḥammad."

Here as in the Dome of the Rock, we translate "our *dīn* is *ᵓislām*" as "our community (both religious and political) is Unity (or Concord)"; *ᵓislām* here defines the (desired) nature of the Arab community headed by Walīd. These two lines make it clear that the Arab state/community has a God of its own, and is expected to be unified in its worship of Him. They are also a test of faith: and how simple, how easy it is to start on the right path! All a man has to do, to qualify as a member of the right community, is to recite them.

We consider, then, that this text was composed specifically for this inscription, and was then included in the Qurᵓān when it was canonized. It documents the difference between ᶜAbd al-Malik's outlook, and Walīd's. It provides the theological justification for the bold deeds that Walīd favored, such as the ostentatious, publicly proclaimed replacement of a church by a *masjid.* And Walīd's addition to the *tawḥīd* + *lā šarīk lahu*: *wa-lā naᶜbuda ᵓillā ᵓiyyahu*—"and none would we worship but Him"—turns an argument of religious position into an obvious battle cry. The resulting longer formula was in fact abbreviated to a real battle cry: *rabunā Allāh lā naᶜbuda illā Allāh*—"Allāh is our Lord, we shall worship none but Allāh"—which appeared the following year in part (A) of the inscription. Indeed, the desire to promulgate this briefer slogan may well have been the main reason for ordering the second inscription, which contains no other theological declaration and otherwise simply repeats verbatim the section on the destruction of the church already given in the first one.

In political terms, Walīd was making an overt break with Byzantium. This was expressed by his religious attitude towards the Christians, i.e., the Rūmī faction. It was under Walīd that the Rūmī élite—such as John of Damascus among many others—found it increasingly difficult to retain their government positions. The point of Walīd's ostentatious anti-Christian policy was to demonstrate publicly that the Arab State could now run itself. By the time of ᶜUmar II, this point had been well made. ᶜUmar had no need of the crisis atmosphere engendered by Walīd in the period of political change—it was clear to everyone that the Christians no longer ran the state.

5

From Monotheism to Islam:
Religious Development in the Popular Inscriptions

Of the many religious inscriptions in Classical Arabic known to exist on desert rocks all over the Middle East, only a few hundred have so far been published.[1] In Part III Chapter 1[2] we surveyed those discovered in the Negev and the relatively few published from elsewhere, divided them into classes, and gave a brief description of each class. These inscriptions provide a window through which we may trace the development of the Arab religion from its initial beginnings, through the appearance of Mohammedanism, to the emergence of something classifiable as Islam. This process, as we understand it, took approximately 150 years, from the general, basic Indeterminate Monotheism of Muᶜāwiyah's days, to the Muslim texts of the late 2nd and early 3rd centuries A.H. It is the aim of this chapter to trace that development.

---

1. About four hundred Kufic inscriptions from the Negev have been published in *AAIN* (1993). About two hundred from the Arabian Peninsula have been published in Grohmann (1962), and about two hundred more from Jabal Usays in al-ᶜUšš (1964). A few more have been published in periodical articles: for example, Baramki (1952) and (1964); Bišah (1983); Donner (1984); Khan and Mughannam (1982); Sharon (1966), (1981), (1985), and (1990).
2. Pp. 197–203.

The inscriptions used as examples in this chapter should be understood as representative. We have included in the Appendix of Inscriptions the Arabic text and English translation of all the non-Negev inscriptions referred to, and a representative selection of Negev inscriptions from each class; for the others, the reader is referred to *AAIN*.

Most of the inscriptions are undated. A few do include dates, and quite a number of the undated ones can be assigned to a general time period as a result: for instance, because their named owner is also the owner of a dated text. Thus the date 85/705 in MA 4265(19) enables us to date nine other inscriptions to the same period; the date 300/912 in BR 5119(31) enables us to assign to that period the entire groups BR and HR, which comprise a distinct cluster in a different geographical area from any of the others, and the majority of which were written by three people named Ibn Tamīm, most probably brothers; the inscriptions in these two groups also share a distinct idiom not found in the other Negev texts.[3] Nonetheless, we cannot put all the texts into anything resembling strict chronological order. But we can classify each text according to religious category—the Indeterminate Monotheism of the Basic Texts, Mohammedanism, or Islam—for this division is based on the religious concepts expressed in the text; it derives from linguistic and content analysis, not from reference to dates. This classification is tentative: it is possible that some texts will be reclassified in the future, when further discoveries have widened or refined the basis for assigning a text to a particular class. Nonetheless, the work on the material amassed to date suffices to show that we do have written sources for this early period, which can shed some light on the initial phases of the development of Islam.

Once the inscriptions have been classified by content, there are usually enough dated texts to enable us to assign a chronological range to each class. This shows us that the Basic Texts continue to be inscribed throughout the entire period; but the other classes have chronologically different ranges, except during late Marwānid times: it is possible that for a certain length of time during this period both Mohammedan and Muslim texts were being inscribed.

We consider in this chapter both the popular inscriptions, and the royal Declarations of Faith. The two reflect different phenomena. The royal

3. See *AAIN*, p. 56 for further details on dating the inscriptions.

inscriptions indicate the development of the official state religion; the rock graffiti show what form of religious belief was known to the general population of the areas in which they were inscribed. This popular religion seems to have lagged considerably behind the official version of the faith in its acceptance of new religious beliefs and concepts. The starting point, Indeterminate Monotheism, is evidenced in both the popular and royal inscriptions of the pre-Mohammedan period. But ᶜAbd al-Malik's introduction of Mohammedanism predated the earliest Mohammedan popular inscriptions so far known by about forty years, and the earliest definitely Muslim popular inscriptions are dated only from 160 A.H.

Linguistically, we can trace some development in the popular texts: with the passage of time they accumulated a richer vocabulary, a more elaborate idiom. Some expressions became fixed formulae; others continued in use but their semantic field changed; yet others were altered or replaced by new ways of saying essentially the same thing. New genres—i.e., ways of dealing with a theme—were also developed; thus a concept previously used axiomatically may later appear in a *ḥadīṯ*. But linguistic evidence can be problematic. Changes of semantic field are often not clear-cut—for instance, expressions which have obvious Muslim content in later texts may not have borne the same religious meaning in earlier ones, but deciding the point may well be a question of interpretation. Again, if phrases from the Qurʾān occur in other texts, it is usually assumed that they are Qurʾānic quotations. We, on the other hand, consider that isolated phrases with "Qurʾānic flavor," and even *verbatim* Qurʾānic verses or expressions, are not evidence that the Qurʾān was their source—both they and the Qurʾān may have had a common source. Nor, more generally, do they prove that an orthodox Islam existed when they were written, either among those who wrote them or anywhere else.

So while linguistic evidence does help us to classify the texts, it cannot by itself justify a major distinction such as that between the Mohammedan and Muslim classes. It is the sudden appearance in the inscriptions *of new concepts* which enables us to classify them as exhibiting Indeterminate Monotheism, Mohammedanism, or Islam. Each new class contains *a cluster of concepts not previously attested.* These are, of course, expressed via new words and phrases, which (unlike the development of older expressions over time, mentioned above) did not develop gradually out of older ways of saying the same thing. Rather, they indicate a certain discontinuity of religious concept: the formulation of a new idea or belief, previously unexpressed by any linguistic means.

The conclusion we reach from this situation, at least regarding the

Negev inscriptions, is that the *idiom* was developed and refined by use inside the desert community, as well as elsewhere. Liturgical use and perhaps doxology are obvious examples of circumstances encouraging the elaboration of religious idiom. But *new religious concepts* were imported from outside; and since they occur first in the royal inscriptions, and only later in the popular ones, we conclude that they represent the adoption, at least by those who wrote these inscriptions, of beliefs promulgated by the state.[4]

Another hint that this is so comes from our observation that the scribes who wrote the Negev Mohammedan texts do not seem to have been indigenous members of the population. Among the Basic Texts found at Sede Boqer is a subgroup with Judeo-Christian traits: these were all written by or on behalf of a relatively small number of individuals over a period of time, perhaps adding inscriptions on successive visits to the Sede Boqer site. The Mohammedan inscriptions, by contrast, were written by a larger number of people who each left a smaller number of inscriptions, often only one each. This suggests that they did not stay long in the area; they were just passing through and did not return. It may well be that Mohammedanism was introduced into the area by such people.

Chart III.5.1 tracks the linguistic changes and the new concepts through all classes and in the Qur^ʾān. It is arranged thematically, and within each general theme, in rough chronological order of appearance of the expressions. The following discussion gives briefly some examples of linguistic development, and then considers conceptual content; both these categories appear together in the chart. Many, but not necessary all, of the inscriptions referred to in the discussion as examples are given, in Arabic and English translation, in the Appendix of Inscriptions.

4. We do not discuss here the obvious role of religious leaders, whether those in the caliph's service or those opposing him, in developing terminology, ritual, and religious law and history. Obviously the fact that a term, concept, or belief was *adopted* and *promulgated* by the state does not mean that the caliph or state bureaucracy *originated* it. But it was the state that decided which of the concepts available should be incorporated into the official religion.

Chart III.5.1: Linguistic and Conceptual Changes in the Popular Inscriptions

Expression/Concept	Basic Texts (BT)		Moham-medan	Early Muslim	Muslim
	undated	**datable to 85**	**112–117**	**160–170**	**300/912**
ʿAbd Allāh (title)	Royal (inscriptions only)				
ʾAmīr al-Muʾminīn	Royal (inscriptions only)				
Basmalah occurs	Y	Y	Y	Y	Y
ʾIslām meaning 'social order'			DOR		
ʾIslām as name of the religion	—	—	??	Royal	Y
SIN AND FORGIVENESS					
ġfr/*ʾġfr* (forgive)	Pervasive	Pervasive	Very common	Occasional	Occasional
Note: In Q., requesting forgiveness for sin is part of expected behavior of those who follow the 'straight path.'					
ḏnb (fault, transgression)	Pervasive	Pervasive	Y	Y	Y
Note: Several formulae are BT only, e.g., *ġafar ḏanbihi* and *ġafar ḏanbihi kullaha*; *kull ḏanb*					
mā taqaddama min ḏanbihi wa-mā taʾaxxara	Very common	Very common	Common: usual *ḏanb formula*	Y	Y
kull ḏanb aḏnabahu (*qaṭṭu*)	Y	Y	—	—	Y
Requests lasting ("pre-ventive") forgiveness:	—	Y?	—	—	—
"Forgive him who writes this inscription"	Y?	—	—	Y	Y
"Forgive him who recites it or says Amen"	Y?	—	Y	—	Y
"Forgive him who hears it (if he has faith)"	—	—	Y	—	—
Requests *maġfarah*	—	Y	—	—	—

Expression/Concept	Basic Texts (BT)		Moham-medan	Early Muslim	Muslim
	undated	**datable to 85**	**112–117**	**160–170**	**300/912**
REQUESTS FOR ALLĀH'S FAVORS	Y	—	Y—long, quite concrete lists	—	Y
"Accept him into Your love"	Y	—	—	—	—
"Be pleased with him"	Y	—	Y	—	Y
"Bestow Your favor on him"	—	—	Y	—	—
Incline (*ṣly ᶜalà*) to him	—	—	Y	Y	Y common
You and Your (two) angels incline to him	—	—	—	—	Y common
DEFINITIONS OF GOD					
Rabb al-ᶜalamīn	Y	Y	Y	Y	Y
Beautiful Names	Y common	—	Y	Y	Y
rabb Mūsà	Y common	Y	—	—	—
rabb Mūsà wa-ᶜĪsà	Y	Y	Y	—	—
rabb Mūsà wa-Ībrāhīm	—	—	Y	—	—
rabb al-nās ajmaᶜīn	—	Y	Y	Y	—
laka al-ḥamdu	—	—	Y	—	—
tawḥīd	—	—	Royal only	Y	Y
Allāh is one, *ṣamad*	—	—	—	Y	Y
širk (denial of)	—	—	Y	Y	Y
You are the Omnipotent	—	—	Y	—	Y
O Compassionate/Merciful One	—	—	Y	—	—
You are the Generous One	—	—	Y	—	—
Note: this is not a Beautiful Name					
You know what is concealed and manifest	—	—	—	—	Y

Expression/Concept	Basic Texts (BT)		Moham-medan	Early Muslim	Muslim
	undated	**datable to 85**	**112–117**	**160–170**	**300/912**
Revealer of sins, receiver of prayers	—	—	—	—	Y
CREATION AND COSMOGONY (Heaven-Earth; Fire and *jannah*; Judgment-Resurrection)					
Allāh created heaven and earth	indirectly	—	as part of ḥadīṯ	Y, not in Negev	Y
kalimah—the Word—as agent of creation	Y	—	Y	—	Y
Death as *al-ẓuᶜūn* (Departure)	perhaps	—	—	—	—
ḥayy-an	—	Y	Y	—	—
ḥayy-an wa-mayyit-an	Y	Y	—	—	—
ḥayy-an ġayr hālik	Y	Y	—	possibly (partly illegible)	—
ġayr hālik	—	Y	—	—	—
ġayr hālik wa-lā mafqūd	Y	Y	—	—	—
jannat al-naᶜīm (not necessarily 'paradise')	Y	—	—	Y, not in Negev	Y
al-jannah (not necessarily 'paradise')	—	Y (added as after-thought?)	Y	Y	Y
jamīᶜu-l-xalāʾiq (all created beings)	—	—	—	Y	concept
jamīᶜu xalqihi (all His created beings)	—	—	—	Y	concept
al-nār (the Fire)	—	Y	Y	Y	Y
al-baᶜṯ (Resurrection)	—	—	—	Y, once in Negev	Y
"Raise him from the dead"	—	—	—	—	Y
yawm al-qiyāmah (Day of Resurrection)	—	—	DOR only	—	Y
Herald phrase	—	—	—	Y	—

Expression/Concept	Basic Texts (BT)		Moham-medan	Early Muslim	Muslim
	undated	**datable to 85**	**112–117**	**160–170**	**300/912**
RELATIONS AMONG GOD, PROPHETS, AND MEN					
Jesus as a prophet	Y	—	Royal only	Y	Y
Muḥammad rasūl Allāh	—	—	Y	Y	Y
Muḥammad al-nabiy al-umiyy	—	—	—	—	Y
Allāh forgive Muḥammad	—	—	Y	—	—
Incline to Muḥammad the Prophet	—	—	Y?	—	Y
Allāh's love and blessing on Your servant Muḥammad	—	—	—	—	Y
bi-raḥmah, bi-raḥmatika	—	—	Y	Y	Y
"Accept him into Your Love"	Y	—	—	—	—
Desire to exclude non-believers from Allāh's blessing/forgiveness	Y	Y	Y	Y	N
Inclusion of all in Allāh's blessing	—	—	—	—	Y
Writer trusts/has faith (*amanah*)	—	—	Y	—	Y
Ṣirāt mustaqīm (the Straight Way)	—	—	Y	Y	—
hudà (guidance)	—	—	Y	Y	—
jahd (zeal, exertion on Allāh's behalf)	—	—	Y	Y, not in Negev	Y but in unreadable context
istišhād	—	—	Y= to do	Y= to testify	—
Testifying to one's faith	—	—	Y	Y	Y
Allāh be pleased with...	Y	—	Y	Y	—
šafāʿah—intercession	—	—	Royal only	tombs only	Y
Allāh as patron (*waliy*)	—	—	Rare	Y	Y

Expression/Concept	Basic Texts (BT)		Moham-medan	Early Muslim	Muslim
	undated	**datable to 85**	**112–117**	**160–170**	**300/912**
Allāh as patron and helper (*al-mawlà, al-naṣīr*)	—	—	—	Y	Y
lā ḥawla wa-lā quwwata...	—	—	Y	Y?	—
kafà bi-llāhi šahīd-an (Allāh suffices as a witness)	—	—	—	Y	Y

PATTERNS OF LINGUISTIC DEVELOPMENT

Continuation with no change

Some phrases start to occur in the Basic Texts and continue unchanged right into the Muslim period. The titles *ᶜAbd Allāh* and *Amīr al-Muʾminīn* are two examples. These are general religious expressions—not even specifically monotheistic, and certainly not Muslim—whose precise meaning would depend on whatever faith their user professed. Another such expression is the concluding phrase *amīn rabb al-ᶜalamīn*, which indicates monotheism of an unspecified variety. It is well attested in Basic Texts—e.g., MA 4132(12); MA 4205(14), first part; MA 4900(27); MA 4210(16)—and eventually became a typical Muslim locution. Another example of the continuation of earlier phrases is the mention in the Muslim era of Jesus as a member of God's retinue (*ᶜabduhu wa-rasūluhu*).

An example of linguistic change: *ḥayy-an wa-mayyit-an*

In inscriptions from the earliest phase (as determined by text analysis and from the personal names in them) we find a very common but somewhat obscure phrase: *ġafira li*-[personal name, hereafter abbreviated PN] *ḥayy-an wa-mayyit-an*: e.g., MA 4137(12); MA 4210(16). The "obvious" translation of *ḥayy-an wa-mayyit-an* is "alive and dead"—i.e., while alive and after his death. But in this context—a request to Allāh to forgive the supplicants' sins—such a meaning is highly problematic. The sins, clearly, must have been committed during life; one could argue that the supplicant is requesting forgiveness both while alive and after his death, but this would mean that the writers of these early inscriptions believed in *baᶜṯ* (resurrection) and *ḥašar* (summoning of the dead for judgment). The latter concept is completely absent from the Negev inscriptions, and the former never occurs in the same inscriptions as *ḥayy-an wa-mayyit-an*, nor indeed in any ascribable to the Umayyad period. In fact it occurs only three times in the Negev inscriptions found to date, once in a Muslim text from ca. 300 A.H.—BR 5115(31)—and the other two in an area where there are signs of activity down to 170 A.H.: AR 271(2) and AR 2100(2), both fragmentary occurrences of the set formula *yawma yamūtu wa-yawma yabaᶜṯu ḥayy-an* "the day he dies and the day he arises alive," Q.19:15. The writers of the inscriptions containing the phrase *ḥayy-an wa-mayyit-an* do not mention *baᶜṯ*, and we have no indication that they believed in a life after death. We consider, then, that the meaning they intended by the formula *ḥayy-an wa-mayyit-an* was "alive until dead," i.e., "as long as he lives and until his death." This reading is suggested also by a doublet locution which sometimes replaces the above phrase. It reads: *ġafira li-*[PN] *ġayr hālik wa-lā mafqūd*, literally "forgive [PN] not dead and not missing," or more colloquially, "alive and well": e.g., MA 4265(19). We also find the expression *ḥayy-an ġayr hālik wa-lā mafqūd* "alive, not dead and not missing": MA 4168(13). This last triple formula explains the meaning of the shorter doublet: *ġayr hālik* here parallels, and in the doublet replaces, the previous *ḥayy-an*, and *wa-lā mafqūd* replaces the *wa-mayyit-an* of the older expression. The triple expression appears to be a variant in the development from *ḥayy-an wa-mayyit-an* to *ġayr hālik wa-lā mafqūd*, and shows that both phrases embodied a similar meaning—as we would expect from their occurrence in the same slot in the inscriptions. Ultimately *ḥayy-an wa-mayyit-an* was no longer employed. In due course the same happened to the expression *ġayr hālik*. Both are non-Mohammedan and were replaced by their equivalent (not equal!) Mohammedan expressions, built around *jannah* and *rahmah* versus *nār*. This is, then, an example of a phrase which underwent change and eventual replacement by a different locution during the Indeterminate Monotheist phase; in the Mohammedan, the concept it expresses—of life as extending only till death, of the lack of an afterlife—disappears, and so too, therefore, do the phrases expressing it. In the late Marwānid texts, references to the Fire, *al-nār*,[5] indicate the concept of death as an introduction into the hereafter, though even here they

5. The concept occurs in the Negev only in inscriptions MA 450(8): "Allāh! You are the Protector/the Shelterer, my Lord who protects from the fire" and MA 4205(11); and in inscriptions from the royal Marwānid residence at Jabal Usays (e.g., JU 72).

are rare. The concept of resurrection, *baᶜṯ*,[6] occurs even later, in the Muslim texts.

Linguistic elaboration: the concepts of Creation, Sin, and Forgiveness

The concept 'Lord of Creation' should be considered a monotheistic constant. It occurs in inscriptions from all three classes—Basic Text, Mohammedan, and Muslim—expressed via the phrases *rabb al-ᶜalamīn* and *rabb al-nās ajmaᶜīn* "Lord of all people," though the latter unlike the former does not occur in the Qurᵓān. In the Basic and Mohammedan texts, these are the only phrases used for this concept. By the time of the Muslim texts, the religious vocabulary has widened to include various other expressions embodying this theme of God as Creator: *jamīᶜu-l-xalāᵓiq*—"all the created beings," e.g., ST 640(34), dated 170 A.H.; and *jamīᶜu xalqihi*—"all His created beings," e.g., EKI 261.[7]

The terminology of sin and forgiveness also underwent linguistic elaboration. In the Basic Texts, phrases containing *ġfr*/*ᵓġfr* and *ḏnb* are the main words used to express these concepts. *Ġfr*/*ᵓġfr* may occur alone or in combination with *ḏnb* in locutions such as *ġafira* [PN] *kulla ḏanb-en aḏnabahu qaṭṭu* ("forgive [PN] all the transgressions he has [ever] committed")—e.g., EL 200C(2), MA 4254(17), and MA 419(8)—and *ġafira* [PN] *ḏunubahu kullahu* ("forgive [PN] all his transgressions")—e.g., MA 4132(12), MA 4371(23). Phrases containing *ġfr*/*ḏnb* also occur in Mohammedan texts, where other formulae appear alongside them; in the 3rd-century Muslim texts, though rarely; and in the Qurᵓān. An inscription from Jabal Tubayq in Jordan exhibits a rarer wording of the same concept: *iġfir* [PN] *mā xalaᵓ min ḏanbihi wa-mā ᶜalā minhi* ("forgive all his past transgressions and the recent ones").[8] In our Negev inscriptions this idea is expressed by the formula *qadīmuhu wa-ḥadīṯuhu* "the old and the recent ones"—e.g., MA 475(09), or in reverse order—*wa-ḥadīṯuhu wa-qadīmuhu*—e.g., MA 4371(23), MA 4288(20)—expressions which continue in use into the Muslim texts. The formula *ṣaġīruhu wa-kabīruhu* "his small and great (sins)" is probably another linguistic variant on this general theme. And

6. Negev texts AR 271(2) in unclear context, and AR 2100(2): "Allāh! Incline unto Xālid bn ᶜUmar the day he dies and the day he is sent forth/comes from the dead alive" (*yawma yubᶜaṯ ḥayy-an*).

7. Not published in *AAIN*; given in Appendix of Inscriptions.

8. Baramki (1952). Our translation differs from Baramki's.

two or more formulae could of course be combined in elaboration, as in MA 4288(20): *ġafira Allāh li-*[PN] *kulla ḏanb-en aḏnabahu qaṭṭu ṣaġīruhu wa-kabīruhu wa-ḥadīṯuhu wa-qadīmuhu* "forgive Allāh [PN] any transgression he may have committed whatsoever, his minor and major ones, his recent and older ones." But the most popular version proved to be *ma taqaddama min ḏanbihi wa-ma taʾaxxara* "the earliest of his sins and the latest."[9] At some point in the pre-Mohammedan period a new formula including the word *ʾṯm*, 'sin,' was introduced: *iġfir* [PN] *maġfirah qaʾīmah ... lā yaksub baᶜduhā ʾiṯm-an* "Forgive [PN] a lasting forgiveness ... [so that] he shall not [ever] commit a sin (*ʾiṯm*) thereafter (*baᶜduhā*)": HL 4911(28). *ʾiṯm* continues in use in later classes of texts.

The *concepts* of 'sin' and 'forgiveness' also underwent considerable change. This aspect will be discussed in the section on conceptual development.

Liturgical elaboration: the Beautiful Names of God

Several of the epithets known in Muslim terminology as the Beautiful Names, *al-asmaᶜ al-ḥusnà*, already occur in Basic Text inscriptions, for instance: *al-samīᶜa, al-ᶜalīm, al-ᶜaliyy, al-ᶜazīm, al-ᶜazīz, al-ḥakīm, al-raʾūf,* and *al-raḥīm.*[10] These are abbreviated maxims: giving a list of epithets is a short way of repeating, "God is Great, God is Powerful, God is Wise," etc. Sometimes there is minimal elaboration of the predicate phrase, e.g.: *ᶜarḥam al-raḥimīn wa-ʾaḥkam al-ḥakimīn* "the most Loving among those who love and the best Judge among Judges": MA 419(8). These predicates are also found strung together in chains, the chain itself constituting a main content of the inscription: e.g., MA 4138(13). Now the communal environment and needs of a particular sect determined the development of such phrases and the uses made of them—their literary context. Such a string of predicates implies that liturgical use was the main avenue of development: elaboration such as "the most Loving among those who love"

---

9. Karbalah inscription, DKI 163:8–9, dated 64/684 from Iraq; MA 4319(21), Basic Text; EL 200A(2):2–3, undated; AR 2101(2):3–4, undated; MA 420A(8):3 of Miḥjan bn Saᶜīd, who also appears (without patronymic) as the owner of inscription MA 4510(25), containing *ġayr hālik*; both undated.

10. Other epithets also occur in the same contexts and used in the same way, but they were not in fact included in the Muslim list of the ninety-nine Beautiful Names of God.

or "the One who knows what is hidden" (MA 4371) may be seen as similarly rooted in liturgy.[11]

In the Qur᾿ān these and similar predicates also occur, but their usage differs. They occur as pausal phrases, e.g., Q.2:209: *fa-᾿aᶜlamu ᾿anna Allāh ᶜAzīz Ḥakīm*, or Q.2:211: *fa-᾿inna Allāh šadīd al-ᶜiqāb*. We may see here the employment for literary ends—to demarcate the component locutions and point their moral, whether actually implicit or attributed to them—of the phrases already familiar from liturgical use and daily speech.

Introduction of a new phrase: *lā ḥawla wa-lā quwwata*

The very famous expression *lā ḥawla wa-lā quwwata illa bi-llāhī al-ᶜaliyy al-ᶜazīm* "there is no strength nor power but through Allāh, the High, the Great" is not Qur᾿ānic but a saying in ḥadīṯ.[12] A very similar phrasing of it occurs in an undated composite inscription, MA 4205(14). Lines 1–4 of this inscription are Basic Text, whereas lines 5–12, written by the son of the first owner, are Mohammedan. The phrase occurs in the second, Mohammedan, part. This expression does not occur in the Basic Texts.

The phrase *kafà bi-llāhi* "Allāh suffices" was introduced at a late stage—it is Qur᾿ānic and Muslim only. In the Qur᾿ān and the Muslim texts it is applied to various aspects of Allāh's relationship with man: thus in Q.4 alone it is used of Allāh as a helper (Q.4:45); one who counts a person's deeds (or money) (Q.4:6); one who knows (Q.4:69–70); and the overlord, the one in charge (Q.4:132). The expression *kafà bi-llāhi šahīd-an* "and Allāh suffices as a witness" is discussed in the section on concepts below.

THE DEVELOPMENT OF CONCEPTS AND BELIEFS

The Religious Content of the *Basmalah*

Long before the introduction of Mohammedanism, the *basmalah* was an ossified initial formula with a general religious meaning "in the name of

---

11. Of course the formulae, and the liturgy, were not initially developed in the Negev: formulae came to the Negev ready-made, though once there, they could be elaborated and further developed: cf. p. 300 + n. 4 above.

12. Lane, *ḥawl*, 2:675, col. 3. The meaning of the word *ḥawl* is nonetheless uncertain; various suggestions have been made; cf. Lane, ibid., p. 676 col. 1. We would suggest the derivation from the Semitic *hyl* (Akk. *ellata*, Aramaic languages *ḥeyla* = strength, might). Thus *ḥawla* = *quwwata*: 'strength, might'.

God." It is comparable to other such expressions, such as "if God wills," "with God's help," and so forth, to be found in all the monotheistic sects, though unlike these it had a fixed position as the invariable initial formula. This was a chancery convention, already old and accepted when the Arabs formed their own Arabic equivalent.[13] The Arabic form thus appears in chancery writing very early.[14] On coins it appears more gradually, at first as *bism Allāh* or *bism Allāh rabbī*. The full *basmalah* was struck on coins only from the Mohammedan issues of ᶜAbd al-Malik, who also introduced it on milestones and papyri protocols. It is thus interesting to find that, while it does occur in the Basic Texts, it is not a characteristic item in them.

Religious Atmosphere: Requesting Forgiveness versus Soliciting Favors

The Basic Texts are typically fear-imbued supplications entreating forgiveness (*ᵓġfr/ġfr*) for transgression (*ḏnb*). But they specify neither the sins committed—their character and magnitude—nor the actual atonement made for them; thus we cannot formulate a typology of transgressions. Nor do these texts disclose the punishment which may befall the unrepentent or unpardoned. In fact they never explicitly mention punishment, as such; but it is implicit in the request for forgiveness of transgression. And we know that when they wrote *ḏnb* they had in mind many transgressions, not just a single fault; these might be old ones (root *q.d.m.*), which still needed atonement, or new, recent ones (roots *a.x.r.*, *ḥ.d.ṯ.*); and "transgressions both new and old" was a formulaic way of referring to all one's transgressions. Thus, as we saw in the discussion of linguistic elaboration above, *mā taqaddama min ḏanbihi wa-mā taᵓaxxara* is a very popular locution in the Basic Texts; it continued on into the Mohammedan ones, and appears also in the Qurᵓān.[15]

In the Mohammedan texts requests for forgiveness are still prominent, though we are apt to notice them less, since there are now many other features attracting our attention. But the atmosphere has changed. The requests are no longer fear-imbued: references to *ḏnb* are slight. Instead, there is optimism, a confidence of procuring, through God's benevolence, temporal as well as spiritual benefits, amounting in all to a very personal

---

13. E.g., the usual 6th- and 7th-century Byzantine Greek formula, *ën onomati tou theou* "in the name of God" (preceded in Greek by the sign of the cross).

14. It already occurs in PERF no. 558 of A.H. 22/643.

15. Al-Fatḥ, Q.48:2.

and quite impressive list of desiderata. Typical phrases include *ᶜarziqhu min faḏlika* "provide for him from Your bounty," *ᵓatimma ᶜalayhi niᶜmataka/niᶜamaka* "bestow Your favor/s wholly upon him," *ᵓajᶜalhu min al-mufliḥīn* "make of him one of the prosperous," and more: e.g., SC 301(3). These may be summed up as "Allāh's favors"—*niᶜam-u Allāh*.

Table III.5.1 gives the frequency of the three words *ġfr* 'forgive,' *ḏnb* 'transgression,' and *ṣly* 'incline towards' in the opening phrase of a representative sample of Basic Text, Mohammedan, and Muslim inscriptions.

This analysis of the opening phrases highlights the conceptual change, for the opening phrase of an inscription served to stress an important concept in it. In the Basic Texts, that concept was invariably forgiveness, and it was still frequent in the Mohammedan texts, though less so. But by the Muslim texts, forgiveness has almost vanished from the opening formula. The root *ġfr* occurs seldom in it; *ḏnb* has practically disappeared from the opening phrase. Allāh is now asked, not just to *forgive* the believer, but to *incline towards* him—*ṣly*[16]—and this became the customary opening word of invocation. The idiom *ṣally Allāh ᶜalà* or *Allāhumma ṣally ᶜalà*

Table III.5.1: Distribution of three key words in the Basic, Mohammedan, and Muslim (3rd c. A.H.) classes of inscriptions. JU = Jabal Usays, east of Damascus, Marwānid period (Walīd-Hišām, A.H. 86–125/705–743). *Ḏnb* in the ossified *taqdīm-taᵓaxīr* formula has been excluded. *Ḏnb* was included to show that *ġfr* stays in Mohammedan texts independently of *ḏnb*, which diminishes much more sharply in frequency.

Word	CLASS			
	BT (Negev)	Mohammedan (Negev)	JU (Mohammedan) (Damascus)	Muslim (Negev)
ġfr (forgive)	100%	83%	67%	10%
ḏnb (transgression)	95%	20%	—	2%
ṣly (incline towards)	—	6%	4.4%	49%

Source: statistical pilot study made on a sample group, 1982, and, for JU, al-ᶜUšš (1964).

16. For *ṣly* = 'incline' see Aramaic *s.l.w.*, e.g., in Jastrow (1903).

occurs in the Dome of the Rock, where it relates to Jesus: *Allāhumma ṣally ᶜalà rasūlika wa-ᶜabdika ᶜĪsà bn Maryama* (DOR B:11). It was, then, part of the official Mohammedan idiom introduced by ᶜAbd al-Malik. The expression does not occur in the Qurʾān—indeed this particular verse is foreign to the attitude of all the Qurʾānic verses relating to Jesus. Like other Mohammedan phrases, it started to occur in the popular inscriptions in Hišām's day: for instance, in HS 3154(6), dated 117 A.H.: *Allāhumma ṣally ᶜalà Muḥammad al-nabī wa-ᶜalà man yuṣalli ᶜalayhi* "Allāh, incline to Muḥammad ... and to the one who prays for him." But it only really penetrated the popular level of the faith with the Muslim inscriptions—e.g., BR 5115(31) and BR 5117(31) from ca. A.H. 300/912—where it is highly frequent.

There are conceptual differences between the two words *ġfr* and *ṣly*. While *ġfr* (related to *kfr* 'to cover, conceal') has the meaning of pleading for a final decision to overlook or forgive evil deeds committed, *ṣly* asks for God's good disposition towards the supplicant; *ġfr* refers to the verdict, *ṣly* to the favorable conditions under which it should be reached. In the Muslim texts, *ġfr* still occurs in the body of the inscriptions, but is clearly just one concept among many. The attitude expressed is optimism, and the confidence of receiving God's grace.

As we might expect from this change of atmosphere, the verb *saʾala* 'to request' is common in the Mohammedan and Muslim rock inscriptions, whereas it is exceedingly rare in the Basic Texts.[17] For instance, in a Muslim text of ca. 300/912 we find *ʾannī ʾasʾalka niᶜamaka* "I request of You Your favors": HR 522(30); and in the Mohammedan part of the composite father-son text from Sede Boqer, MA 4205(14):8, we find *ʾasʾal Allāh al-jannah* "I request of Allāh *al-jannah*."

The concept of forgiveness itself seems to have undergone some change over time. In most of the Basic Texts, the supplicant asks for forgiveness for transgressions already committed, in the recent or distant past. In the second half of the composite inscription HL 4911(28), however, we find a more developed request for a different type of forgiveness: *iġfir rabbī li-*[PN] *maġfirah qaʾīmah lā yuᶜaddu rad[iʾ-an] wa-lā yaksib baᶜduhā lā ʾiṯm-an amīn rabb al-ᶜalamīn* "Forgive [PN] a lasting forgiveness [so that] he shall

17. MA 4138(13) contains *wa-huwa yasʾal Allāh al-majannah* "And he entreats Allāh [to grant him] the/this sanctuary." This text is considered in the section on *jannah* below.

not be counted/considered wicked,[18] and he shall not [commit] a sin thereafter."

This text was mentioned in the section on linguistic change, in connection with use of the word *ʾiṯm*. Here we are concerned with the concept *maġfirah qaʾīmah*. This is a rather precise prayer for a sort of "preventive" forgiveness—one that will change the supplicant from fault-prone to sin-proof. Previous texts asked God to guarantee forgiveness of unavoidable future sins; this one asks God to let the supplicant avoid committing them altogether. This implies that he intends—with God's help—to change his future behavior so as to comply strictly with God's commands: the request for such a "preventive forgiveness" indicates an intention to lead a pious life. This request for aid in leading a pious life which will obviate the need for forgiveness occurs also in a Mohammedan text: DL 6137(34) from Wādī al-Ḥafīr in the Negev.[19]

The Mohammedan texts of Jabal Usays east of Damascus, a site of residence of the Marwānid royal family,[20] provide two other occurrences of this formula;[21] but it is uncertain whether in them it meant the same as in the Negev Basic Texts. The owner of both inscriptions is Sulayman bn Jannāḥ, whose father was a *mawlà* of the caliph Walīd.[22] The first runs as follows:

> *iġfir ... maġfirah lā yuʿaddu radiʾ-an ʾamīn rabb al-ʿalamīn*: "Forgive [PN] a forgiveness [so that] he shall not [ever] be counted wicked. Amen Lord of Creation." (JU 27)

---

18. In HL 4911 this word is not fully decipherable, but can be supplied following the similar expression in DL 6137(34), JU 27, and JU 88.

19. It is noteworthy that in the Qurʾān *ġafarah* does not imply this kind of "preventive forgiveness." The assumption is that people inevitably sin, but Allāh informs them, via His messengers, of what is good and what is bad, and those who obey Him will be forgiven their sins, while those who disregard His warnings will be punished. Thus there is no concept of being able to prevent sin: one should follow the Straight Path but will inevitably sin nonetheless, but Allāh will forgive those who return.

20. Publ. in al-ʿUšš (1964). The site is known in the literature also as Usais and Sais.

21. In al-ʿUšš (1964) three inscriptions include *mġfrh* and entreat "preventive forgiveness." The two discussed here include the same wording, if one accepts our suggested reading for JU 27 and JU 88: *mġfrh lā yʿd rdyyʾ* (= *radiyʾ-an*) instead of al-ʿUšš's *lā tuġ[ā]dir ḏanb-an*. A third inscription, JU 35 (ibid., p. 256) is difficult, but includes the request for *mġfrh* plus an adjective or adverb and the negation [of future evil deeds?] *lā yʿm*.

22. al-ʿUšš (1964), p. 303.

And the second:

> *iġfir li-*[PN] *ᵓamīn rabb al-ᶜalamīn. maġfirah lā yuᶜaddu radiᵓ-an wa-kaf[ā]hu mā <ṣanaᶜahu> wa-ᵓanṣurhu ᶜalà man ᶜād[ā]hu wa-ᶜaᵓinhu*: "Forgive [PN] Amen Lord of Creation. A forgiveness [so that] he shall not be counted wicked, and let <his deeds>[23] suffice for him and make him victorious over anyone who encounters him with enmity, and help him." (JU 88)

In these inscriptions the formula has been copied, but without the word *qaᵓīmah*; it is thus not absolutely clear that Sulayman bn Jannāḥ intended to request a "preventive" forgiveness, i.e., was declaring his resolve to live a pious life and avoid sin, with God's help. In JU 88 the formula is preceded by a self-contained request for forgiveness starting *iġfir* and ending with a concluding phrase, *ᵓamīn rabb al-ᶜalamīn*; it is therefore difficult to read *iġfir ... li-*[PN] *maġfirah* as a continuous phrase. Rather, the formula beginning *maġfirah* starts a list of the "soliciting favors" type, familiar from other Mohammedan inscriptions. The request for *maġfirah* thus seems to be regarded simply as one of those which a supplicant could make of Allāh. This change of meaning probably became general during the Marwānid period. In this inscription, at least, the new atmosphere is unconcealed: the supplicant regards the request as an obligatory formula to be got out of the way at the start, so that he is free to proceed to what really interests him: a wish list of an unmistakeably down-to-earth character. The text as a whole gives the impression that forgiveness is sought, not to enable personal perfection in the ways of God, but for worldly gain. More likely, the request for forgiveness has become little more than an ossified formula, an accepted preamble to a list of requests.

Cosmogony and Creation

In the Basic Texts we find an interest, in general, in the relationship of Heaven and Earth to God: *yā-man fī al-samāᵓ ᶜaršuhu wa-al-ᵓarḍ mawḍaᶜ qadamihi* "He whose throne is in the sky and Earth is His footstool": MA 4254(17). The concept that God created Heaven and Earth is first expressed in the Mohammedan Class: *badīᶜ al-samawāt wa-al-ᵓarḍ*—

---

23. "His deeds" is al-ᶜUšš's suggestion for the word which is obviously missing, although no lacuna can be discerned in the facsimile.

HS 3153(6). We can trace this theme—the greatness of God's creative power—in the Qurʾān too, in the practice of citing examples from nature to prove God's existence (*ayāt Allāh*).[24] In the popular texts, the treatment is axiomatic, the conceptual background that of the Old Testament: it seems to be a paraphrase of Isaiah 61:1: "Thus saith YHWH: The heaven is my throne, and the earth is my footstool"; but it could simply be an age-old literary formula.

A further creation theme—and again, of Judaic/Christian origin—is the concept of "the Word"—*kalimah*—as the *agent of creation*: God creates by speaking, as in Q.2:117: "The Creator of the Heavens and the Earth: when He decrees a thing, He only says to it, Be! and it will exist." The idea of the Word as agent is found in the Basic Text MA 4254(17), partly quoted above: it starts *Allāhumma Yā man tammat kalimatuhu* "Allāh! You whose word was fulfilled/accomplished" and continues as quoted above: "whose throne is in the sky" etc. Here again, the concept is presented in axiomatic form, and the Creation and cosmogony are used as further ways of defining and glorifying Allāh.

Only one "cosmogonic" Mohammedan inscription, HS 3153(6), has so far been found in the Negev, and its treatment of the theme is very different. What was previously an axiom is elaborated as the basis for a *ḥadīṯ*:

There is no God but You	*lā īlah illā ʾanta*
Creator of the Heavens and the Earth	*badīᶜ al-samawāt wa-al-ʾarḍ*
[You are] Majestic and Generous	*ḏū al-jalāl wa-al-karm* [*sic*, for *wa-al-akrām*]
As the Prophet finished his prayer	*fa-lamma qaḍā al-nabī ṣallātahu*
He said: Who is Master of the Word?	*qāla: Man ṣaḥib al-kalimah?*
The Omniscient said *or*: [Allāh] said: the world	*Qāla al-ᶜālam/ᶜalīm:*
I created it.	*ʾana badīᶜuhu.*

This is the type of treatment that Wansbrough, by analogy with Jewish practice, calls "haggadic."

24. E.g., Q.30:20–25, 46.

The Hereafter: *al-jannah*, *al-nār*, and *al-baᶜṯ*

The belief in an afterlife apparently entered the Arab religion relatively late; for a long time the Arab monotheists, like the pagan Arabs, regarded life as ending with physical death. The many pagan inscriptions are silent on the subject of life after death. To the best of our knowledge, no Ṯamūdian or Ṣafaitic text is concerned with the hereafter, nor does the cairn of Haniy[25] or the texts from fifty other cairns[26] include any clues which would support a different interpretation. Death and "funerary situations" are a distinct topic of the Ṣafaitic inscriptions, yet they say nothing of the deceased's lot after leaving this world; they record only the mourners' grief.[27]

The attitude of Indeterminate Monotheism is not basically different. The Basic Text formula limits the supplicant's "life horizon" to his bodily existence, with no reference to the hereafter, and both the earlier *ḥayy-an wa-mayyit-an* and the somewhat later *ġayr hālik wa-lā mafqūd* express this view. The Old Testament preserves similar (non-Rabbinic) notions regarding the validity of this life and the religious insignificance of whatever happens thereafter:

> Be not thou afraid when a man is made rich, when the glory of his house is increased. For when he dieth he shall carry nothing away; his glory shall not descend after him.... He shall go to the generation of his fathers; they shall never see light. (Ps. 49:17 [16 in the AV])
> I will sing unto YHWH as long as I live;
> I will sing praise to my (God) while I have my being. (Ps. 104:33)
> While I live will I praise YHWH;
> I will sing praise unto my (God) while I have any being (Ps. 146:2–4)
> Return YHWH, deliver my soul, save me....
> For in death (there is) no remembrance of thee:
> In the grave [in *sheᵓōl*] who shall give thee thanks? [lit: who acknowledges you?]. (Ps. 6:5 [AV 6:4–5])

In view of this conceptual background, we would not expect to find the concepts of paradise or hell very early in our inscriptions. The term *al-jannah* does occur in three Basic Text inscriptions. Of these, one is dated 85/

---

25. Harding (1953).
26. Winnett and Harding (1978).
27. Cf. J. ᶜAlī's summary of the Jāhilī indifference to the hereafter, as described in the Muslim traditions: ᶜAlī, J. (1970), pp. 128–29.

704, one is dated 112/730, and the third is undated. The term also occurs in two Mohammedan inscriptions, one datable to 112/730 and the other undated; and in two Muslim ones, one undated and one dated 160/776.

The exact references for all occurrences of *al-jannah* in these texts are as follows:[28]

- **Basic Text, dated 85/704**: MA 4265(19). The inscription ends with the common concluding phrase "Amen Lord of Creation, Lord of the people, all of them" followed on the next line by the date: "and it was written in ... year 85." The text of this short line is artificially extended so as to take up a full line, presumably for aesthetic reasons. One would expect that to be the end of the inscription, but on a separate line immediately following this is the request, "Admit him into *al-jannah*." Although the line is in the same hand as the rest, and is obviously intended to refer to the owner of the whole inscription, its position after the concluding phrase and the date raises the possibility that the owner added it to his inscription of 85/704 at a later date.

- **Basic Text, dated 112/730**: GM 389(4). The entire text reads:
  Allāh! Forgive [PN] his transgressions, the earlier ones and the later
  And admit him into *al-jannah*
  Amen Lord of Creation.

- **Basic Text, undated**: MA 4510(25). In a short and scarcely legible inscription, a word that may be *al-jannah* appears on a line by itself. Its connection to the rest of the inscription is not legible.

- **Mohammedan, datable to 112/730**: GM 388(4). The entire text reads:
  Allāh! Incline unto [PN]
  And admit him into *al-jannah*
  With no reckoning [*or*: retribution]
  O Compassionate, Merciful One.

- **Mohammedan, undated: HS 3154(6)**. The entire text reads:
  Allāh! Incline unto Muḥammad the Prophet
  And unto him who prays for him
  And [PN] wrote [it]
  And he asks Allāh for *al-jannah* by His love.

28. For the Arabic, see the Appendix of Inscriptions.

- **Composite Basic Text/Mohammedan inscription, undated:** MA 4205(14). It belongs to a father and son; the reference is in the later, Mohammedan part:

  I request of Allāh *al-jannah*
  I seek shelter in Him from the Fire.

- **Muslim text, dated 160/776**: MA 4339(22). The inscription ends:

  And [PN] wrote it and he
  (year) 160 [The word "year" is barely legible, inserted between the lines]
  [requests] of Allāh *al-jannah.*

In addition to these, MA 4369(23), a Basic Text inscription whose owner left many inscriptions, all Basic Text requests for forgiveness with no trace of Mohammedan or Muslim concepts, includes, "Let [PN] enter *jannat al-na^{c}īm.*"

Finally, the term *mjnh* appears in a Basic Text inscription, MA 4138(13), which combines an extremely clear script with a very difficult text. In our attempt to elucidate the initial, pre-Muslim meaning of the concept *al-jannah*, we will consider this inscription first.

The interpretation of this inscription depends on our understanding of *mjnh*, which we read *majannah* and translate as 'sanctuary' or 'retreat.'[29] The suggested translation follows; the reasons for the translation are argued after it:

1–3 Allāh! forgive Aš^{c}aṯ bn ^{c}Iṣām his transgressions, the earlier ones and the later
3–5 verily You are the Listener, the Omniscient, the One-on-High, the Enormous, the Mighty, the Judge, the Gentle, the Loving/Compassionate One;
5 thus forgive him as long as he lives and until his death [*ḥayy-an wa-mayyit-an*, discussed above].
5–6 And also [*wa*] he entreats Allāh to grant him the/this sanctuary [*al-majannah*] and that he shall not leave sanctuary [*majannah*] until he can depart [lit: until the voyage—*al-ẓu^{c}ūn*—will be possible for him]
7 [in another hand] Forgive my Lord
8 [PN, mostly illegible]

29. *Majannah*: "a place in which one is concealed, hidden, protected, or in which one protects himself" (Lane, 2:464, col. 1).

It is possible to read *al-ẓuᶜūn* as a physical departure, in which case this is a request for sanctuary while the writer is awaiting the opportunity to move to somewhere else. It can also be read symbolically: as the departure from the land of the living. In the first case, his troubles would seem to be of an eminently earthly nature. In the second, this most carefully executed inscription records Ašᶜaṯ's vow to refrain from mundane business and devote the rest of his life to preparing for death while dwelling in sanctuary, i.e., in a retreat.[30] Even in this case, the notion of asylum, of being protected by Allāh, inherent in the term *majannah*, seems to be more important than that of departure. The latter is inevitable; and if, as in this text, no thought is given to a possible hereafter, the idea of departure simply marks the end of life and therefore of the danger of sinning and incurring God's retribution.

So the emphasis is not on the final departure, but on an asylum which protects the supplicant—from physical dangers or from the danger of sinning—during life. To read into this text the paradisaic verses of the Qurʾān is difficult, and probably misleading: it cannot mean paradise, for how then are we to interpret the reference to being "ready to depart" from paradise?

The basic meaning of words derived from the Semitic root *g.n.n.* is well known: 'to protect by surrounding with a fence' or anything else that lessens vulnerability. From this derives the meaning 'to shield' (and in Hebrew the noun 'shield'), and also the meaning 'to conceal, hide, especially by or in darkness (night) or depth'; hence the derivative noun meaning 'a deep place,' and so on. The above meanings are found in all the ancient Semitic languages, and are already attested in Ugaritic texts. The accepted meaning given in Lane's *Lexicon* for *majannah* is clearly part of this conceptual context: Arabic thus shares this basic network of meanings with the other languages of this family.

So considering the basic meaning of this root in Semitic languages, we suggest that the essential meaning of *jannah* was a place where a man could feel protected, with no fear of dangers, troubles, or malice of any sort. The verb *jannah* meant 'to hide and conceal; to keep in safety' (Munjid: *jannah*), and the noun was the place where this activity occurred: 'a hiding-

30. And again, he may be thinking in physical terms: he has left civilization and retreated to a desert community, or in spiritual ones: if Allāh protects him he will be in sanctuary, no matter where he is on Earth.

place, a safe place'; i.e., a sanctuary or refuge. Thus we have, in one of the Mohammedan texts from Jabal Usays:

> *Allāhumma ᵓadxil Muḥammad ᵓbn Walīd bi-ḏimati al-jannah ...*
> *wa-katabahu Bḥr wa-huwa yasᵓal Allāh al-jannah*
>
> Allāh! Admit Muḥammad ibn Walīd into the protection/security of *al-jannah* ... and Bḥr wrote it, and he asks Allāh for *al-jannah* (JU 18, ca. A.H. 120–30/738–48).[31]

Here *ḏimmah* (protection, custody) reveals the meaning of *jannah*. Such protection can only be acquired through God's goodwill towards the supplicant, so that we find the very frequent expression "admit me (*ᵓadxilnī*) to *al-jannah*" or "admit me into *al-jannah* by Your affection/kindness (*bi-raḥmatika*)."

The sanctuary requested "admit me to *al-jannah*" in its variant forms—e.g., "Admit him to the protection of *al-jannah*" (JU 18, given above); "he requests of Allāh *al-jannah* through His love" (HS 3154)—thus does not necessarily imply the hereafter. In the Mohammedan texts it seems to be a request for God's protection from worldly evils and misfortunes. We may compare it with the parallel phrase "admit him by Your love among Your righteous worshippers/servants": *ᵓadxilhu bi-raḥmatika fī ᶜibādika al-ṣāliḥīn.*[32] The righteous—*al-ṣāliḥīn*—and their good deeds—*ṣāliḥāt*—refer here, and even more clearly in the Qurᵓān, to those who live on Earth. The Qurᵓān divides mankind (and Jinn) into two groups: the righteous and the impious (e.g., Q.7:168; 72:11), and Allāh will reward the members of each according to their deeds. This reward comes not just after death, but also during life: "Do those who seek evil (*ᵓijtaraḥū al-sayᵓah*) suppose that We shall make/consider them (*najᶜalhum*) like those who believe and do good deeds (*al-ṣāliḥāt*) in the same measure, in their life and in their death (*maḥyāhum wa-mamātuhum*)?" (Q.45:21). Thus the *ṣāliḥūn* will inherit the earth (Q.21:105).

We consider, then, that the request for admittance to *al-jannah* expressed a desire for protection from the evils *of this world*. Similarly, the request for admittance into the ranks of the 'righteous' expressed a desire to avoid the specific evil of being considered 'impious,' again during one's life.

---

31. See al-ᶜUšš (1964), p. 247 for a consideration of the historical date.
32. Al-ᶜUšš (1964), JU 32 and 43; not given in appendix.

The way to be considered righteous rather than impious (repeatedly voiced in the Qur᾽ān, e.g., Q.40:58; 38:29; 45:21), was to believe in Allāh and do good deeds, thus earning His forgiveness for the evil which no ordinary man could avoid committing.[33] There is thus a conceptual link between forgiveness and *jannah*—those who earn Allāh's forgiveness are protected from worldly misfortune—and the Qur᾽ān expresses this link:

> Compete for your Lord's forgiveness and a *jannah* as wide as the heavens and the earth made ready for those who trust Allāh and His messengers. (Q.57:21, our translation; see also Q.3:132–133 for a similar verse with some variations).

The forgiveness is sought now, while alive—not just after death—and so is the sanctuary from evil. One should not read into it the Muslim paradise.[34]

When *jannah* first appears, in the Jabal Usays Mohammedan inscriptions, it seems to mean a sanctuary, or place of protection from worldly evil. It may also mean—and in the verses from the Qur᾽ān quoted above, does also mean—an unspecified reward for having avoided doing evil, i.e., for being one of the righteous.[35] It is only in later, ᶜAbbāsid, texts that *jannah* clearly means a place in the next world: "Allāh! let me depart from this world sound and wise, and let me enter *jannah* safely."[36]

Another consideration also leads us to doubt that *jannah* meant paradise already from its first occurrence. The conceptual opposite of paradise, in the Judaic/Christian tradition, is hell. The corresponding Muslim term, *al-nār*—the Fire—does not occur until the late Marwānid period, and even then it is very rare. The Marwānid texts that mention *al-nār* come from Jabal Usays, and request *al-jannah* and protection through Allāh from *al-nār*: *᾽as᾽al al-jannah wa-᾽aᶜūḏu bihi min al-nār* "I request

---

33. Cf. Lane's comment that *salāḥ-on* was "not ... an attribute of a prophet nor of an apostle, but only of a person inferior to these" (Lane, *salāḥ* 4:1715 col. 1).

34. Indeed, the Qur᾽ān often describes *jannah* as a physical garden of pleasure with no spiritual overtones.

35. Part of the material preserved in the Qur᾽ān derives from a Mohammedan conceptual universe, part from a more Muslim one. Thus in addition to the verses quoted above, there are, obviously, verses referring to *jannah* as the abode of those who have been judged righteous on the final Day of Judgment (e.g., Q.25:15, 24; Q.26:85; Q.88).

36. Jabal Tubayq, Jordan; undated, assumed 3rd/9th century. Source: Baramki (1952); Baramki's translation.

al-jannah and seek protection through Him from the fire."[37] The phrase *ᵓasᵓal Allāh al-jannah wa-ᵓaᶜūḏu bihi min* [*al-nār*] *is also found in the Mohammedan part of the undated composite father-son Negev inscription from Sede Boqer: MA 4205(14). A little earlier, from ca. 85/704, we have the Negev text: "Allāh! You are the Protector/Shelterer, my Lord who protects/ shelters from the fire"—al-muᶜīd min al-saᶜīr.*[38]

So what *al-jannah* and *al-nār* had in common, at their first appearance, was the concept of *Allāh's protection from evil* of one sort or another: *al-jannah*, embodying the concept of protection from worldly evils, was now paired with a request for protection from the punishment meted out to the impious after death. But they were not yet the polar extremes of reward and punishment—the eternal abode of the righteous versus that of the wicked. No Marwānid text displays such a development into this Muslim concept; but it has been reached, very clearly, in Q.2:81-82: "They who accumulate evil (deeds on their account) ... such are inmates of the Fire, where they will remain for ever; but the faithful (*allaḏīna ᵓaāmanū*) who perform good deeds, they are the inmates of *al-jannah* to remain there forever" (Q.2:81-82, translation following Ben-Shemesh).

So we first find the concept *al-nār*—the punishment received after death for having done evil during this life—in late Marwānid times: in a Negev inscription from ca. 85/704, the last year of ᶜAbd al-Malik's reign, and at Jabal Usays among those attached to the Marwānid court. One could hope to obtain Allāh's protection from this fate[39] by being righteous during life, and through this idea of protection, *al-nār* became linked with the concept of *al-jannah*—protection from evildoing during this life. This opened the way for development of the Muslim meanings of the words *jannah* and *nār*. *Al-jannah*, which earlier meant a (usually earthly) refuge, or sanctuary, expanded to include the concept of paradise—the place of reward for pious deeds, in opposition to *al-nār*, the abode of the wicked.

Clearly, the whole subject of the afterlife received theological consider-

---

37. al-ᶜUšš (1964): JU 72, ca. A.H. 113/732, al-Hišām's reign; also JU 49 (by the uncle of the caliph Abū Jaᶜfar al-Mansūr?); JU 58 (p. 272, not given in the Appendix of Inscriptions) with Shi'ite connotations, mid-2nd century.

38. MA 450(8), datable to ca. 85/704 because its owner left another inscription dated that year.

39. Contrast this with the Qurᵓānic concept: in the Qurᵓān *ᵓaᶜūḏu* 'I seek protection' never refers to protection from *al-nār*; usually it refers to protection from *šaytān*, who causes evil and mischief in *this* world.

ation over a long period. We would tentatively suggest that the last part of the conceptual complex to be adopted was that of resurrection—*al-baᶜṯ*. In our Negev inscriptions it appears only twice, both times in an undated text containing no other phrases or concepts which might classify it as Muslim or Mohammedan: *Allhm ṣally ᶜalà Xālid bn ᶜUmar yawma yamūt wa-yawma yubᶜaṯ ḥayy-an ʾamīn rabb al-ᶜalamīn* "Allāh! Incline to Xālid bn ᶜUmar on the day he dies and on the day he will be resurrected alive, Amen Lord of Creation."[40] We classify the concept of resurrection as Muslim, because elsewhere it appears only in Muslim texts.

"We" and "Others"

Most of the Basic Text inscriptions record a private message—usually a request for forgiveness—from one person to Allāh. The supplications are personal, and the only person mentioned is the owner of the inscription. But in other Basic Texts other people also appear: the *writer*, and not infrequently the *one who reads* (the inscription aloud, i.e., recites it) and the *one who hears* (the reading of the inscription) are included in the plea for pardon: e.g., EL 200C(2). The inclusion of a second, third, or even fourth "companion" to the supplication was taken seriously, as is shown by the care the scribes took to include themselves in the supplications,[41] and the fact that they troubled at all to add words on behalf of the reader and the listener. Considerable labor was involved in inscribing on rocks, often with only primitive tools; and if, as was usually the case, the owner of the inscription employed a scribe, it cost him extra to add words. Thus brevity was the rule. Despite this, in the Basic Texts there are a number of examples where not only was the listener included, but the conditions for his inclusion were listed: *ʾin āmana* "If he trusts/believes" and/or *wa-qāla ʾamīn* "if he says Amen" etc.[42] The writer here expects a brother in faith to stop at the inscription and recite it; anyone near enough to hear should join in the test by also repeating the formula. Those who do not belong to the same

---

40. AR 2100(2); AR 271(2), badly preserved; not given in appendix.

41. In the Basic Texts the scribe does not as a rule give his name but writes "and the one who wrote (it)"—*wa-li-man kataba*.

42. E.g., the Karbalah inscription, DKI 163, dated 64/684, and the Negev inscriptions EL 200C(2), NK 380(4), MA 4319(21) (where the request to include others was added in a different hand at the end), GM 389(4) (which specifies "only if he believes"), MA 458(8), and MA 4283A(20).

religious community are excluded from the forgiveness requested of Allāh for those who do. The owner of the inscription, it appears, was prepared to go to considerable effort and/or expense in order to ensure that only those who declared themselves to be of his own religious community—by reciting the inscription themselves and/or saying "Amen" on reading it—should be included in the request for forgiveness.

This attitude is found in the Mohammedan texts also: "And [forgive] the writer and the reciter and the one who listens and says, Amen"—SC 301(3)—or "and him who recites and him who says Amen."[43]

This custom indicates a degree of concern regarding the unbelievers who lived among the believers or in close proximity to them. The believers, it would appear, do not feel themselves to be the majority: it is not at all certain, their logic goes, that someone passing along the road and seeing the inscription will be one of Us, and God forbid that we should request forgiveness for unbelievers of any type! But by the time of the Muslim texts—such as BR 5102(30), datable to 300/912—this habit of including selected others in the request had widened to an all-inclusive blessing: "Be kind/loving towards him who passes on this path." The inference is that all passers-by are now expected to be members of the writer's religious community.

Muḥammad the Prophet and the Definition of God

We postulate that the particular titles given to God, and especially the method of defining Him via reference to prophets, arose not by chance, but in response to specific needs. In the highly charged sectarian atmosphere of the 7th and 8th centuries C.E., one of the believer's problems was how to declare his religious affiliation. This was not a trivial concern; it entailed distinguishing between Rabbinic Judaism, a non-Rabbinic sect such as the Ebionites or some other version of Judeo-Christianity, Samaritanism, Abrahamism, Indeterminate Monotheism, and any of several varieties of Christianity. The method of definition that the rock inscribers found meaningful was to specify the attributes of their god. Defining one's god resulted in defining one's sect in distinction from all others; and it was a clear function of the opening and concluding formulae, i.e., the set phrases

---

43. SC 305(3), dated 112/730, where the inclusion of others, and the date, were added after the concluding phrase, though in the same hand.

customarily used at the beginning and end of a text, or, in the case of a concluding phrase, to indicate a pause in a longer inscription.

Within the general group of Basic Texts, there is a distinct Judeo-Christian subset whose opening phrases define God by reference to two prophets: "Lord of Moses and Jesus" (or less often: "Jesus and Moses"). The formula "Allāh Lord of Moses" in the opening phrase is also very common. Defining God by reference to a prophet dissociated the worshipper from both Christians and Rabbinic Jews. The former would have defined their faith by invoking the Trinity; the latter, by listing the Patriarchs. But a single prophet could not provide a suitable definition. "Lord of Abraham" was too general, and if taken specifically, would imply Abrahamism. Similarly, "Lord of Moses," if taken specifically, would imply Judaism; "Lord of Aaron," Samaritanism. "Lord of Moses and Jesus" not only dissociated the worshipper from all these, it also pointed to his own affiliations: it is plainly a Judeo-Christian formula, and the reference to one or other of these prophets—the very common "Lord of Moses" or, much rarer, "Lord of Jesus"—should be seen as deriving from it. The latter, in which Jesus fills a slot reserved for a human prophet, could still not be accepted (for opposite reasons) by either Christian or Jew, but it is a much less obvious declaration of Judeo-Christianity than the doublet.

The basic concluding phrase of all the inscriptions was usually *ᵓamīn rabb al-ᶜalamīn* "Amen, Lord of Creation." This is not in itself a sectarian definition, for any monotheist could subscribe to it. This may be why later texts add a "pair of prophets" also to the concluding phrase. We have four examples of Basic Texts whose concluding phrase includes such a formula,[44] but the practice of including prophets in this position became more usual only in the Mohammedan inscriptions.[45] The phrase "Lord of Moses and Aaron" is the most common, perhaps because it would not be a natural choice for either Jew or Samaritan (and of course a Christian would define God in terms that included the Son). Certainly it had a fair length of currency in the sectarian milieu, starting in Hišām's reign, and surviving into the Qurᵓān. Other prophets included in a "pair of prophets" concluding phrase are Abraham and Muḥammad.

44. *rabb Hārūn wa-ᶜĪsà* ("Lord of Aaron and Jesus"), HL 4900(27); *rabb Mūsà wa-Ibrāhīm* ("Lord of Moses and Abraham"), MM 113(1); *rabb Mūsà wa-Hārūn* ("Lord of Moses and Aaron"), SC 303(3) and YA 3112(5).

45. E.g., SC 305(3), dated 112/730.

The Karbalah inscription from Iraq (Basic Text, dated 54/684) defines Allāh as "Lord of Gabriel, Michael, and Isrāfīl."[46] Such a definition by reference to angels is otherwise unknown; but it foreshadows their prominence in later Islam. It is not specifically Judeo-Christian, but is, of course, clearly subordinationist, asserting God's supreme position as Lord over the archangels. It serves to remind us that the term Indeterminate Monotheism includes a wide range of beliefs, different groups emphasizing different aspects; and it hints at sectarian disputes referred to more openly in later, Mohammedan and Muslim texts.

The Basic Texts refer to God as *Allāh, Allāhumma* (*ᵓallhm*), and as *rabb/rabbī* (Lord/my Lord) and *ᵓilāhi* (*ᵓlhy*) (my God). The latter, *ᵓlhy*, is attested as yet only once, combined with *rabb*: *rabbī wa-ᵓilāhi.*[47] In the Basic Texts, the recorded titles in the opening phrase of an invocation are: *rabb, rabbī, rabb Mūsà wa-ᶜĪsà, rabb ᶜĪsà wa-Mūsà, rabb Mūsà*, and *rabb ᶜĪsà*. The concluding phrases usually refer to God only as *rabb al-ᶜalamīn*, though as already mentioned a few cases have been found, so far, where this is followed by a "pair of prophets." Thus in the Basic Class *rabb* is a common appellation for God, and *rabb Mūsà wa-ᶜĪsà* is also quite common as an opening phrase. The word *rabb* appears as *rabbī* in place of the word *Allāh*, but this usage did not continue for long; *Allāh/Allāhumma* are the most common words for the deity. The word *rabb* continued to be used in the formula *rabb al-ᶜalamīn*, and, in later texts, as a construct with a "pair of prophets." The latter usages of *rabb*, as far as we know to date, are usually found only in concluding phrases.

The formulae of the opening phrase indicate Allāh's prophets or messengers, and for a long time Muḥammad does not occur among them. Even after he was introduced into the official state religion in 71–72/690–692, the popular inscriptions continued to ignore him until Hišām's day. Then, suddenly, around the period 112–117/730s, he becomes a constant feature of the rock inscriptions: not as one of a "pair of prophets" in an opening phrase defining God,[48] but in the body of the inscriptions, by himself.

---

46. DKI 163:5–6, in Appendix of Inscriptions.

47. MA 87/10 (field number: not published in *AAIN*), probably late from paleographic and orthographic considerations.

48. Only one inscription has so far been found that combines Muḥammad with another prophet (and perhaps significantly, it is Ibrāhīm) in a definition of God: it is, of course, in a concluding phrase, "Amen Lord of Muḥammad and Ibrāhīm": HS 3155(6), dated 117/735.

However, his role, context, and meaning are as little defined in them as in the Dome of the Rock, forty years before. The supplications refer to him as *Muḥammad al-nabī* or *Muḥammad rasūl Allāh*, and we can infer from them only that, notwithstanding his special relationship with God, he was as human as anyone else, and as much in need of forgiveness:

Allāhumma ṣally ʿalà Muḥammad al-nabī wa-ʿalà man yuṣalli ʿalayhi
"Allāh! Incline towards Muḥammad the Prophet and towards those who pray for him" (HS 3154(6):1–2).

Allāhumma ʾiġfir li-Muḥammad rasūl Allāh wa-li-man kataba hadà[!] *al-kitāb wa-li-man qaraʾahu qul ʾamīn rabb al-ʿalamīn*
"Allāh! Forgive Muḥammad the Messenger of Allāh, and the one who wrote this text and the one who recites it. Say Amen, Lord of Creation" (SC 301(3):4–6).

Interestingly, the Mohammedan "creation *ḥadīṯ* text" dated 117/735—HS 3153(6), discussed earlier—does not mention Muḥammad at all, but refers only to "the Prophet."[49] In this it resembles the Qurʾān, and differs markedly from the other Muslim texts, in which the Prophet is always defined as Muḥammad. This "creation *ḥadīṯ*" may have arisen from the "prophetical" Judeo-Christian background, rather than from the elaborators of the official religion. It was, however, accepted by a Mohammedan. We may perhaps conclude from this that "prophetical logia" were now widespread and accepted by Mohammedans. Certainly Mohammedanism—the original "prophetical" Judeo-Christianity plus the identification of their prophet as Muḥammad—was now accepted by wider sections of the population.

Mohammedan texts such as the above continued to be inscribed in the Negev for some time; those discovered so far express this level of definition, with no further development of the concept of the Prophet. Then, ca. 160/776, the first dated Muslim texts appear in Sede Boqer, bringing with them a new set of concepts. Among these is the attitude to Muḥammad. The popular Muslim texts include reactions to views of Muḥammad that do not appear in the Mohammedan ones—especially, they feel a need to refute the idea that Muḥammad has divine or semidivine qualities: "Muḥammad,

49. Though Muḥammad is clearly mentioned in another inscription from the same cluster, HS 3154(6), where Allāh is requested to "incline to" him.

Jesus and Ezra and all Creation are subordinated worshippers" (*ᶜibād marbūbīn* [=*marbūbūn*]): ST 640(34):4–7, dated 170/786. We see this as a reply to the views referred to in Q.9:30: *wa-qālat al-Yahūd ᶜUzayr ᵓibnu Allāh, wa-qalat al-Naṣārà al-Masīḥ ᵓibnu Allāh*: "The Jews say ᶜUzayr (=Esdras/Ezra) is the Son of Allāh and the Christians say *al-Masīḥ* is the Son of Allāh."[50] This inscription reacts to a nonsubordinationist view of Muḥammad's status. It denies that anyone, Muḥammad included, can be so close to Allāh as to merit the description "Son of God," which implies a share in the Godhead. We know that in the late 1st and early 2nd centuries A.H. there were those who considered Muḥammad to be qualitatively different from the messengers of the past, and awaited his second coming—another Judaic and Christian concept. The *Sīrah*, too, refers to this tendency to attribute to Muḥammad superhuman or divine qualities, in the *ḥadīṯ* concerning the reactions to Muḥammad's death: ᶜUmar rose and said, "Some of the disaffected will allege that the apostle is dead, but ... he is not dead; he has gone to his Lord as Moses ... went and was hidden from his people for forty days, returning to them after it was said that he had died."[51] ᵓAbu Bakr restrained him, and said to the people, "If anyone worships Muḥammad—Muḥammad is dead. If anyone worships Allāh—Allāh is alive and immortal."[52] Thus when the *Sīrah* was composed, or edited, there was an evident tendency to "believe in" Muḥammad; but we do not know if this was in the first half of the 2nd century A.H., when Ibn Isḥāq made the initial draft, or in the second half, when Ibn Hišām edited it. The popular inscriptions, however, give us a slightly narrower time span. In the second decade of that century it finds no echo in them—on the contrary, the Mohammedan inscriptions ask Allāh to "incline to" Muḥammad and plead for forgiveness for him; in 160/776, it is a belief that requires firm refutation.

This was a development at odds with the general spirit of the religion from its inception. The Judeo-Christian background from which Islam

---

50. Esdras/Ezra: i.e., he who, according to anti-Judaic tradition, rewrote the Torah from the memory of the Elders after the copy transmitted by Moses had been lost when the First Temple was destroyed. This allegation is the "fact" upon which was based the claim, upheld in the Qurᵓān, that the book which the Jews call the Torah is not that which Moses transmitted to the Children of Israel.

51. *Sīrah* 2:655; tr. Guillaume (1955), p. 682.

52. Ibid., p. 683.

arose was firmly subordinationist, and as we have seen, Indeterminate Monotheism defined Allāh as Lord of all: *rabb al-ᶜalamīn*. Thus the Basic Text definition of God as *rabb Mūsà wa-ᶜĪsà* is not a *declaration* of the subordination of Moses and Jesus, but a *use* of it—the fact itself, that Jesus like Moses is subordinate, is taken for granted. The Karbalah inscription, DKI 163, dated 64/684, similarly uses the archangels as referents in a subordinationist definition of God. And subordination remained the guiding principle of what became the Muslim definition of God—the *tawḥīd* + *lā šarīk lahu*, introduced with the official declaration of Mohammedanism in the Dome of the Rock. The other main message of that declaration, of course, was *Muḥammad rasūl Allāh*; and these elements, separately or together, henceforth defined the official view of God. Thus the personal inscription on the Qaṣr al-Ḥayr fortress (DKI 211), dated 110/728–29 (Hišām's days), includes the *basmalah*, the full *tawḥīd* including *lā šarīk lahu*, and *Muḥammad rasūl Allāh*.

Of these elements, only *Muḥammad rasūl Allāh* had been accepted by the writers of our rock inscriptions even in Hišām's day.[53] The subordinationist definitions were not accepted: the *tawḥīd* does not appear in any Mohammedan popular inscription from the Negev, nor from the Jabal Usays texts.[54] It appears only with the Muslim texts, starting in the earlier group, that from the central Negev dated ca. 160–170/770s–780s; and becoming especially common in the later group, from the western Negev (Nessana area), dated ca. 300/913.

This casts a certain amount of light on the fact that the Muslim texts find it necessary to reaffirm the principle of subordination, at least

---

53. In one sense, he replaces Jesus: the definition of the latter as Allāh's prophet and worshipper is also absent from the Mohammedan popular texts; in fact there is no Christology in them at all. It is, nevertheless, worth noting that one of the Jabal Usays inscriptions (JU 41, al-ᶜUšš [1964], p. 260, erroneously printed 360) contains, without ascription to any speaker, a verse which the Qurʾān ascribes to the infant Jesus: "I am a servant/worshipper of God, He gave me the Book and made me a prophet and blessed me" (lit.: caused me to be blessed).

54. The Jabal Usays inscriptions do contain the ancient Judeo-Christian formula *lā ilah illā huwa* "There is no God but Him," which occurs also in the Qurʾān: *lā ilah illa huwa al-ḥayy al-qayyūm* "There is no God but Him, the Living, the Everlasting": Q.2:255 = JU 16 (al-ᶜUšš [1964], p. 241), dated 93/711–12; JU 26 (p. 249); JU 51 (p. 268). The phrase *lā ilaha illā huwa* occurs in JU 56 (p. 271); and *lā ilaha illa huwa waḥīd* (not Qurʾānic) in JU 96 (p. 296). These inscriptions are not included in the appendix. And cf. the start of Part III Chapter 4.

against the view that Muḥammad had divine qualities. There are, besides, signs that Muḥammad was not the only one whose position was open to doubt. There are Muslim inscriptions from the Negev in which the supplicant entreats not only Allāh but also His whole retinue to bestow their favor upon him: *Allāhumma ṣally anta wa-malaʾikatuka al-muqaribīn wa-ʾanbiyāʾuka al-mursalīn wa-ʿibāduka al-ṣāliḥīn ʿalà* [PN] "Allāh! You and Your angels who are nigh unto You, and Your prophets who were sent and Your righteous worshippers, be inclined (in favor) unto [PN]": BR 5117(31), ca. 300/912.

This indicates that Allāh's entourage was considered to share some of His power, or, as His agents, to have enough power in their own right (even if delegated by Allāh) to make meaningful a supplication to them as well as to Him. The text dates to the last decade of Ṭabarī's life; and we note that he was concerned to prohibit appeals to Allāh in such terms—cf. his commentary on Q.33:56, the very text which appears twice in the Dome of the Rock.

The official religion saw the belief in Muḥammad's supernatural status as exactly parallel to the Christian claim for the divinity of Jesus and the claim of some Jewish sects for that of Ezra—and firmly discounted all three. Having from the start adopted a stringent form of monotheism, it thereafter refused a share of divine qualities to any mortal, Muḥammad included. It was concerned to develop the figure of the Prophet parallel to that of Moses, along historical, not supernatural, lines. But the evidence so far available suggests that while the official religion remained strictly subordinationist, and even as the late Marwānid and early ʿAbbāsid scholars were developing Muḥammad into a historical figure, opposite tendencies were asserting themselves in the popular form of the religion. The *tawḥīd* did not find ready acceptance in Mohammedan inscriptions, in sharp contrast to the Muslim ones. And although the beliefs in the divine qualities of Muḥammad—and possibly the angels—are not expressed in our Mohammedan texts, they were widespread enough by the 160s/770s–780s to require firm refutation in the Muslim ones. We conclude that during the Mohammedan phase, down to ca. 160 A.H., the popular form of belief was less strictly unitarian than the official form. It accepted Muḥammad the Prophet, but found little use for declarations emphasizing the singularity of God or His lack of associates. And while the rock inscriptions now in our possession clearly regarded Muḥammad as a mere mortal, some forms of the popular religion apparently tended to magnify him beyond human proportions.

We consider that the lack of close definitions of Muḥammad in the

Mohammedan texts (both royal and popular inscriptions), followed by their appearance in already-developed form in the Muslim literature, indicates that the elaboration of Muḥammad into a historical figure, and the accompanying creation of a salvation history, was not a popular development, but the work of scholars. It took place in early ᶜAbbāsid and probably also late Marwānid times, presumably under royal aegis. We think it justifiable to date this activity—the consolidation of the historical and religious aspects of Muḥammad—to the mid- to late 8th century C.E. The aim was to present a coherent historical narrative in which people, homeland, and confessional history—from Abraham to Muḥammad—are complementary parts of a complete world view, illustrating the manifestation of Allāh's will in the real world. In this process, Muḥammad becomes a historical figure set beside the great Judaic prophets—Abraham and Moses—and equal to them. Between these three there is no room for comparison, nor for polemic. The polemic is directed against attacks on the doctrine of strict subordination, advanced by those who considered some prophets—Jesus, Ezra, and Muḥammad himself—to have had divine or superhuman qualities.

OTHER CONCEPTS FIRST INTRODUCED IN MOHAMMEDAN TEXTS

'The Right Way' and 'Guidance'

It will by now be apparent that the Mohammedan texts are much richer in language than the previous classes, and that most of this enrichment derives not just from linguistic elaboration, but from the introduction of new concepts, requiring new expressions to convey them. One concept not mentioned so far is *ṣirāt mustaqīm*—'a Straight Way' or 'the Right Way.' It is connected with the idea of guidance—*hudà*, as in *wa-ʾahdihi ṣirāt-an mustaqīm-an* "and guide him onto the Straight Way," which occurs once in the Negev inscriptions: SC 305(3):2, dated 112/730. As we saw in the previous chapter, 'guidance' was also one concept in the web of meanings attached to the complex Prophet/Muḥammad/Mahdī, and was introduced into the official faith a few years after Muḥammad himself, around 77 A.H., when the phrase "He sent His messenger with guidance and the religion of truth" was introduced on ᶜAbd al-Malik's post-Reform coins. From that time on, this phrase was a part of the official declarations. It appeared, for instance, in the official inscription in the mosque of ᶜAmr at Fusṭāṭ, dated

92/710–11,[55] in the papyri protocols (e.g., that from 98/716–717), and could be expected to occur in every official text thereafter.

It therefore comes as no surprise that the concept of *hudà* first appears in popular inscriptions in a text from Hišām's time, and that it is absent from the earlier inscriptions. Like Muḥammad himself, it entered the popular religion, judging from the inscriptions, nearly forty years later than its adoption into the official faith.

Jahd and *ᵓistišhād*

Another set of new concepts is that of *jahd* 'exertion' and *ᵓistišhād* 'martyrdom.' In the Negev, the first occurrence of both terms is in a Mohammedan text dated 117/735, HS 3155–56(6): *Allāhumma ᵓajᶜal ᶜamalī jihād-an (jhd) wa ᵓajᶜal wāfinī ᵓistišhād fī sabīlika* "Allāh consider my deeds great exertion (*jihād*), and accept my compassion as martyrdom in Your cause." This is the sole instance of *ᵓistišhād* found so far in a Mohammedan popular inscription. The meaning "to give witness, to testify" occurs only in Muslim texts, and will be discussed below.

The concept of Intercession

Intercession is a practice typical of a court of law. The concept already appears in the Dome of the Rock: *wa-taqabal šafāᶜatahu yawm al-qiyāmah fī ᵓummatihi* "And accept [Allāh] his [i.e., Muḥammad's] intercession on the Day of Resurrection for his *ᵓummah*." It is absent from the other royal inscriptions, but this means little, since their context does not lead us to expect it. It does not appear in the Mohammedan popular inscriptions, nor even in the Muslim ones up to 300/912 discovered so far. But it is well attested in the Qurᵓān, where it seems to belong to a conceptual system which groups *šafīᶜ* 'intercessor' with *waliyy* 'loyal friend, protector, ally' and *ḥamīm* 'intimate, bosom friend' (e.g., Q.26:98–101).

We may, however, see signs in the 3rd-century Muslim texts of a concept akin to intercession, yet free of the latter's grimmer associations of Judgment. Most of these inscriptions (groups HR and BR, the majority of them by the bn Tamīm brothers, especially Bašīr bn Tamīm, and dated by BR 5119 to 300/912) are essentially requests to Allāh to be well disposed

55. *RCEA* 19.

towards—*ṣly ʿalà*—the writer and/or others, including Muḥammad the Prophet: e.g., BR 5134(32). Very often the writer petitions not just Allāh Himself, but also His angels or "His two angels" and others who are near to Him. Thus BR 5117(31): "Allāh! Incline You and Your angels who are nigh [unto You] and Your prophets who were sent and Your righteous worshippers unto [PN]."[56] The text may also give a list of expectations or specific requests—as in BR 5115(31)—but in general there is no further clarification as to what the petitioner actually wants. This may indicate that it is a general supplication to secure the *constant* sympathy of God and His retinue. But no actual *intercession with God* can be traced—Allāh is approached directly, with or without members of His entourage. Indeed, occasionally it is Muḥammad the Prophet for whom Allāh's favorable regard is sought.[57]

We conclude that intercession was one of the official concepts of the state religion, connected with the view of the hereafter and the idea of Judgment—also pervasive in the Qurʾān. But the absence of requests for intercession from the popular texts, even Muslim ones, indicates that the popular faith, having exchanged the old atmosphere of sin and fear for a positive, optimistic approach to God, found little use for this concept in its everyday dealings with Allāh, preferring a more direct approach: a general request, made directly to Allāh, to view the petitioner with favor.

MUSLIM CONCEPTS

We have a small body of Muslim inscriptions from the Negev and several from Jabal Usays. All these are distinguished from the Mohammedan inscriptions by various terms and concepts, and in general by their idiom. As mentioned above, the three dated groups of Mohammedan texts found so far—from 112 A.H. and 117 A.H. in the Negev and from the 90s to 119 A.H. in Jabal Usays—neither use the same idiom nor contain the same concepts as the ʿAbbāsid texts.

Firstly, in the ʿAbbāsid texts as a whole—not just the inscriptions—it is always clear that "the Prophet" means Muḥammad. Secondly, the complex

---

56. Cf. a tombstone from Egypt: EMC 14:17–18 (A.H. 190/806), publ. in Hawary and Rached (1932): *ṣly Allāh wa-malāʾikatuhu wa-ruslūhu wa-al-nabiyūn* (the rest is missing) "Incline Allāh and His angels and His messengers and the prophets...."

57. Thus BR 5134(32), BR 5150(32), and BR 5116(31).

of concepts regarding the afterlife—heaven, hell, and final resurrection—now first become developed into their Muslim form. These concepts have been discussed in the section on *al-jannah* and *al-nār* above. We would reiterate here that in our opinion the sudden emergence into the Muslim popular inscriptions of the complex of concepts regarding what happens after death, indicates theological development of this question on another plane—not in the popular religion, but among religious scholars. The resulting crystallization of orthodox belief was then promulgated among the population.

Another Muslim concept is that of *Allāh as overlord (patron) and helper*. There is an initial formulation of this idea in the Jabal Usays Mohammedan texts, e.g., JU 103, dated 108/729: *Allāh walyy* [PN], and JU 34 (not included in the appendix), by the same person: *waliyy al-muttaqīn* "the patron/helper of those who fear God." JU 105, by a different person, includes *Allāhumma kun ᵓanta waliyy* [PN] "Allāh! Be the patron/helper of [PN]". But the definition of Allāh as *al-mawlà*, and the more developed expression *niᶜma al-mawlà wa-niᶜma al-naṣīr*—is Muslim, as in, for example, the Negev Muslim inscription EKI 261, dated 164/780–81. The concept is also common in the Qurᵓān. This exact phrasing is not Qurᵓānic, but the concept of Allāh as overlord (patron) and helper or ally is well attested there, e.g., *ᵓiᶜtaṣimū bi-llāhi huwa mawlākum fa-niᶜma al-mawlà* "Strengthen yourselves with Allāh, He is your overlord (patron), a Gracious Patron."[58] There is also *wa-mā lakum min dūni-llāhi min waliyy-en wa-lā naṣīr-en* "Beside Allāh you have neither ally/overlord (patron) nor helper" (Q.2:107).

Finally, there is the idea of *giving testimony*, referred to above as another Muslim concept. It is, of course, well attested in Rabbinic Judaic and Christian writings, where it is connected with the concept of self-sacrifice for the sake of divine truth.[59] But in the popular religion it first occurs in the Muslim texts, expressed by means of the root *š.h.d.*: to testify, to give witness regarding Allāh. As already noted, this root did occur once in a Mohammedan inscription, HS 3155(6), but there its meaning was 'martyrdom' (for Allāh's cause); the verbal form existed, but not the meaning it later expressed.

---

58. Q.22:78, translation following Ben-Shemesh.

59. Compare *martyreo, martyrion, martys* in Lampe, *Patristic Greek Lexicon*, p. 828 col. 1–p. 830 col. 2; and the various forms of bearing witness regarding particulars of faith, common in the Rabbinic literature.

The notion of testimony—giving witness as the mode of announcing one's faith—marks the Muslim stage in the conceptual development of the religion, and it is a significant aspect of the polemical features of the Muslim texts. It seems not to be earlier than the ᶜAbbāsid period, or late in the Marwānid. Thus in the Muslim texts, the claim "I witness" (*ᵓas̆hadu* or a similar expression) is quite frequent.[60] The Basic Class and Mohammedan texts so far discovered, on the other hand, lack it entirely.

The idea of giving witness is also Qurᵓānic, e.g., Q.6:19: "Can ye possibly bear witness (*tas̆hadūna*) that there are other gods (*ᵓālihāt*) associated with Allāh? Say: I shall not/cannot bear witness (*lā ᵓas̆hadu*). Say: but in truth He is God, one and only" (translation following Alī, A.Y. and Ben-Shemesh).

But the concept of giving witness more commonly attested in the Qurᵓān is that summed up in the phrase *kafà bi-llāhi s̆ahīd-an* "Allāh suffices as a witness" (e.g., Q.48:28). This phrase also does not occur in the pre-Muslim Negev inscriptions, neither in the Basic nor even in the Mohammedan texts. It is a late entrant to the vocabulary, which presumably became current in the popular religious idiom as a result of its incorporation into the Qurᵓān, or into the body of holy literature from which the Qurᵓān was canonized.[61] Its use points a contrast, not with the believer who bears witness, but with the practice, pervasive in the Judaic-Christian sectarian milieu, of referring to Scripture (or other authoritative writings) to ascertain religious authority, i.e., prove the truth of one's assertions regarding God.[62] In the Qurᵓān there is no question of bringing witness from scripture, canonical or otherwise. The Qurᵓān of course acknowledges the existence of the Book/the Books in the context of its discourse with Judaism and Christianity; but those who bear witness from a Book, the *ᵓahl al-kitāb*, are not the True Believers: they are, rather, those who must support their false claims by calling a book to witness. But Allāh Himself gives witness of the

60. Thus BR 5132(32), EDI 261, and ST 640(34). The owner of the inscription "testifies that..." or "testifies unto Allāh that... ." ST 640(34) has several instances of *s̆.h.d.* in this one text.

61. Examples from the Negev texts include BR 5131(32), datable to ca. 300/912; and ST 640(34), dated 170/786.

62. We recall the "Colloquium between the Patriarch and the Emir," examined in Part III Chapter 2: the emir demanded scriptural proof—from the Pentateuch alone—of the patriarch's assertions.

True Faith, through His messenger(s), with no recourse to a book. This may well reflect a situation of intersectarian polemic, current before the Qurʾān was composed out of existing sectarian *pericopae*, in which the adherents of a prophet, lacking a scripture of their own, maintain that under the new dispensation of their prophet such a scripture is in fact unnecessary. It is, in the circumstances, ironic that these phrases found their way into the canon.

6

Scripture and Salvation History

This study has essentially been concerned with the initial stages of the Arab State and the Arab religion: the events which led up to their formation and their early years. It was no part of our original purpose to examine the 2nd century, not even its most important religious achievements: the production of the *Sīrah*, the official Biography of the Prophet, the foundation of a salvation history, and the canonization of a scripture. But having come this far, we feel a need to place these events within the framework of the particular view of history proposed in this book. To attempt such a task within the scope of these few pages is of course absurd; so the following chapter can do no more than offer a few general comments, referring to the material already covered earlier in this work, but foregoing detail for the sake of perspective.

THE DEVELOPMENT OF THE QURʾĀN

The Qurʾān contains material from disparate sources. Some of it is native Arab material, such as the stress on the universally "known fact" of the Arabs' descent from Abraham and the accounts of Arab prophets such as Hūd and Ṣāliḥ. Some was borrowed from the other monotheistic religions: Judaism, Christianity, and especially Judeo-Christianity. Thus the Qurʾān alludes repeatedly to the content of the Pentateuch and the Gospels. But while it is true that more Qurʾānic material is classifiable as "Judaic" or "Christian" than as specifically "Judeo-Christian," nonetheless the influence of the latter is central; for whereas the "Judaic" and "Christian" material consists of references to "known facts," or allusions to, and occasional retellings of, stories and legends, the Judeo-Christian material shaped the Qur᾽ān's *theology*. All the Qur᾽ān's Christology can be derived from Judeo-Christian doctrines—that Jesus was a man, not God or the Son of God; though there was a supernatural element in his birth, he was merely God's servant, i.e., inferior, and His messenger.[1] Other Judeo-Christian themes are also present in the Qur᾽ān, specifically an emphasis on Abraham as the first monotheist. Therefore, just as the Qur᾽ānic material implies the existence (not necessarily in Arabic) of the Pentateuch and the Gospels, so too it implies the existence of a considerable body of Judeo-Christian writings. However, we have no evidence for the existence in Arabic of any coherent Judeo-Christian work or body of collected material in the 6th and 7th centuries C.E. Judeo-Christian material did indeed exist, but in Aramaic (Syriac), in which language it had arisen over a long period out of religious dispute on the major tenets of Christianity. This dispute carried over into the material incorporated into the Qur᾽ān, which is full of allusions to sectarian dispute and persecution whose context is unclear. The *ʿulamā᾽* who formulated the theology of the developing state religion drew on Syriac sources, whose contents they expressed in Arabic.[2] The first extant expression of this Arabic formulation of originally Judeo-Christian theology is the inscription in the Dome of the Rock. Before then, we have Arabic formulae of a general monotheistic nature, which may have been translated from Syriac and perhaps Greek, or which may have been composed in Arabic on general monotheistic models; but we have no hint of Judeo-Christianity in Arabic, nor any connected body of religious literature in that language, not even

1. Cf. Pines (1984), p. 145 para. 2: "The conception that Jesus was a mere man could be found prior to the 7th century in Christianity only in the tenets of the so-called Judeo-Christian sects"—where it was a central theological tenet. It could of course be found also among the Jews, but not in conjunction with acceptance of a supernatural element in Jesus' birth, nor as a central ingredient in the definition of belief. Nor of course did the Jews accept that Jesus was a prophet. All these positions are Judeo-Christian alone. Judeo-Christianity is discussed in Part III Chapter 1.

2. We cannot tell if the resulting Arabic texts were actual *translations* of the original Syriac ones; more probably they were formulations in Arabic of Judeo-Christian ideas known from Syriac texts.

collections of locutions, till the "Christological" text of the inscription in the Dome of the Rock.[3]

There are signs that the "Christological text" of the Dome of the Rock inscription was copied from a papyrus: unlike the rest of the inscription, it has diacritical marks, and they are wide, like those made by a stylus used for writing on papyrus. The well-formulated language and detailed expression of the idea it conveys also show that it originated in written material. We can be fairly confident, then, that by 71/691–92, at least, some Judeo-Christian material existed in Arabic.

Whether there were other bodies of religious literature at this time we do not know. The popular rock inscriptions show only general Indeterminate Monotheism until the early 2nd century A.H.;[4] so do the chancery documents (such as letters on official matters to those under his jurisdiction) of the Egyptian governor Qurrah bn Šarīk, from the very end of the 1st century A.H.[5] But by John of Damascus' time, fifty or sixty years after the Dome of the Rock inscription, the Arabs apparently had several books, at least one of which, "The Camel of God," was not incorporated into the canonized version of the Qur°ān.[6] During these years, then, from ca. 71/690 or a little before to ca. 123/740, the Arabs collected and amplified the available written (and oral?) lore of one or more Judeo-Christian sects, in the process enriching Arabic and developing it into the sophisticated religious language necessary to serve as a vehicle for the thoughts being expressed. They developed new ideas and theses on the basis of the old—for instance, the stress on the "known fact" that the Arabs were descended from Abraham, which became central to the Arab view of history—and they added native Arab material. Gradually they amassed a body of material in Arabic, which would become the Qur°ān.

During these years the other elements of the Arab identity were also developed: the Life of Muḥammad and the historical background of the Arab State. There are, however, clear signs that the scholars responsible for developing this material were not those who developed the religious texts. The historical material is written as narrative, somewhat like the narrative of the Old and New Testaments. The religious texts were not composed as

---

3. Text B of the DOR inscription in the Appendix; discussed in detail in Part III Chapter 4.

4. Discussed in Part III Chapter 5, summarized in Chart III.5.1.

5. Part III Chapter 4, pp. 285–86.

6. Discussed in Part III Chapter 2, p. 238.

continuous narrative, nor was any attempt made, for the most part, to turn them into one continuous narrative when collected into books, nor even when the collection of books was canonized. They remained collections of shorter and longer fragments with considerable repetition, both of ideas and of verbatim texts. The Jewish and Christian scriptures are not the *model* for the Qurʾān, but basic *reference works* to whose content the religious material in the Qurʾān alludes. If that material is to be compared to any part of the preceding scriptures, it most closely resembles the Book of Proverbs: a collection of sayings on a limited number of themes, some of which are repeated verbatim or almost verbatim in several places. Some sections may form a narrative or be thematically linked, but there is no attempt to organize the whole work as continuous narrative. It is this Qurʾānic style and disjointed thematic content which led Wansbrough to propose the existence of different bodies of prophetical *logia*, or uncoordinated pericopes,[7] which, he considered, could have arisen in several sectarian communities, differentiated by geographical region or belief.[8] The inscriptions from the Negev and elsewhere provide some support for the existence of such hypothetical sectarian communities, not coexisting but along a time continuum. The popular inscriptions preserve sets of formulae and allow intermittent glimpses of their development. The Indeterminate Monotheistic texts indicate one (nonprophetical) type of "sectarian community," existing in the late 1st/7th century; the Mohammedan ones, a later (prophetical) one, existing a generation later.[9]

The Judeo-Christian texts whose theology entered the Qurʾān had almost certainly been composed over a long period, and probably in all the areas where Judeo-Christianity had once existed: Palestine, Syria, and Iraq. But in the 6th and 7th centuries C.E. these texts could have been preserved only among remnants of those former Judeo-Christian communities: the Judeo-Christian refugees who had fled to Iraq, and very probably the Nestorian Christians, who seem themselves to have lent an ear to Judeo-

---

7. Wansbrough (1977), p. 2.

8. Ibid., p. 50.

9. Although ʿAbd al-Malik's and Walīd's royal inscriptions indicate that Mohammedanism was the state religion at the same time as the Indeterminate Monotheistic community existed in the Negev, this is not evidence for the existence of a Mohammedan *sectarian community* at that time, i.e., that Mohammedanism was the religion of any sector of the population, as distinct from being the officially proclaimed state creed. Of course it may have been; but at present we have no evidence on this point.

Christian arguments and who were, in any case, in such close contact with Jews or Judeo-Christians that their opponents accused them of being Jewish.[10] Similarly, the leading and most active Jewish community of the time was in Iraq. One cannot specify, from the Christian elements in the Qur'ān, in which geographical area the material in it was composed. But the presence of the Jewish and Judeo-Christian elements in the Qur'ān indicates, in our opinion, that these parts, at least, of the material from which the Qur'ān was formed were written in Arabic, on the basis of existing Syriac texts, in the general area of Iraq.

Those responsible for developing this material were the scholars, the *ʿulamāʾ*, not the caliph and his court. Religious development during the Marwānid period does not seem to have been subject to tight political direction. There would of course have been people with firm views regarding which religious expressions were acceptable; but as long as they stayed within the broad guidelines of the state religion, and were not politically dangerous, the Marwānids allowed them a relatively free hand. ʿAbd al-Malik needed a state religion for political reasons, and the state would not have been averse to issuing directives to the scholars about directions of religious development and enquiry; but neither ʿAbd al-Malik nor the Umayyad caliphs in general seem to have taken too much interest in the matter. The political élite, we suggest, was concerned that the religion be monotheistic, and that it accord with the framework the state had defined; beyond that, they did not pay much attention to the details. We have evidence that several different currents of belief circulated: prophetical and nonprophetical, general monotheistic and more specifically Judeo-Christian, and perhaps others that have disappeared without a trace. ʿAbd al-Malik adopted as the state religion those he found useful: the idea of the Messenger of God and the Christology of Judeo-Christianity. Official pronouncements (on coins, protocols, public inscriptions, etc.) thenceforth had to include the official formulae; but the *ʿulamāʾ* were otherwise free to develop beliefs in various directions, and gradually enriched the emerging Arab religion with concepts not found in its predecessors. As time went by, a religious infrastructure of scholars, places of worship, etc. arose, and religious philosophy developed. One piece of evidence for the relatively free hand granted the *ʿulamāʾ* is that in pre-ʿAbbāsid times there is little evidence for standardization of locutions between Iraq, Syria, and the Negev—as

10. Cf. Part III Chapter 1, section titled, "Judeo-Christianity."

there would have been, had the central political authority taken an interest in the details of religious development.

There are indications in the traditional Muslim literature of friction between the *ᶜulamāᵓ* and the Umayyad caliphs. Part of this is probably ᶜAbbāsid exaggeration—we have the scholars' works only in versions edited under the ᶜAbbāsids. But part is probably historical. It is clear that the *ᶜulamāᵓ*'s scope of activity, and presumably influence, was great, especially in the east. Nonetheless, despite any friction there may have been, the *ᶜulamāᵓ* continued their work of developing the Arab religion and history throughout the Umayyad period.[11]

This work of developing the theology of the Arab religion must have been started at some point before 71/690–91, since the Dome of the Rock inscription is evidence for the existence in Arabic by that time of one or more texts (one of which is reproduced in it) containing a formulation of Judeo-Christian Christology, which were adopted into the official Arab religion. Judging from the material preserved in the Qurᵓān, the texts the *ᶜulamāᵓ* wrote were not fully developed theological treatises or expositions of faith; they were more like notes on points of interest. Some were merely short, disconnected locutions and formulae; others were longer, more connected passages. Some of these texts—notably those that became *sūrahs* 2 to 5 in the Qurᵓān—apparently existed as collections already in the first half of the 2nd/8th century.

But while these texts contained the approved theology of the state religion, they were not, apparently, intended from the start to provide its *scripture*. The Old and New Testaments, *given a particular interpretation*, were originally accepted as Scripture. A few legends, such as that about Ḥajjāj's activities in Iraq, indicate that there may have been some Marwānid attempts to collect together an Arab scripture.[12] But the evidence in general suggests that the Qurᵓān was canonized only under the ᶜAbbāsids. Thus the rock inscriptions initially preserve only non-Qurᵓānic locutions, including some with (to use Nabia Abbott's phrase) "Qurᵓānic flavor." The tombstone inscriptions, which start in the 170s A.H., likewise contain only

11. It is possible that the development of the religious and historical texts occurred in different geographical areas: the religion, we have argued above, in Iraq, and the historical texts in Syria.

12. And in view of what we have said above, it is perhaps significant that such an attempt at establishing an official version of an Arab scripture should have taken place in Iraq.

a few Qurʾānic verses, at least down to 200 A.H.[13] Qurʾānic locutions start to appear in the popular inscriptions only in Muslim texts, and even then they are rare.[14]

The "external" evidence of non-Arab texts also indicates the existence in the mid-2nd/8th century of collections of *Qurʾānic material*, rather than of the Qurʾān as we have it now.[15] The letter purporting to be from the Byzantine emperor Leo III to the caliph ʿUmar II, already mentioned, which should probably be dated not earlier than the 120s/740s,[16] mentions traditions that various people had a hand in composing the Arabs' *furqan*, and that Ḥajjāj, ʿAbd al-Malik's governor of Iraq, had tried to destroy non-authorized versions. This argues for the existence of several versions of essentially the same material. John of Damascus, in the *De Haeresibus*, written around 125–33/743–50, gives the names of the first *sūrahs*, but refers to them as separate "silly tales" invented by Muḥammad, not as part of an Arab scripture. Moreover, one of these tales, "The Camel," is not in the canonized version of the Qurʾān; it may thus be considered part of a body of Arab apocrypha so far largely undiscovered. Our conclusion is that when John of Damascus wrote the *De Haeresibus* several collections of locutions existed, and some at least had been linked to the Prophet, but there was no one official text; the Qurʾān had not yet been canonized.[17] We would tentatively place the date of canonization in the late 2nd/8th century. This is very close to Wansbrough's estimate, made on quite different grounds. He proceeded by textual criticism of the Muslim literary sources,

---

13. Hawary and Rached (1932).

14. The 'guidance' formula (Q.48:28, 63:9) occurs in versions with very interesting divergences from the Qurʾānic form. There are also two inscriptions containing a version of the 'herald' locution, Q.50:41, but again with a significant difference: in the Qurʾān the herald of the Judgment Day will call from an unspecified "nearby place," but in the popular inscriptions he calls "from Jerusalem." (See Appendix A for further discussion of both these formulae). In addition, as discussed in the preceding chapter, one Negev inscription, ST 640(34):4–7, assumes knowledge of Q.9:30.

15. Close scrutiny of the history of those Qurʾānic locutions that also appear elsewhere can, however, throw considerable light on the sectarian milieu and the development of the Qurʾān. An an example, Appendix A examines the development of the 'guidance' formula and associated "victory phrase" from its first partial appearance in official inscriptions, through its forms in the popular inscriptions, to the forms found in the Qurʾān; and discusses the variant forms of the 'herald' formula.

16. Discussed in Part III Chapter 2.

17. The evidence of the *De Haeresibus* is discussed in Part III Chapter 2.

from which he concluded that "establishment of a standard text" was not earlier than the 3rd/9th century[18] or the end of the 2nd/8th.[19] We thus have two completely different paths of enquiry leading to very similar conclusions.

Once the decision to create an Arab scripture had been taken, the actual work of canonization was probably completed in a relatively short time. This work involved deciding what to include, putting the various collections of material (books, i.e., *sūrahs*) together, and editing the language of the whole to form a linguistically uniform text. It did not, however, involve thematic or stylistic editing aimed at forming a long, connected narrative or reasoned argument out of the separate locutions and pericopes which had been freely juxtaposed. This fact indicates that the method of composition by juxtaposition was intentional. One effect of this was that, since the holy texts are not ordered and do not have to tell a story, one could quite quickly create a considerable body of scripture from even a comparatively limited basic store of material.

We therefore see the Qurʾānic material as having existed in an uncanonized form for the greater part of the 2nd/8th century, until the Qurʾān was canonized in the first half-century of ʿAbbāsid rule. We suggest that this was largely because the Marwānids did not feel an overriding need for an Arab scripture. They perceived the problem, rather, as the lack of an Arab national history, and especially one which took into account the Arab Prophet they had proclaimed. Some time around the end of the 1st/7th century, then, they turned the attention of the scholars towards these two problems.

THE *SĪRAH*

Already in late Marwānid times an obvious problem for Mohammedanism, the official state religion, was the Prophet's lack of a history and biography comparable to those of Moses and Jesus. A related political problem was the lack of a national Arab history, presenting the Arabs as one nation, rather than a temporary confederation of independent tribes, and thereby providing the rationale for their existence as a discrete political unit, and for the position of the caliph as its overall head. Both these functions—and

18. Wansbrough (1977), p. 44.
19. Ibid., p. 49.

others—were to be filled by the *Sīrah*. Of course the *Sīrah* had many more specific functions: for instance, the official legitimization of social status. Thus many incidents related in the *Sīrah* are "famous firsts": who was the first to do something (a question which grew into a whole branch of Muslim literature: the study of the *ᵓawāᵓil*, the first ones),[20] or assertions that a particular man (the ancestor of a particular family) had already accepted Islam before he died; or they are based on the need to establish precisely who accepted Islam and when—who is to be accorded the status of a Helper or a Companion of the Prophet. These matters determined the prestige and status of such an ancestor's present-day descendants, and therefore the amount of tax they paid and land they were granted. Each family thus had good reason to claim priority for its own ancestry; traditions arose, and an authoritative source was necessary to facilitate decisions between competing claims. But in general terms the *Sīrah* is, on the one hand, a world history according to the Arabs, which tried to provide for the Arab religion some of the functions the Old Testament performed for Christians and Jews;[21] and on the other, a portrayal of the Prophet as a parallel to Moses.

The portrayal of the Prophet himself derived from various sources. In his role as proclaimer of the True Religion, it was modeled on Abraham: his defiance of his kinsmen and people; his exile. In his role as leader of the persecuted minority, it was modeled on Moses, who successfully moulded from redeemed fugitives a new nation—God's Chosen People, relying on God's help to overcome opposition. Thus Abū Bakr's address to the four generals parallels Moses' instructions to the Jews; the invasion parallels the Jews' capture of the Promised Land; there are parallels between the battle of the Yarmūk and the meaning of crossing the Jordan. Jesus also afforded some parallels. For instance, Muḥammad's demand that the ᵓAws and Xazraj tribes should produce "twelve leaders that they may take charge of their people's affairs"[22] could parallel Moses' organization of the Children of Israel, or the twelve Apostles; the next section makes it clear that the latter is intended: "You are the sureties for your people, just as the disciples

20. For instance: who was the first to shoot an arrow for the sake of Islam.

21. One of these was to document the Arabs' place in the general Near Eastern religious context, as descendants of Abraham, like the Jews—a genealogical derivation already generally accorded them by Christian writers.

22. *Sīrah* I:443; Guillaume (1955), p. 204.

of Jesus Son of Mary were responsible for him, while I am responsible for my people."[23]

This parallelism with the great figures of the other monotheistic religions provided the general plan; the details of the Prophet's life were filled in from the most suitable material available. Bashear (1984, 1985) has shown that some of this material was obtained by retrojecting into the mythical Ḥijāzī past events from the life of a more recent Ḥijāzī leader, Muḥammad bn al-Ḥanafiyyah.[24] *Ayyam* stories of the conquest, and stories and traditions that had grown up around the figure of the Prophet, would have provided further detail. The choice of the Ḥijāz as the original Arab homeland was probably Umayyad; the ᶜAbbāsid conception retained it, and indeed there was available no other unoccupied territory where such historical claims could not be refuted by other peoples.

To provide a biography of the Prophet and root him in Arab history was thus clearly one major function of the *Sīrah*. Another was to link him with the prophetical locutions—the scriptural material either collected or in the process of being collected into several discrete "books" during the first half of the 2nd/8th century. Many of the events the *Sīrah* relates are attempts to provide a historical origin, or reason, for a particular text in the scriptural material. For this material did not in fact link up with either the Ḥijāz or the Prophet's life. Its geographical area was al-Šām and especially Iraq. The northern ecological background of the Qurʾān (such as the references to rain in due season, to vineyards, etc.[25]) is easily discernable when it is read with no preconceptions regarding its supposed Ḥijāzī setting.[26] The links between

23. *Sīrah* I:446; ibid.

24. Cf. Part III Chapter 4, pp. 280–82.

25. E.g., Q.6:99–100.

26. For instance, contrary to Western stereotypical conceptions, the region most notable for date palms is Iraq. On the Roman coin commemorating *Iudaea Capta*, the palm symbolized the Jews of Palestine, just as the camel symbolized the Arabs on that commemorating the liquidation of Nabataea and its redefinition as Arabia. In the Qurʾān, references to date palms are quite frequent—*naxlah* alone occurs twenty times, and the clearly proverbial phrase "the dint on a date stone" or "the thread on a date stone," meaning "the least amount," is quite common (e.g., Q.4:53; 4:124; 4:77; 17:71). Similarly, there are eleven references to vines and grapes. Camels are much less frequently mentioned, and the references to them tend to be imported from other sources, especially the Old and New Testaments. *Jamal* occurs twice, once in Q.7:40 in reporting the New Testament phrase "until the camel passes through the eye of the needle," and once in Q.77:33, where its meaning is obscure: "camel" does not fit the context ("sparks like golden camels"?). *Baᶜīr*, a

Scripture, Prophet, and the Ḥijāz as original Arab homeland needed to be supplied. These links are usually presented as *asbāb al-nuzul*: a description of an event concerning which, it is asserted, God sent down a particular Qur᾿ānic verse or passage. They were presumably arrived at by arguing backwards from the Qur᾿ānic verse to a "historical" incident which could have occasioned it.[27] Much of this material, too, should be seen as *compiled* by Ibn Isḥāq or Ibn Hišām, rather than *originating* with them; and occasionally the *Sīrah* preserves differing versions of the same event, affording us a peep through the keyhole of legend at the processes of formulating the stories about the early days of Islam. One such example is the story of how ᶜUmar became a Muslim.[28] Similarly, the fairly frequent alternative traditions regarding what a Qur᾿ānic verse referred to, show that many such efforts were being made to link Scripture with salvation history.

It is almost certain that by the time Ibn Hišām published the *Sīrah* in the form in which we know it, the Qur᾿ān had been canonized. Otherwise it is hard to see how he could have avoided including, among the many scriptural references, quotations of locutions which were eventually excluded from the canon. And conversely, the material the *Sīrah* does refer to, which obviously must have existed at least by the time of its final revision, ranges over the whole of the canon. In short, by the time the *Sīrah* was finished, Ibn Hišām, at least, knew what material was scriptural and what was not, and was able to refer to the whole of the former and none of the latter. This argues for a canonized form.

We may conjecture—and it can only be conjecture—that much of the work of including Qur᾿ānic reference—of pinning Scripture to salvation history—was undertaken by Ibn Hišām. Ibn Isḥāq probably wrote something quite different, with a considerably different emphasis—

---

camel-load, occurs in Q.12:65 and Q.12:72, in a retelling of the Joseph story; and *rikāb*, a riding camel, in Q.59:6, in the phrase "you urged neither horses nor riding camels"—which cannot be considered specific to a desert people. Finally, there are five references (Q.7:73, 17:59, 26:154–57, 54:27, and 91:13) to a "she-camel of Allāh" sent to Ṯamūd when they asked Ṣāliḥ for a sign that he was a prophet: they were told to let her drink at the well, but they hamstrung her, for which Allāh doomed them to destruction. One is reminded of the lost *sūrah* ridiculed by John of Damascus; but even five references to the same apocryphal story do little to prove the frequency of camels in the Qur᾿ān.

27. Examples are too numerous to list, but see for instance, the chapter "Negotiation between The Apostle and the Leasers of Qurayš," *Sīrah* I:294–314; Guillaume (1955), pp. 130–41.

28. *Sīrah* I:340–42; Guillaume (1955), pp. 156–59.

Marwānid, not ᶜAbbāsid: essentially a national Arab history. But the ᶜAbbāsids were concerned to create a history of adherents to a religion—not of the Arabs as an ethnic group—in line with their emphasis on the concept of the Islamic Commonwealth as the unit of group affiliation. Thus in Ibn Hišām's version, reflecting the ᶜAbbāsid concern for a religious rather than ethnic basic of community affiliation, the *Sīrah* became the salvation history of the Community of the Faithful.

The ᶜAbbāsid view of religion entailed not only formulating a scripture and grounding it in history, but conversely, grounding history in Scripture. At each important point in the history of His community, Allāh must have provided His guidance; and these pronouncements are to be found in the Qurᵓān. Scripture thus becomes the basis for history, and historical analysis becomes the "unfolding" of the Qurᵓān so as to reveal the history concealed within it—a process which started with the *Sīrah* and continued thereafter.

RELIGIOUS DEVELOPMENT UNDER THE EARLY ᶜABBĀSIDS

The ᶜAbbāsids annihilated the Marwānid royal family, but left alone many nonroyal members of the Marwānid élite: governors, civil servants, and religious intellectuals, i.e., members of the *ᶜulamāᵓ*. They could perhaps count on the support of some of these, and seem, in any case, not to have perceived them as a threat. The latter responded with several panegyrics of and lamentations for the Marwānids, and then continued to live and work under the new regime. Religion now played a much more central role in politics. The Muslim (ᶜAbbāsid) traditions reveal a strong attempt to provide a religiohistorical foundation for both the conquest and the ᶜAlid dynasty. For one thing, the inclusion in the *Sīrah* of Muḥammad's move to Aylā and the Tabūk *sariyyah*[29] provided "proof" that the policy of expanding the religion—and the state—originated with Muḥammad, not with Abū Bakr: the conquest was but the continuation, by Muḥammad's successors, of the Prophet's intentions, the uninterrupted sequel to the *maġāzī*. Secondly, the traditions developed under the ᶜAbbāsids placed great stress on the concept of the *ṣaḥābah*: the four *Xulafāᵓ al-Rašidūn* were all Companions and/or relatives of the Prophet, and as caliphs they therefore

29. *Sīrah* III:894–906; Guillaume (1955), pp. 602–608.

directly continued the Prophet's policies and wishes. This physical continuation from the Prophet culminated in ᶜAlī, Muḥammad's son-in-law, who should have been caliph and passed on the caliphate to a son who was also the Prophet's grandson. Muᶜāwiyah's assumption of the caliphate is thus presented as a usurpation both politically and religiously. The traditions as we now have them do not deny that the Sufyānids were the de facto rulers at least from very soon after the Arabs took control of al-Šām. But they present Muᶜāwiyah as merely a governor who rebelled against the Prophet's descendant: he should have continued to serve as governor, under a caliph of the Prophet's house. The *Xulafāᵓ al-Rašidūn* together span the gap between Muḥammad and ᶜAlī, creating an unbroken chain of succession and thereby denying the Sufyānids any legitimate claim to the caliphate.

To complete the picture and legitimize their own rule in religious terms, the ᶜAbbāsids used (or devised) the story that the grandson of Muḥammad bn al-Ḥanafiyyah, being the inheritor of the religious authority of the ᶜAlid line, had transferred it to the ᶜAbbāsids. Muḥammad bn al-Ḥanafiyyah's own link with the ᶜAlids was probably tenuous, but as we have seen al-Muxtār had made much of it for propaganda purposes,[30] and by ᶜAbbāsid times it was apparently a "known fact" that the ᶜAbbāsids could build on.

Thus the invasion, as officially reported, connected the ᶜAbbāsid Arab state with the history of Islam—but not with any particular people. For the main point of the invasion saga was not the warfare and conquests, but the offering of Islam to all, and the repeated promise of equality in everything to everyone who joined the Muslims. This was the main political claim of the ᶜAbbāsid traditions, because in it rested the legitimacy of any non-Arab ruler to reign over the Muslim Commonwealth. In the ideal ᶜAbbāsid scheme Islam was the only paradigm; no other bond should be acknowledged or deemed necessary in the social system. The Arabs were those who spoke Arabic, but what mattered was if they were Muslims or not. The notion of *ᶜArabiyyah* was discarded. Arabic-speaking Christians were aliens and as loathed as any other Christians, while Persian-speaking Muslims were brethren in faith.

It is evident that real topics of taxation and legalities, and other rights, privileges, dues, and obligations are reflected in the historical narrative of the *futūḥ*; but this is peripheral to our present study. What should be

---

30. In Part III Chapter 4, pp. 280–81.

emphasized is the *concept* of a Muslim crusade which offered to all the True Faith, but did not destroy the society and administrative patterns of the Byzantine East. The ᶜAbbāsids took pains to ensure that the facts of the recent past and the present would be seen to be the consequences of a special history, one such as the ᶜAbbāsids deemed should be remembered. They did not deny the Marwānid version of the Arab religion—the revelation by God, in Arabic, to an Arab Prophet in the Ḥijāz—but they emphasized the all-sufficient nature of the bonds of faith, which should override any other bonds.

The result of this outlook was the Muslim Commonwealth: a civilization counted among the greatest achievements of the human genius. It took shape at amazing speed—only about a century after the Dome of the Rock it was in full bloom, from Isfahan to Spain. The Islamic civilization was a huge gathering of wisdom and beauty brought home from every contemporary culture; China was not too far and Greece not inaccessible. The new religion, the search for intellectual content, and the embellishment and refinement of art, architecture, and craftsmanship with fresh new patterns, trends of thought, and aesthetics—these things attracted many talents, and all were privileged to participate. This openness towards different cultures, the zeal in searching for wisdom through learning, and perfection in shaping matter gracefully, were possible because Islam triumphed over *ᶜArabiyyah*. The "true" Arabs could join in this intellectual and aesthetic feast just like anyone else, but through it they lost their Arab identity, becoming simply Muslims like any of the converted *ᶜulūj*.[31]

Another major change in religious philosophy attendant on the new regime was the attitude to scripture. The Marwānids had felt no need for an Arab scripture, only for an Arab history and creed. But the centrality of the religion under the ᶜAbbāsids, and its status as a new faith distinct from and opposed to Christianity, rather than an offshoot of it, meant that the lack of

---

31. The notion of the Muslim Commonwealth also worked perfectly to prevent it from endangering Byzantium. Every now and then one or another Muslim non-Arab leader claimed his right to the title of the Head of the Muslim Commonwealth. As long as he was a Muslim, and life continued to be no worse than people were accustomed to, his right to rule within the limits of the *šarīᶜah* could not and would not be seriously questioned. This situation supported a constant fissuring of the Muslim Commonwealth between competing caliphs or sultans, with the result that there was never a consolidated Muslim empire powerful enough to mobilize the resources of the whole Muslim Commonwealth and confront Byzantium.

a scripture was a handicap. Moreover, the very need for the Prophet had to be justified. One does not need a new prophet with the stature and authority of a Moses in order to call attention to the tenets of an existing scripture from which men have strayed. For that, a lesser prophet would be sufficient—and the result would not be the proclamation of a new religion, but a cry to return to the old one.[32] The more the Arab religion was defined as an incompatible alternative to Christianity, the more pressing became the need for a scripture of its own.

There was, too, the need for a religious basis for law. This again developed with time. Muᶜāwiyah and ᶜAbd al-Malik had been content with de facto use of Byzantine legal conventions, which continued in force in the former Roman provinces,[33] and with the notion of rule by consultation (*šūrah*). One conducted the community's affairs by consulting with all the important people and promulgating a decision. This was in fact the Christian method of conducting affairs—to hold a synod and promulgate canons. The ᶜAbbāsids, by contrast, saw rule of the community as based on consensus—*ᵓijmaᶜ*—one consulted with others, and those who agreed with each other formed a group. This is much more akin to the view of Rabbinic Judaism, a view based on exegesis leading to a decision as to law, on the one hand, plus dissenters from it, on the other. Since, however, it assumes that law is to be found in Scripture, it requires a scripture to serve as the basis for exegesis.[34]

On several counts, then, a scripture was becoming necessary. The need was very probably apparent to the *ᶜulamāᵓ* during late Marwānid times, but under the Umayyads their opinions were not translated into action. But from the middle of that century, when the views of the religious intellectuals were adopted by political circles, the way was clear for the need for a scripture to be satisfied.

This scripture had of course to be compiled from the material available. And what was available was, on the one hand, the collections of material generated and assembled from the late 1st/7th century on, and, on the other, a developing body of *sunnah*—traditions (corresponding, as Wansbrough

32. This was, of course, a dilemma of early Christianity vis-à-vis Judaism, and it was resolved in a similar way.

33. Crone (1987a) is a study of the "relative contributions of Roman and provincial law" to Islamic law, taking as an example the system of *walāᵓ* or patronage.

34. Cf. the meeting between the emir and the patriarch, discussed in Part III Chapter 2.

has pointed out, to the Rabbinic Jewish concept of *halakhah*) about what the Prophet had said and intended. And so the concepts of *sunnah*, as revealing the intentions of the Prophet, and of Scripture as revealing God's will, were pressed into service to provide the foundations of law and authority for the new Muslim Commonwealth.

The first official written pronouncement to have survived regarding *sunnah* and Scripture is the inscription in the Prophet Mosque of Madīnah, dated 135/752.[35] This inscription could not be more different in flavor and subject matter from those of ʿAbd al-Malik and Walīd. It is concerned not in the slightest to define the broad outlines of belief, or the relationship of the Community to other religious communities. Rather, its whole stress is on obeying God, which may be done by obeying His law. This in turn is accomplished by acting in accordance with the precepts of His *kitab* and the *sunnah* of His Prophet. The inscription mentions the specific laws the caliph has in mind. Some of them derive from material found also in the Qurʾān, e.g., to honor the duties imposed by family relationships (*ṣilat al-raḥīm*), and to pay taxes intended to aid relatives, orphans, and the poor:

> *ʾannamā ġanimtum min šayʾ-en fa-ʾanna lillāhi xumsahu wa-li-rrasūli wa-li-ḏiyy al-qurbà wa-al-yatamà wa-al-masākini wa-ʾibni al-sabīli*: "From whatever you gain/acquire,[36] one fifth (should be) assigned to Allāh, to the Messenger, to relatives [i.e., in distress], to orphans, to the needy [plural] and to the wayfarer." (Q.8:41).

The main point of the inscription, however, is that one obeys God by following the servants of God and those who obey Him; and vice versa, that one should not obey those who incite to disobedience of God. In the context of 135 A.H., these exhortations are clearly political in nature. The new regime here proclaims that it is based on God's law and the *sunnah* of the Prophet, and brands its political opponents—the Umayyads—as "those who urge disobedience of God." If we were to sum up the message of the inscription in a nutshell, it would have to be: "Obey me (i.e., the caliph, who ordered the inscription), for I am doing what God wants; conduct your daily

---

35. The text and translation are given in the Appendix of Inscriptions.

36. The usual translation of the root *ġ.n.m.* is "to acquire (in war)" (Alī, A.Y. [1934]), "take as spoils of war" (Ben-Shemesh [1979]). But the meaning was not confined to things acquired by war: cf. Lane, 6:2300 col. 3ff.: "a thing acquired or gained without difficulty, trouble or inconvenience." Lane gives also the meaning "(disinterested) gift" (p. 2301 col. 1) and similar.

lives in accordance with the *kitab* of God and the *sunnah* of the Prophet; and pay your taxes." God's law would of course have continued to be orally propounded to the people by their religious leaders; if these now proclaimed that the law was derived from God's *kitab* and the *sunnah* of the Prophet, so be it. In no sense would the ordinary people have had, or expected, access to written Scripture, any more than they had had before. So we may rephrase the inscription's message as: "Obey me, for I am doing what God wants; conduct your daily lives in accordance with what the religious leaders tell you is God's law based on the *kitab* of God and *sunnah* of the Prophet; and pay your taxes."

This is not, essentially, a religious message. It is a plea for a return to normalcy in the wake of political upheaval; it is the use of religion to provide legitimacy for the new regime; and it is an indication that the views of religious leaders will henceforth carry greater political weight. It does, however, draw very marked attention to the concepts "the *kitab* of God" and "the *sunnah* of the Prophet." They occur at both the beginning and the end of the inscription, which first orders and later invites the people to follow them, in the context of obeying God's law. Both times they are mentioned, the *kitab* and the *sunnah* appear together, as repositories of law.

We should remember that *kitab* did not mean a book in our sense, but more generally, something written. The scribes of the rock graffiti used it, for instance, to refer to their inscriptions: "forgive [person's name] ... and the one who wrote this *kitab* and the one who reads it." *Kitab Allāh* thus meant a written record of what God had said. The inscription in the Prophet Mosque of Madīnah proclaimed that such a record existed.

We suggest that the new regime is here introducing the two concepts, Scripture and *sunnah*, for the first time, and stressing that the law of the state will henceforth be based upon them. It is an attack on Umayyad methods of governing the community, and an announcement that from now on, the whole legal basis of government will follow a different philosophy. This does not necessarily mean that a canonized version of Scripture (or an official collection of *sunnah*) existed at the time—rather, it is a declaration of intent. The existence of such a scripture having been officially proclaimed, its eventual canonization was now inevitable.

It is of course possible to maintain that the inscription in the Prophet Mosque indicates the existence in already-canonized form, in 135/752, of the Qurʾān. If so, it would be possible to date the period of canonization fairly accurately; for as we know from John of Damascus, in 125–26/743 the material was still in the form of separate collections, not all of which survived the process of canonization. Which position one adopts is largely a matter of conjecture; but in view of the linguistic evidence, we prefer the hypothesis that the inscription in the Prophet Mosque represents an initial declaration of intent by the new rulers. Its fulfillment took somewhat longer to achieve: the work of Goldziher, Schacht, and Wansbrough, our linguistic examination of the popular inscriptions, and an analysis of the evidence in non-Arab texts presented in Part III Chapter 2, all indicate that the process of canonization was not completed until late in the 2nd/8th century.

The establishment of the Muslim religion, based on the Arab Prophet, Scripture, and a salvation history, finally achieved its full expression with Ṭabarī's works of history and Qurʾānic exegesis in the late 3rd century A.H.

Appendix A
Qurʾānic and Non-Qurʾānic Versions of Locutions

The Development of the 'Guidance' Formula/'Victory Phrase'

This very famous formula occurs three times in the Qurʾān in two variations; each version can be broken down into three parts, here labeled (a), (b), and (c). The Qurʾānic occurrences are as follows:

Q.48:28

(a) *huwa al-laḏī arsala rasūlahu bi-al-hudà wa-dīn al-ḥaqq*
"He it is who sent His messenger with the guidance and the religion of truth"

(b) *li-yuẓhirahu alà al-dīn kullihi*
"to make it/him victorious over any other religion"

(c) *wa-kafà bi-llāhi šahīd-an*
"and Allāh suffices as a witness."

Q.9:33 and **Q.61:9**

(a) and (b) as above

(c) *wa-lau kariha al-mušrikūn*
"even in the face of the dislike/hatred of the *mušrikūn*."[1]

---

1. *mušrikūn* is usually translated 'disbelievers,' but in Part III Chapter 4 we argue that *šarīk* is one of a number of technical terms used to translate into Arabic the concepts needed for Christological/Trinitarian dispute with the Christians. The concept of *širk*, we argue, was an Arabic equivalent of the Greek *synthetos*—compounding the singleness of God, attributing to Him a composite nature—so that *mušrikūn* means specifically 'syntheists': those who hold this belief, i.e., Christians, not just any non-Muslim.

To understand the development of this locution, we must go back to one that does not actually appear in it: *Muḥammad rasūl Allāh*. As already established, this phrase first appears on an Arab-Sassanian coin, dated 71/690–91. It is enigmatic and unexplained; but from the time of its introduction, it started to be used as an official formula on coins and in papyrus protocols, initially in this brief form with no additions. Around the year 86/705, when Walīd I succeeded ʿAbd al-Malik, a fuller form began to appear on coins and in protocols:[2]

Muḥammad rasūl Allāh arsalahu bi-al-hudà wa-dīn al-ḥaqq
"Muḥammad is the Messenger of Allāh, He sent him with the guidance and the religion of truth."

Publications containing coins bearing this slogan, such as Walker (1956), tend to note that this is Q.9:33 or that the coin has Q.9:33 on it; but in every case where a plate is provided, so that the actual reading of the coin can be checked, the formula on it is actually the Marwānid one above, starting *Muḥammad rasūl Allāh arsalah...*, and not the Qurʾānic version which starts *huwa al-laḏī arsala rasūlahu....*[3] Moreover none of the protocols or coins of this period contain either parts (b) or (c); the formula is a combination of *Muḥammad rasūl Allāh* plus the rest of (a) only.

This Marwānid formula continued in use in Hišām's reign (106–25/724–43)[4] and under the early ʿAbbāsids.[5] The further expanded version, adding the "insulting" part (b), only starts to appear at the very end of

2. Protocols containing this formula: Grohmann (1924), p. XXX no. 3, dating to 86–89/705–708, Walīd's reign; ibid., p. XXVIII no. 2a, p. XXXIII no. 8b, p. XLI no. A6, all dating to 90–96/709–714, Walīd's reign; Grohmann (1934), pp. 21–22, no. 12, dated 86/705, by ʿAbd Allāh bn ʿAbd al-Malik, a governor under Walīd; ibid., pp. 23–24, no. 13, dating from 90–91/709–10, Walīd's reign. Coins containing this formula: Walker (1956), p. 9 no. *11; ibid., p. 186 no. 511; AUK 34, p. 8 no. 5.

3. Similarly the auction catalog AUK 36, p. 76 comments that Q.9:33 is on the coins, but quotes the text of Q.9:33 as *Muḥammad rasūl Allāh arsalahu bi-al-hudà* (etc.)—which is the Marwānid formula that appears on the coin, not in fact in Q.9:33! Clearly one needs caution when accepting assertions that Qurʾānic formulae are on early documents and coins.

4. Protocol: Grohman (1924), pp. XLVIIIff. From the reign of Hišām's predecessor Yazīd II (102–106/720–724) we have Arabic-only protocols that contain only the phrase *Muḥammad rasūl Allāh* without the rest; i.e., we have no surviving instance of the use of the guidance formula in Yazīd's reign.

5. E.g., a coin of al-Saffāḥ (132–136/749–753): AUK 36, p. 80 no. 425 + plate XXVI:425; a coin of al-Hadī (169–170/785–786): AUCS 255, p. 89 no. 112.

Hišām's reign or just after, in a single surviving protocol,[6] and then in the reign of al-Manṣūr (137–158/754–775) on coins and protocols.[7]

In the popular Negev inscriptions there are versions of this formula in two texts dating to ca. 160/776–77 (al-Mahdī's reign): MA 4252(17) and MA 4262(18). The former is very difficult to read and fragmentary, the latter a little clearer, though still unreadable in places. Still, it seems clear that both contained a specific reference to Muḥammad plus the rest of section (a) and section (b) of the formula, followed by the "offensive" version of (c) found in Q.9:33 and Q.61:9. They read as follows (square brackets enclose unclear but probable readings):

MA 4252(17)

ṣally alà [Muḥammad] [arsalahu] [1½ lines of text unreadable] *wa-bi-dīn* [sic] *al-ḥaqq [liyuẓhirahu] alà al-dīn kull[ihi wa-] lau ka[riha al-mušrikū n]*

MA 4262(18)

[Muḥamma]d rasūl Allā[h]
[ar]salahu bi-al-hudà
[wa-bi-dīn] al-[ḥa]qq [liyuẓhirahu]
[alà] al-d[ī]n ku[llihi]
[wa-lau kariha] al-mu[šrikūn]

So in early ᶜAbbāsid times (from around the time of al-Manṣūr), the official version of this formula appears to have been

Muḥammad rasūl Allāh arsalahu bi-al-hudà wa-[bi-]dīn al-ḥaqq li-yuẓhirahu alà al-dīn kullihi

At least one popular inscription from this time (al-Mahdī, 160 A.H.) included also a version that began with a different reference to Muḥammad (*ṣally alà Muḥammad arsalahu*...), but it is still a specific reference to him; and the popular inscriptions included also the "insulting" ending *wa-lau kariha al-mušrikūn*. A version with this ending was included in the Qur'ān (Q.9:33 and Q.61:9), and so was the milder version without it

6. Grohman (1924), p. LXXIII no. 33, date range 124–129/742–747.

7. Coin published in *Israel Numismatic Journal* 3 (1966), p. 38 no. 1; protocol: Grohmann (1924), p. LXV no. 14, date range 142–174/759–790.

was substituted for the "insulting" one. But significantly, all the *Qur'ānic* occurrences of the formula remove the opening phrase which explicitly refers to Muḥammad, and substitute a less specific version which does not mention him by name: *huwa al-laḏī arsala rasūlahu....* Considering that both the official and popular inscriptions of the early ʿAbbāsid period knew only a formula that refers to Muḥammad, this is strange indeed. It looks as if the compilers of the canon were not interested to include a specifically "Mohammedan" formula, preferring a "non-Mohammedan" version that does not make it clear who the Messenger is.[8] It could indeed be argued that two competing sets of prophetical formulae were in circulation: a "general prophetical" one and a "specifically Mohammedan" one, and that the Qurʾān was compiled mainly from the former. Or perhaps the decision was made that the canon of Scripture should not be specifically Mohammedan, but should leave the identity of the Prophet open to interpretation—which itself implies that there were people who believed that the Prophet was Muḥammad and others who did not, and the compilers of the Qurʾān did not wish to make it difficult for the latter to enter the fold.

Finally, at some point after canonization, the Qurʾānic (and now official) version of the 'guidance' formula penetrated into the popular inscriptions too: BR 5131(32), datable to ca. 300/912, contains an exact quote of Q.48:28 from beginning (*huwa al-laḏī arsala...*) to end (*...wa-kafà bi-llāhi šahīdan*). Since we have no inscriptions which include this formula from the period between ca. 160 and ca. 300, we cannot tell when this actually happened. By 300/912 the Qurʾān had existed in its canonized form for a hundred years or more.

The 'Herald' Formula

In the 'guidance' formula we saw a process of preferring to include in Scripture a general reference to an unidentified Messenger, rather than a

8. Q48:28, alone of the three occurrences, is close to a reference to Muḥammad, which occurs in the next verse. But it is plain that this reference connects to the rest of Q.48:29, not backwards to Q.48:28, which ends with a stock phrase used often in the Qurʾān as a "concluding phrase" of an idea or subject: *wa-kafà bi-llāhi šahīd-an.* See Part III Chapter 3 pp. 260–67 for a discussion of the meaning of the term *muḥammad*: we consider that it was not originally the Prophet's name, but had become interpreted as a name rather than an epithet at some point during the first half of the 2nd/8th century. Certainly this was the case by mid-century.

known, common version of the formula which used a specific reference to an identified one. Something similar occurs in the case of the 'herald' formula. The Qur'ānic form is in Q.50:41:

> *Wa-astamiʿ yawma yunādi al-munādi min makān-en qarīb-en*
> "And listen for the day when the herald shall call from a nearby place."

The next verse, Q50:42, explains what this call is:

> "The day [in which] they will indeed hear the Roar (*al-ṣayḥah*), this will be the Day of Coming Forth (*yawm al-xurūj*)"

—i.e., the Judgment Day, when the dead emerge from their tombs to be judged. We cannot tell if these two verses were originally together in this form, or whether Q.50:42 was added later, as a gloss on Q.50:41. The context, however, is clearly apocalyptic.

A similar locution occurs twice in our Negev inscriptions, and the reference is very much more down-to-earth and specific: MA 4339(22), dated 160/776: *yawm daʿā al-munādi min Īlyā* "a day when the herald called from Īlyā" (i.e., Jerusalem); and MA 4387[9] where it is repeated twice: MA 4387A: *yawm yadʿū [sic] al-munādi min Īlyā*, and MA 4387B: *yawm yadʿū bihi al-munādi min Īlyā.*

This version, specifically mentioning Jerusalem as the place from which the herald will call, would seem to have been the accepted form of this locution in 160/776, i.e., the early ʿAbbāsid period. When the formula was included in the canon, a version which did not mention Jerusalem was substituted. It is not difficult in this case to see why those who had painstakingly assembled the material of the *Sīrah* to provide an Arab salvation history and link it to Scripture should wish to erase the original prominence of Jerusalem in beliefs about the Judgment Day.

---

9. Not officially published in *AAIN* and so no plate number, but reproduced with a transcription of the relevant lines in the Introduction, p. 10.

Appendix B
Chronology of al-Šām

Date (C.E. or A.H./C.E.)	Event
4th–5th c.	◦ Provincial reorganization. ◦ Abrahamism in Negev Greek inscriptions; paganism among Beduin.
6th c.	◦ Byzantium allows southern and eastern *limes* to fall into disrepair and withdraws good units from it. ◦ Pagan (Ṯamūdian and Ṣafaitic) inscriptions cease but many nonurban Arabs still pagan. ◦ Pagan Arabs of interface areas placed under Phoinikon's control.
570s	◦ Justin stops subsidies to Ġassānids and other border defense tribes.
584	◦ Maurice abolishes Ġassānid buffer state.
Late 6th c.	◦ Byzantium gradually withdraws northwards.
614–628	◦ Persian campaigns. ◦ Persians remove most Chalcedonians from Jerusalem and weaken their influence.
622–624	◦ Heraclius introduces doctrine later called Monotheletism.
628	◦ Byzantium defeats Persians but does not renew active presence in al-Šām.
11/632	◦ Heraclius stops subsidies to Arab tribes of Maᶜan area (interface between al-Šām and Arabian Peninsula).
13/634 to 20/640	◦ Takeover: initially from Gerasa-Faḥl area northwards to around Ḥimṣ.

Date (C.E. or A.H./C.E.)	Event
633–634	◦ Sophronius the anti-Monothelete made patriarch of Jerusalem.
13/634	◦ Arab raiders make roads round Bethlehem unsafe; Sophronius calls them "godless barbarians."
15/636	◦ Traditional date of the Battle of the Yarmūk.
22/643	◦ Muᶜāwiyah gains control of al-Šām from base in Damascus; no evidence for his control of central Palestine (Amman-Jerusalem-Gaza axis). ◦ Heraclius dies, Constance II becomes emperor. ◦ Muᶜāwiyah receives Egypt by negotiation—process may have started as early as 18 A.H. Cyrus still in Egypt till 23/643–44. ◦ Epigraphic evidence for monotheism among "new" ruling Arabs from this date.
24/644	◦ Colloquium of patriarch and emir: latter accepts only the Pentateuch as Scripture.
31/650 on	◦ Arab coins in Iraq bear slogans indicative of Indeterminate Monotheism.
36/656	◦ Battle of Ṣiffīn: Muᶜāwiyah defeats ᶜAlī.
39/659	◦ Truce with Byzantium, indicated by annual Arab tribute to her.
ca. 40/660	◦ Start of Basic Text (Indeterminate Monotheist) inscriptions in Arabian Peninsula.
40s–50s/660s–670s	◦ Syriac accounts of Takeover do not mention battles and indicate the Arabs met with little resistance.
41/661	◦ Muᶜāwiyah officially becomes caliph: honors and respects Christians throughout his reign.
50s/670s	◦ Coins, construction texts, and popular inscriptions all evidence Indeterminate Monotheism only. Some Negev "Judeo-Christian" Basic Texts may be from this period.
60/680	◦ Muᶜāwiyah dies. ◦ 6th Ecumenical Council rejects Monotheletism and Monophysitism, and indicates final Byzantine rejection of her former eastern provinces.

Date (C.E. or A.H./C.E.)	Event
65/685	◦ ᶜAbd al-Malik becomes caliph (65–86/685–705). ◦ Ibn Zubayr's rebellion.
69/689	◦ ᶜAbd al-Malik renews interest in northwest Negev (Elusa-Nessana area).
70/690	◦ Defeat of Ibn Zubayr in Iraq: ᶜAbd al-Malik firmly in control of al-Šām and Iraq.
71/691	◦ Muḥammad proclaimed on Arab-Sassanian coin minted in Damascus.
72/692	◦ Byzantium sends aid in building Dome of the Rock. ◦ Mohammedanism proclaimed in Dome of the Rock inscriptions: essentially Judeo-Christianity + Muḥammad as God's Messenger: argues a Christological position from within the Judaic-Christian tradition.
75/694	◦ Defeat of Ibn Zubayr in the Ḥijāz. ◦ Ḥajjāj in Iraq: marks consolidation of ᶜAbd al-Malik's control. Traditions survive that Ḥajjāj edited the material that would form the Qurʾān, destroying many texts, especially ᶜAlid ones. ◦ In Negev, inscriptions still evidence Indeterminate Monotheism; some suggest Judeo-Christian influence.
77–78/696–98	◦ ᶜAbd al-Malik reforms coinage: coin inscriptions are Mohammedan. Concept of 'guidance' introduced on them.
80s–90s/ 700s–710s	◦ Papyri protocols are Mohammedan; Qurrah bn Šarīk's letters are Indeterminate Monotheist.
85/704	◦ Earliest dated Basic Class inscription in Negev—still non-Mohammedan.
86/705	◦ Walīd I becomes caliph (86–97/705–15).
86–87/705–706	◦ Damascus mosque inscription defines Arab religion in own terms, not via differences from others. ◦ Religion becomes more self-confident and anti-Christian: display of crosses forbidden, church destroyed to build the Damascus mosque.

Date (C.E. or A.H./C.E.)	Event
ca. 100–110/ 719–729	◦ Start of pagan cultic center at Sede Boqer in Negev. Other smaller pagan centers also flourish in Negev.
105/724	◦ Hišām becomes caliph (105–25/724–43). ◦ Material for a Life of the Prophet being collected, especially by Ibn Isḥāq.
112–117/ 730–735	◦ First dated Mohammedan popular inscriptions in Negev.
125/743	◦ John of Damascus knows of Muḥammad as *name* of Arab leader, and of Qur᾿ānic material as separate collections. Gives names of some of these collections, including one not now in Qur᾿ān.
132/750	◦ ᶜAbbāsids come to power.
135/752	◦ First official mention of "Book of Allāh" and *sunnah* of the Prophet, Prophet Mosque inscription, Madīnah.
160–170/mid-770s–780s	◦ Pagan cult centers in Negev destroyed.
164/780	◦ First dated inscriptions in Negev evidencing a cluster of concepts and beliefs definable as Muslim.

Appendix C
The Inscriptions

INTRODUCTION

This appendix contains all the published "official" inscriptions—those made by command of the caliph or governor, usually on a structure he commanded to be built—and a representative selection of the "popular" rock inscriptions—those left by ordinary members of the local population, usually on rocks. We have included all the non-Negev inscriptions referred to in the text, and have tried to include all the Negev ones; any not here, and many more not referred to in this book, may be found in *AAIN*, which is the official publication of the Negev inscriptions found by Y. D. Nevo.[1] Similarly, a few of the notes to inscriptions in this appendix refer to other that were not included here, but only in *AAIN*. One or two of the Negev inscriptions included here have not been previously published. For all non-Negev inscriptions, popular and official, we give the published source.

THE ARRANGEMENT OF THE INSCRIPTIONS

The inscriptions are divided into two sections: first the "popular" rock inscriptions, then the "official" or "royal" inscriptions. Within each section, they are divided by class: Basic Texts (expressing what we have called Indeterminate Monotheism), Mohammedan, and Muslim. It should be stressed that *this division is made on the basis of linguistic analysis, not the*

1. Available from Prof. Gideon Kressel, Social Studies Unit, J. Blaustein Institute for Desert Research, Ben-Gurion University of the Negev, Sede Boqer Campus, Israel 84990.

date of the texts; thus for instance inscriptions datable to the Mohammedan and Muslim periods, right down to the group from 300 A.H., are classed as Basic Text if they contain only the concepts and formulae of that class. There are a few composite inscriptions, where an original text was added on to at a later period by someone else (for instance, the son of the original owner). Where necessary, we have given the inscription in each class to which it is relevant, with a note specifying which part belongs to this class.

There are so few official inscriptions that no further subdivision of them is necessary. The popular inscriptions are further subdivided, where possible, into undated inscriptions, and those that are either dated or are datable to a specific year or to a range of years. Within each of these sections we have attempted (again, where possible) to group inscriptions containing similar formulae and/or belonging to the same owner, in order to facilitate referral from the discussion in Part III Chapter 5. Since this means that the inscriptions are not in the order of their numbers, we provide an index by inscription number.

PROVENANCE

The majority of the popular rock inscriptions in this appendix come from the Central Negev Desert in the south of Israel. Most are from a well-defined hill area around the Ramat Matred plateau, extending northeast to the site at Sede Boqer (site code MA), where the greatest concentration of inscriptions was found. Two sites of inscriptions (site codes HR and BR) have been found in the Nessana area, close to the Egyptian border; the inscriptions from these sites form a distinct group, datable to ca. A.H. 300/912 C.E.

We also include a number of inscriptions from Jabal ᵓUsays, east of Damascus, a site frequented by the Umayyad nobility; these were published in Al-ᶜUšš (1964). The Jabal ᵓUsays inscriptions as a whole are datable to 86–125/705–743.

The numbering system used for the Negev inscriptions is as follows. The initial two letters are the code for the site where the inscription was found. Although our definition of "a site" should be regarded as no more than an arbitrary way of facilitating the description of locations, nonetheless in several cases our "sites" correspond to clusters of inscriptions close together, e.g. sites SC, GM, HS, and of course MA, and the Muslim-period sites of HR and BR.

The first digit after the site code is likewise a code, indicating the general zone of the Negev in which the inscription was found (we divided the Negev into six zones numbered 1 through 6). The remaining digits are the inscription number. A number in parentheses usually follows them: this is the plate number of the inscription in *AAIN*. Thus MA 4132(12) means "inscription 132 from site MA (Sede Boqer), in zone 4 of the Negev; a facsimile was published in Plate 12 of *AAIN*."

POINTS OF ORTHOGRAPHY

The Arabic and the English translation are arranged side by side on facing pages. We have tried to place notes on the most logical side (Arabic or English), but for ease of reading we have placed long English notes on the English side, even when they refer to points of Arabic.

Square brackets [ ] indicate text that was unreadable or only partly readable. The indication can of course be exact only in the Arabic. If the unreadable text was a personal name, this is indicated by [PN] in the English translation.

The Negev inscriptions were photoreproduced from their original publication in *AAIN*; the others were typeset for the current publication. This inevitably resulted in minor differences of orthography between the two. For instance, the Arabic of the Negev inscriptions is set in a slightly different font than the others; the transliteration of the word 'Allāh' in the Negev inscriptions was not given a long ā.

Allāhumma is translated Allāh! with an exclamation point, in order to distinguish it from *Allāh* in the English translation. Similarly, variant forms of the word "forgive" are distinguished in this way in the translation. The reader is referred to the Arabic text for the exact form of the word.

A. POPULAR ROCK INSCRIPTIONS

I. Basic Text (Indeterminate Monotheist), mostly undated

MM 113(1)

1 اللهم لا غفر [ ]
2 [بـ]ـن جذيمة امـيـ[ـن]
3 ثم امين اله مو
4 سا* وابراهيم

* Note orthography

MA 4132(12)

1 غفر ربي
2 لدحشم بن عمر
3 ذنبه كله
4 امين رب العلمين

MA 4137(12)

1 غفر رب موسى
2 لدحشم بن عمر
3 حيا وميتا

MA 4168(13)

1 غفر رب موسى
2 لوضين بن عبد الر[ ]
3 حيا [غير] ها
4 لك ولا مفقود
5 ماين* [ا]مين [ ] [ ]

* i.e. امين

EL 200A(2)

1 اللهم اغفر لخالد ا
2 بن عمر ذ[نـ]به ما تقدم منه وما
3 تاخر امين رب العلمين

AR 2101(2)

1 اللهم اغفر
2 لسلامة بن نهار
3 ذنبه ما تقدم منه
4 وما تاخر امين رب
5 العلمين

A. POPULAR ROCK INSCRIPTIONS

I. Basic Text (Indeterminate Monotheist), mostly undated

MM 113(1)
1 Allah! do not forgive! [PN]*
2 bn Judaymah Amen
3-4 and once more Amen God (of) Mūsā and Ibrāhīm
* Probably Saᶜīd (MM 105(1):2) or Ḥasan (MM 109(1):3)

MA 4132(12)
1 Forgive my Lord
2 Daḥšam bn ᶜUmar
3 his transgressions, all of them
4 Amen Lord of Creation

MA 4137(12)
1-2 Forgive Lord of Mūsà Daḥšam bn ᶜUmar
3 as long as he lives and until his death

MA 4168(13)
1-2 Forgive Lord of Mūsà Waḍīn bn ᶜAbd al-R[ ]
3-4 as long as he lives, alive and well (lit. "not perished and not lost")
5 Amen Amen [ ] [ ]

EL 200A(2)
1-2 Allah! forgive! Xālid ibn ᶜUmar
2-3 his transgressions the earlier ones and the later
3 Amen Lord of Creation

AR 2101(2)
1 Allah! forgive!
2 Salāmah bn Nahār
3-4 his transgressions the earlier ones and the later
4-5 Amen Lord of Creation

MA 455(8)

1 اللهم اغفر
2 لاشعث بن عصام
3 حيا و[مـ]ـيتا

MA 419(8)

1 اللهم اغفر لاشعث بن عصام حيا وميتا
فاغفر* له كل ذنب اذنبه قط لا
2 ارحم الرحمين واحكم الحكمين**

Note that *fa-* comes in place of *liḏālika* *
**فاصبروا حتى يحكم الله بيننا وهو خير
الحاكمين (Q7:87; 10:109; 12:80)

MA 4288(20)

4-1 [ ]
5 [ ] [غـ]ـفر ربي [لـ]ـحازم
6 [بن] عـ[ـبيـ]ـد
7 [ ]
8 غفر الله لخا[لد] بن [حمر] ان كل
9 ذنب اذنبه قـ[ـط] صـ[ـغيـ]ـره
10 [و]كبيـ[ـر]ه حد[يثه] [و]قد[يمـ]ـه

HL 4900(27)

1 غفر ربي لعمر بن
2 جابر غير هالك
3 ولا مفقود امين [رب] العـ[ـلمين]
4 رب هـ[ـا]رون وعيسى

MA 4283A(20)

1 غفر ربي
2 لمن كتب
3 هذا الكتا
4 ب ولمن قرا
5 ثم قال امين ر
6 ب العلـ[ـمين]

MA 455(8)

1-2 Allah! forgive! Aš^c^aṯ bn ^c^Iṣām
3 as long as he lives and until his death

MA 419(8)

1 Allah! forgive! Aš^c^aṯ bn ^c^Iṣām as long as he lives and until his death thus forgive him all the transgressions he has ever committed do not
2 (You are) the most Merciful of the merciful, the First among the judges

MA 4288(20)

1-4 [ ]
5-6 [ ] forgive my Lord Ḥāzim [bn] ^c^U[bay]d
7 [ ]
8 forgive Allah Xā[lid] bn [Ḥumr]ān
8-9 all the transgressions he has [ever] committed
9-10 [his minor and] major ones, [his recent ones and his earlier]

HL 4900(27)

1-2 Forgive my Lord ^c^Umar bn Jābir
2-3 alive and well (lit. "not perished and not lost")
3-4 Amen [Lord of Creation] Lord of Hārūn and ^c^Īsà

MA 4283A(20)

1 Forgive my Lord
2 the one who wrote/writes
3-4 this document/inscription
4 and the one who recites
5-6 (and) afterwards says Amen Lord of Creation

MA 87/10

1 غفر ربي
2 والهى لمن كتب
3 هذا الكتاب
4 ولمن قراه ثم
5 قال امين رب
6 العالمين

MA 453(8)

1 غفر الله لسعيد بن [ ]
2 كـ[ـل] ذنـ[ـب] اذ[نبه]
3 [ا]لكتاب وقال ا[ميـ]ـن
4 عفـ
5 [ ]ط

EL 200C(2)

1 اللهم غفر* [لسلمة] بن مالك
2 كل ذنب اذنبه
3 قط [و]لمن قرى** ولمن
4 سمع [ثم قال] امين

* Note *ǵfr* not *ʾǵfr* after *ʾAllahm*

** Note orthography with *à* and see also SC305(3):3

MA 420A(8)

1 بسم [ا]لله الرحمن الرحيم
2 اللهـ[ـم] [اغـ]ـفر [لـ]ـمحجن بن
سعيد [ما]
3 تقدم من ذنبه وما تاخر انك
4 انت [السميع]* العليم العز[يـ]ـز
الحكـ[ـيـ]ـم امين
5 رب العلمين غفر
6 غفرا
7 غفر

* See note in the translation

MA 87/10*

1 Forgive my Lord

2 and my God

2-3 the one who wrote this *kitāb*

4 and the one who read it and then

5 said: Amen Lord

6 of Creation.

* Field no., 1987 excavation season.

MA 453(8)

1 Forgive Allah Sa^{c}īd bn [PN]

2 [all the transgressions he has committed]

3 (and the one who recites this) inscription/document and says [Amen]

4-5 [ ]

EL 200C(2)

1 Allah! forgive [Salmah] bn Mālik

2-3 all the transgressions he has ever committed

3 [and] (also) the one who recites (this inscription) and the one

4 who hears it [(and) afterwards says] Amen

MA 420A(8)

1 In the name of Allah, the Compassionate, the Merciful

2 Allah! forgive! Miḥjan bn Sa^{c}īd

2-3 his transgressions the earlier ones and the later

3-4 verily, You are the [Listener]* the Omniscient, the Mighty, the Judge, Amen

5 Lord of Creation [in another hand:] forgive

6 [in a third hand:] forgive

7 [in a fourth hand:] forgive

* Completed according to the formula, e.g., MA 4138(13):4.

MA 4319(21)

1 بسم اللـ[ـه] [ا]لـرحمن الـرحيم
2 الـلـهم اغفر لـمحجن بن
3 [سعـ]ـيد مـا تقدم من ذ
4 نبه ومـا تـاخر انك
5 [ا]نت [ا]لـسميع الـعلـيم
6 [رب] الـعلـمين
7 [ ] [ر]بي لـمن كتب هذا [الـكتب
[ولـ]ـمن
8 [ ]

HL 4911(28)

1 غفر ربي لـمختا[ر] بن عثمـا[ن]
2 غير هـالـك ولا [ ]
3 غفر ر[بـ]ـي
4 لـعبد ا
5 لـعلا بن
6 هدا ب
7 مـغفرة قيمة
8 لا يعد رد[يا]
9 ولا [يكسب]
10 بعد[هـا]

11 [لا]* اثمـا ا[مين]
12 رب الـعلـ[ـمين]
13 لـعبد
14 الـ[علا بن]**
15 هدا ب

This *lā* seems out of place and is perhaps a later addition *
For the name see above, lines 4–6**

Datable to 86-125/705-73 JU 27

1 اللهم اغفر لسليمنٍ بن جناح
2 مغفرة لا يُعَدُّ رديئًا *
4-3 امين رب آلعالمين وكتب

Al-Ušš reads here تغـ[ـا]در ذنبا but is in our opinion mistaken *

Source: *JUI*, p. 250

MA 4319(21)

1 In the name of Allah, the Compassionate, the Merciful
2-3 Allah! forgive! Miḥjan bn [Sa^{c}]īd
3-4 his transgressions the earlier ones and the later
4-5 You are the Listener, the Omniscient
6 [Lord] of Creation
7 [ ] my Lord to the one who wrote/writes this [document/inscription] [and the one]*
8 [ ]

* Line 7 second hand.

HL 4911(28)

This is a composite inscription: lines 1–2 are a separate inscription from the rest, and complete in themselves.

1 Forgive my Lord Muxtā[r] bn ^{c}Uṯmā[n]
2 alive and [well] (lit. "not perished and not [lost]")
3 forgive my Lord
4-6 ^{c}Abd al-^{c}Alā bn Hadāb
7 a lasting forgiveness
8 that he may not be reckoned [wicked]
9 nor shall he [commit] (a sin)*
10 thereafter

11 [no]** blame/sin
11-13 [Amen] Lord of Creation
13-15 ^{c}Abd al-[^{c}Alā bn] Hadāb

* The formula in full seems to be *la yaksib iṯm-an li-rabb al-^{c}ālamīn* and see DL6135(34) and DL6137(34). See the different (erroneous) reading of al-^{c}Ušš in *JUI* no. 27, p. 250, and no. 88, p. 295.
** See note (*) to the Arabic text.

JU 27 Datable to 86–125/705–743

1 Allāh! forgive Sliman bn Janāḥ
2 a forgiveness [so that] he shall not be counted wicked
3-4 Amen Lord of Creation, and [it] was written/wrote [it]...

DL 6135(34)

1 بسم الله الر
2 حمن الرحيم ا
3 للهم اغفر لسعيد
4 بن مسرة مغفرة لا
5 يعد رديئا ولا

DL 6137(34)

1 بسم الله الرحمن ا
2 لرحيم اللهم اغفر
3 لميسرة بن سعيد
4 مغفرة لا يعد رد
5 يا ولا يكسب بعد
6 ها اثما لرب
7 العلمين
8 [ا]مين
9 [ثم امين]

MA 4286(20)

1 [ا]للـ[ـهـ]ـم ا
2 غفر ر[بـ] [لـ]ـحا
3 زم بن [عبيد] وادخله
4 في رحمتك

Karbalah Inscription (DKI 163) from near Karbalah in Iraq, dated 64/683

1 بسم الله الرحمن الرحيم
3-2 الله كبر كبير والحمد لله كثيرا
5-3 وسبحن الله بكرة واصلا وليلا طويلا
7-5 اللهم رب جبريل وميكل واسرنيل
8-7 اغفر لشبت بن يزيد الاشعري
9-8 ما تقدّم من ذنبه وما تاخّر
10-9 ولمن قال امين رب العلمين
11 وكتب هذا الكتب في
12 شوّال من سنة اربع وستين

Source: Grohmann, A. (1971)

DL 6135(34)

1-2 In the name of Allah, the Compassionate, the Merciful
2-4 Allah! forgive! Sa^{c}īd bn Masarrah
4-5 a forgiveness so that he shall not be reckoned wicked
nor shall*

* See also DL6137(34):4 on, and HL4911(28):7 on.

DL 6137(34)

1-2 In the name of Allah, the Compassionate, the Merciful
2-3 Allah! forgive! Maysarah bn Sa^{c}īd
4-5 a forgiveness so that he shall not be reckoned wicked
5-7 nor shall he commit a sin against the Lord of Creation*
8 Amen
9 [and once more Amen]

* See also DL6135(34):4 on, and HL4911(28):7 on.

MA 4286(20)

1-3 Allah! forgive (my) Lord Ḥāzim bn [^{c}Ubayd]
3-4 and accept him unto Your love

Karbalah Inscription (DKI 163) from near Karbalah in Iraq, dated 64/683

1 In the name of Allāh the Merciful, the Compassionate
2-3 Allāh [is] great in greatness and great is His Will
3-5 and prayer/praise to Allāh morning, evening and a long night.
[*Note*: here, in the middle of line 5, is inscribed a rectangle, indicating the end of a set prayer, probably copied from a known source.]
5-7 Allāh! Lord of Gabriel and Michael and Asrafīl,
7-8 forgive Ṯabit bn Yazīd al-Aš^{c}aʾrī [i.e. from Ashar]
8-9 his earlier transgression and his later one
10 and him who says aloud: Amen, Lord of Creation
11 and this document (*kitāb*) was inscribed in
12 Šawāl of the year 64.

Lines 2–5 lack a verb. The accepted translation is to supply verbs according to context: "Allāh and announce His greatness and praise Allāh greatly and pray long to Allāh morning, evening and night." We, as explained in Part III Chapter 3, understand *ḥmd* as "will, desire" and see lines 2–5 as *describing* Allāh.

NK 380(4)

1 بسم الله الرحمن الرحيم
2 [ا]للهم اغفر [لعمر]* [ ] بن عدي ما
تقدم من ذ[نبه] وما
3 تاخر ولمن [قر]ا

* We assume that the name ʿmr was written first and *l* was added to it without changing the ʿAyn. See also SH3101(5):4

SH 3101(5)

1 بسم الله الرحمن الرحيم
2 اللهم
3 اغفر
4 [لعمر]* بن عدي
5 بسم الله الرحمن الرحيم
6 اللهم ارض
7 عن مسرة
8 بن زيد

* See note to NK380(4):2

RB 3170(6)

1 اللهم اغفر
2 لمسرة بن زيد
3 وارضا عنه
4 حيا

MA 4254(17)

1 اللهم يا من تمت كلمته* و[يا]
2 من في السما عرشه و[في]
3 الارض موضع قدمه اغفـ[ـر]
4 [لخالد] [بن] [حمران] كل
5 ذنب اذنبه

* See also HS3153(6):5

MA 4369(23)

1 اللهم يا حليم يا كر
2 يم يا رب العرش العظيم
3 ادخل [خالد]* بن [حمران]*
4 جـنـات
5 النعـيم

* Carefully erased

NK 380(4)

1 In the name of Allah, the Compassionate, the Merciful
2 Allah forgive! [[c]Umar] [ ] bn [c]Adiy
2-3 his transgressions, the earlier ones and the later
3 and the one who recites

SH 3101(5)

1 In the name of Allah, the Compassionate, the Merciful
2-4 Allah! forgive! [[c]Umar] bn [c]Adiy
5 in the name of Allah, the Compassionate, the Merciful
6-8 Allah! be pleased with Masarrah bn Zayd

RB 3170(6)

1-2 Allah! forgive! Masarrah bn Zayd
3-4 and be pleased with him, alive (= while he is alive)

MA 4254(17)

1-3 Allah! You whose word was accomplished and whose throne is in the Sky and the Earth is His footstool*
3-4 forgive! [Xālid bn Ḥumrān]
4-5 all the transgressions he has committed

* Lines 2–3 call to mind Isaiah 66:1. We may ask whether the phrase was not a part of the common stock of monotheistic doxology.

MA 4369(23)

1-2 Allah! O Forbearing One, O Generous One
2 O Lord of the enormous Throne
3 (let) [Xālid] bn [Ḥumrān] enter
4-5 (the) Gardens of Grace/Favor

MA 4138(13)

1 اللهم اغفر لا
2 شعث بن عصام
3 ما تقدم من ذنبه وما تاخر انك انت
4 السميع العليم العلي العظيم العزيز الحكيم الرؤف
5 الرحيم واغفر له حيا وميتا و[هـ]ـو يسل الله [ا]لمجنة ان لا يقوم
6 عن مجنة* حتا يتسن* له الظعون
7 غـ[ـفـ]ـر [ر]بي
8 لـ[ ]ـم

* عن مجنة = مُجَنَّة ; يتسن = يتسنى

Datable to 112/730 GM 389(4)

1 اللهم اغفر لورد بن
2 سالم ما تقدم من ذنبه
3 وما تاخر وادخله ا
4 لجنة امـ[ـيـ]ـن رب العلمين
5 ولمن قرى ولمن سمع الا
6 [ان] امن

II. Basic Text—subgroup with "Judeo-Christian" opening phrase

MA 4204A(14)

1 غفر رب عيسى وموسى لـ[ ]

MA 4340(22)

1 غفر ر[بي]
2 غفر رب [عيسى] و[مو]
3 سى لـ[ ]

MA 4210(16)

1 غفر الله رب
2 موسى [و]عيسى لقـ[ـيس]
3 بن سويد حيا ومـ[ـيتا]
4 امين رب العلمين رب
5 [الناس] اجمعين

MA 4138(13)
1-2 Allah! forgive! Aš^c^aṯ bn ^c^Iṣām
3 his transgressions the earlier ones and the later
3-5 verily You are the Listener, the Omniscient,
the-One-on-High, the Enormous, the Mighty, the Judge,
the Gentle, the Loving/Compassionate One;
5 thus forgive! him as long as he lives and until his death
5-6 and also (*wa-*) he entreats Allah to grant him Sanctuary
and that he shall not leave the Sanctuary until he can
depart (lit. until the Voyage will be possible*)
7 (in another hand) Forgive my Lord
8 [PN]

* This may be read as a reference to a coming journey, or symbolically as a reference to death.

GM 389(4) Datable to 112/730
1-2 Allah! forgive! Ward bn Sālim
2-3 his transgressions, the earlier ones and the later
3-4 and admit him into *al-jannah*
4 Amen Lord of Creation
5 and to the one who recites
5 and to the one who hears
5-6 but only [if] he trusts (i.e. has faith)

II. Basic Text—subgroup with "Judeo-Christian" opening phrase

MA 4204A(14)
1 Forgive Lord of ^c^Īsà and Mūsà [PN]

MA 4340(22)
1 Forgive [my Lord]
2-3 forgive Lord of [^c^Īsà] and [Mū]sà [PN]

MA 4210(16)
1-2 Forgive Allah, Lord of Mūsà [and] ^c^Īsà
2-3 Qa[ys] bn Suwayd
3 as long as he lives and [until his death]
4-5 Amen Lord of Creation, Lord of [the people], all of
them

MA 4269(19)

1 [غـ]ـفر الله رب
2 موسى وعيسى
3 لخالد بن حمران
4 حيا وميتا

MA 4513(25)

1 غفر رب
2 موسى لعبد
3 ا[لله]

MA 4514(25)

1 غفر ربي
2 [لـ]ـعبد الـلـ[ـه]

MA 4516(26)

1 اغفر رب موسى [و] عيسـ[ـى]
2 لعبد الـ[ـله] [ ]
3 غير هالك [ ]
4 امين ر[ب] [العلمين]
5 [ ]

MA 4508(25)

1 اللهم رب مو
2 سى وعيسى اغفر
3 لعبد الله بن [ ]

MA 4509(25)

1 [ر]ب مو[سى]
2 [لـ]ـعبد الله بن
3 [عـ]ـدي حيـ[ـا] وميتا

MA 4269(19)

1-2	Forgive Allah Lord of Mūsà and ᶜĪsà
3	Xālid bn Ḥumrān
4	as long as he lives and until his death

MA 4513(25)

1-3	Forgive Lord of Mūsà ᶜAbd [Allah]

MA 4514(25)

1-2	Forgive my Lord ᶜAbd Allah

MA 4516(26)

1	Forgive Lord of Mūsà [and] ᶜĪs[à]
2	ᶜAbd Al[lah] [ ]
3	alive (lit. "not perished") [ ]
4	Amen [Lord of Creation]
5	[ ]

MA 4508(25)

1-2	Allah! Lord of Mūsà and ᶜĪsà
2-3	forgive! ᶜAbd-Allah bn [PN]

MA 4509(25)

1	[Lord of] [Mū]sà
2-3	ᶜAbd Allah bn [ᶜA]diy
3	as long as he lives and until his death

III. Basic Text—dated or datable to ca. 85/704

Dated 85/704 MA 4265(19)

1 غفر الله لحكيم بن
2 عمرو [غير] ها[لك] ولا مفقو
3 د امين رب العلمين رب
4 الناس اجمعين وكتب
5 في مسـ[ـتـ]ـهل ذي الحجة سنة
6 خمس وثمنين مـ
7 ا[دخـ]ـلـه الجنة
8 [ ]

MA 456(8)

1 اللهم اغفـ[ـر]
2 [لحـ]ـك بن عمر[و] [غير]
3 ها[لك]

MA 4256A(17)

1 غفر الله لحكيم بن عمرو
2 غير هالك ولا مفقو[د]

MA 4256B(17)

1 لا لا غفر الله لحكيم
2 غير هالك و[لا]

MA 457B(9)

1 اللهم اغفر لحكيم بن عمرو ما تقدم
2 من ذنبه وما تـ[ـا]خـ[ـر] ا[نك] على
كل شي قد[ير]
4-3 [ ]

MA 4253(17)

1 غفر الـلـ[ـه]
2 لعبد الله ا[بـ]ـن* [ ]
3 [حـ]ـيا [ ]
4 غفر الله لحكيـ[ـم] بن عمرو
5 غير هالك

* Note ʾbn instead of *bn*

III. Basic Text—dated or datable to ca. 85/704

MA 4265(19) Dated 85/704*

1-2 Forgive Allah Ḥakīm bn ᶜAmr
2-3 alive and well (lit. "not perished and not lost")
3-4 Amen Lord of Creation, Lord of the people, all of them
4-5 and it was written on the first day of Ḏu al-Ḥijjah
5-6 year 85 (filled to end of line with ————ـه)
7 admit him into *al-jannah*
8 [ ]

* The first day of 85 AH was 14.1.704.

MA 456(8)

1-2 Allah! forgive [Ḥakīm]* bn ᶜAmr
2-3 [alive] (lit. "not perished")

* See note to MA412B(7).

MA 4256A(17)

1 Forgive Allah Ḥakīm bn ᶜAmr
2 alive and well (lit. "not perished and not lost")

MA 4256B(17)

1 Do not do not forgive Allah Ḥakīm
2 alive and well (lit. "not perished and [not]...)

MA 457B(9)

1 Allah! forgive! Ḥakīm* bn ᶜAmr
1-2 his transgressions, the earlier ones and the later
2 [You are] The Omnipotent (lit. "You effect everything")
3-4 [ ]

* Contrast with the form of the name in MA456(8):1 above, and see note to MA412B(7).

MA 4253(17)

1 Forgive Allah
2 ᶜAbd Allah ibn [PN]
3 as long as he lives [ ]
4 forgive Allah Ḥakī[m] bn ᶜAmr
5 alive (lit. "not perished")

MA 450(8)

1 اللـهم انك
2 المعيذ ربي
3 المعيذ من [ ]
4 السـ[ـعـ]ـير* ان تغفر لحك بن عمرو
5 ما تقدم من ذنبه وما تاخر

* expected <اسئلك>

MA 4252(17)

3-1 [ ]
4 غفر الله [ ]
5 [لحكيم بن عمرو كل]
6 ذنب ا[ذنبه] [قط]
7 صل على [محمد] [ ]
8 [ارسله] [ ]
9 [ ]
10 [ ] وبدين (*sic*)

11 الحق [ليظهره] على الدين كلـ[ـه]
12 [و]لو كـ[ـره المشركون]

Q9:33; 61:9 and see MA4262(18):1-5

هو الذي ارسل رسوله بالهدى ودين الحق ليظهره
على الدين كله ولو كره المشركون

IV. The Qaṣr Xaranah inscription, dated 92/710

1 اللهم ارحم عبد الملك ابن عمر
2-1 واغفر له ذنبه ما تقدم منه وما تاخر
2 من ما اسرّ وما اعلن
3 وما احد كان من نفسه قابل لك
4-3 الا تغفر له وترحمه ان آمن
4 آمنت برب فمنّ علي انت المنان
5-4 وترحم علي فانك انت الرحمن
6-5 اللهم انني اسئلك ان تقبل منه
6 صلاته وهيابته
7-6 امين رب العلمين رب موسى وهرون
7 رحم الله من قراه ثم قال امين امين

MA 450(8)

1-2 Allah! You are the Shelterer
2-4 my Lord who shelters from the Fire
4 that you will forgive Ḥakīm* bn ᶜAmr
5 his transgressions the earlier ones and the later

* See note to MA412B(7).

MA 4252(17)

1-3 [ ]
4 Forgive Allah [ ]
5 [Ḥakīm bn ᶜAmr]
5-6 [all] the transgressions [he has ever committed]
7 incline unto [Muḥammad]
8 [He sent him] [ ]
9 [ ]
10-11 [ ] and with the True Faith
11 [to make it* victorious] over any other faith
12 even in the face of the [*Mušrikūn*'s reluctance/dislike/hatred**]

* Or "him".
** This is the "offensive" ending of the formula. For the "mild" or inoffensive ending see BR5131(32).

We consider this text to be two distinct inscriptions from different dates. Lines 1–6 are pre-Mohammedan, datable to 85/704; lines 7–12, apparently added in a different hand, are Muslim, datable to 160/776.

IV. The Qaṣr Xaranah inscription, dated 92/710

1 Allāhumma have mercy on ᶜAbd al-Malik bn ᶜUmar and forgive him
2 his transgressions, the earlier and the later ones, the hidden and the disclosed;
3 No one of himself draws nigh unto Thee but that Thou forgivest him and hast mercy upon him
4 if he believes. I believe in my Lord. Therefore bestow on me Thy benefits, for Thou are the Benefactor, and have mercy
5 upon me, for Thou art the Merciful. Oh God, I beg of Thee to
6 accept from him his prayer and his donation. Amen Lord of Creation, Lord of
7 Moses and Aaron. May God have mercy on him who reads it and says Amen, Amen, Lord of Creation,

8-7 رب العلمين العزيز الحكيم
8 وكتب عبد الملك بن عمر
9-8 يوم الاثنين لثلث بقين من المحرم
9 من سنة اثنين وتسعين
10 [شهد (؟)] لام بن هرون
11 واسرح بنا ان نجتمع بنبي ونبيه
11-12 في دنيا والاخر*

* الاخر[ة]

Source: Abbott (1946)

V. Mohammedan Popular Inscriptions

These are not further subdivided; the date is given where known

MA 4282(19)

1 [ا]للهم غفر
2 اللهم اغفر لمحمد [ ]
3 بسم الله الرحمن الرحيـ[ـم]
4 اللهـ[ـم] [ ] بن هـ[ـد]اب اللـ[ـهـ]ـم
5 اللـ[ـهـ]ـم اغفر لـ[ ] بن سليمن ذنبه
6 اللهـ[ـم] اغفر لامر القيس بن سلامة ذنبه
7 كـ[ـلـ]ـه حديثه وقديمه
8 و[صبره وغلبه]
9 [غفـ]ـرب*
10 لمعاو[يـ]ـة [بن]
11 [سـ]ـعيد
12 [ ]

Haplography of *gfr rb[y]* *

JU 88

1 اللهم اغفر
2 لسليمن بن جناح ا
3 مين رب العلمين * مغفرة
4 لا يُعدُّ رديئًا وكفه ما** وا
5 نصُرْه على من عَاده وأَعِنْهُ

* and ** see notes to the translation.

Source: *JUI*, p. 292.

8 the Mighty, the Wise! ^{c}Abd al-Malik bn ^{c}Umar wrote [it] on
9 Monday, three [nights] remaining from Muḥarram of the year two and ninety.
10 [Witnessed by] Lām bn Hārūn.
11 And lead us so we meet with my prophet and his prophet
11-12 in this world and the next.

The translation is based on Abbot, N. (1946).

V. Mohammedan Popular Inscriptions

These are not further subdivided; the date is given where known

MA 4282(19)

1 Allah! forgive
2 Allah! forgive! Muḥammad [ ]
3 in the name of Allah, the Compassionate, the Merciful
4 Allah! [PN] bn Ha[d]āb Allah!
5 Allah! forgive! [PN] bn Sulayman his transgression/s
6 Allah! forgive! Imru al-Qays bn Salāmah
6-7 all his transgressions, the recent ones and the earlier
8 and [make him persevere and overcome]
9 [forgive(my)Lord]
10 Mu^{c}āwiyah [bn]
11 [Sa]^{c}īd
12 [ ]

JU 88

1-2 Allāh! Forgive Sliman bn Janāḥ
3 Amen Lord of Creation*—a forgiveness
4 [so that] he shall not be counted wicked and suffice for him**
5 and make him victorious over anyone
who encounters him with enmity, and help him.

* Here ends what seems to be the text originally intended. Its continuation, though in the same hand, is either a later addition or a "second thought" or the like.

** al-^{c}Ušš completes "and let his deeds suffice..." He points out that without an additional word after *mā* the sentence is defective. His suggestion: "his deeds" is, he notes, tentative only.

Dated 112/730 SC 305(3)

1 اللـهم [اغفر] للورد بن سالم ما تقدم من ذ[نـ]ـبه وما تاخر
2 و[تم] نعمتك عليه واهده صرط* مستقيما امن (*sic*) رب
3 العلمين رب موسى وهرون ولمن قرى** ولمن قا[ل] امين كتب في [ ] [سنة] ثنية عشرة ومـئة عل*** خلفة هشام

* For صرطا
** Note orthography with ى and see also EL200C(2):3 and SC301(3):5
*** Should be علـى, see also GM388(4)

SC 301(3)

1 بسم اللـه الرحمن الرحيم ا
2 للـهم اغفر لنهار بن عامر وارز
3 قه من فضلك وادخله رحمتك وات[ـم] [عـ]ـليه نعمـ
4 تك واجعله من المفلحين اللـهم اغفر لمحمد رسول
5 اللـه ولمن كتب هذ الكتب* ولمن قره**
6 قل امين رب العلمين

* Haplography, or *lapsus calami* which was corrected by an *Alif* under *hḏ*, or is it an *ā*? and see EL200C(2):3 and SC305(3):3
** Note orthography

SC 302(3)

1 بسم اللـه الرحمن ا
2 للـهم اغفر
3 [لعبدة] بن [ ]
4 [ومح*] ذنبه و
5 اشرح لـه
6 صدره
7 وانفعه ما
8 تنفعه

* root *m.ḥ.w.*: to erase, to cancel (sins by God)

Datable to 112/73 GM 390(4)

1 اللـهم صلي
2 علـى مسرة
3 بن زيد

SC 305(3) Dated 112/730*

1 Allah! forgive! al-Ward bn Sālim his transgressions, the earlier ones and the later
2 and [bestow fully] upon him Your favor and lead hin in a straight road
2-3 Amen Lord of Creation, Lord of Mūsà and Hārūān
3 and him who recites and him who says Amen. (It) was written in [the year] 112 in the caliphate of Hišām.

* The first day of 112 A.H. was 26.3.730.

SC 301(3)

1 In the name of Allah, the Compassionate, the Merciful
1-2 Allah! forgive! Nahār bn ᶜĀmr
2-3 and provide for him from Your bounty and accept him into Your love and bestow fully upon him Your
3-4 favors and make him one of the prosperous.
4-5 forgive! Muḥammad the messenger of Allah, and the one who wrote/writes his inscriptions/document and the one who recites (it)
6 say: Amen, Lord of Creation

SC 302(3)

1 In the name of Allah, the Compassionate
1-3 Allah! forgive! [ᶜAbdah] bn [PN]
4 [and cancel] his transgression/s
4-6 and open his breast*
7-8 and let him gain whatever you give him**

* I.e., open his heart/mind (to receive your words, etc.), see e.g., Q.16:106; 6:125; 39:22 and elsewhere.

** The sentence is difficult. We interpret it as meaning that the supplicant has no special requests: he accepts whatever Allah wishes to send him. Contrast with SC301(3) above.

GM 390(4)

1-3 Allah! incline unto Masarrah bn Zayd

GM 388(4)

1 اللهم صلي عل*
2 مسرة بن زيد
3 وادخله الجنة
4 بغير حساب
5 يرحمن يرحيم

* Should be علي, and see also SC305(3):3

HS 3154(6)

1 اللهم صلي على محمد النبي
2 وعلى من يصلي عليه و
3 كتب ثوابة بن معروف
4 وهو يسل الله الجنة برحمته

GM 385(4)

1 اللهم اغفر
2 لرفاعة بن مسلم
3 برحمتك

JU 18

1 اللهم ادخل محمد بن الوليد
2 بذمة الجنة امين رب العلمين وكتبه
3 [...] بحر وهو يسل الله الجنة

Source: *JUI*, p. 244.

JU 72

1 انا حفص بن عبد الله
2 اسل الجنة واعوذ به من النار

Source: *JUI*, p. 281.

JU 49

1 انا عبد الله بن علي
2 اسل الله [ا]لرحمة واعوذ
3 به من النار يو[م الحساب]

Source: *JUI*, p. 266.

GM 388(4)

1 Allah! incline unto
2 Masarrah bn Zayd
3 and admit him into *al-jannah*
4 with no reckoning/retribution
5 O Compassionate, O Merciful One

HS 3154(6)

1 Allah! incline unto Muḥammad the Prophet
2 and unto him who prays for him
2-3 and Tuwābah bn Maʿrūf wrote (it)
4 and he asks Allah for *al-jannah* by His love.

GM 385(4)

1-3 Allah! forgive! Rifāʿah bn Muslim, by/in Your love

JU 18

1 Allāh! Admit Muḥammad bn al-Walīd
2 into the protection of *al-jannah*. Amen Lord of Creation
2-3 And [ ] *Bḥr* wrote it and he requests of Allāh *al-jannah*.

JU 72*

1 I Ḥafas bn ʿAbd Allāh
2 request *al-jannah* and recourse to Him for shelter from the Fire.

* The owner of this inscription also left one dated 119/737

JU 49

1 I ʿAbd Allāh bn ʿAlī
2 request of Allāh *al-raḥmah*
2-3 and have recourse to Him for shelter
3 from the Fire on the day [of reckoning].

Note: al-ʿUšš suggests in *JUI* three equally possible ways of completing the last line, all meaning "the Day of Reckoning" or "the Day of Resurrection."

HS 3153(6)

1 اللهم اني اسلك تبين (= تبيان)
2 كل شي لك الحمد لا
3 اله الا انت بديع السمو
4 ات والارض ذ[و] الجلل (= الجلال)
والكرم (= والاكرام) فلما
5 قضا النبي صلاته قال من صحب الكلمت *
6 الله**
7 قال: العلم (= العالم)
8 انا بديعه

* See also MA 4254(17):1

** See note (***) to the translation

JU 46

1 ومن نبيه غير
2 محـ[ـمـ]ـد

Source: *JUI*, p. 264, erron. printed as 364

MA 4113(12)

1 غفر ربي
2 لامر القيس
3 غفر
4 الله لمحمد ذ[نبه]

dated 108/729, Hišām's reign JU 103

1 الله ولي المخول بن عمّار
2 وكتب في شهر ربيع الاخر
3 سنة ثمان ومئة

Source: *JUI*

JU 105

1 اللهم كن انت ولي يزيد بن عبد
2 الواحد الاسدى

Source: *JUI*

HS 3153(6)

1-2 Allah! I ask You make manifest to me all things* Yours is the Will**

2-4 there is no God but You, Creator of the Heavens and the Earth

4 (You are) Majestic and Generous

4-5 as the Prophet finished his prayer he said: Who is Master of the Word?

6 Allah***

7-8 He said: "The World — I created it."

* *tbyn* = *tabyyinu kulli šay*ᵓ*-en* or *tibyān*. Q16:89: ونزلنا عليك الكتاب تبيانا لكل شيء. Lane: "And we have sent down to thee the scripture to make manifest everything" (Lane, Vol. 1, pp. 286, col. 1 para. 1 and pp. 286 (line 7 from bottom)–287). In our opinion this formula refers to the ability to distinguish between right and wrong, i.e. the supplicant requests guidance to a righteous way of life.

** See discussion in the Introduction.

*** "Allah" was apparently inscribed later by someone who felt that the question "Who is Master..." should not be left unanswered.

JU 46

1-2 And who is His prophet but Muḥammad? [i.e., He has no prophet but Muḥammad]

MA 4113(12)

1 Forgive my Lord

2 Imr al-Qays

3-4 forgive Allah Muḥammad [his transgression]

JU 103 dated 108/729, Hišām's reign

1 Allāh is the patron of *Mḥwl* bn ᶜAmmār

2 and it was written in the month of Rabīᶜ II

3 in the year 108.

JU 105

1 Allāh! Be Thou the patron of Yazīd bn ᶜAbd

2 al-Wāḥid from the tribe of Assad.

Dated 117/735 HS 3155-56(6)

Left column lines 1–7

1 بسم الله الرحمن الرحيم

2 اللهم ا[غفـ]ـر لحسن بن ميسرة ولو

3 لديه* وما ولدا امين رب محمد و

4 ابرهيم اللهم اجعل عملي جهدا

5 واجعل رأفتي استشهد** في سبيلك

6 وكتب حسن يوم

Right column lines 8–11

7 الثلـ[ـثـ]ـة

8 في ثمان بقين من ربيع ا[لا]ول (ربيع
الاول) وفيه توفو

9 بني حا[تـ]ـم يرحمهم الله جميعة***

10 وهو في سنة تْتْبعة عشرة****

11 ومـئة

* See Q29:8; 31:14; 46:15. This phrase is rather common in late inscriptions in the Syrian desert, see BSD No. 2 and *passim*

** استشهادا

*** Should be جميعا

**** Should be سبع عشرة

VI. Early Muslim Popular Inscriptions datable to ca. 160–170 A.H.

Dated 164/780–81 EKI 261

1 الله و[ربـ]ـي(؟) سعيد بن يزيد فنعم المولا ونعم

2 النصير سعيد يشهد الله وجميع خلقه

3 انه لا اله الا الله وحده لا شريك له

4 [drawing ?] وان محمد عبده ورسوله

5 وكتب سنة اربع وستين

6 ومائة

MA 4262(18)

1 [[محمـ]ـد رسول اللـ[ـه]

2 [[ار]سله بالهدى

3 [[وبدين]* الـ[ـحـ]ـق [ليظهره]

4 [[على] الد[يـ]ـن كـ[ـله]

5 [[ولو كره] الـمـ[شركون]**

7-6 [ ] [

* The reading بدين follows MA4252(17):10

** See also MA4252(17):7–12

HS 3155-56(6) Dated 117/735*

1 In the name of Allah, the Compassionate, the Merciful
2 Allah! forgive! Ḥasan bn Maysarah
2-3 and his two parents and their offspring
3-4 Amen Lord of Muḥammad and Ibrāhīm
4 Allah! consider my deeds great exertion (*jihād*)
5 and accept my compassion as martyrdom in Your cause
6-7 and Ḥasan wrote (it) on Tuesday
8 the 22th of the month of Rabiy^{c} al-Awwal, in which passed away
9 Banū Ḥā[t]im may God have mercy on all of them
10-11 and this in the year 117*

* The first day of 117 AH was 31.1.735.

VI. Early Muslim Popular Inscriptions datable to ca. 160–170 A.H.

EKI 261* Dated 164/780–81

1 Allāh and [my Lord(?)]** Sa^{c}īd bn Yazīd, and He is an excellent Patron and an excellent
2 Helper. Sa^{c}īd testifies unto Allāh and the whole of His creation
3 that there is no God but Allāh alone, He has no companion
4 and also that Muḥammad is His servant and messenger
5-6 Written in the year 164.

* From site YT in the Negev, not published elsewhere.
** We suspect a scribal blunder here, and suggest the following reconstruction of line 1: "[This is the testimony of] Sa^{c}īd bn Yazīd: Allāh [is] my Lord, and He is an excellent Patron" etc.

MA 4262(18)

1] [Muḥamma]d Messenger of Allah
2] He sent him with the Guidance
3] [and the True Faith] to make it* [victorious]
4] [over] any other faith
5] even in face of the *Mu*[*šrikūn*'s reluctance/dislike/hatred**]
6-7] [ ]

* Or "him".
** See note (**) to MA4252(17).
] = Edge of wall W309 in MA-D3, the mosque at the site of Sede Boqer.

Dated 160/776*   MA 4339(22)

1 غفر الله [ ]
2 [ ]
3 يوم دعـ[ـا] المناد من
4 ايليا يوم [ ]
5 بعد ما كان فيها من
6 بني ادم [مصطفى]
7 السـما
8 فكتب محجن
9 بن سعيد [و]هو
10 <سنه> ستين ومئة**
11 [يسـ]ـل الله الـ[ـجـ]ـنة

See note to the translation *
Line 10 seems to be an insertion **

Dated 170/786*   ST 640(34)

1 رضي الله عنك
2 يا سعيد هذا
3 ما يشهد سعيد
4 يشهد ان محمد
5 وعيسى وعزير
6 وجميع الخلا
7 ئق عباد مربوبين
8 ويشهد لله وكفا
9 بالله شهيدا ا[نـ]ـه احدا
10 احدا صمد لا والد
11 ولا ولد وكتب
12 في سنة سبعين ومائة

The reading of this text was arrived at with the assistance of Prof. Kister (Jerusalem, Aug. 1986).
See note to the translation *

VII. Muslim Popular Inscriptions: undatable

AR 2100(2)

1 اللهم صلي على خالد بن عمر يوم
2 يموت ويوم يبعث حيا امين
3 رب العلمين

MA 4339(22) Dated 160/776*

1 Forgive Allah [ ]
2 [ ]
3 (a) day in which the herald called from
4 Īlyā (= Jerusalem) day [ ]
5 after he was in it** from among
6 men (*bany adam*) [chosen]***
7 the sky
8-9 and Miḥjan bn Sa^{c}īd wrote it and he
10 ⟨year⟩ 160
11 [requests] of Allah *al-jannah*

* The first day of 160 A.H. was October 19, 776. Note that the date was inserted between line 9 and 11 which belong together.

** "in it" (*fīhā*): in the city of Jerusalem.

*** "chosen" (*muṣṭafà*): this reading is uncertain, see facsimile.

ST 640(34) Dated 170/786*

1-2 Let Allah plased with you *yā*-Sa^{c}īd
2-3 this is the testimony of Sa^{c}īd
4-7 (and) he testifies that Muḥammad and ^{c}Īsà and ^{c}Uzayr and all the created ones are subordinate worshippers.**
8-9 and he testifies unto Allah, and Allah suffices as a witness,
9-10 that He is One, indivisible;*** neither begetting nor begotten
11-12 and (this) was written in the year 170

* The first day of 170 A.H. was July 3, 789.

** Dr. G. Hawting comments (letter January 30, 1990): "is it possible that *lillāh* [in line 8] is intended to follow *marbūbīn* (*^{c}ibād marbūbīn lillāh*)? It seems an unusual formula, altogether Lane has it in his *Lexicon* s.v. *marbūb*".

*** For "indivisable" as the translation of *ṣamad*, see the discussions on p. 277. Traditional Muslim scholarship has reached no consensus on the meaning of this word.

VII. Muslim Popular Inscriptions: undatable

AR 2100(2)

1 Allah! incline unto Xālid bn ^{c}Umar the day
2 he dies and (the) day he is "sent forth"/comes from the dead alive Amen
3 Lord of Creation

AR 271(2)

1] يوم يبعث
2 حيا امين رب العلمين
3 [ ] يوم يمو[ت]
4 وكتب
5 يوم ا[لثلـ]ـث

MA 4205(14)

1 غفر الله لسري بن مـ[ ]
2 غير هلك (= هالك)
3 ولا مفقود امين [ر]ب
4 العـــــلمين
5 صلي الله عـــلى
6 محمد [عـ]ــــليه
7 السلم ورحمة الله
8 اسل الله ا[لجـ]ـنة
9 واعوذ به من النار
10 لا حول لنا ولا قوة
11 الا بالله العظيم
12 ولعبد الله بن سري

MA 4252(17)

3-1 [ ]
4 غفر الله [ ]
5 [لحكيم بن عمرو كل]
6 ذنب ا[ذنبه] [قط]
7 صل على [محمد] [ ]
8 [ارسله] [ ]
9 [ ]
10 [ ] وبدين (*sic*)
11 الحق [ليظهره] على الدين كلـ[ـه]
12 [و]لو كـ[ـره المشركون]

Q9:33; 61:9 and see MA4262(18):1–5

هو الذي ارسل رسوله بالهدى ودين الحق ليظهره
على الدين كله ولو كره المشركون

AR 271(2)

1] The day (he) is "sent forth"/comes from the dead
2 alive Amen Lord of Creation
3 [ ] (the) day when he dies
4 and (it) was written
5 Tuesday

MA 4205(14)*

1 Forgive Allah Sariy bn M[ ]
2-4 alive and well (lit. "not perished and not lost"). Amen Lord of Creation
5-6 Allah incline unto Muḥammad
6-7 (let) peace be upon him with (*wa*) Allah's love
8 I request of Allah *al-jannah*
9 I seek shelter in Him from the Fire
10 there is no strength for us nor power
11 but through Allah the Enormous
12 and to ʿAbd Allah bn Sariy

* Composite inscription: lines 1–4 are complete in themselves and belong to Sariy bn M[ ]; lines 5–12 are in different hand and belong to his son ʿAbd Allah. Sariy bn ___ occur also in MA4336(22).

MA 4252(17)

1-3 [ ]
4 Forgive Allah [ ]
5 [Ḥakīm bn ʿAmr]
5-6 [all] the transgressions [he has ever committed]
7 incline unto [Muḥammad]
8 [He sent him] [ ]
9 [ ]
10-11 [ ] and with the True Faith
11 [to make it* victorious] over any other faith
12 even in the face of the [*Mušrikūn*'s reluctance/dislike/hatred**]

* Or "him".

** This is the "offensive" ending of the formula. For the "mild" or inoffensive ending see BR5131(32).

We consider this text to be two distinct inscriptions from different dates. Lines 1–6 are pre-Mohammedan, datable to 85/704; lines 7–12, apparently added in a different hand, are Muslim, datable to 160/776.

MM 107(1)

1 [عـ]بد [ا]لله شا
2 [هـ]ـد [مـ]حمد بشير
3 الله ويستشهد
4 [قـ]ـلبه [عليه]

VIII. Muslim Popular Inscriptions: datable to ca. 300 A.H.

BR 5134(32)

1 بسم الله الرحمن الرحيم
2 [*]ا ان الله وملئكه يصلون
3 على محمد النبي صلوت الله
4 على محمد وكتب بشير بن تميم

* Another hand

HR 514(29)

1 اللهم صلي ا
2 نت وملئكك
3 على بشر [بن] تميـ[ـم]
4 رحمت الله وبركته
5 على محمد عبد
6 ك

HR 516(29)

1 الهم* صلي ا
2 نت و[مـ]ـلكيك
3 على [حسن] بن زيد

* For more examples of this orthography see HL 4906(28), HR 515(29)

HR 517(30)

1 اللهم
2 اللهم صلي
3 [ا]نت وملئكتك
4 على حرملة بن
5 مغرة هـ
6 د كتب
7 هو يسل الله

MM 107(1)
1-2 ᶜAbd Allah testifies that
2-3 [M]uḥammad (is the) announcer/evangelist (of) Allah
3-4 and his heart yearns to give witness/he mortifies his heart [unto Him]

VIII. Muslim Popular Inscriptions: datable to ca. 300 A.H.

BR 5134(32)
1 In the name of Allah, the Compassionate, the Merciful
2 [ ] that Allah and His angels
2-3 will incline unto Muḥammad the Prophet
3-4 Allah's blessing upon Muḥammad
4 and Bašīr bn Tamīm wrote (it)

HR 514(29)
1-2 Allah! incline You and Your angels
3 unto Bišr bn Tamīm
4-6 Allah's love and blessing unto Muḥammad Your servant

HR 516(29)
1-2 Allah! incline, You and Your two angels
3 unto [Hasan] bn Zayd

HR 517(30)
1 Allah!
2-3 Allah! incline You and Your angels
4-5 unto Ḥarmallah bn Muġirah *h*—
6 *d* wrote
7 he requests Allah

BR 5170(33)

1 اللـهم صلـي
2 [انت] ومـ[ـلـ]ـكيك [علـ]ـى

HR 511(29)

1 اللـهم صلـي انت و
2 ملئكتك علـى مر
3 زوق بن [سالـم] [انـ]ـك
4 علـى كـ[ـل]*
5 غفر [ ]
6 لغـ[ـيـ]ـب [والـ]ـشهدة [كشف]**
7 الحوبت*** قبل الصلـ[ـو]ت
8 [رب] انني اسلك
9 [ان] تغفر لمرزو
10 ق [بن] سالـم

* For the complete formula, see HR522(30):3–5

** For the complete formula, see BR5180(33):2–3

*** *ḥawbat for ḥuwab* pl. of *ḥawbah* = sin, crime, fault. This formula occurs also in HR522(20):6–8

HR 522(30)

1 بسم الله الرحمن الرحيم
2 اللهم اغفر لبشر بن
3 تميم انك علـى
4 كل شي [قـ]ـدير وانك علم
5 الغيب والشهدة
6 كشف الحو
7 بت قبل الصلو
8 ت اني [ا]سلك
9 نعمك
10 لبشر بن
11 تميم

BR 5180(33)

1 [ا]للهم علم ا
2 للهـ[ـم] علـ[ـم] ا
3 لغيب والشهد[ة]
4 غفر لـ[ـبـ]ـشر بن تمـ[ـيم]

BR 5170(33)

1-2 Allah! incline, [You] and Your two angels [unto]

HR 511(29)

1-2 Allah! incline You and Your angels
2-3 unto Marzūq bn [Sālim]*
3-4 You are the [Omnipotent] (lit. "You effect everything")
5 forgive [ ]
6 that is concealed and manifest
6-7 [Revealer] of sins, Receiver of prayers
8-10 [Lord] I request You to forgive Marzūq [bn] Sālim

* See lines 8-10.

HR 522(30)

1 In the name of Allah, the Compassionate, the Merciful
2-3 Allah! forgive! Bišr bn Tamīm
3-4 You are the Omipotent (lit. "You effect everything")
4-5 You are the One who knows all that is concealed and manifest
6-8 Revealer of sins, Receiver of prayers
8-11 I beseech of You Your favors upon Biš bn Tamīm

BR 5180(33)

1 Allah! The One who knows
2-3 Allah! the One who knows all that is concealed and manifest*
4 forgive [Bi]šr bn Tam[īm]

* See also HR511(29); HR522((30).

BR 5102(30)

1 بسم الله الرحمن الرحيم
2 غفر [اللـ]ـه لعباس [بن]
3 سليمن ما تقد[م] من ذنبه
4 وما تاخر امين رب
5 العلمين رحم الله من مر هذه
6 الطريق اللهم صلي انت
7 [ ] [النصر] على|صلي

BR 5116(31)

1 بسم الله الرحمن الرحيم
2 اللهم صلي على من
3 كتب هذا الكتا
4 ب وكتب
5 مرزوق بن سالم صلي الله
6 عله* والملئكة ا
7 جـ[ـمـ]ـعيـ[ـن] اللهم صلي
8 على [مـ]ـحمد ا[لنبـ]ـي الامي
9 افضل ما صليت على
10 [ا]حد من السا[بـ]ـقين

* عليه

BR 5117(31)

1 الله الرحمن الرحيم
2 اللهم صلي انت و
3 ملئكتك المقربين وا
4 نبيائك المرسلين وعبا
5 دك الصالحين على امر الـ[ـقـ]ـيس
6 بن تميم

BR 5115(31)

1 اللهم صلي انت و
2 ملئكتك على بشر [بـ]ـن تميم
3 وتقبل منه [ا]نك على كل
4 شي قدير* اللهم صلي عليه
5 وابعثه مقامـ[ـا] محمودا
6 واكرمنه على اعين الاولين
7 والاخرين

* Compare ر of الاخرين in line 7

BR 5102(30)

1 In the name of Allah, the Compassionate, the Merciful
2-3 forgive [Allah] ʿAbbās [bn] Sulayman
3-4 his transgressions the earlier ones and the later
4-5 Amen Lord of Creation
5-6 Allah, be kind / loving towards him who passes on this road / path
6 Allah! incline, You
7 [ ]

BR 5116(31)

1 In the name of Allah, the Compassionate, the Merciful
2-4 Allah! incline unto him who wrote this document / inscription
4-5 and Marzūq bn Sālim wrote (it)
5-7 incline Allah, and the angels, all of them together, unto him
7-8 Allah! incline unto [Mu]ḥammad *a[l-nab]iy al-umiy*
9-10 more favourably than You inclined unto any one among the former ones*

* I.e., The Patriarchs, Moses, Jesus and all the prophets and messengers of old.

BR 5117(31)

1 (In the name of) Allah, the Compassionate, the Merciful
2-3 Allah! incline You and Your angels who are nigh (unto You)
3-4 and Your prophets who were sent
4-5 and Your righteous worshippers
5-6 unto Imr al-Qays bn Tamīm

BR 5115(31)

1-2 Allah! incline You and Your angels
2 unto Bišr bn Tamīm
3 and accept from him (his prayers)
3-4 You are the Omnipotent (lit. "You effect everything")
4 Allah! incline unto him
5 and raise him from the dead unto a desirable place
6-7 and make him honourable in the eyes of the first ones and the last ones

Dated 300/912* BR 5119(31)

1 لا الـه الا الـلـه
2 وحده لا شر[يـ]ـك لـه
3 [بشـ]ـر بن تميم يتـ[ـو]كل|يتكل
4 علـى الـلـه
5 غفر ا[لـلـه] لـ[ـبشـ]ـر
6 بن تميم كـ[ـل]
7 ذنب اذ
8 نبـ[ـه] [غفر] [ا]
9 لـلـه لـه
10 سنة ثلث مئة

See note in the translation *

BR 5131(32)

1 بسم الـلـه الـرحمن الـرحيم
2 هو الـذي ارسل رسولـه
3 بـالـهدى ودين الـحق لـيظهر
4 ه علـى الـدين كلـه
5 كفى [بـ]ـالـلـه شـ[ـهيد]ا*
6 كتب مرزوق
7 [بـ]ـن سا[لـم]

See note to the translation *

BR 5132(32)

1 هذ ما شهد علـيه بشير
2 بن تميم يشهد لا الـه الا الـلـه
3 وان محمد رسيل (*sic*) الـلـه

B. OFFICIAL ("ROYAL") INSCRIPTIONS

I. Basic Text (Indeterminate Monotheist) Official Inscriptions

1. Mu[c]āwiyah's Dam Inscription near Ṭā'if, dated A.H. 58/677–678

2-1 هذا السد لعبد الله معوية امير المؤمنين
3-2 بنية عبد الله بن صخّر بإذن الله
3 لسنة ثمن وخمسين
5-3 الله اغفر لعبد الله معوية امير المؤمنين
6-5 وثبّته وانصره ومتّع المؤمنين به
6 كتب عمر بن حباب

Source: Grohman (1962), no. 268

BR 5119(31) Dated 300/912*

1-2 There is no God but Allah alone, He has no *šarīk*
3-4 Bišr bn Tamīm relies upon (trusts) Allah
5-6 forgive [Allah] [Biš]r bn Tamīm
6-9 all the transgressions he has committed, [forgive] him Allah
10 year 300

* The first day of 300 AH was 18.8.912.

BR 5131(32)

1 In the name of Allah, the Compassionate, the Merciful
2 He is the One who sent His messenger
3 with the guidance and the True Faith
3-4 to make it* victorious over any other faith
4-5 (and) Allah suffices as a [witness]
6-7 (and) Marzūq bn Sā[lim] wrote (it)

* Or "him," the messenger.
** This is the "mild" or inoffensive of the formula (Q.48:28). For the formula with its "offensive" ending see MA4252(17); MA4262(18).

BR 5132(32)

1-2 This is about what Bašīr bn Tamīm testifies
2-3 he testifies (that) there is no God but Allah and that Muḥammad is the messenger of Allah

B. OFFICIAL ("ROYAL") INSCRIPTIONS

I. Basic Text (Indeterminate Monotheist) Official Inscriptions

1. Muᶜāwiyah's Dam Inscription near Ṭāᵓif, dated A.H. 58/677–678

1 This is the dam [belonging] to the Servant of God Muᶜāwiyah
2 Commander of the Faithful. ᶜAbdallah bn Ṣaxr built it
3 with God's permission in the year 58.
4 Allāh! Forgive the Servant of God Muᶜāwiyah,
5 Commander of the Faithful, confirm him in his position and help him and let the faithful
6 rejoice in him. ᶜAmr bn Ḥabbāb/Jnāb wrote it.

2. Construction text, Fusṭāṭ Canal Bridge, dated A.H. 69/688

هذه القنطرة أمر بها عبد العزيز بن مروان الأمير اللهمّ
بارك له في أمره كلّه وثبت سلطانه على ما ترضى وأقرّ
عينه في نفسه وحشمه أمين وقام ببنائها سعد أبو عثمان
وكتب عبد الرحمن في صفر سنة تسع وستّين

Source: *RCEA*, inscription no. 8. No line divisions are given

3. Milestones text, composite: partially reconstructed from four extant examples

امر بتسهيل* هذا الطريق وصنعة الاميال
عبد الله عبد الملك امير المؤمنين رحم الله عليه
من دمشق / ايليا الى هذا الميل (a number) ميل

See note to the translation *

Source: Grohmann (1971), fig. 48 (a-d)

II. Mohammedan Official Inscriptions

1. The "ᶜAqabah inscription" from a road near Tiberias, dated 73/693 or 83/702

1 بسم الله الرحمن الرحيم
2 لا اله الا الله وحده لا شريك له
3 محمد رسول الله
4 امر بتسهيل هذه العقبة
5 عبد الله عبد الملك امير المؤمنين
6 وعملت على يدى يحيى بن ال...
7 في المحرم من سنت ثلث [either 73 or 83...]

Source: Sharon, M. (1966)

2. Construction text, Qaṣr al-Ḥayr fortress, 110/728–29 (Hišām)

1 بسم الله الرحمن الرحيم
2 لا اله الا الله وحده لا شريك له
3 محمد رسول الله
4 امر بصنعة هذا المدينة
5 عبد الله هشام امير المؤمنين
6 وكان هذا مما عمل اهل حمص
7 على يدى سليم بن عبيد
8 سنة عشر ومائة

2. Construction text, Fusṭāṭ Canal Bridge, dated A.H. 69/688

This is the arch which ^{c}Abd al-^{c}Azīz bn Marwān, the Emir, ordered to be built. Allāh! Bless him in all his deeds, confirm his authority as You please, and make him very satisfied in himself and his household, Amen! Sa^{c}d Abū Uṯman built it and ^{c}Abd al-Raḥman wrote it in the month Ṣafar of the year 69.

3. Milestones text, composite: partially reconstructed from four extant examples

The Servant of God ^{c}Abd al-Malik, Commander of the Faithful—God's love be upon him!—ordered [to straighten?*] this road and to make the milestones. From Damascus [alternatively: from Īlya] up to this mile—(a number) miles.

* *bi-tashīl*: our reconstruction following Sharon's DKI 176 (the Mohammedan "^{c}Aqabah inscription," see next section). It has elsewhere been reconstructed *bi-^{c}imarat*.

II. Mohammedan Official Inscriptions

1. The "^{c}Aqabah inscription" from a road near Tiberias, dated 73/693 or 83/702

1 In the name of Allāh, the Merciful, the Compassionate!
2 There is no God but Allāh alone, He has no *šarīk*.
3 Muḥammad is the messenger of Allāh.
4-5 The Servant of God ^{c}Abd al-Malik, Commander of the Faithful, ordered the straightening of this mountain road.
6 It was made by Yaḥya bn al-...
7 In Muḥarram of the year three [and 70] *or* [and 80].

2. Construction text, Qaṣr al-Ḥayr fortress, 110/728–29 (Hišām)

1 In the name of Allāh, the Merciful, the Compassionate!
2 There is no God but Allāh alone, He has no *šarīk*.
3 Muḥammad is the messenger of Allāh.
4-5 The Servant of God Hišām, Commander of the Faithful, ordered the building of this fortress
6 And this is one of the things the people of Ḥims did
7 [carried out] by Sulaym bn ^{c}Ubayd
8 in the year 110

3. Mosque inscription of ʿAbd al-Malik: Dome of the Rock, dated 72/692

Text A: Outer face of octagonal arcade

	بسم الله الرحمن الرحيم	A1	S
	لا اله الا الله وحده	A2	
	لا شريك له	A3	
Q.112	قل هو الله احد الله الصمد	A4	
Q.112	لم يلد ولم يولد ولم يكن له كفو احد	A5	
Q.3:144, 48:9	محمد رسول الله	A6	
	صلى الله عليه □	A7	
	(6+3+2+1) A		SW
Q.33:56	إن الله وملئكته يصلون على النبي	A8	
Q.33:56	يايها الذين امنوا صلوا عليه وسلموا تسليما □	A9	W
	(2+1) A		
Q.17:111	الحمد لله الذى لم يتخذ ولدا	A10	NW
Q.17:111	ولم يكن له شريك في الملك	A11	
Q.17:111	ولم يكن له ولي من الذل	A12	
	وكبّره تكبيرا	A13	
	6+7 وملئكته ورسله	A14	N
	والسلم عليه ورحمت الله □	A15	
	(3+2+1) A		
Q.57:2, and compare Q.64:1*	له الملك يحيي ويميت	A16	
Q.57:2, and compare Q.64:1*	وهو على كل شى قدير	A17	
	(7+6) A		
	وتقبل شفعته يوم القيمة في امّته □	A18	
	□ (7+6+3+2+1) A		E
	بنى هذه القبة عبد الله عبـ ...		
	the date		
	تقبل الله منه ورضى عنه	A19	
	امين رب العلمين	A20	
	لله الحمد □	A21	
	here begins the inner face of the octagon		
	(3+2+1) A		S
	(17+16) A		
	محمد عبد الله ورسوله	A22	
	(15+7+[9+8]) A		SE

* Q.64:1 يسبّح لله ما في السموات وما في الارض له الملك وله الحمد وهو على كل شئ قدير

The rectangles at the end of each section represent the rosettes in the original inscription. Repeated lines are indicated, after their first occurrence, by line number only, e.g., A(1 + 2 + 3).

3. Mosque inscription of ʿAbd al-Malik: Dome of the Rock*, dated 72/692

Text A: Outer face of octagonal arcade

A1 In the name of Allāh, the Compassionate, the Merciful

A2 There is no God but Allāh alone

A3 He has no associate* [not in Qurʾān]

A4 Say: He is Allāh, One! Allāh—indivisible*

A5 He does not beget nor was He begotten, and no one is of equal rank* with Him [Q.112]

A6 Muḥammad [is the/a] messenger of Allāh [Q.48:9, 3:144]

A7 May Allāh incline unto him [not in Qurʾān]

A1 + 2 + 3 + 6

A8 Allāh and His angels incline unto the Prophet [Q.33:56]

A9 Yea all who trust, pray for him and greet him with peace*

A (1 + 2)

A10 The Will* is Allāh's, and it [lit.: which] does not acquire a son

A11 And no one shares* with Him sovereignty

A12 And He has no relative* from among the low beings

A13 And acknowledge [aloud] His greatness. [Q.17:111]

A14 Muḥammad [is the/a] messenger of Allāh, may Allāh incline unto him [= A6 + 7] and His angels and His messengers

A15 And may peace be upon him and Allāh's love

A1 + 2 + 3

A16 His is the Sovereignty,* He causes to live and He causes to die

A17 And He is omnipotent. [Q.57:2]

A6 + 7

A18 And accept his intercession at the head of/for his *ummah* [not in Qurʾān]

A1 + 2 + 3 + 6 + 7

A19 This dome was built by ʿAbd Allāh [title] in the year 72 Allāh, accept [it] from him and be pleased with him

A20 Amen Lord of Creation

A21 The Will is Allāh's

[Here the outer face of the octagonal arcade ends, and the inner face begins]

A1 + 2 + 3

A16 + 17

A22 Muḥammad [is the/a] servant of Allāh and His messenger

A[8 + 9] + 7 + 15 *and inscription B continues on in the same line.*

* Our translation of key words of this inscription differs from their traditionally accepted meanings; it should be read in conjunction with the relcvant parts of Part III Chapters 3, 4 and 5.

An asterisk in the translation indicates a note on that word. Notes are given by section number on pp. 416–17.

Text B: Inner face of octagonal arcade

Qur'an	Text	Line	Direction
Q.4:171	ياهل الكتب لا تغدوا في دينكم ولا تقولوا على الله الا الحق	B1	E–SE
	انما المسيح عيسى ابن مريم	B2	
	رسول الله وكلمته القيها الى مريم وروح منه	B3	
	فامنوا بالله ورسله ولا تقولوا ثلثة انتبهوا خير لكم	B4	NE–E
	انما الله اله وحد سبحنه ان يكون له ولد	B5	
	له ما في السموت وما في الارض	B6	
	وكفى بالله وكيلا	B7	
Q.4:172	لن يستنكف المسبح ان يكون عبد الله	B8	N–NE
	ولا الملئكة المقرمون	B9	
	ومن يستنكف عن عبدته ويستكبر فسيحشرهم اليه جميعا	B10	
	اللهم صلى على رسولك وعبدك عيسى ابن مريم	B11	NW–N
Q.19:15	والسلم عليه يوم ولد ويوم يموت ويوم يبعث حيا	B12	
Q.19:34	ذلك عيسى ابن مريم قول الحق الذى فيه تمترون*	B13	
Q.19:35	ما كان لله ان يتخذ من ولد	B14	
	[سـ]بحنه اذا قضى امرا فانما يقول له كن فيكون	B15	W–NW
Q.19:36	ان* لله ربي وربكم فاعبدوه هذا صرط مستقيم:	B16	
Q.3:18	شهد الله انه لا اله الا هو	B17	
	والملئكة واولوا تعلم قيما* بالقسط	B18	
	لا اله الا هو العزيز الحكيم	B19	SW–W
Q.3:19	ان الذين عند الله الاسلم	B20	
	وما اختلف الذين اوتوا الكتب الا من بعد ما جاهم العلم بغيا بينهم	B21	
	ومن يكفر بايات الله فإنّ الله سريع الحساب	B22	

*** B13: Q. = يحترون; B16: Q. = ران; B18: Q. = قائما**

Source: Kessler, K. (1970)

Text B: Inner face of octagonal arcade

B1	People of the Book! Do not introduce* [anything] into your *dīn* and do not say [anything] about Allāh but the truth	
B2	*al-masīḥ* Jesus the son of Mary is but	
B3	a messenger of Allāh and His word [which He] gave to Mary, and a ruḥ* of His	
B4	And trust Allāh and His messengers and do not say 'three', desist! It is better for you	[Q.4:171]
B5	For* Allāh is one* God only; blessed be He, [how can it be] that He has a child?*	
B6	To Him belongs what is in the heavens and what is on Earth	
B7	and Allāh can take care of it unassisted*	
B8	*al-masīḥ* is not ashamed* to be a servant/slave to Allāh	
B9	nor are the angels who are nigh [unto Him]	
B10	He who is ashamed* to worship Him, and he who is arrogant, He shall summon both together [for judgment]	[Q.4:172]
B11	Allāh! Incline unto Your messenger and servant/slave Jesus son of Mary	[not in Qurʾān]
B12	and let peace* be upon him the day he was born, and the day he dies, and the day he shall be raised alive*	[Q.19:15]
B13	The following is the truth about Jesus son of Mary, about whom you* dispute	[Q.19:34]
B14	Why should* Allāh acquire* a son?	
B15	Blessed be He! Should He decide a thing, He only says to it become! and it indeed becomes, just like that*	[Q.19:35]
B16	Indeed Allāh is my Lord and yours, therefore worship Him, this is a straight way.	[Q.19:36]
B17	Allāh is the witness* [that] there is no God but He	
B18	and the angels and the *ʾūlū al-ʿilm** justly* confirm [it]	[Q.3:18]
B19	There is no God but He, the Mighty, the Ruler/Wise	
B20	*dīn* with Allāh means unity*	
B21	and those who were given the Book/s* diverged after receiving *ʿilm*,* disputing among themselves*	[Q.3:19]
B22	Whoever denies the evidences* which Allāh [produces], [let him know] that Allāh is swift in reckoning.	

Notes

The translations referred to in these notes as "Ali" and "Ben-Shemesh" are listed in the bibliography as Ali, A. Y. (1934) and Ben-Shemesh, A. (1979) respectively.

A3: *šarīk* meaning "associate" rather than the usually accepted "partner"—see discussion in Part III Chapter 4, section "The Theology of the Dome of the Rock."

A4: *al-ṣamad* meaning "indivisible"—see discussion, ibid.

A5: *kufuʾ* meaning "of equal rank"—the accepted translations emphasize the concept of similarity: thus Ali: "there is no-one like unto Him"; Ben-Shemesh, more closely: "equal to Him." In this Christological context, however, the emphasis must rather be on the concept of subordination, i.e. lack of equality in rank to Allāh: no other being is of the same order as God. Cf. Lane 7:2618 col. 2, *kfaaʾ*.

A9: *salimū taslīm-an* meaning "greet him with peace": see discussion in Part III Chapter 4, section "The Theology of the Dome of the Rock."

A10: *ḥ.m.d.* meaning "Will": see discussion in Part III Chapter 3, section "To Praise." *ʾittaxiḏ* "acquire"—cf. Lane 1:29 col. 3. The context is whether Allāh shares His power with a son, a relative, or anyone else. The verb *ʾittaxaḏa* should here be understood from the context of Q.3:28: *lā yittaxiḏal-muʾminūn al-kāfirīn ʾawliyaāʾ* or Q.3:64: *wa-lā yattaxiḏ baʿḍunā baʿḍ-an ʾarbāb-an dūn Allāh.*

A11: *lam yakun lahu šarīk*: see note to A3. In our opinion *šarīk* conveys the concept of the Greek *synthetos*: partaker in or sharer of the divinity, not simply partnership.

A12: *waliyy* meaning "relative, kinsman"—we adopt here the earlier meaning of *waliyy*: cf. Goldziher (1989) 101ff: *mawlà al-wilādah/mawlà al-yamīn.*

A16: Q.64:1 adds here *wa-lahu al-ḥamdu*, "and His is the Will" (see discussion in Part III Chapter 3, section "To Praise").

B1: *lā taġlū* meaning "do not introduce"—the accepted translation is "commit no excesses in your religion" (Ali) or in different words "Do not exceed the limits of your faith" (Ben-Shemesh). We consider this word to derive from the Syriac and Jewish Aramaic *ʿl*: to enter, find entrance, introduce. For the Syriac see *CSD ʿall*, p. 412 cols. 1–2, and *ēṯʿelel*, p. 412 col. 2; for Jewish Aramaic see Jastrow (1903), *ʿūl* interchangeable with *ʿalal*, p. 1050 col. 1; *ʿalal*, p. 1084 col. 1 and *ʾāʿēl* (*afel* form), p. 1084 col. 1.

B3: *ruḥ minhu—ruḥ* is usually rendered "spirit" in accordance with the Judaic-Christian usage (Heb. *rū(a)ḥ*, Lat. *spiritus*, Gk. *pneuma*). But its theological import in Arabic was apparently unclear, for the Qurʾān is wary of explaining the term: "and they will ask you about *al-ruḥ*. Say: *al-ruḥ* comes/comes to be by my Lord's command, and of *ʿilm* you were given but little." (Q.17:85). We therefore prefer to leave it untranslated rather than to guess at the concept intended.

B5: "For ... only" translates *innamā*.
One: *waḥad*—in the Qurʾān the vocalization is *wāḥid*: sole, singular.
Child: *walad*—commonly translated "son" as befits the Christological context, but we leave the more exact translation "child" because the aim here seems to be to emphasize the absurdity of ascribing to Allāh any physical offspring.

B7: *wa-kafà bi-Allāh wakīl-an*—we see the root *w.k.l.* as cognate with Heb. *y.k.l.*: "able to" etc.

B8, B10: *yastankif* meaning "ashamed." The root, *n.k.f.*, is commonly accepted as conveying the concept "disdain, scorn." But it is also known from Syriac: *n:kef* (*CSD*, p. 340), with the meaning "to blush, be ashamed," and derivatives all convey similar concepts, e.g., *n:keftâ*: "modesty, deference, shame." Lane also recognizes this meaning alongside "disdain," cf. Lane 8, *n.k.f.*, supp. 3038 col. 1. It occurs three times in the

Qur°ān, all in Q.4:172–73 and always in the form *yastankif* and paired with *yastakbir*—to be haughty or arrogant. We see the two parts of this couplet as complementary rather than nearly synonymous: *yastankif* means to deny subordination to Allāh "passively" by *feeling* ashamed of being a servant to Him, whereas *yastakbir* means to deny it actively and openly, by arrogance, i.e., by asserting that to be Allāh's servant is beneath one's dignity.

B12: It is questionable if *slm* (here *al-slm* *ᶜalayhi*, in Q.19:15 *wa-salām* *ᶜalayhi*) should be rendered "peace"—cf. note to A9—but the point is peripheral to our present study.

B13: *tamtarūna*, "you dispute"—Q.19:24 has *yamtarūna*: "they dispute," but in the Dome of the Rock the word is fully pointed and the reading unquestionable (see Kessler [1970], p. 6 for facsimile + n. 47). This is a further indication that this inscription, which starts with the invocation "People of the Book!" was addressed to the Christians, as a contribution to Christological dispute.

B14: *mā kana li-Allāh °an...*: "why should..."—this is commonly translated "it is not befitting..." (e.g. Ali, Ben Shemesh), but in view of B15 the sentence should express astonishment, not just state a fact.
"acquire"—see note to A10.

B15: "just like that" translates *innamā*.

B16: "therefore" translates *fa-*

B17: *šahida*, "is the witness"—thus Ben Shemesh: "Allāh Himself is witness that..." Ali translates "that is the witness of God." The reliance on Allāh as sole witness contrasts with the Judaic-Christian practice of referring to Scripture or other authoritative writings: cf. the end of Part III Chapter 5.

B18: *°ulū al-ᶜilm*: commonly translated "those endowed with knowledge" or "men of knowledge." But it is unclear from the text whether they are indeed just men, or a little nearer to the angels. *ᶜilm* = *gnosis*: cf. Pines (1990).
qym° b°lqsṭ: "justly confirm it," in the Qur°ān *qaā°im-a(n) bi-al-qisṭ*. This has been variously translated as "standing firm" (Ali); "uphold justice" (Ben Shemesh); and "he sees to justice" (er sorgt für Gerechtigkeit—Paret and Rivlin). We understand *qym°* from Aramaic: the Syriac *qayyam*, "to establish, confirm, ratify" (*CSD*, p. 495 col. 1, *pael*) and *°aqīm*, "to confirm, ratify" (*CSD*, p. 495 col. 1, *afel*). The same semantic shading is shared by Hebrew and Jewish Aramaic (Jastrow [1903], *qwm* 1330–1331).
bi-al-qisṭ, lit. "in justice," or "with justice," we read as an adverbial phrase modifying *qym°*.

B20: For *°islām* meaning "unity" or "concord" and *dīn* meaning "the community" or "the regulation of social intercourse," see Part III Chapter 4, section "The Theology of the Dome of the Rock."

B21: Book/s: *ktb* may be *kitab* or *kutūb*; note that B4 refers to "messengers" in the plural.
ᶜilm = *gnosis*: cf. Pines (1990).
bağy-a(n) baynahum meaning "disputing among themselves"—*bağy-an* is usually translated "envy," but this seems to be a derivative meaning; the common Jewish and Christian Aramaic meaning of *bᶜy*, *bᶜ°* is 'to search, enquire, ask, examine' (Jastrow [1930], *Dictionary*, p. 181 col. 1; *CSD*, p. 50 col. 1) and this meaning is shared also by the Arabic (Lane 1:231 cols. 1–2). "Disputing," "arguing" and "examining" are common meanings in the Aramaic. In Syriac *b:ᶜâ* + *ᶜam* conveys the meaning "to dispute, argue." (*CSD*, p. 50 col 1). Text B ends with the assertion that Allāh's community should be unified in belief: the widespread dissonance among the monotheists has resulted from their denial of the *ᶜilm* (*gnosis*) which was bestowed upon them, and their everlasting examining and inquiring and disputing (all derived from root *bᶜy*/°, Arabic *bğy*).

4. Mosque inscription of Walīd I: Damascus Mosque*, dated 86–87/705–6

(A) (the *later* text, 87 A.H.)

1 ربنا الله لا نعبد الا الله
2 امر ببناء هذا المسجد وهدم الكنيسة التي
3 كانت فه عبد الله الوليد امير المؤمنين
4 في ذى الحجّة سنة سبع وثمانين

(B) (the *earlier* text, 86 A.H.)

1 بسم الله الرحمن الرحيم
2 لا اكراه في الدين قد تبيّن الرشد من الغي
3 فمن يكفر بطاغوت ويؤمن بالله فقد استمسك
4 بالعروة الوثقى لا انفصام لها والله سميع عليم
5 لا اله الا الله وحده لا شريك له
6 ولا نعبد الا اياه ربنا الله وحده وديننا الاسلام
7 ونبينا محمد صلى الله عليه وسلم
8 امر ببنيان هذا المسجد وهدم الكنيسة
9 التى كانت فيه عبد الله امير المؤمنين
10 الوليد في ذى القعدة سنة ستّ وثمانين

The layout of the text is ours, but it follows the original sequence *

Source: *RCEA* no. 18

4. Mosque inscription of Walīd I: Damascus Mosque, dated 86–87/705–6*

(A) (the *later* text, 87 A.H.)

1 Our Lord is Allāh, we shall worship none but Allāh!

2-3 The Servant of God al-Walīd, Commander of the Faithful, ordered the building of this *masjid** and the demolishing of the church that was in it*

4 in [month] *ḏu-l-ḥijjah* of the year 87.

(B) (the *earlier* text, 86 A.H.)

1 In the name of Allāh the Merciful, the Compassionate!

2 There is no coercion in matters of *dīn*:* the right way is henceforth distinguished from the wrong/crooked.*

3-4 And he who denies error/nonsense* and trusts in Allāh clings to a firm handhold never to give way; and Allah is an omniscient Listener.

5 There is no God but Allāh alone, He has no *šarīk**

6 and we shall worship none but Him! Our Lord is Allāh alone; our Community is Concord,*

7 and our prophet is Muḥammad, may Allāh incline to him and *salam.**

8-10 The Servant of God, Commander of the Faithful, al-Walīd, ordered the building of this mosque and the demolishing of the church that was in it in [month] *ḏu-l-qaᶜdah* of the year 86.

* For a discussion of this inscription see Part III Chapter 4, section "Walīd's Islam." An asterisk indicates a note on that word, given below.

Notes

A2-3: *masjid* is a common Aramaic term for "a place of worship." The word "mosque" can translate it, provided it is not taken to imply a *miḥrāb*-oriented structure: there is no archaeological evidence that the type of structure we today call a "mosque" existed in Walīd's time.
hadm, "demolishing"—though in fact this church was not entirely demolished: its outer walls were left intact while the *interior* was destroyed and reshaped.

B2: *ġayy*, "crooked"—cf. the Jewish (not Christian) Aramaic *ᶜwy, ᶜwh*, "to be curved, bent, crooked" etc. (Jastrow [1903], p. 1049, cols. 1–2); by extension, "to pervert, to be wrong," opposite of "to be/do right."

B3: error/nonsense: *ṭāġūt*: cf. Hebrew and Aramaic *ṭᶜy, ṭᶜh, ṭʾh* (Bibl. Heb. *tᶜh*, 'to wander, be lost'): Jastrow (1903), p. 542 cols. 1–2; *CSD*, p. 177 col. 2, *ṭᶜâ* Syriac *ṭaᶜyutâ* or *ṭāyūtâ*, *ṭaᶜyūtâ*, "erring, straying, error, folly" (*CSD*, p. 178 col 2 *infra*).

B5: *šarīk* meaning "associate" rather than the usually accepted "partner"—see discussion in Part III Chapter 4, section "The Theology of the Dome of the Rock."

B6: *dīn, ʾislām*: see notes to Dome of the Rock inscription, B20.

B7: *salam*: see notes to Dome of the Rock inscription, A9, B12.

III. Muslim Official Inscriptions

Mosque inscription: Madīnah mosque, dated 135/752 (al-Saffāḥ)

بسم الله الرحمن الرحيم §1
لا اله الا الله وحده لا شريك له §2
محمد عبد الله ورسوله §3
Q.9:33 [هو الذى ارسل رسوله بالهدى ودين الحق ليظهره §4
على الدين كله ولو كره المشركون
امر عبد الله امير المؤمنين بتقوى الله وطاعته §5
والعمل بكتاب الله وسنة نبيه صلى الله عليه وسلم §6
وبصلة الرحم §7
وتعظيم ما صغر الجبابرة من حقّ الله §8
وتصغير ما عظّموه من الباطل §9
واحياء ما اماتوا من الحقوق §10
واماته ما احيوا من العدوان §11
وان يطاع الله §12
ويعصى العباد في طاعة الله §13
والطاعة لله ولاهل طاعة الله §14
ولا طاعة لاحد في معصية الله §15
يدعو الى كتاب آلله وسنة نبيّه §16
والى العدل في احكم المسلمين §17
والقسم بالسوية في لميئهم §18
ووضع الاخماس في مواضعها التى امر الله به لذوي §19
القربى واليتامى والمساكين

Source: *RCEA* inscription no. 38; line division is ours, made for ease of reference. See discussion of this inscription in Part III Chapter 6.

III. Muslim Official Inscriptions

Mosque inscription: Madīnah mosque, dated 135/752

1 In the name of Allāh, the Merciful, the Compassionate!
2 There is no God but Allāh alone, He has no *šarīk**
3 Muḥammad is the servant of Allāh and His messenger.
4 He it is who has sent His messenger with the Guidance and the religion of Truth, to make it victorious over every other religion, even in the face of the *mušrikūn*'s* dislike/hatred!
5 The Servant of God, Commander of the Faithful, has ordered to fear Allāh and to obey Him
6 which is to act according to Allāh's *kitāb** and the *sunnah* of the Prophet, may Allāh incline to him and *salam*;*
7 to obey the moral obligations of kinship,
8 and to amplify Allāh's truth, which the tyrants dwarfed,
9 and to diminish the falsehood which they magnified,
10 and to revive the rightful duties/taxes* which they abolished,
11 and to abolish the wrongful things which they established [lit: "brought to life"],
12 and that Allāh should be obeyed.
13 And he advises the servants [i.e. the people] concerning obedience to Allāh,
14 that is, obedience to Allāh and to those [responsible for?] obedience to Allāh
15 and no obedience to anyone who [incites] to disobedience of Allāh.
16 He calls [the people] to the *kitāb* of Allāh and the *sunnah* of His prophet
17 and to justice in ruling* over the Muslims
18 and to equity in the allocation of their income
19 so that the *ˀaxmās* taxes will be imposed as Allāh has ordered for [the benefit of] close relatives and orphans and the needy.

Notes

2: *Šarīk* meaning "associate" rather than the usually accepted "partner"—see discussion in Part III Chapter 4, section "The Theology of the Dome of the Rock."

4: *Mušrikūn* we understand to be those who associate others with God's divinity: a reference to Christian Trinitarianism, more specific than the usual translation "unbelievers."

6: *Salam*: see discussion of this concept in Part III Chapter 4, section "The Theology of the Dome of the Rock."

6 + 16: Allāh's *kitāb*: see discussion in Part III Chapter 6. *Kitāb* meant a written record, not specifically a "book" in our sense; *kitāb Allāh* thus meant a written record of what God had said or decreed. This is the earliest official reference to such a record.
The *sunnah* of the Prophet: similarly, this is the first official introduction of this concept.

10: Taxes: the context of taxation is suggested by lines 18–19.

17: *ˀAḥkām* could mean "ruling" or "judging." *RCEA* translates the latter, but the context here is legitimization of the new rulers and their program: the right to impose taxes and so forth.

DATED AND DATABLE INSCRIPTIONS

Date	Inscription No.	Contains name/formula	Reason
85/705	**MA 4265(19)**	حكيم بن عمرو	**dated**
Datable to same period:			
	MA 457B(9)	”	same owner
	MA 4252(17)	”	”
	MA 4253(17)	”	”
	MA 4256A(17)	”	”
	MA 4256B(17)	حكيم	partial name
	MA 450(8)	حك بن عمرو	”
	MA 456(8)	”	”
	MA 412B(7)	حك	”
	MA 415(7)	”	”
112/730	**SC305(3)**	ورد بن سالم	**dated**
Datable to same period:			
	SC310(3)	”	same owner
	GM 389(4)	”	”
117/735	**HS 3155(6)**	حسن بن ميسرة	**dated**
160/776	**MA 4339(22)**	يوم دعـ[ـا] المناد من ايليا يوم [ ]	**dated**
Datable to same period:			
	MA 4387A( )*	[يوم] يدعو ب(?) المناد من ايليا يوم	same formula
	MA 4387B( )*	”	”
170/780	**ST 640(34)**	سعيد	**dated**
300/912	**BR 5119(31)**	بشير بن تميم	**dated**
Datable to same period:			
	Group HTR and BR**		

* See facsimile in the the introduction to *AAIN*, p. 10.

** HR and BR form a distinct group of inscriptions, datable by BR 5119 to 300/912:

a) They occur together in a different geographical area from the others – by the Sinai border near Nessana (see *AAIN*, Map 2, p. 3).

b) Many are by three people named bn Tamīm, most probably brothers.

c) These people and some others in the group share a distinct idiom not found in the other Negev texts.

Index of Inscription Numbers

"Popular" inscriptions are from the Negev unless otherwise stated

Inscription no.	Class	Page no.
ᶜAqabah Inscription	Mohammedan: Official	410
AR 271	Muslim (undatable): Popular	400
AR 2100	Muslim (undatable): Popular	398
AR 2101	Basic Text: Popular	368
BR 5102	Muslim (ca. 300 A.H.): Popular	406
BR 5115	Muslim (ca. 300 A.H.): Popular	406
BR 5116	Muslim (ca. 300 A.H.): Popular	406
BR 5117	Muslim (ca. 300 A.H.): Popular	406
BR 5119	Muslim (ca. 300 A.H.): Popular	408
BR 5131	Muslim (ca. 300 A.H.): Popular	408
BR 5132	Muslim (ca. 300 A.H.): Popular	408
BR 5134	Muslim (ca. 300 A.H.): Popular	402
BR 5170	Muslim (ca. 300 A.H.): Popular	404
BR 5180	Muslim (ca. 300 A.H.): Popular	404
Bridge (Fusṭāṭ)	Basic Text: Official	410
Dam inscription (Ṭāᵓif)	Basic Text: Official	408
Damascus mosque	Mohammedan: Official	418
DKI 163 (Karbalah)	Basic Text: Popular	376
DL 6135	Basic Text: Popular	376
DL 6137	Basic Text: Popular	376
Dome of the Rock	Mohammedan: Official	412
EKI 261	Muslim (160-170 A.H.): Popular	396
EL 200A	Basic Text: Popular	368
EL 200C	Basic Text: Popular	372
Fusṭāṭ bridge	Basic Text: Official	410
GM 385	Mohammedan: Popular	392
GM 388	Mohammedan: Popular	392
GM 389	Basic Text: Popular	380
GM 390	Mohammedan: Popular	390
HL 4900	Basic Text: Popular	370
HL 4911	Basic Text: Popular	374
HR 511	Muslim (ca. 300 A.H.): Popular	404
HR 514	Muslim (ca. 300 A.H.): Popular	402
HR 516	Muslim (ca. 300 A.H.): Popular	402
HR 517	Muslim (ca. 300 A.H.): Popular	402
HR 522	Muslim (ca. 300 A.H.): Popular	404

Inscription no.	Class	Page no.
HS 3153	Mohammedan: Popular	394
HS 3154	Mohammedan: Popular	392
HS 3155-56	Mohammedan: Popular	396
JU 18 (Jabal Usays)	Mohammedan: Popular	392
JU 46 (Jabal Usays)	Mohammedan: Popular	394
JU 49 (Jabal Usays)	Mohammedan: Popular	392
JU 27 (Jabal Usays)	Basic Text: Popular	374
JU 72 (Jabal Usays)	Mohammedan: Popular	392
JU 88 (Jabal Usays)	Mohammedan: Popular	388
JU 103 (Jabal Usays)	Mohammedan: Popular	394
JU 105 (Jabal Usays)	Mohammedan: Popular	394
Karbalah (DKI 163)	Basic Text: Popular	376
MA 87/10 (field no.)	Basic Text: Popular	372
MA 419	Basic Text: Popular	370
MA 420A	Basic Text: Popular	372
MA 450	Basic Text (ca. 85/704): Popular	386
MA 453	Basic Text: Popular	372
MA 455	Basic Text: Popular	370
MA 456	Basic Text (ca. 85/704): Popular	384
MA 457B	Basic Text (ca. 85/704): Popular	384
MA 4113	Mohammedan: Popular	394
MA 4132	Basic Text: Popular	368
MA 4137	Basic Text: Popular	368
MA 4138	Basic Text: Popular	380
MA 4168	Basic Text: Popular	368
MA 4204A	Basic Text-J-C: Popular	380
MA 4205	Muslim (undatable): Popular	400
MA 4210	Basic Text-J-C: Popular	380
MA 4252 lines 1–6	Basic Text (ca. 85/704): Popular	386
MA 4252 lines 7–12	Muslim (undatable): Popular	400
MA 4253	Basic Text (ca. 85/704): Popular	384
MA 4254	Basic Text: Popular	378
MA 4256A	Basic Text (ca. 85/704) Popular	384
MA 4256B	Basic Text (ca. 85/704)	384
MA 4262	Muslim (160-170 A.H.): Popular	396
MA 4265	Basic Text (ca. 85/704): Popular	384
MA 4269	Basic Text-J-C: Popular	382
MA 4282	Mohammedan: Popular	388
MA 4283	Basic Text: Popular	370

Inscription no.	**Class**	**Page no.**
MA 4286	Basic Text: Popular	376
MA 4288	Basic Text: Popular	370
MA 4319	Basic Text: Popular	374
MA 4339	Muslim (160-170 A.H.): Popular	398
MA 4340	Basic Text-J-C: Popular	380
MA 4369	Basic Text: Popular	378
MA 4508	Basic Text-J-C: Popular	382
MA 4509	Basic Text-J-C: Popular	382
MA 4513	Basic Text-J-C: Popular	382
MA 4514	Basic Text-J-C: Popular	382
MA 4516	Basic Text-J-C: Popular	382
Milestones (composite)	Basic Text: Official	410
Mosque (Damascus)	Mohammedan: Official	418
Mosque (Madīnah)	Muslim: Official	420
MM 107	Muslim (undatable): Popular	402
MM 113	Basic Text: Popular	368
NK 380	Basic Text: Popular	378
Qaṣr al-Ḥayr fortress	Mohammedan: Official	410
Qaṣr Xaranah	Basic Text (92/710)	386
RB 3170	Basic Text: Popular	378
SC 301	Mohammedan: Popular	390
SC 302	Mohammedan: Popular	390
SC 305	Mohammedan: Popular	390
SH 3101	Basic Text: Popular	378
ST 640	Muslim (160-170 A.H.): Popular	398
Ṭāʾif dam inscription	Basic Text: Official	408

Bibliography

ABBREVIATIONS

AAIN = *AAIN1* = Nevo, Yehuda D., Z. Cohen, and D. Heftman, eds. *Ancient Arabic Inscriptions from the Negev*. Jerusalem: IPS Press, 1993.

AAS = *Asian and African Studies*. Haifa, Institute of Middle Eastern Studies.

Abḥāṯ = *Al-Abḥāṯ*: *Quarterly Journal of the American University of Beirut.*

ADAJ = *Annual of the Department of Antiquities of Jordan.*

AUK = Auction catalogs of Bank Lou AG, Zurich/Numismatik.

AUK 34 = *Mittelalter Neuzeit*. Auktion 34, Zurich, October 11, 1983.

AUK 36 = *Islamic Coins*. Auktion 36, Zurich, May 7, 1985.

AUCS 255 = *Islamic Coins* (special offprint from auction catalog 255). Lucerne, September 18, 1984.

BASOR = *Bulletin of the American Schools of Oriental Research.*

BSOAS = *Bulletin of the Society of Oriental and African Studies.*

CAD = University of Chicago. Oriental Institute. *Assyrian Dictionary*, edited by I. J. Gelb et al. Chicago: Oriental Institute, 1956–84.

Colt I, II, III = Colt Archaeological Institute. *Excavations at Nessana: Report of the Colt Archaeological Expedition*. 3 vols. Princeton, N.J.: Princeton University Press, 1950–62. The Arab papyri are in Vol. III.

CPR3 = Grohman, Adolf, ed. *Allgemeine Einführung in die Arabischen Papyri*, and *Protokolle*. Corpus Papyrorum Raineri III: Series Arabica vol. 1 parts 1 and 2. Wien: Burgverlag, 1924. Bound together.

CSCO = Corpus Scriptorum Christianorum Orientalium. Edited by J.-B. Chabot et al. Section 2: Scriptores Arabici; section 6: Scriptores Syri.

CSD = *A Compendious Syriac Dictionary*. Edited by J. Payne-Smith

(Mrs. Margoliouth), founded on the Thesaurus Syriacus of R. Payne-Smith. Oxford: Clarendon, 1903 and many reprints.

DIS = Jean, C. F., and J. Hoftijzer. *Dictionnaire des Inscriptions Sémitiques de l'Ouest*. Leiden: Brill, 1960–64.

FM = Ibn ᶜAbd al-Ḥakam. *Futūḥ Miṣr wa-Axbaruha*. Edited by C.C. Torrey. New Haven, 1924.

FS = al-Wāqidī, Abū ᶜAbd Allāh Muḥammad ibn ᶜUmar. *Futūḥ al-Šām*. 2 vols. in one. Egypt: Muṣṭafà al-Babī al-Ḥalabī Press, 1934.

GENT = *A Greek-English Lexicon of the New Testament, being Grimms Wilke's Clavis Novi Testamenti*. Translated, revised and enlarged by Joseph Henry Thayer. Edinburgh: T and T. Clark, 1901 and many reprints.

GLIS = *Greek and Latin Inscriptions from Syria*. 3 vols. Princeton, N.J.: Princeton University Archaeological Expedition to Syria, 1899–1909. Volumes are numbered III, IIIA, IIIB. Vol. III is described as the publication of an American Archaeological Expedition to Syria.

IEJ = *Israel Exploration Journal*.

JAOS = *Journal of the American Oriental Society*.

JESHO = *Journal of Economic and Social History of the Orient*.

JNES = *Journal of Near Eastern Studies*.

JRAS = *Journal of the Royal Asiatic Society*.

JSAI = *Jerusalem Studies in Arabic and Islam*.

JSS = *Journal of Semitic Studies*.

JUI (i.e., *Jabal Usays Inscriptions*) = al-ᶜUšš, Muḥammad Abū al-Faraj. "Kitābat ᶜArabiyyah Ġayr Manšūrah fī Jabal ᵓUsays". *Al-Abḥāṯ* 7 (1964):227–316.

L and S = Liddell, H. G., and R. Scott. *A Lexicon abridged from the Greek-English Lexicon of H.G. Liddell and R. Scott*. 3d ed. Oxford: Oxford University Press, 1849 and reprints.

OCLD = *Oxford Classical Dictionary*. Edited by N. G. L. Hammod and H. H. Scullard. 2d ed. Oxford: Oxford University Press, 1970.

ODCC = *Oxford Dictionary of the Christian Church*. Edited by F. L. Cross and E. A. Livingstone. 2d ed. Oxford: Oxford University Press, 1983.

PG = Patrologia Cursus Completus... Series Graeca. Edited by J.-P. Migne.

PL = Patrologia Cursus Completus... Series Prima (= Latina). Edited by J.-P. Migne.

Qaryat al-Fau = Al-Ansary, A. R. *Qaryat al-Fau: a Portrait of pre-Islamic Civilization in Saudi Arabia*. London: Croom Helm, 1983.

QS = Wansbrough, John. *Quranic Studies: Sources and Methods of Scriptural Interpretation*. Oxford: Oxford University Press, 1977.
RCEA = *Répertoire Chronologique d'Épigraphie Arabe*. Edited by Combe, Sauvaget and Wiet. Vol. I. Cairo: Imprimerie de l'Institut Français d'Archéologie Orientale, 1931.
SM = Wansbrough, John. *The Sectarian Milieu*. Oxford: Oxford University Press, 1978.
ZDMG = *Zeitschrift der Deutschen Morgenländischen Gesellschaft*.

PRIMARY SOURCES

This section contains editions of primary sources listed by the author or commonly known name of the source. Editions referred to in the text by editor are also given in the general bibliography, listed by editor.

Al-Azdī. *Futūḥ al-Šām*. Edited by W. N. Lees. Calcutta: Baptist Mission Press, 1854.

Ammianus Marcellinus. *History*. 3 vols. Loeb Classical Library. London: Heinemann, 1960 and reprints. Text and English translation.

Arculf. *Pilgrimage of Arculfus in the Holy Land*. Library of the Palestine Pilgrims' Text Society vol. III. New York: AMS Press, 1971.

Athanasius of Balad. *Letter "to the Effect that the Christians should not Partake of the Sacrifices that the Mhaggaraye now Have*." In Nau, M. F. "Littérature Canonique Syriaque Ineditée." *Revue de l'Orient Chrétien* 14 (1909):128–130.

Al-Bāladurī, Aḥmad bn Yaḥyā. *Futūḥ al-buldān*. Edited by M. J. de Goeje. Leiden: Brill, 1866. First half translated into English by P. K. Hitti as *The Origins of the Islamic State*. New York: Columbia University Press, 1916.

———. *Kitāb Anṣāb al-Ashrāf*. Vol. 1, edited by Muḥammad Ḥamīdullāh. Egypt, 1959. Vol. 4A, edited by Max Schloessinger, revised and annotated by M. J. Kister. Jerusalem: Magnes Press, 1971. Vol. 4B, edited by Max Schloessinger. Jerusalem, 1938. Vol. 5, edited by S. D. F. Goitein. Jerusalem, 1936.

Bar Hebraeus. *The Chronography of Gregory Abu ᵓl-Faraj, commonly known as Bar Hebraeus, being the first part of his political history of the world*. Translated and edited by Ernest A. Wallis Budge. 2 vols. Amsterdam: APA–Philo, 1932, reprinted 1976. Vol. 1: translation; vol. 2: facsimile of Bodleian Ms. Hunt. 52.

Bar Penkayê, John. See under John bar Penkayê.

Chronicon ad annum 705. Translated by Robert Hoyland. In Hoyland, Robert. *Seeing Islam as Others Saw It: a Survey and Evaluation of Christian, Jewish and Zoroastrian Writings on Early Islam*. Princeton, N.J.: Darwin Press, 1997.

Chronicon ad annum 1234 = Chronicon miscellaneum ad annum 1234 pertinens, translated and edited by J.-B. Chabot. CSCO: Scriptores Syri 36 (1920), 56 (1937). Text and Latin translation respectively.

Chronicon miscellaneum ad annum Domini 724 pertinens. Edited by E. W. Brooks. CSCO III: Scriptores Syri 3: Chronica Minora II: 77–155. Translated in Hoyland, Robert. *Seeing Islam as Others Saw It: a Survey and Evaluation of Christian, Jewish and Zoroastrian Writings on Early Islam*. Princeton, N.J.: Darwin Press, 1997.

Chronicon Iacobi Edesseni. Edited by E. W. Brooks. CSCO: Scriptores Syri 5: 261–330 and 6: 199–258. Paris, 1905.

Codex Justinianus. Edited by P. Krieger. Berlin, 1877.

Dionysius of Tellmaḥre. See under Pseudo-Dionysius of Tellmaḥre.

Elias of Nisibis. *Eliae Metropolitae Nisibeni Opus Chronologicum*. Edited by E. W. Brooks and J.-B. Chabot. 2 vols. CSCO: Scriptores Syri 3, vols. 7–8. Paris, 1909–1910. Also reprinted as vols. 62 and 63 of the reprint of this series: Louvain: Durbecq, 1954 and 1962. French translation in Delaporte, L.-J., ed. *Chronographie de Mar Elie bar Sinaya, Métropolitain de Nisibe*. Paris: Librarie Honoré Champion, 1910.

Eusebius. *Ecclesiastical History*. London: Heinemann, 1959–64. Greek text and English translation.

———. *The Ecclesiastical History of Eusebius Pamphili, 265–339*. Edited by William Wright and Norman McLean. Amsterdam: Philo, 1975. Syriac text.

Eutychius of Alexandria (d. 328/940). *Nazm al-jawhar/Annales ecclesiasticae*, edited by L. Cheikho et al. 2 vols. CSCO: Scriptores Arabici 45. Louvain: Imprimerie Orientaliste, 1985. Arabic and German translation.

The Histories of Rabban Hôrmîzd the Persian and Rabban bar-ᶜIdtâ. Edited by Ernest A. Wallis Budge. 2 vols. London: Luzac, 1902. Reprinted New York: AMS Press, 1976. Syriac and English translation.

Ibn ᶜAbd al-Ḥakam. *Futūḥ Miṣr wa-Axbaruha*. Edited by C. C. Torrey. New Haven, 1924.

Ibn Ḥajar. *Kitāb al-Isābah fī Tamyyz al-Ṣaḥābah*. Beirut: Dar al-Fikr, reprinted 1978.

Ibn Ḥazm. *Jamharat Ansāb al-ᶜArab li-Abī Muḥammad ᶜAlī bn Aḥmad bn Saᵓīd bn Ḥazm al-Andalusī*. Edited by ᶜAbd al-Salām Muḥammad Hārūn. Daxaᵓir al-ᶜArab 2. Cairo: Dar al-Maᶜarif, 1961 and many reprints.

Ibn Hišām, Abū Muḥammad ᶜAbd al-Malik. *Al-Sīrah al-Nabawyyah li-ibn Hišām*. Edited by Muṣṭafà al-Saqqā, Ibrāhīm al-Abyārī, and ᶜAbd al-Ḥafīz Ṣalabī. Cairo, 1937 and reprints. English translation: *The Life of Muḥammad: a translation of Ibn Isḥāq's Sīrat Rasūl Allāh*. Translated and edited by A. Guillaume. Karachi: Oxford University Press, 1955.

Ibn Isḥāq, Abū Bakr Muḥammad. *Sīrat Rasūl Allāh*. See Ibn Hišām, above.

Ishoᶜyahb III. *Ishoᶜyahb Patriarchae III Liber Epistularum*. Edited by R. Duval.

CSCO: Scriptores Syri 11–12. Louvain, 1904–1905, reprinted 1912. Syriac and Latin translation.

Jacob of Edessa. *Chronicon Iacobi Edesseni.* Translated and edited by E. W. Brooks. CSCO: Scriptores Syri 5: 261–330 and 6: 199–258. Paris, 1905. There is a newer translation of 7th-century portions in Palmer, Andrew. *The Seventh Century in the West-Syrian Chronicles.* Liverpool: University of Liverpool Press, 1993.

———. *Scholia on Passages of the Old Testament by Mar Jacob, Bishop of Edessa.* Edited by George Phillips. London: Williams and Norgate, 1864.

John bar Penkayê. *Ktābā d-rīš mellē.* Books 10–15 and translation of Book 15 in Mingana, Alphonse, ed. *Sources Syriaques.* Leipzig, 1907. Translation of Books 14 and 15 in Abramowski, Rudolph. *Dionysius von Tellmaḥre: zur Geschichte der Kirche unter dem Islam.* Leipzig: Deutsche Morgenländische Gesellschaft, 1940.

John of Damascus. *Saint John of Damascus: Writings.* Translated and edited by Frederic H. Chase. Washington: Catholic University of America Press, 1958.

John of Ephesus. *Historia Ecclesiastica.* Edited by E. W. Brooks. CSCO: Scriptores Syri 3. Louvain and Paris, 1935–36.

John of Nikiu. *The Chronicle of John (c. 690 A.D.) Coptic Bishop of Nikiu.* Translated and edited by Robert H. Church. London, 1916. Reprinted Amsterdam: Philo Press.

John of Phenek. See under John bar Penkayê.

Khuzestani Chronicle = Nöldeke, Th., trans. and ed. *Die von Guigi herausgegebene Syrische Chronik übersetzt und commentiert.* Sitzungsberichte der Kaiserischen Akademie der Wissenschaften in Wien, Phil.-Historische Klasse, 128. Vienna, 1893.

Maruta. *Life* = Nau, M. F. "Histoire de Marouta." *Patrologia Orientalis* III (1909):52–96.

Maximus the Confessor. *Letter* no. 8. Edited by J.-P. Migne. PG 91, cols. 440–46.

———. *Letter* no. 14. Edited by J.-P. Migne. PG 91, cols. 533–544.

———, Syriac Life of = Brock, Sebastian P. "An Early Syriac Life of Maximus the Confessor." *Analecta Bollandiana* 91 (1973):289–346.

Michael the Syrian. *Chronique de Michel le Syrien, Patriarche Jacobite d'Antioche, 1166–1199.* Edited by J.-B. Chabot. 2 vols. Paris, 1901. 7th-century material is in vol. 2.

Al-Munjid = *al-Munjid fī al-Luġah wa-al-ʾAʿlām.* 27th ed. Beirut: Dar el-Mashreq, 1984.

Nikephoros. *Historia Syntomas.* Edited by C. de Boor. Leipzig: Teubner, 1880.

Nilus. *Narrationes* = *Sancti Nili Narrationes de Caede Monachorum et de Theodulo Filio.* PG 79: cols. 589–694.

Notatia Dignitatum. Edited by Otto Seeck. Frankfurt am Main: Minerva Press, 1962. Reprint of 1876 ed.

Patriarch John. "Discussion with an Arab Emir" = Nau, M. F., trans. and ed. "Un Colloque du Patriarche Jean avec l'Émir des Agaréens et Faits Divers des Années 712 à 716 d'après le Ms. du B.M. ADD. 17193." *Journal Asiatique*, 9th sér., 5 (1915):225–279.

Procopius of Caesarea. *Works*. 7 vols. Loeb Classical Library. London: Heineman, 1914, reprinted 1961.

Pseudo-Clementine *Homilies* = Rehm, B., J. Irmscher, and F. Paschke, eds. *Die Pseudoklementinen*. Vol. 1, *Hamilien*. Berlin, 1969.

Pseudo-Clementine *Recognitiones* = Rehm, B., ed. *Die Pseudoklementines Recognitiones*. Berlin, 1965.

Pseudo-Dionysius of Tellmaḥre. *Chronicle*, 4th part = Chabot, J.-B. *Chronique de Denys de Tellmaḥre, Quatrième Partie*. Bibliothèque de l'École des Hautes Études 112. Paris, 1895.

Pseudo-Methodius. English translation and commentary in Alexander, Paul J. *The Byzantine Apocalyptic Tradition*. Berkeley: University of California Press, 1985.

Pseudo-Nilus. See under Nilus.

Rabban bar-ᶜIdtâ. *Histories* = *The Histories of Rabban Hôrmîzd the Persian and Rabban bar-ᶜIdtâ*. Edited by Ernest A. Wallis Budge. 2 vols. London: Luzac, 1902. Reprinted New York: AMS Press, 1976. Syriac and English translation.

Rabban Hôrmîzd. *Histories* = *The Histories of Rabban Hôrmîzd the Persian and Rabban bar-ᶜIdtâ*. Edited by Ernest A. Wallis Budge. 2 vols. London: Luzac, 1902. Reprinted New York: AMS Press, 1976. Syriac and English translation.

Sebeos: *History of Heraclius* = *Histoire d'Héraclius par l'Évêque Sebeos*. Translated into French and edited by Frederic Macler. Paris: Imprimerie Nationale, 1904.

Simon ben Yōḥay. *Midrash of the Ten Kings*. Partial translation and discussion in Lewis, Bernard. "An Apocalyptic Vision of Islamic History." *BSOAS* 13 (1950):308–338.

———. *Prayer*. Translation and discussion in Lewis, Bernard. "An Apocalyptic Vision of Islamic History." *BSOAS* 13 (1950):308–338.

———. *Secrets*. Partial translation and discussion in Lewis, Bernard. "An Apocalyptic Vision of Islamic History." *BSOAS* 13 (1950):308–338.

Sīrah. See under Ibn Hišām.

Socrates. *Historia Ecclesiastica*. Edited by R. Hussey. PG 67, cols. 556–557. Also published separately: Oxford, 1953.

Sophronius. *Christmas Sermon, 634 C.E.* Greek text: Usener, H., ed. "Weinachtspredigt des Sophronos." *Rheinisches Museum für Philologie* n.s. 41 (1886):500–516. Latin translation: "Sancti Sophronii Hierosolymitani Orationes. Oratio I: In Christi Natalitia." PG 87, cols. 3201–3212.

Sozomenus. *Historia Ecclesiastica*. PG 67, cols. 1408–1413. Greek text. Also published separately: *Sozomenus Kirschengeschichte*. Edited by Joseph Bidez. Berlin: Akademie-Verlag, 1960.

Syndicon Orientale. Translated and edited by J.-B. Chabot. 3 vols. Paris: Imprimerie Nationale, 1902. Vol. 1: Syriac text; vol. 2: French translation; vol. 3: appendices and notes. Page numbering is consecutive throughout the three volumes.

Al-Ṭabarī, Abū Jaᶜfar Muḥammad ibn Jarīr (d. 310/923). *Taʾrix al-rusūl wa-al-mulūk*. Edited by M. J. de Goeje et al. Leiden, 1879–1901. Our page references follow this edition.

———. *Taʾrix al-rusūl wa-al-mulūk*. Edited by Muḥammad Abū al-Fadl Ibrāhīm. 2nd ed. 10 vols. Cairo: Dar al-Maʾarīf, 1968–69. The page numbers of De Goeje's edition are printed in the margins of the Arabic text.

Tacitus. *Germania*. Revised by E. H. Warmington with a translation by M. Hutton. Loeb Classical Library. London: Heinemann, 1970.

Tertullian. *Opera*. CSCO Seria Latina II.

Theophanes. *Chronographia*. Edited by C. De Boor. 2 vols. Leipzig: Teubner, 1883–85.

ᶜUmar II. *Correspondence with the Emperor Leo* = Jeffery, Arthur. "Ghevond's Text of the Correspondence between ᶜUmar II and Leo III." *Harvard Theological Review* 37 (1944):269–332. English translation.

Al-Wāqidī, Abū ᶜAbd Allāh Muḥammad ibn ᶜUmar. *Futūḥ al-Šām*. 2 vols. in one. Egypt: Muṣṭafà al-Babī al-Ḥalabī Press, 1934.

SECONDARY SOURCES

Primary sources referred to in the text by editor and date are listed here in that form; they also appear in the list of primary sources under the name of the author of the text, or the title if there is no author.

Abbott, Nabia (1938). *The Kurrah Papyri from Aphrodito in the Oriental Institute*. Chicago: University of Chicago Press, 1938.

——— (1946). "The Kasr Khrānah Inscription." *Ars Islamica* 11–12 (1946):190–95 and Fig. 1.

Abramowski, Rudolph (1940). *Dionysius von Tellmahre: zur Geschichte der Kirche unter dem Islam*. Leipzig: Deutsche Morgenländische Gesellschaft, 1940. Includes translation of Books 14 and 15 of Bar Penkayê.

Adelson, Howard L. (1962). *Medieval Commerce*. Princeton, N.J.: Van Nostrand, 1962.

Al-Ansary, A. R. (1983). *Qaryat al-Fau: a Portrait of pre-Islamic Civilization in Saudi Arabia*. London: Croom Helm, 1983.

Alcock, Leslie (1971). *Arthur's Britain: History and Archaeology, A.D. 367–634*. Harmondsworth, Middlesex: Penguin, 1971. Reprinted with corrections: Pelican, 1973.

Alexander, Paul J. (1985). *The Byzantine Apocalyptic Tradition*. Berkeley: University of California Press, 1985. Includes translation of the Syriac text of the Pseudo-Methodius, plus commentary.

Ali, A. Y. (1934). *The Glorious Kur'an*. Beirut: Dar al-Fikr, 1934 and many reprints. Text, translation, and commentary.

Alī, Jawad (1980). *Al-Mufassal fī Ta'rīx al-ᶜArab qabla al-Islām* (History of the Arabs before Islam). Vol. 6. Beirut: Dar al-ᶜIlm Lilmalāyyin; Baghdad: Maktabat al-Nah-ah, 1980. In Arabic.

Ashtor, E. (1976). *A Social and Economic History of the Near East in the Middle Ages*. Berkeley: University of California Press, 1976.

Atiya, Aziz S. (1968). *A History of Eastern Christianity*. London: Methuen, 1968.

Avi-Yonah, M. (1974). *Carta's Atlas of the Period of the Second Temple, the Mishnah and the Talmud*. 2d ed. Jerusalem: Carta, 1974. In Hebrew.

Badian, E. (1967). *Roman Imperialism in the Late Republic*. Pretoria: University of South Africa, 1967; Ithaca, N.Y.: Cornell University Press, 1968.

Baramki, Dimitri (1952). "Kufic Texts." *ADAJ* 1 (1952):20–22 and plate VII. Kufic inscriptions collected by Lancaster Harding in Jordan. Palaeographic considerations would date them to the 9th century A.H.

——— (1964). "Al-Naqūx al-ᶜArabiyyah fī al-Badiyyah al-Suriyyah" ("Arabic inscriptions in the Syrian desert"). *Abḥāṯ* 17 (1964):317–346. In Arabic.

Bashear, Suliman (1984). *Muqaddimah fī al-Ta'rīx al-Axar* (An introduction to the other history). Jerusalem, 1984. In Arabic.

——— (1985). *Liqrat Historyah Islamit Aḥeret*? (Toward another early Islamic history?) Jerusalem, 1985. In Hebrew.

——— (1985a). "The Mission of Diḥya al-Kalbī and the Situation in Syria." Paper presented at the 3rd International Colloquium "From Jāhiliyya to Islam," Hebrew University of Jerusalem, summer 1985. *Jerusalem Studies in Arabic and Islam* 14 (1991):84–114.

——— (1985b). *Diḥya al-Kalbī*: The Angelic Messenger in Syria. Published and circulated privately, 1985. Summary and conclusions of Bashear, S. (1985a).

——— (1989). "Qur'ān 2:114 and Jerusalem." *BSOAS* 52 Part 2 (1989):215–238.

——— (1989a). "Yemen in Early Islam: an Examination of Non-Tribal Traditions." *Arabica* 36 (1989):327–361.

Bates, M. L. (1976). "The 'Arab-Byzantine' Bronze Coinage of Syria: an Innovation by ᶜAbd al-Malik." In *A Colloquium in Memory of George Carpenter Miles*. New York, 1976.

——— (1986). "History, Geography and Numismatics in the First Century of Islamic Coinage." *Revue Suisse de Numismatique* 65 (1986):231–261 and plate 31.

Baynes, Norman H., and H. St. L. B. Moss, eds. (1961). *Byzantium: an Introduction to East Roman Civilization*. Oxford: Clarendon Press, 1961.

Becker, C. H. (1911). "Neue arabische Papyri des Aphroditofundes." *Der Islam* 2 (1911):254–268.

Beeston, A. F. L. (1979). "Nemara and Faw." *BSOAS* 42 (1979):1–6.

Bell, H. I. (1911). "Translations of the Greek Aphrodite Papyri in the British Museum." *Der Islam* 2 (1911):269–283.

——— (1911a). Continuation of above in *Der Islam* 2 (1911):372–384.

——— (1912). Continuation of above in *Der Islam* 3 (1912):132–140.

——— (1912a). Continuation of above in *Der Islam* 3 (1912):369–373.

——— (1913). Continuation of above in *Der Islam* 4 (1913):87–96.

Bell, H. I., and C. H. Roberts, eds. (1948). *A Descriptive Catalogue of the Greek Papyri in the collection of Wilfred Merton*. Vol. 1. London: Emery Walker, 1948.

Ben-David, Joseph (1988). *Beduin Agriculture in the Negev: Recommendations for Policy Formulation*. Jerusalem: Jerusalem Institute for Israel Research, 1988. In Hebrew.

Ben-Shemesh, A. (1979). *The Noble Quran, translated from the Arabic*. Tel-Aviv: Massada, 1979.

Berchem, M. van (1920–27). *Matériaux pour un Corpus Inscriptionum Arabicarum*. 2e partie: *Syrie du Sud, Jérusalem*. 3 vols. Mémoires de l'Institut Français d'Archéologie Orientale du Caïre 43–45. Cairo, 1920–27.

Bidez, Joseph, ed. (1960). *Sozomenus Kirschengeschichte*. Berlin: Akademie-Verlag, 1960. Greek text of the *Ecclesiastical History*.

Bišah, Ġāzī (1983). "Naqš ᶜArabī min Qaṣr al-Maštà wa-ʾAhamiyatuhu" ("Arab inscription from Qaṣr al-Maštà"). *ADAJ* 27 (1983):75–77, 135–136 (plates). In Arabic.

Blair, Sheila (1992). "What is the Date of the Dome of the Rock?" In *Bayt al-Maqdis: Abd al-Malik's Jerusalem*, edited by Julian Ruby and Jeremy Johns. Part 1. Oxford: Oxford University Press, 1992.

Bowersock, G. W. (1976). "Limes Arabicus." *Harvard Studies in Classical Philology* 80:219–29.

——— (1983). *Roman Arabia*. Cambridge, Mass.: Harvard University Press, 1983.

Brock, Sebastian P. (1973). "An Early Syriac Life of Maximus the Confessor." *Analecta Bollandiana* 91 (1973):289–346.

——— (1976). "Syriac Sources for Seventh-Century History." *Byzantine and Modern Greek Studies* 2 (1976):17–36. Also reprinted in Brock, Sebastian P. *Syriac Perspectives on Late Antiquity*. London: Variorum Press, 1984.

——— (1982). "Syriac Views of Emergent Islam." In *Studies on the First Century of Islamic Society*, edited by J. Y. N. Boll. Carbondale, Ill.: Southern Illinois University Press, 1982. Also reprinted in Brock, Sebastian P. *Syriac Perspectives on Late Antiquity*. London: Variorum Press, 1984.

——— (1984). *Syriac Perspectives on Late Antiquity*. London: Variorum Press, 1984.

——— (1987). "North Mesopotamia in the Late Seventh Century: Book XV of John Bar Penkāyē's *Riš Mellē*." *JSAI* 9 (1987):51–75. Reprinted in Brock, Sebastian P. *Studies in Syriac Christianity: History, Literature and Theology*. Aldershot: Variorum Press, 1992.

——— (1992). *Studies in Syriac Christianity: History, Literature and Theology.* Aldershot: Variorum Press, 1992.

Brockelmann, Carl (1948). *History of the Islamic Peoples.* London: Routledge and Kegan Paul, 1948.

Brooks, E. W., ed. (1905). *Chronicon Iacobi Edesseni.* CSCO: Scriptores Syri 5:261–330 and 6:199–258. Paris, 1905.

Brooks, E. W., and J.-B. Chabot, eds. (1909–10). *Eliae Metropolitae Nisibeni Opus Chronologicum.* 2 vols. CSCO: Scriptores Syri 3, vols. 7–8. Paris, 1909–1910. Also reprinted as vols. 62 and 63 of the reprint of this series: Louvain: Durbecq, 1954 and 1962.

Brown, Peter (1971). *The World of Late Antiquity: from Marcus Aurelius to Muhammad.* London: Thames and Hudson, 1971.

——— (1978). *The Making of Late Antiquity.* Cambridge, Mass.: Harvard University Press, 1978.

Budge, Ernest A. Wallis, trans. and ed. (1902). *The Histories of Rabban Hôrmîzd the Persian and Rabban bar-ᶜIdtâ.* 2 vols. London: Luzac, 1902. Reprinted New York: AMS Press, 1976. Syriac and English translation.

———, trans. and ed. (1932). *The Chronography of Gregory Abu l-Faraj, Commonly Known as Bar Hebraeus, being the First Part of his Political History of the World.* 2 vols. Amsterdam: APA–Philo, 1932, reprinted 1976. Vol. 1: translation; vol. 2: facsimile of Bodleian Ms. Hunt. 52.

Bury, J. B. (1923). *History of the Later Roman Empire from the Death of Theodosius I to the Death of Justinian.* 2 vols. New York: Dover, 1923, reprinted 1958.

Busse, Heribert (1977). "Die Arabischen Inscriften im und am Felsendom in Jerusalem." *Das Heilige Land* 109 (1977):8–24.

——— (1981). "Monotheismus und Islamische Christologie in der Bauinschrift des Felsendoms in Jerusalem." *Theologische Quartalschrift* 161 (1981):168–178.

Cambridge Medieval History. Vols. 1–4. Cambridge: Cambridge University Press, 1964.

Chabot, J.-B., trans. and ed. (1894). "L'Apocalypse d'Esdras touchant le Royaume des Arabes." *Revue Sémitique* (1894):242–250, 333–47. Text and French translation.

———, trans. and ed. (1895). *Chronique de Denys de Tellmaḥre, Quatrième Partie.* Bibliothèque de l'École des Hautes Études 112. Paris, 1895. This is the Pseudo-Dionysius of Tellmaḥre.

———, ed. (1901). *Chronique de Michel le Syrien, Patriarche Jacobite d'Antioche, 1166–1199.* 2 vols. Paris, 1901. 7th-century material is in vol. 2.

———, trans. and ed. (1902). *Synodicon Orientale.* 3 vols. Paris: Imprimerie Nationale, 1902. Vol. 1: Syriac text; vol. 2: French translation; vol. 3: appendices and notes.

———, trans. and ed. (1920). *Chronicon ad annum 1234 pertinens.* CSCO: Scriptores Syri 36 and 56. Paris, 1920 and 1937. Text and Latin translation respectively.

——— (1934). *Littérature Syriaque*. Paris: Bloud and Gay, 1934.

Chase, Frederic H., trans. and ed. (1958). *Saint John of Damascus: Writings*. Washington: Catholic University of America Press, 1958.

Church, Robert H., trans. and ed. (1916). *The Chronicle of John (c. 690 A.D.) Coptic Bishop of Nikiu*. London, 1916. Reprinted Amsterdam: Philo Press.

Cohen, Rudolf (1981). *Map of Sede Boqer East (168) 13-03*. Jerusalem: Archaeological Survey of Israel, 1981.

——— (1985). *Map of Sede Boqer West (167) 12-03*. Jerusalem: Archaeological Survey of Israel, 1985.

Colt Archaeological Institute. *Excavations at Nessana: Report of the Colt Archaeological Expedition*. 3 vols. Princeton, N.J.: Princeton University Press, 1950–62. The Arab papyri are in Vol. 3.

Conrad, Lawrence I. (1987). "*Kai elabon tēn hēran*: Aspects of the Early Muslim Conquests in Southern Palestine." Paper presented at the 4th International Colloquium "From Jāhiliyya to Islam," Hebrew University of Jerusalem, July 1987.

——— (1987a). "Abraha and Muḥammad: Some Observations Apropos of Chronology and Literary Topoi in the Early Arabic Historical Tradition." *BSOAS* 50 (1987):225–240. Also reprinted in *The Quest for the Historical Muhammad*, edited with translations by Ibn Warraq. Amherst, N.Y.: Prometheus Books, 2000.

——— (1990). "Theophanes and the Arabic Historical Tradition: some Indications of Intercultural Transmission." *Byzantinische Forschungen* 15 (1990):1–44.

Cook, Michael (1981). *Early Muslim Dogma: a Source Critical Study*. Cambridge: Cambridge University Press, 1981.

——— (1983). *Muḥammad*. Oxford: Oxford University Press, 1983.

Crawford, Michael, ed. (1983). *Sources for Ancient History*. Cambridge: Cambridge University Press, 1983.

Crone, Patricia (1980). *Slaves on Horses: the Evolution of the Islamic Polity*. Cambridge: Cambridge University Press, 1980.

——— (1980a). "Islam, Judeo-Christianity and Byzantine Iconoclasm." *JSAI* 2 (1980):59–95.

——— (1987). *Meccan Trade and the Rise of Islam*. Princeton, N.J.: Princeton University Press, 1987.

——— (1987a). *Roman Provincial and Islamic Law: the Origins of the Islamic Patronate*. Cambridge: Cambridge University Press, 1987.

Crone, Patricia, and Martin Hinds (1986). *God's Caliph: Religious Authority in the First Centuries of Islam*. Cambridge: Cambridge University Press, 1986.

Crone, Patricia, and Michael Cook (1977). *Hagarism: the Making of the Islamic World*. Cambridge: Cambridge University Press, 1977.

Corpus Scriptorum Christianorum Orientalium. Edited by J.-B. Chabot et al. 368 vols. in 7 sections. Louvain, 1903–77. Scriptores Arabici = section 2; Scriptores Syri = section 6.

De Vries, Bert (1985). "Urbanization in the Basalt Region of North Jordan in Late Antiquity: the Case of Umm el-Jimāl." In *Studies in the History and Archaeology of Jordan*, edited by ᶜAdnān al-Ḥadīdī. Vol. 2. Amman: Department of Antiquities of Jordan, 1985.

Delaporte, L.-J., trans. and ed. (1910). *Chronographie de Mar Elie bar Sinaya, Métropolitain de Nisibe*. Paris: Librarie Honoré Champion, 1910.

Devreese, Robert (1937). "La Fin Ineditée d'une Lettre de Saint Maxime: un Baptême Forcé de Juifs et de Samaritains à Carthage en 632." *Revue des Sciences Religieuses* 17 (1937):25–35.

Diehl, Charles (1957). *Byzantium: Greatness and Decline*. New Brunswick: Rutgers University, 1957. Translation of the French edition of 1919, reprinted with minor corrections 1926.

Dixon, Abd al-Ameer (1971). *The Umayyad Caliphate*. London, 1971.

Donner, Fred McGraw (1981). *The Early Islamic Conquests*. Princeton, N.J.: Princeton University Press, 1981.

——— (1984). "Some Early Arabic Inscriptions from al-Hanakiyya, Saudi Arabia." *JNES* 43 (1984):181–208.

——— (1986). "The Formation of the Islamic State." *JAOS* 101 (1986):283–296.

Drory, Rina and Josef Drory (1979). "The Arabic Inscriptions at Horvat Berachot." *Dumbarton Oaks Papers* 33 (1979):324–326 and figs. 46–48.

Duval, R., ed. (1904–5). *Ishoᶜyahb Patriarchae III Liber Epistularum*. CSCO: Scriptores Syri 11–12. Louvain, 1904–1905, reprinted 1912. Syriac and Latin translation.

Ephᵓal, Israel (1982). *The Ancient Arabs (9th–5th century B.C.)*. Jerusalem: Magnes Press; Leiden: E. J. Brill, 1982.

Evenari, M., L. Shanan, and N. Tadmor (1982). *The Negev: The Challenge of a Desert*. 2d ed. Cambridge, Mass.: Harvard University Press, 1982.

Fahd, Toufic, ed. (1983). *La Vie du Prophète Mahomet*. In *Colloque de Strasbourg*, October 1980. Paris: Presses Universitaires de France, 1983.

Freeman, Philip, and David Kennedy, eds. (1986). *The Defence of the Roman and Byzantine East: Proceedings of a Colloqium, University of Sheffield, 1986*. 2 vols. BAR International Series 297. Oxford: BAR, 1986.

Frend, W. H. (1972). *The Rise of the Monophysite Movement*. Cambridge: Cambridge University Press, 1972.

——— (1976). *Religion Popular and Unpopular in the Early Christian Centuries*. London: Variorum Press, 1976.

——— (1980). *Town and Country in the Early Christian Centuries*. London: Variorum Press, 1980.

Gibb, Hamilton A. R. (1958). "Arab-Byzantine Relations under the Umayyad Caliphate." *Dumbarton Oaks Papers* 12 (1958):219–33.

Gichon, M. (1971). "The Military Significance of Certain Aspects of the *Limes*

Palaestinae." In *Proceedings of the 7th International Congress of Roman Frontier Studies*, edited by Shimon Applebaum. Tel-Aviv: University of Tel-Aviv Students' Press, 1971.

Goldziher, I. (1889). *Muhammedanische Studien*. 2 vols. Halle, 1889–90. English translation: *Muslim Studies*, translated by C. R. Barber and S. M. Stern, edited by S. M. Stern. Albany: State University of New York Press, 1966 and reprints.

Gordon, Cyrus (1955). *Ugaritic Manual*. 3 vols. Analecta Orientalia 35. Rome: Pontificum Institutum Biblicum, 1955.

Graf, David F. (1978). "The Saracens and the Defense of the Arabian Frontier." *BASOR* 229 (1978):1–26.

Greek and Latin Inscriptions from Syria. 3 vols. Princeton, N.J.: Princeton University Archaeological Expedition to Syria, 1899–1909. Volumes are numbered III, IIIA, IIIB. Vol. III is described as the publication of an American Archaeological Expedition to Syria.

Greek-English Lexicon of the New Testament, being Grimms Wilke's Clavis Novi Testamenti. Translated, revised, and enlarged by Joseph Henry Thayer. Edinburgh: T. and T. Clark, 1901 and many reprints.

Green, Judith and Yoram Tsafrir (1982). "Greek Inscriptions from Hammat Gader." *IEJ* 32 (1982):78–96.

Grierson, Philip (1961). "The Monetary Reform of ᶜAbd al-Malik." *JESHO* 3 (1961):241–264.

——— (1968). *Catalogue of Byzantine Coins in the Dumbarton Oaks Collection*. Washington: Dumbarton Oaks Center for Byzantine Studies, 1968.

——— (1982). *Byzantine Coins*. London: Methuen, 1982.

Griffith, Sidney H. (1980). "The Prophet Muḥammad, his Scripture and his Message according to the Christian Apologies in Arabic and Syriac from the First Abbasid Century." In *La Vie du Prophète Mahomet*, edited by Toufic Fahd. Paris: Presses Universitaires de France, 1983.

——— (1985). "Stephen of Ramlah and the Christian Kerygma in Arabic in Ninth-Century Palestine." *Journal of Ecclesiastical History* 36 (1985):23–45.

——— (1985a). "The Gospel in Arabic: an Inquiry into its Appearance in the First Abbasid Century." *Oriens Christianus* 69 (1985):126–67.

Grohmann, Adolf, ed. (1924). *Allgemeine Einführung in die Arabischen Papyri*, and *Protokolle*. Corpus Papyrorum Raineri III: Series Arabica Vol. 1 parts 1 and 2. Vienna: Burgverlag, 1924. Bound together.

——— (1934). *Arabic Papyri in the Egyptian Library*. Vol. 1: *Protocols and Legal Texts*. Cairo: Egyptian Library Press, 1934.

——— (1952). *From the World of Arabic Papyri*. Cairo: al-Maᶜaref Press, 1952.

——— (1962). *Arabic Inscriptions*. Expedition Philby-Ryckmans-Lippens en Arabie Part II Vol. 1. Louvin: Publications Universitaires, 1962.

——— (1963). *Arabic Papyri from Hirbet el-Mird*. Louvin: Bibliothèque du Museon, 1963.

——— (1971). *Arabische Paläographie.* Band 2 Teil 2. Graz and Cologne: Hermann Bohlaus, 1971. Facsimiles of dated inscriptions, and discussion.

Grohmann, Adolf. *Protocols* = Grohmann (1924), Vol. I, Part 2.

Guillaume, A. (1950). "The Version of the Gospel used in Medina ca. 700 A.D." *Al-Andalus* 15 (1950):289–96.

———, trans. and ed. (1955). *The Life of Muḥammad: a translation of Ibn Isḥāq's Sīrat Rasūl Allāh,* with introduction and notes. Karachi: Oxford University Press, 1955.

Al-Ḥadīdī, ʿAdnān (1975). "*Fulus naḥasiyyah min ʿAmmān*" ("Umayyad Copper Coins from Amman"). *ADAJ* 20 (1975):9–14. In Arabic.

——— (1982–87). *Studies in the History and Archaeology of Jordan.* 3 vols. Amman: Department of Antiquities of Jordan, 1982, 1985, 1987.

Haiman, Mordechai (1988). *Yishuvīm Yisraʾeliyīm be-Har ha-Negev* (Israelite settlements in the Negev highlands). Jerusalem: Hebrew University. Institute of Archaeology, 1988. M.A. thesis. In Hebrew.

Harding, G. L. (1953). "The Cairn of Hani." *ADAJ* 2 (1953):8–49 and plates V–VII.

Hasson, Isaac (1982). *Recherches sur Muʿāwiya Ibn Ali Sufyan, sa Politique Tribale, Militaire et Agraire.* Jerusalem: Hebrew University of Jerusalem, 1982. Ph.D. thesis. In Hebrew with French summary.

Hawary, H., and H. Rached (1932). *Stèles Funéraires.* Vol. 1. Cairo : Imprimerie de l'Institut Français d'Archéologie Orientale, 1932.

Hawting, G. R. (1982). "The Origins of the Muslim Sanctuary at Mecca." In *Studies in the First Century of Islamic Society,* edited by G. H. A. Juynboll. Carbondale, Ill.: Southern Illinois University Press, 1982.

——— (1984). "We were not Ordered with Entering it but only with Circumambulating it." *BSOAS* 47 (1984):228–42.

——— (1986). *The First Dynasty of Islam: The Umayyad Caliphate A.D. 661–750.* London: Croom Helm, 1986.

——— (1986a). "Hudaybiyya and the Conquest of Mecca: a Reconsideration of the Tradition about the Muslim Takeover of the Sanctuary." *JSAI* 8 (1986).

Heather, Peter (1986). "The Crossing of the Danube and the Gothic Conversion." *Greek, Roman and Byzantine Studies* 27 (1986):289–318.

Hendy, Michael F. (1985). *Studies in the Byzantine Monetary Economy 300–1450.* Cambridge: Cambridge University Press, 1985.

Herrin, Judith (1987). *The Formation of Christendom.* Princeton, N.J.: Princeton University Press, 1987.

Hill, D. R. (1971). *The Termination of Hostilities in the Early Arab Conquests.* London: Luzac, 1971.

Hinds, Martin (1983). "'Maghāzī' and 'Sīra' in early Islamic scholarship." In *La Vie du Prophète Mahomet,* edited by Toufic Fahd. Paris: Presses Universitaires de France, 1983.

Honigmann, E. (1951). *Évêques et Évêchés Monophysites d'Asie Antérieure au VIe Siècle. CSCO* 127:2. Louvain, 1951.

Hoyland, Robert (1991). "Arabic, Syriac and Greek Historiography in the First Abbasid Century: An Inquiry into Inter-Cultural Traffic." *ARAM Periodical* 3 (1991):211–233.

——— (1997). *Seeing Islam as Others Saw It: a Survey and Evaluation of Christian, Jewish and Zoroastrian Writings on Early Islam.* Princeton, N.J.: Darwin Press, 1997.

Hütteroth, Wolf D. (1985). "Ottoman Administration of the Desert Frontier in the 16th Century." *AAS* 19 (1985):145–55.

Ibn Warraq, trans. and ed. (2000). *The Quest for the Historical Muhammad.* Amherst, N.Y.: Prometheus Books, 2000.

Isaac, Benjamin (1984). "Bandits in Judaea and Arabia." *Harvard Studies in Classical Philology* 88 (1984):171–203.

——— (1986). "Reflections on the Roman Army in the East." In *The Defence of the Roman and Byzantine East,* edited by Philip Freeman and David Kennedy. Vol. 1. BAR International Series 297. Oxford: BAR, 1986.

——— (1986a). "Līstīm be-Yehuda u-ve-Arabiyyah" ("Bandits in Judaea and Arabia"). *Cathedra* 39 (1986):3–36. In Hebrew.

——— (1988). "Ha-Minhal ha-Rōmī ve-ha-Iyūr" ("The Roman administration and urbanization"). *Cathedra* 48 (1988):9–16. In Hebrew.

——— (1990). *The Limits of Empire: The Roman Army in the East.* Oxford: Clarendon Press, 1990.

Jastrow, Marcus. *A Dictionary of the Targumim, the Talmud Babli and Yerushalmi, and the Midrashic Literature.* 2 vols. London: Luzac; New York: Putnam Press, 1903 and reprints.

Jean, C. F., and J. Hoftijzer (1960–64). *Dictionnaire des Inscriptions Sémitiques de l'Ouest.* Leiden: Brill, 1960–64.

Jeffery, Arthur, trans. and ed. (1944). "Ghevond's Text of the Correspondence between ʿUmar II and Leo III." *Harvard Theological Review* 37 (1944):269–332.

Jones, A. H. M. (1964). *The Later Roman Empire: A Social, Economic and Administrative Survey.* 2 vols. Norman, Okl., 1964.

Jones, J. M. B. (1957). "The Chronology of the *Maghāzī*: a Textual Survey." *BSOAS* 19 (1957):245–80.

Juynboll, G. H. A., ed. (1982). *Studies in the First Century of Islamic Society.* Carbondale, Ill.: Southern Illinois University Press, 1982.

Kaegi, Walter E. (1968). *Byzantium and the Decline of Rome.* Princeton, N.J.: Princeton University Press, 1968.

——— (1969). "Initial Byzantine Reactions to the Arab Conquest." *Church History* 38 (1969):139–149.

——— (1981). *Byzantine Military Unrest 471-843: An Interpretation.* Amsterdam: Hakkert, 1981.

Kawar, I. (1960). "Byzantium and Kinda." *Byzantinische Zeitschrift* 53 (1960):57–73. For later works by this author see Shahîd, Irfan.

——— (1960a). "Procopius and Kinda." *Byzantinische Zeitschrift* 53 (1960):74–78. For later works by this author see Shahîd, Irfan.

Kennedy, D. L. (1982). *Archaeological Explorations on the Roman Frontier in North-East Jordan.* BAR International Series 134. Oxford: BAR, 1982.

Kennedy, Hugh (1985). "The Last Century of Byzantine Syria: A Reinterpretation." *Byzantinische Forschungen* 10 (1985):141–183.

——— (1985a). "From *Polis* to *Madina*: Urban Change in Late Antique and Early Islamic Syria." *Past and Present* 106 (February 1985):3–27.

Kessler, Christel (1970). "ᶜAbd al-Malik's Inscription in the Dome of the Rock: a Reconsideration." *JRAS* (1970):2–14. The only reliable facsimile of this inscription.

Khan, M., and Ali Mughannam (1982). "Ancient Dams in the Ṭāᵓif Area 1980 (1401)." *Aṭlāl* 6 (1982).

Khoary, R. G. (1983). "Les Sources Islamiques de la 'Sira' avant ibn Hisham (m. 213/834) et leur Valeur Historique." In *La Vie du Prophète Mahomet*, edited by Toufic Fahd. Paris: Presses Universitaires de France, 1983.

Killick, Alistair (1986). "Udruḥ and the Southern Frontier." In *The Defence of the Roman and Byzantine East*, edited by Philip Freeman and David Kennedy. Vol. 2. BAR International Series 297. Oxford: BAR, 1986.

King, Geoffrey R. D. (1983). "Survey of Byzantine and Islamic Sites in Jordan. Second Season Report, 1981. Part I: The Field Report." *ADAJ* 27 (1983):385–436.

——— (1983a). "Prospection de Sites Byzantins et Islamiques en Jordanie, 1980–1983." *Syria* 60 (1983):326–329.

——— (1985). "Islam, Iconoclasm, and the Declaration of Doctrine." *BSOAS* 48 (1985):267–277.

——— (1991). "Settlement in Western Arabia and the Gulf in the 6th–8th Centuries A.D." Paper presented at the 2d Workshop on Late Antiquity and Early Islam: Land Use and Settlement Patterns, London, April 1991. Preprint. Also published in King and Cameron (1994).

King, Geoffrey R. D., and Averil Cameron, eds. (1994). *The Byzantine and Early Islamic Near East. Vol. II: Land Use and Settlement Patterns.* Proceedings of the 2d Workshop on Late Antiquity and Early Islam: Land Use and Settlement Patterns, London, 1991. Princeton, N.J.: Darwin Press, 1994.

Kister, M. J. (1962). "A Booth like the Booth of Moses: a Study of an Early Hadīth." *BSOAS* 25 (1962):150–155. Also reprinted in Kister, M. J. *Studies in Jāhiliyya and Early Islam.* Variorum Press, 1980.

——— (1980a). *Studies in Jāhiliyya and Early Islam.* Variorum Press, 1980.

Koren, J., and Y. D. Nevo (1991). "Methodological Approaches to Islamic Studies." *Der Islam* 68 (1991):87–107. Also reprinted in *The Quest for the Historical Muhammad*, edited with translations by Ibn Warraq. Amherst, N.Y.: Prometheus Books, 2000.

Lammens, Henri (1910). "Qoran et Tradition: comment fut Composée la Vie de Mahomet." *Recherches de Science Religieuse* 1 (1910):27–51. English translation in: *The Quest for the Historical Muhammad*, edited with translations by Ibn Warraq. Amherst, N.Y.: Prometheus Books, 2000.

——— (1911). "L'âge de Mahomet et la Chronologie de la Sira." *Journal Asiatique*, 10th sér., 17 (1911):209–50. English translation in: *The Quest for the Historical Muhammad*, edited with translatins by Ibn Warraq. Amherst, N.Y.: Prometheus Press, 2000.

——— (1919). "A propos d'un Colloque entre le Patriarche Jacobite, Jean 1er et ^c^Amr ibn al ^ɔc^Ās." *Journal Asiatique*, 11th sér., 13 (1919):97–109.

Lampe, G. W. H., ed. (1961). *A Patristic Greek Lexicon*. Oxford: Oxford University Press, 1961.

Lane, Edward W. *An Arabic-English Lexicon*. 8 vols. London and Edinburgh, 1863–85. Reprinted New York: Ungar, 1955–56.

Lewis, Archibald R. (1951). *Naval Power and Trade in the Mediterranean, A.D. 500–1100*. Princeton, N.J.: Princeton University Press, 1951.

——— (1969). "Byzantine Light-Weight Solidi and Trade to the North Sea and Baltic." Reprinted in Lewis, Archibald R. *The Sea and Medieval Civilizations: Collected Studies*. London: Variorum Press, 1978.

——— (1978). *The Sea and Medieval Civilizations: Collected Studies*. London: Variorum Press, 1978.

Lewis, Bernard (1950). "An Apocalyptic Vision of Islamic History." *BSOAS* (1950):308–338.

Lewis, Bernard, and P. M. Holt, eds. (1962). *Historians of the Middle East*. London, 1962.

Liddell, H. G., and R. Scott (1849). *A Lexicon Abridged from the Greek-English Lexicon of H. G. Liddell and R. Scott*. 3d ed. Oxford: Oxford University Press, 1849 and reprints.

Livingston, A., M. Khan, A. Zahrani, M. Salluk, and S. Shaman (1985). "Epigraphic Survey 1404/1984." *Aṭlāl* 9 (1985):128–144.

Lopez, Robert S. (1943). "Mohammed and Charlemagne—a Revision." *Speculum* 18 (1943).

Luft, Ulrich (1974). "Der Beginn der Islamischen Eroberung Aegyptens im Jahre 639." *Staatliche Museum zu Berlin Forschungen und Berichte* 16 (1974):123–28.

MacAdam, Henry Innes (1986). *Studies in the History of the Roman Province of Arabia: The Northern Sector*. BAR International Series 295. Oxford: BAR, 1986.

——— (1986a). "Some Notes on the Umayyad Occupation of North-East Jordan." In *The Defence of the Roman and Byzantine East*, edited by Philip Freeman and David Kennedy. Vol. 2. BAR International Series 297. Oxford: BAR, 1986.

——— (1992). "Settlements and Settlement Patterns in Northern and Central Transjordania, ca. 550–ca. 750." In *The Byzantine and Early Islamic Near East*. Vol. 2: *Land Use and Settlement Patterns*, edited by Geoffrey R. D. King and Averil Cameron. Princeton, N.J.: Darwin Press, 1994.

Macdonald, B. et al. (1983). "The Wādī el-Ḥāsa Survey 1982: a Preliminary Report." *ADAJ* 27 (1983):311–323.

Macdonald, M. C. A. (1983). "Inscriptions and Rock-Art of the Jawa Area, 1982: a Preliminary Report." *ADAJ* 27 (1983):571–574 and plates cxxiii–cxxiv.

Macler, Frederic, trans. and ed. (1904). *Histoire d'Héraclius par l'Évêque Sebeos*. Paris: Imprimerie Nationale, 1904.

MacMullen, Ramsay (1988). *Corruption and the Decline of Rome*. New Haven: Yale University Press, 1988.

Matthews, John (1975). *Western Aristocracies and Imperial Court, A.D. 364–425*. Oxford: Clarendon Press, 1975.

Mayerson, Philip (1963). "The Desert of Southern Palestine according to the Byzantine Sources." *Proceedings of the American Philosophical Society* 107 (1963):160–72.

——— (1964). "The First Muslim Attacks on Southern Palestine." *Transactions and Proceedings of the American Philological Association* 95 (1964):155–99.

——— (1975). "Observations on Nilus' *Narrationes*: Evidence for an Unknown Christian Sect?" *Journal of the American Research Center in Egypt* 12 (1975).

——— (1983). "The City of Elusa in the Literary Sources of the Fourth–Sixth Centuries. *IEJ* 33 (1983):247–53.

——— (1986). "The Saracens and the *Limes*." *BASOR* 262 (1986):35–47.

——— (1988). "Justinian's Novel 103 and the Re-organization of Palestine." *BASOR* 269 (1988):65–71.

——— (1989). "Saracens and Romans: Micro-Macro Relationships." *BASOR* 274 (1989):71–79.

Meyendorff, John (1964). "Byzantine Views of Islam." *Dumbarton Oaks Papers* 18 (1964):115–132.

Migne, J.-P., ed. *Patrologia Cursus Completus... Series Prima (= Latina)*. 221 vols. Paris, 1844–90.

———, ed. *Patrologia Cursus Completus... Series Graeca*. 161 vols. Paris, 1857–68.

Miles, G. C. (1948). "Early Islamic Inscriptions Near Ṭāʾif in the Ḥijāz." *JNES* 7 (1948).

——— (1952). "Miḥrāb and ʿAnazah: a Study of Early Islamic Iconography." In *Archaeologica Orientalia in Memoriam Ernst Herzfeld*, edited by G. C. Miles. Locus Valley, N.Y.: Augustin Press, 1952.

——— (1962). "The Earliest Arab Gold Coinage." *American Numismatic Society Museum Notes* 13 (1967):227.

Mingana, A., ed. (1907). *Sources Syriaques*. Leipzig, 1907. Includes text of Books 10–15 and translation of Book 15 of John bar Penkayê.

Mochiri, Malek Iradj (1981). "A Pahlavi Forerunner of the Umayyad Reformed Coinage." *Journal of the Royal Asiatic Society* 113 (1981):168–172.

Momigliano, Arnold, ed. (1963). *The Conflict between Paganism and Christianity in the Fourth Century*. Oxford: Clarendon Press, 1963.

——— (1963a). "Christianity and the Decline of the Roman Empire." In *The Conflict between Paganism and Christianity in the Fourth Century*. Oxford: Clarendon Press, 1963.

Moorhead, John (1981). "The Monophysite Response to the Arab Invasion." *Byzantion* 51 (1981):578–91.

Nahlieli, Dov, and Yigeal Israel (1988). "Naḥal La^{c}anah." *Hadashot Arkhiologiot* 92 (1988):69. In Hebrew.

Nau, M. F. (1904). "Maronites, Mazonites et Maranites." *Revue de l'Orient Chrétien* 9 (1904):269–72.

——— (1909). "Littérature Canonique Syriaque Ineditée." *Revue de l'Orient Chrétien* 14 (1909).

——— (1909a). "Histoire de Marouta." *Patrologia Orientalis* 3 (1909):52–96.

——— (1915). "Un Colloque du Patriarche Jean avec l'Émir des Agaréens et Faits Divers des Annèes 712 à 716 d'après le Ms. du B.M. ADD. 17193." *Journal Asiatique*, 9th sér., 5 (1915):225–279.

Negev, Avraham (1976). "The Churches of the Central Negev: an Archaeological Survey." *Revue Biblique* 81 (1976):400–422.

——— (1981). *The Greek Inscriptions from the Negev*. Jerusalem: Franciscan Press, 1981.

——— (1986). *Nabatean Archaeology Today*. New York: New York University Press, 1986.

Nevo, Yehuda D. (1985). "Sede Boqer and the Central Negev: 7th–8th century A.D." Paper presented at the 3d International Colloquium "From Jahiliyyah to Islam," Hebrew University of Jerusalem, 1985.

——— (1989). "A New Negev Arabic Inscription." *BSOAS* 52 (1989):18–23.

——— (1991). *Pagans and Herders: a Re-examination of the Negev Runoff Cultivation Systems in the Byzantine and Early Arab Periods*. Jerusalem: IPS Press, 1991.

Nevo, Yehuda D., and A. Rothenberg. *Sede Boqer 1983–84*. Forthcoming.

Nevo, Yehuda D., and Judith Koren (1990). "The Origins of the Muslim Description of the Jahili Meccan Sanctuary." *JNES* 49 (1990):23–44.

Nevo, Yehuda D., Z. Cohen, and D. Heftmann, eds. (1993). *Ancient Arabic Inscriptions from the Negev*. Jerusalem: IPS Press, 1993.

Nöldeke, Th. (1875). "Zur Geschichte der Araber im 1. Jahrhundert d. H. aus syrischen Quellen." *ZDMG* XXIV (1875):76-82.

———, trans. and ed. (1893). *Die von Guigi Herausgegebene Syrische Chronik Übersetzt und Commentiert*. Sitzungsberichte der Kaiserischen Akademie der

Wissenschaften in Wien, Phil.-Historische Klasse Band 128. Vienna, 1893. This is the Khuzestani Chronicle.

Ostrogorsky, George (1959). "Byzantine Cities in the Early Middle Ages." *Dumbarton Oaks Papers* 13 (1959):47–66.

Oxford Classical Dictionary. Edited by N. G. L. Hammod and H. H. Scullard. 2d ed. Oxford: Oxford University Press, 1970.

Oxford Dictionary of the Christian Church. Edited by F. L. Cross and E. A. Livingstone. 2d ed. Oxford: Oxford University Press, 1983.

Oxtoby, Willard G. (1968). *Some Inscriptions of the Safaitic Bedouin*. New Haven: American Oriental Society, 1968.

Palmer, Andrew, with Sebastian P. Brock and Robert G. Hoyland (1993). *The Seventh Century in the West-Syrian Chronicles*. Translated Texts for Historians 15. Liverpool: University of Liverpool Press, 1993.

Parker, S. Thomas (1979). *The Historical Development of the Limes Arabicus*. Los Angeles: University of California at Los Angeles, 1979. Ph.D. thesis.

——— (1983). "The Central *Limes Arabicus* Project: the 1982 Campaign." *ADAJ* 27 (1983):213–230.

——— (1986a). *Romans and Saracens: a History of the Arabian Frontier*. Dissertation Series 6. Philadelphia: American Schools of Oriental Research, 1986.

——— (1986b). "Retrospective on the Arabian Frontier after a Decade of Research." In *The Defence of the Roman and Byzantine East*, edited by Philip Freeman and David Kennedy. Vol. 2. BAR International Series 297. Oxford: BAR, 1986.

——— (1987). *The Roman Frontier in Central Jordan: Interim Report on the* Limes Arabicus *Project, 1980–1985*. 2 vols. BAR International Series 340. Oxford: BAR, 1987.

——— (1987a). "The Roman *Limes* in Jordan." In *Studies in the History and Archaeology of Jordan*, edited by ᶜAdnān al-Ḥadīdī. Vol. 3. Amman: Department of Antiquities of Jordan, 1987.

——— (1988). "The *Limes Arabicus* Project: the 1987 Campaign." *ADAJ* 32 (1988):171–187.

Patrich, Joseph (1982). "Issur Pessel u-Tmunah b'qerev ha-Nabbatīm." ("Prohibition of a graven image among the Nabateans."). *Cathedra* 26 (1982):47–104. In Hebrew with English summary.

Peters, F. E. (1988). "The Commerce of Mecca Before Islam." In *A Way Prepared: Essays on Islamic Culture in Honor of Richard Bayly Winder*, edited by F. Kazemi and R. D. McChesney. New York: New York University Press, 1988.

Phillips, George (1864). *Scholia on Passages of the Old Testament by Mar Jacob, Bishop of Edessa*. London: Williams and Norgate, 1864.

Piccirillo, Michel (1985). "Rural Settlements in Byzantine Jordan." In *Studies in the History and Archaeology of Jordan*, edited by ᶜAdnān al-Ḥadīdī. Vol. 2. Amman: Department of Antiquities of Jordan, 1985.

Pines, Shlomo (1966). "The Jewish Christians of the Early Centuries of Christianity According to a New Source." *Proceedings of the Israel Academy of Science and Humanities* 2, no. 13 (1966).

——— (1967). "Jewish-Christian Material in an Arabic Jewish Treatise." *Proceedings of the American Academy for Jewish Research* 35 (1967):187–217.

——— (1984). "Notes on Islam and on Arabic Christianity and Judaeo-Christianity." *JSAI* 4 (1984):135–152.

——— (1990). "Jāhiliyyah and ᶜIlm." *JSAI* 13 (1990):175–194.

Raby, Julian, and Jeremy Johns, eds. (1992). *Bayt al-Maqdis: ᶜAbd al-Malik's Jerusalem*. Vol. 1. Oxford Studies in Islamic Art 9. Oxford: Oxford University Press, 1992.

Rāgib, Yūsuf (1981). "Lettres Nouvelles de Qurrah bn Šarīk." *JNES* 40 (1981):173–187.

Reeland, Adrian (1714). *Palaestina ex Monumentis Veteribus Illustrata.* 2 vols. Trojecti Balavorum, ex lib. G. Brodelet, 1714.

Rehm, B., ed. (1965). *Die Pseudoklementines Recognitiones.* Berlin, 1965.

Rehm, B., J. Irmscher, and F. Paschke, eds. (1969). *Die Pseudoklementinen.* I: *Hamilien*. Berlin, 1969.

Répertoire Chronologique d'Épigraphie Arabe. Edited by Combe, Sauvaget, and Wiet. Vol. 1. Cairo: Imprimerie de l'Institut Français d'Archéologie Orientale, 1931.

Rosen-Ayalon, Myriam (1987). "In Quest of the Early Roots of an Islamic Glazed Ware." *Eretz-Israel* 19 (1987):142–52. In Hebrew with English summary.

Rostovtzeff, M. (1957). *Social and Economic History of the Roman Empire*. 2d ed., revised by P. M. Fraser. Oxford: Clarendon Press, 1957.

Rothenberg, B., and J. Glass (1981). "The Midianite Pottery." *Eretz-Israel* 15 (1981): 85–114 and plates 13–17. In Hebrew.

Rubin, Uri (1986). "The Kaᶜaba: Aspects of its Ritual, Functions and Position in Pre-Islamic and Early Islamic Times." *JSAI* 8 (1986):97–131.

——— (1990). "Ḥanifiyya and Kaᶜaba: An Inquiry into the Arabian Pre-Islamic Background of Dīn Ibrāhīm." *JSAI* 13 (1990):85–112.

Rubin, Z. (1986). "Diplomacy and War in the Relations between Byzantium and the Sassanids in the Fifth Century A.D." In *The Defence of the Roman and Byzantine East*, edited by Philip Freeman and David Kennedy. Vol. 2. BAR International Series 297. Oxford: BAR, 1986.

Sahas, Daniel J. (1972). *John of Damascus on Islam: the Heresy of the Ishmaelites.* Leiden: Brill, 1972.

Sauer, James A. (1982). "The Pottery of Jordan in the Early Islamic Periods." In *Studies in the History and Archaeology of Jordan*, edited by ᶜAdnān al-Ḥadīdī. Vol. 1. Amman: Department of Antiquities of Jordan, 1987.

Schacht, Joseph (1950). *The Origins of Muhammadan Jurisprudence*. Oxford: Clarendon, 1950.

Schacht, Joseph, and C. E. Bosworth, eds. (1974). *The Legacy of Islam*. 2d ed. Oxford: Clarendon Press, 1974.

Schick, Robert (1987). "The Fate of the Christians in Palestine During the Byzantine-Umayyad Transition, A.D. 600–750." Paper presented at the Conference on the History of Bilad al-Sham in the Umayyad Period, 1987.

Schoeps, Hans-Joachim (1964). *Das Juden-Christentum*. Bern: Francke Verlag, 1964.

Seeck, Otto, ed. (1962). *Notitia Dignitatum*. Frankfurt am Main: Minerva Press, 1962. Reprint of 1876 ed.

Segal, J. B. (1962). "Syriac Chronicles as Source Material for the History of Islamic People." In *Historians of the Middle East*, edited by Bernard Lewis and P. M. Holt. London, 1962.

——— (1984). "Arabs in Syriac Literature before the Rise of Islam." *JSAI* 4 (1984):89–124.

Shaban, M. A. (1971). *Islamic History A.D. 600–750 (A.H. 132): A New Interpretation*. Cambridge: Cambridge University Press, 1971.

Shahîd, Irfan (1984). *Rome and the Arabs: A Prolegomena to the Study of Byzantium and the Arabs*. Washington, D.C.: Dumbarton Oaks, 1984. For earlier works by this author see Kawar, I.

——— (1984a). *Byzantium and the Arabs in the Fourth Century*. Washington, D.C.: Dumbarton Oaks, 1984. For earlier works by this author see Kawar, I.

——— (1989). *Byzantium and the Arabs in the Fifth Century*. Washington, D.C.: Dumbarton Oaks, 1989. For earlier works by this author see Kawar, I.

Sharon, Moshe (1966). "An Arabic Inscription from the Time of the Caliph ᶜAbd al-Malik." *BSOAS* 29 (1966):367–72 and plate I.

——— (1981). "Arabic Inscriptions from Sede Boqer." Appendix in Cohen, Rudolf. *Map of Sede Boqer East (168) 13-03*. Jerusalem: Archaeological Survey of Israel, 1981. Photographs, transcriptions, and English translation.

——— (1985). "Arabic Inscriptions from Sede Boqer." Appendix in Cohen, Rudolf. *Map of Sede Boqer West (167) 12-03*. Jerusalem: Archaeological Survey of Israel, 1985. Photographs, transcriptions, and English translation.

——— (1990). *Ancient Rock Inscriptions*. Supplemental volume to Lender, Yeshaᶜyahu. *Map of Har Nafha (196) 12-01*. Jerusalem: Archaeological Survey of Israel, 1990. Introduction, photographs, transcriptions, and English translation.

Simon, Robert (1989). *Meccan Trade and Islam: Problems of Origin and Structure*. Budapest: Akademiai Kiado, 1989.

Smith, Sidney (1954). "Events in Arabia in the Sixth century A.D." *BSOAS* 16 (1954):424–464.

Soden, Wolfram von (1958). *Akkadisches Handwörterbuch*. Wiesbaden: Harassowitz, 1958 on.

Stern, Menahem (1980). *Greek and Latin Authors on Jews and Judaism*. Vol. II. Jerusalem: Israel Academy of Sciences and Humanities, 1980.

Tawab, A. M. (1977-82). *Stèles Islamiques de la Nécropole d'Assouan.* 2 vols. Cairo: Institut Français d'Archéologie Orientale, 1977 and 1982.

Tcherikover, V. (1963). *Ha-Yehudīm be-Miṣrayīm...* (The Jews in Egypt in the Hellenistic–Roman age in the light of the papyri). 2d rev. ed. Jerusalem: Magnes Press, 1963. In Hebrew with English summary.

Thompson, E.A (1966). *The Visigoths in the Time of Ulfila.* Oxford: Clarendon Press, 1966.

Trimingham, J. S. (1979). *Christianity among the Arabs in Pre-Islamic Times.* London: Longman, 1979.

Tsafrir, Yoram (1988). *Excavations at Reḥovot-in-the-Negev.* Vol. 1, *The Northern Church.* Qedem 25. Jerusalem: Hebrew University of Jerusalem. Institute of Archaeology, 1988.

Tsafrir, Yoram, and Gideon Foerster (1991). "From Scythopolis to Baysan—Changing Concepts of Urbanism." Paper presented at the 2d Workshop on Late Antiquity and Early Islam: Land Use and Settlement Patterns, London, April 1991. Preprint. Also published in King and Cameron (1994).

University of Chicago. Oriental Institute. *Assyrian Dictionary.* 14 vols. Edited by I. J. Gelb et al. Chicago: Oriental Institute, 1956–84.

Usener, H., ed. (1886). "Weinachtspredigt des Sophronos." *Rheinisches Museum für Philologie,* n.s. 41 (1886):500–516. Greek text.

Al-ᶜUšš, Muḥammad Abū al-Faraj (1964). "Kitābat ᶜArabiyyah Ġayr Mansūrah fī Jabal ᵓUsays" ("Arabic inscriptions from Jabal Usays"). *Al-Abḥāṯ* 7 (1964):227–316.

Van Ess, Josef (1992). "ᶜAbd al-Malik and the Dome of the Rock: An Analysis of Some Texts." In *Bayt al-Maqdis: ᶜAbd al-Malik's Jerusalem,* edited by Julian Raby and Jeremy Johns. Vol. 1. Oxford: Oxford University Press, 1992.

Vasiliev, Alexander A. (1952). *History of the Byzantine Empire, 324–1453.* 2d English ed. 2 vols. Wisconsin University Press, 1952 and many reprints.

——— (1955). "Notes on Some Episodes Concerning the Relations of the Arabs and the Byzantine Empire from the Fourth to the Sixth Century." *Dumbarton Oaks Papers* 9–10 (1955–56):306–16.

Walker, John (1941). *A Catalogue of the Arab-Sassanian Coins.* London: Trustees of the British Museum, 1941.

——— (1956). *A Catalogue of the Arab-Byzantine and Post-Reform Ummayyad Coins.* London: Trustees of the British Museum, 1956.

Wansbrough, John (1977). *Quranic Studies: Sources and Methods of Scriptural Interpretation.* Oxford: Oxford University Press, 1977.

——— (1978). *The Sectarian Milieu.* Oxford: Oxford University Press, 1978.

——— (1987). "*Res Ipsa Loquitur*: History and Mimesis." 7th Einstein Memorial Lecture, Israel Academy of Sciences and Humanities, Jerusalem, 1986. Jerusalem: Israel Academy of Sciences and Humanities, 1987.

Weber, Carolyn, and Aaron Wildavsky (1986). *A History of Taxation and Expenditure in the Western World.* New York: Simon and Shuster, 1986.

Wheeler, Sir Mortimer (1955). *Rome beyond the Imperial Frontiers.* Harmondsworth, England: Penguin, 1955.

Whittaker, C. R. (1994). *Frontiers of the Roman Empire: a Social and Economic Study.* Baltimore: Johns Hopkins Press, 1994.

Whitting, Philip D. (1973). *Byzantine Coins.* New York: Putnam Press, 1973.

Wilkinson, J. (1977). *Jerusalem Pilgrims before the Crusades.* Jerusalem: Ariel, 1977.

Winnett, Frederick V., and J. L. Harding (1978). *Inscriptions from Fifty Safaitic Cairns.* Toronto: Toronto University Press, 1978.

Witakowski, Witold (1987). *The Syriac Chronicle of Pseudo-Dionysius of Tel-Maḥrē*: A Study in the History of Historiography. Acta Universitatis Upsaliensis: Studia Semitica Upsaliensia 9. Uppsala: University of Uppsala, 1987.

Wright, William, and Norman McLean, eds. (1975). *The Ecclesiastical History of Eusebius Pamphili, 265–339.* Amsterdam: Philo Press, 1975. Syriac text.

Zadok, Ran (1977). *On West Semites in Babylonia during the Chaldean and Achaemenian Periods (an Onomastic Study).* Jerusalem, 1977.

Zarins, Juris, and Zaharani Awad (1985). "Recent Archaeological Investigation in the South Tihama Plain." *Aṭlāl* 9 (1985).

Index

Muḥammad (*continued*)
in Sebeos, 230
in *Sīrah*, 256, 257, 282
in Syrian chronicles, 130–31
traditions about, 255, 256
muḥammad, meaning of, 260, 263–265
in Qurʾān, 265–67
Muḥammad ibn al-Ḥanafiyyah, 280, 281–82
Muḥammad rasūl Allāh (formula), 247, 251 table, 279, 284–85, 329. *See also* Mohammedanism; Muḥammad the Prophet
al-Munḏir (Ġassānid king), 33, 46
al-Munḏir (Laxmid chief), 75, 77
Muslim (term for religion)
in John of Nikiu's *Chronicle*, 233, 234–35
not in 7th-c. texts, 215
Muslim historical sources
view of Arab conquest, 1–2
historicity of, 2, 6–7, 8
Muslim rock inscriptions. *See* rock inscriptions, Muslim
al-muṣṭafà, concept of, 264
Muʾtah, Battle of, 108
al-Muxtār, 280–81

Nabataeans, 177, 177n. 18
Najrān, 68
al-nār, 321–22. *See also* hereafter, the
Nazarenes. *See* Judeo-Christianity
Negev, Avraham, 73n. 14, 79n. 42, 189
Negev "cities." *See* Negev desert, towns in; *and names of specific cities*
Negev desert. *See also* Arabia, province of; Byzantine provinces, eastern; *limes*, eastern; Palaestina Tertia, province of
acculturation of tribes in, 82, 83
Christians in, 82
paganism in, 82–83, 176, 177–85
rock inscriptions in (*see* rock inscriptions)
rural population of, 78, 79, 80
towns in, 3n. 4, 78, 79, 82, 158, 175
Christianity in, 175–76
demography of, 174, 177, 177n. 18
paganism in, 174–176
Nessana, 79n. 42, 158–59, 201n. 86
Nessana papyri, 47, 158, 201n. 86
Nestorian church, 52, 52n. 4, 89
and Arab rulers, 216, 217, 221
attitude to intermarriage, 217–18, 219, 221, 221n. 49
and Judeo-Christians, 191–92
right to judge Christians, 225–26, 228–29
Nestorianism. *See* Nestorian church
Nikephorus (9th-c. chronicler), 99
Nöldeke, Th., 110–12, 113
Notitia Dignitatum, 38n. 34, 42, 42n. 55
Nubia, 54, 160n. 15
numismatic evidence. *See* coins

Oboda, 35n. 19
offering shelves
at Sede Boqer cult center, 180
official inscriptions, 204, 298–99. *See also* rock inscriptions
ʿAqabah inscription, 204–205, 287, 288
in Damascus mosque, 204, 205, 294–95
in Dome of the Rock, 204, 247, 265, 271–72, 275–79
on Fusṭāṭ bridge, 204, 288
in Fusṭāṭ mosque, 331–32
on milestones, 274n. 9
in Prophet Mosque, Madīnah, 204, 205, 352–54
on Ṭāʾif dam, 204, 288
oikoumenē. *See* Byzantine provinces, eastern
Orthodox (Byzantine) church, 52, 59, 61. *See also* Chalcedonianism
break with eastern sects, 62–64
political meaning of allegiance to, 159–60

pagans and paganism
ḥanpê as term for, 213–15
pagans and paganism, Arab, 10–11, 13, 207, 244–45
animal sacrifice among, 182–83
burial customs of, 219
Christian descriptions of, 212–13, 214–16, 217–19
in Negev "cities," 174–76

religious concepts and formulae (*continued*)
in rock inscriptions, 196, 197–98, 199, 200, 298, 299, 335, 357
by specific concept/formula
Allāh's favors, 311, 312, 314
Allāh as overlord/patron, 334
Allāh as witness, 335–36
angels, 326, 333
al-baʿṯ, 305–6, 307, 323
basmala, 250 table, 279, 284–85, 309–10
bearing witness, 334–36
creation themes, 307, 314–15
'guidance' and *al-hudà*, 279, 280–81, 282, 285, 331–32, 343n. 14, 355–58
ḥašar, 305–306
ḥayy-an wa-mayyit-an, 305–306
'herald' formula, 343n. 14, 358–59
hereafter, the, 305–307, 316–23, 334
intercession, 332-33
ʾislām, 234, 278, 294, 295
istišhād, 332, 334–6
jahd, 332
al-jannah, 316–21, 322
kafà bi-llāhi..., 309, 335–36
la ḥawla wa-lā quwwata..., 309
"Lord of Moses and Jesus," 325, 326, 329
martyrdom, 332
Muḥamad rasūl Allāh, 247, 251 table, 279, 284–85, 329, 356
al-nār, 321–22
resurrection, 305–306, 307, 323
al-ṣamad, 277
šarīk, 277, 355n. 1
sin and forgiveness, 305, 307–308, 310–14, 323–24
taslīm, 277
tawḥīd, 271–72, 276–77, 279, 284–85, 295, 329, 330
religious formulae. *See* religious concepts and formulae
religious scholars. *See ʿulamāʾ*
resurrection, concept of, 305–306, 307, 323
riddah campaigns, 97n. 22
ritual destruction of vessels, 181–82
rock inscriptions. *See also* official inscriptions
Basic Text, 197–99, 297–335 passim
in Classical Arabic, 196–200
drawings in, 83n. 53
in epigraphic peninsular languages, 68–69, 174, 176, 195–96
Mohammedan, 199, 297–335 passim
Muslim, 200, 297–333 passim, 333–36
in Negev, 196–200, 297–335
classification of, 197–200, 298, 299, 301–305 chart
dating of, 298
religious formulae in (*see* religious concepts and formulae)
use of, as historical evidence, 8
royal inscriptions. *See* official inscriptions

Sabaean civilization, 68
Ṣafaitic cairns, 174
Ṣafaitic rock inscriptions, 68–69, 82–83, 174, 176. *See also* epigraphic peninsular languages
Sahas, Daniel J., 237, 238
Saint John's Church, Damascus, 193
Salīḥ (Arab tribe), 33, 75
al-Šām. *See* Byzantine provinces, eastern; *limes*, eastern; *and names of specific areas*
ṣamad, meaning of, 277
Samaritans, 194–95, 225
šarīk, meaning of, 277, 355n. 1
Sassanian empire. *See* Persian empire
s.b.ḥ., meaning of, 261–62, 267
Schacht, Joseph, 4, 228n. 64, 241
Scythopolis (Bayṣān), 140, 147 table
Sebeos. *See History of Heraclius* (Sebeos)
Secrets of Rabbi Simon ben Yoḥay, 210–12
Sede Boqer cult center, 178, 179–85, 201–203
date of, 183, 184–85, 203–204
and monotheists, 201–203
similarity to Jāhilī paganism, 182
Sergios (commander at Battle of Dāṯin), 99, 100
Sergius (patriarch of Constantinople), 60
Severinus (pope), 62